MASS COMMUNICATION

The Impact of the Information Age on Everyday Life

AT A GLANCE

✓ The new electronic media provide greater flexibility as to when, where, and how we are informed and entertained.

✓ The traditional mass media are no longer the only organizations that process information to inform and educate large numbers of people.

✓ Our "culture" and our "cultural agenda" are heavily affected by the types of information we receive through the media of mass communication.

✓ One of the major effects of mass communication is to "commercialize" information—to aid the function of marketing cultural goods and services.

✓ Theorists have long attempted to study the *effects* that mass communication has on society and individuals, usually by analyzing the behaviors that result when messages are sent through a channel to receivers.

✓ The P↔I↔C model developed for this book suggests that the interests and the behaviors of consumers help determine the kinds of information that producers offer in the marketplace.

We are living in the *Information Age*, an era when communication media have become central to nearly all that we do. Our tools for sending, transmitting, and receiving information have always occupied an important place in human activity. Today, more than ever before, communication technology has a pervasive impact on our personal and professional lives, our groups and organizations, our own society, and the world community.

Evidence of the impact of new media is all around us. Consider the proportion of the space in department stores and shopping malls allocated to communication and information technology—television, videocassettes, videodiscs, video games, stereo systems, photographic equipment, telephones, electronic watches, calculators, computers, and a variety of other technologies. This is the *hardware*—the physical tools—of the Information Age. Additional space is devoted to *software* such as records, tapes, computer programs, video game cartridges, and a number of magazines and books that relate to the use of these media.

New media appear in nearly all facets of contemporary social and professional activity. In the entertainment industry, cable television, telecommunications, video-gaming, and recording and playback devices have greatly broadened the number of leisure outlets available to us. Increasingly, portable video and audio devices provide greater flexibility as to *when*, *where*, and *how* we are entertained.

At work, word-processing systems, sophisticated photocopying equipment, phone conferences, facsimile (fax) machines, cellular mobile phones, and other media are the accepted standard even for small businesses. Within larger organizations, management information systems (MIS), corporate video, and electronic mail provide decision-makers with access to vital information at the touch of a keyboard.

These same basic information-processing and communication capabilities are also used in medicine to aid in data collection and record-keeping. They facilitate patient diagnosis, care, and treatment. With computers, all medical information about an individual—medical histories, data on prescribed medications, lab test results, copies of all X-rays—can be transmitted electronically or stored on a portable disk. This information can be moved physically or electronically from one physician or hospital to another.

In the news media and the publishing industry, new technologies have changed the way information is collected, processed, and distributed. Writers and editors have access to a variety of databases to supplement information gathered through interviews and other means. Articles are written, revised, edited, and arranged on-screen. The finished product—newspaper, magazine, or book—may be printed in a traditional manner or transmitted via satellite or cable to remote printing sites, as is the case with newspapers like *USA Today* and *The Wall Street Journal*.

Libraries are also being transformed by the new media. The concept of the library as a building where people come to read and check out books and articles is giving way to the view of a service institution that aims to serve the broad-based information needs of its clients. In addition to print materials, patrons at a growing number of libraries have access to audiotapes and videotapes, computers and computer software, and electronic information services. New information systems allow users at remote stations to access documents that were formerly available only in print form in a single or few copies, and were unavailable to others once checked out. Devices like the videodisc also offer great potential for reducing the space necessary for data storage and for increasing ease of access to documents once stored.

> In the 21st Century, we will reap the benefits made possible by the explosion in communications technology.... Already, that technology has accelerated the movement toward a "paperless" office. Electronic mail with messaging and text capabilities has enabled an organization to conduct business instantaneously around the world and around the clock.
>
> —*Ellen M. Hancock, Vice President and General Manager, Communication Systems, IBM* (January, 1990, *IBM Update*)

Chapter 1   The Impact of the Information Age on Everyday Life   5

USA Today's sections are organized to direct readers quickly to the information that interests them.

With developments such as *videotex*, which uses the television or computer monitors to display text and graphic content, information can be transmitted directly to the consumer via cable or phone lines, or to an intermediary computer. But unlike the more familiar uses of television, videotex systems allow audience members to play a role in selecting the information they receive. In this way, consumers can "personalize" what has traditionally been standardized *mass* media programming.

TECHNOLOGICAL CONVERGENCE

At the heart of these advances is the convergence of media that were once distinct in their forms and uses. Newspapers, for example, historically provided their audience with the summary of events of the day. Television, radio, and film were primarily entertainment media. Telephones were used socially and in business contexts, typically as a substitute for short, face-to-face conversations.

Today, many of these traditional distinctions are rapidly becoming obsolete. Those who have television with cable may now select channels for shopping, music, religious programming, weather, comedy, and adult movies. Cable users also have a channel that functions as a local bulletin board or want ad section much like what we find in the newspaper or on the wall of a local supermarket.

With some fairly inexpensive equipment and a flip of the switch, television becomes an arcade game. Connected to a microcomputer, television becomes a book—a self-instructional guide to French, finance, or computer programming.

A consumer buys a mini-cam so that she can become a producer of her own historical record of family and friends.

With some additional hardware and software, the telephone also changes function to become a device for the transmission of alphanumeric and graphic messages to or from another computer.

Together, the computer, telephone, and television can become a newspaper, magazine, game, reference tool, catalog, index, and a variety of other things. When a printer is added they become a typewriter and paper or a card catalog and the stacks of books at a reference library in medicine or law. When connected to a videodisc or videocassette, television becomes a movie screen. When the tapes played are ones recorded by an individual, television is a home movie or a family album.

 INSIGHT

The Multimedia Phenomenon

One of the consequences of convergence in media uses and ownership is that entertainment information may begin as a single-medium event and quickly become a multimedia phenomenon.

"Beverly Hills 90210" began as a popular Fox network television program, but the characters were soon featured on shirts, clothing, bedding, watches, hats, and dolls—similar to the multimedia explosion of images from "Sesame Street" and "Teen-Age Mutant Ninja Turtles." "Sesame Street" began as a television series, but soon spawned books, movies, recordings, toys, and even packaging and advertising for children's vitamin pills. "Turtles" began as comic-book characters, then got their own television cartoon and adventure movies, as well as becoming part of a fast-food chain's advertising campaign.

With these hybrid media and uses, producers and consumers are able to carry out functions that were once difficult, time-consuming, or even impossible. So significant is the impact of media convergence that some have called these developments, "the communication revolution," and used terms like *commputication* (communication + computers) or *telecomputerenergetics* to signal the blending of once-distinct technologies. Commenting on this trend today, Everette Dennis, executive director of the Gannett Center for Media Studies at Columbia University, remarked: "If there is a single concept that marked the last decade, it is surely the convergence—the coming together of communication devices and forms into . . . electronically based, computer-driven . . . systems that retrieve, process and store text, data, sound and image."[1] Over 20 years ago, Edwin Parker observed the beginnings of this trend, which he saw as particularly significant because it would lead to:

1. Increased amounts of information available to the public, and increased efficiency . . . since everything need not be distributed to everyone in the audience.
2. Greater variety in the ways information packages can be constructed.
3. Receiver selection of information (both in content and timing) as opposed to source control of information selection, packaging, and transmission.
4. Improved "feedback" capability (since the individual subscriber can "talk" to the system. . . .
5. Greater convenience to the user.[2]

The Information Age has also been marked by a convergence of news and entertainment-oriented products. Television programs like "A Current Affair," "Phil Donohue," "America's Most Wanted," and "Entertainment Tonight" blur the lines between "information" and "entertainment." The same can be said for movies like "JFK," and for a growing number of TV "docu-dramas." A vivid example was provided by an episode of "Doogie Howser, M.D." that portrayed the show's characters in the emergency room caring for the victims of the rioting in Los Angeles following the Rodney King verdict. The show included a number of videotape segments from actual newscasts of rioting, looting, and burning. The possibility for blurring "reality" and "fantasy" was perhaps most dramatically demonstrated by the Fall, 1992, season-opener of "Murphy Brown" in which the content of an actual speech by Vice-President Dan Quayle criticizing the program's content became central to the show's storyline.

THE INTERNATIONAL SCENE

- The United States and other alliance countries begin air attacks on Iraq while the leaders of these countries and the world community watch live coverage on CNN.
- The starvation-wracked bodies of Sudanese children appear on television clad in T-shirts bearing the names and faces of American television and music heroes.
- Japan integrates the jargon of communication technology into its own language, and for good measure shortens it up a bit. The subject you are studying in this course becomes "masu-komi."

The Cable News Network (CNN) newsroom in Atlanta is the center of a news operation that reaches every part of the globe.

Communication technology has always served to broaden our horizons and extend the range of information available to us. Now, with new and hybrid technologies, global communication on a scale that was only a fantasy a couple of decades ago is fast becoming a reality. TV satellite services have had a dramatic impact on the international scene. To illustrate, Cable News Network (CNN) is available in 90 countries, and MTV (the music channel) is available in 60 million homes around the world. Moreover, newspapers are printed and distributed at various geographic sites around the world via satellite, and the international distribution of books, videotapes, records, and cassettes are realities of life in the 1990s.

The impact of international media is substantial. One of the most vivid examples of the influential role of mass communication and the new media is in the area of East-West relations. There is little question that news and entertainment media have facilitated information flow and understanding among citizens of Eastern and Western countries through increasing exposure to one another's leaders, cultures, and perspectives.

Mass communication has played a more basic yet less direct role in improving East-West relations: Communication media were a stimulant to policies of *glasnost*—openness—and *peristroika*—change—within the former Soviet Union. With today's sophisticated communication technologies, it has become increasingly difficult for leaders of a society to seal off their citizenry from the global community.

Where evolution and revolution lead toward increased citizen participation in government, there is also a corresponding shift away from government control

TECHNOLOGY

CNN Links "Global Village"

The events of "Desert Storm" vividly demonstrated that the global village has already become a reality. CNN is available in 90 countries, and the world—and its diplomatic and military leaders—watched as the air attacks on Iraq and Kuwait were broadcast live. The crisis in the Middle East reminds us that, with today's sophisticated media, even weather information has become a valuable international commodity. Great care was taken to be certain that forecasts on the Persian Gulf area were not broadcast in such detail or with such timeliness that they would strategically benefit Iraq.

---

over content and financing of mass communication institutions. They are being replaced with mass communication systems more like our own, in which the marketplace plays a more central role in regulating and paying for production and distribution. Speaking specifically of the countries in the former Soviet Union, Yassen Zassoursky, professor and dean of the School of Journalism at Moscow University, indicates that there is much to be done. The new structures mean that mass communicators will be far more accountable to their audiences than to the government. Implied also is a more active and meaningful role for consumers. At the same time, assurances of financial support from the government will lessen, as mass communication institutions must compete in the marketplace for funds to support their operations.[3]

In the Eastern European countries of Poland, Czechoslovakia, and Hungary, a number of developments are taking place:

- New laws governing print media are being written.
- Print media are still mainly advocacy publications, connected to governments, political parties, or factions, rather than being completely independent.
- Broadcasting media are under government control, but independent, privately initiated broadcasting is being considered.
- Journalistic quality is mixed, and there is a need for non-communist-oriented schools to provide alternative approaches to the education of mass communication professionals.[4]

In Eastern Europe as in the former Soviet Union countries, the transition will not be an easy one. Notes Janos Elek, journalist and senior specialist at Hungarian Television, after the initial euphoria in Eastern Europe, people in the media have sobered up to the daunting tasks facing them. "We have many questions . . . but very few answers. . . . We are like the man . . . who suddenly learns he can fly, but though he learns to fly, it's also a lot of trouble."[5]

As we shall see in the pages ahead, the developments and consequences of the Information Age discussed thus far are only the tip of the iceberg. New media have given us a number of new options for creating, distributing, and displaying messages, and these new possibilities have also opened the door to innovative ways of thinking about the nature of the mass communication process itself. Where once *mass communication* was equated with *mass media*—such as radio, television, newspapers, and magazines—there is now a need for a broader view, which takes account of new media and other mass communication institutions.

CULTURE: SOCIETY'S INFORMATION BASE

Symbols are basic to the culture of each society. By *culture*, we mean the language, knowledge, ideologies, customs, folklore, heroes, rituals, habits, and life-styles that are characteristic of a society. Culture provides a kind of knowledge or *information base* that links and gives a common identity to members of a particular society.

Spoken and written language are the most basic cultural elements, but other symbols serve this same role. Particular objects, places, people, ideas, documents, songs, and even folktales may be important to a culture. For Americans, the Statue of Liberty, Washington, D.C., Abraham Lincoln, the concept of freedom of speech, the Constitution, "The Star Spangled Banner," and the story of George Washington and the cherry tree are important symbols in the web of culture. All have their own prized meanings, and their shared appreciation unites members of the culture in a common identity. While the specific elements of cultures vary from one society to another, the linking and collective identity functions they serve are comparable within all societies.

THE ROLE OF MASS COMMUNICATION

THE ELECTRONIC CHURCH

From a viewer of the "700 Club":

I was watching [the program] on Christmas Eve and I had an experience, and then I just started watching it all the time. . . . I had seen it before, but I had never really followed it. My hand had just hit the (remote control) button and they were

Many institutions within society contribute to the creation, perpetuation, and evolution of culture. Schools play a very basic part in the creation, distribution, and sharing of culture, as do churches, governments, and the business community. *Mass communication* is the process through which the information base of a culture is created, distributed, and shared. *Mass media* are institutions that are formed specifically to engage in the mass communication process. These mass communication institutions play indispensable roles through the packaging, distributing, popularizing, validating, and commercializing of the cultural information base.

Packaging and Distribution of Culture

In any society, mass communication institutions package and distribute the cultural information base. This information base consists of the news and entertainment programs, public relations, and advertising, along with other information products and services provided by libraries, museums, theme and amusement parks, software producers, database services, art galleries, sports, and even shopping malls.

Mass media such as newspapers, television, and film have long played a fundamental role in packaging and transmitting cultural information. Many other organizations whose primary function is not mass communication in the usual sense of the term now also possess their own facilities for disseminating information to local, national, and sometimes international audiences.[6] For instance, a number of corporations and religious groups have their own telecommunication production and broadcast systems.

Chapter 1   The Impact of the Information Age on Everyday Life   11

> there saying the "sinner's prayer." It was a mistake, really, I hadn't planned on watching it. I must have passed out or something, because suddenly I was crying. I just sat there and cried for fifteen minutes, and then I found myself sitting there talking to them on the telephone.... I didn't even know what had happened. The lady on the phone... explained to me that I had given my life to Christ and that I was now a new person. I was healed of everything, in an instant. I was healed of smoking cigarettes, alcohol, drinking, in a matter of seconds, it went away, just like that.
>
> *Source:* Stewart M. Hoover, *Mass Media Religion: The Social Sources of the Electronic Church* (Newbury Park, CA: Sage, 1988); and Stewart M. Hoover, "The Electronic Church as Therapeutic Community," in Gary Gumpert and Sandar L. Fish, eds., *Talking to Strangers: Mediated Therapeutic Communication* (Norwood, NJ: Ablex, 1990), pp. 214–222.

Televangelist Robert H. Schuller's Sunday morning service from the Crystal Cathedral is carried to millions of homes by television.

Popularizing and Validating Function

While the concept of a cultural information base may seem abstract, its consequences are not. In describing his early years growing up in Harlem, noted sociologist Irving Louis Horowitz provides insights into the subtle yet pervasive impact of communication-based cultural realities:

> Saturdays were special. Between noon and 6:00 p.m. we entered the magic world of the moviehouse.... They all had in common an entrance fee of ten cents.... [T]he films may have been two years old, or even older. But to a mind so young, no films are dated. Cowboys are good, Indians bad.... So Saturday was a crucial day not to be tampered with....
>
> The films had a narcotizing effect on us. I recollect always being stunned walking out into the daylight afterward. It was as if the outside world was an illusion, and the movies inside the realities being left behind."[7]

Through mass communication, concepts of what is real and make-believe, right and wrong are distributed from place to place and from generation to generation, and in the process, are popularized and sanctioned. News, entertainment, sports, and advertising programming tell us stories about people and how they live, provide insights into how people think, and portray the consequences of particular behaviors. In subtle ways, they provide lessons about friendship, family life, war, crime, music, religion, and politics. Whether the topic is sex, violence, drugs, or racial issues, they contribute to the visibility, currentness, and validity of the topics they address.

News and Informational Programming: Agenda of Concerns and Ways of Thinking.
Sometimes intentionally, but more often unintentionally, news and

informational programming have the effect of popularizing and validating particular concerns and ideologies (ways of thinking) by ignoring or discrediting others. Even interviews and public opinion polls contribute to the popularity and legitimacy of certain issues through the choices that information producers make. Interviews and polls, for example, deal with particular topics and questions. Many topics are available, but only some are included. To ask respondents their opinions on environmental pollution, a political candidate, or a governmental policy is to state by implication that these are important topics of the day. Their importance is further underscored when the results of the poll are published. These selected topics are given a visibility and legitimacy that is not afforded to other topics of perhaps equal significance that were not selected for examination.

Mass communication news and informational programming contributes to the popularization and legitimation of culture through the selection of what is and what is not to be "news." It also contributes to the cultural agenda by the interpretation (or lack of interpretation) of news events, and through the way "causes" and "effects" are implied.

Entertainment Programming: Gender Roles and Life-styles. Entertainment programs contribute importantly to the web of culture, often in subtle ways. Few topics inspire interest and controversy as much as discussions of male and female roles, their appropriateness, significance, and origins.

Concerns about the popularizing and validating functions of entertainment are well exemplified in the controversy on "family values" that was triggered by the portrayal of single parenthood on the "Murphy Brown" show. "Who's the Boss" is an example of a television program that has made a direct and forceful statement about gender roles, by reversing stereotypes. Angela, the head of the house, is a tough-minded, independent, detached, no-nonsense professional. Tony, on the other hand, is the supportive, dependent, cuddly, "I'm-here-whenever-you-need-me" housekeeper, exemplifying characteristics more frequently associated with the "traditional woman" stereotype.

Soap operas and call-in shows like "Dr. Ruth" can also be examined in terms of their embedded cultural messages. With their emphasis on interpersonal intrigue, entanglements, and intimate dialogue, they reinforce the idea that intimate conversation and self-disclosure are appropriate ways to cope with personal and social problems. Studies also suggest that "soaps" often portray men as sensitive to interpersonal problems, and women as occupying professional roles with substantial power, which has the effect of giving these behaviors and themes increased cultural legitimacy.[8]

Advertising: Economics and Consumption. In addition to providing persuasive content for particular products or services, advertisements also include more general—and more subtle—cultural messages regarding economics and consumption: They urge us to become consumers. Encouraging consumption is a universal theme in advertising and many promotional efforts. However, rarely is the message "We want you all to get out there and buy all kinds of things and services" made explicit. One area where this theme is apparent is in advertising for credit cards. College students are a prime target of these campaigns. Direct mailings and "take an application" posters urge their audience "to establish your credit now" and assure that the bank will "say yes" when the application is submitted. The implicit economics lesson is a simple one: It is important to be a consumer, it is necessary to establish credit—the sooner the better—and it is good to buy on

Chapter 1   The Impact of the Information Age on Everyday Life   **13**

 RESEARCH

Values Embedded in TV Programs

A study analyzing the content of weekday prime-time shows from the three major networks for two weeks—excluding sports, news shows, cartoons, and movies—found that incidents involving values play an important role in programming.

The researcher identified a total of 1148 value incidents in the programs studied. Of these, 49.4 percent dealt with *values toward others*, such as respect for the rights of all, respect for different views, and compassion for others. About one-quarter (26.3 percent) dealt with *values toward self*, for instance, personal integrity, honesty, and courage to express conviction.

Just over 20 percent (20.8 percent) related to *values toward both self and others*, such as sense of duty and respect for property. The remaining value incidents (3.5 percent) concerned *citizenship values*, like patriotism, citizens' rights, citizens' responsibilities, and legal authority.

The study concludes: "The personal values that are endemic to American culture are deeply embedded in the programming material of its most favored entertainment medium."

Source: Gary W. Selnow, "Values in Prime-Time Television," *Journal of Communication*, 40:2, Spring 1990, pp. 64–74.

THE NEWS IMAGE

In general, news programs implicitly present "an optimistic faith in a good society, [in which] businessmen and women will compete with each other in order to create increased prosperity for all . . . [and] will refrain from unreasonable profits and gross exploitation of workers or consumers."

Source: Herbert Gans, *Deciding What's News* (New York: Pantheon, 1979), p. 46.

credit. For many of us, this particular economics and consumer behavior message is reiterated on a near-daily basis by offers from credit card companies.

When the public decides that particular kinds of advertising are a negative cultural force, pressure for restraint is applied. In such instances, advertising may be regulated by external agencies, as with the bans on television cigarette advertising. Or a sponsor, in an effort to avert the threat of such regulation, may initiate

Is the day far off when hundreds, perhaps hundreds of thousands of people engage in play together through computer links?

RESEARCH

Prime-Time Culture: Sex on TV

How does TV programming today compare with 20 or 30 years ago in terms of the amount of sexual material presented? Research comparing sexual context—references or acts—of today's prime-time television for a sample week in 1989 to a sampling of prime-time shows in the 1950s and 1960s found the following:

- Today's shows had an average of 5.3 sexual incidents per hour compared with 3.5 in 1950s and 1960s programs.
- Fox network programs averaged 9.4 incidents per hour. NBC averaged 6.5; CBS, 5.7; and ABC, 3.6.

Source: Rhoda Estep, California State University, Stanislaus. Paper presented at the Society for the Scientific Study of Sex, San Francisco, March, 1990.

---

pro-social advertising. Messages from beer companies urging moderation in consumption—"knowing when to say when," for instance—do this by presenting what amounts to a kind of "reverse advertising." Perhaps in the future we will see ads by credit card companies promoting moderation in buying on credit and suggesting limiting the number of credit cards consumers apply for.

Sports: Heroes and Villains. Sporting events provide another interesting illustration of the ways in which mass communication products serve as carriers of cultural messages. Dan Nimmo and James Combs in *Mediated Political Realities* discuss how sports programming prepares viewers for political participation in society. Sporting events, particularly when distributed by mass media, are presented as suspense-filled contests with heroes and villains. They present a story of the "triumph of justice or the intervention of fortune, . . . heroic deeds and untimely errors, dramatic climaxes, and the euphoria of the victors along with the gloom of the vanquished."[9] The authors argue that mass media coverage and sports commentators contribute further to the melodramatic nature of sports by introducing rivalries and quarrels among players, salary and contract disputes, fights and fines, winning and losing, romance and death. Sporting events teach about playing by the rules, losing gracefully, sportsmanship, competition, and persistence.

In even more obvious ways, mass communication entertainment and news products and services fulfill this same *cultural popularization and legitimation function* for individuals. The visibility provided by mass communication is a major force in creating celebrity status for certain individuals in sports, politics, religion, the arts, and advertising. And often with popularity comes the legitimating of particular dress, hair, behaviors, and life-styles. Through mass communication, particular heroes, buildings, places, songs and other symbols are also given visibility and currency.

Video Games: Control and Consequences. Video games also provide implicit cultural messages.

> Trees, people, houses, animals, and other cars buzz back and forth across the road in front of your metallic red Porsche 944 as you screech around the turns. Suddenly a bike pulls out in front of you and you are forced to swerve off the road into a ditch, where your car crashes into a brick wall and blows up.[10]

INSIGHT

"Your Sneakers or Your Life"

- Atlanta, September 1988: An unnamed 17-year-old was robbed of a Mercedes-Benz hat and Avia hightop shoes after the boy's companion was shot by the assailant.
- Houston, April 1989: 16-year-old Johnny Bates was shot to death by a 17-year-old after he refused to give up his Air Jordan hightop shoes.
- Anne Arundel County, Maryland, May 1989: 15-year-old Michael Eugene Thomas was found strangled. A 17-year-old acquaintance allegedly killed the boy for his two-week-old Air Jordan basketball shoes.
- Chicago, 1989: 19-year-old Calvin Walsh was fatally shot when he refused to give his Cincinnati Bengal jacket to assailants.
- Atlanta police estimate there were at least 50 cases involving robberies of sportsgear in the first four months of 1990.
- Chicago police indicate that about 50 incidents involving jackets and a dozen involving gym shoes are reported each month.

"These assailants aren't simply taking clothes from their victims. They're taking status. Something is very wrong with a society . . . in which pieces of rubber and plastic are sometimes worth more than a human life. . . . With . . . million-dollar advertising campaigns, superstar spokesmen and over-designed, high-priced products aimed at impressionable young people, [sportswear producers] are creating status from thin air to feed those who are starving for self-esteem."

Estimates indicate that the shoe industry spends some $200 million a year on advertising; Nike alone spent approximately $60 million on TV and print advertising in 1990.

Source: Rick Telander, "Senseless," *Sports Illustrated,* 72:20, May 14, 1990, pp. 36–49.

Is this a problem? Not if the press of a button brings you back to the start of the track in the same shiny Porsche—and this is exactly how things work in the world of video-gaming. One of the strongest messages that video games send is immortality, and the possibility to redo what went wrong without consequence.[11] Home video games come equipped with a "reset" button that allows the player to have a fresh start at any time without consequence. Inserting a quarter in a coin-operated machine accomplishes the same goal. In some games the character on the screen merely needs to swallow a "power pill" to be granted a few additional lives. If you don't like the particular situation you're in, the touch of a button wipes your troubles away. Obviously, these lessons can be a problem if applied to real-life situations:

> It is much easier to rid oneself of a mutant ninja turtle with no regrets than it is to delete a lover or "reset" a relationship. The turtle is much more forgiving, and will have no regrets about playing the same game again with no recollection of the previous interaction. Many video games offer the consumer a pause control. When a player wants to take a break from a particular game, and to return later, the touch of a button makes this possible. When the individual returns, hours or days later, he or she will find the game patiently waiting at the same place it was when stopped, another luxury unfortunately absent in everyday encounters.[12]

Commercializing Function

Mass communication often plays a role in giving commercial value to and helping to sell particular cultural symbols. In this sense, mass communication institutions are part of the cultural industry, which the United Nations Educational, Scientific, and Cultural Organization (UNESCO) describes as an industry involved in the large-scale production, reproduction, storage, or distribution of cultural goods and services.[13]

Herbert Schiller, a mass communication and culture scholar, writes that increasingly, "cultural creation has been transformed into discrete, specialized forms, commercially produced and marketed. Speech, dance, drama (ritual), music, and the visual and plastic arts have been vital, indeed necessary, features of human experience from earliest times. What distinguishes their situation in the [present] . . . era are the relentless and successful efforts to separate these elemental expressions of human creativity from their group and community origins for the purpose of *selling them* to those who can pay."[14]

Mass communication plays a major role in the commercialization of celebrities, brand names, art objects, music, and other elements of culture. This is especially obvious in areas where the popularization of particular individuals through mass communication has given great value to them, their names, and anything associated with them. One example is endorsement of clothes or other athletic gear by sports figures. Another is the selling of autographs—a common practice at baseball card shows and other events. Commercialization also takes place when a celebrity's name is added to other products, services, or ideas as a way of enhancing value or marketability. Ironically, mass communication plays a role in giving celebrities commercial value, and is then used to enhance the value of products or services they endorse.

Not only people, but also fictional characters are commercialized after being created by mass communication: consider Big Bird, Miss Piggy, Mickey Mouse, and the Teenage Mutant Ninja Turtles. So too, mass communication is essential in the commercialization of places such as Disney World, Central Park, Beverly Hills, Fort Lauderdale, Las Vegas, New York, and Paris.

ORIGINS OF THE CONCEPT OF MASS COMMUNICATION

To understand mass communication today and the pervasive role it plays in our lives, it is helpful to have an appreciation of the ways in which our thinking about the process has evolved over the years. It is difficult to determine precisely when the concept of mass communication was first developed, but we can trace the roots of the idea to the ancient Greeks. Greece was then an oral culture, and one had be skilled in speaking persuasively to large audiences in order to carry out basic daily activities. As a result, scholars of the time became interested in studying the art of public speaking.

A Foundation in Public Speaking

Aristotle (385–322 B.C.) was a central figure in early communication study. He regarded communication as both an art to be practiced and a discipline to be studied—a perspective that continues in the field today. Aristotle thought about the process of communication in terms of public communication involving an orator, a speech, and hearers, as illustrated in Figure 1.1. In his terms, "the *orator*

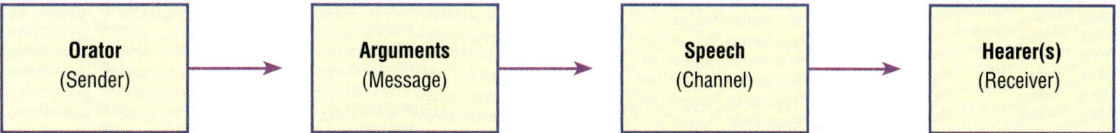

FIGURE 1.1 **Aristotle's Approach** Aristotle saw public speaking as consisting of an orator (sender) who constructs arguments (messages) and transmits them through speech in order to persuade hearers (members of the audience) of the correctness of a particular position.

must not only try to make the *argument* of his speech demonstrative and worthy of belief, he must also make his own character look right and put his *hearers*, who are to decide, into the right frame of mind" (emphasis added).[15] With this notion, Aristotle identified what have come to be the basic elements for many traditional models of mass communication: An *orator* who is the *speaker*, an *argument* that is the *message*, *speech* that is the *channel*, and hearers—a *public audience*—receivers.

The Beginning of Journalism

The area that has contributed even more directly to the heritage of mass communication study is journalism. Historians trace the first practice of journalism to Egypt, some 3700 years ago, when a record of the events of the time was transcribed on the tomb of an Egyptian king. In subsequent years, Julius Caesar had the day's news posted in a public place, as well as having additional copies printed and available for sale.[16]

Predecessors of today's newspapers were a combination of newsletters, ballads, proclamations, political tracts, and pamphlets. In the mid-1600s newspapers in the modern form emerged, with the first paper published in the United States in 1690, *Publick Occurrences Both Foreign and Domestick*. While the roots of journalistic practice are lengthy, interest in journalism as an academic area of study in the United States did not emerge until the early 1900s.

THE CONCEPT EVOLVES: THE IMPACT OF MASS MEDIA

Great advances were made in mass communication theory during the twentieth century. Interest in the mass communication process was influenced by work in the field of speech, and even more so by developments in journalism and by technological advances in the marketplace. The advent of radio, film, and television gave increased impetus to efforts to better understand mass communication, and led naturally to the development of a concept that emphasized the role of *mass media*—including technologies like newspapers and radio, which were capable of disseminating messages to large, geographically dispersed audiences.

The S→M→C→R Perspective

During the late 1940s, the 1950s, and the 1960s, a number of writers contributed in important ways to the advancement of our understanding of the mass communication process as they sought to come to grips with the role of mass media in human communication. One of the major contributors to our thinking about mass communication was political scientist Harold Lasswell. Although Lasswell's view grew out of his studies of propaganda, the model he developed in 1948 provided a broad and useful approach to mass communication more generally.

In essence, Lasswell defined communication as "who says what to whom in what channel with what effect."[17] Mass communication was seen as a fairly straightforward, one-way process whereby a *source* creates a *message*, and transmits it through a *channel* to a *receiver*, thereby bringing about *effects* or *outcomes*, as portrayed in Figure 1.2. In the case of an article on Madonna in *Rolling Stone*, for instance, the reporter/writer of the story would be the *source*, the story would be the *message*, *Rolling Stone* would be the *channel*, and the readers would be the *audience*. The *effect* might be to inform or entertain.

Lasswell's approach reflected a much broader view of communication than that suggested by Aristotle, for whom the major channel was speech. Lasswell's notion of *channel* emphasized the important role played by media in the mass communication process. And, his concept of *effect* suggested that a number of outcomes may result from mass communication. As with the Madonna example above, the Lasswell model suggests that an audience can be informed, entertained, offended, persuaded, or any of a number of other possibilities.

Over the years, theorists expanded on Lasswell's concept, creating other models of mass communication, all of which exemplify, in varying degrees, what may be labeled the S→M→C→R *perspective*. Sometimes termed the *hypodermic-needle approach*, this view sees mass communication as involving a *source* who constructs a *message* and transmits it through a *channel* (or medium) to *receivers*, thereby bringing about specific *effects*, much as a nurse might inoculate patients by injecting them with a vaccine (see Figure 1.3).

Deficiencies of the S→M→C→R Perspective

The S→M→C→R concept of mass communication has been valuable to our understanding in many respects. It has helped to identify the important elements in the mass communication process, clarify the relationship between components, explain the powerful role of mass communication in our lives, underscore some of the important functions served by mass media, and guide research on mass communication process and effects. The framework also has its shortcomings, and these limitations are particularly apparent when we try to apply the models to the interactive media of the Information Age.

S→M→C→R Is Simplistic. Traditional S→M→C→R approaches portrayed mass communication in simple terms. Emphasis was placed on a single mass communication event—a source creating and transmitting a message through a channel to audience members. This way of thinking about mass communication focuses on an instant in time. It "freezes" the ongoing dynamics in much the same way

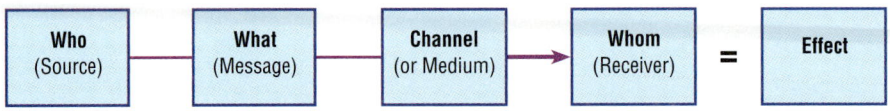

FIGURE 1.2 **Lasswell's Approach** Lasswell saw the communication process being defined by "*Who* (source) says *what* (message) to *whom* (members of the audience) in what *channel* with what *effect.*"

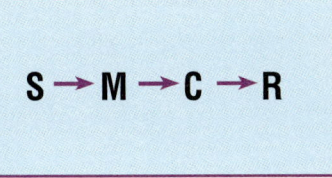

FIGURE 1.3   **The S→M→C→R Approach** The S→M→C→R approach views mass communication as a one-way process in which a source produces and transmits a message or messages through a channel to receivers. Limitations of this approach include presenting a static and overly simplistic view, minimizing the influence of various contexts and levels of communication, portraying audience members as passive, and limiting usefulness for describing mass communication using newer, interactive technologies.

that the "pause" button on a VCR stops the action in a taped sporting event. Unfortunately, this approach tends to obscure the complexity and process-like nature of mass communication. In actuality, people are often engaged in a number of mass communication events more or less simultaneously, with multiple media, messages, and sources. An example is a student reading a book while glancing periodically at a favorite movie on television. Even over the course of five minutes, the nature of mass communication involving this student, the book, and the television may be very complex and variable—far more so than would be suggested by a single "freeze-action shot."

Moreover, a focus on a single mass communication event involving a source, message, channel, and receiver tends to divert attention from complex, continuing processes that occur at an institutional and societal level. A more inclusive perspective is needed to highlight the role mass communication institutions play in the mass production and distribution of news, entertainment, and cultural fashions.

S→M→C→R Ignores Other Influences on Communication.   It is easy to see why theorists might choose to focus on *source, message, media,* and *audience* in their efforts to try to characterize mass communication. However, this perspective fails to recognize how much interplay there is between mass communication and communication in face-to-face, group, organizational, or societal settings.

Face-to-face communication can have a great influence on our use of information provided through mass communication. This would be the case, for instance, if the student we discussed previously is diverted from his reading and TV viewing when his sister enters the room and initiates a conversation. There is also the less obvious, indirect impact of the groups of which we are members, the organizations for which we work, and the society and world community in which we live. These groups can and do have an important impact on the mass communication process. They have an influence on the attitudes, values, and preferences which guide our decisions as to what information sources we pay attention to, and how we interpret and use information. Our reactions to a particular movie are influenced by what we hear others say about the film, and by the values and attitudes we have learned through face-to-face communication with family and friends.

These same influences also shape the kind of mass communication programming that is *created*. The individuals who write, produce, and direct films are also participants in a number of relationships, groups, and organizations, which play an important role in shaping the attitudes and values that permeate their work.

Interpersonal messages—one person trying to reach another—share space with mass communication messages on a campus bulletin board.

Advocacy groups, such as those opposed to violence and sexuality on prime-time television, also influence viewing behavior and may influence advertisers to cancel their sponsorship of programs.

The reverse is also true: Communication in face-to-face, group, and organizational settings is influenced by mass communication. As one example, think of the situation of two individuals who do not know one another starting up a conversation about a basketball game they are watching on a television set displayed in a department store.

S→M→C→R Suggests That Audience Members Are Passive. An S→M→C→R perspective suggests that the source, the message, and the medium exert tremendous influence on the outcomes of mass communication. It may well lead to the conclusion that members of the audience are passive, helpless victims of the process, wholly controlled by the messages of the mass media.

As members of mass communication audiences, we are indeed influenced in ways of which we may be largely unaware. For instance, few of us probably ever have thought much about how we have been influenced to recognize the face of Dan Rather or Vanna White, or the music of Billy Joel or Whitney Houston. That knowledge, like so much other knowledge we have, arises as a consequence of being members of mass communication audiences.

We also know that as receivers we play active, discriminating roles in the mass communication process. As audience members we can and do engage in active decision making about whether to give our attention to particular mass media offerings, and in many instances we can actively and consciously choose *how* to use the information we receive. We are not forced to read a particular newspaper or magazine, watch "Murphy Brown" or "Roseanne," or listen to or buy records

Chapter 1   The Impact of the Information Age on Everyday Life

Buying the Sunday paper is a ritual; sorting out the sections makes the consumer the ultimate editor of the paper.

produced by Prince or Gloria Estafan. These are choices we make as members of the potential audience for particular media products. Whether as an individual or as a member of the collective audience, we can and do play an active, vital, and highly influential role in the process of mass communication.

Interactive Media Do Not Fit the S→M→C→R Model.   With the S→M→C→R concept of mass communication, the content and availability of information products are seen as controlled by the source and media. That was quite appropriate for traditional mass media like television, radio, newspapers, books, or magazines.

The media of the Information Age—VCRs, cable television, and personal computers—are more *interactive*, however. They permit audience members to exert greater control over content, timing, and locale. To take one example, there are thousands of audiocassette tapes available for use at whatever time of day or night we choose to listen. And we may choose to play these tapes at home, at work, in

 **TECHNOLOGY**

Faxing Democracy

The fax machine became an instrument of democracy in 1989, when Chinese students living in various countries used fax machines to flood their homeland with reports of the massacre in Tiananmen Square. In 1990, the same technology was used to facilitate voting by GIs stationed in Saudi Arabia. Normally, when done by mail, it takes at least a month. By fax, voting was completed within 24 hours.

Source: The New York Times, November 2, 1990, p. A-34.

The concert hall in your head takes a mass experience and converts it into a personal experience.

the car, or while walking or jogging. We can "fast-forward" through selections we don't care for, "pause" for interruptions, and "freeze" or "rewind" to repeat portions we particularly like.

S→M→C→R Does Not Explain How Mass Communication Transforms Information. S→M→C→R concepts of mass communication may keep us from realizing that information does not remain intact as it moves from the source to the audience. Every step in the preparation and handling process alters information. Even a source's initial act of preparing a message is a creative act. Two reporters may create very different stories though they have both witnessed the "same" crime scene: One may focus on the victim while the other describes police action in finding the criminal.

As the information created by a source moves along its way to the ultimate audience member, it undergoes a number of transformations. It is altered by each person, and may also be influenced by the channels through which it passes, even with the best of intentions and the highest quality technology.

 **TECHNOLOGY**

Television Consumers Become Producers

Technological advances promise to make broadcast television a far more interactive, viewer-controlled medium. For about the price of a movie channel, cable system subscribers in Montreal are able to play a direct and active role in creating sports and news coverage. With the new system, viewers may select from among four different views of the event on four different channels. In the case of sporting events, one channel provides the traditional "wide angle" coverage. Other channels offer close-ups of players, while yet another provides continuous instant replays. For news programs, the system allows viewers to break away from the standard newscast at various points to receive more in-depth information on a news story of particular interest, and later to return to the "standard" broadcast. Other applications are being developed and market-tested.

A FRAMEWORK FOR UNDERSTANDING MASS COMMUNICATION IN THE INFORMATION AGE: THE P↔I↔C MODEL

New media present new options for mass communication professionals, the industry, and audience members, and these challenge all of us to reexamine our ways of defining mass communication. For us, the result has been the development of what we call the P↔I↔C model, shown in Figure 1.4, and used as the organizing framework for this book. In the model, *P* stands for *Information Producer*, *I* for *Information Products and Services*, and *C* for *Consumer(s)*. Mass communication is defined as

> The process through which information products and services are created and distributed by an organization for consumption by an audience.

The P↔I↔C approach overcomes many of the limitations of the S→M→C→R. As we shall see in more detail in the pages ahead, the P↔I↔C approach emphasizes

P — Production

Description: Mass communication organizations create and distribute information products and/or services

Organizations:
- Television networks
- Newspaper publishers
- Movie producers
- Magazine publishers
- Book publishers
- Record companies
- Advertising agencies
- Public relations firms
- Libraries
- Museums
- Information services
- Etc.

I — Information Products and Services

Description: Information products and/or services are distributed to an audience

Products/Services:
- Television programs
- Newspapers
- Movies
- Magazines
- Books
- Records/tapes
- Ads
- Public relations campaigns
- Documents
- Exhibits
- Research reports/databases
- Etc.

C — Consumption

Description: Information products and services compete for the attention of, acceptance by, and use by audiences

Audiences:
- Individuals
- Couples, families, co-workers, etc.
- Groups
- Organizations
- Societies

Uses/Impact:
- Information
- Entertainment
- Persuasion
- Education
- Diversion
- Motivation
- Deception
- Socialization
- Etc.

FIGURE 1.4   P↔I↔C Model of Mass Communication

the complex two-way nature of mass communication and highlights the influence exerted by consumers as well as producers.

The Process: Production, Distribution, and Consumption

Using the concepts of process, production, distribution, and consumption is quite deliberate. The Industrial Revolution brought an age in which the mass production, distribution, and consumption of *industrial* goods were central to the economic and social fabric of our society. In a similar way, the communication revolution has brought us to an age wherein the basic commodity is *information*, rather than industrial goods.

A *process* is an activity that consists of a number of separate but interrelated steps that occur over time. A consumer product such as an automobile begins as raw materials, which are then transformed through the various steps of manufacture. Mass communication products are also "manufactured." Through a series of interconnected activities of production, distribution, and consumption, raw data and symbols are transformed into usable, meaningful information packages. A politician's press conference is attended by a reporter and taping crew; a script is written and the tape edited; and finally, the information from the politician appears as a two-minute segment on the Six O'Clock News. These products are then sold to consumers, or to advertisers or sponsors who underwrite costs of the production and distribution process.

When we talk about the *production* of information, we mean *the creation, gathering, and/or rearrangement of information*. This description of mass communication includes the work of a broad range of institutions and professionals. For instance, from this perspective we can identify the work of television news departments and newspaper editorial staffs as involving the gathering, reorganizing, and rearranging of information. And, viewed in this way, it is clear that public relations professionals, textbook authors, and even museum curators are engaging in a similar process in their work.

Whereas Industrial Age production involved commodities like automobiles, sewing machines, and washing machines, mass communication in the Information Age involves the mass production of news, entertainment, public relations, advertising, and *popular culture*—symbols, artifacts, fashions, and social practices, which become widely adopted by members of a society.

By *distribution*, we mean the movement of mass communication products from the point of production to the point of consumption. Sometimes the movement occurs immediately, as with a live television broadcast. In other instances the distribution involves substantial time delays, as with magazines, books, films, records, or taped TV programs.

Consumption refers to the uses, impacts, and effects that mass communication can have for a single individual, a relationship, group, organization, or society. For individual audience members, examples include being informed, entertained, persuaded, educated, humored, motivated, or deceived. For a society, the influences of mass communication may be social, political, cultural, economic, or technological.

As in an industrial context, information production and consumption are parts of a single system. The products that surround us have a significant influence on consumption. Without production, there can be no consumption. Conversely, without consumption, production eventually ceases. The availability of fast sports

RESEARCH

Interactive TV Shows Bring Fugitives to Justice

Television shows that feature re-creations of unsolved crimes are credited with playing a significant role in the apprehension of criminals. "Reality-based crime shows"—programs like Fox Network's "America's Most Wanted" and NBC's "Unsolved Mysteries"—encourage viewers to call in tips on a toll-free 800 number. In the case of "America's Most Wanted," 153 of the 231 criminals profiled to date are now in custody, 101 as a direct result of viewer tips to (800) CRIME-90.

Source: Dylan Jones, "Show Brings 101st Fugitive to Justice," *USA Today*, March 13, 1990, p. 5.

---

cars is something we tend to take for granted. However, if no automobiles with high-powered engines were produced, none could be purchased by consumers. On the other hand, if autos with powerful engines were available, but no consumers purchased them, production eventually would be terminated. Similarly, we take the products of mass communication very much for granted. Our consumption of them assumes that they are produced and available to us. If consumers fail to find a use for particular information products or services—if there is no consumer demand—eventually those products or services will cease to be produced.

The *economic relationship* between the consumers and producers may be direct, indirect, or a blend of the two. In the case of movies, for instance, consumers directly underwrite production costs through their purchase of tickets. Television and radio producers and distributors, on the other hand, are supported by advertisers who want to gain access to consumers of those mass communication products. In such instances, consumers provide indirect financial support of production and distribution each time they purchase advertisers' products. With newspapers and magazines, the economic link between consumers and producers is partially direct—through payment of subscription charges—and partially indirect—through the purchase of advertisers' products.

Mass Communication Organizations

Mass communication organizations are to the Information Age what industrial organizations were to the Industrial Age. Industrial organizations mass-produce, distribute, and market industrial goods; mass communication organizations mass-produce, distribute, and market information products and services. The primary product of General Motors is automobiles, while CBS's is news and entertainment.

When we think of the idea of mass communication organizations, the first things that come to mind are *mass* media like television, radio, newspapers, and magazines, so named because they typically reach large (massive) audiences. Certainly, these mass media are our most familiar information-producing organizations. But, as we shall see, book publishers, the recording industry, museums,

INSIGHT

Mass Communication Inventories

INVENTORY: Your Mass Media Day

- Read one local newspaper and one national newspaper.
- Listen to news on the radio while waking up and while commuting.
- Read special-interest magazine aimed at your life-style.
- Scan trade publication for developments in your field of work.
- Watch the evening news on television.
- Enjoy your favorite television show.

INVENTORY: Your Mass Communication Day

- Note billboards and election campaign posters on the way to school or work.
- Read memos circulated to all employees where you work.
- Attend an educational lecture on a topic of public interest.
- Tour a historical exhibit in the lobby of a public building.
- Sort through your mail and respond to the Sierra Club survey.
- Read and discard FAX message seeking volunteers for youth project.

INVENTORY: A Newspaper Editor's Day (Producer Mode)

- Select letters-to-the-editor page for tomorrow's edition.
- Assign team of reporters to cover election campaign rally.
- Write editorial opinion on the importance of recycling.
- Review newspaper's policy on printing names of juvenile offenders.
- Choose color photo for cover of special supplement on education.
- Meet with publisher to discuss expansion of Sunday edition.

INVENTORY: A Newspaper Editor's Day (Consumer Mode)

- Read other newspapers to find out what stories they are running.
- Take calls from readers who disagree with editorial opinion.
- Lunch with Chamber of Commerce to hear mayor speak on crime.
- Watch "Oprah Winfrey" show about "Women Addicted to Soap Operas."
- Absorb trade news in *Editor & Publisher*.
- Visit the shopping mall to see if business is really down.

Inventories help us to understand how "mass communication" can be seen as broader than just "the mass media." Note, too, how the producer of information for a mass audience also must be a consumer of information.

libraries, the advertising and public relations industries, and other new Information Age organizations serve similar functions.

Information Products and Services

Information products are collections of messages that are organized in a particular way for a particular purpose for use by a particular audience. We use the term *information product* in a broad sense to include not only news, but also entertain-

A consumer shopping at a home improvement warehouse store views a videotape demonstration of how to install flooring. The videotape performs some of the roles of a salesperson (usually an example of interpersonal communication) while also serving both as an advertisement and an instruction manual (usually mass communication situations).

ment, public relations and advertising, computerized databases, and even symbolic elements of popular culture. Examples of information products are newspapers and magazine articles, television and radio newscasts or entertainment programs, fiction and nonfiction books, advertisements and public relations campaigns, phone books and computer databases, museum exhibits, and theatrical plays. *Information services* are activities associated with preparation, distribution, organization, storage, or retrieval of information. Information services include news or editorial research, public relations consulting, and electronic information delivery.

The Audience

> If the people who watch Ted Koppel decide they're tired of Ted Koppel, then Ted Koppel is gone.
>
> Ted Koppel, interviewed on "The Power Game" episode of Hedrick Smith's "Behind the Scenes" program (PBS, Channel 13, New York, 8 P.M., Jan. 4, 1989.)

The term *audience* refers to the group of individuals who have potential for being exposed to and using an information product or service. In the terminology of the Information Age, the audience is the *user group*.

Traditionally, when talking about mass communication, "audience" evoked an image of a large, diverse group of viewers or readers all being exposed to the same information at more or less the same time, and all being unknown to the information producers.[18] However, the advent of some of the new technologies like VCRs, CDs, portable cassette tape players, and personal computers suggests the value of a broadened concept of audience. The view of "audience" that we adopt does not presume that the user group must be a specific size or particularly diverse, that all of its members must be exposed to the same information at the same time, or that members of the group must be unknown to the information producers. More basic in our view is the requirement that the information product

INSIGHT

The Information Glut: Literacy for an Information Age

One of the most obvious characteristics of the Information Age culture is the increase in available information products and sources, and in the capacity and speed of devices for its storage, retrieval, and manipulation. That this is the case had led some to describe us as increasingly "information-rich." Unfortunately, for all of the richness of information in our environment, we have not experienced a similar increase in our human capacity to understand, manage, share, and productively use this voluminous wealth of information. Some writers have suggested that we are actually in worse shape now than before the arrival of the Information Age. They point to the fact that the percentage of available information that we are personally familiar with and capable of handling grows progressively smaller. The result is *information overload*, or what some have called "info glut."

An excellent example of sometimes bizarre consequences of the information explosion is a statistical table in the USA Snapshots: "A Look at Statistics That Shape Our Lives" appearing on the front page of the "Life" section of *USA Today*. The statistics compared calories contained in the low-cal dinners provided by the major airlines. From the table, information consumers learn that Continental airlines meals have the lowest average calories (385), followed by American and United (400), Pan Am (527), and TWA (620).*

One can certainly question the pressing individual or social need for or utility of this information. Would passengers select an airline based on the calories in their meals? Would they alter their in-flight eating habits based on this information? Would an airline alter its menus upon learning that its meals averaged 127 calories higher than those of another airline? Is society better served by having this information? Or is this simply an example of the creation, packaging, dissemination, and commercialization of information for its own sake—information that may actually clog the communication arteries through which far more important, relevant, and useful messages should flow?

The challenges—and the problems—of living in this "information-soaked" age are numerous. To cope with the proliferation of communication products and technology we need better skills for processing information as consumers and producers. And this, in turn, implies new ways of thinking about literacy for the Information Age.

Traditionally, definitions of literacy emphasize *the ability to read and write*. Today we need a more generic approach to literacy, one that slices into the problem of literacy at a far more fundamental level, reflecting a new understanding of the nature of communication and mass communication today. We may, indeed, need to develop a new view, one that includes not only reading and writing, but also skills in media literacy including:

- Identifying alternative communication and information products and services;
- Evaluating the usefulness of alternative media, products, and services;
- Accessing and retrieving information;
- Organizing, classifying, and managing information;
- Using computers and other communication technologies;
- Understanding the economics of alternative media, products, and services;
- Assessing others' information and communication needs and tastes;

Continued

> **Continued**
>
> - Developing information and communication systems, policies, and procedures;
> - Preparing information for intellectually, socially, and culturally diverse consumers; and
> - Assessing the impact of information products and services.
>
> As we move rapidly into the Information Age, there can be little doubt that full participation in society as mass communication producers and consumers will increasingly require new communication competencies of us all.
>
> *"A Look at Statistics that Shape Our Lives" *USA Today*, July 6, 1989, p. D1.

or service involved must have been deliberately produced and distributed by a mass communication organization for a particular constituency. A network television program distributed to a mass audience fits this definition, as does a videotape produced for a corporation, a church newsletter distributed to a congregation, or a museum exhibit prepared for local patrons.

THE P↔I↔C PERSPECTIVE

We believe the P↔I↔C model provides a useful framework for thinking about mass communication study and practice in an age of new and changing media. As we shall see in more detail in the chapters ahead, the approach emphasizes

- Traditional mass media and newer technologies;
- Convergence among once-distinct mass communication media, products, and services;
- Interactive capabilities of many mass communication media;
- Active decision-making roles played by mass communication producers *and* consumers;
- Complex individual, social, economic, and cultural dynamics that contribute to the interplay between mass communication producer and consumer groups; and
- General *and* specialized mass communication producers, products, services, and consumer groups.

FUTURE FILE

✓ Your telephone company soon will be able to bring you any kind of information you desire for display on your home computer or television screen. What information do you want to receive?

✓ The new electronic media provide greater flexibility as to when, where, and how we are informed and entertained. If you headed an innovative mass communication enterprise, what kinds of new information products and services would you want to develop?

✓ The P↔I↔C model suggests that consumers have a great deal to say about what kind of information is produced for their consumption. If you were a consultant for the mass media, what methods would you suggest for producers who are trying to *predict* where the consumers are headed?

NOTES

1. Everette E. Dennis, "Director's Commentary," *Communique*, 4:5, (January 1990), p. 2.
2. Edwin Parker, "Information Utilities and Mass Communication, in H. Sackman and Norman Nie, eds., *The Information Utility and Social Choice* (Montvale, NJ: AFIPS Press, 1970), p. 53.
3. Yassen Zassoursky, "Mass Communication in the Soviet Union Today." Lecture at Rutgers University, October 1989.
4. See Everette E. Dennis and Jon Vanden Heuvel, *Emerging Voices: East European Media in Transition* (New York: Gannett Center for Media Studies, 1990) for a detailed discussion of the current state of mass communication in Eastern Europe.
5. "The Rocky Airwaves of Eastern Europe," *Communique*, December 1990, p. 1.
6. Herbert Schiller, *Culture, Inc.: The Corporate Takeover of Public Expression* (New York: Oxford University Press, 1989), pp. 30–31.
7. Irving Louis Horowitz, *Daydreams and Nightmares: Reflections on a Harlem Childhood* (Jackson: University Press of Mississippi, 1990), pp. 31–32.
8. M. E. Brown and L. Barwick, "Fables and Endless Genealogies; Soap Opera and Women's Culture." Paper delivered at the Australian Screen Studies Association Conference, Sydney, December 1986.
9. Dan Nimmo and James E. Combs, *Mediated Political Realties* (New York: Longman, 1983), p. 126.
10. Robbi L. Ruben, "Lessons of Videogaming," Unpublished paper, Rutgers University, November 1989.
11. R. Ruben, 1989.
12. R. Ruben, 1989.
13. UNESCO, *Cultural Industries: A Challenge for the Future of Culture* (Paris: UNESCO, 1982), p. 21.
14. Herbert Schiller, p. 31.
15. W. Rhys Roberts, *Works of Aristotle* (Oxford: Clarendon Press, 1924), p. 1377b.
16. J. F. Frank, *The Beginnings of the English Newspaper 1620–1660* (Cambridge: Harvard University Press, 1961), p. 2.
17. Harold D. Lasswell, "The Structure and Function of Communication in Society," in Wilbur Schramm, ed., *Mass Communications* (Urbana: University of Illinois Press, 1960), p. 117.
18. Charles R. Wright, *Mass Communication: A Sociological Perspective*, 3rd ed. (New York: Random House, 1986), pp. 7–8.

SUGGESTED READINGS

Budd, Richard D., and Brent D. Ruben, *Beyond Media: New Approaches to Mass Communication*, 2nd ed. (New Brunswick, NJ: Transaction, 1988).

Dizard, Wilson P., Jr., *The Coming Information Age: An Overview of Technology, Economics, and Politics* (New York: Longman, 1989).

Mowlana, Hamid, *Global Information and World Communication: New Frontiers in International Relations* (New York: Longman, 1986).

Pool, Ithiel de Sola, *Technologies of Freedom* (Cambridge, MA: Belknap, 1983).

Schement, Jorge R., and Leah Lievrouw, *Competing Visions, Complex Realities: Social Aspects of the Information Society* (Norwood, NJ: Ablex, 1987).

Schiller, Herbert I., *Culture, Inc.* (New York: Oxford University Press, 1989).

Williams, Frederick, *Technology and Communication Behavior* (Belmont, CA: Wadsworth, 1987).

CHAPTER 2

Communication and Information Consumption

AT A GLANCE

✓ Communication between and among humans is complex because we do not all share one set of meanings for symbols.

✓ Of all types of communication, *mass* communication frequently imposes the greatest delay between sender and receiver, and thus possesses the least opportunity for assuring that the message received matches the message that is sent by the producers.

✓ Through information *selection*, each individual determines what messages will be received. Through message *interpretation*, each individual decides what meaning to assign to information. Through message *retention*, each individual decides what value to place on information received.

✓ One of the most important activities engaged in by the consumer is to decide which information has the greatest credibility and utility.

✓ The organization, presentation, and novelty of messages help determine what information will be noticed and retained by the consumer.

✓ Personal *needs* determine what information will have utility for the consumer.

Knowing the dynamics through which messages are produced and consumed is basic to an understanding of mass communication. In this chapter our focus is on the nature of human communication and the processes of information production and consumption.

UNDERSTANDING HUMAN COMMUNICATION

Communication is one of life's most fundamental activities. It is through this process that we are able to coordinate our activities with one another and, more generally, to adapt to the environment in which we live. The process of communication is necessary in order to carry out even the most basic of life's activities. In the same way that we take in oxygen and foodstuffs and transform them into the materials we need to function, we also create, take in, and process *information* that is equally necessary to life. The most fundamental activities—like moving from place to place, learning, courtship, and even reproduction—would be impossible without creating, transmitting, and processing information.

What *exactly* is human communication? To illustrate the complexity of the process, let's contrast it with the communication process that takes place among bees.

Signals, Symbols, and Meaning

When a worker bee locates a desirable food source, it announces the find to other bees in the hive by either a "round dance" or a "tail-wagging dance."[1] Bee communication works efficiently and effectively because it involves *signal language*. The message elements—the dance, the tail-waggle, and its direction—have the same significance, meaning, or information value to all members of the bee society because the meanings of the message elements are apparently genetically "programmed into" the bees. Given this, it is no wonder that the communication activities of bees and many other animals are so orderly and predictable. *A message sent is a message received*. Or, to put it another way, the meaning or information value of the signals is identical for the scout bee and for all its hive-mates.

The contrast between signal language and human symbolic language suggests why human communication is so complex and often unpredictable. The message elements we use in human communication do not necessarily mean the same things to those who create them as they do to those who receive them. Think, for instance, of the range of reactions to the symbolic content of a film, a photograph, or a concert. Human symbols—letters, numbers, words, pictures, or objects that stand for or represent something besides themselves—do not have automatic, innately shared meanings.

The sense that our messages will have depends not on genetic programming, but on the meaning, or information value, we have learned to attach to the particular set of symbols. As humans, we have to "teach" one another what we mean by the symbols we use to communicate. This teaching process goes on all the time, and it is generally so subtle that we are unaware it is happening. Some of the necessary learning, such as how to read, write, and calculate, comes from formal schooling. A good deal of this learning—what is and is not offensive or immoral,

Chapter 2   Communication and Information Consumption   35

You don't have to read Japanese—the McDonald's symbol tells you that this is an American product being marketed in Tokyo.

for instance—comes about informally from experience with parents, friends, colleagues, and as members of a society and world community. All symbols, whether words or visual, are human products. These symbols work for effective communication only if both the information creators and the information users have learned to attach similar meanings to them.

Human communication, then, involves the use of symbols in the creation, transmission, and processing of information. By *information creation* we mean the origination of messages. Information may be created in words in the form of speech, writing, or computer programs; or nonverbally by gestures or appearance, photographs, concerts, or works of art. *Transmission* refers to the movement of information from the source to the receiver. In face-to-face communication, creation and transmission occur simultaneously. The act of speaking or gesturing serves both to create and to transmit. When sender and receiver are removed from one another in time or space, transmission becomes more critical and complex—a situation typical of mass communication, wherein sender and receiver may be separated by hundreds or thousands of miles. *Information processing* involves sensing, making sense of, and using messages about circumstances, objects, and people that surround us in order to adapt to one another and our environment. Communication is *reciprocal* because communication is an ongoing process in which we serve both as information creators/transmitters *and* as information receivers/users. In the ongoing dynamics of face-to-face conversations, for instance, we engage alternately as sender and receiver—creating/transmitting verbal and nonverbal messages, sensing and making sense of other's messages, then again creating/transmitting, sensing and making sense of messages, and so on.

Simple symbols tell drivers what to expect ahead.

Communication Modes and Contexts

Information is created, transmitted, and received through one or more of the *communication modes*: visual (sight), auditory (sound), tactile (touch), olfactory (smell), and gustatory (taste). Each is essential to human communication in one way or another. In mass communication, sight and sound are most significant.

Communication occurs in a number of *contexts*, or situations, ranging from the personal and private to the more impersonal and public, as portrayed in Figure 2.1. On one end of the continuum are situations involving *intrapersonal communication* and at the other, *mass communication*.

- *Intrapersonal communication*: Sending and receiving information that we ourselves create. *Examples*: Looking into a mirror to check your appearance, in-

Personal and Private ←···→ *Impersonal and Public*

| Intrapersonal communication | Interpersonal communication | Group communication | Organizational communication | Mass communication |

FIGURE 2.1 **Contexts of Communication**

specting a cut on your finger to see if it needs bandaging, or talking to yourself about how to act at a job interview.

- *Interpersonal communication*: Sending and receiving verbal and nonverbal messages in relationships and face-to-face contexts. *Examples*: Conversing with a friend, shaking hands with an acquaintance, or exchanging glances with someone across a table.
- *Group communication*: Sending and receiving verbal and nonverbal messages in group contexts. *Examples*: Participating in a decision-making task with a group of friends, conversing at a family get-together, or taking part in a team project.
- *Organizational communication*: Sending and receiving verbal and nonverbal messages in business or organizational contexts. *Examples*: Carrying out a public relations campaign, responding to an interoffice directive, or participating in an annual meeting.
- *Mass communication*: Sending and receiving messages in an impersonal context in which source and receivers are separated from one another in time, space, or both. *Examples*: Creating a television program, reading a book, or listening to a favorite CD.

These contexts of communication are not mutually exclusive; they overlap and interrelate with one another. For instance, you engage in interpersonal communication in an organizational context when you interview for a job. You are involved in group and organizational communication when you work with a team of people in a company to prepare a news documentary for television. When you listen to a radio program and discuss it with members of your family, you are participating in group as well as mass communication.

Teleconferencing in the workplace combines interpersonal, small group, and mass communication.

Dynamics of the Communication Process

When you stand in front of a mirror, you are the *source* of information in an intrapersonal communication event. When you notice yourself, you become the *receiver*. In the ongoing dynamics of interpersonal communication situations, reciprocity is also unavoidable as we alternate frequently between the role of source and that of receiver, as when two acquaintances notice one another on the street and exchange pleasantries.

In other communication contexts, such as in organizational communication and mass communication, there is often a substantial delay between the creation and the transmission of information by one party, and its reception and use by others. For instance, it may take a considerable time for an employee in a remote office of a large corporation to get formal notification of a new institutional policy. Even though there may be a substantial time lag, communication in these circumstances still possesses its reciprocal quality. This would occur when the employee calls the central office to seek clarification on an aspect of the policy, or, in a more subtle sense, when he or she adjusts his or her actions in response to the new policy.

Mass communication typically involves the greatest delays in source/receiver reciprocity. A classic example of a mass communication receiver becoming a sender is when an individual writes a letter to the editor in response to an article that appeared in the newspaper. In some instances, sender/receiver reciprocity does not occur in this direct or obvious way. Such is the case when viewers who believe that the content of a television program is in poor taste choose not to buy the products of the advertisers who sponsor the show.

HUMAN INFORMATION CONSUMPTION

As information consumers, we are each engaged in an ongoing process of choosing among, making sense of, remembering—and sometimes forgetting—mass communication products and services. As simple and automatic as information consumption seems, it is a dynamic process involving a number of factors. *Human information consumption*, or *human information processing* as it is often called, involves three fundamental activities: *information selection, information interpretation*, and *information retention*.

Information Selection

At any instant in time, we are surrounded by a number of information sources that compete for our attention and interest. *Selection* is the process through which we choose to tune in to certain sources and information while tuning out others.

Attention to Mass Communication Sources. In most situations, several forms of communication—interpersonal, group, organizational, and mass communication—serve as sources of information. Where there are multiple sources, we select certain sources and information to attend to while disregarding others. How this occurs is a complex phenomenon that has occupied the attention of scholars over the years.[2]

INSIGHT

The Global Village

Communication technology has always served to broaden our horizons and extend the range of information available to us. Now, with new and hybrid technologies, a number of popular and scholarly writers have pointed optimistically to a future in which citizens of the world would be linked in what we might think of as a "world community" or "global village." The image is of a massive network where individuals would be united through the communication technologies with shared access to the world's information. In this vision, "Communication is the key tool in developing human potential and well-being on a mass scale."*

With global communication come new possibilities: bridging geographic, cultural, and political boundaries; sharing information and a common agenda of concerns; and ultimately, addressing local and global problems in a united way. The present and projected capabilities of today's mass communication systems are making the concept of a global village seem an increasingly feasible reality.

But is the global village really what everyone wants? Some suggest now that the barriers that could be broken with communication technology may be quite important to maintain.

There are several issues here. The United States is one of the world leaders in the production, commercialization, and export of mass communication products and services. Thus, the control of the technology and products for the global networks may well be based in the United States and other highly industrialized nations.

But many are concerned because they see Western culture imbedded in our mass communication products and services. If mass communication products from the United States, Japan, and other industrialized countries are widely consumed throughout the world, the pervasive influence of Western culture may be an inevitable, if unintended, consequence of the creation of a global village.

For a less industrialized country, the prospect of enabling its citizens to be linked to the world community in order to have access to U.S. prime-time television raises some obvious questions. Can a culture hope to preserve its identity, political or ideological integrity, and traditional values when its citizenry is plugged into "Dallas," "The Simpsons," or *Rambo*? Concerned about precisely these issues, French television and movie producers have demanded that a quota be placed on the broadcast of U.S. television programs. The goal is to ensure that at least 60 percent of Europe's TV shows are created in Europe.†

This potential for economic and content dependency raises a fundamental question that will be at the core of discussions in the 1990s: Is it possible for an individual, organization, or society to depend on others economically and technologically, but be uninfluenced by the cultural messages of mass communication products and services? Or does control of information products and information imply power? Commenting on this issue on the societal level a number of years ago, anthropologist and communication scholar Alfred G. Smith offered an observation that remains pertinent: "Today our primary resource is information. Today knowledge is the primary wealth of nations and the prime base of their power."‡ Clearly, the challenge is to reap the benefits of global communication without unnecessarily sacrificing individual and cultural integrity and independence in the process.

---

*Frank Feather and Rashmi Mayur, "Communications for Global Development: Closing the Information Gap," in Howard F. Didsbury, Jr., ed., *Communications and the Future: Prospects, Promises, and Problems* (Bethesda, MD: World Future Society, 1982), p. 343.

†Philip Revzin, "La Boob Tube: Europe Complains About U.S. Shows," *The Wall Street Journal*. October 16, 1989, p. 1-10.

‡Alfred G. Smith, "The Cost of Communication." Presidential Address, International Communication Association, 1974. Abstracted as "The Primary Resource," *Journal of Communication*, 25, 1975, pp. 15–20.

The world is brought to remote locations when a microwave dish receives signals from satellites.

Even when facing a simple decision, we make a number of complex choices of which we are scarcely aware. Consider what happens when we look away from a magazine article to answer a telephone or to respond to a question posed by someone in the room. The act of hearing the telephone or the question involves selection. Triggered by the ringing phone or by a person's voice, we begin tuning ourselves to the information necessary to the events that will follow. In so doing, we ignore other potential information sources—the temperature in the room, the color of the carpeting, the appearance of other people who may pass by, the noise of a nearby copy machine, or the thunderstorm outside.

A classic illustration of the selective reception of information is provided by parties and similar social gatherings. During such affairs it is not at all difficult to carry on a discussion without being overly distracted by other conversations. Moreover, it is possible to tune into an exchange among several persons a good distance away without changing position and while appearing to be deeply engrossed in the conversation at hand. In that same setting, we are also able to tune out the external environment in order to concentrate on our own feelings, decide what we ought to be doing, think about how we are being perceived by others, or decide when to leave. It is also possible to focus on the event in a more global framework, analyzing whether the party is sedate or wild, winding up or down, and so on.[3]

Filtering. Given these kinds of examples, it may seem as though information selection operates much like a *filter*, letting in some sounds, images, or smells, while screening out others.[4] Further examination reveals, however, that the process is often more complex than that. For instance, we know that even when we have tuned in to a particular information source and tuned out others, the "non-selected" sources may, nonetheless, be taken note of. This is the case, for instance, when a news bulletin on television or radio, which was being used only as a source of background noise, suddenly catches our attention.[5]

There is also some evidence to suggest that it is possible to take note of and to attach meaning to messages even when one is unaware of doing so.[6] Some studies have suggested that under hypnosis we may be able to remember information that we were not fully aware of selecting for attention in the first place.[7] Awareness of the complexity of the attention process has led to the adoption of a *modified filter model* as a way of thinking about selection.[8] According to this model, individuals assign priorities to competing information sources and allocate their attention among them, while monitoring other information and perhaps even attending to still other sources—sources unknown even to the individual involved—all with a minimum of conscious awareness.

Information Interpretation

A second facet of information processing is *interpretation*. When we *interpret*, we determine what significance to attach to a word, sentence, circumstance, gesture, or event. We also decide whether to regard the information as true or false, serious or humorous, new or old, contradictory or consistent, amusing or annoying.

The basic issue is one of *meaning*. Each of us must attach meaning to the information sources and the information we perceive. Because this is an individual process, the meanings we assign are unique for each of us.

News and Entertainment. The process of interpretation is essential to mass communication consumption. Mass communication producers draw clear distinctions among news, entertainment, advertising, and public relations. These distinctions are based on their purpose and content. News products and services are *intended to inform* consumers by providing factual and timely information as to significant events going on around them. Entertainment programming is *designed to entertain*—to serve as a source of diversion, amusement, or engagement without particular regard to the accuracy or timeliness of the content. Advertising and public relations are *intended to influence* consumer buying behaviors or points of view through persuasive information.

INSIGHT

Prime Time Deals with Cancer

Entertainment programming often serves informative functions—sometimes unintentionally, sometimes by design. An example of the latter is "Why, Charlie Brown, Why?" produced in association with the American Cancer Society. In the prime-time special, cartoonist Charles Schulz explains the effects of cancer to young viewers and explores possible cures. In the story, Charlie Brown and Linus are concerned about a classmate, Janice, who is suffering from leukemia. Covered topics include chemotherapy treatment and stages of reaction to cancer—hurt, denial, and anger. Explains executive producer Lee Mendelson, "We're in the entertainment medium, but we've also tried to educate from time to time."

Cancer—ovarian cancer, in particular—was also a topic of two episodes of "thirtysomething." Phone requests to the "800" ovarian cancer information line doubled in the period following the programs.

Source: Ray Bobbin, " 'Peanuts' Looks at Leukemia," Tribune News Services, March 11, 1990; *USA Today*, March 21, 1990, p. 1D.

The *Christian Science Monitor*, a venerable national newspaper, has spawned an electronic counterpart: Christian Science Monitor Television.

While these distinctions may be clear and sensible from the producer's perspective, there is no assurance that consumers will arrive at the intended interpretations or derive the intended outcomes. Depending on the meanings consumers attach to particular mass communication products, it is quite possible for entertainment programming to inform or persuade, or for news programming to entertain and so on.

RESEARCH

Our Impressions of the Police: Where Do They Come From?

In a *New York Times* poll regarding police activity, only 4 percent of those surveyed said they formed their impressions from television entertainment-oriented police programs; 57 percent indicated that their impressions were based on news reports, and 37 percent said their knowledge came from personal contacts. Yet, 82 percent of those surveyed who had a favorite police show said they believed it was generally accurate. In contrast, 84 percent of police surveyed said TV programs present an inaccurate view of police work. Mark Penn, a partner in the polling firm, concluded that given "people's answers about the realism they see in police shows, I think they definitely get more of their impressions from TV shows than they are willing to acknowledge."

Source: The New York Times, April 21, 1987, p. B4.

Retention—Memory

Information retention, or *memory*, plays an indispensable role in information consumption. We are able to store and actively use an incredible amount of information—at least several billion times more than a large research computer—and yet we can locate and use it with an efficiency and ease of operation that is astounding.[9]

We have little difficulty accessing the information we need in order to go about our daily routine—to select appropriate clothing and dress, to start and operate an automobile, or to use the many mass communication products and services that surround us. And because of this capacity, most of us can answer questions like "Who is Dan Rather?" "Can you name a New York newspaper?" "Who won the Super Bowl last year?" and "Who were the Beatles?" quickly and with a high degree of accuracy. While these seem like relatively simple questions, it would take a considerable time to locate the answers in a book, library, or even many electronic databases. This capability underscores the sophistication of human memory systems. In recent years, much effort has been directed toward understanding the complex processes by which memory operates.[10]

A good deal of sensory information can be processed within the system at any one time. For example, when you look through the newspaper to determine what movie is playing at a particular theater, not only that information but additional sensory data relating to other items in the paper, such as other movies and other theaters, would also be processed at some level of awareness. The information that is not what is being sought would be lost very rapidly through *decay*, probably within a second or so.

Information that will be further used becomes part of *short-term memory* and is available for a relatively brief period of time—perhaps 15 seconds.[11] Our short-term memory capacity is limited under normal circumstances to a few pieces of information only, such as a phone number or a string of several letters or words. Most of us have had the experience of looking up a number, only to forget it by the time we walked across the room to the phone. Through recitation or rehearsal, however, we can extend the time available to use information. Thus, if we repeat a phone number to ourselves several times as we walk across the room, the likelihood of remembering it for the needed time period greatly increases. Some of the information is further processed and elaborated to become a part of our *long-term memory*.

Generally, the longer that information is available to us in short-term memory, the greater the chance it will become a part of our long-term memory.

The Information-Processing Cycle. Information selection, interpretation, and retention operate in a highly interrelated manner. They function in what we may think of as an *information-processing cycle*, through which incoming information is used as the basis for *description*, *classification*, *evaluation* and eventually, *action* (see Figure 2.2).

In most circumstances—whether we are watching someone walk across a room, viewing a television program, listening to an audiocassette, or reading a book—our initial use of information is for *description*: for determining the nature and characteristics of the sound or image before us.

Based on our descriptions, *classification* is possible. When we classify, we compare our new observations with information stored from previous experience to determine where a sound or image "fits".

> The organization of memory is so efficient that most of the time we are unaware of having to exert any effort to locate and use these materials. Consider the ranges of kinds of information you keep in, and can easily summon forth from, your own memory: the face of your closest friend . . . the words and melody of the national anthem . . . the spelling of almost every word you can think of . . . the exact place where you keep the pliers . . . the name of every object you can see from where you are sitting . . . and enough more to fill many shelves full of books.
>
> Morton Hunt, *The Universe Within* (New York: Simon & Schuster, 1982), p. 86.

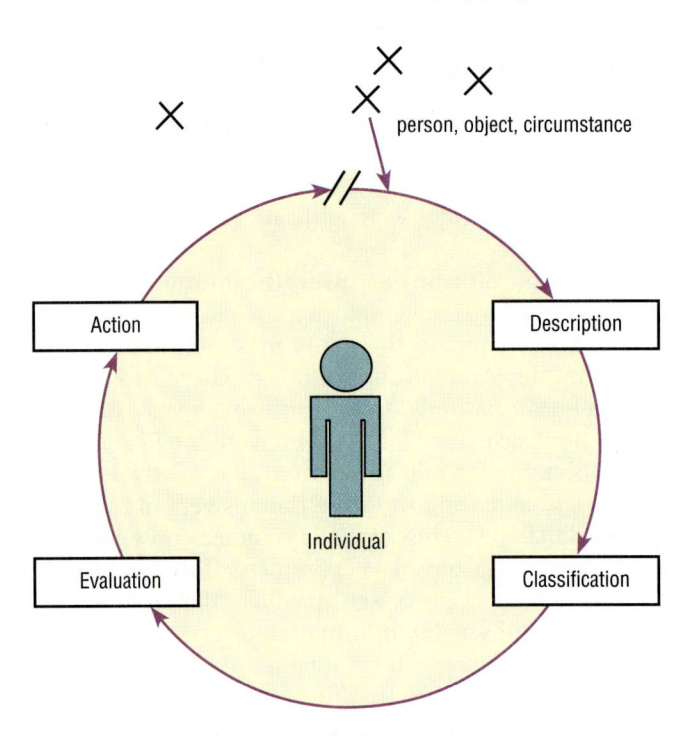

FIGURE 2.2 **The Information Processing Cycle** The X's refer to data or information about a person, an object, or a circumstance. The individual goes through the ongoing process of describing the data, classifying it, evaluating it, and deciding what action is appropriate.

Evaluation is a third phase in information processing. This stage involves identifying the range of possible relationships between us and the sounds and images and determining what, if any, actions or reactions are appropriate and/or necessary. A fourth step in the information-processing cycle is *action* to be undertaken based on our descriptions, classifications, and evaluations.

After acting, we often gather additional information to monitor and assess the impact of those actions. In so doing, we are once again involved in the description, classification, and (re)evaluation and action cycle.

We can illustrate this cycle by considering a very simple activity. Imagine for a moment that you are scanning through television channels looking for something light to fill a free hour before leaving for a meeting. As you begin to flip through the various channels, you notice an image that looks promising. Your first clues are the sound of audience laughter and smiling faces on actors you don't recognize.

Based on the first few audible and visible characteristics of that program you have selected, your interpretative processes, influenced by your memory, lead you to inferences about what the program will be like. As you continue to process information, you eventually classify the program as a "situation comedy", which seems to fit the goal you had in mind, and in the split second that this information-processing cycle requires, you walk over and sit down, in full confidence that the program is appropriate.

With additional information, you find that this show is a rerun, and you decide to look for other options. As you process the information from other channels, your initial objective is to determine "what it is"—to *describe* the content. Perhaps it's two people talking, a group singing, or a man reading. Closely related is the *classification* stage, which involves fitting what you see and hear into some category that helps you make sense of it. Is it a "sitcom," a dramatic program, a news show, a commercial, a music video, or a religious broadcast?

Based on *classification*, you are able to *evaluate* its usefulness for you at that point: Is this "light and entertaining?" A music video station may be perfect given that goal, but the same content would be wholly inappropriate if you wanted to find out what happened to the stock market or to the local football team.

FACTORS THAT INFLUENCE INFORMATION CONSUMPTION

Why do we pay more attention to some information sources than others? Why do some mass communication personalities appeal to us while others do not? Why do some programs seem more interesting and relevant than others? Why do we remember some ads for many years, while others are forgotten almost immediately?

Many factors influence the dynamics of information consumption. Using the P↔I↔C model, we can classify these factors based on whether they are characteristics of the *producers, information products and services*, or *consumers*. In the following sections, we will discuss these three categories, factors that are important in each, and their influence on mass communication consumption (see Figure 2.3).

Characteristics of Information Producers That Influence Consumption

The way we process information as consumers depends to a large extent on the characteristics related to mass communication producers—the professionals who create and distribute information products and services.

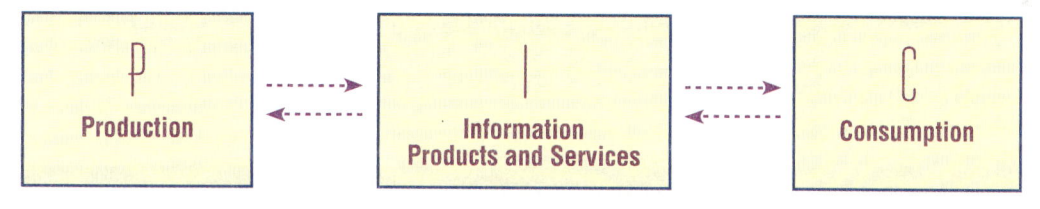

P Production ⇄ **I** Information Products and Services ⇄ **C** Consumption

Producer characteristics:
- Source attractiveness and similarity
- Source credibility and authority
- Source motivation and intent

Product/Service characteristics:
- Media
- Physical characteristics
- Organization
- Novelty
- Repetition

Consumer characteristics:
- Needs
- Attitudes and values
- Goals
- Capability
- Utility
- Communication style
- Context
- Experience and habit

FIGURE 2.3   **Factors That Influence Information Consumption**

> **MEG RYAN BECOMES AN INTIMATE FRIEND**
>
> Women love me now.... Mostly women over 30. They'll talk to me about anything. In aisles and checkout lines in grocery stores and drugstores and stuff, they corner me and reveal the most personal things.
>
> Meg Ryan, following the film *When Harry Met Sally* (*US*, February 19, 1990, p. 6).

Source Attractiveness and Similarity. *Attraction* can play a significant, though often subtle, role in influencing the nature of selection, interpretation, and retention of information. In our first impressions, we are greatly influenced by the dress, physique, manner, and general appearance of those presenting the information. All other things being equal, if we find television news or entertainment personalities attractive, we are more likely to tune to their program—an insight that often influences staffing decisions in the industry.

Generally speaking, the more *similarity* there is between information sources and consumers, the more likely consumers are to pay attention to those persons and what they say.[12] Sometimes similarities that increase interest are basic characteristics like gender, level of education, age, religion, background, race, hobbies, or language capacity. In other instances, we are particularly interested in persons because we believe they share our needs, attitudes, goals, or values. Thus, we are often drawn to mass communication sources who we believe share our gender and race, our political preferences, and our point of view. As a consequence of these perceived similarities, the information such sources provide is likely to be noted more than if the same information came from a dissimilar source.

Source Credibility and Authority. As consumers, we are more likely to attend to and retain information from individuals and/or organizations we regard as having *credibility*—believability, authority, or knowledgeability—than those not so perceived.[13] In most instances, the credibility attributed to a particular person or organization depends on the topic in question. Most of us, for example, are more likely to attend to and retain information on international affairs presented by a network news commentator than to information on the same topic offered by our next-door neighbor. When the topic is insurance, however, we may well attach more credibility to our neighbor who has 25 years' experience working in the field than to an advertisement in the newspaper.

Sometimes, however, mass communication sources may be viewed as credible regardless of the topic. Information provided by physicians, clergymen, professors, or lawyers may be treated as noteworthy, even when the topic is outside their area of expertise. Similarly, celebrities, politicians, and other persons who are in the "public eye" may be given particular attention and significance. Thus, the sports star speaking on politics or the medical doctor lecturing on religion may be accorded more than an average level of attention because of the credibility attached to the person by virtue of education, fame, or visibility.

INSIGHT

Madonna's Credibility Compromised

Madonna's Pepsi ads were pulled from television by the sponsor, Pepsico Inc., after consumers confused the ads with the pop singer's controversial music video of "Like a Prayer." The video, which had been shown on MTV, portrayed Madonna kissing a saint and "receiving Christ-like wounds in her hands." Several religious groups labeled the video "offensive," and prior to the cancellation of the ad, had asked consumers not to patronize Pepsico, which owns Pepsi soft drinks, Frito-Lay snacks, and Taco Bell, Pizza Hut, and Kentucky Fried Chicken restaurants.

Source: USA Today, April 4, 1989, p. 1B.

The importance of credibility was underscored in 1955 in landmark studies by political scientists Elihu Katz and Paul Lazarsfeld. They found that voting information presented in the mass media did not have the universal impact on audience members they had expected. In searching for an explanation for media ineffectiveness, Katz and Lazarsfeld developed an explanation of mass communication that linked face-to-face with mass communication. They concluded that some people were consistently more influential than others, and that "ideas often seem to *flow* from radio and print *to* opinion leaders and from them to the less active sections of the population" in what could be described as a two-step flow.[14]

Like individual information sources, some groups and organizations are regarded as more credible than others. The names of certain international corporations or local businesses, for instance, evoke images of authority and believability, while others inspire precisely the opposite association. A consumer will react quite differently to an explanation as to the "facts" behind an environmental crisis such as an oil spill depending on which type of organization is reporting the difficulty. Similarly, some mass communication producers—news organizations, for instance—are generally regarded as high-credibility sources, while information products created by advertising and public relations organizations may be viewed with less credibility. There are important exceptions to these generalizations depending on the particular mass communication source, the situation, and the consumers involved.

Source Motivation and Intent. The manner in which we react to a particular source and that source's information depends greatly on *motivation* and *intent*—the way we explain a source's actions to ourselves. If we assume, for instance, that we are watching a newscaster whose intention is to inform us, we are likely

Tennis star Jennifer Capriati is a walking advertisement for various products used by the millions who watch her matches on television.

to react quite differently than if we believe the intention is to persuade or to deceive. The journalist, we assume, is motivated by a desire to objectively report the news. Moreover, we assume that he or she has nothing particular to gain based on how we respond. In a case where we recognize a source as an advertiser or public relations professional, we may ascribe different motives and may react differently as a consequence.

Characteristics of Information Products That Influence Consumption

Media. Differences such as whether information is presented via print or illustration, film or microfiche, radio broadcast or the spoken words of a friend can have a direct influence on information reception. Simply in terms of availability, some media provide more exposure to information than others. More consumers watch television than read academic journals, yet each reaches far more people than do electronic consumer databases.

There are other less apparent distinctions among mass media in terms of their impact on information consumption. Recent studies have shown, for instance, that newspapers have been declining as primary sources of national and international news for many individuals. Yet it has also been suggested that newspapers are, in fact, a major data source for local news.[15] Information provided by several media is often more influential than when it is available through a single medium.[16]

During World War II, radio carried debates about America's role in the conflict. Here an audience in New York's Town Hall listens to a discussion that is being carried live on "Town Meeting of the Air."

Physical Characteristics. *Physical characteristics* like size, color, brightness, and intensity can also be important to the consumption of information products and/or services. Information products that utilize large, colored, bright, or intense text or images are more apt to be noticed than those without these characteristics. A large photo or typeface, a four-color advertisement, or a bright light are likely to be attended to before messages without these attributes. A large headline is more noticeable than the small type used to designate the editorial staff of the newspaper or to list political notices. Nudity, explicit sexuality, graphic violence, and profane language may well be noticed and responded to quite differently than information products that do not contain these characteristics.

The manner in which information is presented within a medium can also have a bearing on its reception. In newspapers, for instances, factors such as sentence length, the number of different words used, punctuation, and language level can influence comprehension, credibility, and interest associated with a publication.[17]

Organization. Organization is often an important factor influencing information selection, interpretation, and retention. In any number of situations, the order in which we are exposed to particular information sources can be important. How many times, for instance, do we find ourselves picking up grocery items we had not intended to because we noticed them on our way to get bread or milk? For mass communication consumers, the organization of messages and the ordering of information within a newspaper article, television program, or advertisement may also have a substantial influence on information processing.

For instance, the organization of most news stories follows an *inverted pyramid* format, whereby a summary of the facts relating to "who," "what," "when," "where," "why," and "how" is presented in the first paragraph. This allows readers, listeners, or viewers to get the basics with a minimal investment of time and energy. The arrangement of the contents of newspapers, magazines, and radio and television into predictable sections with predictable order serves this same function.

Likewise, the placement of elements within a picture, the order of paragraphs, or the location of advertisements in a written or audio document can have a substantial impact on the overall impression created, and this knowledge is used as the basis of strategic placement of information by mass communication pro-

RESEARCH

"This Is Your Brain on Drugs"

The use of intense, fear-arousing language is a common tactic used in public service antidrug commercials. One ad depicts an egg in a frying pan, with an announcer's voice saying, "This is your brain on drugs." Research now suggests that this approach may "backfire," and have the reverse effect. It is thought that when messages are too intense, targeted viewers tend to tune out the message or convince themselves that it is not realistic or relevant to them.

Source: Dr. Jay A. Winsten and Dr. William DeJong, "Recommendations for Future Mass Media Campaigns to Prevent Preteen and Adolescent Substance Abuse," Center for Health Communication at the Harvard School of Public Health, *Health Affairs,* Summer 1990. Discussed in *The New York Times,* Friday, Feb. 16, 1990, pp. D-1 and D-17.

ducers. How often, for instance, do we notice a news story or advertisement by chance because of its placement relative to a program we were watching or listening to or its proximity to an article we were reading?

Novelty. Often, messages that are novel, unfamiliar, or unusual stand out and grab our attention. While we may generally devote little attention to the color of automobiles, a pink or purple car is likely to catch the eye of even the most preoccupied motorist. Television viewers take the use of sound and color images for granted in the advertisement of products and services. Thus, ads presented in black and white with no sound or with no images of the product, are likely to attract our attention simply because they violate our expectations.

Repetition. In general, we are likely to take into account and remember messages that are repeated frequently. *Repetition* contributes to the way we learn our native language, our parents' and friends' opinions, the slang and jargon of our associates, and the accent of our geographic region. It is also the means through which we learn advertising slogans and jingles, the names and faces of film and television personalities, and the lyrics of popular songs.

Characteristics of Information Consumers That Influence Consumption

While traditional mass communication theory characterized audience members as passive recipients of information, an understanding of the dynamics of information processing underscores the active and dynamic quality of consumers. Morton

INSIGHT

Repetition

Can you identify the products that go with the slogans?

1. "Just for the taste of it . . ."
2. "The heartbeat of America . . ."
3. "If it's got to be clean, it's got to be . . ."
4. "How do you spell relief?"
5. "Melts in your mouth, not in your hands."
6. "You deserve a break today."
7. "You're in good hands with . . ."
8. "Nobody doesn't like . . ."
9. "The world of little people."
10. "Quality is job 1."
11. "We build excitement . . ."
12. "Coming to you straight from Maine."
13. "The official airline of Disneyland."
14. "Color-safe bleach."
15. "The San Francisco treat."
16. "You've come a long way, baby."
17. "When you care enough to send the very best."
18. "Mm, mm, good."
19. "I heard it through the grapevine."
20. "Kiss a little longer."

1. Diet Coke. 2. Chevrolet. 3. Tide. 4. Rolaids. 5. M & M's. 6. McDonald's. 7. Allstate. 8. Sara Lee 9. Fisher-Price. 10. Ford. 11. Pontiac. 12. Poland Springs Water. 13. Delta 14. Clorox II. 15. Rice-A-Roni. 16. Virginia Slims. 17. Hallmark. 18. Campbell's Soup. 19. California Raisins. 20. Big Red.

Hunt makes this point eloquently in discussing the opening sentence of Gibbon's *Decline and Fall of the Roman Empire*:

> "In the second century of the Christian era, the Empire of Rome comprehended the fairest part of the earth, and the most civilized portion of mankind."
>
> A reader who finds this sentence perfectly intelligible does so not because Gibbon was a lucid stylist but because he or she knows when the Christian era began, understands the concept of "empire," is familiar enough with history to recognize the huge socio-cultural phenomenon known as "Rome," has enough information about the world geography so that the phrase "the fairest part of the earth" produces a number of images in the mind, and, finally, can muster a whole congeries of ideas about the kinds of civilization that then existed. What skill, to elicit that profusion of associations with those few well-chosen cues—but what performance by the reader! One hardly knows which to admire more.[18]

Without doing any injustice to Hunt's intent, we could extend the point to apply equally to the impressive accomplishments of information consumers in general—to a *listener* in a personal, group, public, or mediated setting, or to the *observer* of visual images in an art gallery, baseball game, or television program.

For each of us, a complex set of elements works together to influence our decisions as to which sorts of messages we will attend to and how we will interpret and retain the information that results. Many of these factors have to do with characteristics of individual information consumers.

Needs. Among the most crucial factors that play a role in our information processing are *needs*. Scholars generally agree that our most basic needs, like those of other animals, have to do with the physiological realm: food, shelter, physical well-being, and sex.[19] These basic needs can be powerful forces in directing our behavior. When fundamental needs are not met, our efforts to satisfy them are compelling guiding forces in information reception. To the person who hasn't eaten for several days, for instance, few topics will be as susceptible for selection as information relating to food.

In addition to physiological needs, we have needs associated with our spiritual, psychological, social, and communicative well-being. Perhaps the most basic of these has to do with maintaining and developing one's identity and self-concept. Religious and "talk" (audience call-in) radio and television programming may address these needs directly for some viewers, as would self-help and personal development books, cassettes, and videotapes.

Attitudes and Values. Attitudes—preferences and predispositions about particular topics, people, and situations—also play a critical role in information consumption. Most people will attend to and be favorably disposed toward information and interpretations that support their views before they will consider nonsupportive information.[20] The person who supports candidate or position X, for instance, is likely to pay far more attention to articles and ads about that candidate or position than to items about Y or Z.

Values are basic principles that we live by—our sense of what we ought and ought not do in our relations with our environment and the people in it. As with attitudes, values also can substantially influence our information selection, interpretation, and retention.

The interrelationship of attitudes, values, and information consumption is a complex one. On occasion, information inconsistent with our attitudes or values can lead to more, rather than less, attention. At times, we spend more time reflecting on information that troubles us than on messages that are consistent with our perspective; we may take the latter for granted.

Goals. Most of us are at best only partially aware of our needs, attitudes, and values. We consciously set our *goals*. When we decide to pursue a particular career, the decision requires us to direct our attention toward certain kinds of information and *away* from others. The goal of achieving competence in an area—athletics, for instance—shapes the messages to which the individual attends as well as his or her interpretations. First, the goal increases the likelihood of exposure to print, broadcast, and face-to-face information pertaining to athletics in general and to the chosen sport in particular. Second, the goal may well increase the individual's contact with other people interested in a similar activity, and this will have an additional influence on information consumption. The demands of physical fitness may also play an important role in determining how information about food, drinking, smoking, health, and drugs will be attended to, interpreted, and remembered.

Capability. Our capability regarding a particular topic and our facility with language have an obvious impact on the kinds of information we attend to, and how we interpret and retain that information. The probability of English-speakers spending much time listening to Spanish-speaking radio, watching Spanish television programming, or reading Spanish publications is naturally very low, simply because they lack the capability for meaningful interpretation.

Mass-produced images on the wall of a dorm room remind college students who they are, what interests them, and what links them to other people.

Utility. Generally speaking we will attend to and devote effort to understanding and remembering information that we are able to *use*. To the individual who is thinking about purchasing a new automobile, news articles and advertisements on this subject suddenly become much more relevant, interesting, and memorable than they were prior to the decision to shop for a new car.

Studies of mass communication uses and gratifications point out how uses influence consumers' choices among particular information products and technologies. Viewers of religious television programs, for instance, may be guided by curiosity, habit, or a desire for information, entertainment, a substitute for attending church, companionship, moral support, salvation, or any of a number of other objectives.[21] Creating a video library, replaying music videos, using exercise tapes, time-shifting, and socializing are variously cited as reasons for using VCRs.[22]

Communication Style. Depending on our communication style, we may be drawn to or actively avoid the chance to deal with other people. People who are shy or apprehensive about engaging in verbal communication in a group setting, for example, may avoid such circumstances whenever possible.[23] Such people may prefer to listen to a television program on health or consult a home medical guide for information on a particular illness rather than ask their doctors for information.

Context. Our reaction to information and sources often depends on the *context*—on whether information products are being consumed at home or on vacation; at work or leisure; in an office, a church, or an auditorium.

The presence of others often has a very direct bearing on how we select as well as how we interpret and retain information. How we want to be seen, how we think other persons see us, what we believe others expect from us, and what we think they think about the situation we are in, all shape the way we react in social situations. In our effort to evaluate a particular movie, book, lecture or painting, the reactions of others are often of major significance to our own judgments. If, for instance, we are in the company of an esteemed colleague or friend who gives a very positive report on a new movie we had not planned to see, our plans may well change.

Experience and Habit. As consumers, we develop a number of information reception habits or tendencies as a result of our experiences. We develop preferences for particular media, programming types, and consumption patterns. We may like to listen to news on the radio, watch it on TV, read *USA Today*, or do all of these. We could watch television every night, all day long, on weekends only, or not at all. Perhaps sit-coms are our favorite, or sports, news, soaps, or old movies. We may like to listen to a stereo while we study or we may prefer quiet. We may visit a museum regularly or prefer to spend that time watching rented videotapes. At any moment these habits are probably the most significant factor in our mass communication consumer behavior.

MASS COMMUNICATION: A MIXED BLESSING

Mass communication extends the basic human communication capacity for face-to-face exchanges. We generally think of this extension in positive terms, pointing to the capability of media to traverse time and space in a manner and at a pace

RESEARCH

Habits

Ranking of Activities Engaged in by College Students for More Than 10 Hours per Week

Activity	Percent of Students Devoting 11 or More Hours to Activity
1. Talking informally to other students	31
2. Studying in the library	15
3. Watching television	14
4. Leisure reading	4
5. Participating in organized student activities (other than athletics)	3

Habits can have a major influence on the selection, interpretation, and retention of mass communication products. The activities listed here are ranked based on the percentage of college undergraduates who indicate they spend 10 or more hours per week on each. How might such habits influence mass communication consumption of undergraduates, and how would these patterns differ from other groups?

Source: Ernest L. Boyer, *College: The Undergraduate Experience in America* (New York: Harper & Row, 1987), p. 181.

---

that would otherwise be impossible. However, there are trade-offs. Mass communication is really a mixed blessing, on the one hand enhancing and enlarging the potential for human communication, and on the other limiting and constraining communication with others.

Limited Communication Modes

One limitation imposed by mass communication can be reducing the available range of communication modes. In face-to-face encounters, an individual can process visual, auditory, tactile, olfactory, and gustatory information. Mass communication media limit the number of modalities. In the case of radio or print, one mode is involved. Television and film utilize two.

Any restriction on the number of available modes can be seen as limiting the richness of human communication, but, for many purposes, one or two communication modes may be quite adequate. A newspaper or magazine account of an event in the Middle East can provide consumers with a comprehensive overview of noteworthy events that have transpired during the period in question. However, even the most sophisticated mass communication media cannot transmit to consumers many of the sights, sounds, and smells that were present for the reporter.

At times, this limitation is not a liability, but is in fact a positive and desirable characteristic. A case in point is a work of fiction. In reading a novel, it is often the absence of fully functioning face-to-face communication modes that both requires and allows readers to play an active role in creating the visual images themselves. In such an instance, it can be argued that media constraint actually enhances the richness of the communication experience.

Decreased Control

In contrast with someone in a typical face-to-face communication situation, the mass communication consumer generally has much less influence on the content and directions of interaction. This is particularly true of traditional mass media like television. The only option available to an audience member who wishes to alter the content of communication is to "turn off" the message—an option that at times we might wish were more readily available in interpersonal situations! Mass communication consumers may exercise control by writing a letter or making a phone call to the station—or in the case of print media, canceling a subscription. However, in such instances the controlling feedback from the consumer is delayed, and it is unlikely that any one audience member can exercise great control over the producers or products.

The decreased control afforded audience members by many mass communication situations can foster a sense of detachment, increased passivity, and decreased responsibility for directing the communication process and its outcomes.[24] To a greater extent than in face-to-face encounters, the sense that we are engaged in a human communication act can be lost. Because producers and consumers are removed in time and space from one another, the dynamic nature of the process is obscured.

Information stored electronically on a disc can be accessed anywhere, making computers as convenient to use as a book.

However, consumers are not wholly passive. There is always the option of removing oneself from the audience. Moreover, new technologies, like VCRs, offer consumers greater control, which helps explain their popularity.

From the producer's perspective, mass communication situations often afford *more* rather than *less* control than in face-to-face situations. Ads, television programs, newspaper articles, recordings, and movies may be redone many times before being released. Mass communication producers have the capability of reworking and refining information products at length before distributing them. All face-to-face communication is "live"; there are no opportunities for rewriting, editing, reshooting, retouching, or lip-synching.

Anonymity

In mass communication, audience members may know the producer, reporter, or author by name, but may have little broader knowledge of the individuals involved. Similarly, if producers know their consumers at all, it is generally in terms of their aggregate market characteristics such as age, sex, occupation, political orientation, or brand preferences.

While this limitation may seem to be a liability, sometimes mass communication serves as well as it does for the very reason that the audience members are unknown. The success of listener call-in radio programs can in part be attributed to the anonymity afforded by the medium. Callers need not identify themselves in order to share an opinion about a controversial topic or seek advice on a personal problem. In such instances, mass communication provides a vehicle for mediated therapeutic communication.[25] The attraction of 900 numbers—"dial-a porn" (or a conversation, relationship, or job interview)—for some consumers can also be traced to the anonymity afforded by mass media.

Blending of Work and Leisure Activities

As we noted earlier, the relationship between the functions of transportation technology and those of communication and information-processing technology has always been an important and interesting one. Moving information can be more efficient and economical than moving people, and information technologies provide an increasing number of options. The possibility of substituting communication for transportation is apparent in a wide and growing range of human activities—journalism and mass communication, library work, entertainment, health care, and business.

Nowhere is the blending of transportation and communication more apparent than where it relates to the concept of "home" and "work." "Work" once meant a *place* one went. With today's technologies and an ever-increasing number of citizens employed in information and service jobs, "work" can often be done anywhere appropriate communication technology is available. For a growing number of workers, the idea of an "office" filled with individuals may be replaced with, or supplemented by, an understanding of "office" that means an individual in front of a computer terminal at home, in a hotel room, or on a plane, able by a touch of the keys to have access to the people and information he or she needs.

The distinction between work and leisure may also be eroding, as a screen (TV or computer) serves as the source of images that are used for both. While we can only speculate on the long-term impact of these possibilities, it is clear that the new technologies are giving us new possibilities—possibilities that have the potential to transform the way many of us spend our days.

FUTURE FILE

✓ How can the "delay" in mass communication be minimized using new electronic media, thus reducing the difference in "message sent" and "message received"?

✓ How can the producers of mass communication messages "personalize" information to increase the likelihood that consumers will place a greater value on it, and thus decide to retain it?

✓ Is it possible to reduce the number of different meanings that individuals have for symbols used in mass communication messages, thus increasing the chances that a message will be consumed in the manner that the producer intended?

NOTES

1. Karl von Frish, *Bees: Their Vision, Chemical Senses, and Language*. rev. ed. (Ithaca, NY: Cornell University Press, 1981).
2. Robert T. Craig, "Information Systems Theory and Research: An Overview of Individual Information Processing," in Dan Nimmo, ed., *Communication Yearbook 3* (New Brunswick, NJ: Transaction-International Communication Association, 1979), pp. 99–120; D. Deutsch and J. A. Deutsch, "Attention: Some Theoretical Considerations," *Psychological Review*, 70 (1963) pp. 80–90; Lewis Donohew and Philip Palmgreen, "An Investigation of 'Mechanisms' of Information Selection," *Journalism Quarterly*, 48 (1971) pp. 624–639; and Lewis Donohew and Philip Palmgreen, "Reappraisal of Dissonance and the Selective Exposure Hypothesis," *Journalism Quarterly*, 48 (1971) pp. 412–420.
3. Samuel L. Becker, "Visual Stimuli and the Construction of Meaning," in Bikkar S. Randhawa, ed., *Visual Learning, Thinking and Communication* (New York: Academic Press, 1978), pp. 39–60.
4. D. E. Broadbent, "A Mechanical Model for Human Attention and Immediate Memory." *Psychological Review*, 64 (1957), pp. 205–215.
5. Robert Craig, p. 102.
6. See discussion of "Research on Behavior Without Awareness," in James V. McConnell, Richard L. Cutler, and Elton B. McNeil, "Subliminal Stimulation: An Overview," *American Psychologist* 13 (1958), pp. 230–232.
7. The issue of what is recalled under hypnosis and drugs is relatively controversial. While it was long believed that the information recalled was in its "original, unaltered" form, it is now recognized that memories may be elaborated and distorted by time and circumstance. For a discussion of these issues, see Elizabeth Loftus, *Memory* (Reading, MA: Addison-Wesley, 1980), pp. 54–62.
8. Robert Craig, p. 103.

9. Morton Hunt, *The Universe Within* (New York: Simon & Schuster, 1982), p. 85.
10. For a more detailed description of information-processing stages and dynamics see Geoffrey Loftus and Elizabeth Loftus, *Human Information Processing* (Hillsdale, NJ: Lawrence Erlbaum, 1976), and Peter H. Lindsay and Donald A. Norman, *Human Information Processing* (New York: Academic, 1977).
11. Loftus and Loftus, p. 8.
12. See Lawrence R. Wheeless. "The Effects of Attitude, Credibility, and Homophily on Selective Exposure to Information," *Speech Monographs*, 4 (April 1974), pp. 329–338.
13. Carl L. Hovland and W. Weiss, "The Influence of Source Credibility on Communication Effectiveness," *Public Opinion Quarterly*, 1 (1951) pp. 635–650.
14. Elihu Katz and Paul F. Lazarsfeld, *Personal Influence: The Part Played by People in the Flow of Mass Communications* (New York: Free Press, 1956), p. 32.
15. R. C. Adams, "Newspapers and Television as News Information Media," *Journalism Quarterly* 58: 4 (Winter 1981), pp. 627–629.
16. Steve K. Toggerson, "Media Coverage and Information-Seeking Behavior," *Journalism Quarterly*, 58: 1 (Spring 1981), pp. 89–92.
17. See Judee K. Burgoon, Michael Burgoon, and Miriam Wilkinson, "Writing Style as Predictor of Newspaper Readership, Satisfaction, and Image," *Journalism Quarterly* 58: 2 (Summer 1981), pp. 225–231.
18. Hunt, pp. 119–121.
19. One of the most widely cited classifications in recent years was provided in the writings of Abraham Maslow, "A Theory of Human Motivation," *Psychological Review*, 50 (1943), pp. 370–396. The framework differentiates between basic biological needs and "higher order" psychological and social needs.
20. Lawrence R. Wheeless, "The Effects of Attitude, Credibility, and Homophily on Selective Exposure to Information," *Speech Monographs*, 41 (1974), pp. 329–338.
21. Robert Abelman, " 'PTL Club' Viewer Uses and Gratifications," *Communication Quarterly*, 37: 1 (Winter 1989) pp. 54–66.
22. Alan M. Rubin and Charles R. Bantz, "Uses and Gratifications of Videocassette Recorders," in Jerry L. Salvaggio and Jennings Bryant, eds., *Media Use in the Information Age: Emerging Patterns of Adoption and Consumer Use* (Hillsdale, NJ: Lawrence Erlbaum, 1989), pp. 181–195.
23. Cf. Phillip Zimbardo, *Shyness* (Reading, MA: Addison-Wesley); James C. McCroskey, "Oral Communication Apprehension: A Summary of Recent Theory and Research," *Human Communication Research*, 4 (1977), pp. 78–96; Gerald M. Phillips and Nancy J. Metzger, "The Reticent Syndrome: Some Theoretical Considerations About Etiology and Treatment," *Speech Monographs*, 40 (1973).
24. See Robert Kubey and Mihaly Csikszentmihalyi, *Television and the Quality of Life: How Viewing Shapes Everyday Experience* (Hillsdale, NJ: Lawrence Erlbaum, 1990) for a discussion of the impact of television viewing on passivity.
25. Gary Gumpert and Sandra L. Fish, eds., *Talking to Strangers: Mediated Therapeutic Communication* (Norwood, NJ: Ablex, 1990) provide an excellent collection of articles examining therapeutic uses of communication technologies.

SUGGESTED READINGS

Fiske, John, *Introduction to Communication Studies*, 2nd ed. (London: Routledge, 1990).
Graber, Doris A., *Processing the News*, 2nd ed. (New York: Longman, 1988).
Gumpert, Gary, and Robert Cathcart, *Inter/Media: Interpersonal Communication in a Media World* (New York: Oxford University Press, 1986).
Rogers, Everett M., *Communication Technology* (New York: Free Press, 1986).

Ruben, Brent D., *Communication and Human Behavior*, 3rd ed. (Englewood Cliffs, NJ: Prentice-Hall, 1992).

Salvaggio, Jerry L., and Jennings Bryant, *Media Use in the Information Age: Emerging Patterns of Adoption and Consumer Use* (Hillsdale, NJ: Lawrence Erlbaum, 1989).

Wartella, Ellen, and Byron Reeves, "Communication and Children," in Charles R. Berger and Steven H. Chaffee, eds., *Handbook of Communication Science* (Newbury Park, CA: Sage, 1987), pp. 619–650.

CHAPTER 3

Mass Communication Effects

AT A GLANCE

✓ Producers must identify their audiences and define the characteristics of those audiences in order to know what information consumers want and need.

✓ Feedback is the mechanism by which producers learn how audiences react to information available in the marketplace.

✓ Audience research methods help producers to measure consumer response.

✓ The influence of mass communication may be long-term rather than immediate.

✓ There are various schools of thought about the effects of mass communication.

✓ The technological school holds that the *form* of the media has as much effect on audiences as the *content* of the media.

✓ The effects of the mass communication media are complex and may involve multistep processes that have long-term influence on individual behaviors.

In this chapter we focus on mass communication audiences, their nature and characteristics, and the ways in which audience members influence and are influenced by the mass communication process and mass communication producers.

THE CONCEPT OF AUDIENCE

An *audience* is a group of individuals with a common pattern of mass communication consumption. At the very least, such individuals share in common *access* or *exposure* to the same mass communication products or services.

Audience Access

The accessible audience for a newspaper, an educational cable channel, or a community library would be all those individuals to whom the information products and services were available. For newspapers, the accessible audience would be defined as all individuals who are within the distribution area of the paper. For a cable TV system the audience of access would include all residences within a wired area. For the library, the audience would be all members of the community who could take advantage of the service. Thinking in terms of audience accessibility is particularly useful when analyzing the *potential* market for new or existing mass communication products or services: How many potential subscribers, viewers, or listeners are there?

Audience Exposure

Another way to define audiences is *exposure*: whether consumers saw, heard, or read (were exposed to) particular information products or services. Many mass communication organizations use exposure as the basis for identifying their audience. Newspapers and magazines monitor circulation and readership, radio and television stations track viewership and audience-share, museums record visitors, and libraries calculate circulation. Specific measures of exposure are critical from a marketing and advertising perspective for the purpose of targeting advertising and public messages for particular audiences.

Audience Awareness, Attitude, Opinion, Knowledge, and Behavior

Another way to think about audiences is in terms of whether individuals who have been exposed to mass communication products have developed increased awareness or knowledge, new or reinforced attitudes or opinions, or new behaviors. For instance, do individuals who were exposed to a particular weekly news magazine know what topics were discussed in the last issue? Can consumers identify the products endorsed by particular celebrities? Have undecided voters who watched a series of news programs developed voting preferences? Have readers of an advertisement for a newspaper or magazine taken out a new subscription? In instances such as these, the audience of concern is individuals who have actually become aware or knowledgeable, acquired or reinforced attitudes or opin-

RESEARCH

Imitative Impact of Mass Communication Suggested

Sometimes the mass communicator doesn't know who needs to be reached by a message. "To whom it may concern" messages posted in public places make the connection.

Research suggests that an "imitative effect" influences teenage suicide rates. A study examining 38 nationally televised news or feature reports about suicide from 1973 to 1979 found that the number of teenage suicides jumped by about 7 percent in the 7 days after each of the broadcasts. The result: "nearly 3 extra suicides nationwide per program, or 110 more suicides than would otherwise be expected in the years covered in the study. 'Our study suggests there is a danger period . . . for about a week after news stories on suicide.'"

Source: Erik Eckholm, "Studies Link Teen-Age Suicides, TV," *The New York Times*, September 1, 1986, summarizing research by David P. Phillips and Lundie L. Carstensen, University of California at San Diego.

---

ions, or engaged in particular behaviors as a by-product of exposure to mass communication products.

CHARACTERISTICS OF AUDIENCES

Mass communication audiences can be described in terms of their size, demographics, psychographics, and type. A familiarity with audience characteristics is helpful in understanding, describing, analyzing, and targeting consumers of particular mass communication products and services.

> ### RESEARCH
>
> ## Do you *Zip, Zap, Schiz?*
>
> If your television set has a remote control, you probably do. *Zip, zap, schiz, channel surfing,* and *flipping* are terms that are used to refer to the practice of rapidly changing from channel to channel. Morris Cohen, executive vice president of Music Television (MTV), calls the remote control the "single most important technological breakthrough in the television history when it comes to consumer behavior." Using remote controls, viewers may bypass commercials, attempt to watch two or more programs simultaneously, and fast-forward through commercials when watching previously recorded material.
>
> Studies of remote control use suggest that
>
> - Viewers watching material recorded earlier on VCRs "zap" about 40 percent of the material.
> - 50 percent of 12- to 34-year-old viewers decide what to watch by flipping through channels with a remote rather than by reading *TV Guide* or newspaper listings.
> - Men are twice as likely as women to be "zappers."
>
> "We know they use remote controls, [but] we want our audiences to use those remotes to land on or to at least come back to our channels," says Cohen, executive vice president of corporate affairs and communications of MTV Network (Nickelodeon for kids, Music Television for teens, Video Hits 1 for adults, and family entertainment on Nick at Nite). "Rather than pretend ['flipping'] doesn't exist, we recognize our audience does it, and have incorporated it into our spots to build loyalty. We want our viewers to recognize themselves on networks that belong exclusively to them." MTV tries to establish their channels as "home bases" for their audiences by showing frequent previews of upcoming videos, and working with advertisers to make sure their ads are sandwiched between attractive programming in order to minimize "zapping."
>
> *Source:* Lynn M. Jackson, "Remote Control on the Button" and "Companies Fight Back to Hold onto Fickle Audiences," *Courier-News* (Bridgewater, NJ), April 9, 1989, pp. H1, H2, H7.

Size

Size is an essential characteristic of any audience. The number of viewers exposed to a particular radio or television program or advertisement, subscribers to newspapers or magazines, spectators at a concert, or patrons of a museum or theme park is essential to the economics of production and distribution. Additionally, audience size is one measure of the significance and impact of a mass communication product, service, or event.

Where the goal is awareness, knowledge, understanding, or behavioral impact, the size of the audience is equally important. Here the issue may be how many viewers, readers, or listeners called a "900" number for more information, mailed in an order form, or phoned in a contribution after reading an article.

Demographics and Psychographics

Demographics refers to classifications of consumers based on characteristics such as geographic distribution, gender, age, income, education, occupation, ethnic background, length of exposure, and frequency of exposure. *Psychographic data* are concerned with personal and psychological characteristics of consumers, including such things as buying habits, attitudes, opinions, leisure patterns, political values, and so on. Depending on the purposes and circumstances at hand it may be important to know whether particular audiences are composed of more men or women, Republicans or Democrats, children or seniors, wage earners or unemployed, sports car or truck owners, hunting enthusiasts or Nintendo fans, and so on.

Audience Type

Based on demographic and psychographic profiles, distinctions are often made among *elite, popular*, and *specialized* audiences.[1]

Elite Audiences. Elite audiences are small in size. They are composed of opinion leaders who are affluent and highly educated. Examples of elite audiences include patrons of the arts and early adopters of technologies like cellular telephones or home fax machines.

General Audiences. Composed of individuals representing a broad cross section of society, general audiences are large and diverse. Examples include audiences for mass appeal newspapers, magazines, television programs, and public events.

Specialized Audiences. Specialized audiences are composed of individuals who possess similar demographic and psychographic characteristics. These audiences are comparatively small and include audiences for mass communication products focusing on particular hobbies, products, leisure activities, or interest areas.

Beyond being interesting in their own right, these distinctions are often of strategic value to mass communication producers. Mass communication technologies, products, and services frequently move through stages of adoption beginning with "elite audiences." Acceptance by this audience, composed of individuals who are influential within their communities, provides the basis for later adoption by larger, more diverse, popular audiences. At this stage, products and services are mass-produced and mass-marketed at prices that facilitate broader access. Technologies like VCRs, home computers, CD players, and cellular phones, which were initially affordable and attractive only to small, elite audiences, are becoming increasingly available and attractive to a larger group. A similar pattern occurs when products of the arts and mass media—famous paintings, objects, or writings—which were originally prized only by "elites," are copied, mass-produced, and mass-marketed for a general audience.

AUDIENCE FEEDBACK SYSTEMS

Audiences exert a substantial influence on mass communication producers by means of *audience feedback systems*—mechanisms through which information regarding audience reactions are channeled back to producers. We will examine two such systems: market-based feedback systems and research-based feedback systems (see Figure 3.1).

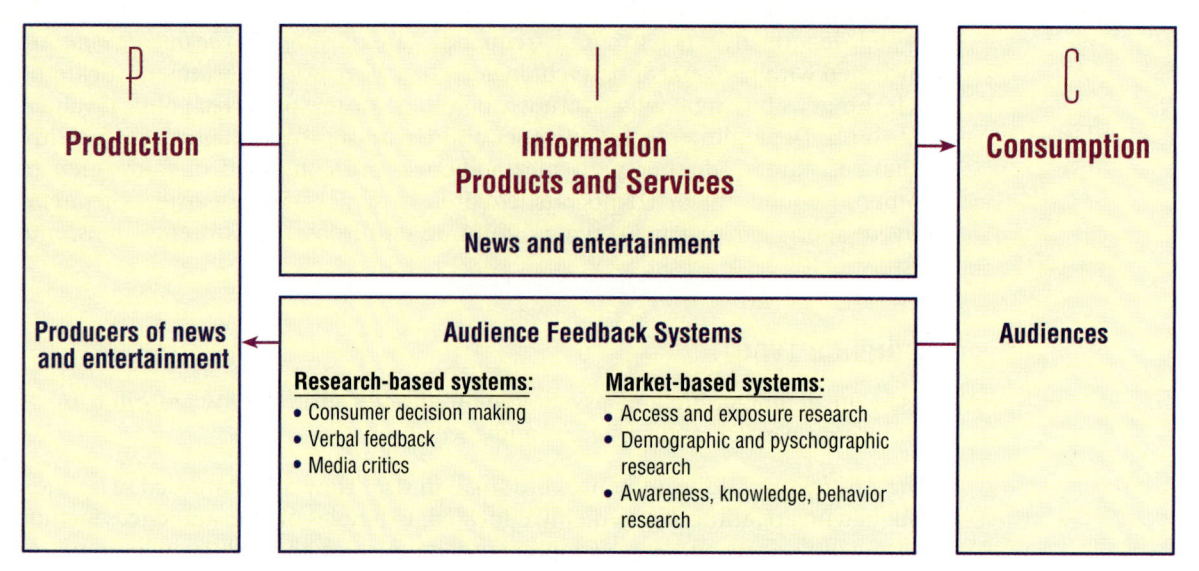

FIGURE 3.1 Audience Feedback Systems

```
┌─────────────┐    ┌─────────────────────────────┐    ┌─────────────┐
│      P      │    │             I               │    │      C      │
│ Production  │───▶│      Information            │───▶│ Consumption │
│             │    │   Products and Services     │    │             │
│             │    │    News and entertainment   │    │             │
│ Producers   │    ├─────────────────────────────┤    │  Audiences  │
│ of news and │◀───│  Audience Feedback Systems  │◀───│             │
│entertainment│    │ Research-based   Market-    │    │             │
│             │    │ systems:         based      │    │             │
│             │    │ • Consumer       systems:   │    │             │
│             │    │   decision       • Access   │    │             │
│             │    │   making           and      │    │             │
│             │    │ • Verbal           exposure │    │             │
│             │    │   feedback         research │    │             │
│             │    │ • Media          • Demographic│   │             │
│             │    │   critics          and      │    │             │
│             │    │                    psychographic│ │             │
│             │    │                    research │    │             │
│             │    │                  • Awareness,│   │             │
│             │    │                    knowledge,│   │             │
│             │    │                    behavior │    │             │
│             │    │                    research │    │             │
└─────────────┘    └─────────────────────────────┘    └─────────────┘
```

Market-Based Feedback Systems

A number of natural, market-based processes exist that provide mass communication producers with information relative to access, exposure, awareness, knowledge, and behavioral impacts. These systems include consumer decision making, verbal feedback, and media critics.

Consumer Decision Making. Consumer decision making is generally the single most significant source of audience feedback. Fundamental decisions by audiences members as to whether to subscribe, attend, view, or purchase mass communication products and services present a poignant message to producers. Audience reactions to mass communication products and services can also be actively solicited. Coupons, rebate offers, bring-this-ad-and-get-a-discount promotions, and the like provide a measure of the impact of particular promotional efforts.

The direct impact of consumer behavior on the economic well-being of mass communication producers varies among different types of mass communication products (see Figure 3.1). At one extreme are mass communication products that are directly supported by readers, viewers, or listeners, without the benefit of subsidies from the sale of advertising. In the case of books, home videocassettes, and cable TV services, for instance, the impact of consumer decisions to buy or not buy are quite direct. For broadcast TV and radio, on the other hand, the majority of operating funds come from advertisers. Here, the impact of audiences, while still critical, may be less immediate and direct. This is even more the case with publicly supported educational television, museums, and libraries. In all of these examples, audience decisions ultimately affect the life of individual products (a particular book, television program, or library, for instance), and influence the mass communication institution (a publishing organization, television station, or library system) (see Table 3.1).

Verbal Feedback. Information created by consumers through verbal feedback on mass communication products or services is another important source of influ-

TABLE 3.1 Audience Role in Providing Economic Support of Mass Communication Producers and Products

	Supported by Audience	Supported by Advertising	Supported by Contributions
Books	X		
Information services	X		
Home videocassettes	X	X	
Cable TV	X	X	
Films	X		
Newspapers	X	X	
Magazines	X	X	
Museums	X		X
Commercial broadcast television		X	
Radio	X	X	
Educational television/radio			X
Libraries			X

ence. In some cases, verbal feedback is provided by casual conversation between employees of mass communication organizations and family or friends. More often, such feedback is provided formally. Mechanisms for feedback are provided by many mass communication organizations. Newspapers and magazines encourage "letters to the editor," television stations offer time for opposing views, and some radio stations provide phone-in opportunities for listeners who want to express their views. Other examples of this form of feedback include unsolicited correspondence or phone calls of complaint or commendation from audience members.

Media Critics. Information created by reviewers and/or critics through published or broadcast evaluations of mass communication products and/or services is another important feedback mechanism. Mass media critics are an "elite audience." Since most of us don't have the time or resources to see every film, watch every program, read every book, or subscribe to every information service, the critics function as surrogates who do it for us, recommending what we should favor with our money and attention. Much as opinion leaders can influence public opinion on political or artistic matters, mass media critics can influence audiences to notice and use particular products. Thus, audience members often find themselves attending the play that gets the favorable review, watching the television show that is recommended by the newspaper columnist, or buying the book a reviewer praises. In the process, critics also provide yet another feedback mechanism to mass communication producers.

We can extend our P↔I↔C model to account for the role of the critic as a specialized audience member (see Figure 3.2). The critic first acts between the producers and general audiences. At this point, the role of the critic is one of calling attention to the availability of information and recommending responses. On the feedback swing, the critic may again be interposed between feedback information and the receipt of that information by the producers. At this point, the critic acts as interpreter of how and why the popular and elite audience members reacted positively or negatively to the information.

Critics, or *reviewers* as they are often called in the mass media, fill several important functions, including:

Gene Siskel and Roger Ebert have refined the art of using one medium, television, to inform consumers about another medium, the movies.

1. Informing audience members about what is new and interesting,
2. Raising the cultural level of the community,
3. Advising audience members on how to use their time and money,
4. Helping artists and performers to understand how their efforts are being received by the audience,
5. Recording the history of the mass communication fields, and
6. Entertaining audiences with their articles and reports.[2]

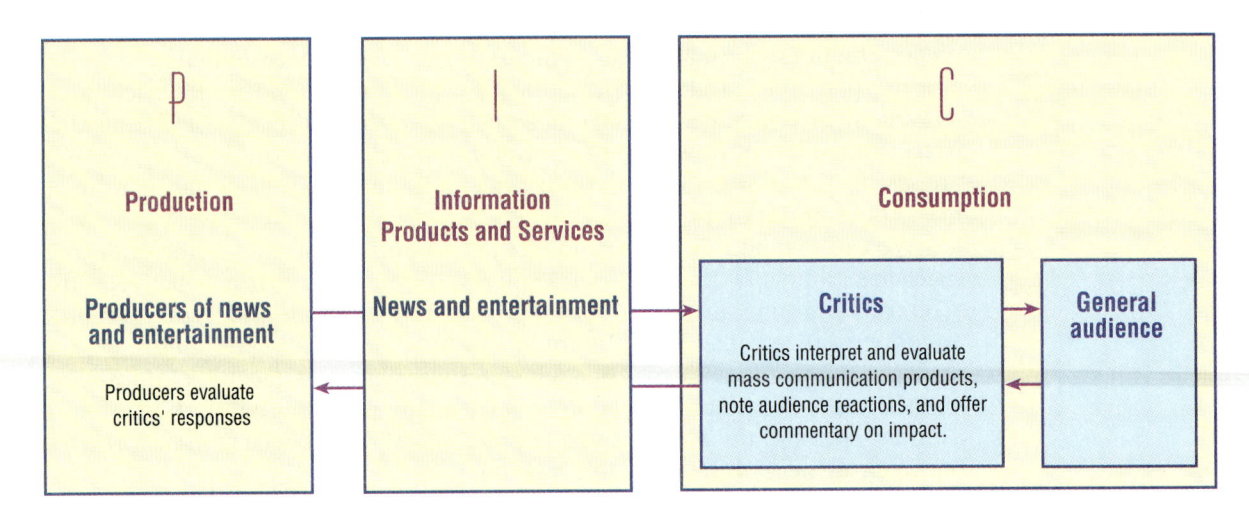

FIGURE 3.2 The Critic's Role

P — Production: Producers of news and entertainment. Producers evaluate critics' responses.

I — Information Products and Services: News and entertainment

C — Consumption: Critics interpret and evaluate mass communication products, note audience reactions, and offer commentary on impact. → General audience

INDUSTRY

Audience Feedback Systems

Producer	Market-Based Feedback Systems	Research-Based Feedback Systems
Newspaper	Subscriptions and cancellations Fluctuating newsstand sales Consumer use of special coupons, special phone numbers Letters to editor Phone calls to editors, reporters	Audit Bureau of Circulation Readership surveys
Magazines	Subscriptions and nonrenewals Newsstand sales Letters to the editor Publicity gained in other media Consumer use of cards, coupons Participation in contests and promotions	Simons Market Research Bureau Mediamark (MRI)
Books	Sales Reviews Mentions and author appearances in other media	Best-seller lists *Publisher's Weekly* sales data
Radio	Calls to deejays Consumer use of special phone numbers in ads Participation in contests Letters to Federal Communication Commission (FCC)	Arbitron ratings
Television	Reviews Emmy Awards Response to special offers only on TV Letters to FCC Use of "equal time"	Nielson ratings Arbitron ratings
Film	Admissions Reviews Academy Awards Word of mouth Publicity in other media	*Variety's* weekly box office figures *Variety's* annual industry report
Recordings	Sales Consumer/parents group reactions Grammy Awards	*Billboard* "Hot 100" chart ASCAP data MCA data
Advertising*	Client decisions Reviews Letters to media and advertisers Consumer inquiries to merchants Use of coupons Sales of products linked to specific promotions	Starch reports on recognition and recall Focus group interviews Shopping mall and store interviews
Theater	Admissions Reviews Word of mouth Publicity in other media	*Variety* box office figures

Continued

Audience Feedback Systems *Continued*		
Producer	**Market-Based Feedback Systems**	**Research-Based Feedback Systems**
Museums, libraries, and popular culture events	Attendance Circulation Admissions Ticket sales Reviews Critiques and suggestions from elite and specialized audiences	Audience surveys Budget reviews by trustee board

*Although advertising is usually part of another medium, it can exist alone and it is subject to its own specific feedback and measurement systems.

Research-Based Feedback Systems

As useful and influential as market-based feedback mechanisms are, the information they provide can be difficult to interpret, and may not represent the audience at large. For instance, the information that 25 subscribers to a community weekly newspaper canceled their subscriptions during the same period is an example of consumer decision-making feedback. But what exactly do these cancellations mean? Were these subscribers unhappy, or are they moving from the community because of a factory closing? If they are displeased, what is the focus of their dissatisfaction? Is it a series that has been running in the paper, the lack of local community news, or the absence of state news? And is the reaction of those who canceled representative of the audience as a whole?

Research-based feedback systems are created to provide systematic information about audience response to particular mass communication products or services.

Audience Access and Exposure Research. Research may have a variety of goals and may utilize any number of methods. Efforts to evaluate access or exposure involve calculating the number of potential or actual members of an audience. Mass communication organizations can gather such data themselves, or, as is more often the case, they may acquire this information from specialized research organizations that produce and market specialized information products and services.

Audience Demographic and Psychographic Research. Information regarding demographic and psychographic characteristics is acquired through telephone or mail surveys of members of the intended audience. When it is difficult to gain access to members of a *target audience* for survey purposes, more indirect methods are used. Researchers may interview a sample of physician's receptionists in an effort to determine whether particular magazine articles or advertisements were noticed by physicians in the office. Indirect methods may also be used when there is reason to doubt that those surveyed would be candid in their responses.

Audience Awareness, Attitude, Opinion, and Behavior Research. In such cases, the goal is to measure consumers' selection, interpretation, retention, and action.

> ### RESEARCH
>
> ## "The Queens Housewife Test"— Public Opinion Pretesting
>
> In July, 1990 a debate among the staff of the NBC Nightly News—the No. 3 rated network newscast—was resolved in an unusual way. The argument was about whether a story on apartheid and its effect on the education of South African children should be included in the nightly news show. Executive producer Steven Friedman insisted that viewers were becoming bored with stories on South Africa, and challenged the staff "to prove it was a piece that would interest a housewife in Queens." In effect, Friedman was asking his staff to provide evidence that the public was interested in this topic. Sofia Perez, a production assistant, rose to the challenge. She said her mother, Josefina, was a housewife in Queens, and she thought her mother would be interested in seeing the story. Friedman decided to let Josefina Perez preview the segment and make the decision for the network. Josefina liked the story, and thought the topic was important. On August 1, the segment aired and was seen by millions of audience members based on Josefina's reaction.
>
> Other producers have tried to solicit viewer opinions as an input to their editorial decision making. Cable News Network, for example, asked viewers to help select stories by calling a 900 number to indicate their interests.
>
> Source: *The Wall Street Journal*, July 7, 1990, p. B-1.

A number of methods are available. One of the most familiar is the public opinion poll, which assesses the opinions and attitudes of a sample of audience members toward particular issues or individuals. Sometimes polls are used on a "one-shot" basis; more often they are administered a number of times in an effort to track changes in the audience's response.

Other forms of research aim at assessing audience attention, comprehension, and retention. Such efforts may begin before the actual mass communication products are distributed in their final form. Studies may analyze textual material in terms of its *readability*—educational level required to comprehend the content. Probable audience reactions to content, organization, and illustrations can also be pretested with a sample of individuals who are representative of the target audience. Post-test research is conducted after individuals have been audience members for particular mass communication products and services.

Often, both pre- and post-tests use a *self-report technique*, whereby audience members are simply asked to describe their reactions to mass communication products in a written survey, in person, over the telephone, or in focus group interviews. Individuals or group members may be asked how much attention they paid to particular information products or services, how they felt about these products, whether their attitudes or knowledge changed as a consequence, or whether they found the event useful, informative, entertaining, and so on.

Other research techniques are more indirect. For instance, audience members could be given a *recognition* test, in which they are presented with a grouping of articles, ads, or program segments, and asked to indicate which they recognize. By including fictitious materials in the group, it is possible to check on the accuracy of their responses. *Recall* techniques ask consumers to describe particular mass

> ### RESEARCH
>
> ## "Garbage Analysis"—A Unique Approach to Audience Research
>
> Sorting through garbage can reveal a great deal about audience members, including products they have purchased, rented, and used. What we might call "garbage analysis," thus, would qualify as a naturalistic, unobtrusive—if messy—approach to assessing consumer behavior. Courts in New Jersey and Hawaii, however, have determined that this technique violates rights to privacy. The most recent decision in New Jersey was issued in 1990 as a result of police garbage searches that revealed drug paraphernalia and traces of illegal drugs. In the decision, the New Jersey Supreme Court rejected the U.S. Supreme Court's ruling on a case in California that concluded "people lose any reasonable expectation of privacy in their trash by leaving it in bags alongside the street." The New Jersey court commented: "Undoubtedly, many would be upset to see a neighbor or stranger sifting through their garbage, perusing their discarded mail, reading their bank statements, looking at their empty pharmaceutical bottles, and checking receipts to see what videotapes they rent."
>
> Source: *Courier-News* (Bridgewater, New Jersey), July 18, 1990, p. A1.

communication products or their contents without the benefit of looking at sample items. Mass communication organizations may gather this information themselves, but often they contract the services of a research organization.

The difficulty of conducting this type of research has itself become a major focus for many scholars and practitioners in the field. As noted earlier, the challenge is twofold: determining precisely how to measure changes that may occur, and deciding how any changes that are identified relate to particular mass communication products and services. Both are complex research problems.

Studies of *behavioral effects* face additional challenges: What consumers are aware of and how they may have interpreted information do not necessarily indicate what they will retain. Moreover, neither selection, interpretation, nor retention will necessarily result in behavioral impact. For instance, we know that audience members exposed to political news and/or advertisements may be aware of a coming election, be convinced of the merits of a political candidate and his or her qualifications, and yet fail to vote. Major difficulties include: (1) defining the behaviors we want to focus on, (2) isolating the influence of particular mass communication products and/or producers from all other sources of information and from all other forms of communication, (3) measuring relevant behaviors, and (4) identifying linkages between mass communication and individual behaviors. In the case of the political scenario, above, suppose the individual did vote: How would we know whether this outcome was necessarily the consequence of the news or ads?

Research Environments. To minimize the possibility of extraneous factors affecting the outcomes of studies, a great deal of control over the research environment is required—an argument for conducting such studies in a laboratory setting. For instance, a group of typical consumers could be shown various candidate ads in a laboratory setting, and then taken into the next room to engage in simulated voting. However, no matter how sophisticated the laboratory research designs are,

With the touch of a number on a Nielsen People Meter, a viewer lets the researchers know who is watching what.

such an approach may be criticized for lacking authenticity and the complexity of everyday situations in which mass communication processes actually operate.

Field research projects, which are conducted in more *natural* environments, are an alternative to laboratory studies. For instance, researchers could observe the processes by which consumers select mass communication products from a newsstand, respond to political candidates' speeches, or talk about their voting behavior. Naturalistic, *unobtrusive* studies can be combined with interview and survey methods in which the individuals studied are asked to explain the reasons underlying the observed behaviors. Here, too, there are obvious difficulties. For instance, the behaviors of particular interest are often undertaken in natural settings—at home or in a voting booth—and at times that make unobtrusive observation virtually impossible.

It is obvious that behavioral effects studies, while potentially invaluable to mass communication producers, are complex, time-consuming, and costly. As a consequence they are used less frequently than other methods discussed. Nonetheless, in the development of some advertisements or other expensive campaigns—and in academic research on mass communication—the benefits of behavior studies are thought to outweigh the costs.

THE EFFECTS OF MASS COMMUNICATION ON AUDIENCE MEMBERS

Now that we have defined audiences and their role in the mass communication process, how can we explain the impact of mass communication on the individual members of these audiences? Broadly speaking, there are two schools of thought.

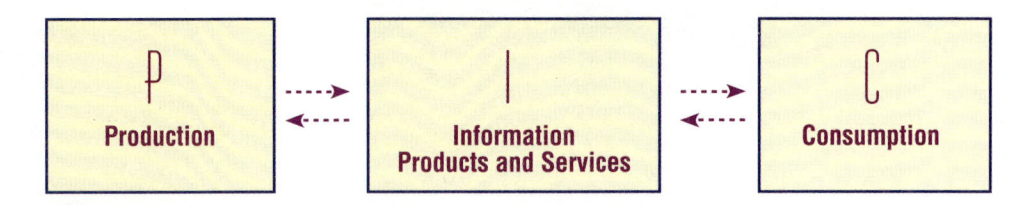

```
    P  --->  I  --->  C
Production   Information   Consumption
             Products and Services
```

Producer and Product Perspectives:

Direct impact:
- Experimental attitude change studies

Indirect, longer-term impact:
- Functional analysis
- The press and pictures in our heads
- Agenda setting
- Cultivation theory
- Spiral of silence
- Technological school
- Modeling theory

Consumer Perspectives:
- Cantril and *War of the Worlds*
- Erie County Voting Study
- Diffusion of innovations
- Uses and gratifications
- Media system dependency

FIGURE 3.3 **Perspectives on Mass Communication Impact**

One perspective emphasizes the role of mass communication producers and products, and the other stresses consumers (see Figure 3.3).

The Producer Perspective

Producer-centered approaches assume that information producers, products, and services exert a controlling influence on human behavior. This way of thinking is suggested by statements such as these: "Teenage violence is a result of watching so much violence on television," and "Decaying morals within society are the consequence of increasingly explicit sexuality on television, records, and music videos." Each implies a *causal relationship* between mass communication on the one hand and individual and/or social behavior on the other.

Experimental Studies of Attitude Change. The Yale Communication and Attitude Change Program, directed by Carl I. Hovland throughout the 1950s, grew out of the study of military training films during World War II.[3] Hovland and his colleagues adapted the methods of experimental psychology for their research and conducted carefully designed experiments in a variety of laboratory settings. Their goals were to understand how attitudes are formed and how they change, and to formulate laws of persuasion. Their guiding assumptions were that media presentations bring about direct and immediate changes in people's attitudes, and that there is a close connection between a change of attitude and a change of behavior. Their studies focused on the influence of mass communicators and messages on short-term attitudes of audience members. The results of these studies lent support to the view that the producer has a powerful influence on mass communication consumption, though some questioned the applicability of laboratory research findings in everyday situations. Hovland and his followers argued

> ### RESEARCH
> ## Evidence of Effectiveness of Drug Ads
>
> Since the Media-Advertising Partnership was formed in 1987, about 75 advertising agencies and 20 to 30 production companies have created approximately 200 antidrug commercials with a value of $430 million, and they have done so at no charge. Based on a three-year research project conducted by Gordon S. Black Corp. of Rochester, N.Y., a highly regarded independent research firm, it has been determined that the ads have been very effective. In communities where the antidrug ads were widely disseminated through print and electronic media, adults reportedly reduced their marijuana smoking by 33 percent, while the reduction was only 15 percent in communities where antidrug ads were seen less often. According to John O'Toole, president of the American Association of Advertising Agencies (AAAA), this is "some of the strongest evidence ever presented concerning the effectiveness of advertising. . . . We are confident that advertising can, indeed, un-sell America on drugs."
>
> *Source:* American Association of Advertising Agencies.

that the research results from the laboratory could be generalized outside the lab. Some critics were convinced; others were not.

Functional Analysis. Other producer-oriented approaches to describing the influence of mass communication have suggested that information producers and products have a *direct* but *long-term* rather than immediate impact.

Based on work by Robert Merton and extended by Charles Wright, the functional approach sought to identify long-term positive consequences of mass communication—*functions*—and negative consequences—*dysfunctions*. Wright described mass media as serving a number of functions for audience members, including (1) surveillance, (2) correlation, (3) socialization, and (4) entertainment.[4]

1. *Surveillance* refers to the role mass communication institutions play in providing a constant stream of news-related information that keeps audience members aware of developments in the environment that may affect them. Surveillance may consist of a *warning function*, alerting members of the audience to danger (example: a hurricane or polluted water supply) and a *status conferral function*, allowing individuals, organizations, and issues that are highly visible on mass media to be seen as significant by members of the audience (example: political, entertainment, or sports figures whose names and accomplishments become common knowledge).

2. *Correlation* applies to the way in which mass communication helps individuals interrelate, assimilate, and interpret information about the events of the day. News stories that provide analysis and synthesis perform this function. Documentaries may serve this goal, as do editorials.

3. *Socialization* relates to the contribution mass communication makes in providing individuals with the information they need in order to participate in society—political, social, and economic information, for instance.

4. *Entertainment* provides mass communication listeners, readers, and viewers with a release and diversion.

Dysfunctions might include mass communication contributing to a threat to existing social order within a particular region or society, fostering unrealistic expectations, heightening anxieties about world conditions, or *narcotizing*—numbing audience members to critical problems by overexposing them to information about these problems.[5]

The Press and the Pictures in Our Heads. In his classic 1921 book, *Public Opinion*, Walter Lippman discussed the role of newspapers in presenting images of the world beyond the reach of the typical American reader, particularly the events in Europe surrounding World War I.[6] Lippman noted that the press seemed very effective at creating representations of reality in the minds of the public, but that often the "pictures in our heads"—pictures that he asserted would shape public opinion and behavior—were inaccurate.

Lippman was concerned that media-based pictures may have little correspondence to "the world outside." One of the reasons for the disparity was the time difference between the occurrence of an event and the availability of subsequent newspaper reports, a lag that was greater in the 1920s than today. But a more significant reason for the disparity was the fact that reports are inevitably based on limited information. Moreover, reports are written from a particular perspective—always a particular physical perspective and often a political or ideological one—and are subject to various practical and economic constraints involved in the final product.

Agenda Setting. *Agenda-setting* theory focuses on the longer-term cognitive impact of mass communication, and on the media's "ability to mentally order and organize our world for us."[7] Research on this topic originated with the work of Maxwell E. McCombs and Donald L. Shaw in the late 1960s. They studied the 1968 and 1972 presidential elections and found a high correlation between the amount of time and space devoted to particular issues in the media and the ranking of these issues in order of perceived significance in the minds of the audience. They concluded that "audiences not only learn about public issues and other matters from the media, they also learn how much *importance* to attach to an issue or topic from the emphasis the media place upon it."[8]

By implication, this theory also suggests that the absence of coverage of particular individuals, events, or circumstances by mass communication media greatly limits the opportunities for them to enter the consciousness of consumers.[9] Much more research remains to be done in this important area to examine variables involved, to explore the relationship between an individual's agenda and his or her behavior, and to examine the more basic questions about the extent to which media coverage creates audience agendas or reflects preexisting public agendas.

Cultivation Theory. Another influential mass communication producer and product-based approach has grown out of research by George Gerbner and his colleagues in the Annenberg School of Communications at the University of Pennsylvania.[10] Since 1967, Gerbner has spearheaded an annual analysis of the amount and content of violence in prime-time television programs. These analyses attempt to determine not only the quantity of violence but also certain qualitative factors such as the sex, race, and age of criminals and their victims. This group of researchers, involved in what is called the Cultural Indicators Project, present their findings in a yearly Violence Profile.[11]

The researchers survey groups of viewers, who are divided into high and low television users, to determine if there are significant differences in the two groups'

> America's media managers create, process, refine, and preside over the circulation of images and information which determine our beliefs and attitudes and, ultimately, our behavior.
>
> Herbert I. Schiller, *The Mind Managers* (New York: Beacon, 1973), p. 1.

Bryant Gumbel interviews presidential candidate Bill Clinton on the "Today Show." Talk-show interviews were the major innovation of the 1992 campaign, upstaging press conferences and debates as a way of reaching voters.

perceptions. Of particular interest is whether the two groups have differing estimates of the level of violence in their neighborhoods, and whether they are involved in violent acts. Findings from much of this research supports the view that television shapes or "cultivates" certain beliefs in the minds of the viewers. Frequent television viewers, for instance, have exaggerated fears concerning the threat of violence.

The Spiral of Silence. Elizabeth Noelle-Neumann has proposed that, over time, media effectively limit the range of ideas or opinions available to the audience.[12] The theory suggests that, from attending to the media, individuals obtain an impression—more than likely a distorted one—of the distribution of opinion in society. If a consumer finds that his or her own opinion on a particular issue coincides with the majority opinion displayed in the media, the individual will be more likely to express and act on this opinion. If, on the other hand, a consumer's opinion is unsupported by media messages, he or she is more likely to keep quiet about it, to refrain from action, and thus to be caught up in a "spiral of silence." Mass media are in this way seen as promoting the consideration and acceptance of certain sets of opinions while at the same time silencing the discussion of others. Noelle-Neumann believes that this influence is especially acute today because of the pervasiveness and repetitiveness of media messages.

The Technological School. In addition to theories suggesting that mass communication products have a *direct* effect on consumers, there are others proposing that this influence is significant but *indirect*. One such group of theorists has focused its research efforts on the impact of the media themselves rather than on the messages they convey. These researchers have been termed the "medium theorists," and together form what could be called *the technological school*. Propo-

> ### RESEARCH
> ## Dukakis Believes His Campaign Was Damaged by Television
>
> Michael S. Dukakis offered the following observation on his unsuccessful bid for president: "I said in my acceptance speech at Atlanta that the 1988 election was not about ideology but about competence... I was wrong. It was about phraseology. It was about 10-second sound bites. And made-for-TV backdrops. And going negative." Mr. Dukakis referred to a study at the John F. Kennedy School of Government at Harvard University comparing TV coverage of the 1968 and 1988 presidential elections. The study found that in 1968 nearly half of all network television sound bites were 40 seconds or more, compared with 1 percent in 1988. in 1968, the candidates spoke for at least one minute in 20 percent of the newscasts, whereas in the 1988 there were no sound bites of that length. "If you couldn't say it in less than 10 seconds, it wasn't heard because it wasn't aired," said Gov. Dukakis.
>
> *Source:* Fox Butterfield, "Dukakis Says Race Was Harmed by TV," *The New York Times*, April 22, 1990, p. 23.

nents of the technological school do not dismiss the idea that particular messages may have various effects on particular individuals, audiences, or behaviors. They contend, however, that the most substantial impact of mass communication lies in the more general and indirect effects of different communication technologies (including writing, printing, and electronic media) on modes of thought, patterns of human interaction, and the structure of societal institutions.[13]

This emphasis can be summed up by saying that "the medium is the message."[14] Marshall McLuhan, author of this memorable phrase, was one of the earliest and certainly the most widely known of the medium theorists, and he and his mentor, Harold Adams Innis, did much to highlight this point of view.[15] Innis argues that Western culture has been deeply influenced by the spatial bias of print media, which he believes has promoted cultural complexity, confusion, and alienation.

McLuhan shared with Innis the conviction that communication media are extensions of the human mind and body. Commenting on his notion that "the medium is the message," he noted, "This is merely to say that the personal and social consequences of any medium—that is, of any extension of ourselves—result from the new scale that is introduced into our affairs by each extension of ourselves, or by any new technology."[16] He considered modern electronic media to be a sort of extension of the human nervous system, an extension that circles the globe and establishes a network of interpersonal involvements that he referred to as a "global village." McLuhan elaborated on and extended these basic ideas in his books *The Gutenberg Galaxy, Understanding Media*, and others.[17]

McLuhan's ideas, as well as his methods and style, have evoked much scholarly controversy over the years. As a consequence he has stimulated a great deal of interest in the implication of communication technology among students, scholars, and the general public—perhaps more than any other modern writer on mass communication.

Other technology-school writers of the late 1950s and early 1960s developed more scholarly ways of describing how the form of communication media can influence individuals and societies. Walter Ong traced this theme through a wide range of aspects and historical periods in Western culture.[18] His early work dealt with the influence of printing on the organization and segmentation of knowledge, both in textbooks and in the mind, during the sixteenth century. Ong's subsequent books have examined the diverse ways in which the history of human communication—from public speaking, to writing, to printing, to the electronic media—is mirrored in the evolution of the human mind.[19]

Joshua Meyrowitz is another thinker who has more recently made a major contribution to the technological school of thought on media effects. His provocative book *No Sense of Place* (1985) examines the influence of electronic media on the construction of particular kinds of cultural environments within which our roles and behavior patterns are played out.[20] The main point that Meyrowitz makes is that "by bringing many different types of people to the same place, electronic media have fostered a blurring of the many formerly distinct social roles."[21] The impact of electronic media is a result of their ability to portray people in roles, situations, and places in a powerful manner that has broad influence on audience members.

Modeling Theory. The idea that people learn particular attitudes and patterns of behavior by observing other people is a widespread and empirically supported assumption. *Modeling theory* is concerned with the ways in which the observation of behavior in mass communication products can encourage corresponding behavior patterns in consumers. The theoretical foundation for modeling theory is the more general social learning theory developed primarily by psychologist Albert Bandura.[22] *Social learning theory* takes as its starting point the observation that people construct images and goals for themselves and engage in behavior that they assume will help them reach these goals. Behavior that is found to contribute to this objective is reinforced and can develop into a habit, while behavior that does not contribute tends to fade away and be forgotten.

The mass media provide an almost limitless source of images and behavior patterns for their audiences to observe and, perhaps, to adopt either unconsciously or consciously. A child might learn to imitate the kindness or aggression displayed by television characters. A young person intent on social acceptance can acquire apparently pertinent attitudes, expressions, and styles of dress from television or magazines. An adult concerned about professional advancement can come to identify with or to practice the behavior of highly successful members of his or her profession as learned through mass communication.

The Evolution of the Producer Perspective. The early S→M→C→R theory was based on the assumption that media and their messages exert an all-powerful influence on audiences. As we have seen, communication researchers applied a widening array of research techniques in field studies of media effects, and failed to find conclusive evidence to support an extreme producer-centered approach to mass communication effects. Wrote Joseph Klapper in his classic 1960 book, *The Effects of Mass Communication*:

> The accumulated literature is vast in scope and varied in regard to topics, scientific validity, and findings. It attests to occasions on which persuasive communication, transmitted by any given medium, has succeeded; occasions on which it has had no impact; and occasions on which it has produced "boomerang" effects.[23]

Theories of effects evolved gradually to take account of the exceptions, nuances, and limitations that were discovered. Increasingly, producers and products were seen as contributing to and *reinforcing*—rather than in and of themselves causing—individual and social behaviors. Thus, for most scholars who emphasize the role of the producer and product, the period from the 1940s through the 1960s marked a shift in thinking. The shift was away from the position that mass communication producers and products are all-powerful, and have *direct, universal, uniform,* and *instantaneous* effects, and toward the position that influence is *more indirect, limited, less universal,* and *less immediate.*

The Consumer Perspective

Consumer approaches emphasize the role *audience members* play in mass communication outcomes. While producer theories may portray consumers as *passive* and *controlled*, the consumer perspective emphasizes their *active* and *controlling* role. This way of thinking is implied in the statement "When a movie gets too violent, he just tunes it out," or "Today's youth are mature enough to enjoy all forms of television, records, and music videos without being unduly influenced."

Cantril and War of the Worlds. One of the earliest research efforts to focus attention on the consumer role was undertaken by Hadley Cantril. The Halloween, 1938, radio broadcast of "War of the Worlds" was one of the most extraordinary events in the annals of mass communication. On that night some 32 million people were listening to radio. Of these, an estimated 6 to 9 million people heard CBS radio's "Mercury Theatre of the Air," and many concluded that alien creatures from Mars were invading the planet, based on the newscast-style presentation of H. G. Welles's science fiction classic.[24] Some listeners were propelled into what has been described as "a mindless panic." Many others "thought the world was ending; terrified people cried, hid, prayed, or fled into the countryside."[25]

Immediately following the "War of the Worlds" broadcast in October, 1938, the Office of Radio Research of Princeton University launched a research program to investigate the nature of the mass-mediated panic. The research was spearheaded by Hadley Cantril and was reported in a book entitled *The Invasion from Mars: A Study in the Psychology of Panic.*[26] Probably the most significant aspect of the study in terms of mass communication theory is that psychological and social differences among listeners were given serious consideration. Cantril found that differences in critical abilities, in levels of education, and in strength of religious beliefs as well as in personality factors such as emotional security and self-confidence were important elements in explaining why some people were frightened while others were not.

The Erie County Voting Study. Additional insights into factors that often intervene between media messages and audience responses emerged from a landmark study of the 1940 presidential election. This study focused on Erie County, Ohio, and was undertaken by Paul Lazarsfeld, Bernard Berelson, and Hazel Gaudet, who reported their findings in *The People's Choice.* One conclusion was that different types of responses to the political propaganda presented by the media corresponded with an individual's membership in various social categories.[27] Another finding, which proved to be even more influential, emerged unexpectedly. In the course of interviewing voters regarding how they arrived at their decisions, the researchers discovered that for many voters, messages from the media were often

Chapter 3 Mass Communication Effects

INSIGHT

War of the Worlds

8:00 P.M. EST, October 30. CBS News Bulletin
"A huge, flaming object, believed to be a meteorite, fell on a farm in the neighborhood of Grover's Mill, New Jersey, twenty-two miles from Trenton."

8:32 P.M. EST, October 30. CBS News Bulletin . . .
It has been determined that the mysterious landing in Grover's Mill, New Jersey was not a meteorite. Accounts indicate that it is a space vehicle carrying alien beings. We take you now to the Secretary of the Interior. "Citizens of the nation: I shall not try to conceal the gravity of the situation that confronts the country, nor the concern of your Government in protecting the lives and property of its people. However, I wish to impress upon you—private citizens and public officials, all of you—the urgent need for calm and resourceful action. Fortunately this formidable enemy is still confined to a comparatively small area, and we may place our faith in the military forces to keep them there. In the meantime placing our trust in God, we must continue the performance of our duties, each and every one of us, so that we may confront the destructive adversary with a nation united, courageous, and consecrated to the preservation of human supremacy on this earth. I thank you."

8:45 P.M. EST, October 30, CBS News Bulletin . . .
The aliens, believed to be from Mars, have apparently overcome military opposition and are advancing toward New York . . . There are reports that the aliens are blanketing the city with poison gas. Announcer Ray Collins was killed by aliens on the roof of the CBS Broadcasting Building. The boats in the New York harbor had been whistling an emergency alert until moments ago when their warnings were silenced. . . .

(SILENCE)

8:55 P.M. EST, October 30, Amateur radio operator in New York City . . .
"2X2L calling CQ." "2X2L calling CQ." "2X2L calling CQ."
"Isn't there anyone on the air?" "Isn't there anyone?"

8:58 P.M. EST, October 30, Orson Welles . . .
"This is Orson Welles, ladies and gentlemen, out of character to assure you that the *War of the Worlds* has no further significance than as the holiday offering it was intended to be. The [CBS] Mercury Theatre's own radio version of dressing up in a sheet and jumping out of a bush and saying BOO!"

"We annihilated the world before your very ears. . . . You will be relieved, I hope, to learn that we didn't mean it. . . . So good-bye and everybody remember, please, for the next day or so, the terrible lesson you learned tonight. That grinning, glowing globular invader of your living room is an inhabitant of the pumpkin patch, and if your doorbell rings and nobody's there, that was NO Martian . . . it's Halloween."

Based on excerpts from the CBS adaptation of "War of the Worlds," broadcast on October 30, 1938, and transcripts and discussions of the event in Hadley Cantril, *The Invasion from Mars: A Study in the Psychology of Panic* (Princeton: Princeton University Press, 1940), and Shearon Lowery and Melvin L. DeFleur, *Milestones in Mass Communication Research: Media Effects*, (New York: Longman, 1983). Emphasis added.

not obtained first-hand from newspapers or radios, but instead were received second-hand. Those individuals who did read and listen to the media and who could then influence the opinions of others became known as *opinion leaders*, and the mass communication process involved was referred to as the *two-step flow*. This study suggested that the actual effects of the media were rather limited, with the primary factors in political decision making being social characteristics and interpersonal influences.

The Diffusion of Innovations. An area of research that also focuses on the role of opinion leaders is the study of patterns through which information about new ideas, techniques, and products spreads throughout an organization or a society.[28] The *diffusion of innovations* was first studied in rural agricultural populations and developing countries, but has since been investigated in a variety of settings. Analyses of opinion leadership have shown that many opinion leaders are regarded as knowledgeable only on certain topics, while other such leaders are looked to for information and advice on a wide range of issues. These investigations have also revealed that the patterns of diffusion and adoption cannot be described accurately as simple, two-step processes, but must be understood in terms of multiple steps and complex interpersonal communication networks. The understanding and reception (or rejection) of a particular idea by individuals has been found to depend heavily on their location in a communication network, on the nature of their links with others, and on other individual and interpersonal factors.

Uses and Gratifications. A number of scholars over the past few decades have argued that the most important factors governing the effects of mass communication are the needs of audience members. They propose that basic human needs motivate individuals to attend to particular forms of mass media and to select and use messages in ways they find personally gratifying.[29] Thus, a given medium, such as television, and a certain set of messages, such as sports information, might be used by different individuals in very different ways depending on the particular needs they are seeking to satisfy. On the other hand, some audience members might have no use at all for this information.

This approach suggests also that consumers may use information products in a variety of ways that are not all that obviously related to the content of the information. These uses include

- Grist for social interaction: One use of mass communication products may be to provide viewers with something to talk about with friends and colleagues.[30] Examples: Events of the day reported on in the local newspaper, the score of the Monday night football game, or events on the latest episode of a popular TV series.
- Means to structure and mark time.[31] Examples: Our mornings may begin by watching the "Today" show or by reading the local newspaper. For many, the day ends with the close of the late news or the David Letterman show.
- Status symbol: Mass communication products and services may also confer status on their owners or users. Examples: A cellular car phone, a portable CD player, or large-screen television set.
- Others: Playing a "boom box" loudly may be a way of attracting attention or claiming territory. A library can be used as a place to sleep or to meet new acquaintances. Listening to a portable cassette player with earphones can be a way to isolate oneself.

In many respects, the uses and gratifications approach is more a general perspective than a specific theory; it represents an attempt to understand audience members as active information consumers, and to place the emphasis not on what media *do to* people, but rather on what people *do with* the media.

Media System Dependency Theory. In an effort to bring together elements of other theoretical perspectives, Sandra Ball-Rokeach and Melvin DeFleur proposed that media impact arises from a complex web of interactions among audiences, the media, and the larger social system. They have said:

> One way to describe media dependency theory is to say that it is an "ecological" theory (in the original meaning of that term): it focuses on relationships between small, medium, and large systems and their components. An ecological theory views society as an organic structure.... The media system is assumed to be an important part of the social fabric of modern society, and it is seen to have relationships with individuals, groups, organizations, and other social systems. These relationships may be conflict-ridden or cooperative; they may be dynamic and changing or static and orderly. They also may range from being direct and powerful to being indirect or weak. Whatever the particulars of the *relationship*, it is the relationship that carries the burden of explanation.[32]

In this perspective, individuals are seen as dependent to varying degrees. Because the media system has control over the information resources many people consider essential for reaching their goals, patterns of dependence become firmly established. The nature of these relationships, of course, is different for different individuals. Some people rely almost totally on television or radio, while others prefer print, and, whereas some viewers watch television primarily to increase their understanding, others watch it mostly as a form of play.

Reconciling Producer and Consumer Perspectives

The relationship between production and consumption is an extremely complex one, particularly as it relates to explaining mass communication effects. Is violence on television the cause of increasing violence in contemporary life? Or is violence in contemporary life the cause of increasing incidences of (and interest in) violence on television? Or are both caused by some third factor? Are morals in America on the decline? If so, are mass communication institutions and programming the cause? If we found that prime-time programming, advertising, song lyrics, music videos, and teenage books and magazines contained more sexually explicit ma-

INSIGHT

"Redrum": Mass Communication Effect?

Reading, PA. (AP) Police arrested two suspects yesterday in the decapitation of a 41-year-old hotel worker whose body was found beneath the word "redrum"—"murder" spelled backward—written in blood. The case attracted widespread attention because the murder scene was similar to one in the 1980 movie "The Shining" which was shown on cable television days before the slaying. In both the movie and the case, the word "murder" was written backward in blood on the walls.

Source: Courier News (Bridgewater, NJ), July 30, 1987.

> **EFFECTS OF TV VIOLENCE: POINT-COUNTERPOINT**
>
> It's gross oversimplification to think all we have to do is substitute Disney for Miami Vice to produce kinder, gentler TV audiences.
> Susan Percy, *USA Today* Guest Columnist
>
> Many in the industry still argue that TV violence does no harm. They claim 25 minutes' exposure to violence has no impact, while 30 seconds' exposure to a commercial has great impact. The obvious answer: TV sells—whether a political product, or a soap, or violence.
> Senator Paul Simon
>
> Source: "No Place for a Sit-com Solution," "An Opposing View: Congress Must Fight Violence on TV," and "An Opposing View: Congress Must Fight Violence on TV," *USA Today*, June 27, 1989, p. 6A.

terial today than it did 10 years ago, would that prove that mass communication is causing this change in society? Or would we perhaps be as accurate to assert that society is causing a change in mass communication? Or both? These are kinds of issues that mobilize, motivate, and at the same time perplex mass communication researchers and practitioners alike. They are not easy questions to answer.

Producer-oriented approaches emphasize the role of producers, products, and services in explaining the effects of mass communication. These perspectives remind us that producers and products of mass communication play an important and influential role in our lives—individually, socially, and culturally. They do so through the creation, packaging, and distribution of the information that fills our environment—information with which we must organize ourselves in order to function as humans.

Consumer-oriented theories stress the role consumers play in explaining the impact of mass communication. They remind us that as consumers we play an active role in the mass communication process and in determining its effects. Individual needs and uses, social dynamics, and preferences of audience members are emphasized.

Can these two perspectives be meaningfully reconciled? Consider the following analogy: "High-powered sports cars cause accidents." It is true that high-powered sports cars are involved in a number of accidents—more accidents than cars lacking such power. Are the cars themselves to blame? Would we eliminate all these accidents if we stopped producing fast cars? To what extent are the drivers to blame?

One can certainly speed and drive recklessly in a Corvette. The car *is* designed for high performance. But these same behaviors are also possible in a Honda Civic, if a driver chooses to *use* it in these ways. However, we can't take this argument too far; without a car, after all, there can be no speeding or reckless driving. We might, therefore, want to conclude that a high-powered sports car *facilitates*, but does not itself *cause*, accidents. Thus, accidents are the result of particular *patterns of consumption in relation to product characteristics and availability*.

For those of us interested in mass communication, the case of high-powered cars is interesting, because it involves an analogous relationship between technology and human behavior. As with cars and drivers, it seems reasonable to assume that mass communication technologies and products facilitate but are seldom the sole cause of audience behavior. Generally, the effects that occur between mass communication producers and consumers are *mutually causal*, or *mutually controlling*—a perspective that is well illustrated with the P↔I↔C perspective.

As with the Corvette, mass communication effects result from *both*

1. The availability of technologies and products with particular characteristics and capabilities, and
2. The uses to which consumers put technologies and products.

They are the result of particular *patterns of consumption in relation to product characteristics and availability*. Mass communication technologies, producers, products, and services play an important role in defining, influencing, and shaping the available options, direction, and limits of those uses—over time, if not at every instant. As consumers we influence the impact that mass communication producers, products, and services have through the choices we make individually and in the aggregate—as audience members.

Additional Concerns About Mass Communication Effects

Concerns about the impact of mass communication in certain areas have been particularly widespread in recent years. In the final section of this chapter, we briefly consider several areas of great concern: violence, sex and pornography, education, and socialization.

Violence. Violence on television has been the focus of controversy since the early 1950s. In the late 1960s two governmental commissions—the National Commission on the Causes and Prevention of Violence, and the Surgeon General's Scientific Advisory Committee on Television and Social Behavior—undertook a series of studies. On the basis of both laboratory experiments and field studies, the Surgeon General's committee concluded, somewhat cautiously, that viewing violence on television contributes to violent or aggressive behavior in viewers. The nature and strength of the causal relationship between viewing televised violence and subsequent aggressive behavior, however, is a major point of contention, and is especially debated by some representatives of the television industry. But these and other research programs and reports, such as *Television and Behavior: Ten Years of Scientific Progress and Implications for the Eighties,* issued in 1982 by the National Institute of Mental Health, have supported a causal connection among social scientists, politicians, educators, and the general public.

Informal discussions of violence often proceed on the assumption that everyone knows what violence is and that they can easily recognize it when they see it. But in order to make progress in understanding scientifically the problem of televised violence, it is necessary to establish precise definitions and reliable methods of analyzing and quantifying this phenomenon. Should "violence" in cartoons be considered equivalent to violence in crime shows? Does true violence include damage to property or only injury to persons? And should accounts of natural disasters such as earthquakes qualify as violence? Researchers have devised a variety of answers to questions such as these. The most ambitious research program is the ongoing Cultural Indicators Project conducted by the Annenberg School of Communication at the University of Pennsylvania. As mentioned previously, these investigators analyze the prevalence or distribution of violence throughout a given sample of programs, the rate or frequency of violent behavior within these programs, and the role of violence with regard to the characteristics of aggressors and victims. The results are combined to form an annual Index of Violence, which has shown that though there are often yearly fluctuations, there has not been a significant change in the percentage of programs containing violence since 1967, though the frequency of violence in particular programs has increased.[33]

Mass communication researchers have proposed that at least four factors may be involved in bringing about the effects of televised violence.

1. The first and perhaps most important factor is *observational learning,* which refers to the process through which people learn to imitate role models and types of behavior, especially if the behavior is perceived as being rewarded. This process seems to be at work not only in the imitation of televised aggression among children, but also in the influence of highly publicized murders, suicides, and prize fights among adults.[34]

2. The second factor is the change in attitudes that often occurs through television viewing. Studies have shown that children who watch substantial amounts of

> **RESEARCH**
>
> ## Public Opinions About Television and Sex
>
> Most people believe that
>
> - Television influences the values and behavior of people who watch several hours of television each day.
> - Television viewing encourages teenagers to be sexually active.
> - Television exaggerates the importance of sex in American life.
> - Contraceptive advertising on television would encourage more teenagers to use contraceptives.
>
> Source: *Attitudes About Television, Sex and Contraceptive Advertising* (New York: Louis Harris and Associates, February, 1987).

television are more likely than less avid viewers to accept aggressive behavior in other children. Other research suggests that violence on television can cultivate attitudes of suspicion and images of an extremely violent world in the minds of its viewers.

3. A third possible factor is *physiological arousal*, the idea that viewers are stimulated by observing violence, to which they may nevertheless become desensitized over time, and that this arousal leads to, or is maintained by, subsequent aggressive activity.

4. The fourth factor involves the process of justification. Many people who watch televised violence may already engage in violent behavior or possess aggressive tendencies, and may then find in television a form of justification for their actions.

Although much research has been done on the effects of violence in the media, many unanswered questions still surround this multifaceted issue.

Sex and Pornography. The production and consumption of sexually explicit material in the form of books, magazines, and movies is a worldwide business of enormous dimensions. Several of this country's most popular magazines are erotic in nature, and the increased availability of soft-core and hard-core pornography on videocassettes has added another source of erotica in the mass media. But while many Americans enjoy a regular diet of such material, others consider it distasteful or even demonic.

With such a wide range of views concerning what is offensive and what is not, it is obviously difficult to formulate definitions of erotica and pornography and a legal concept of obscenity that are widely applicable and acceptable to everyone. Some definitions focus on the intent of the producers; others emphasize the response elicited in consumers.

The courts have attempted, in broad terms, to define obscenity in such a way that local prosecutors, judges, and juries can make rational decisions on whether particular information products enjoy constitutional protection. In deciding *Roth v. United States* 1957, the Supreme Court held that obscenity does not enjoy constitutional protection, but all ideas having "even the slightest redeeming social importance" are protected. The standard the court offered for judging information to be obscene was "whether, to the average person, applying contemporary community standards, the dominant theme of the material, taken as whole, appeals to prurient interests."

Each of those crucial phrases in the Roth decision had the force of requiring a jury to consider not just whether some individuals found some words or images offensive, but whether the entire work violated the norms of the community. In 1966's rerun of the Fanny Hill case (*Memoirs* v. *Massachusetts*), and again in 1973 (*Miller* v. *California*), the wording was revised and revised again. The Miller decision put forth three tests for

1. Whether the average person, applying contemporary community standards, would find that the work taken as a whole appeals to prurient interest,
2. Whether the work depicts or describes in a patently offensive way sexual conduct specifically defined by the applicable state law, and
3. Whether the work taken as a whole lacks serious literary, artistic, political, or scientific value.

The Court later ruled that community standards need not mean just the standards of people living in the precise area where a magazine was sold or a movie was shown. It also held that nudity and sex, in and of themselves, are not obscene. The Supreme Court has not protected those charged with obscenity when the producer's advertisements for the information make it clear that the producer was pandering blatantly to the prurient interests of specialized consumers.

INDUSTRY

Cable Seeks a Middle Ground

Network television, regulated since its inception, practices self-censorship that keeps hard-core pornographic material from the airwaves. The movies, on the other hand have enjoyed great freedom in the past two decades, largely because of the industry rating system designed to prevent children from seeing material considered unacceptable.

Cable television falls between network television and movie theater presentations in terms of the way the consumer finds and uses information. In a monograph on obscenity and cable television, mass communication researchers Denise Trauth and John Huffman summarized the problem:

Audiences of theatrical film are provided with a rating service.... Cable, by contrast, requires that a customer subscribe for a minimum period; the customer then has access to all offerings during this period. This distribution system and the potential for inadvertent viewers in the cable audience—some of whom may be children—require a standard of obscenity for cable stricter than that which would be applied to theatrical film but less limiting than that appropriate for conventional television.*

In its early days, cable television was well known for its late-night offerings of "heavy R-" or even "X-rated" material. The Playboy Channel specializes in such fare. But, in the complicated set of societal balances that seem always to be at work, by the late 1980s cable television, in its bid for larger audiences, is tending toward precisely the middle ground suggested by Trauth and Huffman.

*Trauth, D. and John Huffman, "Obscenity and Cable Television: A Regulatory Approach," *Journalism Monographs*, 95, March 1986, p. 26.

Research on the functions and effects of sexually explicit material in the media began in earnest with the establishment in 1970 of the Presidential Commission on Obscenity and Pornography. Since that time a good deal of study has been done on various aspects of this issue, including the influence of pornography on the image and treatment of women and on the relationship between the sexes, on the physiological effects of viewing such material, and on the possible relationship between pornography and violent crimes such as rape and murder and other forms of aggressive behavior.

With regard to the first of these topics, analyses of the content of pornographic materials have provided some evidence that messages of the supremacy of men over women are often present. Other research indicates that viewing pornography can contribute to attitudes of increased acceptance of violence toward women, but also that sexually explicit material portraying men and women as partners or equals can help to reduce antisocial attitudes. Studies of the relationship between the use of pornography and criminal behavior reveal a positive relationship between high levels of availability and/or consumption of pornography and high rates of rape. But a causal relationship has not been found, and it would be premature to say, on the basis of this research, whether, or how, one causes the other. The relationship between pornography and crime is extremely complex, and involves many cultural, educational, and familial influences.

A number of different theories have been presented to account for the actual or assumed effects of pornography and to describe its role in society. Some writers consider modern pornography to be an aspect of a long-standing and widespread historical tradition of artistic expression, and propose that it serves beneficial functions with regard to sexual communication and education. From a feminist perspective, much pornography is seen as a damaging form of propaganda that grows out of and sustains an unequal relationship between the sexes created by the male domination of women. Pornography has also been analyzed and interpreted from psychoanalytic, Marxist, and a variety of religious points of view.[35]

Education. Questions concerning the educational or intellectual impact of mass communication media have been discussed and debated for centuries. In ancient Greece, Plato warned that writing weakens the mind and destroys the memory. In the fifteenth century, similar complaints were leveled against printing, though many people defended it as an unprecedented means for distributing and increasing knowledge. In the twentieth century, the possible ill effects of radio on home study habits has been discussed, but the major focus of controversy has, of course, been television.

Investigations, beginning in the 1950s, have shown that people who spend a great deal of time watching television have lower IQs than people who spend less time doing so. But this research merely reveals a correlation and at this point it is impossible to state whether heavy television viewing in some way lowers IQ, or whether persons with lower IQs choose to watch more television. Our understanding of the relationship between television viewing and reading behavior also remains uncertain. Some studies have found that a positive correlation shows up over time among younger viewers, while other studies have shown that adults who spend no time reading watch much more television than those who read. Similarly, the nature of the connection between viewing and both academic performance and educational aspiration has not yet been unraveled; so many factors—such as grade level, gender, television content, and type of school subject—seem to be implicated in this very complex relationship.[36]

Researchers have also studied the effects of specific educational programs such as "Sesame Street." These studies provide evidence not only that the content of these programs can help children strengthen certain cognitive abilities such as problem solving, reasoning, language, and arithmetic skills, but also that the form or style of presentation can stimulate the development of other important mental operations. "Zooming-in" on a detail of a larger scene, for example, can encourage the practice of analyzing something into smaller parts, and presenting several different camera angles of an object can represent the cognitive process of considering something from a number of perspectives. The research also suggests that the educational impact of television viewing is affected by the nature of the family and social relationships prevailing in the viewing environment.[37]

Socialization. People are constantly faced with questions concerning who they are, how they fit into society, and how they should act. Such questions are particularly urgent for young people, who find role models not only among family members, friends, and acquaintances, but also among television and movie characters. Content analyses of television programs have yielded a great deal of information on the demographic characteristics of the characters portrayed, and researchers have examined the influence these programs can have on the development of personal identity and on the association of certain attitudes and behavior patterns with particular sexes, ages, races, and occupations.[38]

Many of the men and women characters appearing on television present somewhat stereotyped male and female images. Various studies have shown that children who are heavy television viewers, when asked whether certain activities or occupations would be associated with women or with men, gave answers more in line with television stereotypes than did lighter viewers.

Research also indicates, however, that programs with characters in atypical occupational roles can educate children away from the traditional sexual stereotypes. Additionally, it has been found that boys almost always choose male characters as ideal role models, and that girls sometimes choose female characters but also often choose male ones.[39]

The heaviest viewers of television fall into two age groups—young children and the elderly. Little research has been done on the effects of television on older people, but several studies indicate that younger viewers acquire attitudes about the elderly from television. Research reveals that heavy viewers develop inaccurate and rather stereotyped ideas concerning the health and personal characteristics of the elderly, and that such ideas are especially prevalent among viewers of fantasy-type programs.[40]

Another age-role issue is what has been described as the "disappearance" of childhood, a phenomenon that has concerned numerous social scientists in recent years. It refers to the fact that since many children today tend to speak, dress, and behave more like adults than did their counterparts in previous decades, the boundaries between the roles of children and the roles of adults have faded significantly. Theorists have identified one important factor in this process as the increased access children have to ideas and information that were once considered the exclusive province of adults, a type of access that has been greatly facilitated during the past 30 years by the shift in American society from a book culture to a television culture.[41]

For many Americans, the mass communication products are the primary source of information about racial and ethnic minorities. Research regarding minorities on television has progressed over the years from simple head counts to

> ## RESEARCH
>
> ### Research on Television Effects
>
> 1. Cognitive and Emotional Functioning
>   - Cognitive processing
>   - Forms and codes of television
>   - Arousal
>   - Emotional development and functioning
> 2. Violence and Aggression
>   - Violence in television content
>   - Effects of televised violence
> 3. Imagination, Creativity, and Prosocial Behavior
> 4. Socialization and Conceptions of Social Reality
>   - Sex-role socialization
>   - Age-role socialization
>   - Race-role socialization
>   - Occupational role socialization
>   - Consumer role socialization
> 5. The Family and Interpersonal Relations
>   - Television's families
>   - Television's effects on the family and social relations
> 6. Television in American Society
>   - Production of prime-time television
>   - Public's attitude toward television
> 7. Education and Learning About Television
>   - Educational achievement
>   - Television and reading
>   - Educational aspiration
>   - Learning about television
>
> In 1980, the National Institute of Mental Health classified the nearly 3000 studies dealing with various facets of television effects, outcomes, and uses into these seven categories.
>
> *Source: Television and Behavior: Ten Years of Scientific Progress and Implications for the 80s.* Vol. 10., *Summary Report* (Washington, DC: National Institute of Mental Health, U.S. Department of Health and Human Services, 1983).

more sophisticated content analyses of the types of roles played by minorities, but the relationship between media portrayals and the perceptions and subsequent behavior of consumers remains little understood. Although the presence of blacks in television programs has increased noticeably during the 1970s and 1980s, the appearance of Hispanics, Asians, or Native Americans is still quite rare, and there is little interaction between races. Investigations of the impact of programs such as "Sesame Street," which deal specifically and deliberately with racial images and relations, have shown, however, that young viewers can acquire positive attitudes toward minorities and that minority children can gain confidence and cultural pride.[42]

While an enormous amount of research has been done on the *antisocial* consequences of television, some researchers have also examined its *prosocial* influences. Studies of deliberately prosocial programs like "Mister Rogers' Neighborhood," "Fat Albert," and "Freestyle" provide evidence that such shows can indeed foster positive, constructive attitudes and actions, but that the influence is by no means uniform, is sometimes short-lived, and can be enhanced or diminished by various conditions in the viewing environment.[43]

FUTURE FILE

✓ A producer is interested in designing a new medium aimed at college students. The producer has no idea what the form or the content of the medium should be. What does the producer need to know about the audience of college students?

✓ If the form of the medium has as much effect on the audience as the content, what current media forms may be doomed in the near future because they no longer appeal to the interests or the needs of audience members?

✓ How can producers increase the amount and the quality of feedback they receive so that they can do a better job of providing what it is that consumers want and need?

NOTES

1. This distinction was proposed by John C. Merrill and Ralph L. Lowenstein, *Media, Messages and Men: New Perspectives in Communication* (New York: McKay, 1971), pp. 33–44.
2. Todd Hunt, *Reviewing for the Mass Media* (Philadelphia: Chilton, 1972), pp. 3–8.
3. Carl I. Hovland, Irving L. Janis, and Harold H. Kelley, *Communication and Persuasion* (New Haven: Yale University Press, 1953).
4. Charles R. Wright, *Mass Communication: A Sociological Perspective*, 3rd ed. (New York: Random House, 1986), pp. 3–28.
5. Wright, pp. 3–19.
6. Walter Lippman, *Public Opinion* (New York: Macmillan, 1921).
7. Donald L. Shaw and Maxwell E. McCombs, *The Emergence of American Political Issues* (St. Paul, MN: West, 1977), p. 5; see also Maxwell E. McCombs and Donald L. Shaw, "The Agenda Setting Function of the Mass Media," *Public Opinion Quarterly*, 36:2 (1972), pp. 176–187.
8. Maxwell E. McCombs and Donald L. Shaw, "Structuring the Unseen Environment," *Journal of Communication*, 26:2 (Spring 1976), p. 18.
9. Wright, pp. 154–155.
10. George Gerbner et al., "The Mainstreaming of America: Violence Profile No. 11," *Journal of Communication*, 30 (Summer 1980), pp. 10–29.
11. George Gerbner and Larry Gross, "Living with Television: The Violence Profile," *Journal of Communication* 26 (Spring 1976), pp. 173–199.
12. Elizabeth Noelle-Neumann, "Return to the Concept of the Powerful Mass Media," in H. Eguhi and K. Sata, eds., *Studies of Broadcasting* (Tokyo: Nippon Kyokii, 1973), pp. 67–112.
13. Joshua Meyrowitz, *No Sense of Place* (New York: Oxford University Press, 1985), pp. 16–23.
14. Marshall McLuhan, *Understanding Media* (New York: McGraw-Hill, 1964), p. 7.
15. Harold A. Innis, *The Bias of Communication* (Toronto: University of Toronto Press, 1951); Harold A. Innis, *Empire and Communication*, rev. ed. (Toronto: University of Toronto Press, 1972).
16. McLuhan, p. 7.
17. Marshall McLuhan, *The Gutenberg Galaxy* (Toronto: University of Toronto Press, 1962).
18. Walter Ong, *Ramus, Method, and the Decay of Dialogue* (Cambridge: Harvard University Press, 1958).
19. Walter Ong, *The Presence of the Word* (New Haven: Yale University Press, 1967); *Rhetoric, Romance, and Technology* (Ithaca, NY: Cornell University Press, 1971); *Interfaces of the*

Word (Ithaca, NY: Cornell University Press, 1977); *Orality and Literacy* (London: Methuen, 1982).
20. Joshua Meyrowitz, *No Sense of Place* (New York: Oxford University Press, 1985).
21. Meyrowitz, pp. 5–6.
22. Albert Bandura, *Social Learning Theory* (Englewood Cliffs, NJ: Prentice-Hall, 1977).
23. Joseph T. Klapper, *The Effects of Mass Communication* (New York: Free Press, 1960), p. 13.
24. Shearon Lowery and Melvin L. DeFleur, *Milestones in Mass Communication Research: Media Effects* (New York: Longman, 1983), p. 70.
25. Lowery and DeFleur, p. 59.
26. Hadley Cantril, *The Invasion from Mars: A Study in the Psychology of Panic* (Princeton: Princeton University Press, 1940).
27. Paul Lazarsfeld, Bernard Berelson, and Hazel Gaudet, *The People's Choice* (New York: Columbia University Press, 1948).
28. Everett M. Rogers, *Diffusion of Innovations* (New York: Free Press, 1962); Everett M. Rogers and Floyd Shoemaker, *Communication of Innovations: A Cross-Cultural Approach* (New York: Free Press, 1971); Everett M. Rogers and Ronny Adhikarya, "Diffusions of Innovations: An Up-to-Date Review and Commentary," in Dan Nimmo, ed., *Communication Yearbook 3* (New Brunswick, NJ: Transaction Books, 1979), pp. 67–82.
29. Elihu Katz, Jay Blumler, and Michael Gurevitch, "Uses of Mass Communication by the Individual," in W. Phillips Davison and Frederick Yu, eds., *Mass Communication Research: Major Issues and Future Directions* (New York: Praeger, 1974); Jay Blumler and Elihu Katz, eds., *The Uses of Mass Communication* (Beverly Hills, CA: Sage, 1974).
30. Lee Thayer, "On the Mass Media and Mass Communication: Notes Toward a Theory," in Richard W. Budd and Brent D. Ruben, eds., *Beyond Media: New Approaches to Mass Communication* (New Brunswick, NJ: Transaction Books, 1988), pp. 64–70.
31. Thayer, pp. 64–70.
32. Melvin L. DeFleur and Sandra Ball-Rokeach, *Theories of Mass Communication*, 5th ed. (New York: Longman, 1989), pp. 302–303.
33. David Pearl, "Violence and Aggression," *Society*, 21:6 (Sept./Oct. 1984), p. 21.
34. Leonard Berkowitz and Karen Heimer Rogers, "A Priming Effect Analysis of Media Influences," in Jennings Bryant and Dolf Zillmann, eds., *Perspectives on Media Effects* (Hillsdale, NJ: Lawrence Erlbaum, 1986), pp. 57–81; David Phillips and John E. Hensley, "When Violence Is Reward or Punished," *Journal of Communication*, 34 (Summer 1984), pp. 101–116.
35. L. Lederer, ed., *Take Back the Night: Women on Pornography* (New York: William Morrow, 1980); Neil M. Malamuth and Victoria Billings, "Why Pornography? Modes of Functions and Effects," *Journal of Communication*, 34 (Summer 1984), pp. 117–129.
36. Samuel Ball, Patricia Palmer, and Emelia Millward, "Television and Its Education Impact: A Reconsideration," in Jennings Bryant and Dolf Zillmann, eds., *Perspectives on Media Effects* (Hillsdale, NJ: Lawrence Erlbaum, 1986), pp. 129–140; David Pearl, L. Bouthilet, and J. Lazar, eds., *Television and Behavior*, esp. chap. 9, "Education and Learning About Television" (Washington, DC: U.S. Department of Health and Human Services, 1982).
37. Ball, Palmer, and Millward, pp. 133–134, 136–138.
38. See Stanley J. Baran and Vincent J. Blasko, "Social Perceptions and the By-Products of Advertising," *Journal of Communication*, 34 (Summer 1984), pp. 12–20; Pearl, Bouthilet, and Lazar, eds., esp. chap. 6, "Socialization and Conceptions of Social Reality."
39. Pearl, Bouthilet, and Lazar, eds., pp. 54–56.
40. Ibid, pp. 56–58.
41. Meyrowitz, especially chap. 12, "The Merging of Masculinity and Femininity" and chap. 13, "The Blurring of Childhood and Adulthood."
42. Bradley S. Greenberg, "Minorities and the Mass Media," in Bryant and Zillmann, eds., pp. 165–188; Pearl, Bouthilet, and Lazar, eds., pp. 58–59.
43. Jerome Johnston and James S. Ettema, "Using Television to Best Advantage: Research for Pro-social Television," in Bryant and Zillmann, eds., pp. 143–164.

SUGGESTED READINGS

Budd, Richard W., and Brent D. Ruben, eds., *Beyond Media: New Approaches to Mass Communication*, 2nd ed. (New Brunswick, NJ: Transaction Books, 1988).

Cantril, Hadley, *The Invasion from Mars: A Study in the Psychology of Panic* (Princeton: Princeton University Press, 1940).

Lowery, Shearon, and Melvin L. DeFleur, *Milestones in Mass Communication Research: Media Effects* (New York: Longman, 1983).

NIMH, *Television and Behavior: Ten Years of Scientific Progress and Implications for the Eighties*, Vol. 1: *Summary Report* (Rockville, MD: National Institute of Mental Health, 1982), p. 87.

Wright, Charles R., *Mass Communication: A Sociological Perspective*, 3rd ed. (New York: Random House, 1986).

PART TWO

Influences on Mass Communication, Media, and Messages

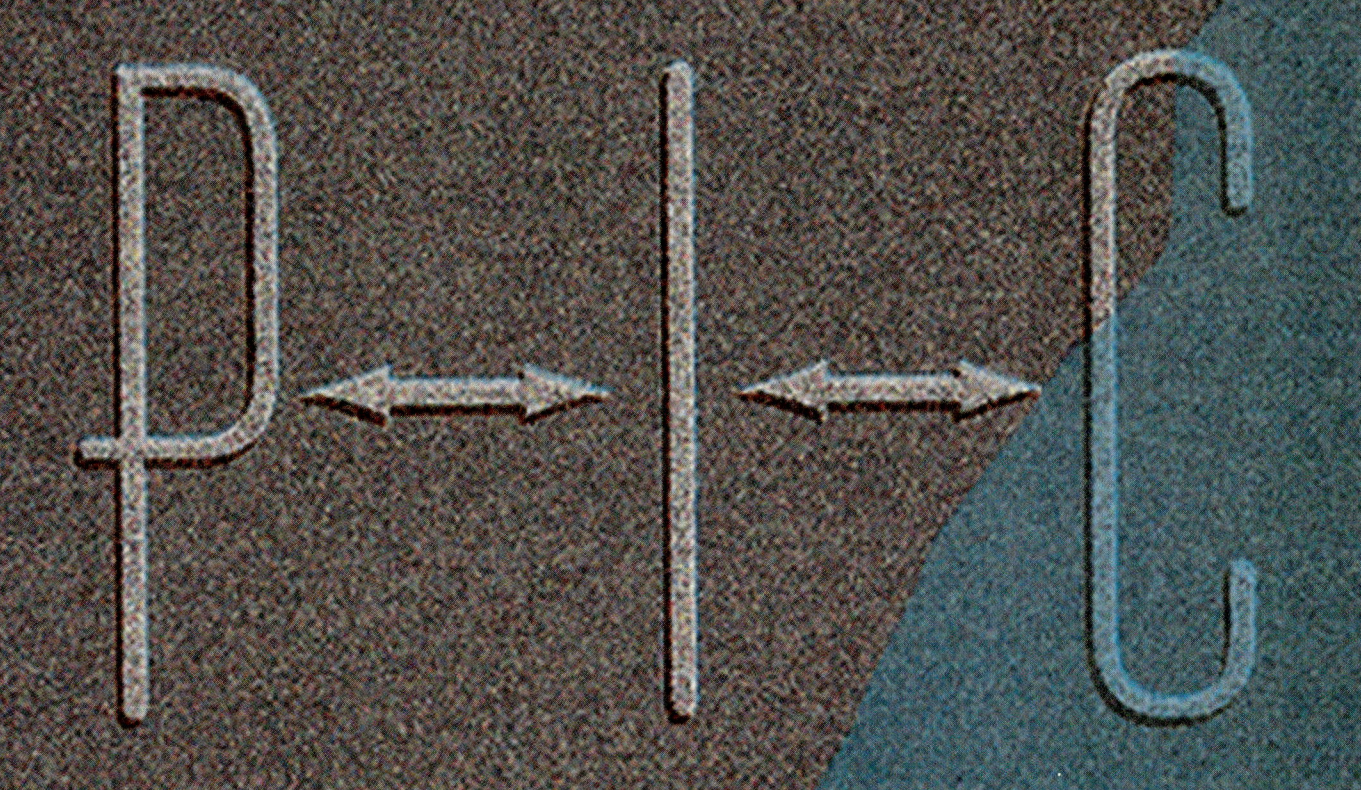

CHAPTER 4

The Selection and Packaging of News

AT A GLANCE

✓ The organization of a news operation delegates responsibility for gathering and preparing certain kinds of news to specialized reporters and editors.

✓ Every journalist functions as a "gatekeeper" who decides what information to pass on to the consumer and what information not to use.

✓ Because gathering news is expensive, press associations and syndicates perform the task at the national and international level on behalf of the local media.

✓ Over the years, generally accepted criteria have developed for deciding what constitutes "news." Objectivity—lack of bias in reporting the news—is strived for, but today the "myth" of objectivity is questioned.

✓ Economic, political, and legal pressures shape the content of the news media. The media are criticized for bending to these pressures that have become part of the institution.

You have looked through your morning newspaper three times and you can't find anything about the charity concert held to raise funds for the homeless, a concert you attended and enjoyed. It raises questions once again for you the news consumer: "How do they decide what to put in the newspaper? Who makes the decisions? Why don't they have the stories that interest me in addition to the many stories that don't interest me at all?"

Before we look at the news and entertainment media in individual chapters, we will ask "What is news?" and "How do producers decide that news will be passed on to consumers?" In the main, our focus will be on newspapers, because historically newspapers have been in the forefront of deciding what is news and how it is packaged. Broadcast media and other information providers have refined the basic definitions of news and the techniques of newsgathering pioneered by newspapers. In later chapters, we will see that such concepts as "newsworthiness" and "the editing function" can be adapted—using the P↔I↔C model—to explain how other information producers select and shape messages according to their understanding of what the consumer needs and wants.

NEWS PRODUCERS

To understand the type of information called "news," we must look first at the roles news producers play, consciously and unconsciously, that affect the process of information selection and dissemination.

Structure of the Newsroom

Newspapers have come a long way from the one-person print shop, where the same individual gathered, wrote, edited, printed, and even helped disseminate information. Like all large mass communication organizations, the news media have become highly structured hierarchies with a myriad of functions performed by specialists. The editor-in-chief of a print publication or general manager of a broadcast operation may have little or no involvement in the actual day-to-day reporting, writing, and packaging of news. Instead, he or she is a manager who directs the activities of supervisory personnel, calls and runs meetings of policy-setting groups such as the editorial board of a newspaper, and represents the news operation to the business side of the company as well as to civic groups, legislators, and other outside interests.

Because the editor-in-chief of a print medium and the general manager of a broadcast medium have responsibility for administration and policy, the day-to-day news operations are supervised by the managing editor of a newspaper or magazine and the news director of a broadcast medium. In a large operation, responsibility is further delegated to editors or directors of local news, wire news, sports, business news, entertainment, and life-style features (society, family, leisure, food, home decorating, etc.).

The *editorial page director* is in charge of overseeing the writing of editorials and the selection of material provided by columnists for the opinion page of the newspaper. Most newspapers have a few columnists of their own to handle local issues, and they buy additional columnists from national syndicates. The editorial opinions of the paper reflect the views of the editorial board, which ordinarily is headed by the *publisher*—the person charged with overall operation of the newspaper. Other editorial board members may include the editor-in-chief, the editorial page director, and two or three other top editors. Note that the editorial page director occupies a special position on the organization chart, reporting to the editor-in-chief and separate from the news organization.

The *city editor* has more duties than editors of the specialized departments of the news organization, because it is the duty of the city editor to assign all local stories to reporters and to oversee the operation of the copy desk, where stories are edited and prepared for use in the newspaper.

Below the managers in the organization are the people with specific duties that involve writing and editing:

Reporters work in the field or on the phone, gathering original information that is the basis for local stories, or seeking local reaction to national and inter-

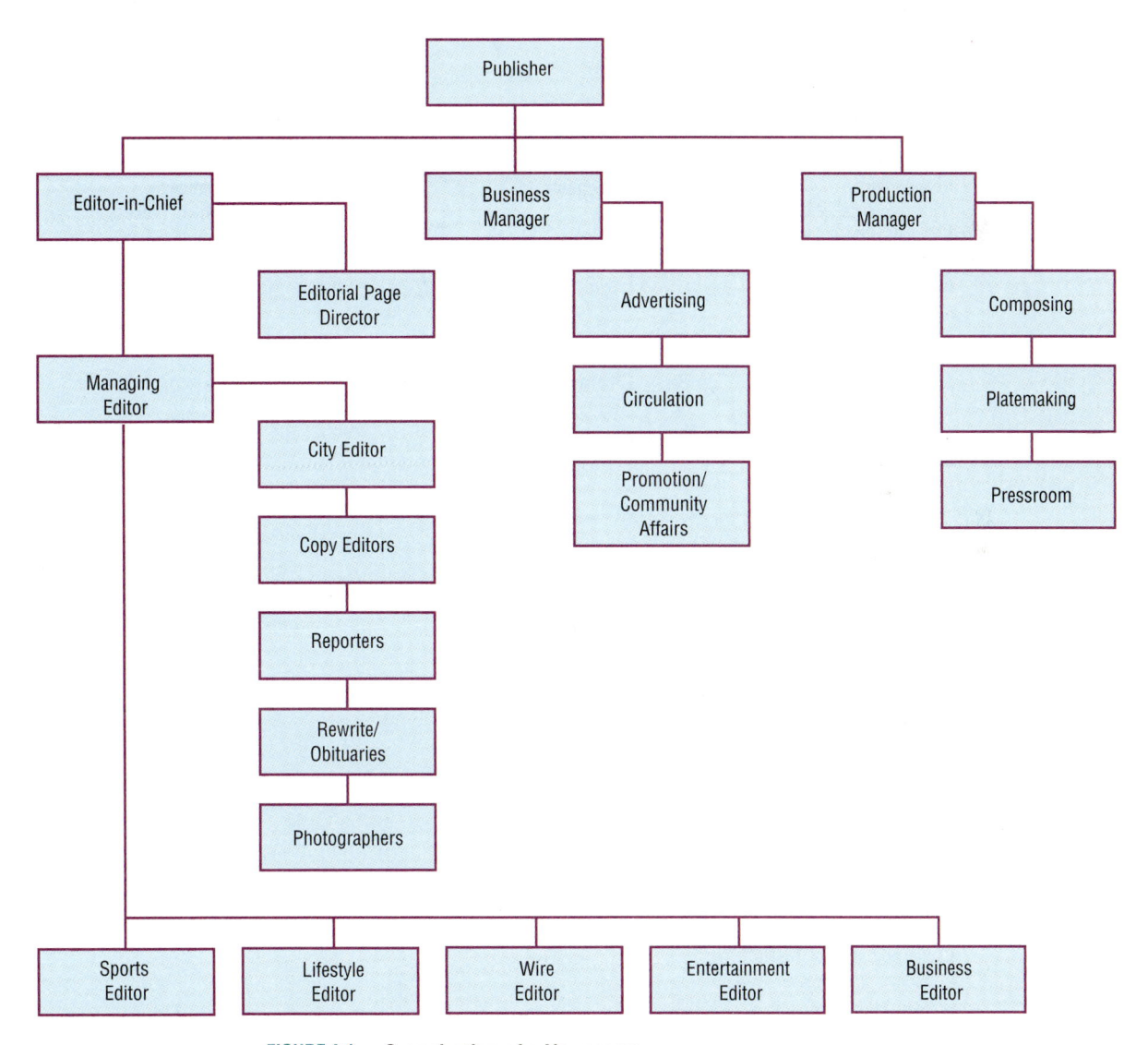

FIGURE 4.1 **Organization of a Newsroom**

national stories. The reporter's assignment comes from the director of a department—the sports editor or the business editor, for example—and that editor or director decides when the story is in proper shape to be scheduled for use.

Copy editors receive information prepared by reporters and are responsible for checking the accuracy of facts, placing the story in proper format, and preparing it for use.

Rewriters take wire copy, news releases prepared by public relations people, and materials prepared by reporters and reshape the material to fit the style and needs of the local medium. They also write the obituaries for local people who die.

Photographers and staff artists, both in print and broadcast, work with editors and reporters to prepare pictures, drawings, and charts or graphs that will illustrate the stories.

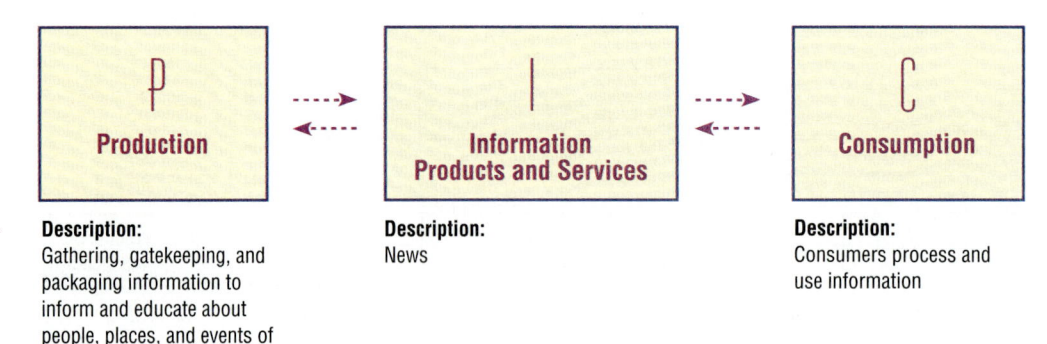

P — Production

Description:
Gathering, gatekeeping, and packaging information to inform and educate about people, places, and events of consequence in day-to-day affairs of consumers

News Producers:
- Reporters
- Copy editors
- Rewriters
- Photographers and staff artists
- Producers
- Production managers

News Packaging Considerations:
- Newsworthiness
- Departmentalization
- Illustrations and graphics
- Style
- Proof

Pressures:
- Manipulation of information
- Commercial control
- Legal and political threats
- Conflicts of interest
- Consumer action

I — Information Products and Services

Description:
News

Characteristics of News:
- Timeliness
- Proximity
- Human interest
- Consequence
- Disaster
- Prominence
- Novelty
- Conflict

Categories of News:
- Hard news
- Soft news
- Straight news
- Spot news
- Enterprise news
- Investigative reporting
- Obituaries
- Databanks

C — Consumption

Description:
Consumers process and use information

Audiences:
- Individuals
- Couples, families, co-workers, etc.
- Groups
- Organizations
- Societies

FIGURE 4.2 P↔I↔C Model of Mass Communication—News

Aided by electronic scanning technology, a compositor in Europe prepares a photo for placement on the layout of a page.

The Production Component

Producers, in the broadcast media, are responsible for the script, continuity, and content of the program, while the *director* "calls the show" and directs the technicians who run the equipment that makes the newscast happen.

The production manager, in the print media, supervises typographers, composers, platemakers, and pressroom operators who accomplish the preparation of printing plates from which the publication will be printed.

Relationship with Business and Advertising

Rounding out the structure of the typical news medium is the business department. In addition to financial controls, including purchasing materials and meeting payroll, the business operation includes the advertising department, the circulation department (in print media), and the promotion department. Advertising typically generates 75 percent of the income for print media, with circulation providing the other 25 percent. Promotion is important to maintain circulation for print media and to keep listenership or viewership high in broadcast media.

News media divide physically and philosophically into the "news side" of the operation and the "business side." Those on the news side tend to believe that, ethically, they must remain oblivious to the fact that a news medium is a profit-making venture; otherwise there might be a tendency to ignore some stories and promote others according to the desires of advertisers.

From the point of view of those on the business side, reporters and editors often seem to use information that offends advertisers. Examples include the investigative story that reveals consumer deceptions by a local auto dealer, or the "trend" story that says local malls are hurting for business. The promotions department usually finds that the news side is not eager to give news space to contests and other promotions sponsored by the newspaper, because the news people believe the news should not be "commercialized."

Consequently, the business side of any print medium usually schedules "house ads"—advertisements paid for by the publication—and does not attempt to involve the news operation in circulation or other business-related operations. (In broadcast, disc jockeys and announcers routinely are used to read "promos" for contests, but newscasters are not.)

The Journalist as "Gatekeeper"

Communication scholar Kurt Lewin used the term *gatekeeper* to describe any person who controls the flow of information to others, selecting what is important and what shall be discarded. In a landmark study published in 1950, David Manning White used the term to describe what wire editors do when they select some items for use in their newspaper and discard others.[1]

The gatekeeping editor in the study, referred to as Mr. Gates, was required to note on each story that came over the telegraph his reason for using or not using it. If the story was local or affected local people, it was more likely to be used than a story from a remote locale, unless the other story had bizarre or unusual twists. Because the paper had to compete with another local paper, Mr. Gates's decision sometimes was based on the feeling that the other newspaper was likely to use the article. Follow-up research 17 years later, after the other newspaper had gone out of business, showed that the gatekeeper no longer gave "competitive pressure" as a reason for using a story. Instead, the shrinking size of his own newspaper's *news hole*—the space available for news—meant that he was more likely to give "no space" as a reason.[2]

All producers function as gatekeepers. From all of the information available, a small amount is selected and most items are rejected. Sources for a news story recount what they remember—or choose to remember—and thus are the first gatekeepers. Reporters sift through their notes and recollections, choosing what, in their opinion, will make the story complete, accurate, and interesting. Editors then scan all of the stories prepared by their reporters or offered by the wire services to select enough material to fill the news hole or the half-hour news broadcast. The consumer is the final gatekeeper, choosing what news to absorb and what items to skip or ignore.

All those who have studied gatekeeping understand that *utility* is the first and foremost reason for letting a news item pass. If the perception is that the audience wants or needs information, that information is likely to be accepted for publication or broadcast. If an item *fits a pattern*—that is, it looks like information previously used, so it is judged to be newsworthy—it may get the green light. If the information is *unusual* in a way that intrigues the gatekeeper, and if the perception is that the item also will amuse, astonish, or intrigue the audience, it may see the light of day. In other words, any gatekeeper, while applying standard criteria, also makes a personal judgment that a story is worth sharing with the consumer.

Editors are confronted with reams of information from which they must select the stories for the next day's paper.

Events or Process?

Traditionally, news media have geared their reporting and editing processes toward covering events as they unfold. These include meetings of public bodies, fires and other disasters, and the pronouncements of officials and celebrities who decide to call news conferences for the purpose of attracting the attention of the press.

Contrary to the idea one gets from consuming the American news media, most stories do not have a neat beginning and ending. Most occur in some context over time and represent the unfolding of some complicated process. They become news stories when an event propels them to the attention of journalists. There has been a slow trend in the American media toward the reporting of what we call *process-centered news*—cultural trends, analysis of economic changes, and background reports on the thinking, arguing, and compromising behind the political headlines.

Event-centered news is gathered by reporters, whose primary skills are efficient observation and bias-free description. Process-centered news may be gathered and presented by writers who have been given the broader license to explain, interpret, and provide a context for understanding the trend or societal change.[3]

Many news media feel that process-centered stories should carry special labels such as "analysis" or "commentary." They may place such articles only in specially labeled opinion sections because they feel reporting should "stick to the facts." Media critics reply that there are few objective facts, and news that is not explained may be misleading to consumers. Election coverage by the television networks has become increasingly process-centered. While cameras still cover pronouncements from candidates' headquarters, anchors and analysts in the studio provide instant interpretation and analysis of the vote.

An example of how the news media ignore a process-centered story until it becomes an event can be seen in the reporting of the problem of homelessness in America. There probably always have been homeless people in the country. However, in the 1980s the problem became front-page news when two events sparked journalistic interest.[4]

First, an association of mortgage bankers issued a news release reporting that mortgage foreclosures the previous year were at their highest since the Great Depression. A careful reading of the report showed that the rise had been small, and such fluctuations were not unexpected. However, the phrase "highest since the Depression" in the news release made the report noteworthy.

At about the same time, the wire services provided stories about a "tent city" that hundreds of homeless people, including whole families, had erected outside Houston, Texas. Television stations jumped at the visual impact of showing Americans who had to live outdoors because they had lost their homes. Houston in the 1980s, of course, was atypical—an oil boom town that attracted thousands of laborers from the North who hoped to glean a share of the economic miracle there. When the boom cooled, some people who had gambled lost their homes.

The news media put labels on the phenomenon they saw in these two stories. *The Los Angeles Times* coined the phrase "the new homeless." *The Washington Post* spoke of "the new victims of homelessness." *The Boston Globe* talked of the "contemporary homeless." *The New York Times* referred to "the new poor."

Foreclosures and homelessness continue to affect hundreds of thousands of Americans, and the causes are the same. However, the story disappeared from the newspapers after a few weeks. The triggering events were over, and the story was not "news" any more. It remained for a magazine, *The Atlantic Monthly*, to provide the process-centered coverage that the other media only hinted at, when author Greg Easterbrook described the root causes of homelessness and analyzed its effect on American society.

The Role of Press Associations and Syndicates

The news media often purchase the information they distribute to their consumers. They share the cost of gathering information, in effect, by using press associations and syndicates that make articles and data available to any and all media, including competing newspapers and broadcast stations. The practice of having a single "pool" reporter cover an event is followed not only for economic reasons, but where it is impractical to permit access to scores of reporters. During the Persian Gulf War in 1991, for example, pool reporters were selected to ride with Desert Storm troops when they made incursions into Iraq from Saudi Arabia. In addition to wire service reporters, the pool usually included reporters from one or more major newspapers and one major television network.

In the few cities where competing newspapers still exist, duplicative efforts exist on the local level as papers compete for exclusive coverage of local events. The wire services are used only to supplement local coverage.

Gathering news for use by diverse media dates back at least to the middle of the nineteenth century. The Associated Press (AP) was formed in 1848 by six New York newspapers that wished to reduce the expenses caused by duplicating efforts at obtaining news from afar. The AP soon discovered that the news from its offices in New York and Washington was eagerly sought by small papers throughout the country that could not afford to maintain a bureau in the major cities, and AP began to sell its news to more newspapers. Soon the telegraph was used to transmit the news, which is why the AP and its eventual imitators became known as "wire" services. Today the press associations use satellite technology.

In its first half-century, AP offered one newspaper in each region exclusive use of its services. Predictably, this led to competition. In 1907, the United Press (UP) was formed by newspaper chain owner E. W. Scripps, who offered his service to clients that could not get the AP wire. In 1909, William Randolph Hearst's International News Service (INS) offered a similar service. The present UPI—United Press International—resulting from a 1958 merger between the second- and third-ranked news associations, has grown increasingly unprofitable and is close to failing. Reuters, the European news agency, is used by some American media, and there are many smaller and specialized press associations.

AP is the largest of the news gathering and disseminating organizations. Unlike other wire services, it is an association. Any newspaper may join and, as a member, may take part in electing the board of directors. Subscribers to the other news services have no such involvement. Fees charged by news services are based on

President George Bush talks to reporters aboard Air Force One on his way to take part in an economic summit meeting.

the circulation of the member newspaper, so the cost of belonging varies greatly for small dailies and large metropolitan newspapers.

The effect of the wire services was to begin the process of homogenizing the American newspaper. Members of AP and subscribers to UP and INS did not want opinionated or slanted news coverage, either because it might differ from their own views, or because they were striving for objectivity and lack of bias in their news stories in order to attract more readers. Journalistic objectivity therefore became the standard, and newspapers increasingly reserved opinions for the editorial page.

Client newspapers also wanted to be able to cut a story to the length they desired, and they had to do it under deadline pressure. So the wire services popularized the *inverted pyramid* format, wherein the main points of the news event are summarized in the "lead" paragraph, and then additional quotes, background information, and facts are presented in descending order of importance. To this day, a typical wire service news story can be cut at any point without causing confusion. (Articles labeled "features" are not meant to be processed hastily either by editor or consumer, however, and they may begin with an intriguing anecdote and then proceed at a more leisurely pace.)

Also of importance to newspapers are the *feature syndicates* that mail packets of articles and illustrations to newspapers on a regular basis. Political columns, cartoons, advice columns, horoscope columns, and full-page illustrated seasonal spreads featuring recipes and food-serving suggestions all are provided by syndicates such as United Features, King Features, and the North American Newspaper Alliance. Leading newspapers such as *The New York Times* also offer their features and columns through syndication. Smaller syndicates specialize in areas such as religion, automobiles, science, sports, coin collecting, and regional news. Fees are charged according to circulation, and many of the items cost only a dollar or two to use. Exclusivity in each city may be granted for certain popular columns and leading comic strips.

The Myth of Objectivity

Partly as a result of wire service domination of the production and distribution of news for use in smaller papers throughout the nation and in other parts of the world, the "objective" story—free of political bias from the publisher and free of personal bias from the reporter and editor—became a hallmark of journalism. It became a code taught in journalism schools, and the myth of "objectivity" permeated journalism training. (A myth is a collective belief that is accepted uncritically.) While the myth of journalistic objectivity was accepted through much of the twentieth century, today it must be examined seriously. Consider these questions about "objective" news reporting:

- Is there a reporter who does not filter information through a set of values developed over time, assigning greater meaning to some facts than others?
- Does the practice of assembling news articles by quoting spokespeople (with differing viewpoints from either side of an issue) guarantee lack of bias?
- Is the entire journalistic system biased by virtue of its situation in the free enterprise system, where information is packaged for sale?
- Are journalists somehow better trained and equipped to sort through and select the facts than judges, clergy, teachers, parents, and lawyers?

> ### INSIGHT
> # The Mass Media Cycle
>
> Acccording to journalism and mass communication scholar Donald L. Shaw, all mass media go through a cyclical rise and fall in popularity and impact. There is a period in which media strive toward maximum audience popularity, then a period in which a particular medium is highly successful, and finally a period of adjustment and downward slide. "Most, like radio, survive, but some, like black and white commercial film, do not." Shaw offers the following observations:
>
> - Change is becoming more rapid;
> - The concept of "mass media" has become obsolete because modern technologies provide so many information and entertainment options for audience members;
> - No medium, once it has slipped from its position of dominance, has ever returned to the top;
> - The content of a medium alone will not attract audiences back once they leave. In addition to content, factors such as convenience, habit, and interest are influential;
> - Media that are flexible in adjusting to change will continue to appeal to a substantial segment of the audience, a segment that advertisers also want to reach.
>
> *Source:* Donald Shaw, "The Rise and Fall of American Mass Media," Roy W. Howard Public Lecture in Journalism and Mass Communication Research. No. 2, April 4, 1991. School of Journalism, Indiana University, p. 20.

The critical consumer necessarily develops a "situational" understanding of just how objective the news media are, can be, and try to be.

PACKAGING THE NEWS

Rarely does the same person gather information, write the story, and decide how the story will be presented. The editor of a small paper now and then may be able to play all of the roles, from reporter to copy editor to layout editor. Occasionally a powerful anchorperson such as Dan Rather of CBS is permitted to think up a story idea, go on location to film the footage, and return to the station to select the shots that he will narrate on screen. But typically the information gathered by a reporter is passed to an editor in the print media or a producer in the broadcast media, who will take responsibility for selecting the material to be used and arranging it for presentation to the audience.

Here are some of the considerations the editor who packages a story for dissemination must take into account:

Newsworthiness. Whether a story will be used in that day's newspaper or that evening's news broadcast is the editor's first decision. Presumably, the decision of newsworthiness can be made objectively by submitting the story to the tests we discussed earlier: Is it timely, does it concern or affect many readers, and is it interesting? The editor's personal bias also can affect the decision, as we noted when we discussed the concept of gatekeeping. Add to this the problem of time and space constraints, and "newsworthiness" becomes more difficult to explain. On a "slow news day," stories that otherwise have little merit may find a place in the mix. In newspapers, a heavy volume of advertising can cause a "tight news hole," meaning a story has less chance of being used. Conversely, if the abundance of advertising causes an extra section to be added to the paper, the editor may find additional open pages to fill. Public relations people who submit a "soft" news release hope the editor will use it because of the need to fill space.

Historical patterns and traditions of the news business may also underlie the decision to use one story and not another. The ritual of identifying the first baby born in an area hospital each new year may not satisfy any test of newsworthiness beyond the fact that it's done annually and the public has come to expect it.

Departmentalization. Because they carry so much information, and because they know the consumer cannot and will not pay attention to all information equally, the mass media put information into sections or departments—the sports report on the local late-night news, for example, or the business page of the newspaper. Many stories could appear in any of several departments. A feature about two senior citizens who started a window-washing business could appear on the business page, in the life-style section, in the Sunday feature section, or even on page 1 if it were a slow news day. A radio news director could decide that the championship victory by the local high school was too important to listeners to save for the sports report, and thus decide to lead the entire newscast with it. Whether to put a story in a department or section usually is the second decision an editor must make, after the critical decision of whether to use the story at all.

Illustrations and Graphics. Anyone trying to place a story in the media knows what "art" can do to sell the story to a print editor or a broadcast producer. The newspaper story accompanied by an interesting photograph has a better chance of being placed above the fold, away from advertising, or in the middle of the page where it will break up the gray field of type. A color slide accompanying a piece submitted to a magazine enhances the chance that it will be used in a department or column. Video footage can make the difference in getting a story on television, where heads talking with no visuals behind them are what every producer tries to avoid. Every reporter is happy when a photographer or camera crew is assigned to his or her story, because once an editor or producer invests in pictures, there is a much greater likelihood the entire package will be used. When a page is laid out or a broadcast is scheduled, the art is placed first, and the words are fit around it.

Style. As the decision to use a piece, where to use it, and how to use it progresses, the editor must consider the question of style. The word is used in two different and important ways. First, each newspaper, magazine, or broadcast report has its formula and format. The assertive, even abrasive, approach is right for "60 Minutes," but wrong for the "Today Show." Disdainful put-downs are permitted and even encouraged on the "Style" pages of *The Washington Post,* but would be frowned on by the editorial page editors of the same newspaper. Every story must be consistent with the personality of its journalistic environment or it will be jarring and out of place. The second definition of *style* involves the rules of punctuation, capitalization, spelling, and typographical format followed by the individual news outlet. Most newspapers follow the *Associated Press Stylebook* in general, but develop their own supplement to cover local usage and terminology particular to the area they cover. Copy editors are responsible for checking style as they routinely edit a story for accuracy, consistency, and completeness.

Proof. Not incidentally, the person responsible for selecting and placing a story must ensure that the story is not libelous or slanderous, that it does not involve unwarranted invasion of privacy, and that it reflects a fair attempt to represent all sides of the issue. If the piece does not meet all of these tests, the editor may reject it. Usually, however, the reporter or the copy editor is directed to provide the missing information or rewrite the passages that could raise legal or ethical questions.

Obviously, editing involves making several judgments in a short time, which is why editors generally are more experienced and more highly paid than the reporters whose stories they select and package.

CHARACTERISTICS OF NEWS

Why is one item "news" when another item doesn't qualify? The item selected as news probably meets one of the following tests:

Timeliness. The item is current. A century or more ago, when news came by ship and pony express, timeliness was not a factor. If it was new to the reader, then it was news. Today, with virtually instantaneous electronic transmission of visual and written information, news is perishable. Editors who are confronted with a day-old story must find a fresh "peg" on which to hang it.

The "Live at Noon" news show on WRAL-TV in Raleigh, N.C., is tailored to the interests of the local area. Celebrities, newsmakers, and area leaders are interviewed by the hosts.

Proximity. The item happened nearby. If two children are killed in a fire in a remote place—Chicago if you live in New York, or New York if you live in Chicago—it is only of mild interest. But if it happened in your town, you wonder: "Have I ever passed that place? Is it somebody I might know?" A high-school basketball team's victory gets front-page attention only in the weekly paper serving the local area. Even the local daily, which covers dozens of suburban communities, probably will judge that the story doesn't interest enough readers to merit a position on the front page.

Human Interest. The item is a compelling example of humanity. You hear on the radio about a little girl who fell down a well in a faraway state. The fact that she is still alive and hundreds of rescuers are racing against the clock to save her life touches the hearts of millions and keeps the story in the media for three days until she is brought out alive—a basic human interest story.

Consequence. The item affects the reader—has consequence on the reader. The incredible fact that the death, injury, or capture of a million souls in the Iran-Iraq war of the 1980s did not attract much attention in the U.S. news media can be attributed to the inability of the consumer to fathom what difference it all made. Not many Americans are of Iranian or Iraqi heritage. Millions of Americans, however, have Irish ancestors, so the report of a car-bombing that kills two people in strife-torn Northern Ireland will get news coverage.

Disaster. Related to consequence, but of greater magnitude, are the attributes of a disaster. When a mudslide roars down a mountain and wipes out a school in Wales, killing 50 schoolchildren, it is the horror of calamity that interests the audience. Follow-up articles—"second-day stories"—for a disaster such as a plane

Lieutenant Colonel Oliver North is sworn in before he testifies at the Senate Iran-Contra hearings. Because of intense public interest, the event was carried live and in full on more than one television network.

crash in which a few passengers miraculously survive can be classified as human interest stories. *Sidebars*—secondary articles running alongside the main article—explain whether a disaster could happen to us in a similar situation.

Prominence.   The people involved are celebrities. If you or your neighbors give a party, it probably will not be reported in the news media . . . unless, perhaps, one of you shoots the other. If the White House gives a party for film stars, we can all read or hear every detail about what was served, who wore what, and what was said by everyone of importance.

Novelty.   The item is unusual. If man bites dog, that's news, according to the old saying. When a hobbyist builds a boat in the basement and then can't get it out without tearing down the house . . . that, also, is news.

Conflict.   The item is an example of our inability to get along: divorce, charges of political corruption, the arrest of a bombing suspect, the snubbing of an American diplomat, or a movie star's complaints about a film critic.

The more of these characteristics that can be found in a story, the more likely the news medium is to decide that the audience will be interested in the story.

CATEGORIES OF NEWS

Rather than speaking of such formal concepts as "surveillance" and "correlation," the working journalist is more likely to refer to the *watchdog* role of the news media, meaning that the actions of politicians and appointed officials must be monitored, and wrongdoing should be exposed.

The categories of news are captured in expressions such as *hard* and *soft* news, *straight* and *feature* story, *spot* and *enterprise* news, along with terms for specialized forms such as investigative reporting, community service, and obituary writing.

Hard news is the factual account of an event that happened within the past 24 hours, reported in summary format to account for the *who, what, when, where, why,* and *how* elements. Traditionally, hard news is reported in inverted pyramid format, meaning that as many of the five *W*s as possible are included in the opening sentence or short paragraph referred to as the story's *lead*—for example, "Paul Simon's *Graceland* last night won the Grammy for 'Song of the Year' in a live telecast from New York City." Then facts and background information are presented in order of importance, eventually accounting for the "why" and "how" elements.

Soft news may be less timely, of less consequence, and written in a style that does not attempt to summarize everything in the lead. An example would be an interview with the winner of the Grammy award for "Song of the Year" in which the reporter recounts in chronological fashion how Paul Simon spent the evening after the award was announced, providing insights into his attitude toward his music, the entertainment business, and the friends who helped his career.

Straight news is a synonym for hard news, but the term refers more to the factual style of writing than to a type of news. Similarly, *feature treatment* means that the writer leans heavily on slice-of-life quotations and descriptions of dress and behavior in order to provide more insight than straight news reporting might include.

Spot news, or breaking news as it is called during broadcast reports, is up-to-the-minute coverage of events that are happening even as the paper goes to press or the newscast goes on the air.

Enterprise news is likely to be labeled "exclusive" by a news medium, because the editor or reporter thinks up the story idea on his or her own, asks questions that may not be obvious to anyone else, and may be able to offer information that has not previously been imagined or reported. An example would be the writer who returns to the college campus, sits in on classes, interviews students and professors, and writes a story reporting that students are getting "back to basics" in their choice of elective courses because of a perception that careers depend on a solid knowledge of math, history, and language skills. If the story has no peg—that is, if it was not triggered by a criticism from the Secretary of Education or a speech by the president of the university—then it is considered an enterprise story.

Investigative reporting involves digging for facts over time, frequently by a team of reporters, in order to expose wrongdoing, crime, or a disturbing trend in society. Because investigative reporting is costly and can lead to lawsuits from those charged with malfeasance, modern newspapers engage in it infrequently and with an eye on capturing awards such as the Pulitzer Prize. Broadcast outlets are most likely to air their investigative reports during the "sweeps weeks," the three periods each year when the ratings services calculate the number of listeners and viewers.

Obituaries, or obits, have a special function and are written to a certain format and style. Written in straight news format, the obituary provides the reader or listener with information that may be used to decide whether to attend a wake or memorial service, to write an appropriate letter, or to make a financial contribution. Smaller news media often treat obits as if they were no different from the death announcements that funeral homes pay to have inserted—dry, factual lists

---

INSIGHT

Will the Real George Bush Please Stand Up?!

The image of George Bush in the U.S. press, 1987:
 Soft-spoken "preppy" wimp doing whatever Reagan asked

The image of George Bush in the U.S. press, 1988:
 Sharp-tongued, mean-spirited bulldog attacking his opponents

The image of George Bush in the U.S. press, 1989:
 Sportsman, family man, regular guy, conciliator, and leader

The image of George Bush in the U.S. press, 1990:
 World leader, foe of naked aggression, cool in face of adversity

The image of George Bush in the U.S. press, 1991:
 Defensive about high appointments, ignoring domestic issues

Did George Bush really change so much as he made the transition from Vice President to candidate to President? Certainly he had to project different capabilities and varied styles to suit new situations. But his "image" changed because the press habitually reduces information to the simplest form, applies labels, and then perpetuates "realities."

of memberships, affiliations, accomplishments, and survivors. Television and the larger newspapers, however, are likely to provide a feature treatment for the deaths of prominent people. Photographs recall the career of the person, quotes capture the personality, and the opinions of others are cited to evaluate the importance or impact of the career and life of the deceased.

Databanks increasingly are offered by both print and video media. Data displays are characterized by graphic style: borders, headings, charts, and typographic devices that highlight information presented in list form instead of prose. *USA Today* has popularized data displays in print, and many television news or sports programs put data displays on the screen during transitions from one part of the program to the next.

PRESSURES ON THE NEWS MEDIA

So far we have concentrated on the decisions made by editors based solely on the criteria of the production system. But the consumers of information, especially enlightened individuals and organized pressure groups, have an important influence on the decision-making process of mass media producers. As much as journalists might like to theorize that there is some pure and rational system of deciding what's news, the reality is that the media are constantly under scrutiny, and their decisions are continually subjected to outside forces.

Manipulation of Information

In a perfect world, news reporters would simply talk to every party involved in an issue, select representative facts and opinions, and record the data with fidelity. Often it is in the interest of others, however, to be selective in providing information to the mass media. Reporters and editors have to contend with a number of systematic means for manipulating information.

Access and Favoritism. News sources decide which media to favor. The President of the United States occasionally holds press conferences at which reporters from the leading national media are arranged in the front row, and representatives of less important media are relegated to the back rows. On almost a daily basis, White House spokespeople make themselves available in the press briefing room. But occasionally the President chooses to allow one or two reporters to have an hour or more of his time on an exclusive basis. Usually if one of the major networks is accorded such a privilege, the others are given a similar opportunity. Occasionally, though, the President will exercise his ability to punish a network he feels has not provided favorable coverage by substituting a major newspaper or newsmagazine at the special interview. The practice of favoring a friendly "lapdog" medium over a "watchdog" one is much more common at the state and local level, where legislators and mayors reward media they view as supportive by granting special interviews or permitting a favored reporter to travel in the plane or car with the elected official and staff. (Where access must be limited owing to cramped quarters, the media prefer to elect one of their own as "pool reporter," with the expectation that all information thus gained will be shared immediately. But elected officials are not required by law to comply with such arrangements.)

Controlled Release. In order to prevent manipulation of information that could affect the price of a stock to the advantage of some and detriment of others, the federal Securities and Exchange Commission (SEC) requires "complete and open disclosure" and "timely release" of information simultaneously to all media. That is a fact of life that corporate financial relations and public relations people adhere to faithfully, lest they be charged with providing "insider information." Agriculture price support information from the government is similarly monitored to prevent speculation. But government officials and corporate managers dealing with nonfinancial information are not bound by any such regulations. Many of them learn that the time and manner of information released to the press can have a great effect on the impact of the story. Most Presidents take advantage of their access to the broadcast media by making important announcements of positive information "live from the Oval Office" during prime-time evening viewing. Less happy information may be parceled out by a lower functionary late on Friday afternoon—too late for the day's newspapers, on too short notice to permit reaction from opponents on the evening news, and thus consigned to Saturday's news, which has a smaller audience. Corporations defend their decision to announce personnel changes and negative earnings reports at the fabled hour of 4 P.M. Friday on the grounds that the stock markets have just closed for the weekend and there will be time for analysts to put the information in perspective in the financial media before the markets reopen on Monday. Another good time for "hiding" information from the media is late Saturday night or early Sunday morning, when the Sunday papers have already gone to press and broadcast audiences are not looking for news reports. Sunday night, however, can be an opportune time to gain media attention, because editors may be struggling to find enough information to fill Monday morning papers and broadcasts after a languorous "slow-news" weekend.

NFL superstar Joe Montana and singer Tony Bennett ride a San Francisco cable car to promote the United Way—an example of a "pseudo event" meant to attract the press.

Pseudo-Events. Historian Daniel Boorstin coined the term *pseudo-event* to describe manufactured occasions that publicists use to focus attention on their clients' causes. The visit of a head-of-state's spouse to a day-care center rarely reflects the spouse's expertise or opinions on day-care; the visit is made rather to portray the spouse as a humanitarian interested in children and to round out the desired image of the visitors as "nice" people. Poor people who erect a shantytown on the lawn of the state capitol to focus attention on the plight of the homeless are creating a visual event for the cameras that may or may not be tied to the provision of substantive information. It is easy for a news medium to ignore a news release or fact sheet on the housing shortage, but hard for them to pass up the opportunity to photograph squatters outside the governor's office.

Disinformation. Outright lying to the press, along with the raising of misleading questions, was labeled *disinformation* by U.S. Department of State officials in the 1980s. The term was first applied to Soviet campaigns such as the repeated allegations that the American government was behind a purposeful spreading of the AIDS virus. Another form of disinformation is the smoke screen that an organization may put up to divert attention from another more serious situation. A company may ballyhoo the roll-out of a new product at the same time as it is quietly laying off some of its workers. A political candidate may go on the attack on some minor issue in order to cover his or her failure to understand a more critical issue. The press may play into such a candidate's hands because the blustery charges about alleged misdeeds of an opponent are "better copy" than would be a story on some issue such as the candidate's position on the U.S. trade imbalance or the problems with financing the Social Security system.

Commercial Control

Reporters tend to be less influenced than editors by pressures stemming from the commercial nature of information enterprises. That's because reporters do not deal with the "business side" of the operation; they have little or no opportunity to

---

INSIGHT

The Press Misses the Story

News analyst Ellen Hume cites several reasons why the press was unable to uncover the savings and loan scandal, which saw billions of dollars lost when savings institutions failed in the late 1980s and early 1990s:

- It was a "numbers" story, not a "people" story—the press doesn't do a good job of understanding and reporting on financial news.
- The story happened all over America, not in Washington.
- The villains were powerful, respected people. The victims were the little people.
- Many of the documents that might have tipped investigators off to the story were kept secret by law.
- Journalists have gotten used to having stories conveniently fed to them, and they aren't prepared to commit the time or energy in investigative reporting.

Source: Ellen Hume, "Why the Press Blew the S&L Scandal," *The New York Times,* Thursday, May 24, 1990, p. A-23.

meet with the publisher of the paper or the owner of a broadcast station. They simply gather the information without concern for its effect on the economic well-being of their employer. Editors, on the other hand, must argue for their budgets, and attend planning meetings where "the bottom line" (profit or loss) dictates what resources are available to the newsroom. Reporters have the luxury of believing the myth that news and business operations can and must be completely separate, while editors and broadcast station managers merely wish it could be so. A basic fact of life for the mass media is *the pressure to lower costs and produce a profit.*

Competition. Few of the mass media have a market all to themselves. (A newspaper in a remote small town where there is no local radio station may be an exception, as is a one-of-a-kind specialized magazine catering to a small number of esoteric hobbyists.) In order to keep their share of consumers, most media have to ensure that the competition isn't offering something they aren't. That means resources are directed one way or the other not because an editor makes a choice, but because business sense dictates it. When the circulation department of one New York newspaper came up with a "Bingo!" game to attract readers with $1000 cash prizes, a competing paper quickly countered with "Wingo!" and another felt pressured to come up with "Zingo!" Editors were forced by their management to put color "teaser lines" across the top of page 1 to promote the contests, and they also had to run feature stories about readers who won. In this case, the newspaper's circulation department was creating its own pseudo-events. A newspaper editor may feel that horoscope predictions are a foolish waste of space, but the business side worries that failure to carry such trivia risks losing a large number of readers. A station manager may feel that devoting five minutes to the weather and hiring a jolly buffoon to point at the meteorological charts is a waste of time and salary, but management will cite the popularity of the competition's weather person, and demand that the weather be reported in an entertaining fashion.

INDUSTRY

The Changing Role of the Journalist

As competition stiffens in the newspaper business—competition from alternative information sources, not just other newspapers—journalists find their rule and their roles changing.

In the past, "editorial autonomy" meant that editors and reporters on the *news side* of the paper resisted any pressures from the *business side* (advertising and circulation) to run certain stories, suppress certain stories, or provide favorable coverage simply because it would please an advertiser or increase sales.

Today editors realize that the very existence of their newspapers may depend on *marketing* principles. That means catering to the interests of advertisers and subscribers with supplements or special sections of the paper that provide *service* articles directly related to the associated advertising.

In the semiannual "Cars and Campers" section, for example, auto dealers who take ads are likely to be mentioned in the articles. The annual "Restaurant and Gourmet Guide" focuses on its supporting merchants.

Journalists who enter the field with visions of a Pulitzer Prize dancing in their heads may wince at this increasingly common practice. But most have come to a grudging understanding that their livelihoods depend on it. Whether this bartering of journalism's credibility makes any difference to the readers is a subject yet to be researched.

Advertising Pressure. Without thinking about the consequences, a business editor gave prominent play in the Sunday paper to a wire service report showing which cars were rated least safe by a government agency. The worst record in crash testing went to the models sold by the newspaper's leading advertiser. The next day the owner of the car agency was on the phone to the publisher canceling his ads, a move that would cost the paper hundreds of thousands of dollars. Another paper agreed with an auto dealer always to place his ad at the bottom of the first page of the Sunday sports section, in return for a guarantee that the ad would run every week of the year—a decision that assured the paper hundreds of thousands in revenue, but negatively affected the sports editor, whose front page was cluttered with an ad. There, in a nutshell, is the dilemma facing an editor. Journalists believe that the objective presentation of the news should not be tainted by commercial pressure, but publishers and station owners see more shades of gray in their desire to accommodate the interests of advertisers.

Sponsorship. A similar problem is created by sponsorship of television shows, events that are covered by the media, and "tie-ins" between the media and products or services. A large manufacturer of electrical appliances who also builds atomic power plants withdrew its sponsorship of a news program that provided a forum for antinuclear spokespeople. When cigarette advertising was banned from television, tobacco companies underwrote various tennis and golf tournaments and paid to put their names on the scoreboards at baseball and football stadiums so that they could inject their message into the programs. Many medium-sized daily newspapers join with local travel agencies and foreign tourist boards to sponsor trips abroad for their readers, thus bringing into question each newspaper's ability to be objective if the travel industry or the country in question becomes involved in negative news.

Companies can get their stories to business editors through the PR Newswire, a computer data base. The technology makes the mailing of printed news releases obsolete.

An obvious way to prevent commercial pressure on a medium of mass information is to find a way to make it noncommercial. One way is government ownership, which is how broadcast media are handled in many European countries. That can lead to stodgy, unappealing programming selected by bureaucrats, and, at worst, it can result in government slanting of or interference with the news. The trend in European countries has been toward a mix of commercial and government stations to provide a variety of information formats and outlets.

Public broadcasting—National Public Radio and television's Public Broadcasting System—have been an important part of the Federal Communication Commission's plan for a mix of information in this country. But not-for-profit broadcasting, still subject to economic realities, must "beg" on the air for viewer donations while it courts large foundations and commercial sponsors for grants. Recent moves to accept "enhanced credits" for sponsorship of PBS programs have brought messages looking very much like ads to a medium that once prided itself on freedom from the inevitable pressures of commerce.

Legal and Political Threats

Most media can survive the loss of an advertiser. In fact, most advertisers who pull out to punish or make a point eventually return because they need the advertising medium as much as it needs them. Legal and political actions, however, can jeopardize the very existence of a newspaper or station.

Lawsuit. Libel and slander laws temper the tendency of the media to attack unfairly or carelessly, and privacy laws protect the ordinary individual from undue scrutiny by the press. Moreover, the very *threat* of using such laws against the media acts as a restraint on editorial judgment. At any one time a newspaper may have two or three libel suits pending, some owing to typographical errors or mistaken identification: It's part of the cost of doing business, and most cases are settled out of court. The occasional major suit, however, goes to trial and results in a judgment of millions of dollars against the medium. Where fault is found, the media hope to reduce the penalty in appeal by showing lack of malice, or by arguing that the amount of the judgment is unreasonably large. Once burned by a lawsuit, the editors may find themselves erring on the side of caution, removing quotes and allegations from reporters' copy to be on the safe side, and sometimes removing the grist of the story in the process.

Legislation. Australian media baron Rupert Murdoch found many a sympathetic ear in 1988 when he charged that Sen. Edward Kennedy had grafted an amendment onto a late-hour piece of legislation that had the effect of forcing Murdoch to divest himself of his Boston and New York newspapers because he also owned television stations in those cities. Murdoch's papers had criticized Kennedy, and many saw the law against dual ownership as the senator's way of punishing the offending media. Cable television entrepreneurs who moved into a totally unregulated field in the 1960s soon found themselves the target of legislation that made basic profitability, let alone great success, much more difficult in the 1980s. Like all businesses, the media must expect excesses to be corrected through the legislative process. The media fear that in extreme cases, punitive legislation can have the effect of stilling voices that threaten the status quo or criticize the excesses of powerful elected officials.

Government Pressure. Government agencies have many ways of retaliating against the media and bringing pressure, beginning with controlling access to in-

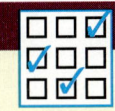

> ## RESEARCH
>
> ### Most Newspapers Have Corrections Policies
>
> Do newspapers take seriously their responsibility to correct errors they have made? Research conducted by the Gannett Center for Media Studies at Columbia University indicates that most papers have a written policy of correcting errors within a day or two and placing the correction under a *standing headline* in a regular position near the front of the newspaper.
>
> "The majority of news corrections are of relatively simple and indisputable factual errors," according to the research report. "Subjective errors—concerning questions of news judgment, fair play, accuracy and the like—are more likely to be acknowledged in the large papers than the small ones, but in both cases editors usually prefer to handle such errors by suggesting that complainants write letters to the editor for publication."
>
> Content analysis of 12 papers showed corrections ranging from a low of 0.11 news corrections per 100 news pages (Daytona Beach, Fla. *Evening News*) to a high of 3.21 corrections per 100 pages (Oneonta, N.Y., *Daily Star*). Correction letters per 100 letters to the editor ranged from none (Hagerstown, Md., *Herald Mail*) to 25 (*Boston Globe*).
>
> *Source:* D. Charles Whitney, *Begging Your Pardon: Corrections and Corrections Policies at Twelve U.S. Newspapers,* Gannett Center Working Paper, 1986.

formation they create. (Freedom of Information Act legislation largely guards against such abuses, however.) Agencies with regulatory or investigatory power can target media for scrutiny when they themselves come under the eye of investigative reporting. Many small weeklies and dailies depend on "legal advertisements" mandated by municipalities and states for a sizable part of their income. Designation as the "paper of record" for purpose of placing such advertisements can be jeopardized by attacking the very officials with the power to make such designation. A small paper that had criticized government handling of waste disposal problems found that when it applied for permits to build a new printing plant it ran into dozens of roadblocks from government agencies empowered to delay or deny permits for handling the inks, cleaning solvents, and other chemicals used in the printing process. A radio station's request to erect a bigger transmitter or antenna can draw unusual scrutiny if the station has been critical of local government policies in the past.

Just the *threat* of legal action is of such concern to many publishers and owners that it can have the subtle effect of intimidation on a news medium.

Conflicts of Interest

Journalists wish to be considered free from the taint of association with individuals or groups that could cause them to inject biased information into their reporting. The goal is laudable, but disassociating oneself from any and all alliances is difficult.

Publishers and station owners are business people. They belong to country clubs, attend Chamber of Commerce luncheons, and socialize with the bankers and lawyers who influence the community. Many media owners and managers find it difficult to keep their involvement with local commerce and politics separate from their role of overseeing the workings of an editorial board that decides news policies.

Confrontations between media owners and their news staffs are common in the industry. Usually the publisher or station manager is persuaded by senior editors or news directors that the special nature of news reporting means that ordinary business or political practices are not appropriate. For example, after a businessman with no media experience, took over a television network in 1987, he advised his new employees that they ought to become involved in Political Action Committees by making contributions. After a public flurry erupted, the head of the network's news division convinced the overzealous new chairman to announce that his directive did not apply to news employees.

Every reporter and editor is also a private citizen who probably chooses to join clubs, support a political party, and get involved in community affairs. The problem comes when a line is not drawn between professional and private activities, or even when outsiders have a perception that there is no line. The *Star-Ledger* of Newark, N.J., was embarrassed when it was revealed that one of its reporters was acting as a public relations counsellor for some of the very groups he was supposed to be covering as part of his beat. The paper quickly transferred him to another position. Other papers and stations have fired staffers who failed to reveal that they were creating potential conflicts of interest through their outside activities.

Journalism and politics do not mix. A newscaster who decided to run for town council resigned his job at the radio station. When his unsuccessful campaign was over, he was not welcomed back to the news media; he sought employment in advertising and public relations. Similarly, a reporter who took a leave of absence to join the reelection campaign of a legislator found that the leave would be permanent unless he agreed to return in a capacity that did not permit him to handle news of politics or public affairs.

The inability of the business side of a news medium to accept the "purity" of the news product can lead to conflict. (From the point of view of the owner, business manager, or advertising director, the inability of the editorial staff to acknowledge the profit motive of the medium is the problem!) A zealous advertising manager may gain the support of the local merchants for a special supplement in a print medium or a week-long promotion in a broadcast outlet. When the news staff is asked to prepare stories that tie in with the promotion—stories they consider "fluff" with no news value—they may balk. Writing and editing material with no purpose other than to attract consumers to the advertising package may rub them the wrong way.

Of course there is a place in journalism for those who have become involved in politics and commerce—as a columnist or commentator, where one's words are labeled clearly as informed opinion. *The New York Times* conservative columnist William Safire's writings reflect his experience as a White House speechwriter. Bill Moyers has made the transition from journalist to presidential press secretary (under Lyndon Johnson) to respected commentator on public broadcasting.

Consumer Action

We have argued throughout this book that consumers are not passive receivers of information. The consumer's response to information received constitutes *feedback*—new information created in reaction to the original information. That feedback often influences the producer of mass messages. While consumer feedback takes many forms, special interest groups and individual activists who act as spokespeople for unorganized groups can apply pressure to news organizations that is similar to legal and political threats. Formal and informal mechanisms also exist for delivering individual complaints to the producer, and the media themselves sometimes attack other media.

Special interest groups include church organizations, politically oriented groups, and coalitions that form around individual issues. The Reverend Jerry Falwell's "Moral Majority" coalition of religious organizations sought in the early 1980s to focus attention on all forms of mass media information that they felt were unwholesome and not suitable for American families. In addition to presenting their views on various religious radio and television programs sponsored by groups belonging to the coalition, the Moral Majority engaged in letter-writing campaigns to legislators and congressional representatives who they felt would be sympathetic to their conservative point of view. They also mounted a grassroots campaign aimed at influencing the Federal Communication Commission. In 1966, the courts ruled that civic associations, professional societies, churches, unions, and educational institutions—even though they had no direct economic stake in the issue—could contest an application to the FCC for license renewal. Action for Children's Television (ACT), originally a group of mothers in Massachusetts, became active in FCC petitioning, along with such diverse groups as the National Association for the Advancement of Colored People (NAACP) and the United Church of Christ's Office of Communications. The publisher of a chain of small weekly newspapers in Wisconsin, who also was the printer for an underground newspaper, was driven out of business when a local machine-tool manufacturer decided the underground paper was obscene. The manufacturer organized a boycott of advertisers, to which the publisher refused to bow in the belief that freedom of expression should not give in to public pressure.[5]

While most special interest groups claim to represent "public opinion" and to be acting for the good of society, producers of mass communication information must decide which complaints are really in the public interest and which represent a special point of view. As an aide to the National Advisory Commission on Civil Disorders noted, "The problem is made harder by the fact that accusations of bias against the media are often based on the bias of the audience itself."[6]

Individual activists often are successful at using the media to focus criticism on media performance. Ralph Nader's well-publicized news conferences often raise questions not only about unsafe products, but also about how those products are portrayed in advertising messages. Before cigarette advertising was banned from the airwaves, a one-person campaign by lawyer John Banzhaf III convinced the FCC to require anticigarette ads on television to counter their effects.[7] Journalists themselves can become critics of the performance of their fellow reporters. Veteran journalist Joseph Alsop returned from a visit to Vietnam during the war to report that some reporters were allowing anti-American bias to creep into their stories, a move that led to the resignation of two *Time* magazine reporters whose superior supported Alsop's view.[8]

Media critics play a role in monitoring the performance of the press. *The Washington Journalism Review*, published at the University of Maryland journalism school, monitors press coverage of affairs centered in the nation's capital. The *Columbia Journalism Review*, published at Columbia University's journalism school, is known for its "Darts and Laurels" department, which praises examples of good reporting and editing, but hits sloppy or biased journalism with zingers. *The Quill*, published for members of the Society of Professional Journalists, presents analysis of news coverage by individual newspapers or stations as well as the entire profession's performance on important issues. Regional press reviews are published in several major cities, and magazines such as *New York* and *The Atlantic Monthly* regularly publish articles examining the role of information producers.

The presses are rolling and *Al Ahram* is about to hit the streets of Cairo, Egypt.

Until recently, publications and stations preferred not to mention the competition, partly to deny them undue publicity and perhaps also because publishers and station owners constituted an invisible "club" with unwritten rules against criticizing one another. That attitude is changing today, however, partly in recognition that mass communication is big business worthy of coverage, and partly because media personalities are inherently interesting to the public. In 1988, for example, *The New York Times* introduced a new department, "The Media Business," and *The Wall Street Journal* instituted a regular column of information about marketing and advertising news.

Individual consumer action can be accomplished in many ways, including the simple action of switching off the television set or canceling a subscription to a publication—decisions that do not let the producer know what your specific complaint might be, but that, in aggregate, may accumulate and spell the end for a banal television program or greatly reduce the profitability of a newspaper that does not satisfy the needs of its audience. The Federal Communications Commission's license renewal mechanism guarantees that broadcast stations pay attention to complaints received from their listeners and viewers, although individual written response to complaints is not mandated. Newspapers, while they are not required by law or regulation to handle feedback in any particular way, view the letters-to-the-editor column on the editorial page, as well as the "corrections" box now found on page 2 or 3 of most papers, as a way of rectifying mistakes and providing readers with an opportunity to differ with views expressed by others, including the paper's editorial board. The National Advertising Division of the Council of Better Business Bureaus in New York receives consumer complaints about advertising, as does the Federal Trade Commission in Washington. The first is an independent association supported by merchants and manufacturers; the second, of course, is a government agency. All the major television networks maintain Audience Service departments in their New York headquarters to respond to viewer concerns about network programming and news. Manufacturing and service companies are sensitive to individual complaints about their advertising messages. *The Wall Street Journal* reported that when Norika Bridges of San Francisco wrote the Florsheim Shoe Co. to complain about slights against Asians in its advertising, the president of the firm wrote back to her, apologized, and said the ad was being pulled.[9]

CRITICISMS OF THE NEWS MEDIA

The background provided so far should enable us to understand better the perennial criticisms of the news media that follow below. Because each of the criticisms hits on a partial truth—and, conversely, because each criticism is based on selected information that may reflect a particular point of view—we shall present each in quotes and attempt to provide pros and cons for every issue that is raised.

"The News Media Are Biased." Anyone who has attended an event and then read or heard an account of it in the news media is aware that reporters usually choose to focus on one aspect of a story. If that aspect happens to be something that we don't feel was the main point, we may come to the conclusion that the reporter was "biased," especially if the account appears to favor the "other side" in a story that concerns politics or controversy. Because reporters tend to be younger than the average consumer, and because their task of exposing wrongdoing tends to place them in an antiestablishment stance, many people perceive that reporters have a *liberal bias.* That is, they are seen as left-leaning politically, and champions of the underdog oppressed by a bureaucratic society. There may be some truth in that on a case-by-case basis, but as mass communication researcher and theorists Ted Glasser suggests, the American press is inherently a *conservative* institution, despite the occasional liberal bent of a reporter.[10] Glasser argues that journalists are wedded to the status quo, they accept and participate in the conservation of society's dominant values, and they proceed from an underlying assumption that the American value system is "right." Nevertheless, journalists and consumers often find themselves at odds when it comes to understanding the role of reporter or editor.

"The News Media Are Too Quick to Jump on the Bandwagon." The pressure of competition causes editors to demand that their reporters get the latest information—even predictions of what is about to happen—and to report it even if they are not 100 percent certain of the facts. From the journalists' point of view, facts can be added to later versions of a story as they become known. But a story that later proves largely in error leaves a bad taste in the consumer's mouth. When a Northwest Airlines MD-82 jet crashed on takeoff from the Detroit airport in August 1987, a CBS reporter told Dan Rather on the CBS Evening News program that "my best guess . . . is that it was a catastrophic failure of the engine, that it literally exploded." Similar speculation among journalists, witnesses, and airport personnel was reported as apparent fact by many major newspapers and broadcast stations.[11] National Transportation Safety Board investigators soon discovered that the cause was something entirely different. A 1986 Reuters news agency report describing a sniper on a New York City rooftop had news media scrambling to get reporters on the scene when the story was exposed as an apparent hoax.[12] After the Iowa caucuses in 1988, the media jumped on the bandwagons of the apparent

> ### RESEARCH
>
> ## Readers' Perceptions Differ from Those of Journalists
>
> Journalists and their readers often find themselves at odds when it comes to understanding the role of the reporter and the editor. Studies conducted by Minnesota Opinion Research, Inc., on behalf of the Associated Press Managing Editors (APME) and the American Society of Newspaper Editors (ASNE) indicate that 70 percent of a scientific sample of journalists believed that their newspapers are highly factual. Only 50 percent of the public agreed.
>
> The studies showed that 85 percent of the journalists consider reporters to be objective, a statement that only 63 percent of the public supported.
>
> Two-thirds of the press but only one-fifth of the public thought journalists should report stories from "off-limits" battle areas during the fighting.
>
> Almost 60 percent of the journalists believed that the public's right to know is as important as the individual's right to a fair trial. Only about 30 percent of the public agreed.
>
> Journalists and their readers agreed on one issue: The vast majority of both groups supported the idea that improving the credibility of newspapers should be a high priority for publishers.
>
> Source: Alex Jones, "Polls Compare Journalists' and Public Views," *The New York Times*, Oct. 30, 1985, p. A-13.

leaders—Dole, Robertson, Gephardt, and Simon—and reported that the campaigns of Bush, Dukakis, and Jackson had been dealt death blows, just the opposite of the way the picture looked slightly more than a month later. After the 1984 elections, the networks swore they would not contaminate the election process by predicting winners based on exit interviews with voters before the polls closed. Halfway through the 1988 primaries NBC jumped the gun and predicted a winner before the polls closed. Endless examples of this type have soured consumers, yet the media appear unable to resist rushing on air or into print with unproven information in the hope that they will be perceived positively as being "on top of the news" and "the first to report."

"The Media Rely Too Heavily on Favorite Sources and Can Be Manipulated by Those Sources." In his book *Moscow Meets Main Street*, Professor Ted J. Smith III argues that a handful of slick Soviet operatives performing as "journalists" in Washington have managed to become frequent sources for news reports on American television purporting to describe Soviet society and Soviet-American relations. He argues that the networks, in their rush to take advantage of the availability and articulateness of these spokespeople, unwittingly have provided a channel for Soviet propaganda.[13] Others have argued that the press anointed the Reverend Jesse Jackson as spokesperson for black people in America, turning to him for his reaction whenever racial or minority issues surfaced in the national debate. Thus the media, without stating such a purpose, helped make Jackson viable as a national political candidate. Editors counter these criticisms by saying they must seek familiar faces whom their audiences can identify as leaders representing a point of view, and that giving certain people repeated exposure in the media does not connote endorsement of their views.

"The Media Are Careless with Information." On any given day, a newspaper has at least a handful of "typos"—typographical errors—that any reader picks up,

Chapter 4 The Selection and Packaging of News

Reporters follow the leader: the White House press corps files its stories from a hotel ballroom in Houston when the president visits that city for an economic conference.

as well as erroneous facts like "hook-shot" instead of "set shot." The sportscaster on TV gets mixed up and reports that Chicago won a baseball game when the graphic on the screen says Atlanta was the winner. We forgive a few of these bloopers, but when we see our own name misspelled in the press, or when we know from experience that someone was misquoted, suddenly we mistrust all reporting. The editor would respond, wearily, that newspapers and broadcast reports prepared under deadline pressure are subject to error, and that the media should be judged for the vast amount of information they transmit correctly.

"The Media Use Sensationalism to Attract an Audience." A scantily clad actress on a magazine cover sells more copies than the portrait of a political leader. During "sweeps weeks," when broadcast ratings are determined, feature stories on prostitution, runaway children, and spouse-abusers suddenly get heavy promotion and extended air time. These are the facts of economic life of the popular news media; in other words, the charge is true. Some media consciously sensationalize the news at all times to attract a wide audience. Publishers counter such criticism by saying, "That's what sells newspapers." Broadcasters can see the results of the ratings in black and white after they trot out their investigative team on a sordid story of vice or crime. The audience, as we have seen, helps decide whether the media will continue to use sex and sensation to attract and hold its attention.

"The Media Are Aimed at the Lowest Common Denominator of Society." Because the mass media need to attract large audiences in order to charge profitable rates from the advertisers who support the media, there is a natural tendency to write and report so that everyone can understand the information. Television's "happy

> **MINORITIES/WOMEN**
>
> ## Built-in Bias Shapes the News
>
> The guests on leading television public affairs shows such as "Nightline" and "The MacNeil/Lehrer Newshour" are most likely to be white, middle-aged men, according to a study by Fairness and Accuracy in Reporting, a liberal watchdog group. The producers of those shows counter that their format calls for society's leaders to appear on the programs, and thus the shows merely reflect social reality.
>
> Blacks, on the other hand, are most likely to be portrayed as outside the social mainstream, according to a *Newsweek* guest columnist, who noted, "Most black Americans are *not* poor. Most black teenagers are *not* crack addicts. Most black mothers are *not* on welfare. . . . Yet one never would deduce that by watching television or reading American newspapers and magazines."
>
> *Source:* Walter Goodman, "Watchdog Group Criticizes 2 News Programs," *The New York Times,* May 28, 1990, p. C-20; Patricia Raybon, "A Case of 'Severe Bias,'" *Newsweek,* October 2, 1989, p. 11.

talk" news presents unthreatening "plain folks" reporters, weatherpeople, and sportscasters who jolly each other through the half-hour so that the experience is pleasant and painless for all. As long as the mass media remain a predominantly commercial enterprise committed to securing the largest possible audience, aiming low intellectually is to be expected.

"The Media Invade the Privacy of Individuals." The widow of a police sergeant slain in the line of duty weeps uncontrollably at graveside. The camera stuck in her face brings her grief into our kitchen; we cannot escape the sound of her sobs and the vision of her total breakdown. Many viewers are horrified by the invasion of privacy—to which the journalist counters: "Grief is natural, it does not reflect negatively on anyone." Besides, the image of a murder's impact on one family may have the positive effect of spurring society to action in fighting crime and violence. Most journalists, however, would not defend the colleague who enters a home under false pretenses to obtain, perhaps by theft, pictures from the family album of a crime victim. Few condoned the actions of the freelance photographer who hounded Jacqueline Kennedy Onassis and her children on the streets outside her home to the point where a judge forbade him to come within close camera range. In a society where most citizens are pleased to catch themselves on camera when television covers the visit of a presidential candidate to our town, and where many of us dream of being interviewed after we win $1 million in the state lottery, privacy is a relative thing.

> **INSIGHT**
>
> ## Fan Mail
>
> The sports editor of the Bridgewater (NJ) Courier-News invites readers to take sides on an issue and offer their comments. The editor then selects a dozen or more of the best replies and fills a half-page of the newspaper with a weekly feature called "Fan Forum: Letters from our readers." Thus the consumers assist the producer in creating the information that others will read.

FUTURE FILE

✓ You have been asked by your employer, a regional phone company, to design a news information service for delivery to home computers. Your task is to ensure that all information displayed is "objective." The material will be displayed as listings, graphics, charts, and so on. Can you assure your employer that the service will be free of "bias?"

✓ In many countries, competing newspapers are owned by political parties, the government, the church, and other social organizations. Will the spread of technology make these partisan news outlets obsolete? Or will they begin to flourish in the United States as people look for alternatives to the homogenized information presented by the mainstream news media?

✓ Computer databases allow individual users to construct their own reality by selecting only the information they wish. Will the news medium of the future be only a *listing* of available information, with the consumer functioning as the editor who assembles the individualized news product?

NOTES

1. David Manning White, "The 'Gate Keeper': A Case Study in the Selection of News," *Journalism Quarterly*, Fall 1950, pp. 383–390.
2. Paul B. Snider, " 'Mr. Gates' Revisited: A 1966 Version of the 1949 Case Study," *Journalism Quarterly*, Autumn 1967, pp. 419–427.
3. Todd Hunt, "Beyond the Journalistic Event: The Changing Concept of News," *Mass Communication Review* 1 (April 1974), pp. 23–30.
4. Greg Easterbrook, "Housing: Examining a Media Myth," *Atlantic Monthly*, April 1979, pp. 10ff.
5. I. Doig and C. Doig, *News: A Consumer's Guide* (Englewood Cliffs, NJ: Prentice-Hall, 1972), pp. 29–31.
6. Hillier Kreighbaum, *Pressures on the Press* (New York: Thomas Y. Crowell, 1972), p. 189.
7. Kathleen Jamieson and K. K. Campbell, *The Interplay of Influence* (Belmont, CA: Wadsworth, 1988), p. 222.
8. Herbert J. Gans, *Deciding What's News* (New York: Pantheon Books, 1979), p. 267.
9. "She Took Pen in Hand, Exacted Her Vengeance," *The Wall Street Journal*, May 5, 1988, p. 35.
10. Theodore Glasser, Talk to students at Rutgers University, April 7, 1988.
11. William M. Carley, "In a Big Plane Crash, Cause Probably Isn't Everybody's Guess," *The Wall Street Journal*, March 19, 1988, p. 20.
12. Larry Rohter, "News Agency Disseminates and Retracts Report of Rooftop Sniper," *The New York Times*, Nov. 4, 1986, p. B-3.
13. Ted J. Smith III, *Moscow Meets Main Street* (Washington: The Media Institute, 1988).

SUGGESTED READINGS

Crouse, Timothy, *The Boys in the Bus* (Westminster, MD: Random House, 1973).
Doig, I., and C. Doig, *News: A Consumer's Guide* (Englewood Cliffs, NJ: Prentice-Hall, 1972).
Epstein, E. J., *Between Fact and Fiction: The Problems of Journalism* (New York: Random House, 1975).
Gans, Herbert J., *Deciding What's News: A Study of CBS Evening News, NBC Nightly News, Newsweek and Time* (New York: Pantheon Books, 1979).
Krieghbaum, Hillier, *Pressures on the Press* (New York: Thomas Y. Crowell, 1972).
Tuchman, Gaye, *Making News: A Study in the Construction of Reality* (New York; Free Press, 1978).

CHAPTER 5

Regulation of the Mass Media

AT A GLANCE

- Regulation is constantly being rethought and reinterpreted, with different rules covering the special situations of different technologies.

- The First Amendment to the Constitution of the United States of America guarantees freedom of speech and freedom of the press.

- Despite constitutional guarantees, many laws, regulations, and court decisions limit freedom of expression in certain situations, usually to guard against abuses or to protect a vulnerable segment of society.

- The Freedom of Information Act (FOIA) allows citizens access to public records and documents in the interest of the free flow of information.

- Professional communication organizations engage in self-regulation when they adopt codes of ethics.

- Specific laws guard individuals against public abuse and protect the rights of the originator to profit from the creation of information and ideas.

- Ownership of the media of mass communication is becoming concentrated in ever-larger organizations that strive to provide every form of information, both print and broadcast, news and entertainment.

Before we look at the development of the various and separate media of mass communication, it is useful to consider the philosophies that underlie the controls or the lack of controls that societies choose to put on those media. Americans take justifiable pride in saying that they enjoy freedom of speech and freedom of the press, unlike citizens of countries where dictators or totalitarian regimes exercise rigid controls over all forms of expression. Yet even we have a considerable body of laws that restrict various forms of mass communication "for the public good"—that is, to protect citizens from excesses and misuses that even an open society chooses not to tolerate.

REGULATION: HOW MUCH? WHAT KIND? BY WHOM?

- Critics contend that Saturday morning children's television is essentially one solid commercial. Many of the programs involve fictional characters who are tied to a line of commercial products.
- Dial-a-porn, dial-a-conversation, and dial-a-date services are readily available to anyone with a telephone.
- Following the State of the Union address by the President, networks provide "equal time" for a speech by a representative of the opposition party.

As these examples suggest, the Information Age has underscored the importance of issues of regulation: How much do we need? What kind? And by whom? As the late communication scholar Ithiel de Sola Pool argued forcefully in *Technologies of Freedom*, the development of new and hybrid media has not occurred in a vacuum, but rather in a specific historical and legal context.[1] When we examine communication systems in a historical and legal perspective, we can distinguish three types—print, common carrier and broadcasting—each with distinctive policies.

1. For print media, the valued First Amendment concepts of freedom of public and religious speech have generally served as guiding principles. The courts have acted to prohibit censorship and licensing of publications.

2. The operation of the mail, telephone, and telegraph systems has been shaped by a very different philosophy and regulatory framework. These have been regarded as *common carriers*—channels to which all should have access.

3. A third regulatory pattern has emerged for broadcasting, where the intent has been to ensure the fair and appropriate use of what were, at least originally, a limited number of usable radio frequencies. In an effort to achieve this end, extensive government regulation has been instituted, including the licensing of station operators based on an assessment as to whether they are operating in the public interest.

An analysis of these three rather distinct regulatory and legal traditions leads to a basic question relative to newly emerging communication technologies: Will the new electronic media be thought about and handled in the protected First Amendment tradition of speech and print, or in the more regulated tradition of the common carriers and, in particular, broadcasting? Pool argues that the shift to electronic communication may be a critical turning point that history will remember.[2]

Chapter 5 Regulation of the Mass Media 131

Artists parade their version of the Statue of Liberty in front of a controversial exhibition of Robert Mapplethorpe photographs to remind would-be censors of First Amendment protections.

Approaches to the regulation of print that we live by today were developed in the seventeenth and eighteenth centuries in Great Britain and America. It seems likely that what we think and do during this present period will serve as an important precedent for the control of mass communication systems for a substantial period of time in the future.[3]

Closely related to questions about regulation are issues pertaining to freedom and the free flow of information. Some writers have suggested that the technologies of the Information Age will naturally promote freedom if they are not regulated by the government or controlled by big business.[4] It is their view that regulation will inevitably minimize freedom, and that centralizing the control of mass communication resources and regulating are inherently negative.

This raises a number of provocative issues regarding the nature and origins of regulation and the impact of regulation and technology on human behavior. In some senses, of course, the idea that regulation inhibits freedom seems obvious; more regulation appears to result in less freedom. On the other hand, there are also some circumstances wherein regulation seems to enhance the free, diverse, and open flow of information. For instance, regulation has led to the development of educational and public broadcasting, and ensured a balance in the presentation of ideas on controversial issues. Even the "rights" to freedom of speech and privacy that we take for granted are themselves the consequence of regulations set forth in the Bill of Rights. It has even been argued that regulation is a "citizen's sole means of exerting influence."[5]

We often assume that media control and regulation are primarily a consequence of government activity, because governmental regulations, rules, and policies are obvious. In addition to governmental regulation, which may lead to prior restraint or censorship, there are two other sources of regulation: (1) the audience for a particular medium on the "consumer" side of the equation, and (2) the media owners and information providers on the "producer" side. By their reading, listening, and viewing choices, mass communication consumers can do as much to limit the diverse and open flow of information as government regulation. Similarly, by their programming choices, producers may also do much to constrain the free and diverse programming. In commercial television, for instance, are the limitations and constraints on media fare more the product of broadcasting regulation or public preferences?

The larger questions are: What are the functions and dysfunctions of regulation? What are the most appropriate agencies and mechanisms of control and regulation? What values should guide our regulatory decision making in an Information Age? The ultimate issue, then, is not whether regulation is desirable or not, but *how much*, *what kind*, and *by whom*?

This chapter addresses major issues of regulation, but it is not exhaustive. We shall encounter several more examples of regulation and self-regulation in the media chapters to come, including the movie ratings by the motion picture industry, the regulation of broadcasting by the Federal Communications Commission, and the ever-changing legislation aimed at controlling ownership, program content, and rates in the cable industry.

FREEDOM OF INFORMATION AND PRIVACY

"Congress shall make no law . . . abridging the freedom of speech, or of the press."

The wording of the First Amendment to the Constitution of the United States is crystal-clear. The right to speak up on an issue or to use the media of mass communication to articulate the ideas and opinions of an individual or group is sacrosanct. (The First Amendment also guarantees freedom of religion and the right to assemble for the purpose of giving or receiving information.)

Moreover, the Freedom of Information Act, passed in 1966 and amended several times, guarantees citizens the right to obtain any unclassified information created or stored by the government. But even in a free and open society, there are constant pressures to deny citizens the right of expression and the right of access to information—often in the interest of protecting other collective and individual rights.

To demonstrate the complexity of First Amendment issues, consider these cases currently being debated in the courts, legislatures, and editorial columns of America:

- *Naming rape victims.* The news media routinely use their access to public records to cover any and all crimes reported by police departments. Names of victims, details of the crime, and identification of those arrested and charged for the offenses are reported in the interest of informing the public. Nonetheless, most news media routinely do not publish the names of rape victims. They withhold

Chapter 5   Regulation of the Mass Media   **133**

The legacy of Thomas Jefferson is that the expressions of "Married With Children," although offensive to some, are protected by the First Amendment to the Constitution.

that information on the grounds that publication would further stigmatize those already victimized by crime. In this case, the press has a freedom, but chooses not to use it for fear that the publication of information could cause great harm to the individual involved. (Should a newspaper decide to publish the name of a rape victim, it is protected under a 1989 Supreme Court decision that a rape victim's privacy must bow to the First Amendment right to publish legally obtained information.)

- *Phone sex.* In a 1989 decision, the Supreme Court upheld the right of "dial-a-porn" companies to provide services where the information dispensed was "indecent," but not "obscene." The decision held that concerns over shielding children from such information should not deny access to the information by adults who desire it.

    The Court held in 1989, however, that the section of the federal law requiring telephone companies to block access to sex-talk services unless a customer asked in writing to receive them was legal. The Justices held that totally banning phone sex had the effect of limiting adults to conversations suitable only for children. After further review, during a period of over two years when the law was not enforced while the issue was studied further, the Court in 1992 reaffirmed its earlier decision and said that Congress had the right to protect children from pornography.

- *Identification of burglary victims.* A law passed in 1989 in Texas prohibited the news media from publishing the names of burglary victims. The intent was to prevent such victims from harassment by salespersons from firms selling burglar alarm systems. It slipped through the state legislature before the news media

Dispensing sexual information by telephone is not illegal, said the U.S. Supreme court, because adults have a right to receive messages that may not be suitable for children.

realized that it effectively curtailed basic crime reporting that was of interest to citizens.

The Freedom of Information Act: A Continuing Saga

Pressed by journalists and consumer advocates alike, Congress passed the Freedom of Information Act in 1966, and it became law—appropriately—on Independence Day, 1967. The new law required that government records be open for inspection by individuals unless specific exemptions were spelled out. The exceptions included protection of the national defense, trade secrets, and certain law-enforcement records.

Immediately government bureaucrats threw up roadblocks. They made indexes of the records inaccessible, charged outrageous fees for photocopying, and limited access to the records to a few hours a week. To prohibit such practices, Congress passed the first of many amendments to the FOIA in 1974.

Later amendments exempted more types of information from the FOIA, including trade information and information about nuclear power plants. The 1986 amendment favored major news organizations with a reduction in fees for research and copying, but access to records for commercial use—that is, by corporations and businesses wanting information of use to them—was made more difficult and the cost higher. Since the bulk of requests to government agencies are from individuals and businesses, the 1986 amendment undermined the intent of the original Freedom of Information Act.

Freedom of information promises to be an area of contention for the foreseeable future, with journalists, librarians, political activist groups, business concerns, and consumer advocates battling government officials for the right to know what data government agencies have compiled on individuals and groups in society.

Impact of the Information Age

In an age when information is increasingly regarded as a commodity to be owned and possessed, we should not be surprised that there are an increasing number of legal arguments about proprietary rights to information. A tension is emerging between the argument for the free flow of information and open access on the one hand, and privacy and security on the other. With new technology, such information as personal credit records, phone numbers, social security numbers, and subscription lists, gathered and stored for a particular purpose, may be sold or used inappropriately in other unauthorized circumstances. For instance, some videotape rental firms keep electronic records of the titles of the videotapes each customer has rented. This information can be sold to other organizations, which will use it to target direct mail advertising. While this use of the information may be little more than annoying, how would we feel about these kinds of records for individuals seeking to run for public office being released to the media?

New communication technologies also facilitate the duplication of print, audio, and video materials and computer software. Whether it be the photocopying of several chapters of a book, the duplication of rented videotapes, or illegal copying of computer software, the "piracy" or theft of copyrighted information has become an issue of increasing concern.

ETHICS CODES AND SELF-REGULATING ORGANIZATIONS

Democratic societies, free enterprise systems, and the social responsibility theory of mass communication all view excessive regulation by the government as something to be avoided. Among the best ways to avoid government regulation is to demonstrate *self*-regulation.

Owners of the mass communication media and professionals in such fields as journalism and public relations exercise their social responsibility and protect themselves from overregulation by adopting *ethics codes* and by forming self-policing associations such as those discussed below.

The leading ethics codes are those devised by media associations, for example:

- Journalists have two main ethics codes. Those who join the Society of Professional Journalists (SPJ) must agree to abide by the strictures of an ethics code that prohibits the acceptance of "anything of value" in return for favorable coverage in a story. Many newspapers adopt the ethics code of the American Society of Newspaper Editors (ASNE), which calls for, among other things, fairness and balance in the reporting of public affairs.

- Information specialists who belong to the Public Relations Society of America (PRSA) or the International Association of Business Communicators (IABC) subscribe to codes that call for agents to reveal the identity of clients on whose behalf they create and release information, and to avoid conflicts of interest when serving their clients.

> ### INSIGHT
> ## The Press: Four Theories
>
> In the 1950s, three leading mass communication scholars proposed that four theories accounted for the varied ways that political systems view the role of the press and control of the institutions of mass communication:
>
> *Authoritarian.* Dictators and totalitarian regimes, afraid or unwilling to trust their people, impose regulations, taxes, and other strictures that make it impossible to publish views or ideas counter to those of the ruling power.
>
> *Libertarian.* At the opposite extreme, based on the philisophies of John Milton and John Locke, is the theory that no information should be barred from the marketplace of ideas unless it interferes with or denies the liberties of another citizen. Milton's *Areopagitica* argued against authoritarian control.
>
> *Soviet.* Marxist regimes held that the one role of the press was to express and disseminate socialist dogma, hand in hand with the ruling socialist party.
>
> *Social Responsibility.* The American system holds that press freedom is guaranteed only if the press serves the functions of informing society, interpreting, and correlating that we outlined in Chapter 3.
>
> While the four theories were developed to explain press roles, it is easy to apply the same definitions to other institutions of mass communication, including entertainment, popular culture, advertising, and public relations.
>
> *Source:* Fred S. Siebert, Theodore Peterson, and Wilbur Schramm, *Four Theories of the Press* (Urbana: University of Illinois Press, 1956).

- The National Association of Broadcasters (NAB) provides leadership on many aspects of advertising practices for members, which include the vast majority of radio and television station owners.
- The Motion Picture Association of America's (MPAA) rating system is aimed at keeping Congress off the industry's back as well as providing guidance for consumers.

All of these groups—and others, such as the Magazine Publishers Association, the Yellow Pages Association, and the Direct Mail Association—disseminate promotional materials that they are prepared to carry to legislative bodies for lobbying purposes if they are threatened by increased government regulation.

THE LEGAL MATRIX

Professional mass communicators, when they prepare for their specific duties, and owners of mass communication media, when they engage lawyers to help them conduct their business, learn to deal with the myriad of laws and rules that affect the most basic aspects of their business. If you continue your studies in the field, you will learn about libel in your reporting and editing courses, about copyright in your magazine writing and book publishing courses, and about the ever-changing sets of regulations governing broadcasting in your radio and television courses.

INDUSTRY

Libel: Is There No Limit?

How do the scandal sheets sold in supermarkets get away with the bizarre stories they run about celebrities? In part, they rely on the fact that celebrities give up much of their privacy. They also know that, while a celebrity might have a chance of winning, the stars don't need the grief that comes from thrusting their names further into the limelight with lawsuits that serve to repeat the untruthful information over and over.

One star who did go to court was comedienne Carol Burnett, who objected to a *National Enquirer* story portraying her as drunk and abusive in a restaurant. Her $1.6 million award was reduced to $200,000, but Burnett expressed satisfaction at having protected her reputation while punishing the publication. She managed to perpetuate the moral lesson by using the settlement money to establish a fund to reward reporters for responsible journalism.

Libel and Slander

Libel is written defamation, and slander is spoken defamation. Defamation has been defined as information that exposes a person to ridicule, hatred, or contempt. However, if a person is seen as a "public figure"—that is, if he or she is an elected official, a celebrity, or a person thrust into the limelight by events—many of the protections of libel and slander may evaporate. The landmark 1964 *New York Times* v. *Sullivan* ruling held that when a public official is defamed by a news report, "reckless disregard for its truth or falsity" is the only grounds for a libel judgment.

Copyright

Prior to 1976, a writer could protect information only by filing forms with the U.S. Copyright Office. Now automatic protection is granted until a work is published. Application must be made and a copyright notice must appear in the work to be protected when it is published. Writers, editors, and information specialists must take special care to avoid violating copyrights held by other mass communicators. In recent memory, notable copyright cases have involved a section of somebody else's published memoirs that author Alex Haley apparently inadvertently included in his book *Roots*, song lyrics that appeared in Beatles songs as well as the music of others, and sections of scholarly works apparently lifted by prominent figures when writing their own dissertations. The lesson learned is that extreme care must be taken when using information "found" in public, because eventually someone may claim and prove ownership. Martin Luther King's "I Have a Dream" speech and the familiar "Happy Birthday to You" song are examples of copyrighted works that have figured in embarrassing legal actions.

Implied Endorsement

Permission must be gained to use the image or sanction of a person or organization if endorsement of a product, idea, or institution is implied. When characterizations of current or past celebrities are used in advertisements, the families and heirs may

French chef Paul Bocuse was not amused when a McDonald's advertisement in the Netherlands used his photo without getting permission from him.

demand payment, or bring suit to prevent the use of a likeness or imitation. Release forms must be signed by individuals (or parents of minors) whose likenesses are used for promotional purposes. The McDonald's hamburger chain ran afoul of this requirement when its agency in the Netherlands used a file picture of four chefs in a humorous ad, only to find later that they were identifiable as the staff of noted French chef Paul Bocuse, who was not amused and sued.

Hate Speech

In the summer of 1992, the Supreme Court ruled that "hate speech"—fighting words of one against another based on racial, ethnic, or sexual orientation—could not be banned by law, no matter how offensive to a group or an individual. The justices gave many varied explanations for the decision, but underlying it all was the feeling that words cannot be punished because of the feelings of those who express them. The decision had the effect of counteracting the many "hate speech" regulations enacted in recent years on college campuses to prevent utterances, writings, and symbolic acts that were considered racist, sexist, or homophobic.

Shield Laws for Reporters

Many states—but still fewer than half of them—have "shield" laws protecting reporters from revealing their sources when they have promised anonymity in order to gather information in an investigative story. In states where there is no shield law, or only limited protection, the reporter who refuses to reveal sources in a court of law may be subject to a citation of contempt and may be required to serve a jail term for the duration of a court case where the judge is seeking the information that the press believes is "privileged." In 1992, reporters from *Newsday* and National Public Radio refused to answer questions from a Senate special counsel investigating leaks to the press of sexual harassment charges brought against Supreme Court nominee Clarence Thomas by Professor Anita F. Hill. Both reporters cited First Amendment protection, which the press believes functions as a federal "shield" law.

Gag Rules

Similarly, a judge may restrain the press by prohibiting reporters from revealing certain details of a case or interfering with the judicial process by seeking information from witnesses and other participants in a case. If the press oversteps the bounds of a gag rule, the judge may find the reporter, photographer, or editor in contempt and assess a fine.

Cameras in the Court

In 1991, television viewers were able to watch the rape trial of a member of the Kennedy family on television—save for the face of the accuser, which was covered by a blue dot. A few months later, a similar trial of boxer Mike Tyson was not permitted on television, and viewers had to be content with pictures taken outside the courtroom. Depending on the jurisdiction, still or television cameras may or may not be permitted, and the practice is still considered "experimental" in most states. Experience indicates, however, that decorum can be maintained when cameras are present, and the main effects of photographic coverage have been greater public attention and increased understanding of the court system.

Coverage of Legislative Bodies

Similarly, cameras have traditionally been excluded from the deliberations of legislative bodies, except for hearings held by committees in situations where public interest is extremely high. Coverage of both houses of the U.S. Congress by C-Span television, however, has shown that business can be conducted in an orderly manner under the watchful eye of television, and legislators do not disrupt business by "playing to the camera." Rules regarding electronic coverage of law-making bodies are rapidly being liberalized.

Antitrust Legislation

In order to prevent monopoly control over information that can result from concentration of ownership, the federal government uses antitrust legislation to prevent one organization from dominating or excluding others from the communication business. Since 1975, communication companies have been prohibited from owning a television station and a newspaper in the same major market in order to assure more than one point of view.

WHO OWNS THE MEDIA OF MASS COMMUNICATION?

As we shall see in Chapter 6, Benjamin Franklin did it all: wrote the material for a publication, set the type, and sold the copies from his print shop. Still today there are small weekly papers and small-circulation specialized magazines for which one person gathers the information, sells the ads, sets the type, sticks on the address labels, . . . and realizes the profit or takes the loss. And there are radio stations in small towns where the news and ads are read from the station owner's breakfast table.

In the American private enterprise system, and in a society such as ours where government controls are regulatory but not political in nature, it is still possible for any individual to enter the business of mass communication for the purposes of disseminating information and making a profit. However, mass media have become Big Business, and increasingly it takes experience, money, and the ability to deal with complex regulations and social demands in order to have a major impact in the world of mass communication.

New Ownership Patterns

In January 1990, a new era began in the information-entertainment industry after the Delaware Supreme Court cleared the way for Time Inc. to gain control of Warner Communications. Thus was born a new company that, in the words of *The New York Times* "would insure Time Warner a place in the 1990s as one of a handful of global media giants able to produce and distribute information in virtually any medium."[6] Time Inc.'s revenue had come primarily from magazines and cable, while Warner produced films, music, cable, and specialized magazines. Paramount Communications Inc. had tried to block the merger, seeking to gain control of Time Inc. in order to join Time's publishing empire and cable services with Paramount's film and television divisions to form an equally formidable world competitor.

The Time Warner development came at the end of a decade that saw the growth of newspaper chains. It had also been a period when large advertising agencies merged into a smaller number of giant advertising combines. The decade that follows promises to see even more merger mania as the world becomes one large market and, in the jargon of the investment community, a few "players" dominate production and distribution of goods and services.

Will it really be necessary to be a *mega*-company, a *super*-giant firm in order to be successful in the twenty-first century? Auto companies, accounting firms, and other businesses apparently think so, for they have been caught up in the fever of mergers and acquisitions. Media companies apparently are no different, for they depend on profits and market domination to convince the other mega-businesses that they can deliver audiences for advertising messages.

According to the annual survey and listing of 100 leading media companies published by *Advertising Age* (see Table 5.1), the nation's top media company in August, 1992, was Time Warner, which edged ahead of Capital Cities/ABC for the first time. Both had more than $5 billion in revenues. Tele-Communications Inc., a cable firm, moved up to fourth place, edging out General Electric (the owner of NBC) and CBS Inc. For the first time in history, companies owning cable dominated over companies associated primarily with network television.

Oklahoma law professor Anita Hill testifies before the Senate Judiciary Committee hearings on the nomination of Clarence Thomas to the Supreme Court. When public interest is high, the workings of legislative bodies are shown on national television.

The Times-Mirror Company of Los Angeles not only publishes newspapers but is an "across-the-board" media company with magazine, books, broadcast, and cable operations. Other major newspaper companies that have diversified into magazine publishing and broadcast or cable include the Knight-Ridder chain, the Tribune Company of Chicago, the New York Times Company, the Cox Chain, the Washington Post Company, and Rupert Murdoch's News Corp.

As the move to bigness continues, it should come as no surprise if CBS and GE (NBC) strike deals to join with one or another of the print-oriented giants. Other major players could include firms such as Whittle Communications of Nashville, which, in addition to being a fast-growing advertising firm, is involved in magazine publishing and specialized video. Increasingly there will be pressure for such firms to find ways to match their capabilities with those of other companies in order to forge a larger presence in the world of mass communication.

Pressures of the Marketplace

We can attribute the pressures to merge and grow to these basic realities of the marketplace:

TABLE 5.1 Leading Media Companies, 1991 (in millions)

Rank 1991	Rank 1990	Company, U.S. headquarters	Total media revenue	Newspaper revenue	Magazine revenue	Broadcast revenue	Cable TV revenue	Other media revenue
1	2	Time Warner, New York	$5,229.0	—	$1,928.0	—	$3,301.0	—
2	1	Capital Cities/ABC, New York	5,172.0	$521.3	321.0	$3,712.0	489.4	$128.3
3	3	Gannett Co., Arlington, Va.	3,382.0	2,629.8	—	360.1	—	392.1
4	7	Tele-Communications Inc., Denver	3,206.0	—	—	—	3,206.0	—
5	5	General Electric Co., Fairfield, Conn.	3,153.5	—	—	3,086.0	67.5	—
6	4	CBS Inc., New York	3,035.0	—	—	3,035.0	—	—
7	6	Advance Publications, Newark, N.J.	3,013.0	1,714.0	859.0	—	440.0	—
8	8	Times Mirror Co., Los Angeles	2,763.3	1,973.8	291.5	94.2	403.8	—
9	9	News Corp., Sydney	2,278.0	164.0	575.0	964.0	—	575.0
10	10	Knight-Ridder, Miami	1,953.8	1,953.8	—	—	—	—
11	11	Hearst Corp., New York	1,947.2	680.0	1,002.0	265.2	—	—
12	14	Cox Enterprises, Atlanta	1,716.0	709.0	2.0	409.0	596.0	—
13	12	New York Times Co., New York	1,703.1	1,274.4	352.7	66.5	—	9.5
14	13	Tribune Co., Chicago	1,636.6	1,141.6	—	495.0	—	—
15	17	Viacom International, New York	1,459.3	—	—	159.1	1,300.2	—
16	15	Thomson Corp., Toronto	1,419.6	645.2	774.4	—	—	—
17	16	Washington Post Co., Washington	1,292.2	642.7	326.5	163.5	159.5	—
18	19	Turner Broadcasting System, Atlanta	1,190.7	—	—	—	1,190.7	—
19	18	E.W. Scripps, Cincinnati	1,161.6	691.0	—	245.4	225.2	—
20	21	Continental Cablevision, Boston	1,127.0	—	—	—	1,127.0	—

Source: "100 Leading Media Companies," *Advertising Age,* August 10, 1992, p. S–2.

1. Firms dealing with their clients want to present themselves as "full-service" companies. They want to be able to say, "We can design your information and place it in any channel in order to reach all the audiences you want to target for your message." That's no different from the claims of an insurance firm that wants to be able to say, "We can take care of all your insurance needs" or the retailer who boasts, "If you need it, we've got it."

2. The buying power of media giants is considerable; they can get the best price for materials they need, and they can spread the cost of gathering information among their various news and entertainment operations. That's no different from the retailer who can claim to offer the lowest prices in town because "we are a volume buyer."[7]

Increasingly the question consumers will have to ask is, "Are we being served as well by the news media giants as we were by the many smaller companies that preceded them?" This is not just a philosophical question; it is an issue that Congress will have to monitor in the twenty-first century. Legislators have always kept an eye on monopolies and passed laws when it appeared that too much control was vested in one firm. As we will see, the original NBC was split in two to end its dominance of broadcasting, and the AT&T telephone monopoly was forced to divest itself of the local operating companies when it wanted to enter other lucrative markets.

Counterbalancing the concern over control of the media by too few firms is the concern that America will lose its dominance of communication to such huge diversified companies as Bertelsmann of West Germany, Hachette of France, the News Corporation of Australia, or Sony of Japan. The loss of dominance in electronics to Japan is a sobering precedent that leads many American media chiefs to be wary of the possibility that they could also lose their dominance in the creation and dissemination of information.

FUTURE FILE

- ✓ You have decided to become the Communications Czar of the twenty-first century. Name the existing company you will buy as the foundation for your information empire. Identify smaller, specialized organizations you will then seek to acquire to round out the mix of media and markets. *Suggestion:* Branch out into some areas not yet included by the current media giants.

- ✓ According to former Supreme Court Justice Warren Burger, this country has twice as many lawyers as it needs. Will many of the top lawyers become the heads of communication conglomerates in the future, sensing that their expertise is more crucial to mass communication enterprises than that of the "creative" and business people?

- ✓ If, indeed, global expansion leads to the evolution of just a few giant mass communication companies, will U.S. firms take the lead, or will we become "satellites" of enterprises owned in foreign lands? What will be the consequences if oil companies in the Middle East control communication enterprises in our country?

NOTES

1. Ithiel de Sola Pool, *Technologies of Freedom* (Cambridge, MA: Belknap, 1983).
2. Pool, p. 10.
3. Pool, p. 10.
4. Cf. Herbert I. Schiller, *Culture, Inc.* (New York: Oxford University Press, 1989); and Ithiel de Sola Pool.
5. Ernest D. Rose, "Moral and Ethical Dilemmas Inherent in an Information Society," in Jerry L. Salvaggio, ed., *Telecommunications: Issues and Choices for Society* (New York: Longman, 1983), p. 21.
6. Floyd Norris, "Time Inc. and Warner to Merge, Creating Largest Media Company," *The New York Times*, March 5, 1989, pp. 1, 39.
7. David Waterman, "A New Look at Mass Media Chains and Groups," presentation to the International Communication Association, San Francisco, May 1989.

SUGGESTED READINGS

Bagdikian, Ben H., *The Media Monopoly* (Boston: Beacon Press, 1987).

Gillmor, Donald, and Jerome Barron, *Mass Communication Law* (St. Paul: West Publishing, 1984).

Merrill, John C., *The Dialectic in Journalism: Toward a Responsible Use of Press Freedom* (Baton Rouge: Louisiana State University Press, 1989).

Nelson, Harold, and Dwight Teeter, *Law of Mass Communication* (Mineola, NY: Foundation Press, 1986).

Siebert, Fred S., Theodore Peterson, and Wilbur Schramm, *Four Theories of the Press* (Urbana: University of Illinois Press, 1956).

Smolla, R. A., *Suing the Press: Libel, The Media and Power* (New York: Oxford University Press, 1986).

FREEDOM OF SPEECH AND FREEDOM OF THE PRESS

CATHERINE PRATT

Catherine Pratt teaches media law, criticism, and public relations. She is the author of several articles on law and ethics.

In 1791, a still-young United States of America ratified the Bill of Rights, the first 10 amendments to its Constitution. These amendments outlined specific freedoms guaranteed to citizens and placed limitations on government action concerning restrictions of those freedoms. Among these 10 amendments is our country's commitment to the free exchange of information, the First Amendment.

In part, this amendment reads: "Congress shall make no law . . . abridging the freedom of speech, or of the press." Its language is more philosophical than legal. Like the other provisions in the Bill of Rights, its interpretation has been varied and, at times, controversial.

Although the First Amendment's language includes the phrase "no law," our guaranteed "freedom of expression" is not absolute. Throughout our history, individuals and groups have been restricted from speaking, or they have been punished after they spoke. Publications have been suppressed and editors jailed for disseminating information that the government deemed improper.

Constitutional law is fluid because it is defined through the interpretations of the sitting Supreme Court justices. While the First Amendment itself has not been altered in its 200 years of existence, judicial rulings on what expression is and is not protected have frequently changed.

One of the most widely argued reasons for flexibility in First Amendment interpretation is that the nature of communication has changed dramatically since 1791. The framers lived in a society without television, telephones, or fax machines. Communicating took a great deal longer and was considered a much more formal enterprise. It has been argued that the free speech and free press clauses of the First Amendment might not have been included in the Bill of Rights if the framers could have anticipated some of the "expression" it now protects. These arguments, however, could be applied to almost any part of the Bill of Rights or the Constitution. We cannot read the framers' minds and we should not be sidetracked by arguments suggesting that anything new is inherently suspect. We don't know whether Thomas Jefferson would be appalled by "Married with Children," and we have no way of knowing whether James Madison would defend *Hustler* magazine's blistering satire of the Reverend Jerry Falwell. What we do know is that the framers left us a legacy of protection for free expression unmatched anywhere else in the modern world—at least in theory, if not always in practice.

The current "state of the amendment" is somewhat clouded. The twentieth century has seen a gradual widening of protection for expression, particularly in the area of political speech. In times of war or armed conflict the collection and release of information is more likely to be impeded or punished.

The war that began in the Middle East in 1991 provided us with an uncomfortable reminder of just how much control government can have over our First Amendment rights. If you look at early newspaper or broadcast coverage of the war, you're likely to see a notation clearly stating that someone in the government had seen and cleared the information pre-

Continued

Continued from page 145

sented in the report. Most people would agree that government censorship of information vital to national security or to troop safety is necessary and acceptable, but we have no way of knowing whether the withheld information was vital to our security or safety. And we had no way of knowing whether specific government officials would widen the censorship net to include information that was embarrassing or negative, but was not a threat to national security.

The major news organizations are in general agreement that current government controls on information in situations like that are extremely broad. We may never know whether that much censorship was justified or was an infringement on our First Amendment free press guarantees.

In recent years, the Supreme Court has regularly used a "right to know" argument to justify protection of certain kinds of expression. The Court has said, for example, that advertising deserves some First Amendment protection, not because the advertiser has free expression rights but because the public has a right to receive the information contained in some advertisements. This emphasis on the consumer rather than the producer has no visible roots in the language of the First Amendment, but the Court has nonetheless relied on this rationale in a number of cases. The problem with this approach, however, is that it seems to be an excuse for withholding First Amendment rights from some information producers. If you grant First Amendment protection to advertising communication only because the public has a right to the information, then you can take away this protection if you don't think the information in the ad is valuable or necessary. The Court has ruled that information about competitive prescription drug prices is valuable for consumers, but information about gambling is not. The former was given First Amendment protection, the latter was not. It doesn't take much imagination to figure out that what some censors think is valuable or necessary may not match what individuals in the public think is valuable or necessary.

Of all the areas of First Amendment concern, the one most prominent is usually message restriction, or limits on First Amendment protection because of the content of the information presented. The recent controversies over the photographs of Robert Mapplethorpe and Andres Serrano illustrate the complexities of this concern. In the case of Robert Mapplethorpe, for example, a photo exhibition of 150 works was legally harassed by individuals and government officials who objected to six of the photos. (Four were homoerotic in nature; two were artistic nudes of children.) The photos were exhibited in galleries where admittance was certainly limited to those interested in seeing the photos. Although Mapplethorpe's photography had been critically praised, the Cincinnati museum that exhibited the work was subjected to a lengthy and expensive legal battle that many would argue has had a chilling effect on free expression.

The Serrano controversy centered on a single photograph of a plastic crucifix in a jar of urine, which the artist said was his commentary on the cheapening of Christianity. The photograph was produced during a year in which an NEA grant had been awarded to the artist. The Serrano photograph and the Mapplethorpe exhibit ignited a backlash against federal funding for the arts. The Martin Scorcese movie *The Last Temptation of Christ* produced a similar call for censorship, and 2 Live Crew's rap music resulted in a court appearance on obscenity charges.

It can be convincingly argued that expression must be broadly protected and that assaults based on taste or offensiveness are dangerous in the long term. Some scholars have a pessimistic outlook about public support for free expression, however, and a few have publicly said that if the First Amendment were put to a referendum today, it would lose. Ulti-

Continued from page 146

mately, the public influences the parameters of First Amendment protection by encouraging or discouraging freedom of expression. The Supreme Court has made some First Amendment decisions that appear out of step with public sentiment, but many more provide a fair reflection of the country's mood. Producers and consumers of information should remember that "the bottom line" on their own personal freedom is a strong First Amendment and a country that encourages healthy debate and tolerates opinions and expression that diverge from the norm.

ETHICS AND MASS COMMUNICATION

DENI ELLIOTT

Deni Elliot is the director of the Institute for the Study of Applied and Professional Ethics at Dartmouth College and teaches in the philosophy department. She edits the book review section of the Journal of Mass Media Ethics.

Ethics is the study of how people act in regard to other people. Different theories present different perceptions of morally ideal behavior, but minimal morality in all cases requires that *one should not cause another to suffer unnecessarily.* In addition, *one should justify one's actions if those actions are likely to lead others to suffer.* Some argue that you can justify causing individuals to suffer if what you are doing will bring about the greatest good for the greatest number. Others say that you can justify causing suffering if you are acting in a way that recognizes individual rights as having priority and gives the trump card to the most vulnerable. But all hold that behavior that violates the general admonishment *"Don't cause others to suffer"* must be justified to be moral.

One twentieth century ethical theory, developed by philosopher Bernard Gert, provides a list of moral rules that follow from the basic idea, "Don't cause others to suffer unnecessarily."[1] These moral rules, in turn, form a basis from which to explain professional responsibility and restraint: (1) don't kill, (2) don't cause pain, (3) don't disable, (4) don't deprive of pleasure, (5) don't deprive of freedom, (6) don't deceive, (7) don't cheat, (8) keep your promises, (9) obey the law, and (10) do your role-related duty. Not every violation of these rules leads to suffering, but it is likely that others would suffer if these rules were not generally followed. For example, it might not cause anyone to suffer if I run a stoplight at 3 A.M. at a deserted intersection (notice how the justification for my action—"late at night, no one around"—is inherent in my description), but others would certainly suffer if people generally disregarded the laws concerning traffic lights. Lacking justification for an exception, everyone should always act in accordance with the moral rules.

Morality and Mass Communication

Being an ethical practitioner means being committed to acting in a way that doesn't cause others to suffer unnecessarily. Practitioners can act on that commitment by following these steps:

Step One: Identify Your Professional Duty

You don't know whether you are acting in accordance with a moral rule (like "Do your duty") if you don't know what it includes. The professional duty is a short statement of what separates one occupation from others. It captures the essence of what it means to be doing this particular job in society, taking nothing else into account.

The formulations of duty I have suggested below are offered as the starting place for discussion. Each practitioner and each student should consider and discuss with colleagues the statement of professional duty.

1. *Advertisers* have a duty, to the best of their ability, to promote their client's products or services to the targeted audience.
2. *Entertainers* have a duty, to the best of their ability, to present programming and products that target groups find enjoyable.
3. *News representatives* have a duty, to the best of their ability, to gather and present people with accurate information that citizens need to maintain a self-governing society.
4. *Public relations specialists* have a duty, to the best of their ability, to promote favorable

Continued from page 148

relationships between their client and the targeted audience.

In each case, "to the best of their ability" is inserted to make it clear that one's duty is *do-able*. Even if real-life practitioners are hampered by their limitations, it is important both within the profession and by lay audiences as well to understand what the practitioner is attempting to do.

Step Two: Follow the Rule "Do Your Duty" Within the Context of the Moral Rules
Doing one's duty doesn't excuse violations of the other moral rules. Lacking justification, it is not acceptable for journalists to break the law as they gather and present the news, for advertisers to promote a product that results in users being disabled or killed, for entertainers to use material that causes individuals pain, for public relations practitioners to lie to journalists on behalf of their client. These are all blatant and obvious instances of practices that would be immoral unless there was good reason for doing them. However, interesting ethical problems arise when people are undecided as to whether a certain action violates moral rules (causes a person to suffer) or when they try to determine whether a recognized violation is justified.

For example, a newspaper publishes a story about tax loopholes used by public officials. Because of the story, legislation is passed that closes the loopholes, and the mayor is forced to pay more taxes. The mayor and his or her family are hurt by the story and resulting action. Did the story cause them to suffer pain (Violation of Moral Rule #2)? Some might argue that the mayor would not have been harmed in this way without the story, but it doesn't follow that the story was the cause of the pain.

By way of analogy, consider what happens when you get the last table at a restaurant when the noontime rush is just beginning. People who come in after you cannot get a table; perhaps, because of limited time for lunch, they have to forgo the pleasure of eating at that restaurant that day. Did your actions deprive them of pleasure? Perhaps. Are you morally blameworthy for causing them to suffer (Violation of Moral Rule #4)? Of course not, unless you violated another moral rule like cheating or deceiving someone to get the table. So, the difficult question for media practitioners (and for other professionals) is in determining under what conditions they are morally blameworthy for the suffering of others.

Step Three: Determine What Kinds of Actions Count as Moral Rule Violations for the Profession
Many of the issues discussed in the scholarly media literature relate to moral rule violations, but since they are not discussed in that language, it's sometimes hard to get a handle on what the ethical problem might be and what needs to be addressed in dealing with it. Here are some of the major ethical issues for media specialists presented in a way that clarifies the morally relevant questions.

Advertising
Special Audiences: Some audiences deserve special consideration—children, for instance. Lacking experiential filters, children are especially vulnerable to advertising messages. Should advertising surrounding children's television shows therefore be limited? Does the advertiser deprive children (or their parents) of freedom by creating need and desire that would not otherwise be there?

Special Products: Should products that are harmful if used as intended be advertised? Tobacco products and alcoholic beverages are the types of products most often cited in this ethical dilemma. Within moral rules talk, one might argue that by creating a desire for the product that might otherwise not be present, the advertiser is at least partly to blame for the pain

Continued

Continued from page 149

suffered by individuals who are swayed by the advertisement to use that product.

Deception: Everyone knows that, lacking justification, it's wrong to deceive people. But what counts as deception in the advertising business, which is based, at least in part, on illusion and fantasy? "Want love? Get Close-Up" proclaimed a singer in a toothpaste commercial from years back. No one would argue that this is deceptive, but it's equally hard to argue against the misleading nature of the connection. The advertiser wants members of the audience to connect a desire for intimacy with using a certain brand of toothpaste.

This connection is far-fetched and unlikely to fool many people. But how many people hear the claim, "the best that money can buy," and confuse that to mean "better than any of the others"? Should advertisers refrain from leading members of the audience to wrong conclusions?

Entertainment

Unintended Messages: It's undeniable that we learn through being entertained. Well over half of a newspaper's nonadvertising column inches are devoted to non-news items—feature stories that give us our villains and heroes, in-depth issue stories that help us understand the plight of disenfranchised groups. We watch to see how our favorite sit-com characters deal with child abuse, extramarital flirtations, and catastrophic illness.

Do the decision-makers in entertainment media have an obligation to be concerned about the consequences of unintended messages? The answer to that depends partly on whether these decision-makers can be considered a cause of suffering as a consequence of the messages carried in entertainment media. For example, are these professionals morally responsible if children believe, after watching Saturday morning cartoons, that violence is acceptable if the result is a good end?

Morally Offensive Material: Does the presentation of offensive material cause individuals pain? if so, then this moral rule violation needs justification; something beyond, "well, other people don't mind." But, the associated question raises a new dimension.

Does society have a right to censor expressions of entertainment or art? Doing so certainly interferes with the freedom of those who wish to make such expressions. Depriving someone of freedom is a moral rule violation. It needs to be justified.

If the entertainers are morally blameworthy for individuals' pain and censors are morally blameworthy for depriving the entertainers of their freedom, then we have a conflict between two moral rules: the moral rule against causing individuals pain and the moral rule against depriving people of freedom.

This is the kind of conflict that we have a lot of practice in resolving. With some kinds of cases, we have decided, as a society, that it's better to deprive people of freedom than to deal with the likelihood that a particular kind of expression of freedom will result in individuals' death, disability, or pain. In other cases, like editorial commentary, we have decided, as a society, that it's better to allow the individuals who are the targets of commentary to suffer than to deprive commentators of the freedom to express themselves.

News Media

The whole truth? The fact that news media ought to give people information that they need to govern themselves does not imply that news media ought to supply everything that reporters find out. On a tightly researched story, reporters will include only about 10 percent of the material that they uncover. Most of the material ends up on the electronic equivalent of the cutting room floor because it turns out not to be relevant to the story being told.

Continued from page 150

But other material, such as a community leader's sexual preference or the stolen answer key to a statewide examination, is tempting to publish because many members of the audience would like to know that information. Yet publishing it may violate moral rules. Pulling a gay notable from the closet by way of a news story will undoubtedly cause that person pain, and publishing the answer key to a statewide exam prior to the testing date will cause a variety of people a variety of problems, but it doesn't follow that the news organization has acted unethically.

Some people have argued that it is wrong to attribute moral blame to the "messenger." Within this understanding, it is no more wrong for the news organization to publish such information than it is for someone to take the last available table at a restaurant. It is consistent for news organizations to escape responsibility for the consequences of their negative stories only if they refrain from taking credit for the effects of their positive stories. They can't take credit for publishing if they aren't willing to take blame as well.

Relationships with sources: What does a promise of confidentiality mean? Breaking a promise violates a moral rule, but is it justified if the source has lied or, from behind the shield of confidentiality, charges that someone else has leaked that information?

Reporters get more information from sources that like them than from sources who don't, so what's wrong with developing a close friendship or intimate relationship with one's source? Does it cause someone pain to be used in this way?

On the other hand, if a source is not going to be forthcoming with information, is it justified for a journalist to act deceptively? When is going undercover or lying about what is already known a justified violation of the moral rule "Do not deceive"?

Public Relations

Loyalty: The duty of public relations practitioners is to promote their clients' causes, but doing so can conflict with other moral rules. What should a public relations person do when asked directly by a journalist (or by a relative) if the company for which he or she works is planning to lay off workers? The response, "I can't answer that," will be assumed to mean "Yes." "No" may be a direct lie. Furthermore it is impracticable to the company not to tell him or her such information prior to public dissemination since the public relations practitioner is a vital part of the team that decides *how* to distribute such information.

Consequences: Like people who work in entertainment and advertising, public relations practitioners must consider the consequences of what they promote. If the services they promote cause harm—financial, emotional, or physical—they cannot deny responsibility on the basis that they were only following directions.

The answers to these questions lie not in appeal to law and regulation, but in interpretation of the moral rules and understanding of what makes an exception to the rule justifiable.

Law cannot provide the answer to questions of ethics. Law tells us not to lie to the IRS, but it is ethics that tells us not to deceive a friend.

Media are in a special role in that practitioners spread their understandings and misunderstandings of ethics throughout the public realm. They have the power to shape the public discussion of ethics, they can model how to discuss moral questions, and they can also model when and how to publicly justify making exceptions to the moral rules.

Note

1. B. Gert, *Morality, A New Justification for the Moral Rules* (New York: Oxford, 1989).

PART THREE

The Production of Information: Print and Broadcast Media

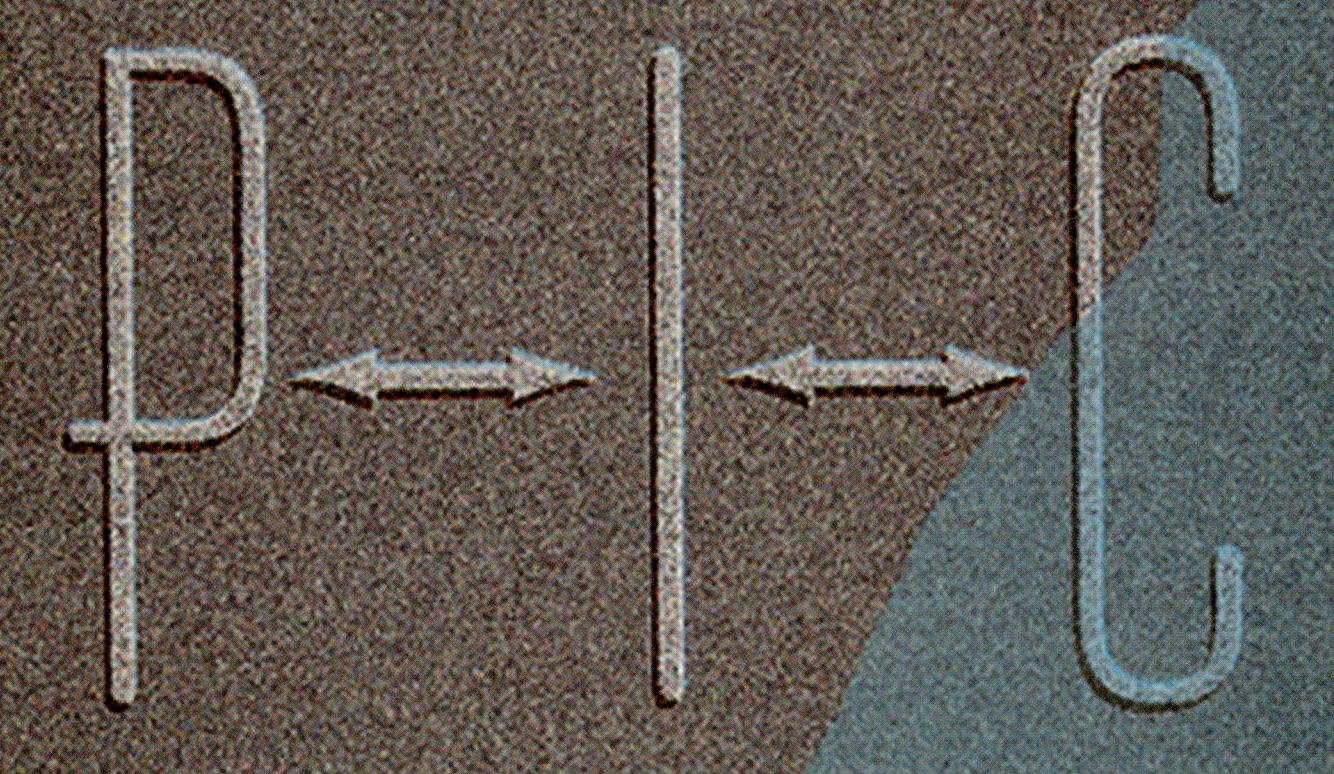

CHAPTER 6

Books

AT A GLANCE

✓ The printing "revolution" began in the sixteenth century, when large numbers of literate people could read information of their own choosing.

✓ Benjamin Franklin was a pioneer in colonial publishing and understood that books and periodicals could both be published by the same entrepreneur.

✓ The book industry has become much more diverse since the 1960s, as paperbacks have become more popular and many specialized categories of books have grown in popularity.

✓ Chain bookstores use the latest marketing techniques to sell books in large quantities, but independent bookstores still flourish by catering to the heavy consumer of books.

✓ Pricing, packaging, and promotion are the keys to marketing strategies that keep print media, especially books, alive in the age of electronic information.

Most of the traditions of mass communication grew out of the revolution that began when people first reproduced and disseminated information through the printed word. Books were the first print medium. Newspapers and magazines have a common historical origin—book printers began producing both as diversions and as ways of supplementing their income.

THE DEVELOPMENT OF A PERMANENT RECORD

In an oral culture, the history and experiences of the people must be passed on carefully from one keeper of the chronicle to another, who may or may not remember the facts and their significance with fidelity. Remote cultures in Asia, Africa, and South America depend on the storyteller to preserve mythic tales of forebears. Even today, Native American tribes value the passing of legend from generation to generation by spoken word.

Eventually, however, there is pressure to preserve history and to advance knowledge by storing information in some form that will enable succeeding generations to begin with the society's accumulated knowledge and experience. Thus, the culture is able to survive and make advances that will improve the lives of all its members.

From Clay to Paper

Early records were kept by forming tablets of dried mud and straw, then carving symbols in these panels so that information could be recalled. As anyone who has carried a heavy book bag across campus can imagine, clay tablets had the advantage of permanency, but they were hardly portable or convenient to use.

By 2000 B.C., in the ancient cultures of Egypt, Rome, and Greece, scrolls that could be rolled up and stored conveniently were in use. Papyrus plants were made into watery pulp, pressed into long rolls, dried, and then inscribed with handwritten symbols. Scrolls allowed records to be preserved, laws to be set down, and proclamations to be issued for rereading throughout the land.

In the first century A.D., parchment began to replace papyrus. The use of animal materials made possible folding and stitching of the writing surface, thus making rudimentary bound books with heavy wooden covers possible for the first time. The Chinese used a combination of vegetable materials including bark, rags, and husks to make the first true papers for artistic purposes. The making of paper spread to Europe during the Middle Ages, where it was used by monks to inscribe Biblical material. Handwritten books became available to the very rich, but the arduous task of copying precluded wide dissemination of written material.

Gutenberg's Contribution

Although the Chinese were engaged in printing before Johann Gutenberg's first efforts in 1450, Gutenberg is associated with the "invention" of printing because he brought the various printing technologies together in a way that made quality reproduction of books and pamphlets possible with greater speed and lower cost. In his shop in Mainz, Germany, Gutenberg adapted the wine press, which had a giant screw that could be tightened gradually down against a flat surface. Instead

Chapter 6 Books

TIME CAPSULE

Books

1456	Gutenberg Bible printed using movable type.
1476	William Caxton establishes printing press in England.
1500s	Books become the first mass-produced form of communication.
1640	Harvard College publishes first book in the Colonies, *Bay Psalm Book*.
1733	Ben Franklin publishes *Poor Richard's Almanac*.
1788	The Federalist Papers are published in book form, with additional essays arguing for a strong central government.
1790	First copyright statute enacted by Congress.
1817	Harper Brothers founded, forerunner of HarperCollins.
1836	*McGuffey's Eclectic Reader* becomes standard text in U.S. schools.
1852	Publication of *Uncle Tom's Cabin* contributes to sentiment for war between the states.
1867	Horatio Alger publishes his first "rags-to-riches" book.
1906	Upton Sinclair's *The Jungle* exposes corruption in the Chicago meat packing industry and begins the era of exposé novels.
1922	Emily Post's *Etiquette* becomes a best-seller for generations.
1926	Book-of-the-Month Club and the Literary Guild of America are founded; book clubs spur publication and reading of best-selling books.
1930	Sinclair Lewis is first U.S. author to win Nobel prize for literature.
1939	Pocket Books introduces consumers to popularly priced paperbacks.
1957	Supreme Court's *Roth* v. *U.S.* decision liberalizes obscenity standards. (Further defined in 1973 *Miller* v. *California* decision.)
1978	Congress revises copyright law to protect works for 50 years after the death of the author instead of a specific statutory term.

of pressing grapes into wine, he pressed sheets of paper against ranks of raised movable type arranged in words and locked into a flatbed form.

Gutenberg's technique prevailed for centuries. Even after the evolution of high-speed rotary presses and, still later, electronic photo-offset techniques that rendered raised metal printing obsolete, Gutenberg's basic concepts survived. Today some specialized printing is still performed on flatbed presses modeled after Gutenberg's.

Gutenberg died a personal failure, and his son-in-law Johann Fust actually carried out the printing operations that made Gutenberg famous. That printing operation ignited the imagination of others, who set up similar presses and gave birth to the craft of printing in Europe. Guilds of craftsmen controlled production in the mid-fifteenth century, and the acceptance of printing as a recognized craft was another step in the printing "revolution."

The Printing "Revolution"

The term *revolution* suggests that the basic functions of society are changed radically. This can be accomplished when one faction overthrows another and insti-

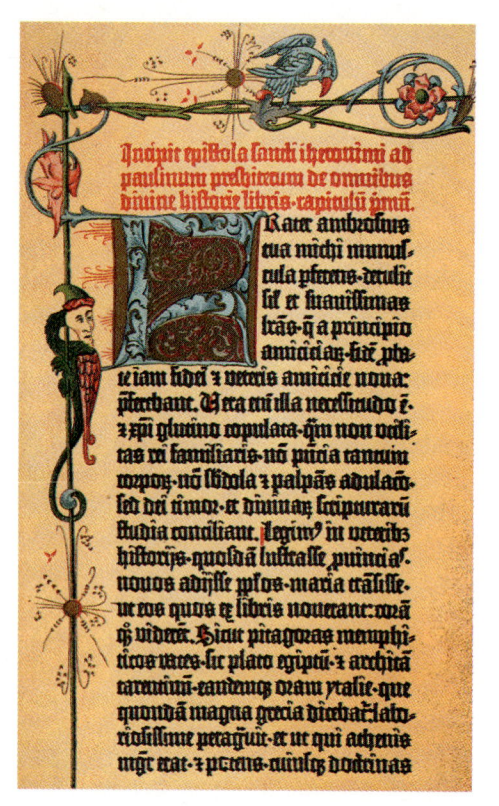

A page from one of the 46 existing copies of the Gutenberg *Bible* printed in Mainz, Germany, between 1450 and 1456.

tutes a new social order. However, revolutions can occur without bloodshed and without the obvious overthrowing of established order. Such revolutions occur when innovation explodes, captures the fancy of the masses, and reworks the fundamental ways that a society receives, distributes, and processes information.

Such a revolution occurred when printing was introduced. By the beginning of the sixteenth century, books printed in common language were available throughout Europe. Literate people, whose numbers were growing, could read material that was not controlled by the state or church or available only to the learned. The availability of such information created a greater demand for it. And the ability of the masses to "read for themselves" instead of being informed by priests, academics, or lords meant that individuals could make interpretations and raise questions on their own. Society thus was reshaped.

Today we understand that information can fuel revolution. But when printing was first introduced, no one could understand what changes it would work on society.

Books Spread to England

An Englishman, William Caxton, learned from the European craftsmen and set up his country's first printing press in 1476. Caxton is credited with printing the first books in English, but he did so only at the pleasure of the rulers and the patronage of the wealthy. They wished to see Caxton's press bring the literature, and thus the culture, of other lands to England. However, they feared that an unrestrained printer also could bring new ideas hostile to the current form of government.

Thus, as printing spread in England, it was carefully controlled. Henry VIII had time between his many courtships to ban the publication of books not on an approved list, including most foreign titles. Eventually the Stationer's Company was organized to license and control publishers, and the Star Chamber Court was instituted to punish those who defied the orders. Not until a general revolution broke out in 1640 did publishers routinely begin to defy the ever-changing laws regulating written expression.

PUBLISHING IN THE NEW WORLD

The first printing press to cross the Atlantic went not to the British Colonies, but to Mexico City, where the Spanish archbishop authorized the printing of religious works beginning in 1539.

A mere 20 years after the Pilgrims landed in the Colonies, bringing their Bibles with them, the first printing press at Harvard College in Cambridge, Massachusetts, was used to publish Bay Psalm Book: *The Whole Booke of Psalms* in 1640. The audience for books was limited by common illiteracy, the small size of the colonial population, and little leisure time among the first settlers. Thus the press was used primarily for publishing *folios*, 16-page pamphlets, many of which could be assembled by the reader into a cumulative collection not unlike the Time-Life Library series so popular today.

Early publishers, centered in Boston, Philadelphia, Baltimore, and New York, were not concerned with the masses, who had neither the education nor the money for books. The cultured few—in effect, the colonial aristocracy—were avid collectors of books from Europe as well as the new land. But local governments, controlled by the landowners, placed restrictions on the distribution of books. The laboring class was not encouraged to read, nor were many of the settlers who pushed westward. It was more than a century after the first press was in operation that books finally became a popular medium in the United States of America.

Early Hybrid Forms of Books

Shorter publications—neither newspapers nor magazines, yet hardly substantial enough to put between hard covers—were created and fed an appetite for information even in colonial days. The most celebrated of these was Benjamin Franklin's *Poor Richard's Almanac*, a compendium of planting information, wise sayings, quips, commonsense health tips, tide tables, and comments on manners and morals. Franklin's almanac appeared in the 1730s and was published annually for a quarter-century. By then other almanacs had appeared. Many were published for profit by printers, and many more were given away or sold at low cost by merchants and manufacturers who used the publications to advertise their wares.

Franklin is credited with establishing the first subscription library scheme. As we shall see, this most ingenious of our founding fathers was instrumental in the development of book publishing that spurred reading in the new land, as well as a pioneer in newspapering and publication of the forerunners of the magazine.

> **INSIGHT**
>
> ## A New Appetite for Books
>
> In early colonial days, literacy was limited to the aristocracy. But in the 1700s, literacy grew in colonial America, and, by contrast with Europe, reading was not an activity limited to the few. Tom Paine's *Common Sense*, published in 1776, is estimated to have sold 300,000 copies in a population of three million people, or 1 for every 10 colonists. The equivalent in today's terms would be a publication that sold 25 million copies in a short time, which is unheard of!
>
> Source: Daniel J. Boorstin, *The Americans: The Colonial Experience* (New York: Vintage Books, 1958), p. 22.

Books in the Colonies and Early America

Indisputably the best book collection in early America was assembled by Thomas Jefferson—a collection that provided the foundation for the Library of Congress.

As America grew, education was put at a premium, and the new school systems created new readers. Cities began to provide more services for their citizens, including free libraries. Book reading and publishing began to surge.

By the 1850s, books were being written by American authors for consumption by a mass audience. Among the most popular were the dime novels, which literally sold for 10 cents, a few hours' pay for a laborer. The "Luck and Pluck" series written by Horatio Alger, Jr. in the 1870s, like his earlier "Ragged Dick" and "Tattered Tom" series, appealed to recent immigrants who longed to pull them-

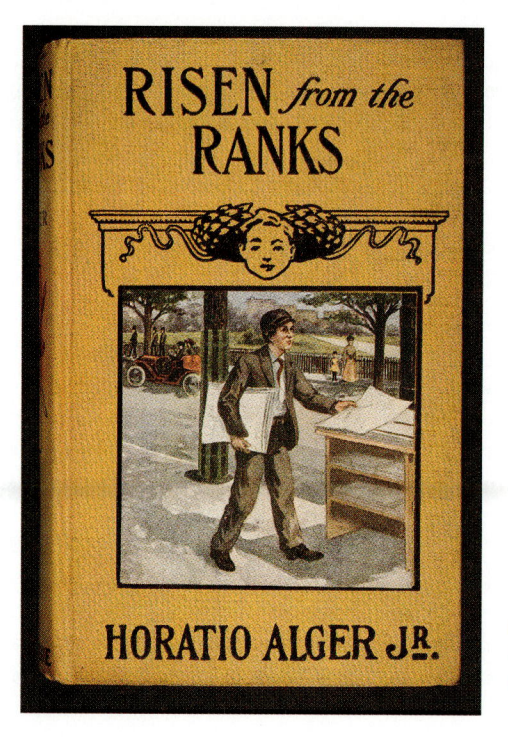

Horatio Alger's *Risen from the Ranks* chronicles the rise of a newsboy who aspires to be the editor of the newspaper—and of course he succeeds, through luck and pluck.

selves up by their bootstraps in the land of opportunity. Alger and other popular authors extolled the virtues of hard work, honesty, and willingness to try again in the face of adversity. Thus they gave shape to a uniquely American value system.

Around the middle of the century, textbook publishing was spurred by the success of the McGuffey Eclectic Readers. Also during this period the American novel came into its own with the publication of such classics as *The Scarlet Letter* by Nathaniel Hawthorne and *Moby Dick* by Herman Melville, ending a dependence on Europe for quality fiction.

The Civil War spurred book production because there was a great demand for reading material from the troops, who spent months and years far from home, often with little to do except read. Wars often have a profound effect on publishing because of the hunger for new information from those who have seen new places and things, and the intriguing subject matter created by conflict and human misery.

After the Civil War, paperback books, many published as a sideline by metropolitan newspapers, became extremely accessible to the mass audience; their low cost was due in large part to the fact that American publishers were reproducing European classics and new titles without paying any royalties (compensation to the authors). An international copyright law requiring the payment of royalties ended the first heyday of the paperback for a half-century.

The Literate Society

The U.S. literacy rate had reached 90 percent by the beginning of the twentieth century, and soon it began to seem as if writing the "Great American Novel" had become the goal of every college-educated American who was exposed to the writings of Dos Passos, Faulkner, Hemingway, and Steinbeck. Publishing and reading fiction would remain popular until television wrought its change on the American use of leisure time.

By the 1940s, a new kind of paperback was creating a sensation: 25-cent "pocket" books sold on newsstands, at train and bus stations, as well as in bookstores. During World War II the government urged publishers to issue slimmed-down "pulp" (made from cheap paper) versions of books for the troops to carry with them.

INDUSTRY

Profile of the Audience for Books

- Sources of books for most people are not primarily libraries. Most readers *own* the book they read: 42 percent bought the last book they read, 27 percent received it as a gift, and 8 percent used a book bought by a member of the family. Only 18 percent said they borrowed the book from a library, and 3 percent borrowed it from a friend. (Source: Gallup annual report on book buying, 1989.)

- The size of audience for books has not declined in the television era. Almost one in four people today say they have read a book recently, contrasted with one in six when television was first introduced into homes. (Source: Gallup annual report on book buying, 1989.)

By the 1950s, the boom in paperback sales had begun, and today the majority of books sold in the United States are softcover.[1] By the 1970s, paperback reprints of the previous year's best-selling novels were setting publishing records, with titles like *Jaws*, *Shogun*, and *The Godfather* selling as many as ten million copies—unheard of for a hardcover edition.

THE BOOK INDUSTRY RESTRUCTURES ITSELF

Until the 1960s, book publishing was a fairly stable industry, with the large houses headed by editors such as Bennett Cerf (Random House) and Ken McCormick (Doubleday). The editors, not the business people, decided what kinds of books would be published, and they worked with authors to nurture them. Of course book publishing was always a business, but in the era of the great editors the myth persisted that the quest for literature was what drives book publishing. Today, publishers call the tune. Although the chairman of Simon & Schuster denied that corporate pressure from parent company Gulf and Western, caused the cancellation of a particularly violent novel in 1990, the industry saw it as another indication of decisions of taste being dictated by the sensibilities of a conglomerate rather than an editor.[2]

Hardcover or Paperback?

As a true mass market for paperbacks developed, publishers began to look at the softcover as the main profit center, rather than merely a means of adding to the financial success of the original hardcover edition. Sales of hardcover books dropped from 54 percent of all books sales in the late 1970s to less than half in the 1980s, with paperback sales increasing by a reciprocal amount, according to the nonprofit Book Industry Study Group.[3] To counter the trend, publishers of hardback books selected sure-fire "blockbuster" books, printed them in large quantities, and then discounted them heavily, making them competitive with paperbacks.

Eventually the surging sales of paperbacks convinced publishers that many books were more appropriately published in softcover. Many light entertainment and self-improvement books fall into this category today, along with the "instant books" that organizations with large staffs and resources such as Dell, Bantam, and *The New York Times* can assemble and print within days after an election, testimony before a congressional committee, a historic space flight, or the assassination of a leader. Many travel volumes, how-to books, humorous works, and cookbooks now originate as paperbacks.

In the 1980s, the publishers of novels by new writers and books aimed at younger adult readers—genres that are not usually very profitable—tried simultaneous publication of hardcover and softcover editions, with the paperback selling at about half the price of the hardback. Readers who prefer the more durable book have that option, but readers with less to spend on books need not wait a year for the cheaper version. The experiment met with considerable success: Paperback sales did not detract substantially from hardcover sales.

Best-selling hardback books are no longer the key to the market. Books, like the other print media, have become specialized. One customer enters a bookstore

> ## ECONOMICS
>
> # Economics of Publishing a Book
>
> When you pay $25 for a book, where does the money go?
>
> *Overhead:* The publisher must pay fixed costs for rent, storing books in a warehouse, postage and telephone, salaries for editors and consultants, and other day-to-day costs. $4.00.
>
> *Composition:* A typesetting company must take the author's manuscript, as edited by the publisher, and set it in type with headlines and charts and photos. Artists and photographers and designers must prepare all of the art and photographic materials. $3.00.
>
> *Manufacturing:* A printer takes the typeset material, creates plates, and prints the pages. A binder joins the pages and adds the hard cover. $3.00.
>
> *Promotion:* Advertisements are purchased in trade and general media. Review copies are sent to editors of trade and general media. Display units are prepared for retailers and sales materials are sent to representatives in the field. $1.00.
>
> *Royalties:* The author or authors receive from 10 to 20 percent of the net price—the price charged to bookstores. $1.50
>
> *Profit:* The publisher realizes a gain from the activity. $1.50
>
> *Markup:* Retailers may choose to sell the book at full price, which means that they will realize the full profit potential. $11.00
>
> Sources: *Publisher's Weekly, The New York Times* and other industry figures.

and goes directly to the "health and fitness" section. Another is interested in a genre such as romance, gothic, or horror fiction. Still another looks only for a new cookbook. Today's book mart is as complex as a major department store, thanks in part to the proliferation of the paperback.

The increased importance of the paperback has given rise to new jargon in the book publishing industry. The "hard-soft deal" refers to the simultaneous acquisition of a book by a hardcover publisher and a softcover publisher, usually with the paperback publisher agreeing to market the book approximately a year after publication of the hardcover edition. Sometimes the two publishers are independent of one another, but increasingly they come under the same corporate umbrella, as with Simon & Schuster and Pocket Books, both units of Gulf & Western.[4]

"Trade paperbacks" are books published originally in paperback format, in a size larger than regular "mass-market," rack-size paperbacks, and at about half the price of a hardcover book. While few major novelists have agreed to let their works begin as trade paperbacks, the format is becoming the leading choice for travel, diet, and cook books. The reason for the phenomenon is strictly economic: Consumers are more likely to spend $12.95 for a softcover book than $29.95 for a hardcover version.[5]

Big Business Means Big Publishers

Editors of serious books and quality fiction viewed with alarm the trend in the late 1980s for book publishers to be acquired by publishing conglomerates. Few

INDUSTRY

A Publishing "Empire"

Murdoch's Divisions United

Book Businesses	Divisions/Imprints	Book Businesses	Divisions/Imprints
Trade/U.S.	HarperCollins HarperCollins San Francisco Harper Paperbacks Harper Perennial Basic Books HarperCollins Children's Books Collins Publishers Harper Audio Harper Business	Trade/Australia Religious/U.S. Religious/Britain Religious/Australia School/U.S. College/U.S.	Angus & Robertson Zondervan HarperCollins San Francisco Collins Marshall Pickering Collins Dove Scott, Foresman Collins HarperCollins Scott, Foresman Little, Brown
Trade/Canada Trade/Britain	HarperCollins Publishers Grafton Collins Times Books Thorsons Bartholomew		

In 1990 publisher Rupert Murdoch moved to create a global publishing empire when he bought Britain's Collins Publishers and merged it with Harper & Row, which he had bought in 1987, and Scott, Foresman, which he acquired in 1989. The list of imprints now published under the HarperCollins name includes trade books, college titles (including, of course, the book you are reading!), religious books, school books, and, until recently, medical books as well. The billion-dollar annual income of HarperCollins places it on the same level of other giants of worldwide book publishing.

publishing houses have escaped merger-mania. The Hearst Corporation bought William Morrow and Avon Books; Random House bought Crown Publishers as well as Knopf, Pantheon, and Ballantine; Harcourt Brace Jovanovich bought CBS Educational and Professional Publishing, including Holt, Rinehart and Winston; in 1990 Harper & Row became HarperCollins by merging with a British publisher, and acquired Scott, Foresman & Co., which had been a division of Time Inc.; Bantam Doubleday Dell (formerly the names of three large independent publishers) became a European-owned firm that includes Delacorte Press; Simon & Schuster, itself owned by Gulf & Western, also owns Prentice-Hall, Pocket Books, and others.

Time Inc. merged with Warner Communications to form Time Warner, bringing along its book division, which included Time-Life Books, the Book of the Month Club, Little, Brown & Co., and Oxmoor House. The book publishing wing of Time Warner accounts for about 20 percent of the parent firm's revenues (about half the income the company's magazines generate).

Book publishers used to stand alone in their own industry. Now most of the houses are parts of conglomerates that include magazines, cable television, film production and distribution companies, and even sports teams. So far there appears to be little pressure to publish books that tie in with these other businesses. The main purposes of consolidation appear to be financial: centralizing control and maximizing profits by becoming an industry leader. Some fear, however, that corporate mentality could lead to a book company being directed to purchase a manuscript because the parent company wants to exploit it also as a film, a television series, or with product tie-ins—regardless of whether it has literary merit or fits the book publisher's list of titles.

Bookselling: Personalized Services or Mass Marketing Chains?

Bookselling, like publishing, is dominated by financial concerns. To this day, some bookstores make a profit by offering personalized service to individual customers. Oxford Square Books in Oxford, Mississippi, and the Elliot Bay Book Co. in Seattle are examples of independent bookstores that maintain a huge backlist (meaning books that have been in print for a year or more), which account for more than a third of their annual sales.[6]

Americans who shop mainly in malls are more familiar with Waldenbooks, B. Dalton, and Barnes & Noble (Dalton is now owned by Barnes & Noble). Dalton and Waldenbooks, with nearly 1000 outlets apiece, account for 35 to 40 percent of all books sold in the United States. Whereas the shopkeeper with the "book nook" on a small-town main street orders books by the ones and twos, Waldenbooks and Dalton order by the hundreds or thousands, keeping track of the inventory daily by computer. Their decisions to stock a book and display it, to discount it in order to create sales, or to "remainder" it at bargain price can have a great influence on whether it sells well. Chains place their stores in high-traffic urban and suburban shopping centers, and they promote and advertise heavily.

Publishers and authors may lament the clout the bookstore chains now wield, but at the same time they acknowledge that modern merchandising methods introduced by the chains have increased the sales of the most popular books. The large independent bookstores with their extensive backlists have managed to compete with the chains by using computers to keep track of their titles.

Chains of bookstores are such a dominant force in the publishing industry today that they sometimes seem like elephants at the watering hole—shoving smaller creatures aside, if only inadvertently because of their huge size. In 1988, the largest chain informed the smallest publishers that it would not handle their books unless these publishers distributed their product through a larger publisher or a wholesaler. For a large chain, dealing with tiny publishers simply isn't cost-efficient. Small publishers love the idea that getting their book in a chain guarantees 1000 outlets, but the chains find that more than half of the books from small publishers have to be returned unsold.[7]

Mass marketing of books in mall stores such as this B. Dalton outlet has changed publishing in America.

At the beginning of the 1990s, Waldenbooks and B. Dalton were still adding outlets at the rate of 100 stores a year. But the publishers, unhappy with many of the practices of the big chains, stopped giving them bigger discounts than the independent booksellers get. And competition from videos, Nintendo games, and other forms of electronic entertainment—along with the soft economy of the early 1990s—suggests that the heyday of chain store growth may be nearly over.[8]

Textbooks: An Important Sector

Because textbooks and educational materials are enumerated in various categories by the Association of American Publishers (AAP), one might miss the point that college, elementary, and secondary texts (plus test materials and educational audiovisual items) account for nearly one-third the revenue of the publishing industry—greater than either trade books or professional books. Consider, too, that the category of "professional" books enumerated by the AAP includes volumes needed for continuing education. Textbooks, in short, are a major category of book publishing.

Custom textbook publishing—assembling texts for individual course instructors by offering chapters and excerpts from many print sources—has grown in popularity, with photocopying firms leading the way in producing the texts. A 1991 decision against Kinko's for violating the Copyright Act has had the effect of clamping down on wholesale photocopying of protected materials. Book publishers, responding to the need for custom texts, have set up computerized operations

ECONOMICS

Publishers' Group Charts Sales by Category

Sales of books in the United States reached $15.5 billion in 1990, an increase of 5 percent over the previous year. Sales figures are estimated by the Association of American Publishers, which uses 13 categories to account for the variety of items sold by book publishers.

AAP Estimated Industry Sales 1989–1990

	Millions of Dollars 1989 $	Millions of Dollars 1990 $	Percentage Change from 1989
Trade (Total)	3623.5	3892.8	7.4
Adult Hardbound	1745.4	1808.2	3.6
Adult Paperbound	976.6	1063.5	8.9
Juvenile Hardbound	665.1	761.5	14.5
Juvenile Paperbound	236.4	259.6	9.8
Religious (Total)	737.1	788.0	6.9
Bibles, Testaments, Hymnals & Prayerbooks	201.0	229.9	14.4
Other Religious	536.1	558.1	4.1
Professional (Total)	2592.8	2765.9	6.7
Business	481.7	527.9	9.6
Law	883.0	947.5	7.3
Medical	490.5	526.3	7.3
Technical, Scientific, & Other Professional	737.6	764.2	3.6
Book Clubs	704.0	725.1	3.0
Mail Order Publications	796.8	731.4	8.2
Mass Market Paperback Rack-Sized	1094.5	1148.6	4.9
University Presses	227.0	245.8	8.3
Elementary & Secondary Text	1983.6	2025.8	2.1
College Text	1842.1	1991.3	8.1
Standardized Tests	119.4	127.6	6.9
Subscription Reference	509.4	540.5	6.1
AV & Other Media (Total)	223.7	237.2	6.0
Elhi	178.6	186.1	4.2
College	17.4	20.0	14.9
Other	27.7	31.1	12.3
Other Sales	211.3	217.6	3.0
Total	14,665.2	15,437.6	5.3

Source: Publishers Weekly, August 9, 1991, p. 10.

that allow individual instructors to select from materials in a large database to request textbooks that reflect the material taught in their courses.[9] Despite the passing of the baby boom that populated the school systems in the 1970s and 1980s, the textbook market is expected to continue as a major sector of American book publishing.

CATERING TO THE CONSUMER'S INTERESTS

A few generations ago, the terms *literature* and *publishing* might have been considered synonymous. Respected publishing houses led their lists with major novels from the nation's best-known writers. Biography, history, humor, inspirational works, cookbooks, and travel guides complemented the fiction.

As television filled the hours once devoted to reading, and as some writers turned to the more lucrative visual media, the novel waned in importance. The offerings from the book industry changed, catering to specific needs of narrow audiences. In the 1970s, *Time* magazine coined the term "nonbook" to refer to booklike publications that sell in bookstores but focus on trivial or transient topics and are of questionable literary value. *The Preppy Handbook*, *Real Men Don't Eat Quiche*, and *100 Things to Do with a Dead Cat* are examples of nonbooks. Of course, some of these works sell a million copies or more.

The New York Times Book Review used to publish two best-seller lists: fiction and nonfiction. In response to the way books are marketed today, the *Times* now publishes several best-seller lists in each week's Book Review section. Hardbacks and paperbacks are separated. "Advice, How-to and Miscellaneous" have their own list, separate from other nonfiction. With the self-help categories and nonbooks removed, the nonfiction best-seller list is dominated by biographies of celebrities.

The Marketing Mentality

In today's business environment, *marketing* is the word that has replaced *literature* in book publishing decisions. Publishers argue that they will have the capital to publish worthwhile but unprofitable books for the elite public only if they successfully satisfy the needs of the masses who want sensational entertainment, help in flattening their abdomens, or schemes for making millions quickly.

Let us look at an example of the impact of marketing mentality on contemporary publishing. The respected Boston publisher Little, Brown came out with *Is Salami and Eggs Better Than Sex?*, subtitled *Memoirs of a Happy Eater*. The book was by television and stage personality Alan King, and reviewers noted that he plundered many of his stand-up comedy routines for the material in the book. A coauthor was enlisted to flesh out the concept. She was Mimi Sheraton, former restaurant critic for *The New York Times*, who tossed off cutesy introductions to each chapter and provided unusual recipes to end each chapter. In show business terminology, she was an "opening act" intended to build excitement for Mr. King's comic turn. The advertising for the book featured quotes from radio comedians Bob and Ray as well as singer Frank Sinatra, whose quote "I have never known a couple who checked into a motel for salami and eggs" apparently provided the title for the book. Although these marketing ploys did help increase attention for the book from the mass media, none was sufficient to make the book a major success.

General versus Specialized Publishers

A few of the largest publishing houses still are known for their eclectic, well-rounded lists of books that cover the spectrum of interests. Doubleday and Random House are examples of such "general" publishers. The era of the general

---

I SAW THIS GREAT BOOK ON TV LAST NIGHT

There is something chilling about a culture in which the purpose of a book is no longer presumed by many to be tied up with the reading of it. More than ever, books are status symbols, fashion accessories, interior-decorative touches, matching gewgaws: they accent the coffee tables of our consciousness. . . .

When Kirk Douglas was on the *Tonight* show recently, guest host Jay Leno thanked him for an inscribed copy of Douglas's autobiography, *The Ragman's Son*, not by saying, "I look forward to reading it" but by saying, "It'll go right up there on my bookshelf."

Richard Rosen, "Bullcrit: The Reading Disorder of the Library Fast Lane," *New York*, Feb. 6, 1989, pp. 44–47.

publisher is on the wane, however, and many houses prefer to specialize in an area where they can capture a large share of the market by limiting their expertise and building a reputation as having a strong list of titles. Specialization also helps the publisher to train sales personnel, and to associate with the sales outlets that are best suited to its list of offerings.

Among the areas of specialized book publishing are these:

Reference—Directories, dictionaries, compendia of historical data, bibliographies. These expensive volumes are purchased mainly by libraries, businesses, and specialists.

Professional—Knowledge esoteric to a specific field of business or trade, and directories or handbooks necessary for conduct of business. These often are sold through professional associations or by direct mail, as well as in retail outlets.

Textbooks—Designed to fit the specific needs and time frames of primary, secondary, and higher education. Sold to school systems and, in college, to individual students through campus bookstores.

Children's books—Picture books, early readers, science and learning, and juvenile fiction. Parents are the prime purchasers, and many children's books are purchased as gifts. Libraries also are an important market.

Technical, scientific, law, and medical—Volumes updating the specialized knowledge in fields where information about innovations must be disseminated rapidly.

Entertainment, self-improvement, how-to, religious, erotica, hobby—Works that cater to the special needs of the individual.

Of course this is only a general and partial list. Some publishers handle mainly poetry, and others have a political slant. Moreover, each large publishing house today maintains several colophons (identifying symbols of individual printing houses) or divisions for the purpose of printing one or another of several specialized types of book. In other words, the big publishers (like General Motors in another area of marketing) want a chance to sell you precisely the kind of product that matches your needs and life-style.

"Vanity Press" Offers Self-Publishing

The author whose manuscript is rejected by every other publisher in the field need not forgo a literary career. *Writer's Market*, the guide for freelance writers, lists "subsidy book publishers" in a special section of its directory. There are at least a dozen, of which the best known is Vantage Press in New York. Known by the pejorative "vanity press" because they produce books for otherwise unpublished authors, the subsidy publishers require the author to pay for the entire venture. The books produced under this system may be perfectly competent in terms of physical production, but except for a single listing in a small ad, the publisher probably will not publicize the book. Vanity authors usually end up being their own best customers, although some vanity publishers can point to one or two books they've published that managed to find an audience and return the cost of production.

Marketing Calls for Innovation

How do you sell books? With a certain amount of daring and imagination:

- The Waldenbooks chain builds excitement, and "traffic," in its stores with displays of nonbook items: tapes, calendars, and posters. The firm's chief executive advises publishers on the timing, design, and marketing of their books, and he sometimes reads manuscripts in order to help new authors.

- The Association of American Publishers has developed Pubnet, an electronic computerized book-ordering system, to help bookstores get stock quickly when there is consumer demand.
- The author of a novel mentioned specific products in her book . . . and then arranged for displays featuring her book in fashionable stores (such as Giorgio on Rodeo Drive in Beverly Hills) that sell the products she mentioned.
- Publishers of romance novels, popular with women, advise authors to alter the formula to include divorced and widowed heroines, reflecting the marital status of the consumers.
- One paperback publishing firm requires all of its top editors, art directors, and other executives to take part in cover-selection meetings because its books are "impulse purchases," where the consumer makes up his or her mind to buy on the spot, with no influence other than personal reaction to the picture and the promotional "blurb" on the cover.

Studies indicate that only half of the reading-age public buys and reads books. "Heavy readers"—especially those aged 25 to 44—account for a third of the reading population and 90 percent of general book sales. Mysteries are the most popular form of fiction, accounting for 17 percent of fiction sales. The top-selling nonfiction category is autobiography-biography.[10]

Garfield creator Jim Davis appears at a book fair to autograph his books.

The book industry used to experience the bulk of its sales in the autumn, leading up to the Christmas gift-giving season. That's still the leading period for sales of expensive gift books, and novels still sell well in the summer when people have more time to read. But book publishing less and less is seasonal, owing partly to the promotions of bookstore chains that want to promote books aggressively all year long and book clubs that want to offer attractive choices every month. Whereas January and February used to be shunned by publishers on the theory that few people bought books after the holidays, now those months are as likely to see a major book published as any other time of year.

Where Do Books Originate?

Some books have a smooth, quick road to acceptance by a major publisher. The sports hero or movie star who decides to pen a reminiscence, a fitness manual, or a cookbook usually can find an agent who will close the deal and arrange for a ghostwriter as well. Authors with proven track records usually develop a personal relationship with a senior editor at a major publishing house—someone proven in the business who can handle the ego and the special needs of a major writer. Under such circumstances, publication is merely a matter of delivering a satisfactory manuscript; going through normal copy editing procedures to check for grammar, style, and accuracy; and then waiting four or five months for typesetting, printing, binding, and delivery to the bookstores.

Such success stories are not representative of the process. More than 40,000 books are published in the United States each year, but hundreds of thousands of unsolicited manuscripts—books written by new authors and submitted for consideration—float from author to agent to publisher and back. The agent, working on a commission from the author's earnings, works with authors to prepare manuscripts for submission to publishers. Experienced writers normally prepare an outline or table of contents and a sample chapter, which they send to their agent or directly to an editor in hopes of getting encouragement.

Book editors must sift through these myriad submissions and proposals. They select the ones they feel have merit either on the basis of sales potential, "importance," or "fit" with the publisher's list for the next year. The editor then becomes an advocate for the manuscript within the publishing house and a devil's advocate with the author, arguing for larger production and advertising budgets on one hand and at the same time prodding the author to sharpen the content of the book to make it read better.

The production of most books takes a year or more to move from nearly completed manuscript to publication date. Memoirs, technical works, major novels, and, yes, textbooks like this one, may take several years of work by the authors. Then the editorial, design, and marketing staffs must perform their skills. It can be a frustrating and lengthy but rewarding process.

New Strategies for Reaching Readers

Book publishers once depended on publicity, good reviews, and favorable word of mouth to sell books. In the consumer-driven information market of the 1990s, however, the book industry increasingly bases its decisions on what book buyers seem to want.

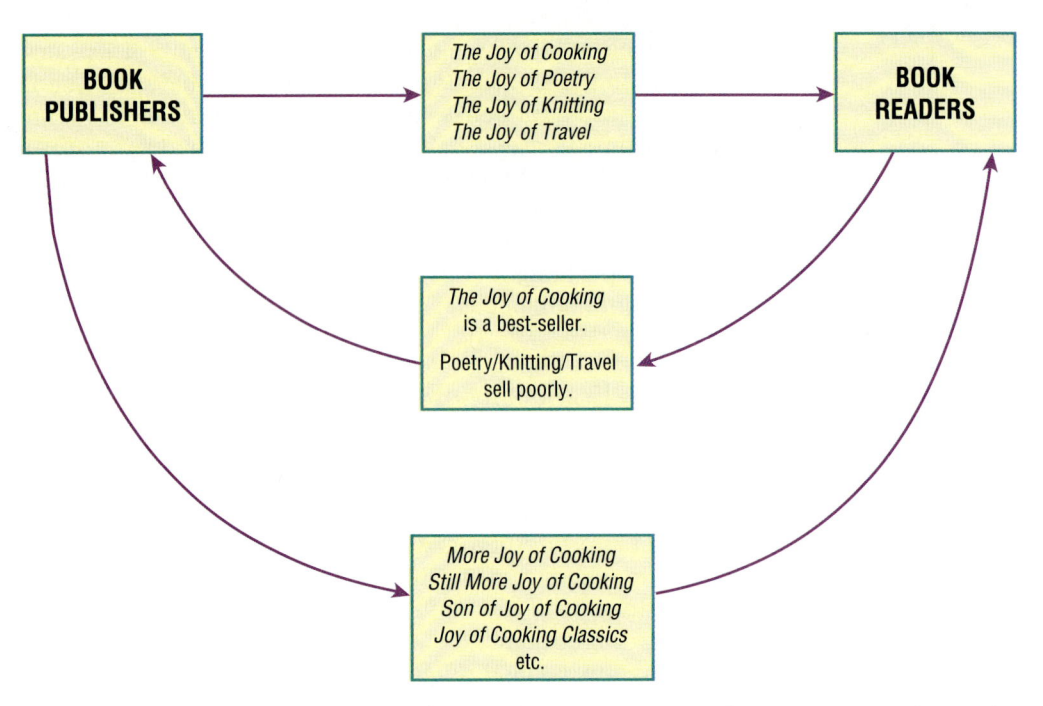

FIGURE 6.1 **Consumer Response Controls Producer's Decisions** The book publisher tries a series of hobby and craft books. The readers embrace one of the volumes in the series, thus encouraging the publisher to "repeat the success" with sequels. In the P↔I↔C model, readers' responses to the publishers' first attempts dictate what will follow.

When a book like Norman Mailer's *Harlot's Ghost* costs $30 in hardback, for example, only the avid—and affluent—reader regularly buys hardback novels. Others have to depend on paperbacks. In order to broaden the market for hardbacks, publishers are experimenting with novels and biographies costing as little as $12.95. At that price, many readers accustomed to paying $3.95 for paperbacks and $7.95 for quality paperbacks are willing to make the move to hardbacks. The publisher has to control cost and publish a larger quantity at that price, but just as retailing shifted from the big old department stores to the discount stores, publishing may be shifting to those houses that can provide quality for less.

In the age of television and *USA Today*, many readers don't want to spend two or three weeks plowing through a 500-page novel. That's why some publishers are encouraging their authors to aim for under 200 pages—the "quick read" that attracts busy readers.

Why Buy a Book? Why Read a Book?

Your boss tells you: "I read a great book on the plane back from Chicago. It's called *The One-Minute Manager*. Makes a lot of sense for anyone who wants to get ahead in business these days." On your lunch hour you pick up a copy of *The One-Minute Manager*.

A friend asks: "Have you read the latest Dick Francis mystery? It's his best one yet. . . . He really outdoes himself this time." The copy at the library is on a long waiting list, so you splurge on your own copy and plan to read it at the beach this weekend.

We've just described the two main reasons why people decide to buy new hardcover books: because the books have immediate and important utility, or because they'll keep you current with "what people are reading."

Sensational biographies of celebrities; history written by recent world leaders; mysteries set in exotic locales; novels that rip the curtain away from the world of entertainment, politics, or business; books that reveal new secrets of beauty, dieting, or fitness—these are some of the categories most likely to stimulate discussion among those who read.

Of course many books are bought and never read, because the urge to *buy* a book is often stronger than the urge to *read* a book. The term "coffeetable book" was coined in the 1960s to describe the oversized volumes, usually full of color photos, that are presented as gifts, especially at Christmas time. Coffeetable books display prints from art museums, recipes, travel photos, antique autos, architecture, or historical points of interest. They make impressive gifts.

Unread books also include many self-improvement volumes, whose purchasers vainly hope to change their appearance, life-style, or success on the job, but for whom the urge to buy the book is stronger than the energy needed to read the book. Best-selling novels mentioned on television shows also may gather dust despite the good intentions of the buyer, who quickly forgets the reason for his or her enthusiasm over the subject.

Countless volumes of encyclopedias go unread, reference books remain unopened, art books gather dust, and instructional volumes await their first reading. All were purchased in the expectation that enlightenment would follow quickly, but the difficulty of finding time to read a book defeats the good intentions of many a book purchaser.

People often write their names in new books, reflecting the expectation that the content of the volume will have a deeply personal relevance and the book itself will remain a treasured possession. (We rarely write our names on newspapers, magazines, or videotapes.) People often remember the names of the authors of the books they read. (They rarely know or recall the names of the people who create television shows, computer programs, or magazines.)

Consider some of these observations about book buying and book reading as you explore the other print and electronic media described in the following chapters. All media have something in common . . . but each medium is used in unique ways by each of us, according to our needs and orientation.

Illiteracy Poses a Threat

Believing literacy to be universal in the United States, publishers hardly expected to lose potential readership to the problem of illiteracy. But in urban America today, the school dropout problem and waves of immigrants from Third World countries have resulted in an alarming increase in nonreaders. Publishers are among many organizations striving to combat the problem through programs in schools and through community groups. In fact, materials to help tutor the illiterate are a new field of specialized publishing.

In 1991, President Bush signed into law a measure that earmarked more than $1 billion to be spent over four years to fund anti-illiteracy programs. Included in the programs were the distribution of books to poor children, establishment of literacy resource centers, assistance for small businesses that establish on-the-job training for literacy, and literacy training in correctional facilities.[11]

FUTURE FILE

✓ You have only one goal in mind: to write next year's best-selling book. Would it be a novel, a biography, or a self-help book? What's the gimmick that will make it sell? Failing that, what celebrity will you team up with to realize your publishing ambition?

✓ More and more information services are being delivered by electronic screen, as part of a video or computer system. What categories of book will lend themselves best to delivery in this mode?

✓ Will it be important to be known as an author—a writer—in the future? Or will people remember only the information, not the creator of the information? Is the heyday of the great novelist and the great biographer over because consumers have grown accustomed to absorbing large amounts of printed information without ever thinking about who created it?! (Right now, can you even name the authors of the text you are reading?)

NOTES

1. Edwin McDowell, "Turmoil in the Racks: The Second Paperback Revolution," *The New York Times,* Book Review section, Sept. 29, 1985, pp. 35, 52–53.
2. Edwin McDowell, "Many Houses Find Images Are Blurred," *The New York Times*, Nov. 19, 1990, p. D-8.
3. Edwin McDowell, "Resurgence in Hard-Cover Printings," *The New York Times*, Oct. 22, 1985, C-13.
4. Edwin McDowell, "Competition Growing in Paperback Business," *The New York Times*, July 18, 1988, p. D-8.
5. Edwin McDowell, "Trade Paperbacks Gaining in Role of a Happy Medium," *The New York Times*, Oct. 17, 1988, p. D-8.
6. Ralph Tyler, "Backlist as Backbone," *Publishers Weekly*, Oct. 26, 1990, p. 25.
7. Joseph Barbato, "Small Publishers Get Their Books into B. Dalton and Waldenbooks Chains," *Publishers Weekly*, Aug. 24, 1990, p. 18; Cynthia Crossen, "B. Dalton Plans to Shut Out Small Publishers," *The Wall Street Journal,* April 22, 1988, p. 35.
8. Roger Cohen, "Jitters in a 'Recession-Proof' Trade," *The New York Times*, Dec. 12, 1990, p. D-11; John Mutter, "A Chat with Bookseller Len Riggio," *Publishers Weekly*, May 3, 1991, p. 33.
9. Robert E. Baensch, "Wither Custom Textbook Publishing?" *Publishers Weekly*, June 21, 1991, p. 27.
10. Rebecca Piirto, "I Love a Good Story," *American Demographics*, July 1989, pp. 36–41.
11. Howard Fields, "$1.1 Billion Literacy Spending Bill Becomes Law," *Publishers Weekly*, Aug. 16, 1991, p. 7.

SUGGESTED READINGS

Compaine, Benjamin M., *The Book Industry in Transition* (White Plains, NY: Knowledge Industry, 1978).

Dessauer, John P., *Book Publishing: What It Is, What It Does* (New York: Bowker, 1981).
Madison, Charles G., *Book Publishing in America* (New York: McGraw-Hill, 1966).
Tebbel, John, *Between Covers: The Rise and Transformation of Book Publishing in America* (New York: Oxford University Press, 1987).
Tebbel, John, *A History of Book Publishing in the United States,* vols. 1–4 (New York: Bowker, 1972, 1975, 1978, 1981).

CHAPTER 7

Newspapers

AT A GLANCE

✓ Early colonial newspapers were allowed to exist only if they enjoyed the patronage of the colonial governor. James and Benjamin Franklin were pioneers in developing the newspaper that included essays, opinions, and articles that exposed government wrongdoing.

✓ By the end of the nineteenth century, the sensationalism of some newspapers had been labeled "yellow journalism." Excesses in reporting crime stories and speculation about the misdeeds of the famous continue to this day, especially in daily newspapers and supermarket weeklies.

✓ Journalism became a profession when organizations aimed at improving the writing, editing, and publishing of newspapers emerged in the twentieth century.

✓ Local news reporting in daily papers has declined, with weekly newspapers picking up the slack. *USA Today* may be the prototype of the new daily newspaper that provides wide national and international coverage for a regional, state, or national audience.

✓ Computer technology has changed the newspaper newsroom. The entrance of phone companies into the information business raises the question of whether newspapers can adapt to the electronic age, or whether they are doomed to die.

Newspaper reading is a ritual for most readers. There's a regular pattern for scanning the contents of the paper and selecting what is to be read—or, if not read, at least glanced at for a few seconds. A newspaper is not really meant to be read in its entirety. For every person who spends half an hour reading the paper from front to back, there is another who finds one or two personally important nuggets of information and discards the paper in little more than a minute.

Consumers are the newspaper's final editors, selecting what interests or affects them. Most newspaper readers have definite personal agendas that cause them to jump from department to department, which they are able to do because of the way the modern newspaper is organized. The investor moves quickly to the stock market listings, then checks out stories that tell what companies are introducing new products or considering merger offers. The sports buff can't be bothered with anything else until the line scores of last night's games have been absorbed. *Doonesbury* fanatics whip right past accounts of the real Washington events on which the comic strip is based because they have to get their daily dose of wit before they can face the news.

The newspaper is a complex institution, not only in terms of the speed with which so much information is gathered and presented, but in the myriad ways each consumer finds to make special use of the product.

THE EVOLUTION OF THE AMERICAN NEWSPAPER

Newspapers began as a mere "sideline" enterprise for printers and gradually developed into the main source of a fresh commodity called news—notice of current events in local areas as well as far-flung places, news of interest to readers not only for its usefulness but also for its unusualness. For well over a century the medium enjoyed this role until the age of electronic media changed the ways people receive news.

Broadsheets: A Profitable Sideline

Until the early 1700s, few printers gave any thought to being the purveyors of the tidbits of trivia and gossip and happenings about town that usually were passed by word of mouth in the community. Printing was a slow and laborious process that did not lend itself to speedy distribution of the latest talk. Besides, governments did not look with favor on those who disseminated frivolous information not approved by the powers in control.

Yet when a technology is available, entrepreneurs will think of ways to use it to cater to the public. And as a society forms, expands, and has more time and money to spend, a market develops for new products. In colonial America, these conditions occurred in the early 1700s, where the presses stood quiet after the books and government publications had been printed. Eventually, printers realized they had a salable commodity in the letters they received from Europe, particularly when the communications dealt with calamity, changes in government, or rumors about people remembered from "the old country." Excerpts from letters were a staple of a new kind of publication, the earliest form of newspaper, called

INDUSTRY
Profiles of the Audience for Newspapers

- The focus of readers today appears to be less local than in the past. "National" newspapers such as *USA Today*, *The Wall Street Journal*, and *The New York Times* enjoy the healthiest circulation growth, while papers that offer a "regional" focus grow slightly and papers with a "local" focus stagnate in circulation. (Source: Audit Bureau of Circulations data reported in *Advertising Age*, 1991.)

- Canadian readers continue to read newspapers to a greater extent than their United States counterparts. Circulation of newspapers in Canada nearly doubled between 1946 and the end of the 1980s, while circulation of newspapers in the United States was up only about 30 percent. (Source: Statistical summaries published by the American Newspaper Publishers Association, 1990.)

- Sunday newspapers attract more readers even though newspaper readership in general is stagnant. While the number of daily newspapers has remained at about 1750 for the past 20 years, the number of Sunday editions increased from 634 in 1973 to 830 in 1989. (Source: Newspaper Advertising Bureau, 1990.)

- Lack of time for reading newspapers is the main reason people give for canceling their subscriptions. (Source: American Society of Newspaper Editors, 1989.)

- Illiteracy threatens newspaper readership. Owing to immigration and also to school dropouts among poor minority innercity youth, America will soon be gaining more than two million illiterate adults each year. By the year 2000 the total number of illiterate adults may reach 90 million—all of them unable to read a newspaper. (Source: U.S. Department of Education, 1989.)

- Older readers are increasingly the main readership of newspapers, and they have specific demands. They want articles about topics that interest them, such as health and finances on a retirement budget. They have failing eyesight and want more legible type. And focus group research shows that they are impatient with getting dirty from the ink that rubs off the newspaper. (Source: The American Society of Newspaper Editors, 1990.)

- Quick-reading summaries between the headline and the first paragraph at the tops of stories convinced a third of the readers of the Portland *Oregonian* that the front page contained more news. (Source: *Oregonian* study cited in *The Next Newspapers*, a study on the future of newspapers published by the American Society of Newspaper Editors, 1990.)

broadsheets, so named because they were single-page impressions made from the full width of the printer's press.

Other broadsheets arrived from England, and printers on this side of the Atlantic quickly combed them, as well as other periodicals, for tidbits of information that would interest colonial readers. The concept of "reporters" was to come much later. Printers merely relied on what they could crib from other sources or what walked in their door in the form of gossip from friends and employees.

This information was set in columns of type, without illustration, graphic devices, or anything but the most rudimentary headlines. The broadsheets were printed in quick impressions on the single page, or, at most, four pages when a single sheet was folded. These papers were sold at the printer's counter or hawked outside in the street by an apprentice or a child.

Early Colonial Newspapers

The publication usually acknowledged as the first newspaper in the colonies was *Publick Occurrences Both Foreign and Domestick*, published in Boston in 1690 by Benjamin Harris. In form, it was a newspaper. The content, however, was offensive to the government because of its disrespect for the established order. It never had a chance to become a periodical because it was banned instantly by the governor.

True newspapers, appearing with regularity, can be traced to the introduction of the *Boston News-Letter* in 1704. The publisher, John Campbell, was the postmaster; thus, he not only had government approval, but he could also distribute his publication through the mails. Because Campbell's paper was "approved," however, its content was of little interest to the people. Consequently, it never achieved the success of later endeavors such as the *Boston Gazette*, introduced in 1719. That paper was printed by Benjamin Franklin's older brother James on behalf of Campbell's successor as postmaster, William Brooker.

When James Franklin decided to publish the *New-England Courant* on his own in 1721, newspapers were beginning to play a bigger role in the community. They mixed information from the town and neighboring villages with essays, opinion pieces, columns, and even "exposés" like those enjoyed today by viewers of "60 Minutes." The Franklin brothers were not afraid to take risks; Benjamin willingly

TIME CAPSULE

Newspapers

1620s	Sheets with foreign (European) news sold on London streets.	1851	*The New York Times* published by Henry Raymond.
1665	*Oxford Gazette* is first English-language newspaper.	1868	First female reporter hired by *New York Sun*: Emily Verdery Bettey.
1690	Benjamin Harris prints *Publick Occurrences*, first newspaper in America.	1883	*St. Louis Post-Dispatch* publisher Joseph Pulitzer buys the *New York World*.
1704	First regularly appearing newspaper in America: *Boston News-Letter*	1895	San Francisco *Examiner* publisher William Randolph Hearst buys the *New York Journal*, touching off competition with Pulitzer's *World*.
1721	*New England Courant* published by James and Benjamin Franklin.		
1735	John Peter Zenger acquitted of libeling government.	1907	United Press begun by E. W. Scripps.
1827	First black newspaper published: *Freedom's Journal*.	1909	International News Service started by Hearst.
1833	Benjamin Day's *New York Sun* is first of the penny papers.	1958	UPI formed from merger of United Press and International News Service.
1835	James Gordon Bennett's *New York Herald* founded.	1971	Minnesota Press Council founded to protect consumers from inaccuracies.
1841	Horace Greeley's *New York Tribune* joins list of penny papers.	1972	*Washington Post* reporters expose Watergate scandal.
1848	Associated Press formed by six New York newspapers.	1982	*USA Today* founded by Gannett.

> **IN PRAISE OF THE NEWSPAPER**
>
> 'Tis truth (with deference to the college) Newspapers are the spring of Knowledge. The general source throughout the nation, Of every modern conversation.
> *New York Gazette,* 1770
>
> *Source:* Neil Postman, *Amusing Ourselves to Death: Public Discourse in the Age of Show Business* (New York: Penguin Books, 1986), pp. 34–35.

operated the irreverent paper on the occasions when James found himself in jail for an indiscretion.

Eventually Ben Franklin left Boston, finding Philadelphia more to his liking. There he took over the *Pennsylvania Gazette* and molded it into a lively, entertaining, literate, and provocative flagship paper for a chain of small local newspapers in eastern Pennsylvania. Newspapers were springing up and dying quickly, but Franklin showed that the medium could survive and become dependable as a conduit for information and ideas.

Probably the greatest contribution of the colonial newspapers was the forum they provided for discussion of the important issues that seeded the revolution. The *Federalist Papers,* written by John Jay, Alexander Hamilton, and James Madison, saw light of day in various newspapers to which they were distributed by the authors. However, it would be misleading to call the colonial newspapers a true mass medium because they circulated primarily to the literate populace who had leisure time and money to spend on publications. It was several decades after the American revolution and the founding of the new republic before cheap newspapers were read by the average citizen and were considered a necessity for keeping in touch with the world.

The 1800s: Development of the Popular Press

The introduction of the rotary press, with its revolving cylinders printing at many times the speed of flatbed presses, made possible the cheap mass production of newspapers. In 1833, Benjamin Day founded the daily *New York Sun,* and within a few years he was using the new technology to produce 30,000 copies each day. The paper sold for a mere penny (in relative value, about the equivalent of what we spend for a daily newspaper today). Thus began the era of the penny papers, the first truly popular newspapers.

Just two years after Day founded the *Sun,* James Gordon Bennett introduced the *New York World* and combined the technology used by Day with a new technique called reporting. He sent people out on the streets to visit the police halls, to observe comings and goings at the piers, and to chronicle the daily occurrences of a busy commercial city. With the New York dailies providing a model, daily newspapers sprang up in major cities around the country in the mid-1800s.

Bennett's success with the *Herald* led to competition. Horace Greeley founded the New York *Tribune* in 1841, hiring the legendary managing editor Charles A. Dana to oversee the news-gathering operation while Greeley concentrated on developing the editorial page's interpretative function. A decade later, in 1851, Henry J. Raymond founded *The New York Times* and emulated *The Times* of London in offering foreign coverage, in-depth reporting, and serious-minded editorials. *The New York Times* continues today as the paper that sets an example for completeness in public affairs reporting.

After the rotary press, other new technologies wrought similar changes on the newspaper industry, resulting in circulation increases for ever-improving products. One was the wire service, which brought stories from afar by telegraph to newspapers that shared the costs. The first, the Associated Press (AP), was formed in 1848 by six New York newspapers as a way to reduce the expenses caused by duplicated efforts to obtain news from afar. (Duplication of effort on local stories was viewed as useful because each paper was competing for an exclusive report on events that directly affected its readers.) The formation of the

AP also served to widen the horizons of smaller papers that could not afford their own correspondents around the country and abroad.

Wars speed the development and use of technology. The value of the telegraphic wire services in speeding news from the Civil War battlefronts to the big-city newspapers was a spur to readership and circulation. Faster printing methods were developed that enabled papers to increase daily circulation and offer large Sunday editions with preprinted feature sections. Newspapers in the South and the Midwest grew and improved as they fed the readers' appetite for information about the war. Following the war, westward expansion led to growth of newspapers in the mountain and Pacific states. By the 1870s the New York newspapers were rivaled in quality by important regional papers such as Joseph Pulitzer's St. Louis *Dispatch*, the Chicago *Tribune* edited by Joseph Medill, William Allen White's *Emporia Gazette* in Kansas, the *Courier-Journal* in Louisville, and the Portland *Oregonian*.

Photography Illustrates the Stories

Before and during the Civil War, sketches made by artists and reproduced through woodcuts generally served as pictorial representation of the events reporters wrote about. Thus, the scenes from the battlefields existed for most Americans as a result of pen and ink work. But photodocumentation of the epic struggle between the Union and the Confederacy by the renowned Matthew Brady was widely exhibited after the war, spurring interest in the use of the photograph to capture true images of important events.

The civil war introduced a new sensation to newspapers: photographic coverage from the battlefield. This 1863 photo by Alexander Gardner shows a newspaper vendor serving the Union camp in Virginia.

In the 1870s, the first use of photographs by newspapers heralded the day when totally realistic representation became a basic part of visual news coverage. By the 1890s, the techniques had been developed for halftone engravings—the system for translating photos into small "dots"—and photos began to appear regularly in the New York newspapers. Wire transmission of photos was not possible until 1924, and it was 1935 before AP established a regular Wirephoto network to supply pictures to its members.

Yellow Journalism

By the end of the nineteenth century, a distinct pattern emerged among major city newspapers: Strongheaded owners built booming businesses out of newspapers by sensationalizing stories concerning crime, abnormal behavior, and government wrongdoing. These newspapers complemented their coverage of human behavior with an eagerness to crusade against wrongs in government, while lauding the spirit of the common working person who plunked down a penny or two for a copy.

The era provides us a term still used to describe journalistic excesses. *Yellow journalism* is any sensational attempt at selling newspapers by depicting the seamier side of life, such as exposés of bordellos or prying into the lives of celebrities. The term comes from a comic strip, "The Yellow Kid," popularized in Joseph Pulitzer's *New York World*. Among the stunts and gimmicks favored by Pulitzer to sell papers was the sponsorship of Nellie Bly's around-the-world trip in quest of

The "high priests of yellow journalism" were mocked in this 1909 cartoon by Joseph Keppler, Jr.

the fictional 80-day record popularized by Jules Verne in his book *Around the World in Eighty Days.*

William Randolph Hearst is the publisher most often associated with this period of the first press barons. His *New York Journal* attempted to outdo Joseph Pulitzer's *World.* Legends abound of the lengths to which Hearst went to buy, plant, or control a story. His competition with Pulitzer to dramatize and place blame for the sinking of the *Maine* in Havana Harbor in 1898 fed the flames of nationalism that led to involvement in the Spanish-American war. Elected to Congress in 1902, Hearst lusted for higher power—perhaps even the presidency of the United States—but his romantic life, personal spending, and ruthless control of his enterprises worked against his ambitions. Orson Welles's classic film *Citizen Kane* is a barely fictionalized account of the excesses of Hearst.

During the yellow journalism era banner headlines, the comics, puzzles, sports sections and other innovations were developed to please the consumer.

NEWSPAPERS IN THE TWENTIETH CENTURY

Yellow journalism has never entirely gone away. As long as there were three or more competing newspapers in the big cities, at least one stayed with the tradition of printing sensational headlines and pictures of bathing beauties.

When magazines developed the exposé story—*McClure's* ran a critical look at Standard Oil by Ida Tarbell in 1902 followed by Lincoln Steffen's series, "Shame of the Cities" (1903–1905)—newspapers followed suit with articles that exposed wrongdoing and corruption. An angry President Theodore Roosevelt labeled the practice "muckraking."

One of the resurgences of yellow journalism came in the 1920s, when several new tabloids were published in New York City, each trying to outdo the other with crime stories, lurid photographs, coverage of scandals involving the rich and famous, and sex escapades. The period came to be known as the era of jazz journalism because it seemed in tune with the raucous music of the time.

The economic woes brought on by the Great Depression cut heavily into newspaper profits and effectively ended the last major wave of yellow journalism's popularity. Nevertheless, as recently as the 1970s, Australian publisher Rupert Murdoch was buying tabloids and injecting them with new doses of yellow journalism—stories about the "killer bees" advancing on the United States from South America, for example—in an attempt to hold readers lured away by television and other entertainment media. Muckraking became more sophisticated and eventually gained a more respectable label: investigative journalism.

Supermarket checkout "newspapers" such as *The Star* and *The National Enquirer* use modern-day yellow journalism with their headlines proclaiming "Elvis Is Living with Martians" and "Baby Born Wearing Sunglasses." But the sensational tabloids aren't really newspapers at all in the traditional sense.

Newspapers of Record

Beginning in 1896, under the leadership of Adolph Ochs, *The New York Times* started to carve out a niche for itself as the "newspaper of record," first for its city, and then for the entire nation. Increasingly, newspaper publishers saw that they could ensure profitability by offering readers a responsible information package based on reporting of public affairs in the circulation area, along with a mix of national and international news, sports, entertainment features, social news, and coverage of local business.

The "newspaper of record" plays the role of an agenda-setter, helping decide which issues will move to the forefront of national debate. In addition to *The New York Times*, newspapers that have attracted national audiences include *The Washington Post, The Wall Street Journal, The Los Angeles Times,* and *The Christian Science Monitor*. Many newspapers grew into roles as leading voices in their state or region; *The Atlanta Constitution, The Chicago Tribune, The Des Moines Register,* and *The Miami Herald* are examples.

The Opinion Function

In the nineteenth century, flamboyant editors used their news columns to wage political battles and attempt to influence national debate. Increasingly in the twentieth century, the opinions of the publisher, editors, columnists, and letter-writers were reserved for the editorial page. Expanded space was made available for exchanges of views in the "op-ed" (opposite editorial) page and even in entire opinion sections, especially in Sunday newspapers. The National Conference of Editorial Writers (NCEW) was founded in 1946 to foster appreciation of the role of editorial pages among both journalists and readers.

Journalism as a Profession

Movies and plays in the 1920s and 1930s portrayed newspaper editors and reporters as chain-smoking, hard-drinking, coarse, street-wise individuals driven by an obsession to yell "stop the presses . . . I've got a scoop!" While the portrait offered by the classic farce *The Front Page* was not entirely fictional, the reality was that newspaper editors and reporters in the twentieth century were beginning to view themselves as professionals rather than craftsmen.

The American Newspaper Publishers Association (ANPA), formed at the end of the nineteenth century as a trade association, emerged in the twentieth century as an organization dedicated to improving newspapers through its research institute, regular publications focusing on business practices and law, and an information service for the profession. In 1909, Sigma Delta Chi was formed as a secret fraternity, only to emerge as an association serving the needs and interests of working journalists. Now known as the Society of Professional Journalists (SPJ), it holds an annual convention, publishes a monthly professional magazine, and lobbies for freedom of the press.

Both SPJ and the American Society of Newspaper Editors (ASNE), formed in 1922, have a code of ethics governing behavior by journalists. The ASNE's *Canons of Journalism*, issued a year after formation of the organization, is a code of conduct for journalists and a ringing statement of principles that include protection of the freedom of the press and the people's right to know. The ASNE has a number of standing committees that monitor journalistic practices, issue publications, and work for professional standards.

The Newspaper Guild, the journalists' trade union, also is concerned with improving the profession. Tired of working long and odd hours for little pay, journalists formed the guild in the 1930s. Today, however, only some 32,000 of the nearly half-million employees of newspapers are guild members, and in the days of automation and computers, the union poses virtually no strike threat to publishers. Wage increases accepted by the union in the 1980s actually lagged behind gains made by other professional workers.

While membership in all these journalism organizations is voluntary, they speak for the field, advance its welfare, and have enhanced its respect.

A Medium at the Crossroads

While the book industry has developed new strategies almost yearly to adapt to a changing marketplace affected by telecommunications, newspapers traditionally have been slower to make adjustments. But by the 1980s a general alarm had been sounded in the newspaper publishing industry. The number of newspapers, the size of the publications, and their impact all have been waning.

The rush of technological developments and changes in the habits of readers (and, increasingly, *non*readers) are causing publishers to be uncertain about the future. In the 1970s, meetings of the ANPA and ASNE included only an occasional panel discussion on technology and its effects. Now entire conferences are built around the question of "Is There to Be a Future for Newspapers, and If So, What?"

The total number of daily newspapers, as monitored by *Editor and Publisher*, the industry trade journal, shrank from 1763 in 1945 to 1680 in 1985, a loss of 87 newspapers, many in large metropolitan areas and some with circulations in excess of half a million. U.S. Bureau of Census figures show a circulation gain for daily newspapers from 45 million to 63 million in that same 40-year period, but those figures can be misleading. A closer look shows that several large and healthy leading regional papers have posted the major gains, while many mid-sized papers show little or no growth. (*The Star-Ledger*, for example, serves the entire northern half of New Jersey as well as the single city it once served, Newark, while smaller dailies in New Brunswick and Trenton show little circulation gain.) In just a six-month period ending March 31, 1989, *The Chicago Sun-Times* lost 11.3 percent of its daily circulation.[1]

During the post–World War II period, the population of the United States was growing at a much faster rate than newspaper circulation. Thus the more revealing figure is the circulation of newspapers per household. In the first half of the twentieth century, circulation averaged 1.3 newspapers per household, meaning that one out of three homes subscribed not only to one paper but to a second one. In the 1980s, circulation per household declined to 0.7, meaning that one out of three homes do not subscribe to a newspaper.

Sunday Papers Show Growth

The one bright spot in newspaper circulation has come in that venerable American institution, the Sunday newspaper. At the beginning of the 1990s, 820 Sunday editions were being printed in the United States, contrasted with 634 at the beginning of the 1970s. Sunday circulation totaled 60.8 million copies in 1988, up from 51.7 million in 1973.[2] About half of the dailies published in the United States, now have Sunday papers.[3] Several papers have dropped their Monday or Saturday editions in favor of adding Sunday.

Sunday papers have always provided a review and summary of the week's news, along with feature stories that are not so timely as those in the daily editions.

Increasingly, readers find that reading a Sunday newspaper is sufficient for keeping up with local news beyond the headlines they hear on the radio while driving to work. In households where two adults work, there is less time for daily newspaper reading. Sunday is the day when two-income families have time to read, compare notes, and plan purchases for the coming week based on local advertising in the Sunday papers. Households that previously read only one Sunday paper—the large metropolitan paper from the center city—appear to be changing their habits to include at least one small daily's Sunday edition in addition to the metro leader. (See Table 7.1.)

The Shrinking Newspaper

The physical size of the daily newspaper has contracted by about 10 percent in page dimensions and also in the number of pages per issue, as publishers wrestle with ever-higher costs for newsprint. The average time a reader spends with his or her newspaper has declined precipitously, from nearly half an hour a day a generation ago to about a quarter of an hour today. Another dramatic change is the ratio of advertising to news content, up from 53 percent advertising in 1946

TABLE 7.1 Top 25 Newspapers by Circulation

Rank	Newspaper	Circulation	Percentage Change	Sunday Circulation	Percentage Change
1	Wall Street Journal	1,795,448	(3.3)	—	NA
2	USA Today	1,491,844	4.5	—	NA
3	Los Angeles Times	1,177,253	(1.6)	1,529,609	0.8
4	New York Times	1,114,830	0.6	1,700,825	0.8
5	Washington Post	791,289	1.4	1,143,145	0.5
6	Newsday	763,972	7.0	875,239	22.7
7	New York Daily News	762,078	(30.6)	911,684	(34.9)
8	Chicago Tribune	723,178	0.3	1,107,938	0.5
9	Detroit Free Press	598,418	(5.9)	1,202,604	(3.0)
10	San Francisco Chronicle	553,433	(1.7)	705,260	(0.7)
11	New York Post	552,227	8.2	—	NA
12	Chicago Sun-Times	531,462	0.8	537,169	(2.0)
13	Boston Globe	504,675	(3.2)	798,057	0.8
14	Philadelphia Inquirer	503,603	(3.1)	974,697	(0.4)
15	Newark Star-Ledger	470,672	(1.2)	700,237	1.0
16	Detroit News	446,831	(10.8)	—	NA
17	Cleveland Plain Dealer	413,678	(3.3)	544,362	(2.9)
18	Mpls.-St. Paul Star Tribune	408,365	0.2	677,753	1.6
19	Dallas Morning News	406,768	2.3	618,283	5.5
20	Miami Herald	398,067	(4.0)	510,549	(1.8)
21	Rocky Mountain News	355,940	1.6	425,443	4.9
22	St. Louis Post-Dispatch	350,350	(8.4)	562,700	0.2
23	Orange Co. Register	347,675	(1.7)	400,375	(1.6)
24	Boston Herald	345,564	(3.7)	227,040	(5.0)
25	Arizona Republic	338,562	2.4	531,180	2.7

Note: Figures in parentheses indicate a circulation loss.

Source: Advertising Age, Nov. 4, 1991, p. 48. Ratings based on Audit Bureau of Circulations information. Figures are for six months ending Sept. 30, 1991.

to more than 68 percent advertising in 1985. The picture that emerges is a newspaper that is a "quick read"—and is read as much for the advertising as for the news.

Growth of national advertising—ads placed by the manufacturers of products rather than the stores that sell them—is much slower in newspapers than in other media. Publishers find an increasingly large part of their advertising revenue comes from local merchants and services. Weekly newspapers, whose growth has led that of daily newspapers in the second half of the century, tend to serve the local merchant because they can deliver a circulation that matches the store's service area. Thus, publishers of daily newspapers serving a city or region find themselves in a squeeze between national media and neighborhood weeklies, and the shrinking of advertising dollars seems destined to continue.

In the 1980s, daily newspapers were able to compensate for the loss of display advertising because of an increase in classified advertising "linage" (advertising rates are calculated on the number of lines, with each line equalling one-fourteenth of an inch, one column wide). At the beginning of the 1980s, classifieds accounted for 32 percent of newspaper revenues; by the end of the decade, the figure was 43 percent. But at the beginning of the 1990s, a soft real estate market accounted for a slowdown in classified ads.[4]

More Casualties: Extras and "PMs"

When was the last time you saw an EXTRA! edition of a newspaper? Probably on your television screen, in a late-night black-and-white movie. As late as the 1940s, when most workers took public transportation to the downtown area of a city during the day, street sales of newspapers were still important. If someone assassinated a major official, a train crashed, or war broke out, the presses would be stopped so that a special front page could be made up with a banner headline and the bare details of the breaking story. People might even emerge from movie theaters in mid-evening to find newsboys hawking newspapers with the familiar cry: "EXTRA! EXTRA! Read all about it!" But changing work patterns, the move to the suburbs, and the constant availability of broadcast news sounded the death knell of the EXTRA!

In the 1990s, yet another staple of print journalism has all but disappeared: the afternoon daily. People come home to watch up-to-the-minute news broadcasts, not to sit down with a "PM" paper full of hours-old items. Most journalists now work overnight to put out "AMs" or "all-day" papers that are ready for delivery by 6 A.M. If yesterday's events are to have utility during the working day, they are better absorbed in the morning. Thus do the producers of daily newspapers adapt to the changing life patterns of the consumers.

The "Metro" versus the Suburban Newspaper

According to their critics, newspapers habitually focus on bad news, only reluctantly noting the good news. If so, the main headline summarizing the trend in American journalism in the past two decades might read:

BIG CITY NEWSPAPERS FAIL OR MERGE AT ALARMING RATE

and the smaller type below would say:

But Suburban Dailies, Weeklies Are Booming

A study of New Jersey's daily newspapers pinpoints the reason for their failure and decline: the inability or reluctance to shift the focus of coverage from the inner city to the suburbs where the more affluent readers have moved.[5] Papers that tried to maintain their printing plants and delivery systems in decaying city centers have withered. Those that moved to the burgeoning suburbs flourished.

In the past generation, five New York City newspapers merged and finally folded, leaving the city with one healthy daily and two struggling ones (the *Post* and the *Daily News*). Meanwhile, *Newsday* on suburban Long Island grew to be one of the region's preeminent dailies, challenging *The New York Times* and the *Daily News* in the boroughs of Brooklyn and Queens. The suburban *Record* of Hackensack, N.J., and the Newark *Star-Ledger* similarly expanded on New York's western flank. At one level, the New York newspaper market appears to have dried up . . . if you look only at the number of papers published in Manhattan. Include the suburbs, where the people who work in New York City have migrated, and the newspaper situation looks considerably more healthy.

"The migration of the middle class and of retail activity to the suburbs helped spur circulation and advertising growth for the suburban papers," notes the author of a special report in *Advertising Age*.[6] Now there are indications that even suburban newspapers that once seemed destined to take over from declining metropolitan dailies are entering a transition phase. The reasons: Growth in the suburbs has slowed, the suburban areas now have many of the same problems as the inner cities, and life-styles continue to change.

As little as a decade ago, according to the researchers and marketing experts interviewed by *Advertising Age*, the suburbs still were dominated by traditional school- and home-oriented families, which meant that they needed information

INSIGHT
Coverage of Local News Declines

Newspaper editor and television executive Michael Gartner criticizes the increasing tendency of local news media to send reporters off on far-flung assignments instead of covering stories close to home:

Instead of going off to Pakistan, why don't they devote that money and time to disclosing that the local grocery chain charges more money for food in the poor parts of town than the rich? Instead of heading to the Super Bowl, why don't they report and investigate the alarming number of football injuries at the town's high school?

. . . In many towns, courts and courthouses go almost uncovered. In many towns, school boards get covered only when there's a fight over spanking. . . . No one is reporting how textbooks get chosen, how lawsuits get settled, how zoning gets waived, how judges get chosen.

Gartner blames the lack of local coverage on editors who don't make their towns the prime focus of their entire careers: "The best editors and TV news directors are long-termers, men and women who have developed an understanding of their towns and affection for the people, a belief in the local way of life. They are neither boosters nor scolds; rather, they are the conscience of the community."

Because daily newspapers now circulate in so many suburbs, each with its own government and social services, the job of recording what goes on in the community is left to the local weeklies.

Source: Michael Gartner, "Local Newspapers Ignore Their Own Main Streets," *The Wall Street Journal*, Feb. 2, 1989, p. A-9.

about the community. Now the suburbs are populated by an increasing number of older adults and younger couples without children who buy houses or condominiums in the area but orient themselves toward the center city, or toward no particular community. They have little interest in the civic affairs covered by the local papers and instead seek out life-style publications and career communication networks.

As a result, "metros" and suburban papers alike are moving away from coverage of weddings, social activities, and local chit-chat and toward features on hobbies, life-styles, travel, cooking, entertaining—in short, the same fare that magazines and other publications with diverse audiences tend to offer.

Television Changes Newspapers' Focus

A sign on the television set prominently situated in one newspaper's newsroom says: "Do not turn off this television! It must be kept on 24 hours every day!" That paper had first learned of the Challenger space shuttle disaster when a reporter at home called to say he had heard and seen it on television.

Keeping on top of breaking news isn't the only reason newspaper editors now must tune in to what television is doing. Because television is what a Gannett editor called "the one shared experience Americans have," print editors have to know what their readers know.[7]

RESEARCH

You Want a Different Paper from Mom and Dad's

The Newspaper Advertising Bureau constantly monitors reader preference for news, newspapers, and news formats in order to advise newspapers how to promote their products and to convince advertisers that newspapers are alive and well. Surveys conducted for the Bureau by independent research firms show that reading patterns for young people differ considerably from those of their parents.

The majority of older readers prefer a news-oriented paper, which they will read from front to back. Younger readers pick and choose what they want to read, and they favor features over news, which they feel they can digest in summary format. In other words, young people want newspapers to be more like television.

Source: Leo Bogart, *An Update on Readership*, research report prepared by the Newspaper Advertising Bureau, Inc., 1988.

Reading Style	All Readers	18- to 24-Year-Olds
Start with front page, go right through	45%	19%
Turn first to other section, go through rest	18%	21%
Read some sections, skim the rest	14%	21%
Only read certain parts, skip the rest	20%	39%

What Kind of Paper Is Preferred		
Mostly news, some features	53%	26%
Mostly features, plus news summary	22%	50%
Want a balance	25%	24%

Some newspapers feel that television spares them the task of describing every detail about the world's earth-shaking events and shifts their responsibility to *explaining* those events. *USA Today* editors, on the other hand, feel that their job is to "preview the news"—to give readers a feeling for what is going to happen and why. One way or the other, newspapers have fit their product to a world in which television is the dominant entertainment and information medium for most people.

USA Today: Prototype of the New Newspaper?

Until the Gannett Co., Inc.—the nation's largest and fastest-growing newspaper chain—introduced *USA Today* in the fall of 1982, newspapers were the only nonnational medium in the United States, and the United States was one of the few countries in the world without a national newspaper. (*The Wall Street Journal* and *The New York Times* have editions that circulate throughout the country, but it can be argued that both are specialized papers appealing to a specialized audience rather than true national newspapers aiming at the widest number of potential readers.)

Research by Gannett in the 1960s showed that more and more Americans didn't want a completely local newspaper, mainly because they had moved to their current home from somewhere else. They wanted to keep in touch with the sports and weather from places where they used to live.

USA Today, while it circulates throughout the nation, does not function as a strong editorial voice in the nation's political and social arena. What it does well, however, is to provide capsulized information that can be digested quickly by busy consumers with an interest in national trends. The paper is as much a "databank" as a news vehicle. Easy-to-understand color graphics put statistics and facts in a form that can be read quickly. Printed as a newspaper, *USA Today* has much in common with the computer-accessed databases that busy executives use to keep abreast of the latest trends and developments.

Detractors have called it "McPaper" because—while it is cheap, convenient, and easy to find in any urban area—its brief stories are to traditional journalism what a fast-food burger is to steak. Initially, advertisers warmed slowly to the new medium, not sure exactly what it was and how it served its audience. Other newspapers, however, were quick to imitate the colorful graphics and quick-reading charts, starting with the giant multicolored weather map.

Four years after its debut, advertising revenues were up 40 percent over the previous year. At that time the gamble appeared to have paid off; the paper was beginning to succeed with advertisers as well as readers. Still, the paper has not consistently shown a profit. John Curley, who succeeded *USA Today* founder and chairman Allen Neuharth as president and chief executive officer, blamed the continuing red ink on two traditional bugaboos of the newspaper industry: rising costs for newsprint and reduced spending by major advertisers. The failure of *USA Today* would not bring down Gannett, but its success could establish Gannett as a true national newspaper publishing force.

Not content with merely inventing a new national medium, Al Neuharth, who shepherded the project from drawing board to financial success, said he envisions an information network that includes television, radio, computer databases, and virtually any other medium into which information gathered by the Gannett system can be channeled. More than any other publisher, he appears to have realized

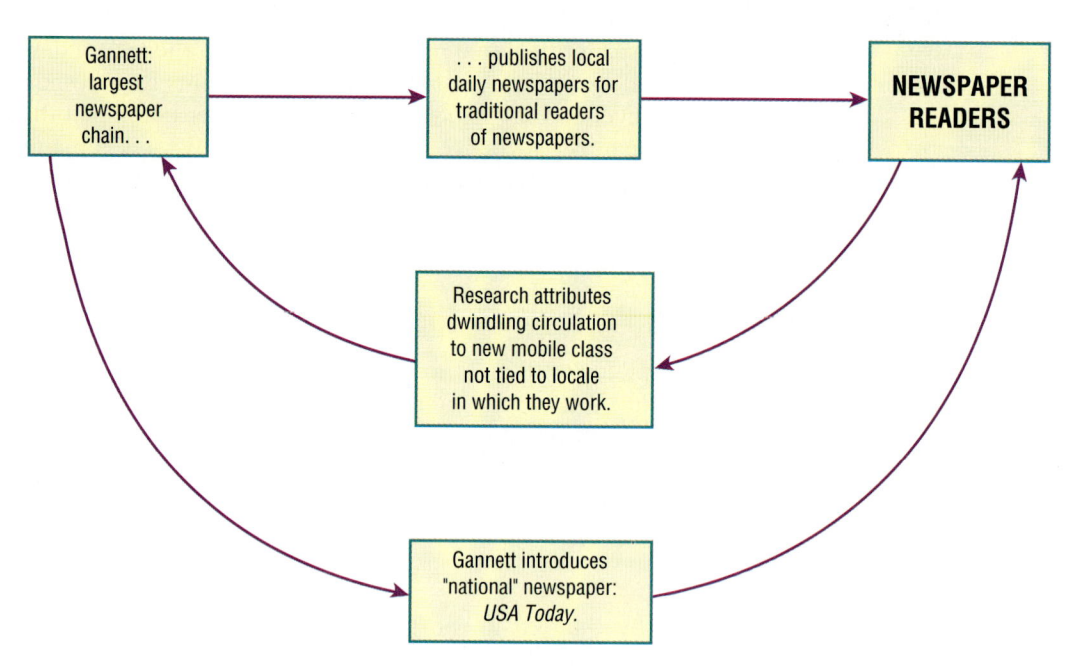

FIGURE 7.1 Producer Detects Need for New Medium. Gannett, as a producer of conventional newspapers, used research to detect that its audience had new and different needs. The consumers' behaviors led the producer to venture a new product: *USA Today*.

that the newspaper in the twenty-first century will be just part of a complex information system.

The headline in *Advertising Age* on *USA Today*'s fifth anniversary offered a prognosis for the new style of newspaper: "Here to Stay."

COMPUTERS CHANGE NEWSPAPERS... AND THE NEWS

While wrestling with the problems of defining their audiences and the interests of the readers, newspapers also have had to acclimate themselves to the computer age. The changes have caused some pains, along with considerable savings of cost and time.

The efficient role played by the computer, however, raises an intriguing question: Can computer technology speed news to its readers more efficiently without the outmoded intervening technology of ink on paper? In other words, has the computer all but made the newspaper as we know it obsolete? That question may be answered early in the next century.

According to a survey by the American Newspaper Publishers Association, there were 23 video display terminals in American newsrooms in 1970. A decade later there were 40,000. Today virtually every reporter, editor, and technician involved in the creation, editing, or storage of news and advertising for daily newspapers—and most weekly newspapers—works with a computer.

In just a short span of time, the newsroom has changed from a mechanical process where people wrote and edited on paper, to a centralized system where information is created, moved, edited, typeset, and prepared for printing entirely within the computer system. Newsrooms and typography shops used to be grimy, bustling places populated by hordes of technicians. Now they are quiet, carpeted places, and the number of jobs has been reduced by the efficiency of a system that translates information into type in a mere fraction of a second.

One of the long-time myths of the newspaper business was that news was generated out of the hustle and bustle of a newsroom presided over by knowing editors who took tips over the phone and shouted at waiting general assignment reporters and rewrite people. Colorful literature of yesteryear—the classic play *The Front Page*, for example—helped to keep that legend alive. But, as *Los Angeles Times* science writer Lee Dembart discovered:

> A number of industries have noticed that after computerization of their operations, there is much less need for employees to gather in one central location to work. A terminal can be set up anywhere and connected by telephone line to the main office. So, too, have reporters noticed that with computer terminals there is less need for them to work in a city room, especially if they are on long-term projects that do not require regular discussions with an editor.[8]

Sports reporters now carry portable computers to the press box, compose their stories as the game unfolds, and telephone the material back to the newspaper's main computer over ordinary phone lines, using a modem. Many columnists, critics, and editorialists who do not need to check in regularly at the office work at home or use a modem to "phone in their work." The lack of competition in one-paper cities means that reporters can put a premium on researching and writ-

INSIGHT

Will Newspapers Lose Classified Ads to the Phone Companies?

Traditionally newspapers have thought of their competition as other newspapers and other news and advertising media, especially the broadcasters. Although the Yellow Pages are a major advertising vehicle, newspapers never really thought of themselves as being in competition with the "Baby Bells" created when the federal government oversaw the breakup of the American Telephone and Telegraph Company.

All that changed when several decisions by a federal judge (made between 1988 and 1991 and upheld on appeal in 1991) allowed the phone companies to deliver electronic information. That included such services as "phone-in yellow pages" in which a caller hears a recorded advertisement that, unlike yellow pages, can be changed at any time according to the wishes of the advertiser. The service could render classified ads in newspapers obsolete because electronic ads would be easier to create, store, and retrieve.

The classified advertising business accounts for nearly 40 percent of the $30 billion spent on newspaper advertising—the most profitable type of newspaper advertising, inch for inch. Newspaper publishers say they are not about to give up that lucrative market without a fight, even if it means developing voice information services of their own.

Sources: Keith Bradsher, "Judge Allows Phone Companies to Provide Information Services," *The New York Times*, July 26, 1991, p. A-1; "Bells Ready to Roll" and "How Publishers Will Battle Bells," *Advertising Age*, Oct. 14, 1991, p. 3.

ing a story well rather than rushing back to the newsroom to make a deadline and create a "scoop" on the competition.

The news provided to newspapers by wire services is now in computer format, reducing the number of people needed to process it before it is set in print. Public relations agencies that deal regularly with newspapers are also capable of transmitting information to the computerized media over phone lines.

Pagination: From Computer Screen to Printing Press

The emphasis in printing technology has always been on reducing the number of steps needed to make "raw copy" ready to print. Today, *pagination* eliminates the need to send material out to a "back shop" where technicians set each story in type, place the story physically in a form or on a layout, prepare a "proof" and send the proof back to the newsroom for corrections.

Pagination is an electronic system for assembling all of the materials created by writers, editors, and graphics specialists on the computer screen and converting computer-screen images directly to a printing plate. The main requirements are

1. A screen large enough to hold all of the information for one page of the publication, and
2. A computer program for calling up all text and graphic materials and positioning them on a visual layout that can be transferred to the printing plate.

Merely by pressing buttons or moving a small electronic pencil over the surface of the electronic layout—much as you might use a "mouse" to create a document—the editor can manipulate the size and position of every element in the layout until the desired result is achieved.

"Paperless, Interactive Newspapers"

Pagination makes a "paperless newsroom" possible. But the end product is a newspaper printed on paper, and those newspapers still must be trucked through crowded streets for delivery to individual subscribers. Obviously the technology now found in the newsroom can be extended to deliver the news product directly to computer terminals in the home.

One such system has been demonstrated experimentally in Columbus, Ohio, to homes served by the interactive Qube cable television system.[9] Viewers could express their support or opposition concerning the issue being presented by pressing numbers on their home keypad, and they could help "edit" a program by indicating what kinds of topics they wanted to learn more about. The desired information would then be supplied to them on the screen.

A small newspaper experimented with an interactive system that enables subscribers to get information at home using a personal computer.[10] Community "micronews" that could be selected included school honor rolls, zoning board actions, and local sports.

The Knight-Ridder chain conducted an experiment with teletex news delivered on home computers but abandoned it when not enough subscribers showed interest.[11] The NewsRetrieval system offered by Dow Jones carries news stories, files of stories from Dow Jones wires concerning many of the companies listed in the major stock markets, and current quotes on stocks and bonds. The News-

Retrieval system also permits the subscriber to check the current value of his or her stock portfolio.[12]

IS THE NEWSPAPER DOOMED?

The advent of computerized electronic transmission of the news and advertising content directly to the home screen raises an obvious question: How long will the newspaper as we know it today exist? Until all homes are equipped with computers—at least ten years in the future—delivery of the printed newspaper will continue to have utility. Experiments in Europe and the United States indicate that not all consumers are ready to receive "news" by computer screen.

Those involved in the Columbus experiment, including the Associated Press, believe that the local newspaper will not be bypassed by electronic information flowing directly from national centers to private homes. The reason is that subscribers are concerned with local affairs, and especially local advertising—information that is best gathered and prepared locally.

Thus the local news producer is bound to survive, even if the newspaper as an artifact eventually disappears. Publishers must reevaluate how the information they now gather can be packaged for electronic transmission. Writers and editors must learn to think in terms of "frames"—the amount of information that can be shown on a screen at one time. Technicians must work on ways for frames containing items that the consumer wishes to save for later use—coupons and special offers, for example, or news items that mention family members—to be printed quickly and cheaply on simple home printers.

Reasons for Optimism

While the number of daily newspapers and their circulation has remained constant, the population of the United States has been rising. So, while newspaper circulation equaled nearly 100 percent of all households in 1970, it had dropped to about 70 percent of all households at the beginning of the 1990s. At that rate, it would equal only about 60 percent of all households by the year 2000.[13] Throughout the 1970s and 1980s, advertising linage remained fairly constant, with small gains in some years offset by losses in succeeding years.[14]

Such data would seem to indicate a stagnant industry; still there are optimists. A study conducted at the University of Missouri School of Journalism found communication professors and media executives divided into three groups: those who think the electronic media will take over, undying traditionalists who believe the newspaper industry will not change much, and a middle group who believe newspapers will find a revised role in an electronic world.[15]

American Newspaper Publishers Association consultant Jon G. Udell, a professor of business at the University of Wisconsin, is one of those who sees newspapers finding new roles. He noted in a speech to the Wisconsin Newspaper Association that the coming population bulge in the 35-to-55 age group will provide an expanding market for newspapers. Like many of those in the Missouri poll, he also believes that electronic transmission of news and information can help newspaper editors to improve their product.[16] Many experts point to the increase in the number of Americans seeking higher education as an indicator that more people will be using print information in the future.

Even in the face of stiff competition from new technologies, newspaper executives believe that print has a future. A survey by a company involved in both newspapers and electronic media showed that almost two-thirds of the top print media executives think newspaper readership will not decline seriously. According to the results, reported in the trade magazine *Editor & Publisher*, respondents split almost evenly when asked whether video technology was "complementary" or "competitive" with print technology.[17]

The strengths of the newspaper in the face of video competition were seen as "portability," "browsability," and "retention of message." Two-thirds of the media executives surveyed said they believe that newspapers can adapt and compete . . . but most indicated that other print media, including newsletters and special interest magazines, are better suited to adaptation.

Newspapers Seek to Adapt and Innovate

In the interim between the newspaper as we know it and the electronic news service of the not-too-distant future, publishers are experimenting with ways to speed the process of printing on paper.

A few newspapers have tried a process long used in the packaging industry called flexography. It uses water-based ink that is easier and speedier to apply than oil-based ink, and it won't come off on the reader's hands![18] Another innovation that may be adapted to newspaper use is ink-jet printing, already de-

---

MINORITIES/WOMEN

A *Nuevo* Approach to the Hispanic Reader

In most American cities with large Puerto Rican, Mexican, or Cuban populations, Spanish-speaking readers have to be content with reading a small Hispanic daily, while the large English-language metropolitan papers ignore them as potential consumers.

The Miami *Herald* realized that it was missing a significant segment of the community simply because its news and its advertising were in English. The publisher of the paper introduced *El Nuevo Herald* as a supplement to the regular paper available to any subscriber who requested it. One out of every four consumers of the 400,000-circulation paper receives *El Nuevo Herald*. In addition to increasing the newspaper's circulation, the move has sharply increased advertising from Hispanic businesses.

The content of the Spanish-language supplement is not merely a translation of news items from the parent paper. Articles and opinion pieces take a strong viewpoint (often more virulently anti-Castro than the *Herald* itself). The paper within a paper may run to 40 pages, and the graphic design often makes it the most attractive part of the package.

The success of the *El Nuevo Herald* could lead to similar ventures in New York, Los Angeles, and other cities with large Hispanic populations.

Source: Albert Scardino, "Giving Miami the News in Both of Its Languages," *The New York Times*, Jan. 17, 1989, p. C-20.

veloped for high-speed computer printers. Computer-controlled nozzles spray ink at the paper in the shape of letters, characters, pictures, or any other graphic information. In addition to speed, the system makes it possible to change information periodically during the press run without stopping the presses. (Thus robbing journalism of another of its mythic sayings: "Stop the presses!") So far newspapers are only using ink-jets to print mailing labels, but some believe the process has promise at the main printing system.[19]

Perhaps the most notable impact *USA Today* has had is that over half the newspapers in the United States have been redesigned to imitate its use of full-color photographs and lavish "spot color" graphics around boxes and charts. At the same time as all these improvements in design are being made, however, the soaring cost of newsprint—prices more than doubled between 1975 and 1988—has put pressure on newspapers to use lighter paper.[20] Gains made in use of color, ink, and graphics may be offset by the loss of quality when images show through thin paper and consumers react to the strange feel of lighter paper.

Speed Is the Key

Faced with electronic competition, publishers of newspapers will have to convince consumers that they can deliver the news quickly and efficiently. The publisher of Canada's *Globe and Mail*, published in Toronto, sees his publication becoming a "print and electronic hybrid" in the 1990s, providing summaries and analysis in the print newspaper, and sending statistics and details to home computer screens.[21]

Newspapers began experimenting with facsimile transmissions of news digests at the beginning of the 1990s. *The Hartford Courant* was the first to create a daily

---

INSIGHT

Newspapers Must Exploit Their Strengths If They Are to Survive

For its special issue on "the challenge of the 90s," *presstime*, the magazine of the American Newspapers Publishers Association, asked Everette Dennis, executive director of the Gannett Center for Media Studies at Columbia University, what newspapers need to do to maintain their health.

Dennis's prescription:

Promote the opinion pages. No other medium offers as much free exchange of ideas as the editorial and "op-ed" pages of newspapers. "Newspapers don't do much to promote opinion sections, yet these pages may be their most important and distinguishable asset."

Make greater use of the databases. Newspapers gather great amounts of information and use only a small part of it in the publication. Information can be recycled and repackaged for use in specialized newsletters and other data services, bringing more revenues to the newspapers.

Source: Everette Dennis, "A Prescription for Economic Health," *presstime*, January 1990, pp. 20–21.

fax edition; soon Knight-Ridder's *Journal of Commerce* began a daily "Datafax" edition, *The New York Times* began TimesFax, and *The Los Angeles Times* announced a NewsFax four-page issue to be beamed to Moscow.[22]

Not to be outdone, Pan Am shuttle flights began, in 1990, to offer hourly newspapers to their busy business travelers. *The Latest News*, issued in the afternoon and early evening hours, aimed to bring executives up to the minute on developments during the day since the morning newspapers. Published by UPI and *Financial World* magazine, the free newspaper was supported by advertisers such as IBM and AT&T.[23]

Realizing that consumers now expect to receive information instantaneously by dialing 900 numbers, newspapers began to market their weather information, sports results, and other tidbits of information through "audiotex" services. Instead of thinking of the printed newspaper as their single product, newspapers are beginning to realize that all the information stored in their computers constitutes a "database" that can be exploited in many ways beyond printing a newspaper and delivering it to the door.[24]

CHANGING PATTERNS OF OWNERSHIP

Until recently newspapers were predominantly an independent medium in terms of ownership. Many were still the property of the heirs of their founders—family-run papers as small as the smallest weeklies and dailies and as large as *The New York Times*. Most chains had no more than a dozen small- or medium-sized papers and were regionally concentrated.

The pattern is changing rapidly. Gannett has not only purchased dozens of independent newspapers, it has bought entire chains, raising the number in its fold to 86 in 1991, or 1 out of every 20 dailies in the United States. Gannett trains its managers by rotating them within the chain. It centralizes many aspects of management, but does not interfere with local editorial policy and allows considerable autonomy in other areas. Cost savings are realized through the use of its own Washington news bureau.

Worry about Gannett's dominance of such a large segment of the newspaper market, especially when the circulation of *USA Today* is included, has been voiced by many critics of American journalism. To date, however, admiration for Gannett's ability to run papers profitably has far overshadowed serious concern about any desire to control the market.

Criticism of another ownership trend has been much louder: the purchase of newspapers by owners who appear merely to want to squeeze profits out of them, with little concern for quality or the integrity of the product. The acquisition of papers across America, including the floundering *New York Post*, by Rupert Murdoch was viewed with alarm by many journalists who decried his formula of crime coverage, sensational reporting, and gossip as news. Many advertisers were wary of the lowest-common-denominator audiences attracted by such newspapers.

But at the beginning of the 1990s, critics grudgingly conceded that Murdoch and recently deceased British "press lord" Robert Maxwell saved many newspapers that might otherwise have died. John Fisher, president of Southam, Inc., one of Canada's two largest newspaper chains, moved to increase profitability by making publishers more accountable to the parent firm, causing some local publishers in the chain to voice concern that eventually editorial independence would be threatened by cost-cutting management.[25]

The phenomenon of newspapers being sold to other newspapers is viewed as a consolidation of power within the industry. Of even greater concern to some is the sale of newspapers to broadcast media companies that want to diversify, and to noninformation producers who buy into the information business. The president of the Newspaper Guild, the union for reporters and lower-level editors, warned of the dangers of "an industry dominated by bankers and big investors" as well as the threat of concentrated media power being used for "political propaganda purposes."[26] To prevent news monopolies, the Federal Communications Commission forbids a newspaper to own and operate a television or radio station in the same community served by the newspaper—the so-called one-to-a-market rule.

In 1970, newspaper publishers convinced Congress to pass the Newspaper Preservation Act, enabling them to cut costs—and save failing newspapers—by merging business and printing operations (but not news and editorial operations) in cities where there still was newspaper competition. Both small and large papers have taken advantage of the law. In tiny Manteca, California, a 6500-circulation daily merged with a twice-weekly. Early in 1990, Detroit's two 650,000-circulation papers, the *Free Press* and the *News*, finally got the go-ahead to join business operations after a lengthy legal battle. As the nation's ninth- and tenth-largest newspapers by circulation, both Gannett's *News* and the Knight-Ridder *Free Press* were losing money for the parent companies, which are the nation's largest and second-largest newspaper companies. The joint operating decision did not solve the papers' problems, as advertisers rebelled against sharply increased advertising rates and subscribers complained about a joint Sunday edition that combined sections and features from each of the papers. All factions could agree that the merger had one benefit: 2000 jobs were saved because neither of the papers had to fold.[27]

In some areas of the country, healthy papers have moved to broaden their circulation by "invading" the territory of others. Long Island *Newsday* now competes for the turf once owned by the Manhattan dailies. The St. Petersburg *Times* is moving into Tampa *Tribune* territory. The Minneapolis *Star-Tribune* and the St. Paul *Pioneer Press* have forgotten their gentlemen's agreement of the past and are fighting for dominance in the Twin Cities.

While daily circulation stagnates, consumers are supporting weekly papers in greater numbers, raising circulation by nearly 25 percent in the 1980s according to the National Newspaper Association.[28] Large chains such as Ingersoll Publications and Media General have bought weeklies, but so have individual entrepreneurs lured by the pretax profit margins of 20 percent for the most successful papers. At the beginning of the 1980s almost 90 percent of the weekly newspapers in the United States were independent; at the beginning of the 1990s approximately half were owned by chains.[29] Some chains merge the operations of as many as 75 weeklies and market them as "zoned editions," with some news running in all editions and other news running only in the community where it is relevant. Such management techniques have made chains of weeklies every bit as strong as many of the dailies whose territories they share.[30]

THE ROLES OF WOMEN AND MINORITIES

A national study released in 1989 confirmed what women journalists have long suspected: The newspapering field is dominated at the top by men. Only 6 percent of publishers and presidents of newspapers are women. Only 8 newspapers over 100,000 circulation in the United States have female editors. Thirty-six percent of reporters are women; only in advertising sales is the number of women proportionate to the population: 55 percent.[31]

Studies by the American Society of Newspaper Editors indicate a similar bias against minorities: they hold only 4 percent of executive positions and less than 7 percent of the reporting jobs. There is hope for improvement, however, because 15 percent of newspaper employees under 25 are minorities.

Few newspapers represent women proportionally to the population in bylines, appearances in photographs, or reference in stories. Does it matter whether women and minorities are represented in newspapers in proportion to their presence in society? Linda Grist Cunningham, editor of *The Daily Record* in northern New Jersey, told *USA Today*:

> If you ask readers specifically, "Do you care whether your reporter is male, female, black, white, Asian, or Hispanic?" I don't think they're going to say, "Yes, I care." What they care about is a newspaper that reflects their interest, culture, lifestyle. They want to feel that umbilical cord between the reader and the newspaper. So if you don't have a newsroom that reflects the community that it's serving, that umbilical cord gets frayed. What readers care about is the result of a diversified newsroom.[32]

In the 1960s and 1970s, responding to the feminist movement, newspapers did away with "women's pages, replacing them with "family" or "life-style" sections. Traditional female audiences had to turn to magazines for content aimed

MINORITIES/WOMEN

Gannett Leads in Minority Hiring

Minorities, although they constitute 22 percent of the U.S. population, accounted for only 7 percent of the country's 55,000 journalists at the end of the 1980s, up from 4 percent at the end of the 1970s, according to statistics gathered by the American Society of Newspaper Editors. At newspapers owned by the Gannett Co., however, 20 percent are minorities, including 15 percent of managers.

In 1979 the firm launched a Partners for Progress program that systematized minority recruiting, hiring, and training. Gannett not only sought minority personnel aggressively, it used bonuses to reward managers who met the hiring goals.

In addition, it began to monitor how individual papers in the chain cover minority news and required reporters to seek out minority leaders to obtain their comments and reactions on stories concerning economics and politics as well as obvious minority issues.

Source: Johnnie L. Roberts, "Gannett Surpasses Other Newspaper Firms in the Hiring and Promoting of Minorities," *The Wall Street Journal*, May 11, 1988, p. 23.

specifically at them. A Scripps Howard study in the mid-1980s showed the number of female frequent newspaper readers dropped 26 percent in a five-year period, contrasted with 16 percent for men.[33]

In order to recapture the female audience, newspapers will have to fit their content to the new realities that find two-thirds of married women with children in the work force, double the number a generation ago. One Knight-Ridder executive suggested that newspapers should respond to the needs and interests of working women with more coverage of issues such as childcare and family management, more information on balancing a career and home life, and more service features written and displayed for a consumer with increasingly less time for reading a newspaper.[34]

FUTURE FILE

✓ The owner of a newspaper chain likes you and is willing to make you the publisher of a new newspaper, provided that you identify the right audience for the newspaper. Would you propose that the chain begin a weekly or a daily newspaper, and what type of consumer should the paper target? Would it be a general newspaper or a specialized one like *The Wall Street Journal*?

✓ What kinds of information already produced and disseminated by newspapers could be modified for use in electronic systems where the consumer calls a toll-free 800 number, or a system where the consumer calls information up on the home computer screen? How can the newspaper ensure that consumers will want to obtain this information from the local newspaper's electronic services rather than the phone company?

✓ Can the argument be made that, no matter what the technological advances, enough people will want a print newspaper to make it feasible to continue publication of dailies? Or will the newspaper of the future be a local weekly newsprint version of what *Time, Newsweek,* and the "News of the Week in Review" section of *The New York Sunday Times* do on a national basis?

NOTES

1. Ira Teinowitz, "Big Dailies Singing Circulation Blues," *Advertising Age,* May 8, 1989, p. 70.
2. *Advertising Age,* March 6, 1989, p. S-2.
3. Joe Sharkey, "More Newspapers Plan Sunday Editions," *The Wall Street Journal,* Jan. 19, 1989, p. B-1.
4. Walecia Konrad, "As Price Tags Shrink, So Will the Daily Newspaper," *Business Week,* July 3, 1989, p. 44.
5. David Sachsman and Warren Sloat, *The Press and the Suburbs* (New Brunswick, NJ: Rutgers University Center for Urban Policy Research, 1985).
6. B. G. Yovovich, "Changes in Suburbs Call for Rezoning News," *Advertising Age,* Aug. 16, 1984, p. 14.
7. P. Weiss and L. Zuckerman, "The Shadow of a Medium: How TV Has Transformed the Telling of the News," *Columbia Journalism Review,* March/April 1987, pp. 33–39.

8. L. Dembart, "Computers: A Newsroom Revolution," *The Los Angeles Times,* Feb. 2, 1983, p. C-1.
9. Ray Laakaniemi, "The Computer Connection: America's First Computer-Delivered Newspaper," *Newspaper Research Journal,* 2:4 (July 1981), pp. 61–68.
10. Ray Laakaniemi, "Electronic Newspaper Part Two: Computer Retrieval Comes to the Small Daily," *Newspaper Research Journal* 3:4 (July 1982), pp. 36–40.
11. Jerome Aumente, *New Electronic Pathways: Videotex, Teletext and Online Databases* (Newbury Park, CA: Sage, 1987), p. 55.
12. Todd Hunt and Michael Cheney, "Dow-Jones NewsRetrieval: An Alternate Information System for Communication Education." Paper presented to the Association for Education in Journalism and Mass Communication, Boston, August 1980.
13. "Black and White and Not Read All Over," *The Wall Street Journal,* April 27, 1988, p. 29.
14. Johnnie C. Roberts, "After Heady Growth, Newspapers Face Tighter Times," *The Wall Street Journal,* Sept. 21, p. 6.
15. C. Holahan, "Experts Say Future of Newspapers Looks Good," *Newspaper Publisher's Auxiliary* 121:22 (Nov. 4, 1985), p. 1.
16. Jon G. Udell, "Trends and the Competitive Outlook for U.S. Newspapers." Speech to Wisconsin Newspaper Association fall conference, October 1985.
17. David Astor. "Media Leaders See Positive Future for Newspapers," *Editor & Publisher,* Sept. 14, 1985, pp. 1, 56.
18. "Flirting with Flexo," *Editor & Publisher,* Jan. 7, 1984, pp. 36–38.
19. "An Elusive Technology Finds a Home," *Editor & Publisher,* Jan. 28, 1984, pp. 64–66.
20. Alan Freeman, "Some Dailies Adopt Lighter Paper, Trim Pages to Cut Newsprint Costs," *The Wall Street Journal,* March 10, 1988, p. 30.
21. Michael T. Malloy, "Roy Megarry, Globe & Mail Publisher, Aims to 'Reinvent' the Paper for the '90s," *The Wall Street Journal,* Aug. 10, 1989, p. B-4.
22. Patrick M. Reilly, "Newspapers Warily Study Fax Editions," *The Wall Street Journal,* Dec. 8, 1989, p. B-1.
23. Pat Guy, "Hourly Newspaper for Pan Am Fliers," *USA Today,* March 12, 1990, p. 2B.
24. Jim Lessersohn, "Readers Are Dialing Their Daily Newspapers to Hear the News That Is Most Important to Them," *ASNE Bulletin,* May/June 1989, pp. 12–14; Christine Sabo, "Information Systems Work Their Magic," *Newspaper Marketing,* June, 1989, pp. 4–13.
25. Gary Lamphier, "Past Presses Newspaper Chief in Canada," *The Wall Street Journal,* Feb. 3, 1989, p. B-7.
26. K. Rothmyer, "Hot Properties: The Media-Buying Spree Explained," *Columbia Journalism Review,* November/December 1985, pp. 38–43.
27. Linda Greenhouse, "Linking of 2 Detroit Papers Upheld by Court in Tie Vote," *The New York Times,* Nov. 14, 1989, pp. D-1, D-20; Joseph B. White, "Newspaper Monopoly Fights to Pass Go," *The Wall Street Journal,* Jan. 25, 1990, pp. B-1, B-4.
28. John K. Emshwiller, "Want to Run a Newspaper? Try Starting Up a Weekly," *The Wall Street Journal,* Nov. 11, 1988, p. 11.
29. Alex S. Jones, "The Weekly Newspaper Becomes a Hot Property," *The New York Times,* May 15, 1989, p. D-6.
30. Joe Sharkey, "Weekly Newspapers Challenge the Dailies," *The Wall Street Journal,* April 13, 1989, p. B-6.
31. Cathy Trost, "Women in the Media Making Slow Progress, Study Finds," *The Wall Street Journal,* April 10, 1989, p. B-1.
32. Barbara Reynolds, "Diverse Work Force Can Benefit Readers," *USA Today,* June 6, 1989, p. 11A.
33. Janet Meyers, "Papers Re-Invent Women's Sections," *Advertising Age,* April 16, 1990, p. 57.
34. Scott McGehee, "Newspapers and American Women," *The Next Newspapers: Future of Newspapers Report,* ASNE Foundation, April 1988, pp. 17–18.

SUGGESTED READINGS

Bagdikian, Ben, H., *The Information Machines: Their Impact on Men and Media* (New York: Harper & Row, 1971).

Bogart, Leo, *Press and Public: Who Reads What, When, Where and Why in American Newspapers* (Hillsdale, NJ: Lawrence Erlbaum Associates, 1981).

Chancellor, John, and Walter R. Mears, *The News Business* (New York: Harper & Row, 1983).

Rankin, W. Parkman, *The Practice of Newspaper Management* (New York: Praeger, 1986).

Rivers, William, *News in Print* (New York: Harper & Row, 1984).

Talese, Gay, *The Kingdom and the Power* (New York: NAL World Publishing Co., 1969).

CHAPTER 8

Magazines

AT A GLANCE

✓ While magazines are related historically to books and newspapers through their printing methods, magazines historically have been the print medium most likely to experiment with new forms and styles of presenting information.

✓ Mass-circulation magazines provided information and entertainment for the broadest possible audience, and thus became attractive advertising vehicles for products aimed at the masses.

✓ Television drew advertisers away from magazines, forcing the collapse of the great mass-circulation magazines and leading to the founding of "special-interest" magazines that were efficient advertising vehicles for reaching particular groups of consumers.

✓ The most successful magazines are those that know their readers and cater to a particular life-style or need for information.

✓ Specialized magazines, especially "trade" magazines aimed at those in a particular profession or business, are successful because they aim to meet the information needs of their consumers.

✓ Research on their consumers' interests and needs enable magazines to succeed in a competitive marketplace.

In its final years as a mass-circulation magazine, the original *Saturday Evening Post* cut its subscription list to eliminate subscribers in ZIP codes that did not fit the profile of the desired "upscale" reader that the magazine hoped to attract in order to satisfy advertisers. Among the subscribers who were dropped was the mother of the publisher.

As we shall see in this chapter, most magazines today no longer try to appeal to a wide readership. Instead they try to target very specific interests, thus delivering an audience with definite characteristics and interests that advertisers want to reach.

In fact, we have reached the day when the producer can tailor copies of the magazine to the needs and interests of the individual consumers. The cover of the November 26, 1990, issue of *Time* magazine greeted each subscriber by name: "Hey (John Doe), Don't miss our really interesting story on the junk mail explosion." Ads in Time Warner publications—*Time*, *Sports Illustrated*, *People*, and *Money*—have carried not only the subscriber's name, but the names of the stores nearest to the subscriber's home that sell the product or service advertised. The match-up is accomplished by the magazine's computer.

MAGAZINES: THE DEVELOPMENT OF SPECIALIZED PUBLISHING

Earlier we saw that book publishing divided into two streams: publishing houses that maintain a general list with "something for everybody" and specialized publishers that cater to a specific audience's interests. Magazine publishing also evolved from primarily general-interest publications to highly specialized and targeted media.

Storehouses of Information

The word *magazine* comes from the French word "magasin" or storehouse. The earliest magazines were, indeed, storehouses of information. *The Gentleman's Magazine*, which appeared in England during the 1700s, was a compendium of letters, planting tables, essays, reprints of business and political documents, gossip, and selections from current or forthcoming works of poetry and fiction. Colonial magazines in the new land followed suit.

One of the particularly American contributions to the concept of a magazine was the almanac, which offered a wealth of useful and intriguing information, both homespun and exotic. Many of the almanacs were given away free or sold cheaply by companies such as Armour, the midwestern food and meat packing firm, whose *Armour's Farmer's Almanac* served as an advertising vehicle for the company's products and, with its year-long utility, brought continuing goodwill to the company from its rural customers.

The magazine differed from the early newspaper in that it was set up more in book format, the content was less tied to current events, and the writing was more sophisticated. Today these same characteristics place magazines somewhere between newspapers and books, a gap-filling role that is well suited to the periodical in its special role of appearing weekly or monthly.

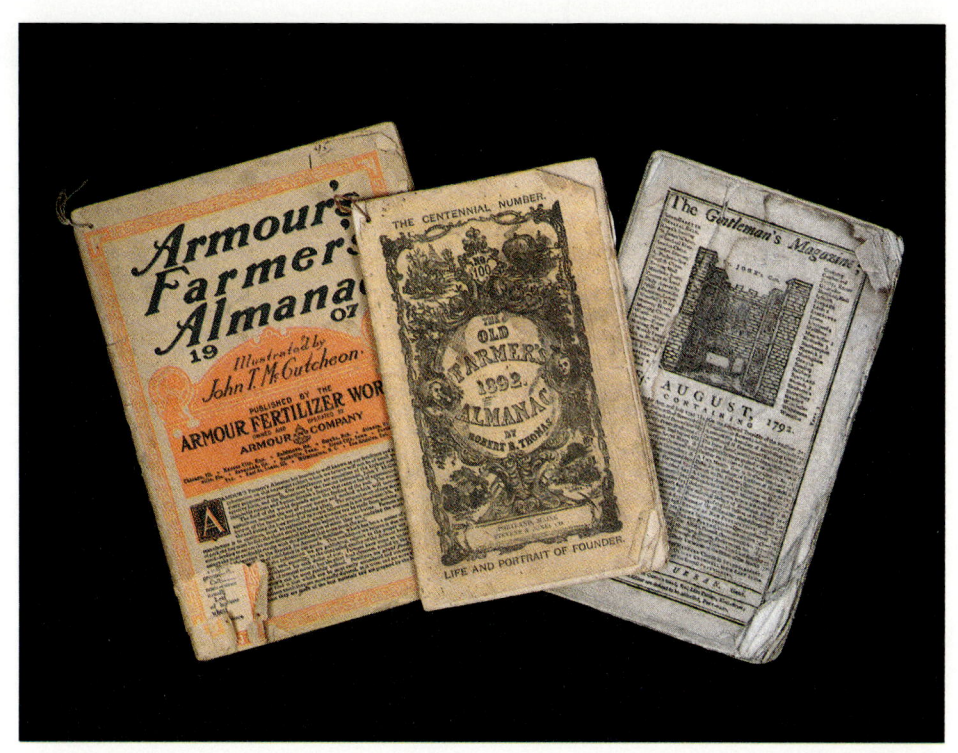

The almanac was a popular hybrid form of magazine at the turn of the century, mingling data, predictions, planting tables, recipes, and short articles together in a storehouse of information. The almanacs were similar in size and format to *The Gentleman's Magazine* which appeared in England in the early 1700s.

Providing Food for Thought

Early magazines were book-sized, approximately six inches wide by nine inches tall, because the publishers printed them on book presses, using the same full-width single column or half-width double-column format as books. Eventually, however, printers tried new styles, and the size of the magazine page grew from being twice as big as book pages to nearly as large as tabloid newspapers.

Magazines have always had a more "experimental" quality than either newspapers or books. From colonial times until the present, editors and publishers have continually tried new concepts or gimmicks for fresh and exciting ways of writing and displaying information to attract audiences. In the late 1800s, for example, *Peterson's Magazine* for women included fashion plates—large fold-out illustrations of the latest dresses and gowns, each individually hand-tinted to add a splash of color to the black-and-white publication. The practice is outmoded, but the term *fashion plate* endures as an expression meaning one who wears the latest styles.

Most of the magazines founded in colonial times lasted only a few issues or a few months. It was the mid-1800s before readers could select from several magazines with proven records. Many of the most popular magazines in the middle of the nineteenth century could be classified as "literary" periodicals: *Harper's Monthly*, *The Atlantic Monthly*, *Century*, and *Scribner's*. In fact, the more successful magazines were published by book companies that used the periodicals to build interest in their forthcoming books by printing excerpts and carrying advertise-

TIME CAPSULE

Magazines

1704	First English-language magazines published in England.
1731	*The Gentleman's Magazine* in England is first to use name "magazine."
1741	First magazines published in America, including one by Ben Franklin.
1821	*Saturday Evening Post* founded.
1830	First women's magazine: *Godey's Lady's Book*.
1850	*Harper's Monthly* founded; other Harper's magazines follow.
1893	*McClure's* and *Munsey's* are the first popular, inexpensive monthlys.
1903	Beginning of the muckraking period.
1903	*Ladies' Home Journal* is first magazine to reach one million in circulation.
1922	*Reader's Digest* founded.
1923	*Time* founded by Henry Luce: first newsmagazine.
1936	*Life* is first picture magazine.
1945	*Ebony* founded to cater to black audience.
1948	*TV Guide* founded.
1953	Hugh Hefner's *Playboy* begins era of the special-interest magazine.
1954	*Sports Illustrated* broadens the concept of the special-interest magazine.
1967	*Rolling Stone* is the first magazine catering to "counterculture" audience.
1969	Television kills *The Saturday Evening Post* and other mass magazines.
1972	*Ms.* becomes first of many new magazines catering to professional women.
1974	*People* magazine is first television-era fan magazine.

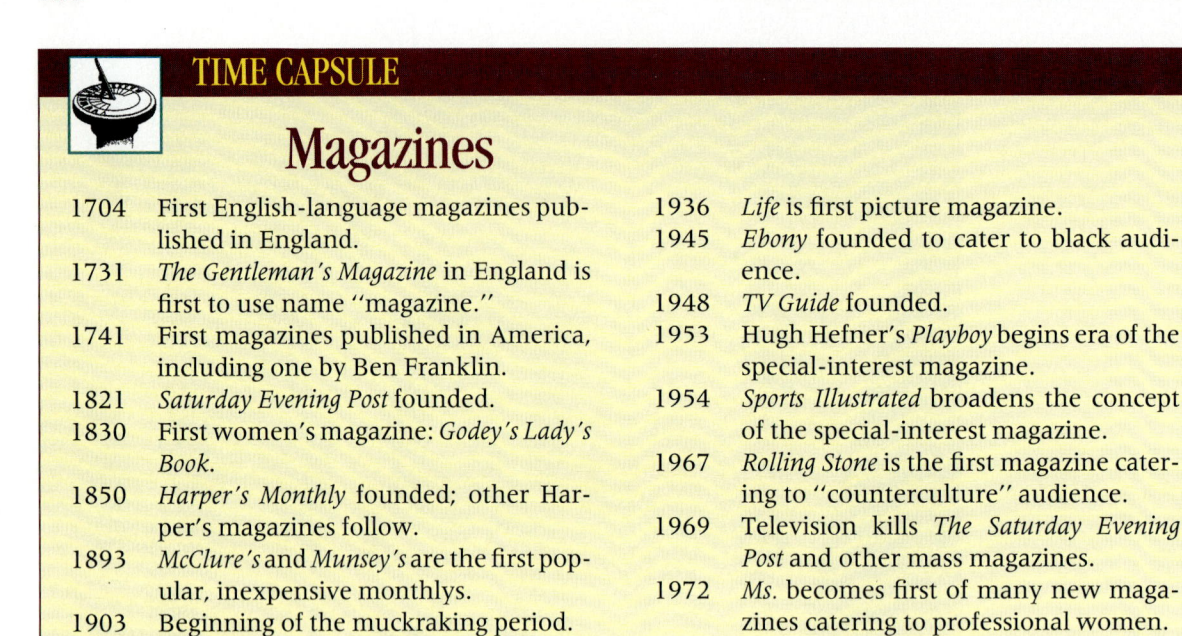

ments for the new titles. Charles Dickens's books, for example, were serialized and appeared in Harper's. The link between quality magazines and book publishing was much stronger and more direct than it is today.

Beginnings of the Mass Audience Magazine

The muckraking popularized by newspapers toward the end of the century also appeared in the large-circulation magazines of the time. Because magazines enjoyed national distribution, they had more impact than newspapers that served only one city. The magazine format, with fewer articles than a newspaper and more pages for each topic, also lent itself to fuller treatment of exposés of government and business wrongdoings, complete with illustrations—at first cartoons and drawings, and eventually photographs—that helped tell the stories in dramatic new ways.

Although *The Saturday Evening Post* liked to trace its history way back to Benjamin Franklin, the truly mass-appeal version of that magazine was developed in the late nineteenth century by its publisher, the Curtis Publishing Company, and flourished until the middle of the twentieth century. The formula developed by *Post* editors served as a model for *Colliers*, *McClure's*, and dozens of imitators: entertainment that included adventure fiction, travel pieces, biographical features about celebrated figures, humor, pictorial essays, and human interest stories. Occasionally they included investigative stories that "blew the lid" off scandals in

Washington and other capitals. Writing was simple and direct, always using vocabulary easily understood by the average citizen. By catering to the lowest common denominator, magazine publishers found they could sell a million or more copies. Consequently they could provide a truly national advertising medium. The resulting financial support enabled publishers to keep the price of their colorful and splashily illustrated magazines very low.

The Saturday Evening Post was a true family magazine. The writing level and line-drawing illustrations made the content accessible to anyone who was literate. More important, the mix of articles appealed to various tastes: They included fact and fiction, humorous articles to balance the "serious" pieces about government or science, and lots of profiles of movie stars, sports heroes, historical figures, and world leaders. Above all, the magazine with the homespun Norman Rockwell covers and the cartoon featuring saucy and wise "Hazel" (the maid near the last page of each issue) was consistently wholesome, informative, and lively—something to curl up with on Saturday night before television was introduced.

While *The Saturday Evening Post* provided plenty of good reading in the pre-television era, it also was a "quick read." Readers could browse through it quickly because the cartoons and the simple layout kept the eye intrigued. This "quick read" formula was further refined when *Life* magazine appeared in 1936, and later *Look* magazine. The line drawings of the earlier magazines were replaced by emotion-provoking pictures taken by the leading photographers of the day and accompanied by punchy captions and cutlines—the line or paragraph of explanation below a photo. *Life*'s articles were short and easy to read, but it was the impact of the stunning photo layouts that attracted the audience.

The general-interest magazines were the leading national advertising vehicle of their day. Soaps, toothpaste, kitchen appliances, cigarettes, automobiles, and eventually alcoholic beverages were the source of huge advertising revenues. Since each copy of *Life, Look,* and *The Saturday Evening Post* was read by several people (that is, they had what magazine publishers call a high pass-along rate), the advertised products had to appeal to almost everybody to make the magazine an efficient advertising vehicle. Ironically, when the first advertisements for home television sets appeared in the mass circulation magazines in the early 1950s, it marked the beginning of the end of the era of general-interest periodicals.

One of the few general-interest magazines to endure today is the *Reader's Digest.* Begun in 1922 by DeWitt and Lila Wallace, originally it merely condensed and reprinted articles from other magazines in a readable format void of interruptions by illustrations or other graphic elements. Today it mixes original articles with reprints, plus departments featuring inspirational ideas, slices of life, and down-home humor. Articles on health and marital relations frequently are bannered on the promotional stickers added to the covers to boost sales at the supermarket checkout counter.

Time Begets the Modern Newsweekly

When *Time* magazine appeared in 1923, it was not the first periodical to present the news of the week accompanied by illustrations and commentary; *Harper's Weekly* had done it half a century earlier, and the *Literary Digest* flourished as the leading news magazine of the early twentieth century.

Nevertheless, the birth of *Time* can be looked on as an important turning point in magazine history. Its innovative techniques became the benchmark for the modern newsweekly, a magazine dedicated to summarizing the week's news in capsule form, categorizing it to fit in departments such as "The Nation" and "The World," and accompanying it with sidebars—shorter pieces that provide background context or commentary. *Time* summarized the main points in a story with brevity, a service to busy readers that was further refined six decades later by Gannett's *USA Today*.

Henry Luce, cofounder of *Time* with Briton Hadden, stamped his personal style on the magazine: breezy, pushy, irreverent, and even smart-alecky. Luce encouraged his writers and editors to coin their own phrases (such as the pejorative "nonbook" noted in the chapter on books). His magazine was presumptuous enough to select its "Man of the Year" for the first issue every January and promote the choice as if the Nobel Prize had been awarded. The slogan of *Time* for many years was "Curt, Concise, Complete." Magazine historian Frank Luther Mott attributes the success of the new venture to its ability to deliver on that promise.[1]

Since World War II, *Time* has had a fiercely competitive relationship with *Newsweek*. Like the attempts for many years of Ford to compete with General Motors by offering "me-too" products, *Newsweek* often appears to be imitating *Time*, and *Time* responds by making sure that it does not miss anything *Newsweek* contains. The third magazine in the field, *U.S. News and World Report*, like Chrysler among the auto makers, is left to work different territory. *U.S. News* offers longer articles focusing on government, economics, and society, leaving the more frivolous pieces on entertainment, sports, and life-styles to the Big Two.

The Impact of Television on Magazines

When television appeared on the market in the late 1940s and found a place in almost every American home in the 1950s, magazine publishers suddenly realized that the formidable new competitor was drawing advertising dollars away from the other national media. After all, television gave advertisers the ability to *demonstrate* their products rather than merely show them or talk about them. The new medium also provided entertainment that was easy for the consumer to use: All you had to do was sit back and watch and listen—no need to turn pages, read . . . or think!

Advertisers of soaps, cigarettes, food products, automobiles, and beer virtually abandoned the general-interest magazines such as *Life*, *Look*, and *The Saturday Evening Post*, sounding their death knell, even though they hung on until the 1960s. Only special-interest magazines that targeted affluent consumers with advertising particularly of interest to them survived the advent of television.

Of course, one magazine profited immensely from the advent of television. *TV Guide* was founded in 1948 to carry program listings, a job it does so well and in such convenient format that the magazine survives today even though newspapers have imitated the listing format in supplements to their Sunday editions. Articles featured on the cover, the handy digest-sized format, and the ease of picking up a copy at the supermarket checkout are reasons for the longevity of *TV Guide*.

INSIGHT

Magazines Provide Three Services

Magazine historian Frank Luther Mott believed that magazines perform three basic services to society:

"They provide a democratic literature which is sometimes of high quality." Mott acknowledged that, in catering to popular tastes, magazines often provide frivolous fare, but that is balanced by the fact that most serious authors at one time or another have contributed to magazines because of their wide audience and undisputed impact.

"The magazine has played an important part in the economics of literature." That role is somewhat diminished contrasted with a century ago, but magazines still provoke interest in serious reading when they print excerpts from forthcoming books.

"Periodical files furnish an invaluable contemporaneous history of their times." By way of proof, the reference rooms of most libraries give prominence to the *Readers' Guide to Periodical Literature*, and it is there that many scholars begin their inquiry into research topics.

Beginning his five-volume history of magazines, Mott observes that no less a personage than George Washington reputedly wrote the editor of a magazine about his product: "I consider such easy vehicles of knowledge as more highly calculated than any other to preserve the liberty, stimulate the industry, and meliorate the morals of an enlightened free people."

Source: Frank Luther Mott, *A History of American Magazines*, vol. 1 (Cambridge: Harvard University Press, 1968), pp. 1–3.

MAGAZINE PUBLISHING: MATCHING TODAY'S LIFE-STYLES

As we have seen with books and newspapers, publishers have to understand and cater to America's ever-changing life-styles if they wish to survive. Magazine publishers now realize they must do more than merely bow to taste: They must "embody" the life-style of a very specific reader. They must be at, or preferably just a step ahead of, the current interests, ideas, and identifications of their very specific audience member—a person who belongs to as small a segment of society as a few hundred thousand people.

Special-Interest Magazines Target Audiences for Advertisers

Time magazine editor Henry A. Grunwald noted:

> The national audience is becoming more fragmented. . . . Nike now makes more than one hundred styles of running shoes. Nationally advertised brands of beer have increased from 76 to 176 in seven years. In the same period, the number of new products of all kinds has nearly doubled. The total number of magazines has increased as well. . . . Special interest magazines are sprouting everywhere.[2]

In other words, increasingly specialized products require increasingly specialized marketing, and magazines that find their "niche" will attract ads.

The shift from general-interest to special-interest magazines began with the television era. When *Life* ceased publication as a weekly in 1972, its parent company, Time, Inc., well understood that the magazine business was changing profoundly. It had already introduced *Sports Illustrated*, which not only narrowed its area of coverage to sports, but did it in a manner that interested "upscale" readers, not the beer-drinkers in the corner bar who were watching wrestling on TV.

Another successful Time, Inc. magazine, *Money*, doesn't aim at the readers of *Fortune*, *Forbes*, or *Business Week*. It speaks to professional people who may not understand economics or big business, but who need and use the nuts-and-bolts investment, saving, and consumer tips that the magazine presents in clear language with easy-to-understand examples using real people's finances to illustrate the points.

In the 1980s, Time, Inc. spent tens of millions of dollars to market-test specialized magazines. *Picture Week*, which could not find a niche that differentiated it from *People* magazine, was folded, as was *TV-Cable Week*. Other titles developed successfully by Time, Inc. show just how narrow the focus must be to convince advertisers they are getting a specific target audience: *Real Estate*, *Home Office*, *Cooking Light*, *Women's Sports & Fitness*, *Southern Living*, *Leisure*, and *Parenting*.

The first major magazine launch of the 1990s was *Entertainment Weekly*, published by the conglomerate formed when Time, Inc. and Warner merged to form Time Warner. *Entertainment Weekly* was conceived as a consumer's guide to television, movies, video, music, and books for the affluent "yuppies," or young urban professionals. Discount and gift promotions helped the magazine find 600,000 subscribers in the first few months, but advertising agencies warned the advertisers that the magazine would have a difficult time holding its target audience. That was because several less expensive local magazine and newspaper sections already were serving the special needs of those seeking reviews and previews of entertainment fare.[3] After extensive redesigning in the first year, the magazine managed to survive.

In a special report on the effect of the "baby boom" generation on magazines, *Advertising Age* suggested that *Bride's* magazine is the ultimate special-interest publication: "The typical reader is intensely interested in the magazine for the six months or year before her wedding, but she rapidly loses interest afterwards and is replaced by someone from the next batch of brides to be."[4] Actually, mothers who have more than one daughter and who are interested far before and long after a particular wedding account for subscriptions that are renewed year after year.

Young adults who are beginning their careers and establishing their households seek information on the proper ways to set and achieve their goals. They find the formulas in such magazines as *Gentlemen's Quarterly*, *Glamour*, *Architectural Digest*, *Working Woman*, *Self*, *Savvy*, *Bon Appetit*, and *House and Garden*. (Some of these magazines, of course, hold their readers well into middle age and beyond.)

Does Your Magazine Know Who You Are?

One of the biggest leaps toward segmented marketing of a magazine came with *Playboy*'s introduction in 1952. Both advertising and editorial content were aimed at one gender and age segment—men 18 to 30 years old—and a higher-than-average level of education and potential income. The venture was hugely successful, generating a business empire as well as inspiring imitators.

TABLE 8.1 The Top 25 Magazines by Circulation

Rank	Publication	Circulation	Percentage Change
1	Modern Maturity	22,450,000	0.0
2	Reader's Digest	16,306,007	(0.6)
3	TV Guide	15,353,982	(3.1)
4	National Geographic	9,921,479	(2.6)
5	Better Homes & Gardens	8,003,263	0.0
6	Family Circle	5,151,534	(0.2)
7	Good Housekeeping	5,028,151	(1.5)
8	McCall's	5,009,358	0.0
9	Ladies' Home Journal	5,002,900	(0.4)
10	Woman's Day	4,751,977	3.2
11	Time	4,248,565	(0.2)
12	Redbook	3,841,866	(2.7)
13	National Enquirer	3,706,030	(7.8)
14	Playboy	3,498,802	1.8
15	Sports Illustrated	3,444,188	(1.8)
16	Newsweek	3,420,167	6.0
17	People	3,235,120	1.9
18	Star	3,207,951	(11.3)
19	Prevention	3,109,562	2.8
20	American Legion Magazine	2,984,389	4.4
21	Cosmopolitan	2,679,356	(1.3)
22	AAA World	2,630,944	6.4
23	Scholastic Teen Network	2,591,130	(4.4)
24	First for Women	2,393,722	(13.4)
25	Southern Living	2,385,058	3.9

Note: Figures in parentheses indicate a circulation loss.
Modern Maturity, the top-circulating magazine, goes to all members of the American Association of Retired Persons. Fourth-place *National Geographic* and *The American Legion Magazine* are also membership publications. *National Enquirer* and *Star* are supermarket tabloids categorized as magazines. *Reader's Digest* and *TV Guide* are both special-format publications. Thus the field of women's interests may be considered the largest "conventional" magazine market. Audit Bureau of Circulation figures are for the first half of 1991, compared with the same period in the preceding year. Note that 80 percent of the top magazines dropped in circulation during that period.

In 1985, *Games* magazine, another property of Playboy Enterprises, made another huge leap toward tailoring the publication to the individual. Each of the magazine's more than half-million subscribers found his or her name printed on the front cover of the initial issue. A Chevrolet advertisement inside was similarly personalized. The same issue had a 32-page catalog insert in copies going to people known to have ordered frequently from catalogs before, and abbreviated 16-page catalogs to "sometimes" catalog buyers. The computerized method of targeting subaudiences within the readership of a single magazine is called Selectronics and was introduced by the R. R. Donnelly Company, a major printer.[5]

Selective binding—inserting certain material only in copies of a publication going to a target population—makes possible ads tailored to individuals. Information obtained at the time you subscribe and other data available from research firms and your credit card company enable a magazine distributor's computer to identify you by age, income, sex, occupation, interests, and purchase patterns. That means the copy of *Newsweek* you get at school could be quite different from the one your

> **INDUSTRY**
>
> ## *Newsweek* Tailors Issue for Specific Consumers
>
> Selective binding—including special supplements in some, but not all, issues of a magazine—has been in use for a decade. Special-interest magazines such as *Farm Journal*, *Modern Maturity*, and *Smithsonian* have used the device, mainly for special supplements sponsored by advertisers.
>
> Beginning in 1992, *Newsweek* is offering subscribers the option of paying $5 more a year for an advertising-free supplement each month. The consumer may choose a nonfiction book excerpt, expanded international coverage, a section on money management, or science news—whatever the reader's interest is. As the individual consumer's copy of the magazine comes off the press and before it is stapled together, a scanner reads the address label and know whether to drop a supplement into that issue.
>
> If the concept works for *Newsweek*, "custom" editions of magazines may become commonplace in the near future.
>
> *Source:* Deirdre Carmody, "Special Newsweek Editions Will Be Sold to Subscribers," *The New York Times*, Dec. 13, 1991, p. D-1.

parents get at home. The selection process for big magazines may be limited to identifying ZIP codes where affluent people live. But more specialized magazines have used this device: in *American Baby* magazine, a Gerber baby food ad began "Hello, Mrs.———" and greeted the subscriber by name.[6]

Categorizing Magazines

Just to get a better understanding of how specialized magazine publishing has become, let's look at some of the major categories of publication:

Association, club, and fraternal—These include magazines such as *Kiwanis* and *The American Legion Magazine* that go automatically to all members of an organization as one of the benefits of belonging to the group.

Business and financial—National publications fall into this category, such as *Forbes* and *Fortune*, and regional ones like *California Business*.

Children's—They range from *Children's Playmate* for the very young, to *Ranger Rick's Nature Magazine* for children in the 5 to 10 age group, to *Discoveries* for a still older child.

College, university, and alumni—Each institution has at least one; major institutions may publish a separate monthly or quarterly for each college and division.

Ethnic and religious—*Ebony* aims at blacks, *The American Zionist* covers politics in Israel and the Middle East, and *The Christian Athlete* is published by the Fellowship of Christian Athletes.

Health—*Men's Fitness*, *In Health* (formerly *Hippocrates*), and *Prevention* are examples. The first focuses on exercise workouts and diet for a young male audience, the other two on healthier life-styles for families.

Chapter 8 Magazines **215**

MINORITIES/WOMEN

Black Publisher's Empire Thrives

While other magazines experience declining circulation (see Table 8.1) *Ebony* grew from 1.3 million copies in 1980 to nearly 2 million in 1990. John H. Johnson—the owner of *Jet* and *EM*, a monthly for black men, as well as *Ebony*—owns the second-largest black business in the United States, the Johnson Publishing Company. He came to Chicago in 1942 with a $500 loan from his mother in Arkansas and built a publishing company that today is worth a quarter-billion dollars. Johnson credits his magazines not only with showing that minorities can be successful entrepreneurs, but also with changing racial attitudes by depicting blacks in a positive light.

Hobby and craft—They are as diverse as *American Antiques, Model Railroader,* and *Scott's Monthly Stamp Journal.*

Home and garden—Familiar titles include *House Beautiful* and *House and Garden,* but there are more esoteric periodicals such as *House Plants and Porch Gardens.*

In-Flight—Seat-back-pocket magazines like *The American Way* and *TWA Ambassador* keep a passenger's mind off delays and bumpy landings.

The newsroom of the *Hollywood Reporter* is a bustling place.

Literary—Antioch Review, *Black Scholar*, and *Kansas Quarterly* are examples.

Men's—Esquire, *GQ*, *Playboy*, and dozens of imitators cover fashion, sports, ethics, cars, careers, and relations with the opposite sex.

Women's—Seventeen aims at older girls, *Mademoiselle* and *Cosmopolitan* focus more on the concerns of the young as they complete their education and begin a career, *Redbook* addresses the young mother, and *McCall's* is meant for the older woman who may work inside or outside her house. Among the many other women's magazines are *Lear's, Ms., Working Woman,* and *Mirabella*.

Other specialized magazine categories include art, automotive, aviation, confessions, consumer, detective, food and drink, history, humor, military, music, photography, politics, regional, retirement, science, science fiction, sport and outdoor, teen, theater, and trade union. And, of course, categories are arbitrary. *Rolling Stone* could be categorized as a young adult magazine or a music publication, but its advertising suggests that it defies attempts to fit in neatly with a single age group or life-style.

Trade Magazines

Most of the magazines in the preceding categories are considered "consumer" magazines, meaning that individuals subscribe for their own reasons, using their own money. An entirely different category is "trade" magazines, to which business people subscribe in order to keep up with their field or profession. Often these magazines are delivered to the workplace, and the subscriptions to them are paid for by the subscriber's employer. Whereas publishers of consumer magazines usually try to keep the subscription price under $25 for a monthly and under $50 for a weekly, trade magazine publishers may charge between $50 and $250 per subscription. Companies are willing to pay that much to put up-to-date, specialized knowledge in the hands of their managers.

Examples of specialized trade magazines include

Advertising Age, for those in the advertising and marketing industry

Video Business, for operators of video stores

INSIGHT

Perception versus Reality

Many magazines decide to aim consistently at one age group, knowing that consumers who *grow out* of the publication will be replaced by those who *grow in*. *Rolling Stone* magazine grew with its audience, changing from a 1960s counterculture publication to a more mainstream magazine interested in music, politics, and popular culture. The problem is that advertisers don't always know the difference. *Rolling Stone* was unlikely to attract advertisers for cars, liquors, and clothes intended for people over 25 unless it could convince those advertisers that its audience was growing more mature . . . and affluent. The "Perception/Reality" advertising campaign run in trade publications brilliantly explained, mostly in visual terms, how the producers and the consumers had changed together.

Chapter 8   Magazines

John Lennon November 9, 1967	Tiny Tim July 6, 1968	The Beatles October 26, 1968	Elvis Presley July 12, 1969	Woodstock September 20, 1969	Kent State June 11, 1970
Muhammad Ali March 18, 1971	The Beach Boys October 28, 1971	Jane Fonda May 25, 1972	Mick Jagger July 6, 1972	Richard Nixon September 27, 1973	Prisoners of War March 28, 1974
Evel Knievel November 7, 1974	Led Zeppelin March 13, 1975	David Bowie February 12, 1976	Star Wars August 25, 1977	The Sex Pistols October 20, 1977	Bob Dylan January 26, 1978
The Blues Brothers February 22, 1979	Bette Midler December 13, 1979	John Lennon, Yoko Ono January 22, 1981	E.T. July 22, 1982	Eddie Murphy July 7, 1983	MTV December 8, 1983
Bruce Springsteen December 6, 1984	David Lee Roth April 11, 1985	Live Aid August 15, 1985	Rock and Roll Hall of Fame February 13, 1986	Madonna June 5, 1986	Pee-wee Herman February 12, 1987

Rolling Stone reached its twenty-fifth anniversary milestone because, unlike other magazines oriented to music and politics, it "grew with its audience" over the years, reflecting changing tastes and attitudes.

Farm Futures Magazine, for those interested in the financial aspects of "agri-business"

Auto Laundry News, for carwash operators

Christian Bookseller, for owners of religious bookstores

American Glass Review, for manufacturers, fabricators, and distributors of glass and glass products

Apparel Industry Magazine, for executives in the clothing business who are interested in equipment, government regulation, training, and management

Microwaves, for microwave engineers and engineering managers

Hardware Age, designed for manufacturers, wholesalers, and retailers

Seeking the College Audience

During the 1960s and 1970s, several publishers, convinced that there was a market for information tailored to the interests of young consumers, launched magazines aimed primarily at college students. Most failed because they could not identify the advertisers who want to reach college students.

Eventually magazine publishers, many of them young entrepreneurs, discovered which advertisers do want to reach college students. Certain advertisers, such as credit cards, beverages, automobiles, and computers, are willing to pay a premium to reach college students because they want to influence buying or career patterns that may last a lifetime. The publishers also learned that the key was not subscriptions. Instead, they developed free magazine inserts distributed in campus newspapers or directly to campus living units. *Newsweek on Campus* and *Business Week Careers* were examples of special editions that acquainted collegians with publications to which (it was hoped) they would eventually subscribe. *Campus Voice* (formerly *Nutshell*) and *Dorm* focused on campus life-styles, and *Ampersand's Guide to College Entertainment* looked at music and movies.

It has been calculated that the seven million full-time undergraduate college students in the United States have about $11 billion available for "discretionary spending"—far too big a market for advertisers to ignore.[7] But habits, interests, and life-styles of college students change faster than those of any other consumer group. Magazine publishers so far have found the college student to be the most elusive consumer in the marketplace.

Targeting Women

Magazines aimed exclusively at women have been around for over a century. Until recently, however, it was assumed that a woman's magazine targeted the mother at home, whose responsibilities were child-rearing, preparation of meals, and anchoring family life. An exception is the fashion magazine aimed at the sophisticated urban woman.

Women's magazines introduced in the 1970s and 1980s focus on the professional whose concerns include looking good on the job, competing with men for career advancement, and filling the dual role of mother and income-provider. The names of magazines catering to these women reflect the life-styles of the readers: *Ms., Self, Savvy,* and *Working Woman.*

Most of the "old-line" women's magazines have circulations of more than five million. Advertisers of food, appliances, and cleaning products seek this mar-

INDUSTRY

Profile of the Audience for Magazines

- Magazines are read by 9 out of 10 adults each month, and each reader reported sees an average of 9 different copies of magazines each month. The average magazine copy is read for 62 minutes by 4.26 different readers. Each reader is exposed to 89 percent of the advertising pages. (Source: *Magazine Newsletter of Research*, published by the Magazine Publishers Association, 1989.)

- Magazines fit readers' profiles (except for men who did not graduate from high school) better than any other medium. Audience members tend to be in more thoughtful and information-seeking moods when reading magazines than when attending to any other mass medium. (Source: Opinion Research Corporation students conducted for the Magazine Publishers Association, 1990.)

- Women spend more time looking at individual copies of magazines than do men. (Source: Audit & Surveys, Inc., study for the Magazine Publishers Association, 1990.)

- The thicker the magazine, the greater the number of newsstand buyers—"because readers believe they are getting more of what they pay for," reports the president of Condé Nast magazines after reviewing the research. (Source: *The Wall Street Journal*, 1990.)

ket. Most of the newer magazines aimed at careerists have circulations of between half a million and one million, and their ads are more likely to be for cigarettes, liquors, cars, and products aimed also at successful men, as well as feminine hygiene and beauty products.

Another type of magazine emerging in the 1990s is represented by *Lear's* and *Mirabella*. These periodicals aim to interest older and mid-career women who identify with neither the homemakers who read the traditional women's magazines nor with the newer publications mentioned earlier. Advertisers' and publishers' assumptions about the women's market are gradually shifting as women's interests and spending habits change.

TECHNOLOGY

Computer Service Claims to Be a "Magazine"

Prodigy—the advertising-supported computer service developed by IBM and marketed by Sears, Roebuck & Co.—requested validation of its "circulation" by the same company that monitors magazines, the Audit Bureau of Circulation. Prodigy even asked the bureau to reclassify the computer service as a magazine.

"We are a magazine, only we don't have paper," said Prodigy's marketing manager. He contended that the computer service competes for the same advertisers as print magazines and needs to document its penetration of the same market.

Source: Bradley Johnson, "Prodigy 'Magazine'?" *Advertising Age*, Nov. 11, 1991, p. 2.

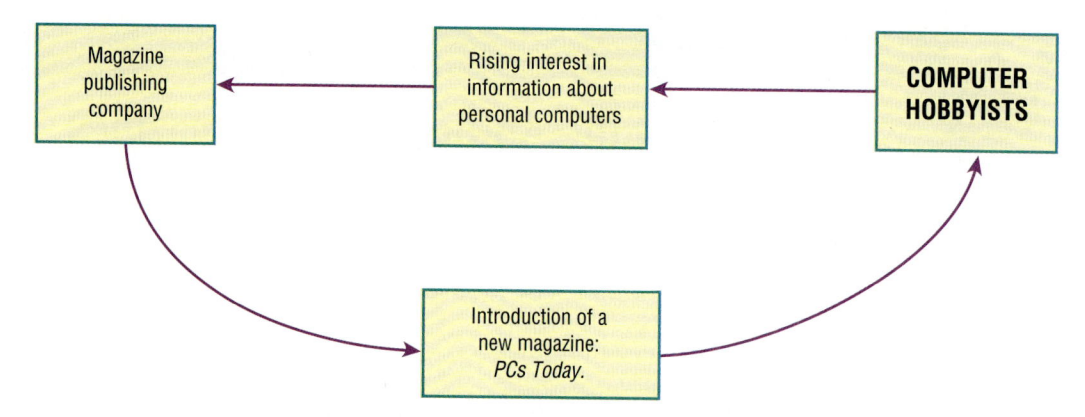

FIGURE 8.1 Consumer Interests Lead to Creation of a New Magazine Note the direction of the arrows. A magazine publishing company that publishes a magazine with a column or department about personal computers notes increased interest from readers, along with increased requests from advertisers who want their ads to appear near that column or department. This signals the publisher to develop a magazine that meets the increased specialized needs of the readers and advertisers.

Creating a New Magazine

Despite the difficulty of correctly identifying an audience and designing a publication that meets its needs, new magazine "launches" are happening virtually every week. Some are created from scratch, but many evolve from other publications. Figure 8.1 uses the P↔I↔C model in an interesting way to show the creation of a new publication out of features of an existing magazine in response to consumer interest.

ENSURING THE FUTURE OF THE MAGAZINE

Because the mass media depend on advertising revenue to make a profit, they must engage in continuous and sophisticated audience research. They need to know who the audience members are, when they use the media, what messages attract their attention, and *why* they make those choices.

Since magazines are so carefully targeted to specialized segments of the mass audience, it is not surprising that magazines are one of the most extensively researched media. The clearinghouse for information is the Magazine Publishers Association (MPA), which cites studies by Opinion Research Corp. and other testing agencies to make the claim that 37 percent of adults feel magazines are the medium that best fits their life-styles—that is, their consumer needs—contrasted with 33 percent for television and 20 percent for newspapers.[8]

Owners of all media are concerned with the "demographics" of their medium, meaning the characteristics of audience members such as age, education, sex, income, type of household, geographic location, and other factors that can be measured using census-type data. Magazine publishers go even further than other media, using research that attempts to measure the values and life-styles of their readers—VALS for short, also referred to as "psychographics." This approach to enhanced demographics takes all of the available data about buying habits and other characteristics of the mass audience into its computers and matches it with the content and circulation data about various magazines. What emerges is a profile of "what kind of people use what kind of media, and why."[9]

Various research organizations have developed different labels for categories of audience members, such as *achievers* (those who set high goals for themselves and are primarily concerned about success in their careers), *belongers* (those whose values and concerns relate to the interest of the groups they join, including school, church, and profession), and *narcissistics* (young, impulsive, individualistic, self-centered people whom one firm characterizes with the phrase "I-Am-Me"). (The categories are arbitrary, and many individuals may fall into more than one category.)

According to VALS research, certain of these groups are more likely to rent a car, buy film, or take an air trip. Members of some groups are heavy users of shampoo and hair conditioners. One research firm has found that *survivors* (poor, depressed, out of the cultural mainstream) are the heaviest viewers of television, and the *societally conscious* group constitutes the lightest viewers of television. *Belongers* and *achievers* are thought to be the largest categories of regular magazine consumers. The MPA contends that VALS research shows magazines to be the medium that can attract the readers who are the most likely to spend money on what advertisers want to sell.

Reader Loyalty Concerns Magazines

All the media try to convince advertisers that a large audience is reading, watching, or listening to their products. Magazines additionally must convince advertisers that the audience is loyal, meaning that the readers pay attention to the product because it is an integral part of their life.

Some magazines point to the fact that most of their circulation is in newsstand sales, which means that the reader makes a choice each week or month to buy the magazine. Others point to their renewal rates as proof that readers want to continue reading the magazine. Many magazines strive for a balance of newsstand sales and subscriptions. Magazines that succeed in attracting the loyalty of readers are said to be "hot" because they have created a very specific "environment"—an aura or feeling with which the reader identifies.

The environment of *GQ* (short for *Gentlemen's Quarterly*) became hot because the perception of advertisers was that the editors and readers alike were hip, tuned in, eager to succeed, and, most important of all, willing to spend whatever is necessary to look good. Conversely, the *Reader's Digest*, with over 17 million circulation and estimated annual profits of $100 million, must spend millions each year promoting itself to advertisers who view the magazine as stodgy and undynamic. One advertising agency head suggested that *Reader's Digest* continues to exist because it is an American institution and people subscribe out of habit, not because advertisers are enthusiastic about its environment.

Many magazines are shared or seen by multiple readers—the pass-along rate. Two to three readers per copy is about standard for magazines like *Time*. Some very personal magazines are seen mainly by the purchaser, such as *Playboy*. Magazines commonly found in waiting rooms at beauty shops and doctors' offices, like *People*, may have an exposure rate far higher than the average. Some magazines have tried basing advertising rates on actual size of audience, which takes into account the pass-along rate.[10] But advertisers appear more comfortable with rates based on circulation, assuming that at least one person reads each copy in some depth.

"What kind of man reads *Playboy*?" asks the house ad in each issue. "She's the Cosmo girl" say the trade ads for *Cosmopolitan*. In each case, the people described in the promotional copy are idealized. The actual consumer of the magazine is less affluent, less glamorous, and less successful, but the advertisers hope the reader will see their products or services as the key to becoming the ideal person. In the well-aimed specialized magazine, the reader may not even make a distinction between the advertisements and the editorial material—all are part of the same well-focused information package.

Shifting Economic Realities

Anyone concerned about inflation and the upward creep of prices should consider the American magazine. In the past decade, as paper costs rose and as magazines grew thicker than ever with full-color information, the subscription price of most magazines has remained steady or lower than in the past.

Consider *GQ*, which is popular with men college age and up who are, or will be, affluent enough to afford most consumer products. Buy all 12 copies on the newsstand at $3 each and the annual cost is $36. But a subscription is just $19.97, which comes to $1.66 a copy. Given the number of pages, often over 400, that's a better bargain than *USA Today*, at 50 cents for a few dozen pages.

The trend for magazines aimed at the truly affluent—those who travel frequently and purchase big-ticket luxury items—is toward free distribution. Publishers guarantee advertisers "full penetration" of affluent neighborhoods, all the holders of a premium credit card, or groups identified by profession. Whittle Communication places half a dozen slick magazines exclusively in selected doctors' offices at no cost to the reader or the doctor—advertisers foot the bill.

Publishers of paid-circulation magazines contend that "free" publications don't have the loyalty or generate the interest advertisers want. The free magazines, on the other hand, don't have to waste money building circulation through promotions and advertising campaigns; they merely target the audience they think advertisers want to reach.

One of the continuing controversies in the magazine publishing business concerns the debate over whether newsstand sales are preferable to subscriptions. The pro-newsstand argument says that when consumers show interest in a magazine by going to the newsstand each week or month and spending their money, advertisers know the readers are interested in the issue and are likely to look at the ads. But according to the pro-subscription reasoning, when consumers want a magazine badly enough to subscribe, advertisers know that the readers are loyal to the magazine, and loyal readers are more likely to pay attention to the ads. Analyzing the subscription versus newsstand ratio of the top magazines doesn't prove the superiority of one point of view. Magazines depending almost entirely on newsstand sales include *Woman's Day, Cosmopolitan,* and *Penthouse*. Magazines whose readers mainly subscribe include *Reader's Digest, Ladies' Home Journal,* and *Good Housekeeping*. *Playboy*, unlike rival *Penthouse*, gets only a quarter of its circulation from newsstand sales. *TV Guide's* sales are fairly evenly balanced.[11]

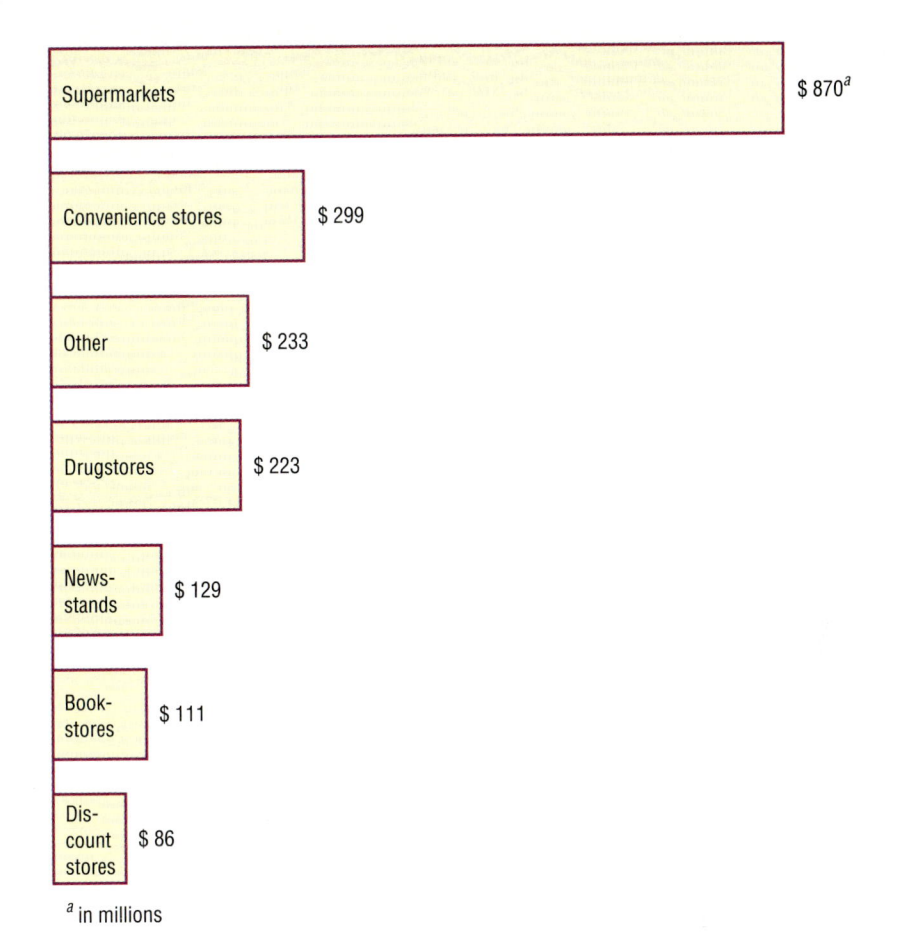

Outlet	Sales
Supermarkets	$870[a]
Convenience stores	$299
Other	$233
Drugstores	$223
Newsstands	$129
Bookstores	$111
Discount stores	$86

[a] in millions

FIGURE 8.2 **Where Magazines Are Sold** The decline of the newsstand as an outlet for magazines can be seen in these 1989 magazines sales figures from the Periodicals Institute. Nearly half of the single-copy sales occur in supermarkets. Convenience stores and bookstores also account for many sales. Wholesalers today carry as many as 3000 magazine titles, but most retailers have limited space and carry only the magazines that are most in demand. Only about half the copies on display are sold; the rest are returned to wholesalers for credit. (Source: Deirdre Carmody, "Newsstands Dwindle, But Some Still Thrive," *The New York Times*, October 29, 1990.)

Controlled Circulation Accounts for Success

For nearly two decades *Reader's Digest* had the largest circulation of any magazine in the United States. During the 1980s, *Reader's Digest* and *TV Guide* were neck-and-neck in the circulation derby. Suddenly, in 1988, both were passed by *Modern Maturity* (see Figure 8.1).

Modern Maturity? Most college students have never heard of the magazine. This is not surprising, since it is a controlled-circulation publication not available on the newsstands. The only way to receive it is to be over 50 years old and a member of the American Association of Retired Persons (AARP). A membership costs only $8 a year, making it also the least expensive magazine available.

Trade ads for *Modern Maturity* explain to advertisers that "Americans over 50 are more likely than others to consider purchases carefully. With the experience of maturity, they analyze in order to buy wisely." *Modern Maturity* has a circulation of more than 21 million, contrasted with about 16 million for the second- and third-highest circulation rivals.

The fourth-largest circulating magazine in the country, with over 10 million member-subscribers, is another specialized publication not available at the newsstand and heavily supported by older subscribers: *National Geographic*. Clearly mature readers have emerged as a major market for magazines. And when their subscription to the magazine is part of a membership package, renewal costs are less than those of ordinary consumer magazines.[12]

FUTURE FILE

✓ As an entrepreneur, you feel most comfortable catering to the needs and interests of your peer group. What magazine will cater to the needs and interests of your classmates in the years immediately following graduation? If you prefer, target a segment of your classmates—the ones "most likely to succeed."

✓ After decades of decline, newspapers are dying as a medium. Assuming that you are a rising star in a media conglomerate, would you advise management that magazines are the next medium to decline and disappear? If not, what do you think will ensure their future?

✓ Information stored in computer databases will be delivered through phone lines for display on computer terminals or television monitors in the home and the office. What role will magazines play in this immediate electronic future?

NOTES

1. Frank Luther Mott, *A History of American Magazines*, vol. 5 (1905–1930) (Cambridge: Harvard University Press, 1968), pp. 304–305.
2. Henry Grunwald, dedication address, the George J. Delacorte Center for Magazine Journalism, Columbia University, March 20, 1985.
3. Patrick Reilly, "Time's Entertainment Weekly Falters, Hitting Market Glutted with Magazines," *The Wall Street Journal*, April 17, 1990, pp. B-1, B-7.
4. B. G. Yovovich, "Getting a Reading on the Baby Boom," *Advertising Age*, Oct. 18, 1985, pp. 11–12.
5. Philip H. Dougherty, "Tailoring of Games Magazine," *The New York Times*, Oct. 31, 1985, p. D-23.
6. Joanne Lipman, "Ads in Magazines Get Personalized Touch as Time, Others Test High-Tech Process," *The Wall Street Journal*, Oct. 27, 1988, p. B-1.
7. "Special Report: College Magazines—The Next Generation," *Advertising Age*, Feb. 6, 1989, pp. S-1ff.
8. "Readers: Knowing Who They Are and How to Reach Them Can Help You Sell Products," *The Magazine Magazine*, Fall 1985, pp. 4–9.
9. "VALS—As a Media Evaluation Tool," *Magazine Newsletter of Research*, 40, October, 1982.
10. Philip H. Dougherty, "Advertising: A Year of Very Big Deals," *The New York Times*, Jan. 2, 1986, p. D-13.
11. "How Much Emphasis Should Be Put on Newsstand Sales When Making a Media Buying Decision?" and "Data Bank: Top 20 Magazines in Single Copy Sales," *Advertising Age*, Oct. 24, 1988, p. S-32.

12. Ira Teinowitz, "Modern Maturity Wins Top Spot in Circulation," *Advertising Age*, Aug. 22, 1988, p. 12.

SUGGESTED READINGS

Compaine, Benjamin M., *The Business of Consumer Magazines* (White Plains, NY: Knowledge Industry, 1982).

Elson, R. T. *Time, Inc.: The Intimate History of a Publishing Enterprise*, vols. 1 & 2 (New York: Atheneum, 1973).

Mott, Frank Luther, *A History of American Magazines*, vols. 1–5 (Cambridge: Harvard University Press, 1966–1968).

Peterson, Theodore, *Magazines in the Twentieth Century* (Urbana: University of Illinois Press, 1964).

Tebbel, John, *The American Magazine: A Compact History* (New York: Hawthorn, 1969).

Wolseley, Roland E., *The Changing Magazine* (New York: Hastings House, 1973).

CHAPTER 9

Radio

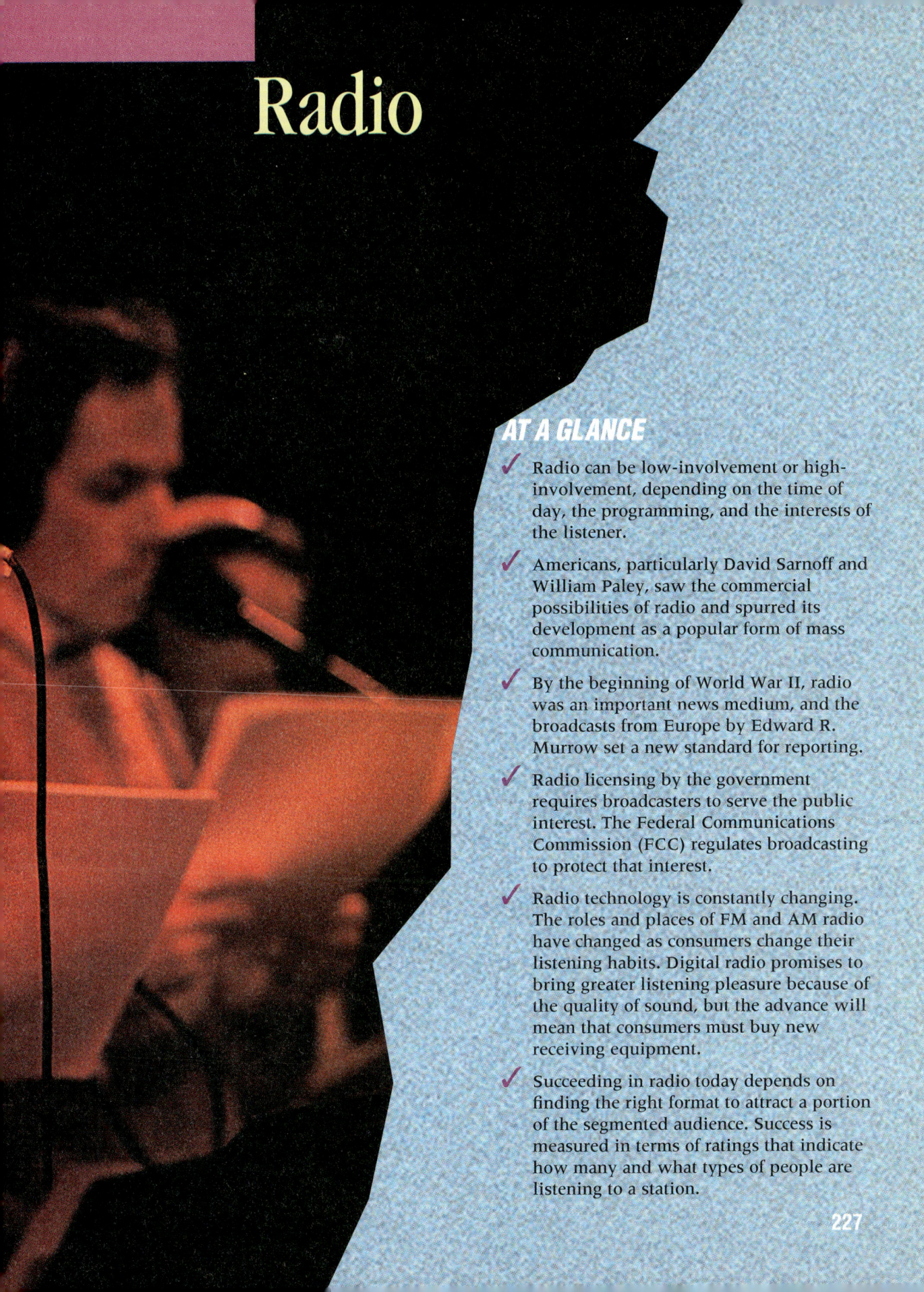

AT A GLANCE

✓ Radio can be low-involvement or high-involvement, depending on the time of day, the programming, and the interests of the listener.

✓ Americans, particularly David Sarnoff and William Paley, saw the commercial possibilities of radio and spurred its development as a popular form of mass communication.

✓ By the beginning of World War II, radio was an important news medium, and the broadcasts from Europe by Edward R. Murrow set a new standard for reporting.

✓ Radio licensing by the government requires broadcasters to serve the public interest. The Federal Communications Commission (FCC) regulates broadcasting to protect that interest.

✓ Radio technology is constantly changing. The roles and places of FM and AM radio have changed as consumers change their listening habits. Digital radio promises to bring greater listening pleasure because of the quality of sound, but the advance will mean that consumers must buy new receiving equipment.

✓ Succeeding in radio today depends on finding the right format to attract a portion of the segmented audience. Success is measured in terms of ratings that indicate how many and what types of people are listening to a station.

Mass communication theorist Marshall McLuhan argued that radio is rich in information, and thus requires little involvement on the part of the consumer.[1] On the other hand, the Radio Advertising Bureau contends in its promotions that radio requires the listener to "complete the picture" and thus requires greater involvement than either television or the print media. Indeed, radio often serves as part of the background "ambience," providing music or chatter that does not require much thought. But, as Figure 9.1 shows, the consumer can move from one level of attention to another with ease.

USING THE AIRWAVES TO COMMUNICATE

People have long speculated on the possibility of transmitting sound over distance. In the 1880s, Heinrich Hertz, a German scientist, demonstrated the properties of airwaves as carriers of sound. In the 1890s, Italian Guglielmo Marconi built radio devices that transmitted signals without the use of wires.

In 1901, Marconi successfully sent wireless signals across the Atlantic Ocean. Soon thereafter he formed companies in Britain and America to market his radio devices, emphasizing that they would replace telegraph wires for sending mes-

7:00 A.M.	Awoke to the clock radio, set on All-News Radio. Heard in five minutes what happened in the world since yesterday, plus two-minute sports capsule and one-minute weather.
7:05 A.M.	Dragged down the hall to the bathroom and shaved while listening to Zany Morning Man on "Radio Yahoo!" Finished waking up laughing at his recipe for low-calorie sundaes.
7:30 A.M.	Grabbed cup of coffee and jumped into car for 20-minute commute to Center City. Traffic helicopter warned about overturned tractor-trailer on Expressway, so took back route.
7:55 A.M.	Punched up Easy Listening station on FM radio in office that plays in background.
4:30 P.M.	Back in car for Drive-Time Jive-Time music-information-news on commute home.
6:00 P.M.	Giants and Dodgers are Game of the Week on Hometown Station; listened while reading newspaper and helping Junior build model train.
11:00 P.M.	Fell asleep to "What's on Your Mind?" listener call-in show. Last thing I remember was lady in Brentwood who thinks either martians or communists are behind the law requiring five-cent deposit on soda bottles and cans . . .

FIGURE 9.1   Diary of a Typical Listener

Enrico Caruso's tenor voice was carried to a larger audience than any other singer had ever enjoyed because of radio.

sages. In 1906, Lee de Forest's addition of a vacuum tube to act as an amplifier made voice transmission possible. In 1910, to demonstrate the capability of the new technology, he broadcast the singing of the great Italian tenor Enrico Caruso from New York's Metropolitan Opera House.[2]

In the early 1900s, governments began to realize the importance of radio communication and wrote laws requiring that radios be used by ships at sea. Ironically, radio messages warning the Titanic of icebergs were ignored because the radio operator on that ship was more concerned with sending personal messages ashore from well-to-do passengers—a real novelty at the time.[3]

The American credited with realizing the potential of radio transmission as a way of bringing information and entertainment into the home is David Sarnoff, a Russian immigrant who worked for the Marconi company during World War I. When that conflict ended, in 1919, Sarnoff was instrumental in bringing together the resources of General Electric, Westinghouse, and American Telephone and Telegraph (AT&T) to form the Radio Corporation of America (RCA).

Sarnoff saw that radio sets could be sold if people were convinced that radio was an effective means of bringing music into the home. In the early days of radio, the music carried on the medium was live, with full orchestras and bands performing in the radio studio. The broadcasting of music spurred sales of records, because consumers went to the stores to buy recordings of the tunes they heard first on the radio. The history of broadcasting and the history of music recording are intertwined, as we shall see when we look at the music industry in a later chapter. (When cable television became popular in the 1980s, music videos shown

> ### TIME CAPSULE
>
> ## Radio
>
> | | | | |
> |---|---|---|---|
> | 1901 | Transmission of first trans-Atlantic wireless signal by Marconi. | 1938 | Orson Welles' "War of the Worlds" is broadcast and panics public. |
> | 1919 | Radio Corporation of America (RCA) is founded. | 1939 | First FM radio station established in New Jersey. |
> | 1920 | First fully licensed station goes on the air: KDKA, Pittsburgh. | 1941 | "Mayflower Decision" prohibits editorializing by broadcasters. |
> | 1926 | RCA's subsidiary NBC is split into "red" and "blue" networks. | 1941 | FCC "Chain Broadcasting" report limits network control of affiliates. |
> | 1927 | Columbia forms third network, later to become CBS. | 1942 | "Voice of America" established to broadcast U.S. propaganda abroad. |
> | 1927 | Federal Radio Act is passed to regulate airwaves. | 1942 | Musicians strike interrupts music production; new fee structure results. |
> | 1933 | FM radio patented by Edwin Armstrong. | 1950s | Radio begins to lose listeners and program formats to television. |
> | 1933 | First "fireside chat" by President Franklin Delano Roosevelt. | 1960s | New formats established: deejay talk, segmented audiences. |
> | 1934 | Mutual Broadcasting System is fourth network. | 1970s | All-talk radio and all-news radio emerge in large markets. |
> | 1934 | Federal Communication Commission (FCC) formed to regulate broadcasting. | 1980s | FM is dominant force in radio; AM adds stereo broadcasting. |

on MTV were at the forefront of new programming in that medium. Again, consumers went to the music stores to buy albums after enjoying the performances on an electronic medium of mass communication.)

The Beginnings of the Network

At first radio broadcasts were occasional, occurring when broadcasters had information of interest to offer an audience. In 1920, Westinghouse obtained a license for KDKA in Pittsburgh, the first "station" offering scheduled transmissions at a regular frequency. Soon other stations were introduced for the purpose of broadcasting weather, news, music and occasionally live coverage of public events. By the mid-1920s, so many people were experimenting with broadcasting that the airwaves were literally jammed with overlapping information, much as is the case today with "ham" radio and citizens' band (CB) transmissions.

We saw earlier that newspapers formed the first wire service in order to spread the cost of gathering information. It soon became apparent that radio broadcasting would be more profitable if several stations shared the expenses of producing and transmitting programs—that is, if they joined in a network.

AT&T was among the first to realize the potential of the new medium as a way of "selling space" to those who wanted to communicate with each other. But in 1926 AT&T gave up on establishing a radio network and sold out its interest.

David Sarnoff, chairman of the board of the Radio Corporation of America, testifies before Congress, encouraging the legislators to fund a radio network to fight propaganda from the Iron Curtain countries after World War II.

That same year, the National Broadcasting Company, an RCA subsidiary, started two networks at the urging of David Sarnoff. The first network was created by linking RCA-owned stations and was identified as the "Red" network; the second was created by joining the stations formerly owned by AT&T and became the "Blue" network. (Legend has it that the color of two pens used in a meeting arbitrarily became the colorful designations.) Seventeen years later the Blue network was sold and became the American Broadcasting Company (ABC). In 1927, the Columbia network, eventually known as the Columbia Broadcasting System (CBS), was created out of a merger of the United Independent Broadcasters network and the Columbia Phonograph Record Company. In 1934 the Mutual Broadcasting System became the fourth radio network. As its name suggests, Mutual was not centrally owned; it constituted a programming cooperative among individually owned stations.

The networks provided music and information services to interconnected stations throughout the country. Advertising was one of the prime motives for linking radio stations. National manufacturers relished the idea of reaching thousands, even hundreds of thousands, of listeners to music and entertainment programs, who would then be captive to messages about the soaps, cereals, cigarettes, and other products they wished to sell. William S. Paley, the son of a cigar company owner, urged his family to use broadcasting as a means of selling products; he is known today as the long-time chairman of CBS.

Early radio was a potpourri of music interspersed with chit-chat and announcements, with occasional live coverage of special news. The concept of "programming," with specific types of information or entertainment beginning and ending at half-hour intervals, developed slowly.

Freeman Gosden creates his brash Kingfish character who argues with Charles Correll's Andy in the popular "Amos 'n' Andy" show. The white actors played their characters in blackface when the show moved to television, but later black actors replaced them in the roles.

> **BASEBALL ON RADIO: A SENSE OF URGENCY**
>
> In the late 1930s, following a baseball team meant listening to the radio. Radio stimulated the imagination and made you want to see the game with an urgency unknown to the television generation. Baseball was not an escape or entertainment; it was life itself.
>
> Irving Louis Horowitz, *Daydreams and Nightmares: Reflections on a Harlem Childhood* (Jackson: University Press of Mississippi, 1990), p. 38.

"Amos 'n' Andy" was the first serial comedy show, introduced in 1928. In the 1930s the variety show with comedians, bands, and singers evolved. By the end of that decade, the majority of the nation's households had radio sets, listening habits were forming around the program schedules, and advertisers had accepted radio as a major marketing tool.

Radio's Emergence as a News Medium

News events such as presidential inaugurations, baseball's World Series, and Charles Lindbergh's arrival in Paris were covered in the 1920s. However, it was not until the mid-1930s that regularly scheduled news programs were offered to the affiliates by the networks. "Newscasts" amounted to little more than the summaries that would be the headlines in the morning newspapers. Newspaper publishers used their influence to block the sale of news by the press associations (AP, UP, and INS) to radio, foreseeing the competition that broadcasting would provide to the print media. Eventually the publishers permitted a Press-Radio Bureau to furnish brief newscasts. By 1940, that compromise ended when the wire services began selling news to radio stations.

The networks, understanding the importance of broadcast news, developed their own capabilities for reporting worldwide and national events. By the outbreak of World War II, radio had become the first way that people heard of important news from Washington and abroad. Americans felt isolated by the events

CBS radio's Edward R. Murrow, here broadcasting the news in 1954, set the standards for reporting from the war front and later for investigative reporting.

in Europe and the Far East, and the voices of correspondents from abroad "brought home" the wars Americans traveled thousands of miles to fight.

Edward R. Murrow of CBS was in Europe when World War II broke out. He assembled a string of reporters on the continent and reported the news they gathered in his nightly broadcast from London. His broadcasts had an immediacy, urgency, and honesty that changed the concept of broadcast news forever. In the two decades that followed, Murrow became the model not only for CBS news reporters, but for all investigative reporters and political correspondents. His blunt, no-nonsense style gave Americans a new image: the reporter who puts a microphone in front of a politician, general, or corporate leader and relentlessly asks the difficult questions that may lead to the truth. That "Sixty Minutes" and its imitators are still among the most important television programs in the 1990s is a tribute to the man who changed broadcast news in the 1940s.

Radio had the power to galvanize Americans into action. Popular singer Kate Smith urged people to buy war bonds, and they did by the millions. Bandleader Glenn Miller aired a farewell show, then took his musicians off to be with the troops. And listeners glued themselves to their radio sets nightly to hear the words: "This is Edward R. Murrow . . . in London."

THE NEED FOR REGULATION

Early experiments demonstrated that one radio signal could interfere with another broadcast on the same frequency, depending on the atmospheric conditions. It

Musical variety and comedy shows performed before live studio audiences were popular in the 1930s and 1940s. Here comedian Jack Benny joins singer Kate Smith on her show.

became clear that if broadcasting were to develop as a viable economic enterprise, some controls would have to be exercised over the new medium.

The Radio Act of 1912 in the United States required anyone operating a radio transmitter to obtain a license from the federal government. The prime concern of the first piece of broadcasting legislation was safety: The law was written to ensure that amateur transmissions would not interfere with transmissions from ships at sea that might be calling in distress to other ships or to land.

As we saw, the first regularly operating radio station began in 1920. The following year, Herbert Hoover became Secretary of Commerce, and he is credited with realizing the need for regulation of what promised to become a booming new industry. It was Hoover who argued for radio stations to be operated by private enterprise rather than government, and to this day that differentiates the United States from the majority of the countries in the world. Hoover oversaw the growth of the radio industry. During his tenure, the practice began of assigning frequencies on the radio spectrum so that signals would not interfere with one another.

In 1923 the National Association of Broadcasters (NAB) was formed—an industry association dedicated to the free-enterprise notion that "self-regulation" was preferable to government interference. The NAB worked out its "standards of good practices," which eventually evolved into the NAB Code, covering a wide range of advertising and programming practices. A major impetus for forming the NAB was the need for broadcasters and music composers to unite over the issue of whether and how much to pay for permission to broadcast copyrighted music.[4]

The Radio Act of 1927 brought the Federal Radio Commission into being. Subsequently, the Communications Act of 1934 established the Federal Communications Commission (FCC) to regulate radio, telephone, telegraph, and—eventually—television and cable. These two pieces of legislation helped shape broadcasting in the United States. They stipulated that broadcasting should be conducted "in the public interest, convenience, and necessity." They strengthened Hoover's concepts that broadcasting should be privately owned, and that the role of government regulators was to ensure that frequencies were assigned to operators who met the technical requirements and performed in the broad definition of "public interest."

What constitutes "the public interest"? In terms of our P↔I↔C model, the needs and interests of the consumer must be met, particularly the need for news of public affairs. The FCC has had to interpret "the public interest" on a case-by-case basis. If a complaint is brought against a broadcast licensee, the FCC must decide whether the case is worthy of a hearing or whether it can be disposed of administratively, either by cautioning the licensee or by explaining its regulations to the person who brought the complaint.

If a hearing or review at license renewal time indicates that the broadcaster is not serving the public interest, the FCC may revoke the license or refuse to renew it. That has happened in fewer than 200 cases since 1934, indicating that the license renewal is virtually automatic. In some other cases—but again, a small fraction—the FCC has put a broadcaster on notice by granting a probationary renewal for only one year. The FCC also has the power to levy a fine for serious or repeat offences of up to $20,000—not a big sum for the larger stations. In fact, the FCC's two strongest enforcement tools are psychological in nature: the *threat* of losing the license and the *indication* that it is considering cracking down on

INSIGHT

Section 315 Affects Candidates for Office

Perhaps the best-known part of the Communications Act of 1934 is Section 315, which stipulates that if a broadcast licensee permits one legally qualified candidate for public office to use a broadcasting station, equal opportunity shall be afforded to all other candidates. The licensee has no power of censorship of material broadcast under provisions of Section 315, nor does that licensee have any obligation to allow the use of the station by any candidates.

Subsequently the act was amended so that appearance by a legally qualified candidate on a bona fide newscast, news interview, documentary, or spot coverage of news events is not covered by the provisions of Section 315.

Every four years, Congress usually passes special legislation exempting presidential contests from the provisions of Section 315 so that national debates can be held without affording "equal opportunity" to fringe candidates who have no realistic chance of garnering enough votes to be serious contenders.

Section 315 applies only to appearances by the candidates themselves, not their supporters or discussions of their views or platforms. When a candidate is a movie or television star, broadcast stations refuse to run the candidate's entertainment material for the duration of the contest. For that reason, none of Ronald Reagan's old movies were shown on television during his campaigns.

licensees who are not serving the public interest. Both techniques, but especially the latter, have been used by the FCC to convince licensees to avoid broadcasting obscene or drug-oriented lyrics.

In 1941 the FCC announced the Chain Regulations, which permit stations to reject any network programs and also to carry programs from other networks than the one with which they were affiliated, if it is in the public interest. Thus, while the FCC has no power over the networks, by regulating licensees it is able to affect network policies. When the networks challenged the Chain Regulations as unfair, the Supreme Court rejected the networks' objections and affirmed the FCC's powers to enforce such regulations.[5]

The FCC's concern over monopoly ownership has led it to institute rules against ownership by a single entity of two AM stations, two FM stations, two television stations, or a broadcast station and a daily newspaper in the same market. In addition, a single owner may not control more than 12 AM, 12 FM, and 12 television stations—a regulation aimed specifically at the networks.

In the spring of 1992—reacting to the failure of more than 300 stations owing to the weak economy—the FCC announced its intention to allow licensees to own as many as 30 AM and 30 FM stations, including up to three of each in large urban markets. Under Congressional pressure, the agency stepped back, indicating that it might instead allow small business owners and minorities to own more stations than other owners. Clearly the issue of multiple ownership will be a fluid one throughout the 1990s.

RADIO'S GOLDEN AGE

The 1930s and 1940s were radio's heyday. Producers tried to adapt every dramatic and entertainment form they could from other media and fit it to radio's technology.

Early programming assumed that listeners were only hearing music and voices, as they could with a phonograph. Eventually, however, scripting radio programs to provide "visual" cues through sound effects and descriptive narration enabled the medium to present play-by-play sports coverage, drama, and other events the listeners could "see" in their heads. Consumer response to experimentation helped the operators of radio stations learn what people wanted from the new medium.

Early developers saw radio as a way of enabling all Americans to enjoy the concert hall, even if they didn't live in major cities. New York's Philharmonic and the Metropolitan Opera became national, rather than regional, institutions because of their exposure on the radio; regular Saturday afternoon broadcasts live from the Met continue today, still sponsored by Texaco. NBC created its own symphony orchestra, and conductor Arturo Toscanini became a leading classical recording artist. CBS countered with André Kostelanetz and the Columbia Symphony Orchestra recording on the Columbia label, and promoted Kostelanetz as "music's leading man." Big bands of the 1930s and 1940s headlined variety shows, and the top tunes of the era were featured each week on "Your Hit Parade"—the forerunner of today's top hits shows, like "Rock in America" and MTV's daily listeners' choice top 10 countdown feature.

Early Murphy Brown? No, here Candice Bergen, daughter of ventriloquist Edgar Bergen, lets Charlie McCarthy sit on her lap while singer Andy Williams looks on. Dummy Charlie's wisecracking had radio audiences in stitches—and on radio it didn't matter if Edgar Bergen moved his lips.

When the "Amos 'n' Andy" show, originally produced locally in Chicago, went on the NBC Blue Network, its success in the 7 P.M. EST slot was so great that families built mealtimes around it, plant closings were adjusted to get workers home in time for the program, and even the President altered his speaking schedule to avoid conflict with America's new love.[6] Radio took over from burlesque as the new showcase for comedians. Among those who achieved national fame were George Burns and Gracie Allen, Bob Hope, and ventriloquist Edgar Bergen with Charlie McCarthy.

In the 1932 election campaign, most broadcast owners were as conservative as their newspaper publisher counterparts, and they opposed Democratic candidate Franklin Delano Roosevelt. But they sold him air time. He was able to carry his message "directly to the people" without editing or journalistic emphasis, and he was elected. His inaugural speech, broadcast coast to coast, aimed at convincing Americans to join in pulling the country out of the Depression and included the memorable statement "The only thing we have to fear is fear itself."

President Roosevelt recognized the power of radio to carry information, ideas, and persuasive messages to the people. His "fireside chats" with the people of America in the 1930s and 1940s allowed him to use the warmth and firmness of his voice to reassure listeners that the resolve of the people and their government would turn the country around. Sometimes he alluded in the broadcasts to the presence at his side of his wife Eleanor and his faithful dog Fala, making them celebrities as well.

In the 1980s, President Ronald Reagan revived the idea of regular presidential messages to the people. His short commentaries were broadcast on Saturday at midday, virtually assuring that his remarks would receive coverage in the well-

President Franklin Delano Roosevelt used radio broadcasts from his home in Hyde Park, NY, to speak directly to the American people.

read Sunday newspapers. The Democrats offered a "reply," but it rarely had the impact of the President's familiar voice. Reagan, who disliked press conferences, found the one-way medium of radio well suited to his abilities to persuade and his discomfort at fielding questions from reporters.

Other developments during the Golden Age of Radio:

- Drama got a shaky start on radio, because ordinary plays lost something in translation to the aural medium. Scriptwriting and acting for radio were new art forms developed on such popular dramatic series as the "Lux Radio Theater" and the "Mercury Theater of the Air."

- Serialized daytime dramas aimed primarily at women were sponsored by the large soap companies, hence the term *soap opera*. "The Romance of Helen Trent" and "Portia Faces Life" were the quintessential soap operas, as their titles suggest. Listeners came to think of the soap opera characters as members of their own families, writing them letters and sending gifts.

- Cops and robbers shows such as "Gangbusters" along with detective shows such as "Mr. and Mrs. North" caught the imagination of listeners. They thrilled to the mysteries of "Inner Sanctum." Perhaps the ultimate mystery adventure show was "The Shadow," featuring a detective whose invisibility permitted him to observe people who were unaware of his presence. This show originated the famous line: "Who knows what evil lurks in the hearts of men? *The Shadow* knows!"

> ### INDUSTRY
> # Profile of the Audience for Radio
>
> - The average American listens to between 20 and 25 hours of radio each week. (Source: Birch Reports, 1990)
> - People in their cars constitute 24.3 percent of "drive-time" listeners and 17.7 percent of all listeners at midday. (Source: *Advertising Age*, 1991)
> - The majority of radio listening is not done in the home. In addition to automobiles, people listen at work and they hear radio playing in stores, at swimming pools, and in other public places. (Source: *Advertising Age*, 1991)
> - Country music fans may or may not be a big segment of the radio audience. Arbitron ratings indicate that 7 percent of Americans listen to country radio, but other surveys have placed the audience at more than one in five listeners. (Source: Arbitron, Associated Press, 1990)
> - In 1940, each home in the United States had 1½ radios; by 1950 each home had 2 radios. Today each American home has between 5 and 6 radios. (Source: U.S. Census figures)

- The quiz show involved members of the studio audience ("I have a woman in the balcony") who tried to "name that tune" or answer the "$64 question." The home audience felt involved as they rooted for ordinary people to win the prizes by answering questions that ranged from trivial to mind-bending.

Involving the Consumer

Initially, consumers of radio were passive listeners. More and more, however, comedians and variety entertainers began to address the public as if entertainers and audience could actually interact. Eventually audience participation shows were developed to build on this feeling of involvement. Amateur-hour programs brought singers, tapdancers, and whistlers to the airwaves, and listeners were encouraged to call local numbers to vote for the prizewinners. "Truth or Consequences" required contestants to perform stunts in order to win prizes—sometimes even requiring them to leave the studio, accomplish a task that might involve listeners to the program, and return the following week. It was the beginning of gimmicks like the call-in contests popular in today's drive-time shows.

TELEVISION AND FM CHANGE AM RADIO'S ROLE

When a new medium of mass communication is introduced, it has no content of its own, so it adapts the content of an older medium.[7] That leaves the old medium with the problem of finding new information to offer in hopes of holding a share—albeit a smaller share—of the audience.

With the coming of television, many of the programs developed for radio, including "Amos 'n' Andy," moved to the new medium through the 1950s and 1960s, taking their audiences with them. By the mid-1960s, there were virtually no continuing serials, comedies, or variety shows on radio: They had all fled to television. Network and independent radio stations alike fell on hard times.

During the same period, FM (frequency modulation) radio began to usurp AM (amplitude modulation) as the vehicle of choice for quality music. FM was ready for introduction in the 1940s, but two FCC requirements delayed its popularity. First, the regulatory body required that all programming carried on FM be "simulcast" on AM, thus diminishing the motivation for consumers to pay extra for FM receivers, unless the higher fidelity FM offered was important to them. The second blow to FM came when the FCC moved FM to a higher point on the broadcast spectrum to make room for additional television channels.

AM broadcasters, in order to create excitement in the 1950s, hired brash and breezy disc jockeys—"deejays" for short—to play the Top 40 hits over and over. That format, and later all-talk radio in the 1960s and 1970s, enabled radio to hold about a third of its audience after the Golden Era came to an end.

Radio has always had a close relationship with the music industry, because radio depends on recorded music for theme songs and transitional music as well as programming. The music industry depends on radio to promote its products and sell recordings. (See Chapter 14 for a discussion of the role of music in mass communication.)

As radio became synonymous with recorded music, the FCC lifted the "simulcast" requirement, and FM gradually emerged as the choice for music programming. Only 100 new AM stations were introduced in the 20 years from 1968 to 1988. During that period, AM's share of the radio audience fell 25 percent as FM attracted listeners with its high fidelity transmissions.

Competition Leads to New Formats

Responding to competition from FM, AM stations tried new formats: all-Asian music in California; an all-medical news station in Denver; an all-self-help station in Pompano Beach, Florida; an all-children's station in Little Rock; and, in Virginia, an all-horse format. In August 1988, Cincinnati listeners to former country station WCVG-AM woke up to the sound of nothing but "The King"; the country had its first all-Elvis format.[8]

All-news stations in the major markets did well on a format of news reports at least every half-hour, interspersed with features, sports, weather, drive-time traffic reports, and occasionally a sporting event or live coverage of presidential addresses and other important breaking news. An all-sports station, not surprisingly dubbed WFAN, made its debut in New York in the late 1980s, taking over the important spot on the AM band formerly assigned to WNBC. The National Broadcasting Company's radio flagship station was sagging in the ratings, and died when NBC shut down its radio network.

Talk Show Hosts Wield Power

When Congress decided to vote itself a hefty pay raise early in 1989, activist Ralph Nader called Boston talk-show host Jerry Williams at WRKO-AM in Boston. Williams decided to take the issue to his listeners—and to other talk show hosts as well. A network of talk show hosts across the country sprang up to pursue the issue.

Chapter 9 Radio

241

Larry King is best-known for his talk show on Cable News Network. But he pioneered the format, including listener questions for his guests, on radio during three decades on the air.

The popular cause proved to be just the shot in the arm the talk shows on AM radio needed. The sentiment early in 1989 was decidedly against a pay raise for Congress. "The only people right now capable of mobilizing the public are talk show hosts," said one beleaguered representative, whose phone was ringing all day long with angry protests against the pay hike.[9]

Of course radio talk shows alone didn't force Congress to back down on its proposed raise. Representatives from urban districts, where talk shows are popular, received much more pressure than rural representatives. But the issue showed that there still is an audience for AM radio, and on occasion it can be mobilized to action. At one point some of the 50 talk show hosts involved in the campaign were even interviewing each other on the air as "sources" for the grass-roots political discussion.

New Hope for AM

Early in 1990, the FCC, at the urging of the National Association of Broadcasters, came to the rescue of AM radio with a set of engineering changes that would give AM more space on the spectrum, enabling it to offer clearer signals, especially at night when radio waves travel farther and are likely to interfere with one another.[10] Congress, the regulators, and the broadcast industry all agree that AM radio should and will be maintained as a viable medium of mass communication.

INDUSTRY

Next on the Horizon: Digital Radio

The sound quality of compact discs will be possible over the radio airwaves when "digital" systems now being developed replace the "analog" systems used in AM and FM broadcasting. Digital music is already being carried over cable systems in test markets. The U.S. government is exploring the possibility of using satellites to carry digital radio worldwide.

Whereas analog systems store and reproduce actual sounds, digital systems represent sounds and music using series of numbers. In addition to eliminating most of the noise associated with analog systems, the digital technology uses much less power for transmission, which makes it attractive for future use.

There is a major technical drawback to digital radio. Because of the large amount of information to be carried, the amount of the spectrum needed for a digital broadcast is many times wider than what is needed for an FM station. And there's an economic concern. If digital radio catches on, all of the 500 million radio sets currently in use in the United States will be obsolete. (Similar drawbacks existed when FM was introduced, but eventually the new technology gained acceptance.)

Source: Andrew Pollack, "Next, Digital Radio for a Superior Sound," *The New York Times,* July 11, 1990, pp. D1, D5.

THE RADIO SPECTRUM

In this and the following chapter, the "spectrum" will be mentioned from time to time. This refers to the radio spectrum, which is the term for the electromagnetic airwaves used for all kinds of broadcasting, including television. These radio waves are in a spectrum that also includes infrared rays, ultraviolet rays, X-rays, gamma rays, and cosmic rays.

Every wave has a length and a frequency, the latter being a measure of the number of cycles in one second from the crest of one wave to the crest of the next measured through a base line and a negative peak. As wavelength increases, frequency decreases. At any one time, thousands of airwaves are occurring at one time. Their range is referred to as the "spectrum."

Waves are labeled in terms of the thousands of cycles per second, once known as kilocycles but now called *kilohertz* (kHz) in honor of the German physicist who developed radio theory. Each spot on the spectrum is identified by the number of kilohertz observed at that point. AM radio channels are at the low end of the spectrum, in the lower frequencies. FM radio is higher, in the very high frequencies (VHF) that are also assigned to the main television channels. Higher numbered television channels are in the ultra high frequencies (UHF).

Ordinary consumers receive information on a limited segment of the radio wave part of the spectrum, the part their radio and television sets are equipped to receive. The rest of the radio spectrum is reserved for military and police use, emergency services, air control, experimental, and secret government uses. The FCC is constantly reassigning parts of the spectrum, responding to consumer demand for different types of broadcast information.

RADIO IS "TRANSNATIONAL"

Most media of mass communication can be restricted to distribution in home countries if the producer wishes, or if other nations forbid certain types of information. But broadcast communication, by its very nature, can fly the airwaves across national borders.

As early as the 1920s Germany was broadcasting propaganda messages to peoples of bordering nations, and other nations soon followed suit. Radio Luxembourg, emanating from one of the smallest countries in Europe, began carrying programming in several languages in the 1930s. Soon after World War II broke out, the U.S. State Department founded the Voice of America to carry democracy's messages to people in occupied or enemy lands. Despite jamming after the war, VOA programs were heard by the Soviet people and contributed to the eventual lessening of restrictions and the end of the so-called Cold War.

In Europe especially, competition for space on the spectrum is intense, and the International Telecommunication Union handles allocations. In most European countries, government ownership of the broadcast media is dominant, but independent commercial stations now are permitted in several nations. Where there is a government monopoly, popular "pirate" stations operated at sea often enjoy the listenership of consumers who want an alternative to official views and dull programming.

Whereas Americans own two radios per person and consume radio as a "personal medium," in developing countries there may be only one radio per several hundred people, and programs must be heard in bars and other public places.

FINDING THE RIGHT FORMAT

People accustomed to leaving their radio at 660 on the dial in the New York City market for WNBC's mixture of talk, news, comedy, and Top-40 were warned in advance by one of the more outspoken deejays. Nonetheless, it came as a shock one Monday morning when the old programming was switched to all-sports radio. What had happened was that the parent company, General Electric, found the old "variety" format to be increasingly unprofitable. Rather than try to install a better-focused concept that a particular audience could identify with, the owners simply sold their spot on the dial to WFAN, which previously operated higher on the spectrum and with fewer kilowatts of power.

The WNBC-WFAN switch was big news because of the size of the players and the radical change in programming. But flip-flops are common in the radio business today. Earlier in the same month an FM station in the same market abruptly dropped its contemporary format and began playing a mix of jazz and new age music. Another FM station went overnight from Top-40 to soft rock.

Imagine a newspaper, believing its mix of news and features wasn't getting a large enough audience, suddenly deciding to become a financial and business publication, or a magazine opting to change its focus from working women to the craft and hobby industry. Among the major public media that depend on advertising for support, only radio has the flexibility to make such rapid adjustments to the changing consumer picture, with a reasonable expectation of finding a new audience or strengthening its hold on an old one as a result of the change.

Country and western stations, numbering almost 2500, account for a quarter of the total stations in the United States. A vast majority of the C&W stations are in the South and border states, as is the case with religious stations, which rank fifth among the favorite formats. Adult contemporary featuring established artists is the second-most popular format, with about 2400 outlets. Like Top-40 and MOR (middle of the road—neither hard rock nor soft rock) which are third and fourth in number, adult contemporary is more likely than C&W to be found in urban centers and is spread more evenly across the country.[11]

Some categories listed in *Broadcasting/Cablecasting Yearbook* are quite specific: French, Greek, Polish, Spanish, and "Other Foreign Languages" account for 5 of the 30 formats. "Big Band" and "Golden Oldies" might sound similar, but they are quite distinct. The former means music of the 1930s and 1940s; the latter refers to rock hits from the 1950s and 1960s.

In describing some of the most popular formats, we'll try to identify the specific consumers for whom producers are tailoring the information:

All-News. No music, no deejays, just news "round-the-clock." One New York station's slogan is "Give us 21 minutes and we'll give you the world." The half-hour or 20-minute segment is anchored by the 3- to 5-minute news summary. The reminder of the period is devoted to a mix of local news reporting and features. Another New York station, for example, has regular three-times-a-day spots on "Fitness and Health" and "Your Dog." The audience for all-news radio is the busy professional who wants to catch up on events during the commute to work. Few listen for an extended time at home because of the repetition of information.

All-Talk. The all-news format has been modified to consist of twice-hourly news reports followed by talk show hosts who may be on the air for only a half-hour when the topic is specific (sex, family, finances) or as much as four hours if the host takes listeners' calls on any subject of interest to the audience. A hybrid form is the aforementioned WFAN, which, when it is not broadcasting live sports events, reverts to all-talk with a mixture of celebrity interviews and listener call-in. The audience for all-talk stations includes commuters, the majority of them nonprofessionals. The most avid consumer, however, may be the shut-in, retiree, or anyone else whose only window on the world consists of listening to stimulating, sometimes aggravating, chatter on the radio.

Black-Oriented. Some sources list the format simply as black, assuming that African-Americans are drawn to it just as Hispanics are drawn to Spanish-language broadcasts. Indeed, the African-American public affairs and informational shows attract primarily a minority audience. But the "black-oriented" label better accounts for the fact that often the music carried on the station attracts a nonblack audience as well.

Classical. In smaller cities, the one classical station that plays chamber music, opera, and symphonic works often is affiliated with nonprofit National Public Radio and/or with the local college or university. The audience is educated and affluent, but the format may not attract advertisers because the sedate atmosphere is considered not particularly well suited for selling products. Usually only the larger markets or towns boasting more than one institution of higher education can support more than one classical station.

Country and Western. Not surprisingly, the category represented by the most stations comprises several subformats. Some C&W stations focus on the current hits, while others have a playlist that devotes equal time to the old standards. In small to medium urban markets where there is only one C&W station, certain hours are devoted to bluegrass, Nashville, and "crossover" hits that are heard on rock stations as well. In large markets, and throughout the South and border states, some stations specialize in bluegrass alone. The audience lives, or yearns to live, on a "Country Road" and wants, like John Denver, to yodel "I'm a country boy!"—even if they live in the big city.

Middle of the Road. MOR stations aim at the young adult who doesn't want the din of heavy metal and has grown too sophisticated for the fast-talking deejay. Out of MOR have grown other formats. *Album-oriented rock* plays songs not popularized by the Top-40 stations and features hosts who provide context for the selections. *Soft rock* stations guarantee their middle-aged listeners that the needles on the volume indicator won't jump into the red zone. *Beautiful music* stations can be heard in elevators and dentists' offices, as well as in the homes and cars of older people who need to eliminate stress from their lives.

Religious. Religious radio carries many nationally syndicated programs of an inspirational nature, as well as sermons and music. Some offer intervals of secular classical music to attract a wider audience than those who seek religious messages. Other stations are run by specific denominations or even specific religious institutions such as seminaries. Evangelists, with their mix of preaching, inspirational music, testimonials, and fundraising, have found radio to be an effective tool for spreading the gospel and supporting their ministries.

Shock Radio. Looking for new formats to attract urban listeners, especially middle-aged males, some stations in large markets have turned their morning and afternoon drive-time programs, as well as late-night call-in shows, over to deejays who specialize in raunchy talk about sex, sometimes interspersed with sketches or cuts from comedy records that are irreverent and often tasteless. For every advertiser who shies away from the shock radio format for fear of offending consumers, there is an automobile dealer, tire company, or beer supplier who is delighted to find that the consumers of his or her products can be found at these hot spots on the radio dial.

Top-40. If ever there was a consumer-driven format, it is Top-40, because the playlists are dictated by what is selling in the record stores and what the listeners are requesting. The top two or three hits are played at least once an hour, and a countdown from number 40 to number 1 is aired at least once a week. There's room for an occasional past hit or one that is "rising toward the charts," but the deejays must whip things right along at breathtaking speed so the listener knows his or her current favorite will be coming up any moment. While the increasing variety in formats means that Top-40 doesn't dominate today as it did in the 1960s, it still has the effect of generating records sales, as do the music video formats on television.

Categories of radio formats, like amoebas, are constantly shifting and splitting. Country and western stars like Randy Travis and Dolly Parton can be heard in any of a dozen different formats. And formats fade in and fade out, as jazz does; just when someone laments, "There are no jazz stations in this town anymore," overnight a languishing MOR station rediscovers its jazz library and reclaims an audience. (See Figure 9.2.)

NETWORK AFFILIATION: CHANGING REALITIES

In the 1930s and 1940s, when soap operas, comedies, and variety shows were the mainstays of radio programming, the leading local radio stations often chose to become "affiliates" of one of the networks. As a network affiliate, the station was guaranteed programming that would attract a large audience.

After television drew away most radio shows and radio stations converted to music or news and information formats, affiliation with a network was less important to local stations. Today, rather than three or four large networks providing broad services, there are more than two dozen specialized networks offering news, public affairs programming, sports, talk, and musical events. WFAN, the all-sports AM station in New York, for example, uses the CBS sports network for NFL games, but turned to the NBC radio news network for foreign coverage during the Gulf War.

PUBLIC RADIO PROVIDES ALTERNATIVE CHOICE

Commercial radio stations depend on advertising to exist. An alternative to commercial broadcasting is *public broadcasting,* found in radio as well as television. Approximately 1300 of the more than 10,000 radio stations in the United States are nonprofit stations. They receive their income from grants made by foundations, from the federal Corporation for Public Broadcasting, and from listener contributions.

The term *educational* was once applied to public radio, because many of the programs were prepared by colleges and public school systems as a means of extending the campus to listeners everywhere. College professors were among the first to tinker with broadcasting technology in the 1920s, and educational programs emanated from campuses throughout the 1930s. But licenses were snapped up quickly for profitable use. The light entertainment of commercial radio attracted a much larger audience than the lectures, discussions of current events, and cultural programs on the handful of educational stations. Despite pressure from educators, the FCC felt in the 1930s that commercial radio provided sufficient education to the public. Requests that a percentage of the airwaves be reserved for educational stations fell on deaf ears. Many universities compensated by preparing programs for broadcast over commercial stations in the early morning or on Sundays, when the audiences were too small to interest advertisers. Gradually the FCC bowed to pressure, however, and in the 1940s the commission set aside approximately 20 percent of the radio spectrum for use by educational institutions.[12]

Few of the programs today are instructional in nature, however, and many are pure entertainment. The creation of the Corporation for Public Broadcasting (CPB) in 1968 brought the word *public* into vogue and spelled the end of the

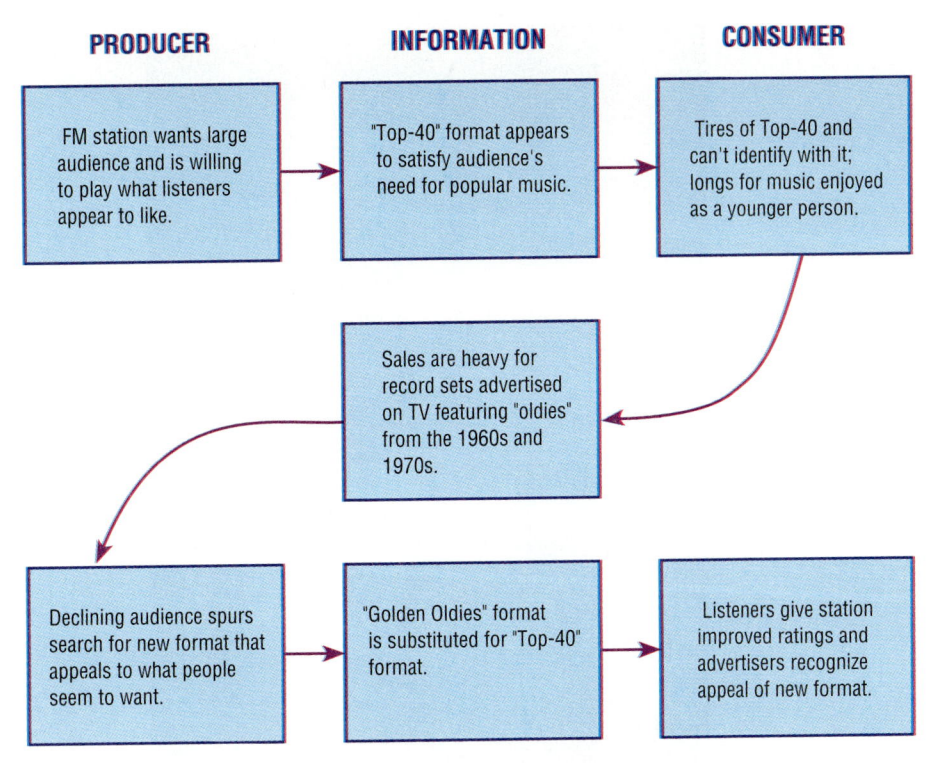

FIGURE 9.2 Consumer Behavior Helps Direct Change in Format for Station The P↔I↔C model here represents a trend at the beginning of the 1990s toward appealing to so-called "baby-boomers"—those in the 25-to-54 age range—with music from their youth. In some markets, "Golden Oldies" stations have taken over first place in ratings. Even where such stations remain in second or third place overall, they may be the first choice of the most affluent sector of the community—and that appeals to advertisers.

"educational" radio era. CPB created the Public Broadcasting Service (PBS) and National Public Radio (NPR) network to facilitate sharing of programming by non-profit stations. As in the early period of commercial network radio, NPR originally required that affiliated stations carry all of its programming, but pressure resulted in the "unbundling" of services in 1988, meaning that member stations can pick and choose what to buy from NPR in order to round out their local programming.

One of the most popular programs carried by public stations is "All Things Considered," a 90-minute nightly public affairs program that mixes in-depth news, business and economic reports, science and health information, cultural features, and interviews. The show is carried to participating stations through a satellite network operated by NPR in Washington, D.C.

The largest distributor of public radio programs is American Public Radio based in St. Paul, known for the success of Garrison Keillor's "American Radio Company." Another program begun by American Public Radio in 1989 is "Marketplace," a collection of news and features about business designed for ordinary people rather than investors. By contrast with commercial radio, such programs are freer to take their time to pursue topics and develop them through interviews with experts and opinion leaders.

Although the audience for public radio is smaller than that for commercial radio, its impact is large. The five million people who listen to NPR's news broad-

Garrison Keillor's homespun Minnesota humor is a hit on public radio, where his "American Radio Company" airs.

casts are highly educated and more affluent than the average listener, and they are extremely loyal consumers who send donations and write their leaders in Congress to urge government support of public radio.[13] Public radio has had special impact in rural areas, where the choice of radio stations is limited and serious news and commentary are eagerly sought by isolated listeners.

MEASURING THE AUDIENCE

Until "people-meters" were tried in the late 1980s as a means of determining which members of a household were watching which programs, television ratings services were able to report to broadcasters and advertisers only which *households* were watching what. That made sense as long as television viewing was a family affair. But as long ago as the late 1940s, radio broadcasters and advertisers had demanded ratings based on *individual people* listening to the radio. That's when listening patterns began to change, and consumers tended to use radios singly rather than in family groups.

Arbitron, one of three broadcast ratings companies (the other two are Nielsen and AGB), dominates the radio ratings game with its weekly diary and follow-up phone call system that measures audience behavior in more than 200 markets.

TABLE 9.1 Top Billing Stations

Rank	Station	Billing ($000,000)
1	WGN-AM, Chicago	$37.4
2	KABC-AM, Los Angeles	35.0
3	KIIS-AM/FM, Los Angeles	31.7
4	KOST-FM, Los Angeles	28.8
5	KPWR-FM, Los Angeles	28.7
6	WINS-AM, New York	25.0
7	WLTW-FM, New York	24.0
8	WCBS-FM, New York	23.5
9	KRTH-AM/FM, Los Angeles	22.4
10	KLOS-FM, New York	22.0
11	KMOX-AM, St. Louis	21.7
12	KNX-AM, Los Angeles	21.5
	WCCO-AM, Minneapolis	21.5
	KGO-AM, San Francisco	21.5
15	KVIL-AM/FM, Dallas	21.0
	WJR-AM, Detroit	21.0
	WHTZ-FM, New York	21.0

Source: Duncan's Radio Market Guide, 1990.

Arbitron's smaller competitors use day-after interviews involving recognition of a list of stations and their formats to determine which stations people are listening to. At one time the Hooper ratings were determined through phone calls at the same time people were listening, but that system was used only in the top markets.

The "ARBs," as they are known in the trade, are all-important in setting advertising rates. Stations in smaller markets get their ARBs annually, while those in the top markets receive new figures four times a year. Mostly "the numbers," as they are referred to knowingly by station manager and advertising representatives, are for trade use, but occasionally a deejay will crow on the air about moving up on the competition. When there is a new market leader, it often is cause for a heavy advertising campaign directed at both advertisers and the listening public. (See Table 9.1.)

If your family's telephone number is selected randomly from a list to be an Arbitron radio household, everyone living under your roof who is age 12 and over will be given a diary to keep. There are spaces on the diary sheet to note the time of day, the call letters of the station, and the place where the listening was done: at home, in a car, or some other place. Even if the individual is merely present at a place where the radio is being played—at work, by the swimming pool, or in a shopping center—the station is noted. Demographic data about the sex, gender, and employment of each individual are included on the weekly sheets.

Deciphering the Data

The tabulated results of the measurements are complicated pages of data that take some practice to decipher. Here's what you'd be looking for if you were the person in charge of programming decisions for a radio station:

Dayparts. The day is broken into *dayparts* such as 6 A.M. to 10 A.M. weekdays, 10 to 3, 3 to 7, 7 to midnight, and midnight to 6 A.M., as well as 6 A.M. to midnight on weekends. The 6 to 10 A.M. and 3 to 7 P.M. dayparts include both commuters and people at home, and thus have the largest audiences. Dayparts help advertisers know they are reaching the most people or the right people.

Sex and Ages. The numbers are further broken down to men and women in six different age groups. These data are extremely important, because programming formats are intended to appeal to specific groups, and advertisers of certain products buy specific time slots in order to get their messages to the target consumers.

Metro and Total Areas. Because stations with different power levels reach wider markets, the numbers are shown both for the smaller *metro* area and the larger *total* market area.

Quarter-Hours and Cumes. The station can determine from the numbers the *quarter-hour estimates* of the people listening, or the cumulative (*cume*), which indicates the total number of people tuning in during a daypart.

Rating and Share. Finally, the numbers are expressed in the *average-persons rating*, which measures actual listenership against the potential number of listeners in the market, and the *share*, which indicates the percentage of potential audience members who were actually listening at the time. Average-persons rating would be important for cumes and for drive time. A high share would be sufficient when measuring the performance of a specific program or time slot.

With all these different ways to "read the numbers," it is not surprising that most of the stations in a market can find data to convince their advertisers that they are reaching an audience. What is not measured by the ratings service, of course, is qualitative information such as whether people actually hear the advertisements, believe them, and make purchases based on the information received. Advertisers desiring that kind of information must use focus groups and telephone surveys to supplement the Arbitron ratings.

MAKING A PROFIT IN RADIO

Unlike the print media, which obtain part or all of their income from consumers who purchase books or subscribe to periodicals, the broadcast media "give their product away free" to consumers. That means they are totally dependent on advertising support for their income. In effect, radio producers "sell an audience" to advertisers. A station may "deliver" 100,000 18- to 24-year-olds to the manufacturer of a brand of jeans, or 250,000 men aged 40 to 55 to an insurance company with a retirement plan for the head of the household.

Through the 1980s, radio station owners could expect on average a healthy 7 percent profit margin. Radio income from advertising topped the $8 billion mark for the first time in 1989, placing radio in a tie for fourth place (with the Yellow Pages) among advertising media. (By comparison, newspaper advertising income was four times as great, at $32 billion; television ads brought in $27 million; and direct mail was third, at $22 billion.[14]) (See Figure 9.3.)

Overwhelmingly, *local* advertising pays the bills for radio stations, accounting for approximately 75 percent of income. National advertising is divided into *net-*

Chapter 9 Radio

How many of these people do you think are reading a newspaper?

For safety's sake, we hope none. The eyes should be watching the road. The ears, on the other hand, are listening to the radio. Which is why your ad should be on the radio. And when you consider that people spend three hours a day listening to the radio and only 39 minutes reading the paper, radio makes even more sense. If you'd like to reach people who don't have time to read the newspaper, call us at 1-800-252-RADIO. **RADIO ADVERTISING BUREAU**
304 Park Avenue South, New York, NY 10010

A print ad prepared by the Radio Advertising Bureau, designed for use in advertising trade magazines, contrasts the amount of time consumers spend with radio to the time spent with newspapers.

work, which accounts for only about 1 percent of income, and *national spot* advertising, which accounts for about a quarter of the income at the typical radio station.

National spots may be the same ads carried on the networks, or they may be special ads produced for and aimed at regional, state, or even particular city consumers. They are called "national" spots because manufacturers of products sold nationwide pay for them, and the purchase of air time is made through the media-buying department of a national or regional advertising agency. National spots are used to target markets that a client finds important; the manufacturer of iced tea, for example, may target southern states.

A 75/25 split also occurs in expenses. Technical costs for running the typical station and the cost of purchasing programming amount to about 25 percent; administration, sales, and promotion account for 75 percent of expenses.

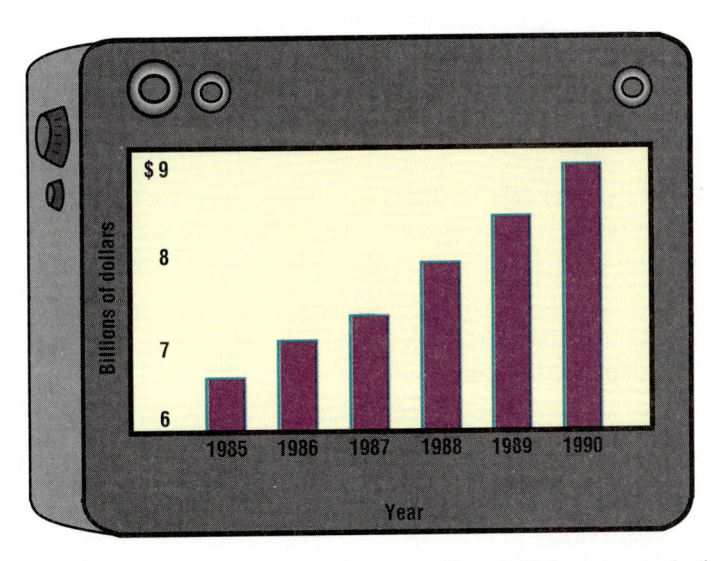

FIGURE 9.3 **Radio Advertising Revenues** Note: 1990 figure is a projection.
Source: Radio Advertising Bureau.

Small Field, Low Pay

Of the 100,000 people working in radio, slightly under 60 percent may be found at commercial (for-profit) stations. Radio is a field dominated by professionals, with a small number of service personnel. Of the white collar jobs at a radio station, managers account for a quarter, sales personnel about 20 percent, and fully a third of the jobs are in the area of putting programs on the air: reporters, announcers, researchers, and the production staff.

Many big-name radio personalities in New York, Chicago, and Los Angeles—especially drive-time deejays and those who can syndicate their Top-40 shows to a string of stations—command salaries exceeding that of the president of the United States (which, after all, is only $200,000). But even when the big salaries of the few genuine stars of radio are added to the national average, the salary picture is low because the vast majority of radio stations are in small markets. The average AM and FM station has just 17 employees. The national average salary for an on-air personality or news reporter is about $15,000 to $20,000. Salaries for experienced personnel vary widely depending on the size of the market—only $30,000 average for a general sales manager in a small market, contrasted with twice that for the equivalent job in a large market. The annual employee turnover rate in the industry is around 25 percent.[15]

A survey of salaries at 200 radio stations in 1988 by a Los Angeles–area accounting firm showed that morning personalities are paid an average of twice as much as their afternoon counterparts, whereas five years earlier the salaries were roughly equal. In early 1989, at least two Los Angeles morning show hosts had five-year contracts paying a base annual salary of $2 million. The reason for the outsized paychecks? Audiences that tune in to the morning personality are likely to stay tuned to the station all day long, thus accounting for increased advertising revenues.[16]

FUTURE FILE

✓ If your campus has a radio station that meets the needs of college students, it probably doesn't sound like any other station on commercial radio because it plays cuts from albums that are not yet "commercial" or mainstream. Is there a place among radio formats for the music that college students like? What would it take to make the format viable beyond the college campus?

✓ Nostalgia keeps reruns going on television for years, but there is no equivalent in radio. Is there an audience for the programs of the "Golden Age of Radio" and, if so, how could a format be built to recycle these programs?

✓ For all the variety in formats and audiences, radio does not offer many of the choices that cable television has introduced. What cable formats might be adaptable to radio: comedy, home shopping, C-SPAN's coverage of Congress?

NOTES

1. Marshall McLuhan, *Understanding Media: The Extension of Man* (New York: McGraw-Hill, 1965).
2. Lynne S. Gross, *Telecommunications: An Introduction to Electronic Media* (Dubuque, IA: Wm. C. Brown, 1988), p. 31.

3. Eugene S. Foster, *Understanding Broadcasting* (Reading, MA: Addison-Wesley, 1978), p. 44.
4. Foster, p. 52.
5. Foster, pp. 219–222.
6. Gross, p. 46.
7. This is a distillation of one of Marshall McLuhan's theories, frequently expressed in his talks and writing.
8. Andrea Adelson, "What's New in AM Radio: Elvis Every Morning, Evening and Nighttime, Too," *The New York Times*, Nov. 20, 1988, p. 13.
9. E. J. Dione, "Waves on Airwaves: Power to the People?" *The New York Times*, Feb. 15, 1989, p. A-20.
10. Mary Lu Carnevale, "FCC Approves Plan to Tune Up Ailing AM Radio Band," *The Wall Street Journal*, April 13, 1990, p. B-1.
11. *Broadcasting/Cablecasting Yearbook* (Washington, DC: Broadcast Publications, 1987).
12. Foster, pp. 374–375.
13. Eleanor Blau, "National Public Radio Gets By with Help from Its Friends," *The New York Times*, Feb. 27, 1989, p. D-13.
14. McCann-Erickson data reported by *Advertising Age*, May 14, 1990, p. 12.
15. Barry L. Sherman, *Telecommunications Management: The Broadcast and Cable Industry* (New York: McGraw-Hill, 1987), pp. 93–94.
16. Andrea Adelson, "In Radio, an Expensive Battle at Sunrise," *The New York Times*, Jan. 30, 1989, p. D-10.

SUGGESTED READINGS

Barnouw, Eric, *History of Broadcasting in the United States* (New York: Oxford University Press, 1966–1970), 3 volumes.

Buxton, Frank, and Bill Owen, *The Big Broadcast: 1920–1950* (New York: Viking, 1972).

Fornatale, Peter, and Joshua Mills, *Radio in the Television Age* (Woodstock, NY: Overlook Press, 1980).

Gates, G. P., *Air Time: The Inside Story of CBS News* (New York: Harper & Row, 1978)

Routt, Edd, James McGrath, and Fredrich Weiss, *The Radio Format Conundrum* (New York: Hastings House, 1978).

Sterling, Christopher, and John Kitross, *Stay Tuned: A Concise History of American Broadcasting* (Belmont, CA: Wadsworth, 1978).

CHAPTER 10

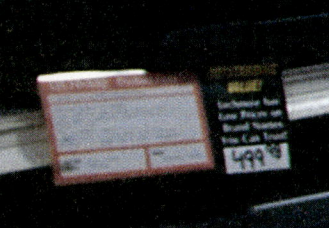

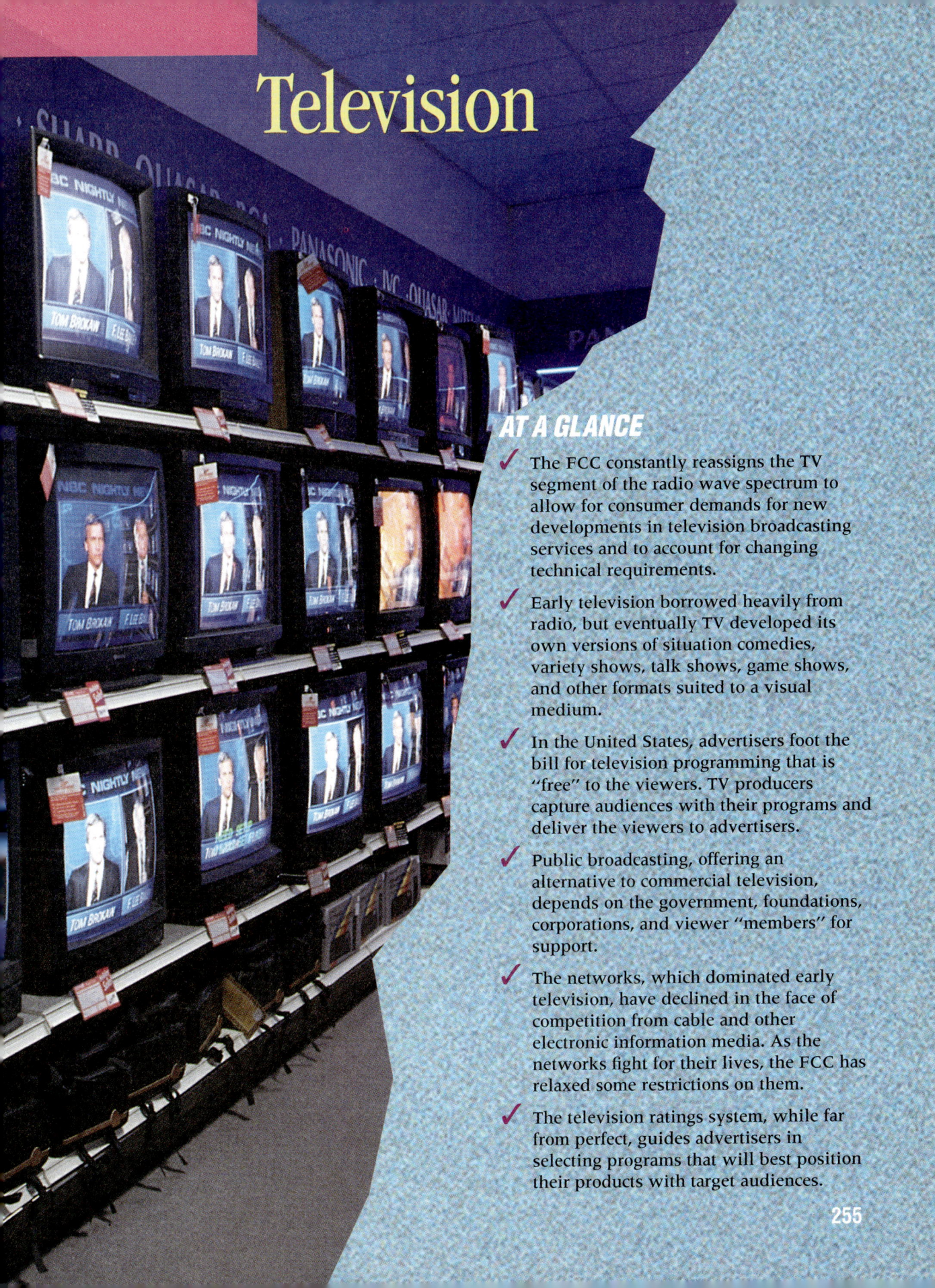

Television

AT A GLANCE

- The FCC constantly reassigns the TV segment of the radio wave spectrum to allow for consumer demands for new developments in television broadcasting services and to account for changing technical requirements.

- Early television borrowed heavily from radio, but eventually TV developed its own versions of situation comedies, variety shows, talk shows, game shows, and other formats suited to a visual medium.

- In the United States, advertisers foot the bill for television programming that is "free" to the viewers. TV producers capture audiences with their programs and deliver the viewers to advertisers.

- Public broadcasting, offering an alternative to commercial television, depends on the government, foundations, corporations, and viewer "members" for support.

- The networks, which dominated early television, have declined in the face of competition from cable and other electronic information media. As the networks fight for their lives, the FCC has relaxed some restrictions on them.

- The television ratings system, while far from perfect, guides advertisers in selecting programs that will best position their products with target audiences.

In the preceding chapters covering the print media and radio, we did not feel it necessary to define the medium being discussed. Not too many years ago, we would have said the same about television. The term merely referred to programs broadcast electronically over the airwaves to receivers in the consumers' homes. At most, we might have broken "television" down into the networks, the independent stations, and public broadcasting.

Today the picture has changed dramatically. The same receivers on which we receive broadcast programming have been modified so that we can hook them up to the local cable company in order to view programming not available over the airwaves. We have attached videocassette recorders so that we can play back pre-recorded movies and other programs. And we find video screens in the work place, carrying business information rather than entertainment programming. *Television* has become almost too general a term because it covers so many applications and involves consumers in myriads of ways.

Thus we shall restrict ourselves in this chapter to the development and uses of *broadcast* television—TV carried over the airwaves. In the following chapter, we shall examine cable and new uses for video information.

We also will be talking about the medium of television in a way that goes beyond a description of the technology and the programming content. We will discuss not just the machinery, but the social context of television, its message, its uses, and the sense we make of it.

THE ADVENT OF TELEVISION

TECHNOLOGY OR MEDIUM?

Mass communication theorist Neil Postman of New York University makes a critical distinction between "technology" and "medium":

We might say that a technology is to a medium as the brain is to the mind. Like the brain, a technology is a physical apparatus. Like the mind, a medium is a use to which the physical apparatus is put. A technology becomes a medium as it employs a

Tinkerers had been working to put pictures with radio since the late 1800s, and by the 1920s Allen B. Dumont was developing the cathode-ray tube and Vladimir Zworykin patented the iconoscopic tube—scanning mechanisms that made possible the breaking down and reconstruction of pictures to be transmitted as electronic information. By 1930, General Electric, Westinghouse, and RCA were demonstrating early television designs in New Jersey laboratories, and in 1939 RCA demonstrated its system at the New York World's Fair. Some hailed it as a technology that would change the American home, but others, including *The New York Times*, described it as a gimmick without useful applications.

Only a handful of stations with fewer than 10,000 viewers went on the air in 1941 when the Federal Communications Commission (FCC) decided that the techniques of black-and-white transmission were well enough developed to be introduced to the public. Then the first of two impediments to the growth of television occurred: The outbreak of World War II diverted the resources of electronics companies to the war effort.

A Freeze on Station Applications

The second delay occurred after the war, when the FCC stepped in to prevent confusion over which color television technology would become the national standard—CBS's *mechanical* system, which was incompatible with black-and-white, or RCA's *electronic* system, which was compatible.

Fewer than 50 television stations were on the air when the FCC decided to "freeze" all license applications in 1948. The government regulators hoped to sort

> particular symbolic code, as it finds its place in a particular social setting, as it insinuates itself into economic and political contexts. A technology, in other words, is merely a machine. A medium is the social and intellectual environment a machine creates.
>
> Source: Neil Postman, Amusing Ourselves to Death: Public Discourse in the Age of Show Business (New York: Penguin Books, 1986), p. 84.

out the problem in six months, but it took more than three years. During that time the number of stations grew to more than 100, because several license applications had been approved prior to the freeze. Most of the largest cities had one or two stations throughout the freeze. Television sets cost $1000 (at a time when a Chevrolet cost $2000) and so most Americans waited for television to come down in price.

The freeze was lifted July 1, 1952, and in 1953 the FCC approved the color system developed by the National Television Systems Committee, an organization of engineers who worked for the electronic manufacturers that were anxious to get production of television sets going.[1] The compromise system, like the RCA system after which it was patterned, was electronic and compatible, meaning consumers who already owned televisions could receive color programming in black-and-white. The cost of television sets began at once to come down thanks to mass production and competition, and the size of the screen grew from 7 inches measured diagonally to more than 14 inches.

Allocating the Spectrum

Whenever a new broadcast technology is introduced, the FCC has to reallocate the finite points on the radio-wave spectrum. When the freeze was lifted, the government provided for over 2000 station assignments in almost 1300 communities. Earlier the FCC had allocated 12 spaces on the spectrum in each market for very high frequency (VHF) stations. After the freeze, there was sufficient allocation for more than twice as many ultra high frequency (UHF) stations as well as 242 allocations nationwide for nonprofit educational stations.[2]

We call 1948 the big freeze . . . but it was not the last. In the summer of 1987, the FCC enacted a freeze limited to the top 30 markets. The issue once again was technical standards, this time the introduction of "high-definition" television. The new technology, expected to be introduced first in major markets in the 1990s, provides better image quality, but requires more of the spectrum.

Other reallocation moves in the past decade have concerned the licensing of low-power television stations meant to serve communities outside the reach of major markets. In addition to bringing local programming to towns outside the sphere of major urban areas, low-power allocations provide an opportunity for smaller entrepreneurs to gain entry to television, including members of minority groups. Thus allocation of the spectrum is intended to meet not only technical needs, but social needs as well. The needs of one community, or even one group within the community, may have to be weighed against the needs of others when allocations are made.

DISCOVERING THE PROGRAMMING FORMULA

Think about it for a moment: What kinds of programs that you see on television are actually happening as you watch them? Newscasts, by definition, are live. Many sports events are, including major football and baseball games. But many of the minor sports were recorded earlier for editing and fitting into one-hour time slots. Most of the entertainment and information programming is prerecorded.

TIME CAPSULE

Television

1923	Television camera tube developed at Westinghouse by Vladimir Zworykin.
1927	Philo Farnsworth applies for patent on electronic television.
1939	Television demonstrated at New York's World Fair.
1941	FCC authorizes commercial television, but World War II intervenes.
1947	"Howdy Doody" is first major children's television program.
1948	NBC and CBS networks offer evening news and entertainment programs.
1948	Licensing of television frozen (until 1952).
1950	Iowa State University begins first educational television station.
1951	Senate hearings on organized crime are carried live on television.
1951	First coast-to-coast television from New York to San Francisco.
1952	"The Today Show" ushers in the new talk-news-interview format.
1953	Eisenhower inauguration is first to be carried live on television.
1954	McCarthy hearings shown live; Edward R. Murrow responds with "See It Now."
1956	First extensive coverage of presidential conventions and campaigns.
1959	Quiz show scandals causes networks to revamp prize giveaways.
1960	Nixon-Kennedy debates change presidential politics.
1961	First live television coverage of a presidential news conference.
1963	Regular programming interrupted after assassination of Kennedy.
1963	First live television broadcast from United States to Europe by means of satellite.
1967	Corporation for Public Broadcasting is established.
1969	Live coverage of moon landing.
1970	Public Broadcasting Service formed.
1978	FCC approves national "superstations."
1980s	Cable and videorecorders cut into network share of television market.

That is one of the main differences between television today and television in the early years.

Early radio programs—variety shows, dramatic productions, comedies, and quiz shows—were performed live for simultaneous transmission throughout the country. So important was the supposed dynamic of a "real" event that announcers at one radio network were required to wear tuxedos: The management was convinced that this made them speak with distinction and moreover it both impressed the studio audience and sparked their earnest participation.

When many of the most popular radio programs and formats moved to television, the tradition of presenting them live continued, if for no other reason than because it was quicker and cheaper than filming and editing them. "Amos 'n' Andy" had to be recast with black actors. Newscasters had to learn to look at the camera from time to time, but basically they were the same radio news readers with a microphone and a sheaf of papers in front of them, with little in the way of graphics or film footage to illustrate what they were reporting. Variety shows were presented live from a hastily refurbished Broadway theater with an announcer standing in front of the curtain and ballyhooing the next act much as a vaudeville host might have done.

Chapter 10 Television

Early Television Invents Itself

The programming we take for granted today had to be appropriated for television, adapted for television, and in some cases invented for television.

Sports events are complicated in terms of camera placements, following the action, and cutting from close-ups to the entire field of action. But they were quickly embraced by television programmers because they attracted large audiences, they were fairly inexpensive to produce, and advertisers liked the tie-in with popular hometown teams. In addition to baseball, which radio had covered for decades, television elevated professional football to new stature. It also brought wider popularity to boxing ("The Friday Night Fights"), professional wrestling (which changed from a sport to pure show business with television exposure), bowling, and even marginal sports-entertainment attractions such as the roller-derby team roller-skating competition.

Variety shows were a natural for television. Whereas radio had been limited to presenting musical acts that could be appreciated by the ear alone, television could use baton twirlers, jugglers, tap-dancers, wire-walkers, puppeteers, and animal acts. Ed Sullivan's "Toast of the Town" long reigned as television's quintessential variety show. "Arthur Godfrey and His Friends" was an extended family of young performers chaperoned by a father-figure host, while Milton Berle's popularity stemmed from the comedian's willingness to go to any extreme to pull off a ridiculous skit. Jack Benny and the comedy duo of Burns and Allen opened and closed their shows working before a stage curtain, then acted with their supporting sidekicks from radio in simple little sketches set in the living room or perhaps a corner of a restaurant. "Your Show of Shows" launched the careers of Imogene Coca, Sid Caesar, Carl Reiner, and an ensemble troupe of regulars who

> A demonstration of television was conducted in 1927 by one of its many inventors, Philo T. Farnsworth. He needed some simple and familiar graphic object to depict on the television screen. Prophetically, he chose a big dollar sign.
>
> David Marc, "Understanding Television," *The Atlantic Monthly*, August 1984, p. 35.

As host of CBS's "Toast of the Town" variety show, columnist Ed Sullivan introduced television viewers to the hottest new acts in show business, including Elvis Presley and, here, the Beatles.

developed their own characters, much as "Saturday Night Live" would do a generation later.

Radio drama had been fairly simple to produce live, because actors only needed to sound like the characters they played, and sound effects took care of setting the scene. Nonetheless, drama made the move to television with considerable success. A new generation of playwrights, directors, designers, and actors presented high-quality original hour-long and 90-minute plays weekly on such shows as "General Electric Theater," "Playhouse 90," and "Studio One."

Some lament the passing of live dramatic television. But a look at those old shows reveals that their production values were quite basic, and the look was flat in texture. Today we expect more polish and excitement from prerecorded programs.

NBC pioneered the talk show format, wherein personalities provided a blend of entertainment, information, and service material. "Today" was the prototype for the early morning news-weather-feature-chatter wake-up format, and "The Tonight Show" paved the way for countless desk-and-couch late-nighters in which a genial host does an opening monologue, interviews a handful of celebrities, banters with the band and the audience, and bumbles through a topical comedy sketch.

Early television broadcasting was carried for only a few hours each day, mainly in the evening when whole families could watch. As programming was expanded into the daylight hours, children's programming was added. Sitting on bleachers or benches in tiny, cramped studios, an audience of a few dozen kids would be entertained by puppets, perpetually cheerful adults, a clown, and a few zany characters. Buffalo Bob was the host-sidekick to the freckle-faced "Howdy Doody," and "Kukla, Fran and Ollie" required nice-lady Fran Allison to interact with two puppets that were the forerunners of the popular "Sesame Street" characters.

Developing Durable Products

Television producers learned how to develop programs that would produce income reliably and repeatedly. Chief among these was the situation comedy that portrayed a set of likable characters in a familiar setting.

The economics of early radio and television were based on the assumption that a show aired once. That meant keeping costs down by rehearsing the show for a week and then presenting it live. When producers saw the possibilities of filming material for television and then distributing it in other countries, rebroadcasting it in the summer, or, eventually, syndicating weekly programs for showing years later in daily "strips"—the same time slot five days a week, much as old episodes of "M*A*S*H" appear today—the shift to prerecording began.

"I Love Lucy," the most popular situation comedy of the 1950s, was the first to be filmed. The show pioneered the three-camera setup, with one camera in the center used for the "establishing shot" of the Ricardos and their neighbors in the living room, and the other two focusing on the faces of Lucy and the person with whom she was speaking. To this day, notice how often the "situation" in a situation comedy is that a family or group of characters is gathered around a familiar artifact—the living room couch or a bar or table—and the three-camera set-up moves the action along swiftly in a manner that is easy to follow on the small screen.

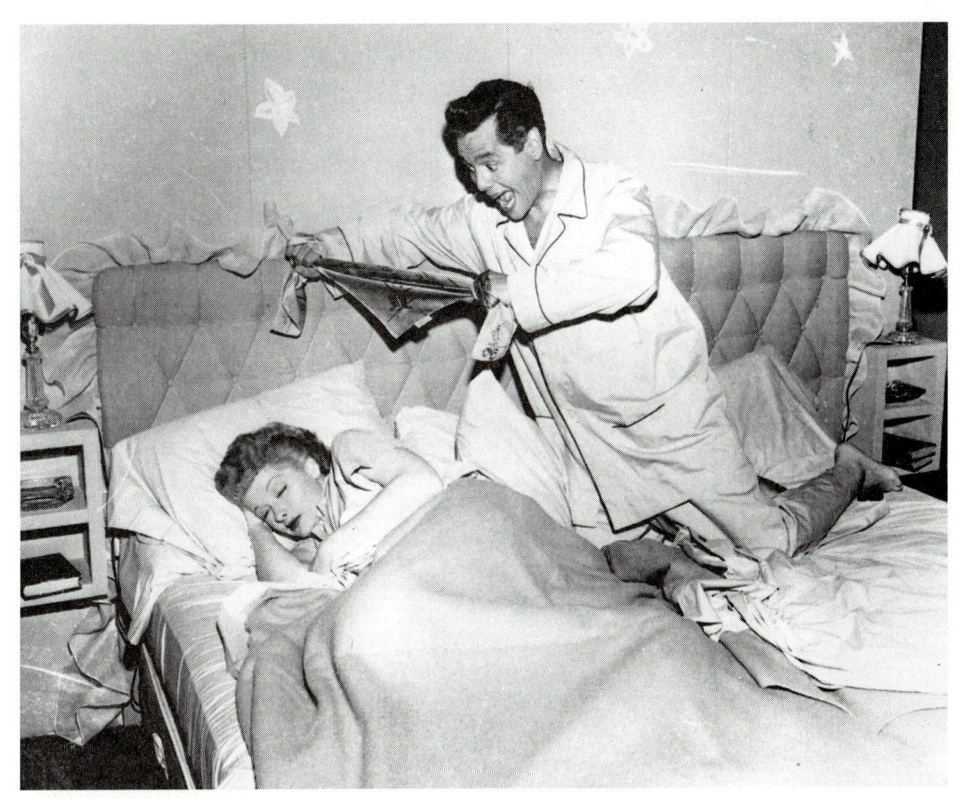

Lucille Ball and Desi Arnaz continue in reruns as America's most popular husband-and-wife comedy team. The network censors allowed the couple to be shown in bed on the "I Love Lucy" show because they were married in real life.

Soon detective shows and westerns filmed on location and edited into a one-hour format, with commercial breaks nicely worked in at planned pauses in the action, joined sitcoms as the main programming for prime-time television. Networks and their advertisers wanted to train audiences to watch the same program regularly, so they encouraged producers to develop familiar and likable characters that could be shown in standardized yet slightly different situations week after week.

The Game Show: Made for TV

There had been quiz shows on radio, such as the one that posed the then-high-paying "$64 Question." The audience had to visualize the contestant excitedly jumping up from the studio audience to try his or her luck with a bit of trivia knowledge. On television, the agony or glee of the contestants could be seen in all its human glory. The games became not just words, bells, and buzzers, but giant boards with flashing lights, handsome hosts, and maybe even a former Miss America modeling the mink coat someone might win.

One early television game show producer believed that the prize giveaways were popular with consumers because Americans had always dreamed of winning big lottery jackpots as Europeans could in the Irish Sweepstakes.[3] Suddenly, there on the screen every night were ordinary people naming that tune, spinning that wheel, winning cars, vacations . . . and not just $64, but $64,000!

For a short while game shows disappeared from television when it was discovered that some contestants on the most lucrative nationally telecast nighttime shows, including "The $64,000 Question," had been "prepared" in ways that enabled them to answer complex or obscure questions. But the tarnish did not last long. Today the game show is so popular that "Wheel of Fortune" has both a daytime and nighttime version, and is an international hit as well. However, the networks are out of the business of producing and broadcasting game shows. "Jeopardy" and the many daytime quiz and game shows are syndicated, which means they are produced by independent companies and sold directly to television stations for use in a "strip."

The Soaps: Escaping Worldly Cares

Another format that made the transition from radio to television was the soap opera. Radio fans had thrilled to "The Romance of Helen Trent" and other programs aimed at allowing the housewife to transport herself from a humdrum existence to the glamorous life of more urbane characters. When the soaps moved to television, the same assumptions were made about the audience, and initially the characters were of interest to young and middle-aged women. But many men became big fans of the television soap operas as well—college students, for example, and those with night jobs.

The addition of the visual component to the soap opera meant that several story lines could be followed at once. Along with the usual middle-aged characters developed in the radio format, television added story lines involving more glamorous young people. Finally, in the 1980s, producers made the move to nighttime, where more mature themes could be explored. "Dallas" was quickly followed by "Dynasty" and "Falcon Crest."

MINORITIES/WOMEN

Does Television Demean Women . . . and Men?

Women are depicted on television as "half-clothed and half-witted," according to a study of the 1989–1990 television season conducted by the National Commission on Working Women. The study found that fewer women than men were portrayed on prime-time shows, and those women tended to be under 40 and rich, which hardly matches with true demographic profiles of real women. The study also criticized the lack of women in decision-making production positions in the television and film industries.

Does that mean men have it better on television? Not according to CBS news correspondent Bernard R. Goldberg. He points out that television shows and commercials portray men as jerks, chauvinist pigs, wimps, incompetents, and clumsy and irresponsible know-nothings.

In its attempt to entertain and to sell, television spares neither sex.

Sources: Andrea Adelson, "Study Attacks Women's Roles in TV," *The New York Times*, Nov. 19, 1990, p. D19; Bernard R. Goldberg, "TV Insults Men, Too," *The New York Times*, March 14, 1989, p. A21.

The prime-time super-soaps are popular not only in America but around the world: Even the natives in a remote village in Peru watch "Dynasty." Just as American movies did, the soaps fulfill the need for heroes and scapegoats—larger-than-life figures against whom the audience members can measure their own success or failure. The images of scheming millionaires in the oil or winery business are exotic and overdrawn, but no more so than the John Wayne vision of the cowboy hero that once personified America for itself and the rest of the world. The super-soaps can be viewed as a continuation of the American tradition of depicting ourselves brawling and swaggering for the entertainment of the whole world.

In the early 1990s, the prime-time soap opera began to wear out its welcome, probably because of the appetite for "new" evening programs. Popular shows like "Falcon Crest" played their last episode. The daytime soaps continued to attract large audiences, however.

TELEVISION RENEWS ITSELF

There is much truth in the complaint that TV feeds on itself, creating a culture wherein the occasional successful new show leads to "spinoffs" (characters from the original show getting their own series) and "clones" (shows that have precisely the same elements as the original one, see Figure 10.1). With so many hours to fill and the pressure to hold audiences they have captured with early evening lead-in shows, programmers fall back on the device of offering more of the same, as the evenings wear on. A study conducted at the Annenberg School of Communications at the University of Pennsylvania showed that, over time, evening television programming presents a remarkably consistent portrayal of the world across program genres and offers few scheduling alternatives to the viewer who might have wanted to avoid sitcoms or violence-laden adventure programs.[4]

But television survives and endures by reinventing itself, usually not smoothly but in fits and starts. Television surprises its consumers just often enough to keep them coming back when it looks as if they are about to drift away.

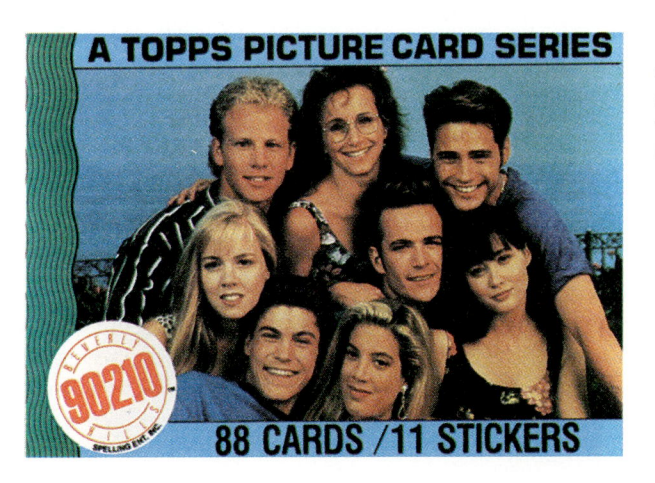

It had to happen: now fans can collect trading cards featuring shots of their favorite stars from television shows like "Beverly Hills 90210."

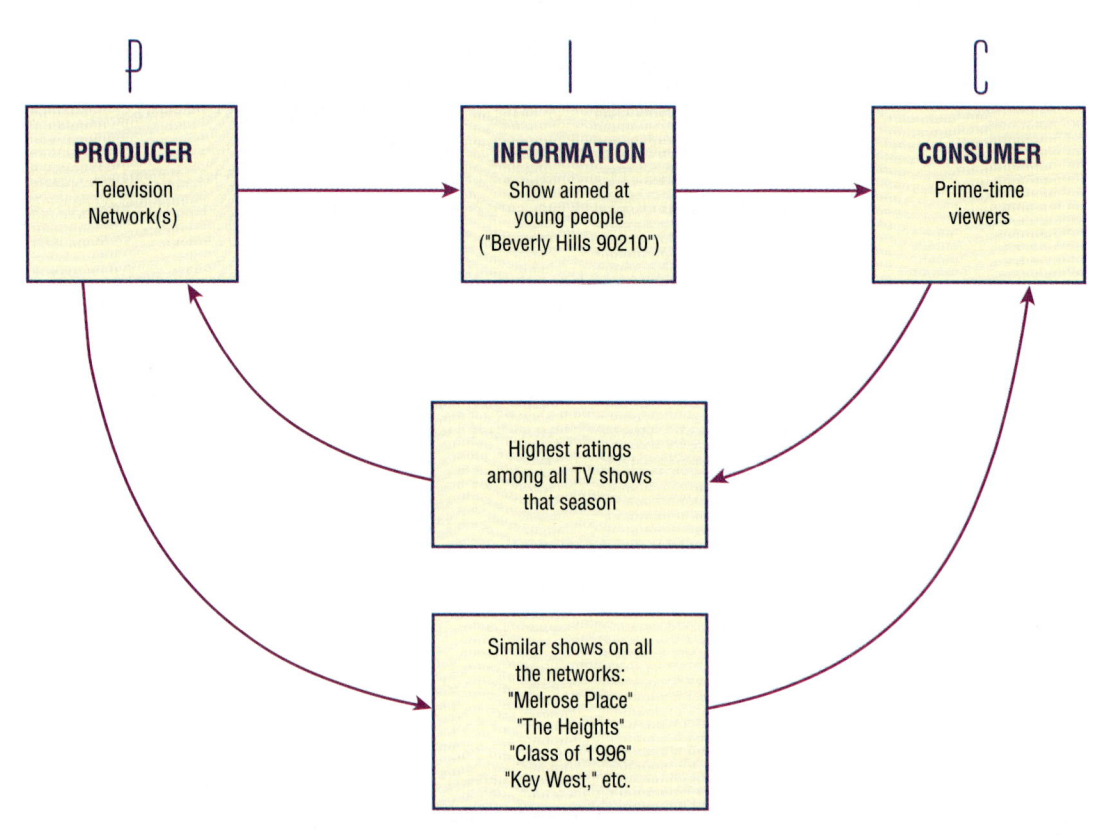

```
      P                          I                          C
┌──────────────┐         ┌──────────────┐         ┌──────────────┐
│   PRODUCER   │────────▶│  INFORMATION │────────▶│   CONSUMER   │
│  Television  │         │  Show aimed at│         │  Prime-time  │
│  Network(s)  │         │  young people │         │    viewers   │
│              │         │("Beverly Hills│         │              │
│              │         │    90210")    │         │              │
└──────────────┘         └──────────────┘         └──────────────┘
```

Highest ratings among all TV shows that season

Similar shows on all the networks:
"Melrose Place"
"The Heights"
"Class of 1996"
"Key West," etc.

FIGURE 10.1 Producer and Consumers Influence Each Other to Create Hit TV Shows The P↔I↔C model shows how one producer takes a gamble on a youth-oriented show, "Beverly Hills 90210," and—when the viewers respond favorably—spinoffs and similar shows follow in quick order.

A Hybrid Format: The Docudrama

The difference between news and entertainment programming has been blurred in recent years by a hybrid form known as the *docudrama*. Based on factual material taken from recent news stories, the docudrama uses fiction techniques to help condense and intensify a story. The producers hope that the program will be of greater interest to the audience because "it really happened," but they make sure the story works by telling it in the dramatic form of a movie.

"The Raid at Entebbe" was a docudrama about Israel's rescue of its citizens held in a plane highjacked to a hostile country. Another docudrama recreated the events when terrorists killed a passenger on the cruise ship Achille Lauro. Each of these shows was more like a movie than the news story from which the situation was adapted.

The reconstructed, or invented, dialogue in a docudrama enables viewers to observe conversations and other events that happened outside of the news event as it originally appeared on television, such as scenes in which the background situation and the motivations of the characters are revealed. The docudrama tries to make a story more comprehensible, sometimes by compressing the time line or by combining into a single pivotal character several characters who played similar roles in real life.

Some of the participants in the real-life stories feel that the docudrama constitutes an unnecessary reopening of past events, often in a way that invades individual privacy. Another criticism of the docudrama is that the producers and their writers often impose a point of view or bias that was not found in the original news accounts.

Other participants welcome the docudrama as a means of focusing attention on an event they feel needs more discussion. "The Atlanta Child Murders," broadcast by CBS in 1985, was hailed by some relatives of both the victims and the alleged murderer as a much-needed reopening of a case that they contend was hastened to a conclusion in order to calm a community horrified by a string of murders. But municipal leaders saw the docudrama as a slur on the city and its justice system. Still others attacked the program as being merely commercial exploitation of recent history. Criticism from local groups was so intense that the network agreed to run a disclaimer before and during the program, explaining that the show was not a documentary, but a drama based on certain facts and including events and characters that were fictionalized for dramatic purposes.

Critics maintain that television blurs the line between fact and fiction, and that even disclaimers before a program are not sufficient to warn an audience. Others argue that the docudrama is a valid way of interesting an audience in social issues and current events. ABC stimulated debate about the hazards of nuclear war in "The Day After," a series that portrayed America under Soviet control after the explosion of an atomic bomb. In order to help consumers appreciate the value of "The Day After," ABC and other media prepared the audience to watch the program with study guides, and they provided panel discussions immediately after the show to foster an exchange of opinions.

Some experts suggest that we expect too much of television. A television producer asked in a letter to *The New York Times*, "Why pretend that television news is anything but entertainment?" He argued that even the straight news presented on television is selected for its dramatic quality, not its real impact on people.[5]

The issue, then, may not be whether the docudrama is a valid television information format, but how the docudrama should be presented to consumers in order to perform a useful and socially responsible service. In any case, the docudrama continues to be a format that enables television producers to create interest and attract audiences.

Blending Formats: "Infotainment" and "Infomercials"

When television was first developed, broadcasters made the distinctions among different types of information crystal-clear to the audience. There were three distinct types: entertainment, news, and commercials. A moment of black screen, and often the words "we'll be back after this message" signaled the beginning of a commercial. Newscasts were dry and straightforward, with serious journalists sitting rigidly at news desks. Entertainment was signaled with distinctive theme music.

Changes began to appear in the 1970s. News readers with charming personalities and good looks replaced journalists. The members of the local "news team" (who sometimes acted more like a "family") included a congenial mix of men and women, a jolly weatherperson, and a zippy sportscaster. Some labeled it "happy talk" news.

At about the same time, commercials were allowed to flow into the news or entertainment program without breaks, so that the audience could not anticipate them and turn their attention elsewhere. Television comedian Johnny Carson instituted the word "blend" to describe information that flows seamlessly.

In the 1980s, "infotainment" was the hot new format. Programs such as "Entertainment Tonight" presented "soft" news about Hollywood, television, and rock stars. The fast-moving, easily digested format blended the structure of a news program with the easygoing style of a talk show. The anchorpeople were encouraged to be personalities themselves, and to feature the same stars that the audience read about in *People* and similar news-gossip magazines.

Fitness and cooking shows are other examples of "infotainment." The hosts not only show their viewers how to exercise or how to prepare a stuffed goose, they promote their books, show clips from their videotapes, wear the clothing viewers can buy, and endorse lines of equipment they developed or use.

Guests on talk shows always have taken the opportunity to promote their books and public appearances. But eventually companies saw the daytime talk shows as an opportunity to work a subtle commercial pitch into the information being presented. A cooking lesson might include the mention of ingredients made by a certain manufacturer. A demonstration of "how to dress for success" could include a style show featuring the fashions of a particular designer.

In hours outside prime time, television has taken to using "infomercials"—spots lasting anywhere from 5 to 24 minutes that present useful information and make clear who the "sponsor" is, even though the program is not considered a commercial message. An insurance company, for instance, sponsors a series of short "family financial planning" programs, each mentioning the firm's insurance plans as examples. The bulk of the program is useful information, giving the "soft sell" additional credibility.

Broadcast television, slow to change, has made limited use of infomercials, but cable has embraced them enthusiastically. That puts competitive pressure on broadcast TV to become cozier with advertisers, offering them "mentions" on programs, and perhaps guaranteeing manufacturers exclusive use of their products in entertainment programs—only Coke and Chevrolets are used by the actors in a popular sitcom, perhaps. It happens already in the movies, and television producers feel the pressure to make more profits for their stockholders.

WHO PAYS FOR TELEVISION PROGRAMMING?

The viewing audience for television grew rapidly throughout the 1950s. Prices for television sets dropped from $800 to $500, and then below $300 for a 19-inch black-and-white set, well within the means of almost everyone. Eventually even color television came as low as $300. In the 1950s, "picture tube insurance" was sold for $39 to $79 a year, because set owners were warned in advertisements on television that tube blowout could be expected, and replacement would cost nearly half the price of the entire set. But by the beginning of the 1960s the quality of television sets proved to be such that the concept of insuring the tube beyond the normal warranty all but disappeared.

More important than the question of how much television sets cost was the issue of who paid for the programming received "free" on that set. Radio had set a precedent for television in the United States. It was assumed from the start that broadcasting would be commercial in nature. This assumption traces to the belief of President Hoover and others that government should not control the content of broadcasting, as well as to the manufacturing community's recognition that radio was a marvelous medium for selling products. Advertising revenues would more than cover the cost of producing programs so that broadcasters could make a profit.

That wasn't the case in most European countries, where the government controlled the broadcast media and a fee was charged at the time a radio or television set was purchased. That fee, along with an annual user's fee and revenue raised by taxes, enabled governments to subsidize broadcasting—a system that continues in many countries. (Recently, Britain has been moving toward abandoning the annual fee, deregulating television, encouraging commercialism, and putting its cherished BBC on the same footing as America's viewer-supported public television.)

Television, with its need for sets, taking film crews on location, editing, and postproduction of sound and graphics, proved to be much more expensive to produce than radio. Advertisers had to foot a much larger bill, but most thought it would be worth it. After all, now you could show the product in use, literally speak directly to the consumer, and create visual excitement appealing to the emotions. Moreover, you could blend the advertising message right into the programming. Avoiding commercials would not be as simple as "flipping the page" in a magazine.

While "free" TV expanded rapidly, some in the industry felt that many kinds of programming would be of sufficient interest that consumers would be willing to pay extra for the privilege of watching them without commercial interruption.

"Channel One" brings the world to the classroom—in return for a few minutes of advertising aimed at students.

Movies, sports events, and concerts were among the events that might be sold this way. In the early 1950s, the FCC authorized and tested the concept of pay TV, with viewers in selected cities paying a "toll" or subscription fee to receive special events programming. The idea never proved viable on broadcast television, however, because of the complexities of promotion and billing. It remained for cable television in the late 1980s to launch successful pay-per-view systems, which will be discussed in the following chapter.

During the 1989–1990 school year, Whittle Communications introduced classroom television news programs that included commercials, a scheme that immediately caused heated debate. New York, California, and Rhode Island banned Whittle's innovative "Channel One" broadcasts because of the commercials. Cable News Network (CNN) offered a similar free educational news service called "CNN Newsroom." For every educator who criticized the commercialized service, another lauded its efforts to make news interesting and relevant to high school students. (The Whittle system also included free video production equipment for participating schools.) Educators who defended the Channel One concept pointed out that students were so accustomed to viewing commercials that their presence on the educational programs did not affect the value of the learning experience.

PUBLIC BROADCASTING'S ROLE

There has always been another, noncommercial view of television. A segment of society criticizes commercial broadcasting for offering mostly "lowest common denominator" programming intended only to capture the attention of the widest possible public and lull them to the point where they will passively receive messages that try to convince them to buy consumer products they don't really need or want. The option for people with that view is to watch and support public broadcasting. That is why, before we return to the realities of commercial broadcasting, we will look once again at the role of "public" broadcasting.

The advent of television was hailed as an opportunity for new and unparalleled efforts to educate the masses with the new technology. But TV channels were limited in number and promised to be even more lucrative than radio stations. Therefore, commercial interests were strongly opposed to reserving part of the spectrum for educational television, so educational forces had to pressure the FCC in a systematic and sustained way. By the time the "freeze" was over in 1952, the FCC had agreed to reserve one channel out of every eight for noncommercial use.

Finding Financial Support

Universities sponsored the first educational television stations, and they immediately ran into two problems: Financial support was difficult to find, and audiences avoided what they considered dull programs.

The Ford Foundation, which helped educators bring pressure on the FCC, continued its support by underwriting National Educational Television (NET), a consortium of nonprofit stations that formed their own sort of network. Rather than feeding programs electronically from a central location, as the commercial

ECONOMICS

Spending on Public TV: How the United States Compares

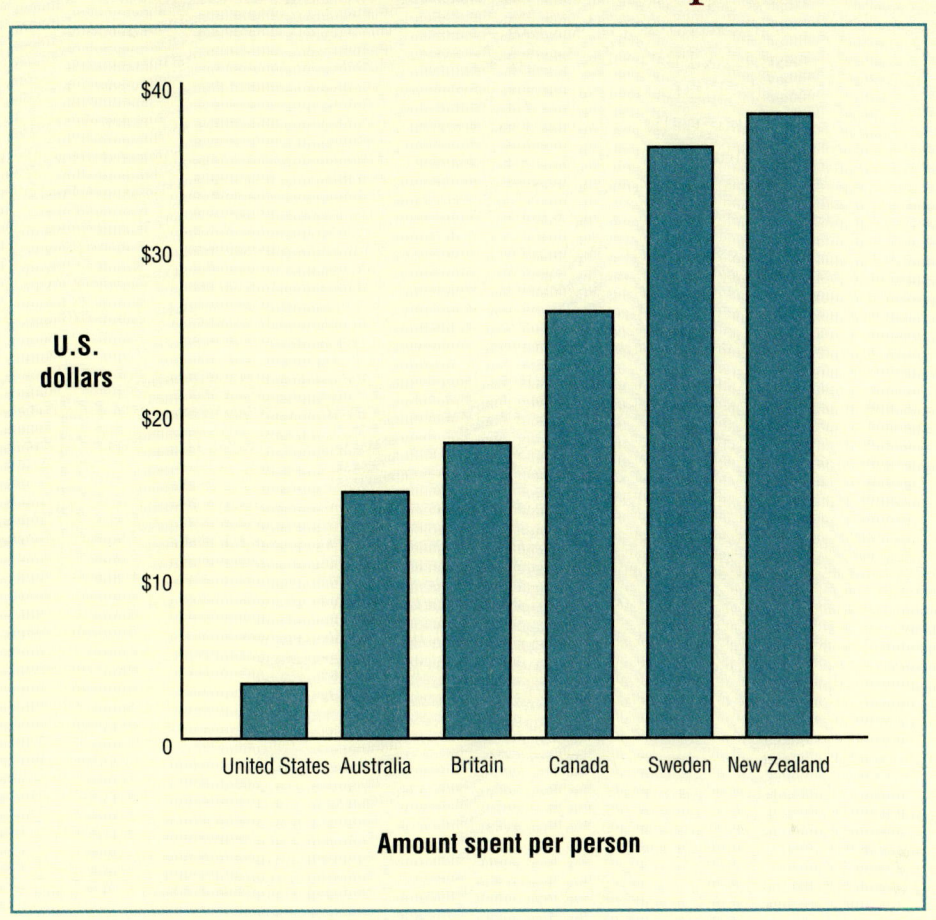

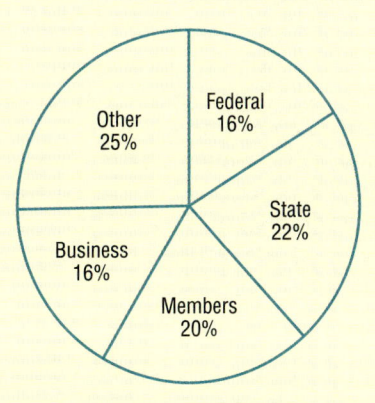

U.S. dollars

Amount spent per person

(United States, Australia, Britain, Canada, Sweden, New Zealand)

Pie chart:
- Federal 16%
- State 22%
- Members 20%
- Business 16%
- Other 25%

The $3.33 spent for each U.S. citizen begins with just 54 cents from the federal government, or 16 percent. State governments pay 22 percent of the cost, "members" cover 20 percent, and business 16 percent. The remaining 25 percent must be raised from foundations or other large donors.

Source: Facts About PBS, Public Broadcasting Service fact sheet, 1985.

networks did, they merely mailed or delivered recorded programs to one another for rebroadcasting.

By the late 1960s, there were nearly 200 educational television stations, and it was apparent that they needed to be put on a sounder footing. The Public Broadcasting Act, passed by Congress in 1967, created the Corporation for Public Broadcasting (CPB) to foster the growth of the nonprofit radio and television stations and facilitate their linkage for the purpose of sharing programming costs. Two years later, the Public Broadcasting Service (PBS) was created specifically to facilitate nonprofit television programming. Congress did not build any permanent appropriations into the act, so CPB and PBS have had to fight for funds—and their very existence—ever since. Nonetheless, educational broadcasting had turned the corner and been given a new, less restrictive identity: "public" broadcasting.

The Public Telecommunications Financing Act of 1978 requires the CPB to submit to the President and Congress a "comprehensive and detailed inventory of funds distributed by federal agencies to public telecommunications entities." In the 1980s, the departments of Commerce and Education awarded the most grants to public broadcasting. Other funding came from the National Endowment for the Arts, the National Endowment for the Humanities, the National Science Foundation, and the United States Information Agency.

Throughout the 1980s, however, federal support for public television was seriously cut back. More and more, public television turned to underwriting from the business community. To make such sponsorship more attractive, many public stations now allow "enhanced credits." While they do not promote the attributes of specific products, these announcements are very much like the "institutional" advertisements seen on commercial television that promote the reputation of a company. Pressured by lagging income, in 1988 PBS changed its rules to permit the mention of one specific product each time a corporation received credit for underwriting a program. Companies support public broadcasting because it enhances their "image" by placing the firm in an "elite environment," to use the jargon of the advertising world.

The public television stations also use on-air fundraising promotion to attract support from "members"—viewers who are willing to pay $35 or more a year to help defray the cost of the programs they watch. Consumers who prefer "NOVA," National Geographic specials, "Hallmark Playhouse," "Masterpiece Theatre," and "The MacNeil-Lehrer Report" have grown accustomed to two-week periods every three or four months when the programming is interrupted by ten-minute phonothon appeals to support the station. Eventually viewers grew tired of the endless begging. Armed with "zappers," they flipped around the dial during the on-air fundraising. In the process, some stayed with other programming instead of returning to public broadcasting. Some stations have responded with shorter breaks and announcements that are not so annoying.

The Challenge for Public Broadcasting

In 1986, members of Congress were charged with pressuring CPB to keep a weekly series called "The Lawmakers," which reflected positively on the work of Congress, in order to keep CPB funds from being cut.[6] To prevent such interference and to assure public broadcasting of federal support, an industry coalition is seeking measures to protect public television from government interference.

At the beginning of the 1990s, public broadcasting stands at a crossroads. The CPB's ongoing national survey of the educational uses of television, radio, and computers in the classroom indicates that there is a continuing need in the schools for educational material received through the electronic media; that need has been reported to the FCC.[7] Public broadcasters also point to the fact that they typically put more emphasis on minority training and hiring than do the commercial stations. Owing to their non-union status, many public stations are able to provide hands-on internships and entry-level jobs for young people interested in learning all facets of broadcast production.

But Congress and the FCC, in the spirit of deregulation, have signaled public broadcasting that it should emulate commercial television in the marketplace to find what programming and means of support are viable, instead of looking for continued government support. Public broadcasters countered with the argument that having to seek sponsorship from the business community leads to programs that are likely to be less controversial, less probing, and more acceptable to conservative interests. Indeed, in the spring of 1990, the programming chief for PBS acknowledged that she was considering adding sitcoms and game shows to make public broadcasting more relevant and popular.[8]

THE RISE AND DECLINE OF THE TELEVISION NETWORKS

The demonstration of television at the 1939 World's Fair in New York captured the imagination of many consumers, but the commercial introduction of "radio with pictures" had to wait nearly a decade owing to the interruption of World War II. Each of the major radio networks entered the television business in the late 1940s, with NBC and CBS signing up affiliates in most of the 100 major markets, while ABC and Dumont—the long-forgotten fourth network—lagged far behind. Dumont dropped out of the competition in the mid-1950s and ABC became a "weak third" in the network field, a role it would hold until its ascendancy in the 1970s as the premier sports network.

There was insufficient programming for round-the-clock broadcasting, and television viewing habits, as we noted at the beginning of the chapter, were more like movie-attending rituals or family radio listening. Typically, the station of the late 1940s and early 1950s came on the air with a "test pattern" around 5 P.M., carried one or two local programs including the reading of the news in the early evening, and joined the network with which it was affiliated for three hours of programming—the beginning of the concept of "prime time." That paralleled radio network programming, and the format remained the heart of the network-affiliate concept even after the networks began to provide soap operas and game shows during the daytime hours.

Because the art of television production would take time to develop, each network carried movies that filled almost the entire three-hour prime-time slot at least one or two evenings a week. Each network began to work with advertisers and film producers to develop continuing half-hour and one-hour programs. Soon certain nights took on a distinctive flavor. Saturday emerged as comedy/variety night, with CBS's popular "Jackie Gleason Show" and NBC's "Your Show of

Shows." CBS established several situation comedies on Tuesday night and the other networks virtually ceded it domination in that segment of programming. Families got locked into habitual viewing: "Mondays we watch the ABC movie, Tuesdays we watch the comedies on CBS. . . ."

The networks gradually developed the capability of filling every night of the week with original programming, and they had to do it 52 weeks of the year because they had no ability to store and reuse television programs. Filmed "kinescopes" of television programs were useful for archival purposes, but they were not of broadcast quality. The introduction of videotape—an electronic means of recording and storing television programs—meant that the networks could make just 26 episodes of a weekly program and show "reruns" in the spring and summer.

The television boom of the 1950s appeared to spell doom for the movie business, because the film audience stayed home to watch "free" television. But the film business did not disappear, it merely adjusted to the new marketplace. In addition, many of its writers, producers, and technicians became employees of production companies and syndicates that developed programs for first-run showing on the networks and later syndication for showing five days a week on independent stations or on affiliates during non-network hours.

By the 1960s, the networks had developed the practice of introducing most of their new shows one or two weeks in the middle of September. Shows that did not find an audience fairly rapidly were canceled and replaced with other programs whose "pilot" episodes shown the summer before did not win them a slot in the opening fall line-up. The networks structured their formats, but it soon became clear that the consumers made the final choices that dictated the prime-time program schedule for network television.

FCC Eyes the Role of Networks

Ever-mindful of its mandate to prevent monopoly control of the information carried on the public airwaves, the Federal Communications Commission began the first of several inquiries into program production and distribution in the late 1950s. (Adding to the concern were the quiz-show scandals of 1959, when it was discovered that producers were hyping the shows by tipping off some contestants so they would win prizes as large as $100,000. That spurred the networks into taking over control from the producers of the game shows they aired.)

In 1970 the FCC passed the "Financial Interest and Syndication Rules," which forced the networks out of the business of syndication. A network could no longer control the profits from reruns of its shows, known as syndication. Shortly thereafter, antitrust suits aimed at curtailing network control of programming were filed by the federal government. By the end of the 1970s, all three networks had signed consent decrees that limited the number of programs they could own. Syndication and program control were profitable for the networks, so the FCC limitations, while they prevented a monopoly, also precipitated the decline of network revenues.

Indeed, by the beginning of the 1990s, as the share of audience and the revenues for the networks plummeted, the FCC began to relax its restrictions on the networks. The Fox Broadcasting Company, bidding to become the "fourth network," was granted a waiver by the FCC to program 18½ hours a week without being subject to the syndication rule. Fox was well on its way to meeting the FCC's definition of a network: 25 stations in at least 10 states offering at least 15 hours of programming each week.

In 1991, the FCC made some concessions to the networks, allowing them to keep resale rights to as much as 40 percent of the programming they produced, and to earn royalties on reruns of other programming. But some lucrative types of programs were excluded, and the main beneficiaries of the 1991 rules were the movie studios that produce television programming. Later in 1991, the FCC began yet another review of television ownership and programming in light of the inroads cable was making against the broadcast networks.

Japanese ownership of communication companies raises questions of whether foreign financial interests will exercise control over the information that American consumers receive. The networks sounded the alarm in 1990 after the Matsushita Electrical Industries Corporation of Japan bought MCA, the parent of Universal Studios.

Networks Lose Viewers and Advertising Revenue

The networks began the 1980s with a combined share of 91 percent of the television viewing audience. By the early 1990s they had about 60 percent. That means that one out of three people who once watched network shows shifted to other programming. It translates into lost advertising revenues, because shrinking audiences put the advertisers in a much stronger bargaining position when they haggle with networks over "upfront" sponsorship of shows—committing themselves in advance to pay for advertising that will put a show on the air.

The 17-week strike of the Writer's Guild of America in 1988 further crippled the networks. The absence of new shows in the first half of that season accelerated the flight of viewers to other forms of video information.

Stopping the Slide

The networks had to find ways to increase profitability. In the 1990s they cut the budgets of their evening news shows from what they spent in the heydays of the 1970s and the 1980s on the theory that they can satisfy viewers without using so many highly paid reporters and far-flung film crews. Ratings for the first part of 1990 showed that the audience for the networks' nightly newscasts, once their most important shows, fell 14 percent in just a matter of months, contrasted with 2.2 percent for prime-time shows and 8.1 percent for daytime programming during the same period.[9] The networks have made up some of the shortfall with syndicated shows that feature topics related to the news, such as "Geraldo," "Oprah Winfrey," and "Donahue." These shows are more cost-effective than the evening news, and they have proved they can deliver large audiences.

The Networks Fight Back

"The Networks Fight Back, Finally." Under that blunt headline, *The New York Times* outlined the steps the networks were taking at the end of the 1980s and are expected to continue in the 1990s to at least halt their losses of audience and revenues to other forms of television, even if they can never regain their dominance of the field.[10] The measures include:

- Cutting costs by reducing staff, except in the area of marketing, where more personnel are needed to work with advertisers.
- Forming a trade association among the networks, unheard of in an earlier era when competition between the networks was too fierce to permit cooperation.
- Promoting new shows in "upscale" magazines to attract the upper-income audience to programming aimed at them instead of the lowest common denominator.
- With the relaxation of syndication, returning to production of more of their own programming, since much of the profit in television comes from syndication of reruns and sales abroad.

At one time the networks used promotions on their own stations to build interest in their shows: It cost them little, and they already had the attention of the potential audiences. Now they realize they have to use other media to lure their audiences back. They've even tried putting ads for their shows on rental videocassettes for movies aimed at the same audience—a move that angers video retailers. In the new scramble for television dollars, the networks have to be imaginative and aggressive if they are to survive.

In June of 1992, the FCC moved to provide relief to the networks. It approved a plan whereby the networks can buy local cable systems, but not in markets where they already own a station. The FCC hoped to foster a new partnership between cable and network television. The decision created anxiety for local affiliates, who may find that the network with which they are affiliated is, in fact, a local competitor as well. The FCC commissioners acknowledged that their new regulation raises many questions, which means that further decisions will be needed throughout the 1990s to sort out the balance between the various players in the television-cable marketplace.

DEVELOPING THE NEWS FUNCTION

Today we are not surprised by the ability of network and local news departments to provide complete coverage of presidential election nights, hostage situations, visits of foreign leaders, space launches, inaugurations, and natural disasters. Yet these functions were developed in just one generation.

Early television was capable of providing little more than the 15-minute reading of the news that radio offered. Gradually the ability to project still pictures behind the news-reader's head was added, and then film footage. Finally, reporters working live from remote locations could be included in the news format, using mini-cameras and micro-dish transmission.

Because of the addition of visual images, news broadcasts were allotted more time. At one time the 15-minute national news and the 15-minute local news made up a half-hour package; eventually each went to 30 minutes. But the desire of the networks to lengthen their evening news shows to an hour met resistance from affiliates who preferred to control the advertising time during their own expanded news shows. In some large urban markets today the local news runs two hours—one hour of "soft" feature news, and the second hour of "straight" news. Public television's "MacNeil-Lehrer Report" expanded to a full hour in the late 1980s to permit fuller treatment of two or three main stories.

Political Conventions Launch New Careers

Radio's top newscasters who gained prominence during World War II did not rush to television. Edward R. Murrow, Howard K. Smith, and Eric Sevareid looked at television as a less serious medium than radio. Rather than spend time in a TV studio preparing to go before the camera, these men preferred to develop their stories in a highly personalized way, polish them at a typewriter much as a print reporter would, and then depend on their carefully cultivated speaking styles to inject the proper drama and highlight the importance of the facts.

What changed the radio newscasters' minds was the decision by the networks to cover the 1948 nominating conventions with television cameras. Here now was an opportunity for the broadcast newsmen who had gained their fame on the European battlefront to sit in another type of arena and explain to their live audiences what was going on. That role was attractive to the newscasters, and when they saw the impact televised coverage could have in allowing the American people to see democracy in action, the venerable Douglas Edwards (CBS) and John Cameron Swayze (NBC) agreed to read the news on television.

The nominating conventions proved to be testing grounds for the new generation of news talent. Positive consumer reaction to the coverage of Chet Huntley and David Brinkley won that team the anchor chairs at NBC after the 1956 conventions, just as Walter Cronkite had moved into the anchor post at CBS after 1952. After covering its first few conventions from the gallery, television moved onto the floor with portable cameras. Tough-minded journalists like CBS's Mike Wallace made their reputations with confrontations that revealed what was happening behind the scenes.

The nominating conventions of America's political parties are now made for television, with all major events carefully "orchestrated" for prime-time viewing. Even the lighting, the color schemes, and the placement of press boxes are tailored to the medium.

Until television news invited itself to the party, national political conventions lacked order and decorum. The organizers hoped more or less to nominate candidates one day, vote the next day, and anoint the winners on the last day. But if there were long demonstrations, fights over the party platform, or the need for several ballots, the conventions could go into the early morning or the agenda might be carried over to the next day.

Television made the nominating conventions a prime-time show. Just as the World Series and the Miss America Pageant reshaped themselves to fit the needs of television, so did the political conventions. The site of the convention must meet the needs of the media. The hours of convention sessions are tailored to fit the main events into prime time. The length, content, and visual look of all speeches and events must meet the dictates of commercial television. Several film segments may be "prepackaged" for showing directly on TV as well as in the convention hall.

CBS executive producer Don Hewitt bemoaned the fact that time-consuming convention floor fights have been eliminated because of the needs of television. "If you want to see a real fight at a political convention," he told a National Press Club audience, "let CBS News's sign be an inch bigger than NBC's. Now you'll see a fight."[11]

Because of their prominence at historic events, the network anchors were elevated to positions of power and respect unusual for anyone in American society. While Gallup surveys in the 1980s showed President Ronald Reagan with a "believability rating" of around 67 percent, the anchors on the three networks had an average rating of about 75 percent.

That's why Cronkite, who consistently had the highest believability ratings before his retirement from the anchor seat in 1981, came to be known as "Uncle Walter." The consumers felt he not only brought them the news, he in fact *embodied* the news. During his coverage of the early manned space launches in the 1960s and 1970s, Cronkite's involvement with the story was so great that he made the study of manned flight his hobby. When the first spaceship landed on the moon, his comments included "Golly, just look at that!" and "Wow, what a thrilling moment!" Far from discrediting him as a journalist, that human touch helped his viewers share the experience much better than if someone had merely recited the facts to them.

The era of the newsreader was over. The participant journalist was now the norm on TV. The "anchors" and other on-air personalities didn't have to remain tied to the New York or Washington studio. Instead they could be expected to travel with the President to a summit, attend the Olympic Games, and even visit the war front as Cronkite and others did during the Vietnam conflict.

Television also changed other facets of national politics. In the 1960 presidential election, candidates Richard Nixon and John F. Kennedy met in the first live television debates. Kennedy's vitality, directness, and careful preparation won out over Nixon's poor makeup, hesitant speaking style, and lack of poise.

HOW TV NEWS DIFFERS FROM PRINT NEWS

As television news coverage expanded and evolved, it became apparent that television news differs from radio news because of the addition of pictures. It differs even more fundamentally from print news, although the typical consumer usually doesn't stop to think about it. Let's look at some key differences:

Time of Exposure to the Story. The consumer of print information can control time of exposure to print news. If an article has utility, the reader can read it thoroughly, reread key facts, and pause to evaluate. There is no way for the consumer to edit or slow down a television news report or, conversely, to speed it up when the topic seems irrelevant (unless the viewer watches a news program recorded earlier on a VCR, which is not the usual viewing pattern for news).

The Reporter's Personality. The byline on a print story might tip the reader off as to the sex and ethnic background of a reporter. The reporter's reputation might be known to the reader. But usually a consumer of print news doesn't notice the byline or attach much importance to it. In television, on the other hand, the reporter's looks, dress, personality, demeanor, speaking style, and mannerisms help the viewer decide whether the information being presented is trustworthy, accurate, and complete. Even if the tests of credibility are met, the viewer's personal like or dislike of the person presenting the information could affect the viewer's evaluation of the report.

Time Constraints. The print reporter fights for space, much as the broadcast reporter must plead for 10 extra seconds to cover another dimension of the story. But those 10 seconds are added to a television story only 50 seconds long. The six or seven paragraphs more that a print reporter requests, when added to a 24-paragraph story, make possible the inclusion of several more facts or quotes that can increase the depth of the reader's understanding.

Type of Data. With those six or seven extra paragraphs, the print reporter is able to add facts, figures, quotes, and background information. Traditionally, print journalists cite numbers, dates, and other specific information to give the reader a picture of "reality." Television reporters have only enough time to provide capsule summaries: "The average family in Our town cannot afford a new house, and so unhappiness is building among young couples who see no hope of owning their own property." That sentence, if it appeared in a newspaper, would be buttressed by quotes from home-buyers and bankers, along with citations of prices, interest rates, and statistics for home ownership by age group. On television, the generalization often is the word of the reporter, which explains why credibility is so important.

Television's Need for Visual Images. As we saw earlier, television has moved away from the "talking head" newsreader. Television must have pictures to hold the attention of its audience. Preferably those pictures should include action, drama, and conflict. Stories about financial trends, political ideas, and other relative abstractions are anathema to TV. Footage of a mother tossing her babies out of a burning building seems always to take precedence over a government official explaining why price supports for grain should be increased. Print is more likely to be able to use both—the fire story on page 1, and the less visual story on an inside page.

Television's Predisposition to Package a Story. The first New Year's baby born in Peoria, Illinois, in 1989 was the illegitimate child of a 14-year-old, delivered in an ambulance. Local TV crews sent to the hospitals chose to ignore that story. They featured the first child born in a hospital as the area's "first baby of the new year." Station managers defended their decision on the ground that the traditional story is supposed to be a happy one. Local newspapers, however, reported the true story (without using the mother's name) on the grounds that births to unwed mothers are an important trend, happy New Year's tradition notwithstanding.[12] Television tends to be bound to format more than print media. Print media are more likely to play a story as the facts and situation dictate.

A print reporter who attended a session on the credibility of the news media sponsored by the Poynter Institute for Media Studies in St. Petersburg, Florida, transcribed an entire evening news broadcast, set it in type and put it in newspaper format. The entire broadcast filled the equivalent of one newspaper page.

Despite the relative completeness of print, many consumers prefer television news because it is easy to understand. Some kinds of information that seem cold and immaterial on the printed page take on greater meaning when spoken by an apparently trustworthy, concerned individual and illustrated in human terms with realistic film footage.

HOW DOES TV PROGRAMMING TAKE SHAPE . . . AND WHY?

The growth in a variety of technologies in the last quarter of the twentieth century means that the home screen is an outlet for not only broadcast television, but also cable, videocassettes, and even home movies made by the consumer's own videorecorder. Sometimes it's useful to deal with the newer technologies separately, since cable television and videocassettes offer many features that broadcast television does not. But as Les Brown, editor of *Channels* magazine, pointed out:

> It all comes down to programming. With everyone chasing the heavy users of television—that so-called mass audience—the difference in distribution systems becomes quite meaningless. Once the technologies enter the household, they are taken for granted, and what they present, however it may get there, is considered television.[13]

So we return now to programming, which we described in discussing television formats earlier in this chapter. Now, however, our emphasis will be on how the programs are selected, and what needs they fill for the producers and for the consumers.

Pressures on the Networks

The chief programmer at each of the three major networks spends a lot of time studying the scheduling board on the office wall that shows the three hours of prime-time programming—8 to 11 P.M. in the East, 7 to 10 P.M. elsewhere—for seven nights a week—21 hours for each network to fill, 63 hours of programs in total. Because about half will be 30-minute episodes of situation comedies and dramas, and each network offers at least one 2-hour movie each week, the total number of prime-time programs each network offers at any one time is around 30.

Trying to decide what will constitute an effective lineup of shows each night in terms of holding an audience from one show to the next is complicated enough. The problem is compounded by the necessity of competing with two other major networks, an up-and-coming fourth network (Fox), independent stations, public broadcasting, and cable. But *scheduling* is only part of the complex business of network programming. There are other pressures on the chief programmer, all of them pushing the network toward decisions that result in "lowest common denominator" programming that makes it difficult for anything but mediocre programs to survive the process.[14]

Among the groups that affect the networks' decisions are

- Advertisers
- Affiliated stations
- Government regulators
- Advocacy groups and television "watchdogs"
- The competition—all television, not just other networks
- Packagers—studios and independent producers of programs
- Artists and creative people, many of whom control their own shows
- The viewers

Any of these groups, when and if they become actively involved, have, in effect, a veto power over the network. When you are dealing with such a large audience and such high production costs, you cannot afford to ignore or offend any segment of society. That's a dilemma that confronts network television more than any other mass medium.

Advertisers want popular programs that attract everybody and offend nobody. The stations that affiliate with the network have much the same outlook. In addition, the affiliates often have concerns that are regional: Stations in the conservative, religious South are more likely to drop a network show with too much emphasis on sex and violence, while outlets in the major urban centers might complain about programs that don't provide enough "mature" interest.

Networks used to produce many of their own dramatic and variety programs. Now they get the majority of their shows from outside producers. With the rise of independent stations and cable, these producers have many more outlets with which to bargain.

Star demands and writer burnout both force programmers to move in new directions. Like athletic heroes who quickly change from thankful rookies to demanding prima donnas, many television stars eventually realize that they carry a show. As their contract clout improves, they demand certain directors, refuse scripts they don't like, insist that their characters' roles be beefed up, and ask for huge raises. Their off-screen involvements can also make a network or independent producer nervous, which may explain why CBS canceled the popular "Lou Grant" show when Ed Asner's leftist politics and support of a union strike against the networks caused letters from viewers, cancellations from sponsors, a sag in the ratings, and uneasiness in the industry.[15]

The relentless demand for a fresh episode each week means that writers eventually burn out. They repeat plots and situations, and eventually they are replaced by less talented writers who resort to recycling old material in a less appealing way.

INSIGHT

The Sports Dome: Stadium or . . . Family Room?

Television enhances the revenues of major league sports teams and many of the larger college teams. But it also provides an incentive to stay home instead of battling the elements in a stadium or ball park. In addition to the creature comforts of home, the television broadcast adds many useful features to the fan's appreciation of the game: color commentary, instant replays, and graphic displays of interesting statistical information.

To lure fans away from the cozy family room, sports promoters had to invent the dome—a sort of family room for 50,000 people.

In addition to the protection from weather, the dome offers seats with backs, not the benches and bleachers of old stadiums.

And up there at the end of the "room" is the giant television, complete with instant replays and statistics. The computer-generated images shown between plays even tell the audience when and how to cheer. Without the assistance of television, today's dome fans might find the game hard to follow because they've been trained to expect an "overlay" of electronic information to supplement the unadorned reality they observe on the field of play.

Video technology makes sports events more exciting, and allows fans to see instant replays just as they would on the home screen.

Figuring Out the Viewers

Complicated as the other problems may be, the television executive's most difficult task is figuring out who the viewers are, what they want, and why they behave the way they do.

At the most basic level, people use television simply as something to do in order not to be doing nothing—a phenomenon sometimes known as being a "couch potato." A study by our Rutgers colleague Robert Kubey indicated that less affluent and less educated viewers, along with divorced and separated individuals, watched television to avoid the negative moods that often coincide with solitude and unstructured time. "As some TV viewers grow dependent on the structured stimuli of television, they may become increasingly incapable of satisfactorily filling leisure time without it," Kubey suggested.[16]

At another level, some people seize on a particular channel or service as "their" television. A woman donating blood at a downtown Red Cross center was not pleased to find the television in the recovery room tuned to CBS's afternoon soap opera lineup: "I watch ABC!" she informed the attendant indignantly, identifying herself as a member of a particular television "family." Others watch only MTV (the music television channel), only cable news, or only sports programs. Television networks and cable services often try to develop a "lead-in strategy" that attempts to capture an audience with a popular program of a certain genre and then hold that audience through the evening with a flow of similar programs. At one time CBS firmly established Saturday night as comedy night. Another night "Falcon Crest" followed "Dallas" because CBS figured to have a particular audience hooked.

Programmers must know who watches on which nights. Adult viewing is heaviest on Sundays and Mondays, then tapers off through the rest of the week. Friday and Saturday nights are known as "babysitter" nights because so many adults are not watching television. More and more, the promotions for programs and reviews in the daily newspaper convince many adults ahead of time to watch or to miss a program. Men much more than women lack loyalty to specific programs and will skip their usual favorite if something sounds more interesting, such as a sports event, on another station.

Just as manufacturers of soap, soft drinks, potato chips, and hair sprays test their products in selected markets, television producers have developed methods of pretesting programs. Tourists visiting New York and Los Angeles are encountered on the street and invited to attend screenings of pilots for TV series held in

INDUSTRY

Profile of the Audience for Television

- Fewer than 50 percent of the people who are asked to participate in survey research designed to measure television audiences are willing to participate. The poor "cooperation rate" threatens to undermine studies of the attitudes and behaviors of television viewers. (Source: Statistical Research Inc. report commissioned by the networks and the National Association of Broadcasters, 1988.)

- Sunday night is the most popular time of the week for viewing television. On any evening, the most viewed evening half-hour is 8:30 to 9 P.M. in the Eastern time zone. (Source: National Association of Broadcasters, 1990.)
- Women view more television than men. Older men and women view more than other age groups. Younger children view more than older children and teenagers. (Source: A. C. Nielsen Co., 1990.)

specially equipped theaters. Holding a button in each hand, they are asked to press one if they like what's on the screen, the other if they don't. In this manner producers have been able to judge whether characters should be kept in a show, and whether the show as a whole is likely to attract an audience. Questionnaires and focus group interviews are also used to debrief viewers that the producers hope represent a cross section of viewers. "Made-for-TV-movies," also known as "pilots," are another way that a network can expose a concept and a set of characters to the mass audience and then conduct surveys to find whether response warrants continuation of the show in series format.

At the beginning of the 1990s, American television producers noted that the viewers, armed with remote control mechanisms "increasingly decided that flipping through the dial—grazing—was a potentially more satisfying experience than watching one program at a time."[17] None of the programming practices developed to capture and hold audiences has proved successful in counteracting the habits of the channel-switcher armed with a remote control device.

WHAT DOES THE CONSUMER MAKE OF TV?

Mainly we have looked at the content of television and why the audience is given more of some kinds of programming than others. But there is more to television than that. Marshall McLuhan's contribution to our understanding of the dynamic of mass communication was the phrase "the medium is the message," meaning that we watch *television*, not just television programs. To understand television's powerful hold on its audiences, it is helpful if we look beyond individual episodes, plots, and characters to the familiar and recurring structure that keeps viewers in front of the tube for hours on end.

On the long-running sitcom "The Mary Tyler Moore Show," Mary uttered the same lines week after week:

"Mr. Grant, may I speak to you?"

"Murray, will you be serious?"

"Ted, where are you going?"

"Rhoda, of course he respects you."

"Sue Ann, don't you dare."

As mundane as they are on the surface, those phrases say everything about Mary's personality and her relationship with the other people in her life. If you haven't caught a "Mary" re-run lately, you can look for similar sets of recurring lines on "M*A*S*H," "Leave It to Beaver," or "Gilligan's Island." Eventually the regular viewers don't *watch* a sitcom so much as they *join* it, like members of the family. (Most of the family members we all know have their standard lines for standard situations, and we can all anticipate them before they are uttered.)

The talk shows also become like extended families for the viewer. There's the studio announcer (an uncle figure) over on the couch chuckling at everything the host (a father figure) says, and eventually we all have a laugh at the expense of the bandleader (a goofy cousin figure). Then cut to the advertisement where a woman we know from her former dramatic series (a mother figure) tells us why we should buy the brand of spaghetti sauce she uses.

RESEARCH
TV and the National Character

A survey of the French public revealed that they would rather not know some things about their leaders. They opposed publication of information about the past personal behavior of public officials by a margin of 49 to 41 percent. Only one in six Frenchmen wanted to know about the finances of candidates for the presidency.
—Louis Harris research cited in Daniel Cohen, "Paris: Newsroom Politics," *The Atlantic Monthly*, April 1983.

In America, candidates for office are obliged to reveal not only their income tax statements, but the state of their health and that of their families, as well as any past misdeeds, however minor. The prying eye of television demands that everything be open to discussion. During the 1988 presidential campaign, drug use by the wife of the Democratic candidate was scrutinized mercilessly by TV, and the Republican vice-presidential candidate's teachers in college were interviewed by TV news reporters wanting to know whether his family had brought pressure to get him into law school. During the confirmation hearings for President Bush's cabinet nominees in 1989, Senator John Tower's past drinking and "womanizing" were the leading television news story for more than a month. The hearings on Supreme Court nominee Clarence Thomas in 1991 centered on allegations of sexual harassment. In an earlier era, President Johnson was goaded into showing reporters a scar on his belly after an operation, and President Carter's beer-drinking brother's high jinks frequently made the evening news.

Do Americans genuinely want such information, or do journalists only assume they do? Is it because television has so many hours to fill and needs exciting pictures, not just the facts, with which newspapers can content themselves? The French watch only half as much TV as Americans. Analysis of the research suggests they have not been desensitized to the notion of personal privacy.

Professor Neil Postman of New York University argues that the talk shows discourage reflection or thinking—activities more likely to occur when reading a book, which would allow for pauses in the information-gathering process. By filling all of the consumer's time with endless babble, Postman says, television destroys the viewer's ability to talk coherently.[18] In other words, our entire lives are in danger of becoming "TV formula" if we succumb to the medium's constant presence.

Professional wrestling's popularity on TV confounds anyone who tries to analyze it at the surface level. It has been debunked as pure entertainment with planned outcomes, and thus it is not covered by the sports pages of most serious media. While it is considered vulgar, antisocial, and harmful by some, *The New York Times* television critic credited its appeal to the fact that it has "all the virtues and none of the faults" of real-life dramas we see on the news and in serious television programs.[19] There is a clearly good side and a clearly bad side. The audience knows they are being had. But it's fun to watch, and, when it's over, the posturing of the participants makes it clear that nobody really was hurt and the whole thing can begin over again next week. That provides welcome relief for viewers who have grown weary of news about taxes, the Middle East conflict, and political squabbles.

RESEARCH

An Antidote to Loneliness?

Research conducted at Rutgers and the University of Chicago found television viewing to be a passive and relaxing low-concentration activity that is often used as a substitute for social interaction. Subjects were given automatic paging devices; each time the beeper went off, they filled out self-report forms. The study showed that loneliness and negative experiences during the day typically preceded heavy television viewing in the evening. Other findings:

- Television can cause a "passive spillover effect." Some viewers report feeling more passive and less alert after viewing. People reported that it was somewhat more difficult to concentrate the longer they viewed, as well as after watching television.

- Television becomes less rewarding the longer it is viewed. Satisfaction drops off for some viewers, and television appears to provide relief from stress and tension only during viewing.

- Heavy viewing perpetuates itself and causes psychological dependence in those who grow accustomed to having their experiences structured for them.

Source: Robert Kubey and Mihaly Csikszentmihalyi, *Television and the Quality of Life: How Viewing Shapes Everyday Experience* (Hillsdale, NJ: Erlbaum, 1990.) pp. 171–173.

TV "Immediacy" Can Be Real or Manufactured

Television allows its consumers to "be there" when important events happen. We are at Cape Canaveral for a space launch. We are in the hearing room when senators question a high government appointee. We are in the stands for every strike and ball of the World Series.

Except for breaking news and sports events, however, most of television is prerecorded. Producers want to have control over the information, they want to shape it to fit the format and time available, and they want to have it prepared ahead of time so that it can be moved electronically without a hitch at the appointed air time. Nonetheless, the producers have learned how to manufacture the prerecorded product so that it has the same immediacy as a live event. When Pat Sajak, host of "Wheel of Fortune" says "Here's Vanna!," it fires up the audience just as does the playing of the national anthem before a ball game.

Game shows have no *when* (the date is never mentioned). They have no *where* (we only know that they come from somewhere in the Los Angeles area, but it could just as well be Chicago or New York). And they have no *why* (except for the annual "Jeopardy" tournament to select a champion, the contestants aren't selected because of any record or proven ability).

Producers of sports pseudo-events such as "American Gladiators," "Battle of the Network Stars," and "Challenge Tractor-Pulling" competitions rely on the readiness of the audience to accept an "immediacy" and reality that is concocted through fast-paced prepackaged video inserts, replays, and hyped-up "color commentary" from celebrity hosts.

The Medium of Confrontation

"Shut up, you creep, I've had just about enough of your lip," sneered the self-proclaimed loudmouth talk show host Morton Downey, Jr. His audience loved it—for a short time. Phil Donahue changed television talk from the civility of sitting on a couch to the more exciting format of walking around, shoving a microphone at people, and demanding, "How do you respond to that?"

Atlantic Monthly author Gregg Easterbrook contends that television works best when it acts as a medium of confrontation. Why? Because complicated discussions are hard to follow. But on television "the viewer can immediately pick up on what's happening . . . confrontations have human story lines that can be grasped by someone who just walked into the room".[20]

One of the events that propelled the presidential candidacy of George Bush in 1988 was his confrontational live interview with CBS's Dan Rather, in which Bush turned on the newscaster with a personal remark recalling the time when Rather stalked off his own program in anger. The standout moment of the televised debates in that same campaign was vice-presidential candidate Lloyd Bentsen's jab at Dan Quayle: "You're no John Kennedy!" to which the response was a flabbergasted "That was uncalled for!"

The television audience is passive: It cannot really join in the discussion on the screen. But it can become more involved if the talk is accompanied by action, as Geraldo Rivera learned when an audience member broke Rivera's nose with a chair during a heated confrontation. Not incidentally, the ratings for "Geraldo" zoomed after that audience-involving incident.

LIVING OR DYING BY THE RATINGS

Every mass medium has a method for measuring the size and composition of its audiences. Audited circulation figures enable advertisers to know how many people read a newspaper or magazine, and surveys provide specific information about which people make up the audience. Box office figures measure theater attendance, and theater producers can observe the house to know which segments of the audience are responding to the program.

But broadcast media, as we saw in the previous chapter, pose a special problem because the consumers can change the station they are watching from minute to minute, and there is no way for the broadcaster to observe or calculate which family members are in the audience for particular programs. A special form of research, then, is needed to measure who is watching what. In order for the information to be useful, it has to be quantified quickly for programmers and the advertisers they must satisfy.

What Is a "Rating"?

The firms that measure the reach and penetration of television programming know how many homes in the country have television. It is against this total number of *potential* viewing units that the ratings are calculated. The ratings for a given half-hour never add up to 100 percent, since 100 percent of homes with television aren't viewing at any one time. The top program in prime time may

Weatherman Willard Scott answers a viewer's dare by dressing up as the late singer Carmen Miranda while doing his job on the "Today Show." (The viewer donated $1,000 to charity.)

have a 30 rating, and all of its competitors in that time slot may have a combined 40 rating, for a total of 70—meaning that 30 percent of the sets in the area measured were *not* turned to any program. (See Table 10.1.)

Ratings, therefore, are most significant in evening prime time, when most people are likely to be at home and free to watch television. This is the period when the major manufacturers of consumer goods and services want to reach the largest possible audience. Ratings are far less significant in the middle of a weekday morning, when as few as 5 percent of households use television.

At times of the day other than prime time, the measurement known as the *share* is more significant. It is possible for a local show to have a rating of only 7, which means that 93 percent of the area homes with television were not tuned in. But the show could have a 40 share, meaning that 4 out of every 10 sets that *were* turned on at that time were tuned to the program.

National advertisers of cars, soaps, and soft drinks that want to reach every consumer probably will not be impressed with a 40 share when they discover that it is coupled with a 7 rating. But a station that has the most popular program in the cheaper time slot will attract plenty of local and specialized advertisers.

Development of the Ratings Systems

The first ratings systems, developed for radio use in the 1930s, involved telephone interviews ("What program are you listening to at this time?), face-to-face interviews at the door ("What stations have you listened to in the past 24 hours?"), and even postcard reply surveys ("Please check off which stations were listened to this past week, and by which family members"). All of the systems relied on

TABLE 10.1 Comparing Program Ratings: Arbitron Readings

	Women 18–24			Men 18–24		
Rank	Shows	Station	Ratings	Shows	Station	Ratings
1	Living Color	WYNY	33	Living Color	WNYW	30
2	Married with Children	WYNY	29	Married with Children	WNYW	27
3	A Different World	WNBC	22	Get a Life	WNYW	21
4	Ferris Bueller	WNBC	21	Fresh Prince	WNBC	15
5	Growing Pains	WABC	21	Ferris Bueller	WNBC	14
6	Get a Life	WYNW	20	Doogie Howser	WABC	14
7	Fresh Prince	WNBC	19	Cheers	WNBC	13
8	The Simpsons	WYNY	19	Growing Pains	WNYW	13
9	Bill Cosby	WNBC	18	The Simpsons	WNYW	13
10	Cheers	WNBC	18	Good Grief	WNBC	13
11	Who's the Boss	WABC	18	Different World	WABC	12
12	Full House	WABC	17	Who's the Boss	WABC	12
13	Family Matters	WABC	17	Bill Cosby	WNBC	11
14	NBC Mon Movie	WNBC	16	Wonder Years	WABC	11
15	Grand	WNBC	16	NFL Mon Ftbl	WABC	11
16	Roseanne	WABC	16	Roseanne	WABC	11
17	Doogie Howser	WABC	16	Married People	WABC	10
18	The Wonder Years	WABC	15	P Lws Cnt Ls	WYNY	10
19	Head of Class	WABC	14	Perfect Strangers	WABC	9
20	Perfect Strangers	WABC	14	Hidden Video	WYNY	9

Note: Advertisers and programmers pour over the ratings figures to determine which programs are delivering which audiences to the advertisers. These figures, for one week in October 1990, show what men and women aged 18 to 24 were watching in the New York market. "Living Color" was the top-rated show for both sexes, but note that men in this age group viewed in smaller numbers than women. "Doogie Howser, M.D." rated high with young men, lower with women. "Monday Night Football" rated fifteenth with young men, but not in the top 20 for women, who were watching the NBC Monday night movie instead.

Source: CBS Television Network compilations.

the cooperation of those who responded, and on their recall ability. Clearly a system that monitored broadcast consumption as it occurred would be preferable.

The A. C. Nielsen company acquired the rights to a device, invented by two professors at MIT, called the audimeter, which could record when a radio set was turned on and to which station. When a family agreed to be one of the 1000 Nielsen families across the country, they were visited monthly by a technician who removed the punched tape carrying the listening information. The data might be nearly two months old by the time Nielsen could assemble them for use by broadcasters and advertisers.

By the time television was introduced for home use, however, the audimeter had been improved so that the consumer could remove the tape and mail it in. Nielsen shifted from radio measurement to rating the television programs, and by the 1960s the technology had improved to the point where data were automatically fed to the company over phone lines, making the data available to the producers within a few days. (Both Nielsen and its main competitor, Arbitron, supplement electronic data with the phone surveys in major markets when "overnights" are demanded by the industry at the beginning of the new television season, or when special programming such as a blockbuster miniseries attracts the special interest of networks and advertisers.)

Critics of the Nielsen technique point out that a television set may be put in use merely to provide background sound, to keep a pet or baby company, or to convince burglars that someone is home—with nobody really "watching" television, and thus no consumer paying attention to the advertising messages. The rival Arbitron system requires family members to make notations in a diary concerning the times when the set is on, to which channel, and, most importantly, which members of the family were watching. Critics question whether the diaries are kept carefully and accurately.

Neither method measures "why" or "how intently" the program is being watched, or what value the audience puts on the message after they have viewed it. That is why the ratings firms augment their usual measurements with the telephone surveys that go into greater detail.

The "People Meters" Experiment

In the mid-1980s, the National Association of Broadcasters informed its members that the ratings companies were readying a new system that would overcome some of the mechanical and behavioral problems with the existing methods. "People meters" were introduced at the beginning of the 1987 television season by Nielsen and a new British rival, AGB Research.

With people meters, each member of a household had to push a button when entering or leaving the room. That information, along with the data on which channel was being viewed, enabled producers to know the age, sex, ethnic group, and education of the audience for each show, because demographic information was obtained at the time the people meter was installed.

The data from the new people meters sent shock waves through the television industry. The networks learned that their audiences were smaller than they had thought—down 15 percent for CBS, slightly less for NBC and ABC.[21] Since the networks promise a certain number of viewers per dollar spent by advertisers, they found themselves having to provide "make-good" slots to sponsors who had overpaid. A few programs, including the "CBS Evening News," learned from people meter data that they had larger audiences than the previous systems had indicated.

Viewing patterns, according to the people meters, also weren't what the networks had supposed. More men were watching "Monday Night Football" and some of the evening soap operas than other ratings systems had indicated. But fewer women were watching the evening soaps, resulting in ratings as much as 23 percent lower for "Dallas."[22] Children and young adults were not represented in the viewing audience to the extent expected. Anxious advertising agencies with clients who manufactured children's products did their own research and discovered that kids, unlike adults, just couldn't be bothered pushing the buttons on the people meters in their homes as they entered or left the room. Agencies handling products aimed at college-age young adults attacked the people-meter data because it measured consumers in households, whereas many young people view television in dorms and public places such as bars and clubs.

At the end of the 1987–1988 television season, AGB Research suspended its U.S. ratings service, conceding defeat in its attempt to replace Nielsen. Of the three networks, only CBS had subscribed to AGB, citing its dissatisfaction with Nielsen. Arbitron announced that it would introduce its own version of people meters. Reluctantly, the television industry had to learn to live with the new measuring

News anchor Dan Rather, told that he appears too stiff to the viewers, occasionally dresses casually in order to project a friendly image.

technique, although it continued to press for improvements that would account for the "missing audiences." Nielsen admitted that its system failed to account for those who watch in bars, hotels, and college dorms. In response to complaints from the networks, the ratings firms are developing systems that will combine people meters and other measurement techniques for greater accuracy. And Nielsen is developing a "passive" people meter with an image-recognition device that can sense which family members are in the room with the television at any one time, doing away with the need to punch in.

In 1991, Arbitron introduced ScanAmerica, a more sophisticated and more costly ratings service than Nielsen's. But by the fall of 1992 it had withdrawn the service, conceding dominance in the television ratings market to Nielsen. Studies had shown variances in the ratings obtained by the two systems. Clearly advertisers preferred one set of figures—however flawed—rather than two sets of figures.

Experiments are being conducted with the passive systems that require no input by the viewer. As early as 1987, a heat-sensor device called the Voxbox 1200 was tested in 600 New York households. The system constantly monitors the room to determine whether viewers actually are in front of the set when a commercial airs. It cannot tell whether they are paying attention.[23] Infrared sensors and electronic identification tags or bracelets for each member of the family are also being experimented with by the testing companies. The ultimate goal is a system that would measure constantly for attention, comprehension, and believability—a tall order.

The skirmishing promises to continue through the 1990s until all the parties can agree on a fair and equitable means of establishing and passing along the high costs of delivering viewers to advertisers.

During the 1990–1991 television season, the networks, their advertisers, and the ratings services—especially Nielsen—were in what the trade journals called a "war" over ratings and the advertising rates tied to them because networks and advertisers so distrusted the ratings. ABC announced plans to conduct its own ratings, and the other networks gave support to the idea. NBC, then ABC and CBS, backed away from their former willingness to "guarantee" advertisers a certain size of audience. Advertisers began to balk at the idea of the networks doing their own audience measurement and then not yielding on rates when smaller-than-expected audiences resulted. After the 1990 World Series between Oakland and Cincinnati resulted in smaller-than-expected audiences, CBS threatened to pay less than its contract with organized baseball called for because of the diminished audience.

Nielsen did manage to win the approval of "Monday Night Football" producers when a new measurement of "away-from-home viewing" began to account for the many sports fans who watch their favorite games in bars and restaurants. Over a million men, previously uncounted in the ratings, were found to be watching sports in public places.

What's Wrong with the Ratings System?

The star of a cancelled television series goes on a late-night talk show and laments: "We thought we would find an audience if our show had been allowed to run, but the ratings killed us off in the first few weeks." The host sighs sympathetically, and the audience is bewildered. How can ratings work so fast to knock shows off the air? Then comes the clincher. Either the guest or the host voices the common complaint: "And to think that just the few thousand people who were surveyed could decide what the whole country will watch!" The studio audience groans in disbelief.

The system is not evil, un-American, or foolish, however. It simply does the job advertisers ask of it. Using scientific methods similar to those that enable pollsters to predict elections with remarkable accuracy, the survey firms can provide the data networks and their sponsors need to know as to whether a show is attracting a large enough audience or whether it needs to be replaced with something that might be more competitive. True, a larger sampling would yield more accurate results. But for the advertiser's purposes, the sampling of 1700 to 4000 households generates data that are good enough to tell them whether they are reaching the numbers and types of people they wish to target with their messages.

The weaknesses in the system come not from the statistical methodology, but from other facts such as the cooperation rate of sample households. As many as a third of households selected at random to represent a segment of the entire population in the ratings surveys do not agree to participate. That can mean that certain types of households, such as minority families, are less likely to be represented. Research indicates that African-American households, for example, are heavy users of television, so underrepresentation of African-Americans in the sample could skew the data.

Another fault of the system is that ratings in most markets are taken during periodic "sweeps" of four weeks' duration, three or four times a year. Stations

Chapter 10 Television

RESEARCH

Charting the Nielsen Ratings

Week 13: December 20–22

	ABC		CBS		NBC		FOX	
FRIDAY		12.3/22		9.5/17		9.4/17		5.9/11
8:00	Family Matters	**12.9/23**	Charlie Brown (R)	9.6/17	Matlock	11.5/21	America's Most Wanted	7.0/13
8:30	Step By Step (R)	12.0/21	Wish That Changed Xmas	9.3/16	(12.2/22)	**12.9/23**	(7.2/13)	7.4/13
9:00	Perfect Strangers	**11.7/21**	Moonstruck (R)	9.3/17	**Pacific Station**	8.4/15	Totally Hidden Video	4.9/9
9:30	Baby Talk (R)	10.8/19	(9.5/17)	9.7/17	Dear John	7.7/14	Best of the Worst (R)	4.2/8
10:00	20/20	**13.5/25**		9.6/18	Reasonable Doubts	7.5/14		
10:30	(13.3/25)	**13.2/25**		9.4/18	(7.8/15)	8.1/16		
SATURDAY		6.7/13		9.6/18		**12.1/23**		5.6/10
8:00	Who's the Boss? (R)	6.7/13	Scrooged	9.0/17	Golden Girls	**12.0/23**	Cops	7.2/14
8:30	Growing Pains	7.5/14	(10.3/19)	10.1/19	Walter & Emily	**10.5/20**	**Charlie Hoover**	4.6/9
9:00	In Concert '91 Presents	4.6/8		10.8/20	Empty Nest	**13.9/25**	Cops II	6.4/12
9:30	(5.0/9)	5.3/10		11.2/20	Nurses	**12.8/23**	Get a Life	4.3/8
10:00	The Commish	7.5/14	P.S.I Luv U	8.1/16	Sisters	**11.7/23**		
10:30	(7.9/16)	8.3/17	(8.2/16)	8.4/17	(11.6/23)	**11.5/23**		
SUNDAY		12.2/21		**15.7/27**		8.2/14		8.0/13
7:00	Life Goes On (R)	7.0/13	60 Minutes	**19.6/35**	Eerie, Indiana (R)[a]	5.3/10	True Colors	5.5/10
7:30	(7.5/13)	8.0/14	(19.4/34)	**19.1/32**	Torkelsons	5.1/9	Parker Lewis	6.2/11
8:00	Home Videos	**13.1/22**	Murder, She Wrote	12.8/21	Hot Country Nights	7.3/12	In Living Color	10.8/18
8:30	Raiders of the	12.2/20	(13.5/22)	**14.1/23**	(8.1/13)	9.0/15	**In Living Color (R)**	11.9/19
9:00	Lost Ark (R)	13.8/22	Baby of the Bride	**14.0/23**	A Mom For Christmas (R)	8.8/14	Married...Children	12.1/19
9:30	(13.9/23)	14.4/23	(15.0/26)	**14.9/25**	(9.3/15)	9.3/15	Herman's Head	8.0/13
10:00		14.9/23		**15.3/26**		9.5/16	Sunday Comics	5.2/9
10:30		14.1/24		**15.8/30**		9.6/17	(4.8/8)	4.5/8

[a]Eerie, Indiana began 8 minutes late due to football.

Variety, the international entertainment weekly trade paper, charts Nielsen ratings for prime time across the four networks. Note in the sample here that both the rating and share are provided—12.9/23 for "Family Matters" means that the show was seen in 12.9 percent of the country's homes and in 23 percent of the homes where the television was on. The figures across the board never add up to 100 percent because some of the audience are watching non-network broadcast television. Note that the "winning" shows in each time slot and the top network for each night are shown in boldface.

Source: Variety, Jan. 6, 1992, p. 26.

know when these periods occur and can schedule especially attractive programs in hopes of tilting the ratings. Thus the ratings may not reflect the usual state of affairs when stations expend only the usual resources and engage in normal promotional activity.

The economics of network television are such that the ratings have become increasingly important as the price of producing a prime-time series escalates and the number of people watching decreases. A study of costs and ratings over 15 years showed that the cost of producing a series nearly quadrupled, while the median rating for a new series dropped from approximately 19 points to 15 points in the same period. Thus each rating point gained by a program today is much more costly—and likely to determine the show's longevity—than was the case 15 years earlier.[24]

When shows with marginal ratings are knocked off the air early, other shows take their places and survive, ironically, with similar ratings. If a sitcom with high-paid stars and a large cast is replaced with a relatively inexpensive factual show produced by the news department, the new show can survive. It will attract advertisers, although not the biggest brands that want to sponsor the hit shows.

Measuring Likability: The Q-Rating

While Nielsen provides ratings of the shows, advertisers look for other ways to measure the impact of the content of those shows. Before they spend millions of dollars to sponsor a series, they check the "Q-rating" of the stars of the show as well as the spokespeople who will appear in the commercials. The "Q" represents the likability quotient of a personality, as measured in questionnaires mailed to families by the TVQ testing firm.[25]

Bill Cosby, who munches Jell-o convincingly with kids, had the highest Q-rating long before he also had the top-rated situation comedy show. When "CBS Evening News" anchor Dan Rather took his wife's advice and started wearing a V-neck sweater under his jacket, his Q-rating went up. Even a person in the news, such as Marine Lieut. Col. Oliver North testifying before congressional hearings on illegal aid to Nicaragua, can test high for the likability quotient.

For years the Huxtables were television viewers' favorite family on "The Cosby Show." Here they meet Stevie Wonder in a recording studio.

TECHNOLOGY AND EXPANSION ARE KEYS TO THE FUTURE

The evolution of television continues with what industry calls "downsizing" becoming a fact of life for the networks. The networks are trimming resources and staff while seeking viable programming that will enable them to hold onto audiences large enough to interest major advertisers. At the same time they must assess how emerging technologies and the expanded world market will affect the role of all of the "players" in the television business.

Low-Power Television

In order to permit a diversity of broadcasters to enter the television business, and in order to make local television possible in communities outside major urban areas, the FCC in 1982 approved the issuance of licenses for low-power television, or LPTV—at the low end of the TV portion of the spectrum. The FCC hoped that LPTV would open the door to minority broadcasters and would help to serve minority and ethnic consumers better than conventional television does. While more than 400 licenses were granted by the end of the 1980s, half in the remote areas of Alaska, the cultural diversity was slow to materialize. The economic realities of trying to sell local television advertising for a limited market proved a deterrent to many entrepreneurs who applied for licenses.[26]

In the 1990s, however, low-power television shows signs of taking off, just as cable did in the preceding decade. Channel America, a chain of 14 stations in the eastern half of the country, is affiliated with another 42 affiliates to which it transmits its programming.[27] Los Angeles has a Silent Network, which runs captioned programming for the deaf. RFD-TV in Omaha bills itself as the "all-rural" network, offering programming of interest to farmers and people living in small towns. The Telemundo Group offers Spanish-language programming and advertises itself in trade magazines as the top medium for reaching America's growing Hispanic population.

Some LPTV stations have disappointed consumers by running "more of the same" programming that duplicates cable and broadcast information already available. Other stations are functioning the way the FCC intended, offering coverage of city council meetings and covering community events as diverse as the high school graduation ceremony, the Veterans Day parade, and a fashion show put on at the shopping mall by local merchants.

High-Definition Television

It took nearly a generation for color to become the standard in the United States because so many families had invested in black-and-white sets. By the same token, Americans have not shown much interest in what promises to be the next big technological improvement: high-definition television, or HDTV. The current price tags of $20,000 and up for 40-inch or bigger screens put HDTV out of the reach of the ordinary consumer.

Already, European and Japanese television is broadcast with higher definition—625 horizontal lines of information per screen and thus greater sharpness

MINORITIES/WOMEN

Spanish-Language TV Is on the Rise

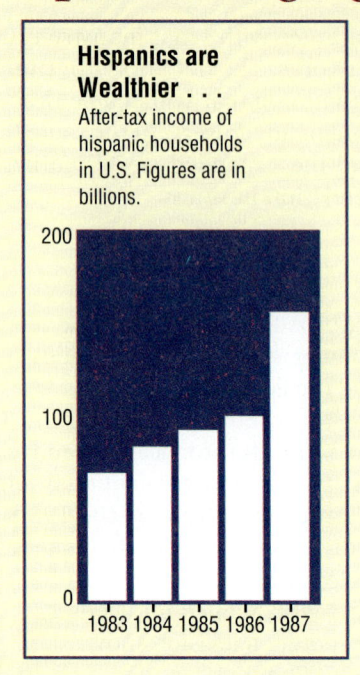

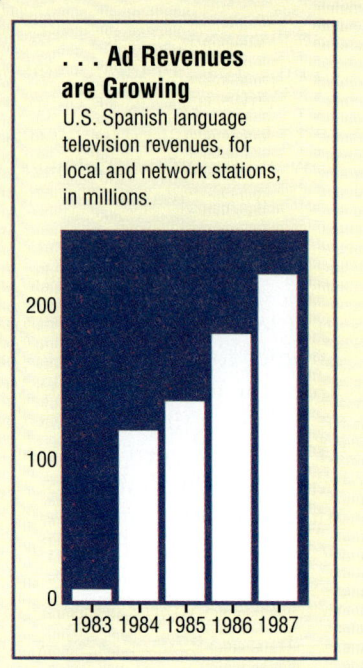

Hispanics are Wealthier...
After-tax income of hispanic households in U.S. Figures are in billions.

...Ad Revenues are Growing
U.S. Spanish language television revenues, for local and network stations, in millions.

Until the mid-1980s, what few Spanish-language stations there were could be found only in the less popular UHF spectrum, mostly in California, New York City, and Miami and along the Mexican border. Major advertisers weren't interested in making a special effort to reach Hispanics.

Now more than 400 Spanish-language television stations form the Univision network. They can cite impressive statistics from the U.S. Census Bureau: Between 1990 and 2010, Hispanics will account for 42 percent of new population growth, doubling their numbers from 20 milllion to 40 million. According to *Hispanic Business* magazine, the income of the average Hispanic family doubled in the 1980s. Revenues of Spanish-language television stations went from a few million dollars in 1983 to more than $200 million in 1988. Today all of the nation's top 25 advertisers spend heavily in Hispanic television.

Univision is owned by Hallmark Cards Inc., which also owns Hispanic stations in 10 major markets. The other major Hispanic network, Telemundo, is run by another non-Hispanic owner, Reliance Capital Corp. Once the Hispanic stations had to import variety shows and *novelas*—soap operas—from Latin American nations; now the U.S. networks are producing many of their own shows for their growing audience.

Sources: *Hispanic Business* (various); Richard W. Stevenson, "Spanish Language TV Grows Up," *The New York Times*, July 7, 1988, pp. D-1, D-22; "Special Report: Marketing to Hispanics," *Advertising Age*, Feb. 13, 1989, pp. S-1ff.

---

of detail—than the U.S. standard of 525 lines. The next generation of television sets promises to achieve the clarity of a good-quality 35 mm snapshot, and manufacturers want to assure themselves of a global market by lobbying for an international standard.

TECHNOLOGY
Changing Times, Changing Technology

"This is your Woodstock," promoters told the tens of thousands of young people who attended the Live Aid concert to benefit African famine victims in the summer of 1985. The rock concert in Philadelphia's John F. Kennedy stadium did bear some resemblance to the huge 1969 event held on a farm in upstate New York. Both concerts featured top artists, and both had a celebrative air.

But there were differences. Woodstock had spontaneity: people came not knowing what to expect. Performers and audience alike improvised as they went along. Live Aid was a media event, presold to television. That meant it was timed down to the minute, like the "Miss America Pageant" or a football half-time show. Commercials appeared at regular intervals. Commentators in television booths were able to tell beforehand exactly what was scheduled to happen next. And the day-long program ran only a few minutes longer than planned.

Those in the stadium could see close-ups of the performers on giant TV screens, as well as live remote images from the twin concert in England's Wembley Stadium. The only people who saw Woodstock live were the 500,000 who went to Woodstock; others had to wait to view the documentary film. "Live Aid," on the other hand, could be seen simultaneously by audiences around the world.

What changed in 16 years to make the events so different? The electronic media had spread "rock culture" from a more specialized audience to a general audience. And satellite transmissions had created a "global culture" where all information is available to all people at the same time.

The Pentagon is eager to see an improvement in the quality of television images because it uses TV graphics for computer simulations, intelligence analysis, and mapping.[28] In 1988 the FCC announced its technical guidelines for HDTV. As it did earlier when color was on the horizon, it assured that no existing set would be obsolete when the new technology comes in. But, apparently wishing to favor American manufacturers, it did not match its requirement for 1100 lines to the Japanese HDTV manufacturers' 1125 lines. Thus a global standard has not been set, unless the Japanese and Europeans decide to adjust to the new American standard.

HDTV research in America is being financed by five different groups. Field tests began in 1989.[29] However, computer developments are helping make the definition in existing TV sets better, so consumer demand for better images is not great. The HDTV screens promise to be large—what are now called "projection" size—but many consumers today favor the individual-sized set 20 inches or smaller. Recent excitement in the market has focused on miniaturization of television, not movie-quality transmission.

The battles to introduce and popularize HDTV promise to be as prolonged and confusing to the consumer as the introduction of television itself over 40 years ago. But *The Wall Street Journal* commentator Robert Goldberg noted, on struggles within the government to decide *who* should develop HDTV, and *when*:

> There's another lobby that hasn't been heard from—the biggest lobby of all, American consumers. They haven't seen high def yet, but once they get their eyes on this new technology, there'll be no stopping them. The talkies couldn't be

stopped. Color television couldn't be stopped. So let me just say what any other red-blooded American in my place would: We want our HDTV. We want it now.[30]

In the spring of 1992, the FCC presented its plan for making the transition to HDTV in the United States. The FCC announced that it expected to make a decision on the system that will be the standard for HDTV by 1993. That would signal the beginning of a 15-year transitional period, at the end of which HDTV will have replaced the current technology. To accomplish this goal, the FCC decided to issue a second channel to each licensee, enabling a station to broadcast its programming simultaneously in the new and the old technologies. After the end of the 15-year transition, in 2008, the station would use only the HDTV license, and consumers should have replaced their old televisions with the new ones. Thus, the FCC hopes to spur the technology without harming viewers who might buy a new television in the mid-1990s.

FUTURE FILE

✓ You are serving as an intern at the headquarters of one of the TV networks. You overhear a top executive saying: "Television is a mix of the old and the new. What we need to do in order to survive is to give our audience something they have always wanted and enjoyed, but packaged in an entirely new way." This is your chance to break into the TV business big time. Describe the old wine that you will sell in new bottles.

✓ For all its promise, public broadcasting has remained a poor cousin of commercial broadcasting. Perhaps the key to its revival will be the return to the original concept of offering *educational* television. How can your university extend its services to consumers by forging a new partnership with public television?

✓ Television viewing is largely a passive activity, giving rise to the description of heavy viewers as "couch potatoes." Interactive television gives viewers the opportunity to participate in programming by sending information back to the producers as the program is in progress. Suggest the format for a program that would increase the participation of your community in local television.

NOTES

1. Eugene S. Foster, *Understanding Broadcasting* (Reading, MA: Addison-Wesley, 1978), p. 111.
2. Foster, p. 112.
3. Norman Blumenthal, *The TV Game Shows* (New York: Pyramid Books, 1975), p. 13.
4. Nancy Signorielli, "Selective Television Viewing: A Limited Possibility," *Journal of Communication*, 36:3 (Spring 1986), pp. 64–75.
5. Peter Sturken, "Docudramas Are No Worse than TV News," *The New York Times*, Nov. 12, 1989, p. 22.
6. John Wicklein, "Time for a Public Broadcasting Overhaul," *The New York Times*, Feb. 28, 1986, p. B-4.
7. *Corporation for Public Broadcasting 1984 Annual Report* (Washington: CPB, 1985).
8. Meg Cox, "PBS Looking at Sitcoms, Game Shows and Promotions to Enliven Network," *The Wall Street Journal*, March 23, 1990, p. B-1.
9. *The Wall Street Journal*, May 4, 1990, p. B-5.

10. Eileen Prescott, "The Networks Fight Back, Finally," *The New York Times*, March 5, 1989, p. D-4.
11. Don Hewitt, excerpts from speech of Feb. 25, 1986, *The New York Times*, Feb. 28, 1986, p. B-4.
12. Toby Eckert, "The New Year's Baby Who Wasn't News," *Columbia Journalism Review*, March-April 1989, p. 6.
13. Les Brown, "Five Tumultuous Years," *Channels 1987 Field Guide*, December 1986, p. 9.
14. Todd Gitlin, *Inside Prime Time* (New York: Pantheon, 1985).
15. Gitlin, pp. 3–8.
16. Robert W. Kubey, "Television Use in Everyday Life: Coping with Unstructured Time," *Journal of Communication*, 36:3, Spring 1986, pp. 108–123.
17. Merrill Brown, "The Boom That Wasn't," *Channels 1989 Field Guide*, December 1988, p. 27.
18. Neil Postman, *Amusing Ourselves to Death: Public Discourse in the Age of Show Business* (New York: Penguin Books, 1986).
19. John Corry, "Wrestling on TV a Kind of Virtuous Docudrama," *The New York Times*, Aug. 10, 1985, p. C-25.
20. Gregg Easterbrook, "What's Wrong with Congress?" *The Atlantic Monthly*, December 1984.
21. A. C. Nielson data as of April 10, 1988, cited in *The Wall Street Journal*, April 18, 1988, p. 30.
22. Peter J. Boyer, "New TV Ratings Device Registers Fewer Viewers of Network Shows," *The New York Times*, Dec. 24, 1987, p. 1.
23. Verne Gay, "TV's 'Holding Power' Tracked," *Advertising Age*, Nov. 16, 1987, p. 42.
24. David Atkin and Barry Litman, "Networks TV Programming: Economics, Audiences and the Ratings Game, 1971–1986," *Journal of Communication*, 36:3 (Spring 1986), pp. 32–50.
25. Lynne S. Gross, *Telecommunications: An Introduction to the Electronic Media*, 3rd ed. (Dubuque, IA: Wm. C. Brown, 1989), p. 381.
26. Michael Couzens, "Low-Power TV: They Jes' Keep a-Growin'" *Channels 1987 Field Guide*, December 1986, p. 54.
27. "Low-Power TV Gains Strength," *The New York Times*, May 14, 1990, p. D-1.
28. Bob Davis, "Pentagon Seeks to Spur U.S. Effort to Develop 'High-Definition' TV," *The Wall Street Journal*, Jan. 4, 1989, p. B-2.
29. Calvin Sims, "HDTV: Will U.S. Be in the Picture?" *The New York Times*, Sept. 21, 1988, p. D-7.
30. Robert Goldberg, "A Rosy, Rectangular View of the Future," *The Wall Street Journal*, June 5, 1989, p. A-12.

SUGGESTED READINGS

Barnouw, Eric. *Tube of Plenty: The Development of American Television* (New York: Harper & Row, 1970).

Gitlin, Todd, *Inside Prime Time* (New York: Pantheon, 1985).

Greenfield, Jeff, *Television: The First Fifty Years* (New York: Crescent, 1977).

Kubey, Robert, and Mihaly Csikzentmihalyi, *Television and the Quality of Life: How Viewing Shapes Everyday Experience* (Hillsdale, NJ: Erlbaum, 1990).

Marc, David, *Demographic Vistas: Television in American Culture* (Philadelphia: University of Pennsylvania Press, 1984).

McCabe, Peter, *Bad News at Black Rock: The Sell-Out of CBS News* (New York: Arbor House, 1987).

Newcomb, Horace, ed., *Television: The Critical View* (Oxford: Oxford University Press, 1982).

Postman, Neil, *Amusing Ourselves to Death: Public Discourse in the Age of Show Business* (New York: Viking, 1985).

QUESTIONS FOR PUBLIC BROADCASTING

MICHAEL CHENEY

Michael Cheney is dean of the School of Journalism and Mass Communication at Drake University. His research interests include media and politics, communication technology, and popular culture. He has worked for public broadcasting as a producer/director.

In September 1990, public television broadcast "The Civil War" for five consecutive nights. Not only did the program receive critical acclaim, it also received the highest ratings ever for a series on public television. Yet during that same week in September, 67 of the 92 programs broadcast had higher ratings than "The Civil War." Of these 67, more than half a dozen would be canceled by the end of the fall season.

By public broadcasting standards, "The Civil War" was an outstanding critical and ratings success, yet by the standard used by the commercial television networks, the program was a failure. In one of its brightest moments, public television highlighted what is still the basic question underlying the future for telecommunications in this country: Is success measured by attracting the largest possible audience, or by attracting a specialized audience?

The Question of Audience

A comparison of the kind of programming offered by commercial television stations and the kind offered by public television stations reveals different philosophies about the kind of audience that each tries to attract. Commercial television stations offer a flow of programs from morning to evening that appeal to the widest common denominator. Morning news programs, talk shows, and game shows are followed by midday soap operas, late afternoon talk shows and syndicated programming, evening news, prime-time programs, late news, and late night programming. The programming philosophy is to offer programs that will be attractive to whomever might choose to tune in and see what is on the air.

Public television stations, in contrast, broadcast programs of a decidedly educational or instructional nature, such as "Sesame Street," "Mr. Rogers' Neighborhood," and "This Old House"; general audience programming such as "Masterpiece Theatre" and "NOVA"; and special offerings such as "The Civil War." While occasionally running blocks of similar programs, public television stations have schedules that offer a mosaic of different programs with different appeals and different intended audiences. In their programming philosophy, the audience is expected to seek out the program at the intended time of day. Viewers of one program are not expected passively to flow into the next program. In all likelihood, the next program will have a different appeal and be of interest to a different audience.

Cable television's growth in the past 10 years offers a third programming philosophy. In contrast to commercial television's programming philosophy of reaching the largest number of individuals with broad-based appeals and public television's programming philosophy of reaching a segmented audience at a particular time, cable television's programming philosophy is to offer programming that will appeal to a segmented audience at any time. MTV, CNN, and ESPN offer their distinct programming any time of the day or night.

Of the three philosophies, public television's philosophy presents the greatest challenge. The commercial television audience is considered to be primarily passive, while the cable television viewers need only be active enough to seek out the proper channel to find the appropriate type of programming. The public television audience is extremely active, not only seeking out the channel, but also seeking out the specific time of the desired programming. With an abundance of program material available, whether this philosophy is appropriate for public television today is an open question.

Continued

Continued from page 298

The Question of Mission

While both cable television and commercial television have as their first objective profit, public television and public radio's mission is less well defined. In 1967, to help provide the needed direction and focus for educational television, the Carnegie Commission sponsored an inquiry into the state of educational television. The result of their work was a report, *Public Television: A Program for Action*, which coined a new phrase—public television—to describe what the mission should be of these educational television stations.

With suggestions from the Carnegie Commission for resolving the matters of national organization, interconnection, and funding, the future for public television began with a stronger sense of mission and purpose than had earlier educational broadcasting efforts. However, since the report was published, the fields of broadcasting and education have changed dramatically. While public television continues to define itself by the language of the 1967 report, changes in the structure of public television have made the earlier answer to the question of mission less certain.

The Question of Programming

During the early years of public television, a system was developed in which individual stations offered up program proposals for consideration by other public television stations. All stations selected their choices for the next year from these proposals of new and returning shows. After a round of selections, the costs to produce the chosen programs were prorated across all interested stations. The process continued for several additional rounds as stations sought to use funds given them by CPB/PBS and other sources to obtain a program schedule. After each round, programs that did not receive significant interest or had too high a cost were dropped from future consideration. Stations, likewise, had the option to select new programs and change their previous selections during each round. Consequently, previously popular programs such as "Sesame Street" or "Masterpiece Theater" were usually fairly inexpensive when most, if not all, of the stations selected those programs. Newer or more controversial programs were not as popular and cost more. The result was a lot of familiar programs and few opportunities for new programs.

The National Programming Service

In the early 1990s, this decentralized system of program selection was changed and the responsibility for choosing programming for the public television stations fell to the newly created National Programming Service (NPS), whose program director makes decisions on programming with approval from a board. This director chooses which programs to continue to fund and also chooses how to allocate any remaining dollars for new program development.

The shift toward a more centralized structure for program selection reflects a shift in the overall structure of public broadcasting. While educational broadcasting began as a decentralized collection of radio stations with little organization, the most recent changes with the NPS, CPB, and PBS bring public broadcasting much closer to the structure of commercial broadcasting. Whether this structure is best suited to the needs of public television in the 1990s is a question that has yet to be answered.

The Question of Public Broadcasting

What is the future of public broadcasting? Throughout its history, public broadcasting has answered questions of audience and mission in ways that differentiated it from commercial broadcasting. Specifically, public broadcasting seeks to provide specialized programming for specific audiences. Against commercial broadcasting, public broadcasting does that well. However, the mission of public broadcasting and its audience runs into potential trouble when faced with newer technologies—not only cable, but also videodisc, videotape, and even low-power television. These technologies provide increased opportunities for reaching specialized audiences more efficiently and inexpensively than over-the-air public broadcasting.

Whether these newer technologies mean a less important role for public broadcasting will tell us a great deal about what we expect from our media system producers and what we want from our media system as consumers.

CHAPTER 11

Cable and Video

AT A GLANCE

✓ Cable began as a system for bringing clear signals to remote locations, but it rapidly developed into a system for bringing consumers more varied information, much of it at premium rates.

✓ Cable has moved from being a virtually unregulated information industry to being heavily regulated, and eventually to being a mixture of regulated and unregulated practices as the FCC decides what roles cable will play in the information mix.

✓ The greatest challenge to cable's success in winning consumers away from broadcast television may come from the entry of the telephone companies into the electronic information industry.

✓ Cable's strength is the variety of services offered to the consumer. On the horizon are interactive services that allow the consumer to participate in the programming being shown on the screen.

✓ Cable News Network (CNN) and C-SPAN have changed the role of television in covering the government and the world.

✓ The video age, which is only beginning, has given the individual consumer as well as businesses hundreds of new ways of choosing and using information.

One Sunday afternoon in November 1988, the NFL football game carried on a broadcast television network had three prime advertisers: a make of automobile, a beer, and a financial service. Later that evening the final NFL game of the day, which was carried on cable's ESPN rather than broadcast television, also had as its leading advertisers a car, a beer, and a financial service. On the broadcast channel, the car was Chevrolet, the beer was Budweiser, and the financial service was the Sears Discover card. On the cable channel, the car was Mercedes Benz, the beer was Michelob, and the financial service was American Express.

"Upscale" viewers—well-off people whom the producers of higher-profit products and services want to reach—have switched their viewing habits from network television to cable. For those who can afford the extra charges, cable offers more variety and choice.

The broad term *video* refers to products and services that give consumers even more personal control over their use of television information. That's why we are treating cable and other forms of nonbroadcast television in a chapter separate from network TV.

CABLE: CONNECTING YOUR HOME TO THE WORLD

The concept of *broad*casting is an exciting one because information is beamed out for reception by one and all—a true and democratic *mass* communication system. But there are problems with broadcasting. The signal goes only so far, depending on the power of the transmitter. Signals can be lost if mountains or tall buildings intervene. The number of signals that can be carried on local airwaves is limited. Within 30 years of the advent of broadcasting, it was clear that technical improvements were needed in order to ensure that clear and adequate signals could be supplied to every consumer.

INDUSTRY

Network TV Share of Audience Decreases While Cable and VCR Ownership Increases

	1982	1989
Network TV share of audience	83 %	67 %
Percentage of households with VCRs	4 %	65.5%
Percentage of households with cable	33.3%	55.6%

Source: Nielsen Media Research. Based on "The '80s: Plugged in to TV," *USA Today*, December 1, 1989.

How Cable Works

At its simplest, a cable system consists of

- An *uplink*—the earth station that sends signals carrying programming up to a satellite. The satellite may then beam the information to yet another satellite serving another sector of the globe.
- A *headend*—the electronic center where signals are captured by an antenna. When satellite transmissions are involved, the headend is a *downlink*. Signals at the headend may be scrambled to prevent unauthorized use by anyone who is not a subscriber.
- *Trunk lines* that carry the signals into districts—a neighborhood, community, or small town—where feeder cables go down each street either on poles or underground, generally wherever the telephone lines are.
- A *drop line* to the individual customer. Inside the subscriber's house, a converter attached to the television set transforms the electronic signal into an unscrambled picture.

Transmissions take barely a fifth of a second, and thus "superstations" in Atlanta, Chicago, and New York—broadcast stations that decided to serve the entire country instead of just their local broadcast area by offering themselves to cable operators—can be viewed in places thousands of miles apart. Entertainment and news services also are fed to foreign countries, so the same movie, sports event, or 24-hour news can be viewed simultaneously on a Caribbean island and in Detroit, Seattle, or Calgary.

Cable Begins as CATV

By 1950, community antenna television (CATV) was bringing signals to remote areas and those previously cut off from broadcast centers by intervening terrain, such as the mountains of Colorado. CATV entrepreneurs erected tall antennas to capture distant or blocked signals, then ran coaxial cable to the homes of subscribers who were happy to pay for the service. Eventually CATV operators began to "import" programs from beyond the area served by their antenna, and the concept of cable television began to develop (see Figure 11.1).

The first technical problem came when the fledgling cable companies went to string their wires. Some planned to run the cables from house to house, but that was feasible only in areas of dense settlement. The obvious solution was to use the poles owned by the telephone company, as other utilities have done. But telephone companies set rates in many areas that added greatly to the cost of cable. Managers of the AT&T system forecast correctly that cable—far from being just a means of improving the television signal—was an alternative means of bringing many kinds of information into homes electronically. That put the cable companies in potentially competitive conflict with the phone companies.

Growth Starts Slowly. The flurry of interest in cable distribution of programming in the 1950s led some to predict that the entire nation soon would be wired. But 50 percent penetration of American homes was not realized until 1988, and 100 percent cable availability may not be a reality until well into the 1990s. Just as it did with broadcast television, the FCC has had to work its way through several

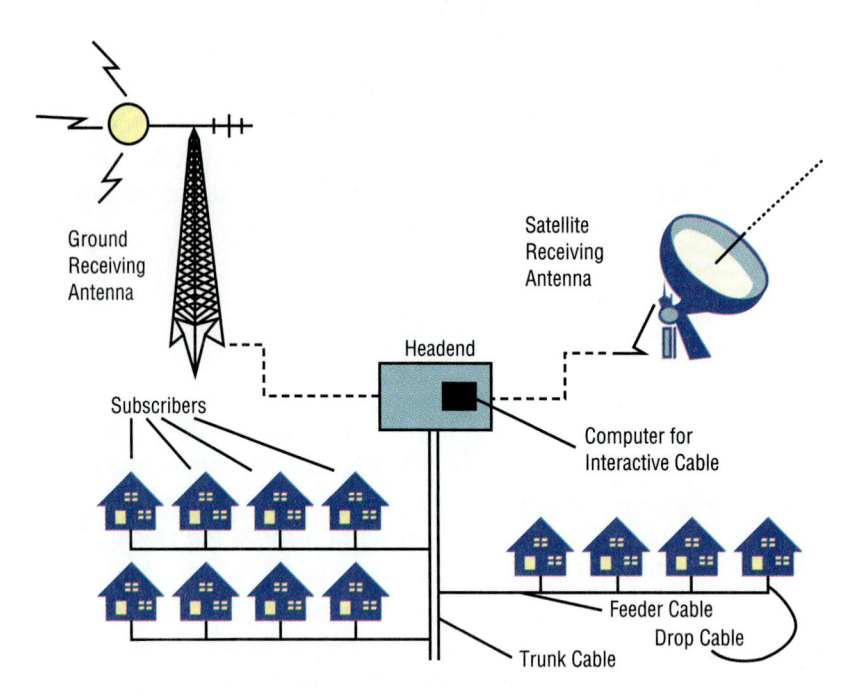

FIGURE 11.1 **How Cable Systems Operate** A cable television system, showing an antenna for receiving satellite programs, and a computer for interactive services. Source: Everett M. Rogers, *Communication Technology: The New Media of Society* (New York: Free Press, 1986), p. 56.

difficult issues to ensure that all customers are served adequately and fairly, and to guard against domination of the field by any one economic group or interest.

In 1959 a U.S. Senate subcommittee considered legislation to require licensing of CATV operators, who were not regulated by any agency. Lacking information about the scope of cable and unsure of the many ramifications of the new technology, the legislators argued the bill to death. At that point, states and municipalities jumped into the regulation of cable, forcing owners to obtain local franchises in order to string wires through or under the streets and requiring them to return a percent of the income to the municipality in return for that franchise. Symbolic of the chaos and uncertainty is the fact that while the borough of Manhattan was among the first areas to be served by cable because its tall buildings make broadcast reception difficult, many areas of New York City still do not have cable even where franchises have been awarded, because of the enormous costs. In some suburbs, a family with cable may live across the street from a family that doesn't, simply because one lives in a wired town and the other doesn't.

Regulating Cable

The FCC did not get involved in regulating cable until 1965, when it ruled that programs imported from more than 60 miles away could not duplicate any local broadcast in the preceding or following 15 days. That prohibited a cable operator, for example, from using a satellite to pick up a concert that was broadcast live in another market but that was scheduled to be shown on tape locally at a later date. This "syndicated exclusivity" regulation pleased the broadcasters but angered the cable operators, who joined to lobby against it. They succeeded in convincing the

FCC to shorten the exclusivity period to just one day. It was the first event in an ongoing struggle that saw the cable operators gaining strength and forcing the FCC not to automatically favor the longer-entrenched broadcasters.[1]

In 1968, the U.S. Supreme Court rejected the argument by cable operators that cable was not interstate and therefore not subject to regulation by the federal government. Moreover, it said FCC regulation of cable was necessary in order to carry out the mandate of Congress to develop the dissemination of electronic information in the best interests of the public. That decision laid the foundation for the FCC to get more heavily into regulating cable.

In the 1970s, cable companies began to offer programming they themselves originated, and they further broadened the information they could offer by receiving signals from satellites. Now homes wired to cable could receive programs from anywhere. When cable differentiated itself as the *multichannel* medium with the most variety to offer, it became attractive even to those in populated areas who did not need CATV in order to receive a signal.[2]

The 1972 Regulations. The FCC issued a set of regulations in 1972 that put cable's house in order, superseding earlier decisions as well as a jumble of state and municipal regulations.[3] Among the most important provisions were these:

Certificate of Compliance. While municipalities could still franchise cable owners, each system operator was required to obtain a "certificate of compliance" from the FCC. The granting of the certificate was virtually automatic, but the process alerted the FCC to verify that the operator was capable of providing service and that the municipality stayed within guidelines in setting reasonable franchise fees.

"Must Carry" Rule. To ensure that cable operators would not carry just the most popular and profitable programs, all local signals had to be carried on cable if the local stations requested it. The "must carry" rule was popular with stations but unpopular with cable operators who preferred to pick and choose among local stations and use the rest of their channels for the most popular services and the lucrative premium channels.

Importation of Signals. Cable operators were permitted to "import" signals in order to carry all three major networks and adequate independent stations. There were several rules governing how many stations could be imported, and operators could not "leapfrog" to bring in a network affiliate hundreds of miles away that was available closer to the home region.

Antisiphoning. Cable systems were allowed to offer pay channels carrying movies, sports, and concerts. However, "siphoning" of events and programs that previously appeared free on broadcast television was prohibited. The FCC had moved in 1968 to prevent the expropriation for exclusive viewing on pay television of popular broadcast programs such as the Super Bowl, the World Series, the Olympic Games, and the Miss America Pageant.

Multiple Ownership. Owners of television stations could not operate a cable franchise in the same community, and the television networks were prohibited from owning cable stations.

Local Origination. Cable operators were required to provide "local origination" programming. In the 100 largest markets, these included "access" channels available to individuals or groups who wanted to get their information on the air.

TIME CAPSULE

Cable

1950s	Community Antenna TV (CATV) brings signals to remote locations.	1977	U.S. manufacturers introduce VHS videorecording format.
1956	Ampex demonstrates first videotape recording system.	1977	Warner introduces "interactive" QUBE system in Columbus, Ohio.
1957	Pay television tested on cable system in Bartlesville, Oklahoma.	1979	C-SPAN brings U.S. Congress to cable subscribers.
1958	FCC declines to regulate cable television (CATV).	1980	Black Entertainment Network is first cable network for minorities.
1964	"Subscription television" offered in Santa Monica, California.	1980s	Impact of cable cuts network audience by nearly a third.
1965	Launch of communication satellites makes cable feasible.	1982	Home Shopping Network is first to use advertising as programming.
1967	CBS fails to attract consumers for "Electronic Video Recorder."	1984	Cable Communications Act.
1968	FCC approves pay-TV.	1984	INTELSAT V satellites launched in synchronous orbits to serve world.
1972	FCC issues first rules for cable television.	1985	"Must carry" rule struck down by courts.
1975	Sony introduces its Betamax videorecording system.	1988	Many groups begin studying ownership patterns of cable services.
1975	Home Box Office introduces first satellite pay network system.	1991	Courts approve FCC go-ahead for phone companies in cable industry.

The 1972 regulations required cable operators to provide original material "to a significant extent," but start-up costs did not permit the building and equipping of studios. In the large markets where local access was required, franchisers provided little more than a rented storefront equipped with one or two cameras and tape recorders supervised by a single technician. Harangues by minor politicians, "artistic" presentations by those with marginal talent, and even sexually oriented material have been carried by the public access channels in some large cities because there were no limitations on the participant consumers. On the positive side, schools and colleges were encouraged to create programs using their own television production facilities.

Most smaller cable systems used one channel for a computer-generated graphics display of time, weather, news announcements, and advertising messages, usually with a local music radio station providing the background sound. A technician and a single camera are all that is required for this service, which only someone trapped in a hotel room in a strange city might actually *watch*.

Deregulation Gives Cable Greater Freedom. The 1984 Cable Communications Act that eased regulation of the industry came after lobbyists for cable owners successfully convinced Congress to shield them from controls by municipalities and states. The owners argued that the prime responsibility of the operator should be to the subscribers of cable television, not to government bodies, and that the market would determine the prices people wanted to pay for various services.[4]

In 1985, the "must carry" rule that had stood since 1972 was struck down by a federal court and the FCC did not fight the move. The chair of the FCC said the decision "takes the first step toward a true marketplace for the distribution by cable systems" and "represents a positive step toward full First Amendment protection for all forms of electronic media."[5] The "must carry" rule died finally when Supreme Court Chief Justice Warren Burger refused to heed the call of broadcasters, especially owners of the smaller UHF stations, who wanted to ensure that cable had to carry their programming.[6] The president of the National Association of Broadcasters called the action "a blow to the localized system of broadcasting in this nation." Even some FCC staff members feared that greedy cable operators would ignore local needs and offer only the most profitable programming. New York City cable operators immediately dropped the New Jersey public broadcasting station, although many New Yorkers work or travel in New Jersey and are interested in news and programs from their neighboring state.

Cable operators say they will continue to fight regulation by the FCC and other authorities on the grounds that they should have all the freedoms accorded to the print media. They argue that they must have the flexibility to find programming that is different from broadcast fare, and also different from the movies that can be rented for viewing on a VCR. They also want to explore the concept of "narrowcasting"—offering channels for specialized audiences such as children, rock music fans, sports enthusiasts, and hobbyists.

In 1988, the Reagan Administration released a report by the Commerce Department's National Telecommunications and Information Administration that called for even further deregulation of cable in order to foster more competition. The report was aimed at ensuring that a few large companies would not dominate the industry. While it did not suggest that telephone companies should be allowed to enter the cable industry, it did suggest that telephone lines could be used as "common carriers" to help more cable companies gain access to information.[7]

Reregulation or Continued Deregulation? In 1990, the head of New Jersey's Board of Public Utilities called cable television in that state a monopoly and suggested that permitting more than one cable company to operate in a town would benefit subscribers by giving them a choice of providers and lower rates. Cable companies argued that federal deregulation precluded states and communities from interfering with their franchises. While cable rates and programming policies cannot be dictated by states or communities, local authorities can set service requirements for utilities. New Jersey has strengthened rules that require quicker response to service outages and billing credit when service outages occur.[8]

Bills working their way slowly through Congress at the beginning of the 1990s would allow cities to regulate rates in areas without two or more cable operators, limit the number of subscribers nationally that any one cable operator could serve, regulate the prices of "premium" channels, and reinstate the "must carry" rule.[9] Cable operators, who argued that they had spent extraordinary amounts to develop almost a million miles of system in just one decade, nevertheless prepared themselves for some form of reregulation. In the summer of 1991 the FCC reinstated local rate regulations for many cable operations. Working in favor of the cable companies was the fear on the part of many in Congress that allowing states and municipalities to control rates and decide on the number of franchises would lead back to the corruption and chaos that marked the early days of cable regulation.

In the fall of 1992, the pendulum continued its swing back toward regulation of cable when both houses of Congress passed a bill to regulate rates for basic cable services and spur competition. Consumer groups and broadcasters were among the biggest supporters of the measure, which passed with sufficient majorities in both houses to override the expected veto from President Bush.

Nevertheless, in January 1992, the Senate handed cable operators a setback by passing legislation that would strengthen both local and federal regulation in order to limit the increases in cable rates. Siding with broadcasters, the legislators wrote into the law a requirement that cable operators pay for programming produced by the broadcasters.

Phone Companies Loom as Competitors for Cable. No industry, save perhaps newspapers, responded with such concern as the cable business when, in 1991, the courts upheld the FCC's decision to allow the Bell operating companies to enter the information services business. What the FCC has in mind is an entirely new technology that uses the video screen to display data transmitted over the phone lines rather than being broadcast or carried on cable wires.

Talking yellow pages, shopping services, theater directories, menu planning services, interactive language lessons, and remote control of home appliances are among the innovations being considered by the telephone companies. Shopping for an automobile using the new information services might mean looking at pictures of the various models on the screen. When the consumer sees a desirable product, the press of a few buttons on the remote control touchpad could bring up such information as prices, options, and the names of local dealers. Calling a dealer, making an offer or counteroffer, and perhaps even financing the car through the local bank or credit union all could be accomplished using the new service, bringing new meaning to the slogan "let your fingers do the walking."

In the worst-case analysis, according to some in the cable industry, the phone companies eventually could dominate everything that is seen on the home screen. Opponents see that as the very kind of information monopoly that was avoided by the breakup of AT&T in the 1980s. From the consumer's point of view, however, the convenience of linking so many electronic services may be highly desirable.

Early in 1992, the New Jersey legislature passed a law enabling New Jersey Bell to wire the entire state with fiber optics capable of carrying any kind of electronic information. The measure was adamantly opposed by cable operators because the new system will render cable technology obsolete and will be capable of carrying many more kinds of information products and services than cable can.

Is Cable a "Freeloader"? Cable's detractors include the networks and production companies that see the new medium as a "leech" on broadcasting, sucking profits from the work of others. Cable networks produce little of their own programming, preferring to profit by recycling the creative work of others.

In 1990, the two groups that protect the rights of music composers—ASCAP (the American Society of Composers, Authors and Publishers) and BMI (Broadcast Music Inc.)—began filing suits against cable networks like HBO as well as individual cable companies. They charged that cable operators were making only token payments or no payments at all for much of the music they were using. ASCAP and BMI—which collect royalties from shopping malls, theaters, and even bars that use music—insisted that cable pay its fair share.

Chapter 11 Cable and Video   **309**

ECONOMICS

Charting Cable's Rapid Growth

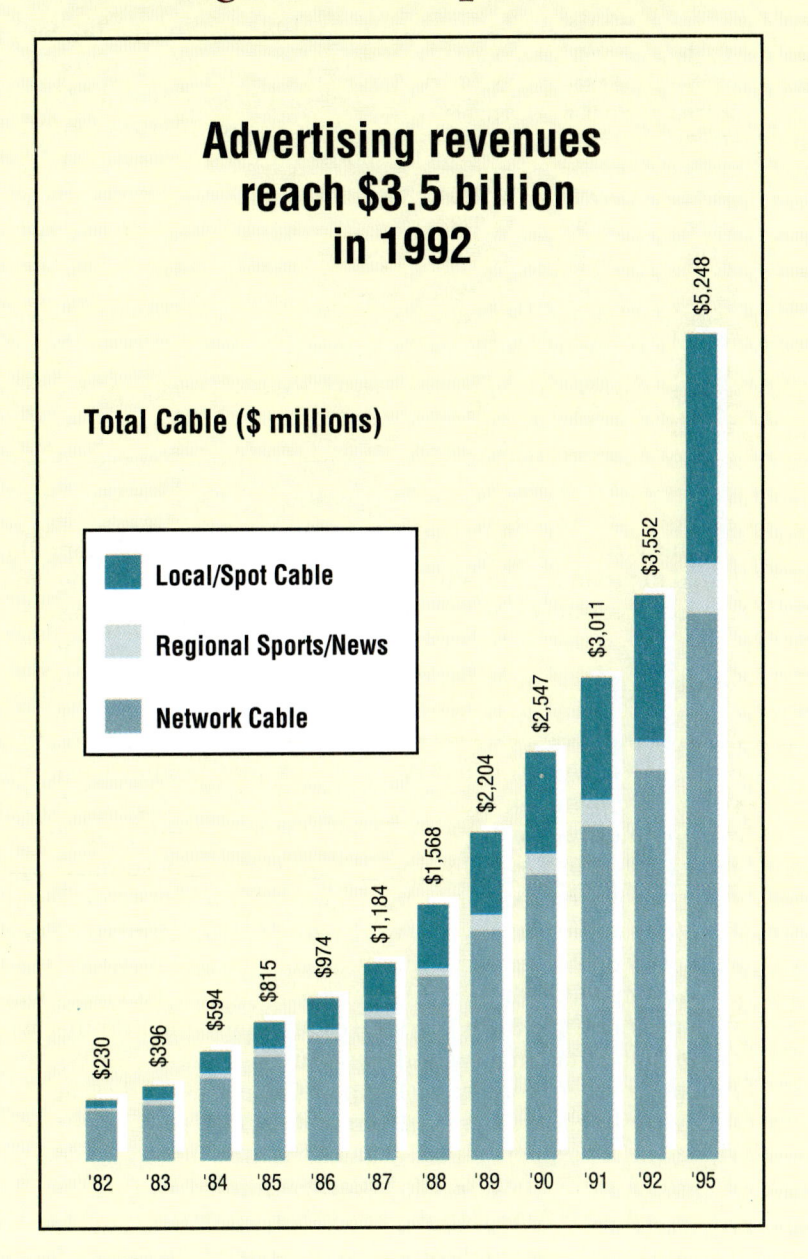

Advertising revenues reach $3.5 billion in 1992

Total Cable ($ millions)

- Local/Spot Cable
- Regional Sports/News
- Network Cable

Year	Total
'82	$230
'83	$396
'84	$594
'85	$815
'86	$974
'87	$1,184
'88	$1,568
'89	$2,204
'90	$2,547
'91	$3,011
'92	$3,552
'95	$5,248

In the decade from 1982 to 1992, cable's advertising revenues increased by 15-fold, and the prediction is for much greater growth.

Source: Advertising Age supplement "An Advertiser's Guide to Cable," February 24, 1992, p. C-2.

INDUSTRY

Cable Penetration Climbing

Year	Homes Passed (Millions)	Cable Subscribers (000)	Household Penetration (%)	Pay Subscribers (000)
1990	83.0	54,871	59.0	26,906
1989	80.3	52,564	57.1	28,643
1988	76.8	48,637	53.8	28,114
1987	74.9	44,971	50.5	27,600
1986	67.3	42,237	48.1	23,709
1985	63.5	39,873	46.2	24,165
1980	NA	17,671	22.6	7,599
1975	NA	9,197	13.2	NA

By 1987 half of the homes in America received cable. The "penetration" of cable approached 60 percent in 1990 and is expected to include two-thirds of American homes by the mid-1990s.

Source: "Advertisers' Guide to Cable," supplement to *Advertising Age,* February 11, 1991, p. 22.

This leads to another set of issues for cable reregulation: Should cable be required to produce a certain amount of its own programming, and should cable be required to compensate others for programming it carries now without payment?

Cable Matures as a Business

Through the 1980s, cable grew like mushrooms after a rain. More than 4000 new systems were launched in that decade—a new system virtually every day. Initially many were owned by local entrepreneurs. Some had media experience, others were businesspeople eager to make a buck, and still others were engineers who had expertise in the technology. Eventually many of those that didn't have an understanding both of the technology and the business sold out to companies that did. Many of the new owners were parts of chains, and some of the largest chains were owned by large communication companies.

Westinghouse, the electric manufacturing company, for example, entered the cable business in 1981 by buying Teleprompter, the firm that wired the northern half of Manhattan in New York City. Just five years later Westinghouse put Teleprompter's parent company, Group W Cable Inc., on the sales block and turned a profit. Westinghouse management had decided to concentrate on broadcasting, where the investment offers a quicker return to stockholders.[10] Warner Communications (now part of Time Warner) formed Warner Amex, but a few years later bought out American Express's share in order to form a new cable venture with Viacom. Ownership patterns were in a state of flux throughout the 1980s as communication companies tried to figure whether cable belonged in their "mix."

Eventually chain ownership became the norm. The government's encouragement of further deregulation at the end of the 1980s was based partly on a concern that a few companies were cornering a large segment of the market. The largest, Tele-Communications Inc., had 20 percent of the nation's 42 million cable customers.[11] Deregulation was seen as encouraging more players to enter the market.

Cable Becomes Profitable. Among the largest cable services, only one was profitable in 1983: TBS, the Atlanta-based Turner superstation. Five years later, however, most of the top advertiser-supported services made money, led by TBS, Turner's Cable News Network, and ESPN. In fact, each of those top three cable services made more profit than CBS and ABC combined.[12] Under deregulation, the networks were free to enter into ventures with cable services, and so the combination of players was constantly shifting at the beginning of the 1990s.

So profitable was cable that systems have been sold at the equivalent of $2000 for each subscriber. New owners are willing to pay that much because they believe more services can be sold to consumers. At one time the average consumer paid less than $10 a month for cable. Many now pay a basic rate over twice that much and add premium services that may bring the monthly bill to $50. In 1988, when the Consumer Price Index rose only about 4 percent, the cost of cable television rose almost 14 percent.

Eventually—assuming that the FCC decides to require competition in the market—cable will approach 100 percent penetration of the American market and consumers will draw the line on how much they are willing to pay and how many services they need. When that happens, the cable industry will "shake out," meaning that many companies will exit because they cannot make a profit, and the remaining companies will solidify their holds over the segment of the market they control. Rather than being "producer-driven" the industry will be equally "consumer-driven." In terms of our P↔I↔C model, there will be an equilibrium, with information being created, priced, and delivered by the producers according to the needs and interests of the consumers.

Users Shape the Medium. Most mass media have to poll their audiences to find out what they like and don't like. Cable gets constant indications of the popularity of its services. Subscribers call to add the Disney Channel or drop Cinemax. They write across their bills to say that they would like to see their service add C-Span, which covers Congress, or perhaps an all-weather channel. They realize they have more control over the information they receive than they do with most other mass media.

Some cable operators are questioning the concept of offering a "basic service" for a fixed rate. That system means that for one price the consumer gets 20, 30, or more "free" channels. Each additional "premium" channel costs more. Instead, cable in the future may be sold in *tiers*, which means that subscribers would package their own services by choosing to pay for several groups of two or three related channels. That would make "buying cable" more like buying books, records, or videotapes—each consumer pays only for what he or she wants, not for a grab-bag of items.

Other cable operators, however, point to recent research indicating that consumers are not staying in their niches. In fact, many viewers are watching the broadcast network-type programming on such services as USA Network and the CBN Family Channel more heavily than the narrowly focused programming designed for well-defined audiences.[13] Convinced that consumers really do like network-type shows, TBS has experimented with running sitcoms in blocks when the broadcast networks are showing news or public affairs programs, so that viewers who want "mind candy" can find it on cable when it isn't on the networks.

The Most Popular Services. Most cable systems offer at least 9 or 10 of the most popular "free" channels as part of their Basic Service, plus 2 or 3 superstations

> **INDUSTRY**
>
> ## Profile of the Audience for Cable
>
> - Viewers prefer more informational and "how-to" shows such as cooking lessons and tips on making home repairs. Cable, with more diversity than network television, can fill that need. (Source: McCann-Erickson special report 1988.)
> - Local programming is of least interest to cable subscribers, mainly because of the low quality. (Source: *Advertising Age* special report, 1990.)
> - Sixty percent of consumers report repeated or prolonged interruptions in their cable service, which is ironic because a clear signal is what cable originally was meant to offer. (Source: *The New York Times*, 1990.)
> - The average bill for monthly cable services in the United States was $25 in 1990, double what it was in 1980. (Source: *The Wall Street Journal*, 1990.)

and a dozen or more channels they think will interest viewers in their area. The most popular services present a variety of programming.[14]

ESPN—48.8 Million Subscribers (Established 1979). Programs college football and basketball, NFL Sunday night games, and other sports. Operates 24 hours a day by showing tape delay and prepackaged sports events. Started by Getty Oil but now owned by Capital Cities/ABC.

CNN (Cable News Network)—47.1 Million (1980). Round-the-clock news. Summaries on the half hour, followed by features and in-depth reports. Frequently goes live for full coverage of space launches, important congressional hearings, and other breaking news. Owned by Ted Turner, whose TBS "superstation" also is carried as a basic service by many operators. CNN Headline News, established simultaneously in 1980, is carried as a separate channel by many operators and ranks thirteenth with 33 million subscribers.

USA Network—46.2 Million (1980). Broad range of programs, including syndicated shows, children's shows, health programs, and sports events. Owned by Paramount Pictures and MCS Inc.

CBN Family Channel—43 Million (1977). Owned by the Christian Broadcasting Network. Religious and inspirational shows, plus documentaries and entertainment suitable for the entire family. The cost of producing some shows is underwritten by viewer contributions made directly to the producers.

MTV—42.6 Million (1981). Music videos, music news, concerts, occasional comedy and quiz shows, plus occasional live coverage of popular events involving young people such as Mardi Gras, Spring Break, and the Grammies. Originally a Warner-Amex company, now owned by MTV Networks, a subsidiary of Viacom, which also offers VH-1, with the same format but aimed at an older audience. VH-1 ranks fifteenth, with 28 million subscribers.

TNN (The Nashville Network)—42 million (1983). Country and western concerts and variety programs, classic western movies, and auto racing. Started by Westinghouse, now owned by Opryland USA, a subsidiary of Gaylord Broadcasting.

Nickelodeon—41.4 Million (1979). Children's programming, including variety and

Senator George Mitchell of Maine on the Senate floor during the debate on authorizing President Bush to use force in the Persian Gulf. C-SPAN's full coverage of Congress allows citizens to watch their government at work.

audience participation shows. "Nick at Night" programming is aimed at an older crowd. Begun by Warner-Amex, now an MTV Networks (Viacom) service.

Lifetime—41 Million (1984). Informative programming for women. Jointly owned by Capital Cities/ABC, Viacom, and Hearst.

C-SPAN—38 Million (1979). Live coverage from the floor of the U.S. House of Representatives and congressional hearings. Public affairs programming during hours and days when Congress is not in session. Operated by the nonprofit Cable Satellite Public Affairs Network, supported in part by the cable companies. C-SPAN II, with 14.2 million subscribers, covers the U.S. Senate.

Arts & Entertainment Network—36 Million (1984). Focusing on the performing arts, including recorded symphony concerts, ballets, and operas, plus classic films and dramas. A joint venture of Capital Cities/ABC, Hearst, and NBC.

Other leading services include the Discovery Channel (science and technology), the Weather Channel, Comedy Central, and BEN (Black Entertainment Network). Some are supported entirely by advertising; others charge cable operators anywhere from 15 cents to 50 cents per subscriber.

NBC entered the cable business in 1989 through a joint venture with Cablevisions Systems Corp. to establish CNBC, the Consumer News Business Channel. With an initial subscriber base of 13 million, the service offers 24-hour consumer-oriented news, market reports, and investment advice. Its competitor, FNN (Financial News Network), was more oriented toward businesses than consumers. Ultimately, there was not enough advertising support for two business-oriented services and FNN was absorbed by CNBC.

With the exception of SportsChannel, the pay services show mostly movies. Operators package from two to five of the premium services at a price lower than the average price of about $10 if the consumer bought them individually, so many families choose among HBO, Cinemax (owned by HBO), the Movie Channel, or Showtime, plus perhaps the Disney Channel, Bravo (cinema classics), or the Playboy Channel, depending on their tastes and interests.

What Is Cable Offering Consumers?

In the early 1980s, the average "basic rate" a cable company charged its customers for a clear signal carrying local channels plus "basic services" (so-called "free" channels) was about $8. At the end of the decade it had doubled to an average of about $16. Similarly, the average total cable bill when so-called premium (extra-charge) channels were added in doubled, from about $12 to about $25.

Costs of each channel to the cable company increased over the decade, but more important, cable companies kept adding new services, including the lucrative home shopping networks, additional sports services, and a business channel. By 1990, each carrier felt the pressure to add a comedy channel. In each case the cost of providing more information had to be passed along to the consumer in the form of rate hikes. Consumer complaints to lawmakers during the first half of the 1980s overwhelmingly concerned disruption of service, improper billing procedures, and the failure of cable companies to answer their telephones. But during the late 1980s, mail and calls to Congress and state legislatures shifted, and the main complaint was increasing charges for basic services.

Some cable companies attempted to mollify customers by asking them in "bill stuffers" to vote for the type of programming they preferred. When costs for sports programs escalated, many cable companies threatened not to carry the events at the increased cost. Complaints from viewers were then used to pressure the providers of sports programming to cut back on price increases. The cable companies thus tried to convince their customers that the cable company itself was a consumer and had to fight rising prices for programming.

Complaints about costs aside, most cable customers realize, especially when their service is out temporarily and they have to hook up the old "rabbit ears" to pull in broadcast signals, that the richness of information is something they value. CNN and C-SPAN are examples of a new kind of useful information that only cable is providing.

CNN—"Always There." Ted Turner's Cable News Network is the convenience store of news: always there when you need it. CNN is carried 24 hours a day not only in the United States but throughout the world. Even in poorer countries where few homes are wired for cable, corporations, hotels, government agencies, and the national broadcast authorities receive CNN. In Poland, coverage from Soviet TV throughout the 1980s was balanced with items taken from various CNN reports.

In an era when broadcast television is criticized for presenting 15-second "sound bites" that merely give the flavor of government and politics at work, Cable News Network presents "gavel-to-gavel" coverage of political conventions and the complete proceedings of important testimony before congressional committees.

Only about half of the homes with cable receive CNN, so its ratings are not as large as the broadcast evening news programs. But considering that people are tuning in from time to time all day long, the cumulative audience for CNN in terms of minutes of news watched may mean that it has as much or more impact than the network news programs.[15]

C-SPAN—"A Seat in the Gallery." In an ideal democracy, citizens would be spectators watching as elected representatives debated the issues of the day. In a country as large as the United States, a citizen is likely to have such an experience

---

CNN PLAYS ROLE IN GLOBAL POLITICS

Ted Turner's CNN Gains Global Influence and 'Diplomatic' Role

When U.S. troops invaded Panama in December, the Soviet foreign ministry's first call went not to the U.S. Embassy, but to the Moscow bureau of Cable News Network.

A hastily dispatched CNN camera crew found spokesman Vadim Perfilyev eager to read on camera a sharp statement condemning the invasion—before the statement had run on the official Tass news agency and hours before it was repeated at a press briefing.

The Wall Street Journal, Feb. 1, 1990, p. 1.

TECHNOLOGY

CNN Leads Gulf War Coverage

This graphic was shown to CNN viewers as Peter Arnett filed his dispatches from Baghdad during the Desert Storm bombings.

Probably the most enduring image of the Persian Gulf War was the still photo CNN put on screen as millions of Americans and millions more around the world listened to the voice of Peter Arnett speaking live from Baghdad while American planes bombed Sadam Hussein's war machinery. The picture shows the newsman using a "flypack" earth station for his uplink to a satellite. Because CNN has so many worldwide correspondents, and because they are equipped with portable technology that frees them from using stationary equipment, the cable network drew viewers away from the more established broadcast networks and won a new following among consumers who appreciated the immediacy of the reports.

Source: Fred Williams, "The Shape of News to Come," *The Quill,* September 1991, pp. 15–17.

---

only once—perhaps on a school's class trip to the nation's capital. C-SPAN changes all that by giving the cable subscriber a seat in the gallery as the Congress debates a bill or a committee holds hearings. When legislative bodies are not in session, C-SPAN carries prerecorded coverage of topical events such as the appearance of a foreign dignitary before the National Press Club or a panel discussion among academics and professionals on tax policies.

C-SPAN's service now also includes coverage of the British Parliament, enabling Americans to watch the Prime Minister defend his or her policies in the House of Commons. The Canadian House of Commons also is now covered. Eventually viewers may be able to look in on the new European Community government in action as well.

C-SPAN has broadened its original mission of showing Americans how their government operates. The ultimate goal is to allow the people of all nations to understand better the workings of other political systems.[16]

Will the Consumer Pay for More?

We saw that growth in cable television spurted in the 1980s, with most basic services in place by 1985 and 57 percent penetration of American homes by the late 1980s. In the 1990s the maximum possible penetration will be reached and consumers will be paying for as many basic and premium services as they feel they need on a regular basis.

The industry believes that future financial growth for cable, therefore, lies in pay-per-view television, or P-P-V as it is shortened in the trade publications. The basic concept is that viewers are willing to pay $5 to $8 to see a first-run film that isn't available yet on the movie channels, $10 or more to see a "live" concert, and $25 to $50 to see a major sporting event such as a heavyweight prize fight. Wrestling "shows" pitting the top 30 fighters in the ring at one time already have appeared on P-P-V.

Showtime, the second-largest of the movie channels, introduced a Viewer's Choice channel in 1985 to carry pay-per-view programming, and a second channel was added a year later. Promotional brochures included with the consumer's monthly bill alert subscribers to the feature films, concerts, and sports events to be carried on P-P-V during the next calendar month. Starting times for the movies may be twice during the day and twice in the evening. The sports events usually are one-shot affairs. To "reserve" the program, the viewer may have to call a toll-free 800-number, unless the cable company has provided an "impulse decoder" that permits instantaneous ordering of a program. The program is unscrambled at the appointed "feed" time, and the consumer is charged on the next monthly bill.

INSIGHT

Consumers Can Help Shape Cable

Viewers have formed local and regional groups to exchange information about cable, and they have banded together to pressure operators into changing their practices. The Cable Users Association of New Jersey, for example, holds workshops on how to use access channels, screens prize-winning videos made by independent producers at its annual meeting, and uses its newsletter to apprise members of their rights under cable regulations. Consumers who are unhappy with signal quality, rates, or programming choices and who have not been satisfied with the response to complaints made to their cable operator find that they can work with the association and local government officials to bring pressure. The association also maintains ties with education. It urges the state Department of Education to fund projects for the development of instructional modules to be carried on cable, and it shares information about innovative cable and video projects going on in schools throughout the state.

Will All Sports Be Pay-per-View? How many people the viewer invites over to view a major sports attraction is anybody's guess. The $50 cost for a championship bout isn't outrageous if 10 people make an at-home event out of watching it. Sports promoters and the cable companies are studying the World Series, and, of course, the Super Bowl as candidates for pay-per-view transmission before the year 2000. Instead of people's watching those programs individually, the price may virtually guarantee that most people will have to build a party or large family get-together around the events (which, of course, is what many people already do for the "free" Super Bowl).

When NBC bid a record $401 milion for the rights to cover the 1992 Olympic Games in Barcelona, it counted on a P-P-V venture with Cablevision Systems to recoup at least a quarter of that amount. The "Triplecast" offered cable viewers three channels—Red, White, and Blue—covering major events such as basketball, swimming, and gymnastics completely, without cutting away from the action, in a 12-hour cycle that was repeated daily. Packages labeled "Bronze, Silver, and Gold" enabled consumers to buy a week of viewing, weekends only, or the complete package at a top price of $170. Initially the option of buying only one day's worth of programming was not available. When consumers ignored the Triplecast packages, a $29.95 per day price was offered, but too late to attract many viewers. The Triplecast was an artistic success, which suggests that better packaging and promotion might make the concept work in the future.

In the New York Market, the majority of NFL football games are still on free network TV, the exception being ESPN's Sunday night game. Mets and Yankee games in recent years have moved to cable, but there is resistance to showing all the games on cable because advertisers want to reach the larger broadcast audience. Consumers are slowly being conditioned toward the idea of paying for professional sports. Cable operators hope eventually to be able to sell sporting events to consumers on a game-by-game basis.

Cable coverage of major sports could mean a schedule in which something is being shown at almost any hour of the day—especially if the NFL fields new franchises in Europe and elsewhere, as is anticipated. Recently uprooted fans who would rather not be restricted to the local team can pay to see their favorites from back home play.

The initial reaction to the move of sports from "free" television to cable was an outrage among working-class fans. For affluent consumers, however, it means more programming and more choice.

"Interactive TV" Changes Producer's Role. Most television viewers have to be content with watching the shot the director of the sports event selects for them—sometimes a close-up of one player, sometimes the width and breadth of the entire action. The individual viewer's interests might be different from what the director thinks the audience needs to see.

Subscribers to an interactive cable system in Montreal were given another option in a January, 1990, ice hockey game between the Canadiens and the Quebec Nordiques. They could use a hand-held remote-control device to make their own choice of pictures from among four being offered simultaneously: the shot going out to all viewers, two close-ups on players from each team, or a continuous delayed replay.[17]

In terms of the P↔I↔C model, the role of the producer has been changed by the new system. The producer provides an array of possibilities, and the consumer acts as coproducer to make a personally tailored version of the game.

In 1990, a two-month experiment was conducted with selected cable customers in Springfield, Massachusetts, to see whether they would choose to spend more time with cable programs that allow them to interact with their television sets. One of the programs allowed viewers to play blackjack against a dealer on the screen; another took the responses of viewers to quiz questions and let on-screen contestants play against the viewing audience. Initial response indicated that many viewers gave the games a try, but the novelty soon wore off. Programmers who try such experiments feel that it may take more substantive material to keep consumers coming back.

Earlier experiments in Columbus, Ohio, and Mountain View, California, showed that interactive systems have great potential for attracting audiences, but, again, consumers quickly lost interest and questioned whether the added expense was worthwhile. "Voting" on the performance of candidates at a debate and giving office-seekers instant audience feedback to their stands on the issues may have a benefit to democratic society, but that alone will not attract consumers to interactive television. If the ability to select from several shorts to "self-edit" your own version of a live event catches on, that may be the best chance for the success of the experimental system.

European countries have developed cable to varying degrees, with Germany leading the number of homes receiving cable services. A unified Europe began to emerge in 1992, along with expectations that transnational cable services may eventually prove valuable.

THE VIDEO EXPLOSION

The American public's rapid embrace of the videocassette recorder, or VCR, paralleled the rise of cable television. At the same time that the amount and type of information coming into the home was increased by quantum jumps, the technology for saving, storing, and replaying the information was introduced. Consumers might have been expected to be overwhelmed by such an outpouring of goodies. Initially they were. Then the market fairly exploded. Suddenly everyone seemed to be watching "videos."

Video actually is a term that describes the picture component of a televised image, as opposed to the *audio* or sound component.[18] But quickly it became the colloquial word meaning the artifact the consumer rented, taped from broadcast or cable television, or maybe even purchased. Videotape was demonstrated in the 1950s. In the 1960s it began to be used by the television industry to create football's instant replays. At that time the effect of showing the viewer instantaneously what had just happened moments earlier was a sensation; now it's so common that viewers take it for granted as a built-in capability of the technology.

A Market Battle: Betamax versus VHS

Japan's Sony Corporation pioneered the development of recorders in the 1960s and took the market lead with its Betamax format. However, it was incompatible

Chapter 11 Cable and Video

College students prepare a video program.

with the VHS format being developed in the United States by the Ampex Corporation. Just as with color television, two rival systems vied for public approval. Both systems are still available, but VHS clearly dominates the market.

The average cost of a videocassette recorder dropped from $728 in 1981 to $420 in 1985,[19] and soon thereafter they could be purchased for as little as $200. The 1985 machines had many new features: They were cable-compatible, they could be remote-controlled, and they offered several different recording modes. Not surprisingly, sales took off at a rate of 25,000 units per day in the United States. Over 12 million units were sold, 50 percent more than in the previous year. At the end of 1987, the 50 millionth VCR had been sold in the United States. Today as with cable, videocassette recorders are found in more than 60 percent of the homes in the country.

The pattern of VCR ownership, in other words, mirrored the pattern for the ownership of television sets a generation earlier. TV sales began slowly, then increased over a five-year period before spurting to the point where 98 percent of all homes had television. Just as television sets changed from a novelty to an essential component of American family life within a decade, the VCR went from a toy for the wealthy to another basic component in the family system for providing entertainment and information.

Initially, cable operators, fearful that VCRs would be used only to show rented movies, tried to convince VCR purchasers that the systems were not compatible. When the cable operators discovered that VCR owners were taping off cable in great quantities, their fears lessened and they began to stress cable and VCR compatibility. A survey of VCR owners showed that only about a third of VCR owners rent movies regularly, while half of them record television programs to view later.[20]

Changing Movie Habits

Many a shopping list today ends with "milk, eggs . . . *movie.*" Videocassettes of films are available at the supermarket courtesy counter. Membership in a video club means privileges such as first choice on the waiting list for popular recent releases. People who rarely go to movie theaters have increased movie-viewing because picking up a video is logistically simpler than planning an outing to the theater. The rental charge is only about $2, compared with $6 to $8 per person for a theater. So even if a rented movie is viewed only in part by one or all members of the family, the relative cost is seen as trivial. That's why some parents feel they can afford to "pick up" three to five movies for a weekend.

The easy availability of videos means that people who had gotten out of the movie-going habit are seeing more films. The films they tend to see are those that have received promotion in the media or by word-of-mouth. Just as shoppers in a supermarket pick out products they recognize and trust, shoppers in the video stores are more likely to pick out *Rocky 16*, *Jaws 10*, or the latest Kevin Costner film because it's a product they recognize. The film critic for *The New York Times* worries that the new distribution pattern for films means that "sleepers" (films that audiences and critics gradually discover) won't have a chance because they will suffer the fate of a book that doesn't get rave reviews right away.[21]

One of the surprising patterns of videocassette usage has been the proportion of X-rated "adult" films available in suburban rental shops. A large segment of society assumed that pornography was one of the trappings of decaying inner cities, made for the gratification of the proverbial "dirty old man." Rental patterns indicate, however, that people in many age, income, and education groups have been satisfying their curiosity or needs through the convenience of rental and home viewing. Adult videos account for about 10 percent of rentals in the stores where they are available.

In the mid-1980s VCR owners who wanted to purchase videocassettes of movies had to pay between $69 and $79 for a feature-length film. But informational tapes such as aerobics workout demonstrations soon came down to $39 or less. In 1985 the popular film *Beverly Hills Cop* was released in quantity at $29.95 instead of $79.95. Sales were brisk. The message was not lost on Hollywood: It is possible to make as much money selling a movie to individuals cheaply as it is to sell it to rental stores at a higher first-sale price. In 1991, millions of copies of *Home Alone* were sold at $14.95 or less. (Philosophically, we are not used to *renting* mass communication media. Most of us want our own copy of a newspaper, magazine, or book, even if we know we'll only glance at it or read it once.)

Purchases of films on videocassette differ considerably from rental patterns. Action-adventure films and science fiction—escapist fare—account for almost half of rentals. Each of the other types of dramatic film accounts for about 10 percent of rentals: children's, adult X-rated, comedies, dramas, and horror films. The all-time best-selling video is "E.T.: The Extra-Terrestrial," which has sold over 15 million copies at $24.95. Disney's "Bambi" has sold over 10 million.

VCRs are responsible for a new hobby: old movie and TV program collecting. Some fans have built libraries containing every episode of various shows. Others specialize in documentaries and historical tapes. Several newsletters enable tape hobbyists to communicate with each other in order to fill out their collections.

By 1985 the $4 billion that Americans spent on rentals and purchases of videos equaled the amount they spent at movie box offices.[22] The numbers attending movie theaters declined as rentals increased. Consumers appeared to be opting for the convenience of take-home videos over the enjoyment of watching films on a large screen with quality sound and sharing the experience with a live audience.

Hollywood was not destroyed by the video revolution, however. The increased home use of movies had the effect of building audience interest in what was new and current at the local theaters. The lower price of movies available for sale rather than rental also assured film producers of a larger share of the proceeds from film distribution. Theater owners raised admission prices to compensate for video competition.

Nielsen Tracks Videocassette Viewing

At first producers of videocassettes were content to use the *sales* of their products as an indication of the audience size. But now that videocassettes carry commercial messages before and after the entertainment information, producers want to know more about which members of the household are watching, and how often. Therefore, in 1989 Nielsen began regular tracking of the use of prerecorded cassettes in the home by adding *Priam*—"prerecorded identification and measurement"—to its national sample. Ads placed on tapes are encoded so they will trip the data recorder on people meters and let advertisers know whom they are reaching.

In a pilot study, Nielsen used the homes already equipped with its people meters to track videocassette viewing. The research showed that 85 percent of the viewers watched the commercial if it appeared at the beginning of the program. When Nielsen tested the film *Young Guns* for Vestron Video, the estimate was that the advertisement placed on the videocassette was seen by an audience of 25 million, contrasted with the average of 21 million people who see an advertisement on a prime-time network television series.[23]

INDUSTRY

Profile of the Audience for Video

- VCR ownership has exceeded 60 percent of all American homes, with urban, college-educated viewers who earn more than $25,000 being the most likely to purchase a VCR and use it to record cable services. (Source: Nielsen, 1990.)

- If an advertisement is added to a videotape, 85 percent of the viewers will watch the commercial, according to Nielsen data. (Source: *Advertising Age*, 1990.)

- Forty-one percent of recordings are made during prime time, and 67 percent of all recordings are of network programs. Most recordings are made while the television set is off. (Source: Nielsen, 1989.)

Specialized Uses of Video

Print media can change their technology when the producers choose, adding color to a black-and-white publication, changing the printing system, or using computers to lay out the pages. The consumer isn't concerned with the problems of changing the technology, as long as the product arrives on time, at the expected price, and with more or less the same content.

Similarly, when television introduces new technology at the production end—for example, when the introduction of the minicam made it possible for live reports to be brought from street locations to the evening news audience—nothing is required of the consumer except to take passing notice of the improvement.

However, when television makes changes in the technology at the receiving end, it must move slowly and carefully because consumers are resistant to innovations that cost a great deal and drastically alter the form of the message. That's why today's television sets are not radically different from those used 25 years ago, save for the addition of remote control, fine tuning, and cable/VCR readiness.

A feature available to cable viewers receiving the music video channels is stereophonic sound, which can be heard through auxiliary speakers rather than the tiny, tinny audio systems in the standard television set.

Closed captioning, which makes "subtitles" visible to hard-of-hearing viewers equipped with decoder machines, began in 1980. The networks voluntarily provided the service and split the cost of writing and adding the subtitles with the federal Department of Education and commercial sponsors.

Video innovation has not been concentrated primarily on the television set, but on uses that can be made of the existing technology. The remainder of this chapter looks at new and emerging applications. Some are designed for the at-home consumer and are tied to cable, others aim to give consumers an opportunity

INDUSTRY

"Quickie" Videotapes Provide Mementos

Paperback publishers found an eager market for books produced in a few short weeks to commemorate the Great Power Blackout in New York City, the Pentagon Papers, the release of the Iranian hostages, and the Gulf War.

The same kind of limited market is emerging for videotapes that provide "live-action" mementos of events that glued viewers to their tube for hours or days on end.

The first was ABC's cassette using footage of its coverage of the 1984 Olympic Games in Los Angeles. More than 120,000 copies were sold at $29.95.

ABC tested consumer interest again in 1986 with a cassette costing half that much that documented the four-day Liberty Weekend festival in New York Harbor commemorating the centennial of the Statue of Liberty.

If quickie documentary videotapes prove successful, they may become a sideline product for the networks' news divisions and other producers who realize that information can be packaged and distributed in a variety of ways.

> **TECHNOLOGY**
>
> ## Codes in TV Listing Simplify VCR Programming
>
> Many consumers who were delighted at the prospect of letting their magical VCRs tape their favorite shows while they were away from home discovered to their dismay that they were recording the wrong show at the wrong time. Programming the recorder proved nearly impossible to many people.
>
> Now newspapers in major markets and *TV Guide* put code numbers like "20651" along- side the program listings to simplify the process. For the consumer who owns a Gemstar VCR Plus+ (sold at electronic stores for $59.95), it's merely a matter of entering the code number into the gadget. Because the code number is imbedded in the opening second of the program information, the VCR turns on automatically and records the desired show.

to be their own video producers, and still others are used by business to facilitate internal communication and to enhance external information programs. (Experiments with teletext, videotex, and on-line databases—print information that joins television technology with computers—will be discussed in Chapter 16, where the focus is on specialized electronic communication systems that go beyond the realm of video.)

Miniaturization. When Sony revolutionized the audio field by introducing the Walkman, its personal sound system, it was inevitable that the market eventually would see Watchman, a hand-held TV-VCR. The $1000 units introduced in 1988 were novelty Christmas gifts for the wealthy. But Sony, which has lost dominance in the video field to Korean competitors, hopes that "personal video" will become as popular and necessary as the personal radio is today. So far, though, sales do not suggest that consumers feel a strong need for the product.[24]

Videocorders. The postwar affluence that began in the 1950s put home movie cameras and projection systems within the price range of the middle class. Super-8 film, which offered the same clear image as 16-millimeter but in a compact unit, spurred a boom in home movie-making in the 1960s and 1970s.

The Polaroid Company introduced "instant movies" during this period, but the system was expensive and unreliable. Besides, small-format video, using half-inch tape, had come to schools and industry, and it was obvious that the home video outfit was just around the corner. Interest in film technology dropped off.

When sales of VCRs accelerated, so did purchases of small video cameras and sound recorders. Consumers discovered benefits that made films obsolete. First, it is possible to view videotapes immediately—no need to wait a week for them to come back from the processing laboratory. Second, it is much easier and more convenient to pop a tape into a VCR than it is to thread a projector and darken the room for movies. Movies tend to jam in the projector, and projection lamps can burn out at inopportune moments, but video is practically foolproof. Video stores now do a lucrative business transferring old home movies onto tape for more frequent and enjoyable viewing.

Because of film's cost and special requirements, it has always been used primarily to record special occasions. Personal video, with its ease of operation, is finding broader applications. It can be used casually because, by contrast with film, unwanted information can be recorded over and the tape can be reused.

Many schools now have a choice between the traditional print yearbook and the video yearbook. The video version is "more alive" and includes the sounds as well as the sights of the school experience. Many schools routinely tape class plays, the senior class trip, the prom, sports events, and graduation ceremonies. Videotapes are also used for orientation purposes, such as "How to use the library" and "Clubs and activities you can join." Even "pen pal" projects between individuals and schools now involve videotapes rather than letter writing.

Just as film was downscaled in size at no loss of picture quality, the video standard of ½-inch tape eventually may give way to ¼-inch tape, which is called 8-millimeter video, an allusion to the popularity of Super-8 film. It is already being used by sales personnel at trade shows and in calls to potential buyers. Manufacturers hope to bring the price down to the point where schools and small businesses, as well as individuals, will see the smallest-format video as a cost-effective means of creating sound-and-picture messages for situations when they might earlier have settled for slides or a display of still pictures. Because so many people have invested in ½-inch VCRs, however, the switch may have to wait until consumers are ready for the innovation.

Business Applications. When Johnson & Johnson, the manufacturer of Band-Aids, Tylenol, baby oil, and other health care products, built its new worldwide

Business meetings are enhanced by video messages, including live connections with participants at other locations.

headquarters in the early 1980s, it included a television studio in the basement. J&J has the equipment and staff to turn out broadcast-quality ¾-inch cassettes. The reason J&J put such a premium on video is that it's simpler to hold a "briefing" in its studios and then mail copies to its family of 170 companies around the world than it is for teams of managers to trek off carrying the same messages in person.

J&J also uses video as a powerful sales tool for its products used in intricate medical operations. A competitor's salesperson might talk at length and provide print brochures that explain how a new suture works in microsurgery. The J&J salesperson hands doctors a videotape they can play on the hospital's VCR to see the product being used under actual conditions.

Many companies now document their meetings, including the critical annual meeting of stockholders, on videotape. Three important objectives are realized by making a video record of the event: (1) management can study the tapes to learn how to make the meeting more efficient in the future, (2) the historical record may be used to document the company's development on future anniversary occasions, and (3) employees and managers at locations far from the main headquarters can be sent copies of the meeting so they will know what went on.

Live video hookups are being used for meetings of far-flung executives of the Ford Motor Company; Sears, Roebuck; Hewlett-Packard; and other companies. The chief executive and the top management staff are "on-camera" from the studio at the head office. Managers in branch locations are connected by telephone. In a more expensive hookup, more than one location may be linked visually as well as aurally.

Videoconferencing (or *teleconferencing*, as it is called in industry) makes it unnecessary for busy people to spend a day getting to and from a central conference center. The major hotel chains offer sophisticated videoconferencing equipment in order to lure companies that do not have their own video capability to conference center motels.

The technology that makes videoconferencing possible is the microwave dish, a contraption like a tilted kettle lid that stands atop or alongside most industrial locations and motels today. The television signal is bounced up to a satellite, and then back down to receiving dishes around the country or the world that are tuned to the same frequency.

Business and higher education are developing teleconferencing partnerships that bring industry people "back to the campus" for refresher courses—except that they may not actually set foot on the campus where the telecourse originates. Instead they go to the nearest university, which hooks up with the originating university. Lesson plans and packets are mailed out ahead of time to participants. During some parts of the teleconference, students at the remote university have the opportunity to question professors at the originating facility. At other times discussions are held among the students and coordinators at the remote location.

On-the-Job Training and Interviewing. Videotape is also used by industry to interview job applicants. Sending a recruiter around to college campuses or hotels for endless interviews with hundreds of applicants can be expensive and wasteful. Pointing to the $10,000 average a company spends on hiring a managerial-level employee, the Corporate Interviewing Network, Inc. cuts that cost considerably by preparing interview videotapes based on questions supplied by the hiring firm. Recruiters screen the tapes to select finalists.[25]

Melvin Goodes, chief executive officer of Warner-Lambert, discusses his interview on the set of "Come Make It Happen," a recruitment video produced for the company's human resources division.

Another useful application of videotape is for training speakers, from the president of the company on down to the sales force. Playback of rehearsals can help speakers, with the assistance of communication specialists, to make their style of presentation more dynamic and to learn better control of voice, posture, and gestures.

The videodisc, similar in appearance to a long-playing record album, lost out to VCRs and videotape in the home market, but business discovered the advantages of the videodisc's computerized ability to jump back or ahead quickly according to the keyboard commands of the user. That makes them ideal for training. A worker can use a video lesson at his or her own pace, trying different options, returning to trace over areas where mistakes were made, or jumping back and forth for quick reviews. J. C. Penney uses the system to teach inventory control because classes and books were considered boring, and the Ford Motor Company found videodiscs the only way to keep up with the huge task of training its thousands of mechanics.[26]

Video Art. The benefits of video technology have been discovered by artists. Because there is a shortage of art teachers qualified to teach figure study, videotapes have been prepared that allow an art student to study a nude model, then stop the live action on a still frame and draw directly from the screen.

Kodak has introduced a "video imager" capable of making a still picture from one frame of video information. The machine, which costs $700, makes prints in just two minutes, at about $1 a print. Artists can find and use any video image they desire to incorporate in a montage or collage. Laser video makes it possible for artists to store copies of all of their work on a single disk for reference and reprinting. Some artists are exploring video, computer graphics displayed on video, and video storage and retrieval as art forms in themselves.

Targeted Political Messages. Candidates for national office used to have to hope that they could create a major "media event" that would attract the networks and wire services, so that news of their views could trickle down to the nation's smaller media through the services of the major media. Satellite video technology has changed that. Speeches, debates, and public appearances by presidential candidates now are made available to media throughout the country directly by satellite hookup that bypasses the networks and wire services. Using small "electronic newsgathering" transmitters, candidates can record and send material directly to any medium that has a receiving unit. Smaller news outlets that used to rely on the networks and wire services now can receive original material, select what interests their audiences, and edit it according to their needs. The staffs of presidential candidates, for example, can phone editors and station managers around the nation to say: "Tune to this frequency and you'll hear and see our candidate explaining how his tax reform proposals will affect the farmers living in your state." Thus, there is a shift away from the generalized information served up by the national media for a national audience toward information that meets the needs of specific consumers.

Interactive Shopping Services. In July of 1985, the Home Shopping Network was introduced to about 8 million households as a live, 24-hour-a-day direct response service selling 25,000 items a day, ranging from jewelry and clothing to small appliances and exercise equipment.[27] Soon Home Shopping Network II, Cable Value Network, and other shopping services blossomed.

In 1986, retailers began using video catalogs—*videologs*—to show consumers the latest fashions or to demonstrate the benefits of household goods. Some charged $10 for cassette videologs, with price applied to the first purchase. Others put their videologs on cable television for viewers to see. Sears, Roebuck was the first mass merchandiser to test the technique, followed by mail-order houses such as Spiegel, and eventually even the exclusive Neiman-Marcus department store.[28]

The first videologs were passive: The consumer viewed the tape, then had to turn to the telephone to order the material. The J. C. Penney Company, however, has market-tested an *interactive* videolog for introduction in the 1990s. Viewers use push-button phones to enter an "electronic mall" displayed through their

INSIGHT

Next: Supermarket CNN

Like American Express, CNN would like to be able to say "Don't leave home without it!" TV monitors showing eight-minute segments from CNN Headline News and two minutes of commercials were placed at supermarket checkout counters in 13 stores across the country during a six-week test in the fall of 1990. Turner Network officials and the ActMedia advertising firm that set up the system are analyzing consumer reaction. ActMedia predicts that if the system goes nationwide, the advertising revenue, which would be shared by CNN and the supermarkets, could reach $100 million a year.

Home shopping networks allow consumers to view demonstrations of a product, then place an order by phone using their credit cards.

cable system. More than 30 stores are included. Shoppers "page through" and stop to select what they want from each store. In the test markets, the most popular service has been a grocery store that delivers food electronically selected by the consumer. Working parents with little time to shop have been the prime users of the service.[29]

Food stores discovered that print ads placed on shopping carts were another effective way of calling shoppers' attention to products. Not surprisingly, then, the "VideOcart" made its debut in 1989: a tiny television set mounted where the consumer can see short "loops" demonstrating products. Eventually the system may be so sophisticated that sensors placed strategically in supermarket aisles will trigger the playing of the appropriate tape just as the shopper enters the area where a certain product is displayed.

Advertisers also use video to get their messages before consumers who are biding their time. Health Club TeleVision Network pays health club operators to put their ad-supported programming on screens in front of stationary bicycles and stair-climber exercise equipment.[30] Healthcare Television Network targets another captive audience: people in doctors' waiting rooms, who view health programs and associated advertising.[31]

Innovation Continues

The front desk at hotels may disappear in the future if cable/computer experiments being conducted for such chains as Marriott and Hyatt prove viable. Instead of approaching a registration desk, the traveler merely walks up to an electronic *kiosk*,

TECHNOLOGY

Creating the "Video Environment" (Or . . . What *Can't* They Do with Video?)

Most consumers think of television or video as a single screen carrying a solitary piece of programming meant to be given full attention. But just as the slide show grew into multiprojector montages that created visual excitement, multiscreen video is coming into vogue as a marketing tool that creates an environment by enveloping the viewer and bringing all the senses into play.

The IMTECH Video Wall fills an entire side of a display area with coordinated images that bombard the consumer with a variety of angles on new fashions, a travel location, a housing community, or whatever the client wants to promote. Envisioned for trade shows, it may eventually appear in department stores and airline terminals as a traffic-stopper. The latest twist is a videowall that is activated by the movement of the consumer passing by and incorporates his or her image into the collage of information being shown.

Innovative auto manufacturer and distributor Malcolm Bricklin is planning a new kind of auto showroom where the potential customer steps into a video booth and is surrounded by myriad images that give the feeling of driving the car.

Sources: Cyndee Miller, "Interactive Videowall Unveiled by IMTECH," *Marketing News*, Feb. 27, 1989, p. 17; Associated Press, "Glitzy Video Booths Proposed to Replace Car Showrooms," *Marketing News*, Feb. 27, 1989, p. 5.

---

inserts a credit card, then selects the services and accommodations needed and waits a few seconds for the computer to assign a room. The consumer's credit card serves as a room key.

At checkout time, there's no need to wait in line at the cashier's desk. While readying to leave the room, the guest calls the room bill and charges up on the screen of the hotel's television set using the telephone and the in-house cable system. If everything is in order, there's no need to check out: Everything will be billed automatically to the credit card.[32]

The newest television sets come with electronic wands like those used at checkout counters in some stores. Consumers will be able to wave the wand over bar codes printed in the newspaper to program their televisions to turn on and record the shows they want to see or to show them the prerecorded ads for prod-

INSIGHT

Unwind Before You Rewind this Video

Stressed at the end of a hard day? The American Express Card Video Service offers cardholders a videotape called "The Reef." It has no narration, just music by Mozart and Brahms and 60 minutes of fish swimming around a coral reef.

Video on video—Nintendo video competitions are carried on cable television.

ucts they want to buy. TV listings soon may include such bar codes to facilitate program selection.

The ultimate computer-television service, now being developed, is the television that knows what you want to watch and makes sure you don't miss it. Some systems require viewers to enter information into the computer about the types and categories of information they want. "Smart" television can read electronic data about your current viewing habits and select shows to record for you that you may not even realize were being shown.

Sound cues carried as part of television commercials can mimic the sounds of a touch-tone phone and automatically dial a number. If the consumer wants to order a product being shown on television or get more information about it, the television can place the call.

The technology for interactive television that permits input and feedback from audience members during the show may also be used for interaction during the commercials. Advertisers are already experimenting with messages that ask the viewer to watch in order to receive a special incentive. At the appointed moment in the commercial the viewer may receive a coupon, place an order at a special price, or become eligible for a prize drawing by activating a touch pad or by using the telephone to respond to the information on the screen.[33]

To attract the consumer to this service (and to convince viewers to pay a few hundred dollars for the electronic interactive unit), advertisers may convince cable producers to extend the interactive capability to the related entertainment programming as well. We may be attracted by the thought of voting *yes* or *no* on

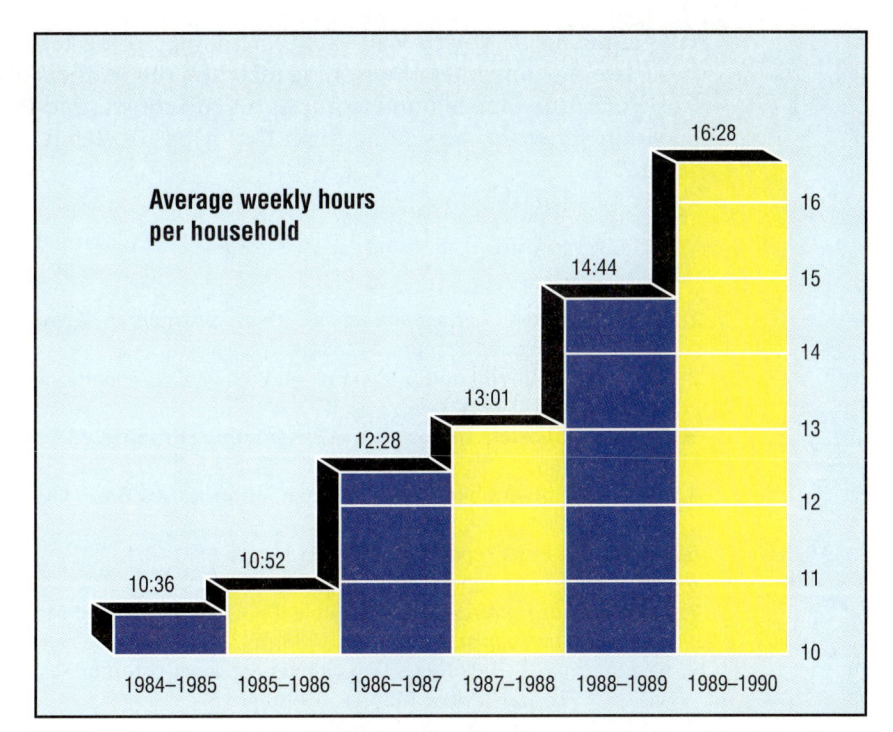

FIGURE 11.2 **Time Spent with Cable is Growing** Source: Cablevision Advertising Bureau, 1991.

whether a Michael Jackson video or a George Michael video should be shown next on MTV—and then we'll stick around to let Michael know that we want the Pepsi coupon, or ask George to send us a Coca-Cola T-shirt.

What is the effect of all these new video services? They turn many *interpersonal communication* situations into *mass communication* situations. We used to have to speak to another human to express our preferences. More and more we may choose to "interact with images" in order to conduct our "public" lives. (See Figure 11.2.)

FUTURE FILE

✓ Think of the aspect of shopping for products or seeking information that most aggravates you. From what you know about the potential of cable and video technology, how could a future electronic information system make shopping or information-seeking easier for you?

✓ Phone companies provide itemized bills that account for each call. They explain what service was provided, for how long, and at what rate. If the phone companies become major providers of electronic information services in the future, what will the itemized bill look like? Will we become accustomed to seeing printouts that account for every minute and dollar spent on our academic research, our shopping, our game-playing, and our consultations with lawyers?

✓ The ultimate decadence of ancient Rome was the bloody games in the Coliseum, where spectators signaled the fate of combatants by holding their thumbs up or down. Will cable technology bring consumers the power to dictate the outcomes of wrestling matches, the winners of domestic battles on sitcoms, the time allotted to guests on talk shows, and the fate of a new television show the very same night that it has its debut? Will that be good or bad?

NOTES

1. Lynne S. Gross, *Telecommunications: An Introduction to Electronic Media* (Dubuque, IA: Wm. C. Brown, 1988), pp. 133–134.
2. Thomas F. Baldwin and D. Stevens McVoy, *Cable Communication* (Englewood Cliffs, NJ: Prentice-Hall, 1988), p. 6.
3. Eugene S. Foster, *Understanding Broadcasting* (Reading, MA: Addison-Wesley, 1978), pp. 360–366.
4. Maurine Christopher, "CATV Deregulation Raises Basic Questions," *Advertising Age*, Oct. 22, 1984, p. 68.
5. Associated Press report, Aug. 2, 1985.
6. Associated Press report, Sept. 10, 1985.
7. Laura Landro, "Agency Urges Cable-TV Changes to Give Market New Competition," *The Wall Street Journal*, June 15, 1988, p. 30.
8. Ted Sherman, "BPU Hears Debate over Stricter Customer Service Rules for Cable Television," *The Star-Ledger*, May 16, 1990, p. 18.
9. Alyson Pytte, "Cable TV: The New Big Kid Confronts Re-Regulation," *Congressional Quarterly*, Dec. 9, 1989, pp. 3361–3363.
10. Geraldine Fabrikant, "The Allure of the Cable System," *The New York Times*, Dec. 5, 1985, p. 1.
11. Landro, p. 30.
12. Geraldine Fabrikant, "For Cable Networks, the Road Gets a Little Steeper," *The New York Times*, Feb. 26, 1989, p. 6.
13. Eileen Becker Salmas, "Who's Going to Pay?" *Cable Television Business*, Feb. 15, 1989, pp. 42–44.
14. Rankings based on the last issue (1989) of the now-defunct *Channels Field Guide* series.
15. John Marcom, Jr., "Increase in Channels Abroad Opens Market for TV News," *The Wall Street Journal*, April 12, 1988, p. 37; Andrew Rosenthal, "Watching Cable News Network Grow," *The New York Times*, Dec. 16, 1987, p. A-32.
16. Kristin Wennberg, "C-SPAN's Next Decade," *Cable Strategies*, March, 1989, pp. 40–45.
17. "Pay-per-View Likely for Canadians," *Variety*, Jan. 11, 1989, p. 119.
18. Jarice Hanson, *Understanding Video* (Newbury Park, CA: Sage, 1987), p. 12.
19. Electronic Industries Association data cited in *Media Matters* newsletter, July 1986, p. 11.
20. Lisa E. Phillips, "Time-Shifting Top VCR Use," *Advertising Age*, Aug. 18, 1986, p. 82.
21. Vincent Canby, "Those VCRs Are Causing Something Momentous," *The New York Times*, Dec. 1, 1985, p. 19.
22. R. Lindsey, "VCRs Bring Big Changes in Use of Leisure," *The New York Times*, March 3, 1985, p. 1.
23. Ira Teinowitz, "Nielsen to Track Videos," *Advertising Age*, Feb. 27, 1989, p. 28; Wayne Walley, "Nielsen Ratings Hit Home Videos in Fall," *Advertising Age*, May 8, 1989, pp. 2, 8.
24. David Sanger, "Hand-Held TV/VCR Unit: Breakthrough or a Gimmick?" *The New York Times*, Nov. 20, 1988, pp. 1, 22.
25. E. Gowler, "Careers: New Twist in Video Interviews," *The New York Times*, Dec. 10, 1985, p. D-30.
26. J. Main, "New Way to Teach Workers What's New," *Fortune*, Oct. 1, 1984, pp. 84–94.

27. Michael Kaplan, "Shoppers Tune in National Cable Network," *Advertising Age*, March 6, 1986, p. 35.
28. Judith Graham, "Neiman-Marcus Tries Video Catalog," *Advertising Age*, March 21, 1988, p. 68.
29. Ira Teinowitz, "Penney's Video Catalog Test Expands," *Advertising Age*, Feb. 6, 1989.
30. Scott Donaton and Kate Fitzgerald, "New Media Concepts Grow," *Advertising Age*, May 14, 1990, p. 4.
31. Judith Graham, "Grey Eyes Ties to Maker of Waiting-Room Videos," *Advertising Age*, May 1, 1989, p. 79.
32. Glenn Eichler, "Check Yourself Out," *Esquire*, February, 1989, p. 66.
33. Joanne Lipman, "Coming Soon: A Chance to Tell Your TV What's on Your Mind," *The Wall Street Journal*, Feb. 23, 1989, p. B-10.

SUGGESTED READINGS

Baldwin, Thomas F., and D. Steven McVoy, *Cable Communication* (Englewood Cliffs, NJ: Prentice-Hall, 1988), p. 6.

Charren, P., and M. W. Sandler, *Changing Channels: Living Sensibly with Television* (Reading, MA: Addison-Wesley, 1983).

Grant, William, *Cable Television* (Reston, VA: Reston Publishing Company, 1983).

Hanson, Jarice, *Understanding Video* (Newbury Park, CA: Sage, 1987).

Jesuale, N., and R. L. Smith, eds., *The Community Medium* (Arlington, VA: The Cable Television Information Center, 1982).

Jones, Kensinger, Thomas F. Baldwin, and Martin P. Block, *Cable Advertising: News Ways to New Business* (Englewood Cliffs, NJ: Prentice-Hall, 1986).

CHAPTER 12

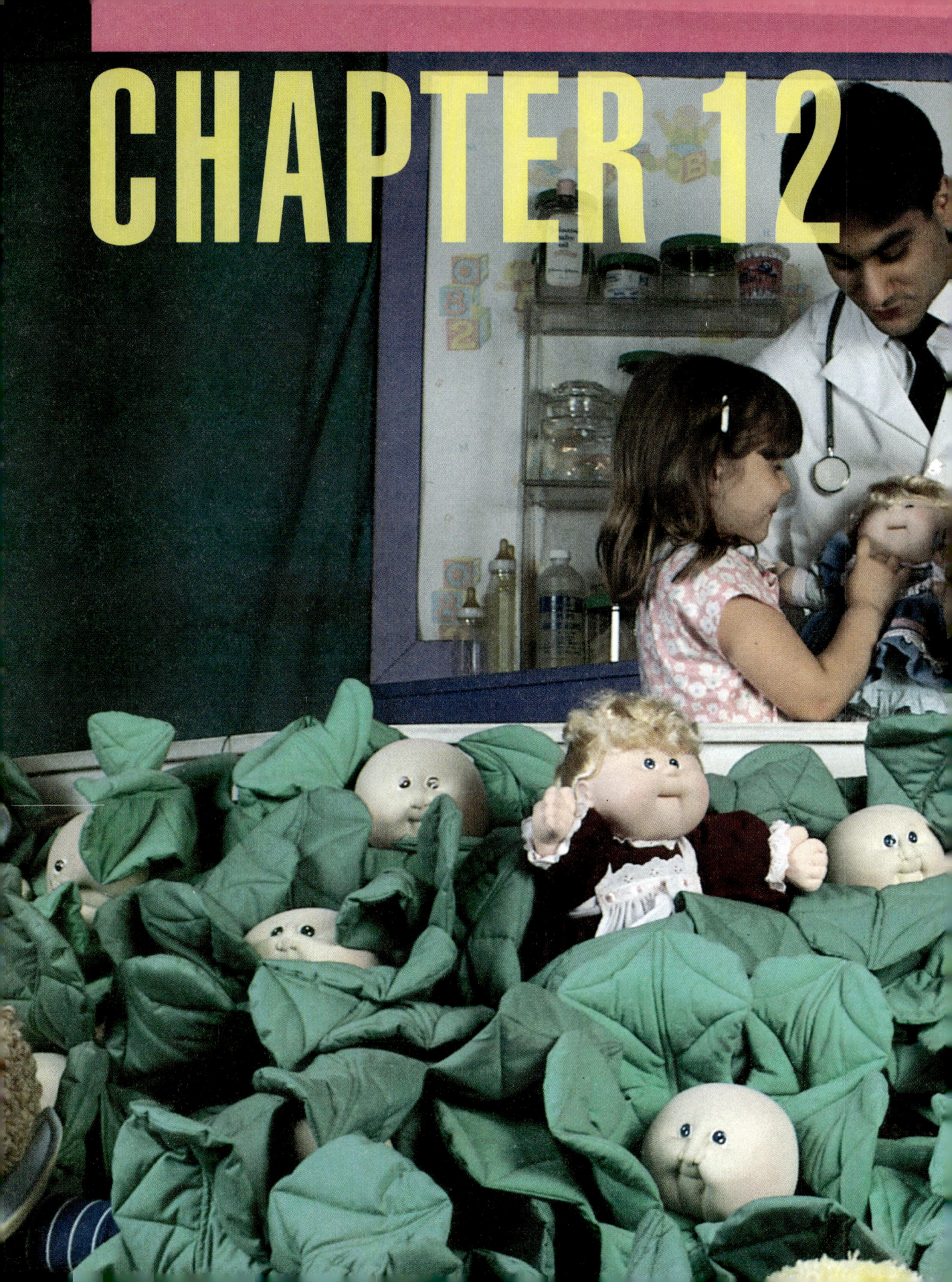

Public Relations

AT A GLANCE

✓ Persuasion techniques practiced in ancient times and in the American colonies laid the groundwork for the field now known as public relations.

✓ Edward Bernays laid the foundations of modern public relations with his books on public opinion and propaganda in the 1920s, and continued for the rest of the twentieth century to define the roles and practices of the field.

✓ Identifying key publics—and planning programs aimed at satisfying their information needs—underlies the concept of two-way symmetric communication that is the most modern definition of public relations.

✓ Relations with the news media are extremely important in public relations because the media carry public relations messages to many of the publics targeted by information campaigns.

✓ Corporations depend on their public relations departments to have crisis communication plans for the inevitable accidents and situations that make publics question the ability of the organization to function properly and efficiently.

Many of the preceding chapters have examined the functions of specific news and entertainment media. The subjects of this and the following chapter—public relations and advertising—are not media in themselves. Instead they serve as *facilitators* of the mass media. That is, public relations and advertising make the creation and distribution of mass media possible because, directly or indirectly, they underwrite the cost of disseminating information cheaply to large audiences.

Advertising, as we shall see in the next chapter, provides the cornerstone of financial support by purchasing time or space in the mass media. Public relations similarly provides what some have called a "subsidy" by providing information free that the media otherwise would have to pay to gather.

Without the support of public relations and advertising, the media would be astoundingly expensive. Imagine a daily newspaper that cost a dollar or two instead of 25 or 50 cents. Magazines could cost $10, and "free" television might cost a dollar or more per half-hour program without the subsidy provided by those who want to persuade the consumer to buy a product or support a cause.

Another compelling reason for studying public relations is that the field, far from being static in terms of growth as many other mass media fields are, provides increasing numbers of entry-level jobs for college graduates.

FACILITATING THE FLOW OF INFORMATION

One of the most discussed books in communication and business professional circles in the 1980s was *Good-bye to the Low Profile,* written by Herb Schmertz shortly before he left his position as vice-president for public affairs of Mobil Oil to form his own public relations firm. Subtitled *The Art of Creative Confrontation*, the book described the changing role of public relations.[1]

Schmertz, who is well known for instituting Mobil's long-running series of advertisements appearing on the "op-ed" pages (opposite the main opinion page) of American newspapers, once was considered controversial among public relations practitioners because of his willingness to inject his own forceful personality into the debate on oil companies and their policies. For years it had been assumed that PR people worked quietly behind the scenes, avoiding conflict and managing the fantasy that events happened naturally without the assistance of public relations. As the title of his book suggests, Schmertz believed it was time to acknowledge the role of public relations in fostering open and full debate on public issues.

While all PR professionals may not agree with his assertive techniques, most appreciate that public relations, once considered an apologist and publicist for "big business," has become a force for building alliances, influencing discussion of public issues, and facilitating the flow of information between producers and consumers of products, services, and ideas. The counsellor for a public relations agency still deals with clients who think a new "image" is the key way to success. But most public relations clients need more sophisticated programs that call for research and persuasive campaigns.

Chapter 12 Public Relations

Pump prices and tax collectors—III

From time to time, we feel called upon to point out in messages like this that when gasoline pump prices go up, we are often subject to criticism. So, occasionally, we also feel called upon to note that a constantly larger chunk of what motorists pay at the pump goes directly to tax collectors of the federal, state and local governments.

Here we go again.

In the chart below, listing major markets where Mobil does most of its business, we have provided the taxes motorists pay for a gallon of gasoline. The lowest number we can find is just under 28 cents. That's in St. Louis. On the higher end of the scale is 46 cents in some New York State locations and 54 cents in Chicago.

Now, as we head into the Memorial Day weekend this year and some serious driving time, it's possible increased demand could affect prices around the country. One thing's for sure. In certain parts of the country, state and local taxes will definitely add to the price you pay at the pump.

We're not saying state and local governments shouldn't be adding to your tax bill; that's a question for the citizens in those areas to decide. But we do think you ought to know how much of the price you pay at the pump goes into government coffers. We would also remind you once again that while market conditions sometimes drive our prices down, gasoline taxes always seem to go in only one direction.

On May 1, the average tax per gallon for the metropolitan areas listed was 39.5 cents—up more than 2 cents a gallon since July 1 of last year. If the national average is close to that number, it means that gasoline users are now paying $43.5 billion a year in direct taxes.

Gasoline taxes in cents per gallon in some key locations:

METROPOLITAN AREA	FEDERAL TAX*	STATE EXCISE TAX	OTHER STATE AND LOCAL TAXES**	TOTAL
St. Louis	14.45	13.0	–	27.45
Newark	14.45	10.5	4.04	28.99
Dallas	14.45	20.0	.59	35.04
Philadelphia	14.45	12.0	10.35	36.80
Baltimore	14.45	23.5	–	37.95
Phoenix	14.45	18.0	1.00	33.45
Detroit	14.45	15.0	5.49	34.94
Washington, D.C.	14.45	18.0	2.64	35.09
Boston	14.45	21.0	.50	35.95
Miami	14.45	4.0	21.80	40.25
Tampa	14.45	4.0	22.80	41.25
Los Angeles	14.45	16.0	10.76	41.21
Providence	14.45	26.0	–	40.45
New Haven	14.45	26.0	5.28	45.73
Albany	14.45	8.0	24.16	46.61
Buffalo	14.45	8.0	25.45	47.90
Long Island	14.45	8.0	26.10	48.55
Chicago	14.45	19.0	20.46	53.91

AVERAGE OF THESE AREAS: 39.5

* Includes federal excise taxes, Superfund tax, and the federal underground storage tank tax.
** Includes sales taxes, gross receipts taxes, local government excise taxes, underground storage tank taxes, and other non-income taxes. (Sales taxes, expressed in cents per gallon, assume a pre-tax dealer price of $1 per gallon.)

Mobil®

One in a series of Mobil op-ed page advertisements discussing issues that concern the company and its publics.

THE ORIGINS OF PUBLIC RELATIONS

Aristotle's *Rhetoric* could be considered one of the earliest volumes on public relations, for in that book the ancient Greek defined rhetoric as the "art of oratory, especially persuasive use of language to influence the thoughts and actions of listeners."

While the term *public relations* probably is less than a century old, one finds ample instances of such activity among the ancients. The authors of the first major public relations textbook indicate that "Caesar carefully prepared the Romans for his crossing of the Rubicon in 49 B.C. by sending reports to Rome on his epic achivements as governor of Gaul."[2] Others suggest that the gospels (*gospel* means "good news") were written "more to propagate the faith than to provide a historical account of Jesus' life."[3]

American colonists, including Benjamin Franklin, Thomas Jefferson, and John Adams, used propaganda techniques familiar to today's public relations practitioners. Samuel Adams spelled them out:

- Formation of an activist organization,
- Using many media,
- Creating events and slogans,
- Orchestrating conflict, and
- Sustaining an information campaign over time until the minds of the public were won over to the cause.[4]

From Press Agentry to Public Policy

Andrew Jackson, the first "common man" to assume the presidency, felt more responsible to the masses than had previous presidents. Distrustful of those who traditionally held power, he surrounded himself with a "kitchen cabinet" of advisors more in tune with his populist views. Among his confidants was Amos Kendall, a former newspaper editor who took on many of the duties now associated with the White House press secretary.

Kendall's approach was that of press agentry—catering to the needs of the press. He wrote speeches for Jackson to deliver, conducted straw polls on public opinion, acted as "advance man" whenever the president went on the road, and built Jackson's "image" as an honest and resourceful president. In addition to shaping the way Jackson was represented in the press, Kendall managed to have an effect on the formation of the president's policies.[5]

By the beginning of the twentieth century, the term *public relations* had come into use. It generally was interpreted to mean the way business explained itself to the people and attempted to convince them that it was working for their general welfare. American Telephone & Telegraph Company president Theodore Vail, who developed many modern business practices, directed that the company's 1908 annual report should be titled "Public Relations," thus giving the term legitimacy. The publication focused on the firm's responsibility to make a fair profit, to treat its employees well, and to answer any questions that could reduce conflicts between itself and its publics.[6]

BIBLIOGRAPHY

P. T. Barnum: Press Agent Extraordinaire!!!

P. T. Barnum's hyped-up publicity for Jumbo the elephant and offspring Baby made the animals so popular that they were featured on a patent medicine trade card in the 1880s.

The use of the extraneously extravagant word *extraordinaire* followed by not one but *three* exclamation points is only fitting when it comes to describing what Phineas Taylor Barnum, in his later years of Barnum and Bailey Circus fame, did for the American art of promotion. Modern public relations practitioners sometimes wince to realize that the excesses of P. T. Barnum are still what some people think "PR" is and does.

As the press agent for his own shows mounted from 1840 through the 1880s, Barnum was concerned only with filling the circus tent, attracting crowds to his museum, and—to facilitate all this—hoodwinking the press into printing believable stories about the odd and amazing attractions he brought before the American people.

In the case of tiny General Tom Thumb, Barnum merely hyped reality by adding to the reputation and legend of his midget attraction. In the case of the Cardiff Giant, a supposed prehistoric relic, and Joice Heth, reputedly a 160-year-old living woman whom the eventual autopsy proved to be only half that age, he shamelessly faked the stories. He fed the newspapers information that was so intriguing it was impossible for editors to pass it up, especially since the public loved it. Barnum coined many phrases, not the least famous of which was "There's a sucker born every minute."

Ivy Lee: Informing the Public

As the twentieth century began, American business was under attack as a force that dominated society and trammeled individuals. Magazine "muckrakers" took industry to task for dehumanizing the work place and putting worker comfort and safety second to profits. As a result, unions organized and legislators began to enact laws to limit business practices. A former New York newspaper business reporter saw the need for industry to explain itself better to society. Ivy Ledbetter Lee's message to business was: "Let the public be informed!"

Business has always had a penchant for secrecy, but Lee advised that openness could help win the support of distrustful publics, including legislators. He opened one of the first publicity agencies specializing in providing information about business to the media. He provided to clients and media alike his Declaration of Principles, spelling out how his firm intended to give editors accurate, complete information and to answer inquiries from the press as swiftly as possible.[7]

Lee provided news on behalf of the coal operators to counter information supplied by local labor unions. He convinced John D. Rockefeller to visit the family's mines in Colorado to offset criticism in a labor dispute. Eventually he was able to change the senior Rockefeller's image of aloofness to one of a charitable and concerned leader of business.

TIME CAPSULE

Public Relations

1787	Publication of *Federalist Papers* molds public opinion favorable to federal movement.
1829	Andrew Jackson appoints Amos Kendall to handle his public relations.
1860s	P. T. Barnum uses publicity to promote his shows.
1904	Ivy Lee establishes first "news bureau" public relations agency.
1907	New AT&T president Theodore Vail establishes public relations dept.
1922	First college course in public relations offered at New York University.
1923	Edward Bernays publishes landmark *Crystallizing Public Opinion*.
1923	Bernays coins the term *public relations counsel* to describe himself.
1948	Public Relations Society of America is formed to promote profession.
1952	First textbooks in public relations are published.
1954	PR News Association formed in New York to distribute news releases.
1980	U.S. Census shows more than 100,000 people working in public relations.
1984	Research by James Grunig establishes importance of two-way symmetric PR.
1985	Burson-Marsteller and Hill and Knowlton dominate U.S. public relations.
1988	"Spin control" is euphemism for shaping presidential campaign issues.
1991	Pentagon uses "Desert Shield" and "Desert Storm" information campaigns to label Gulf War and build support for allied actions.

Edward Bernays: Shaper of the Profession

The name Edward L. Bernays is synonymous with the shaping of public relations as we know it today. More than any other work, his *Crystallizing Public Opinion*, published in 1923, ushered in the era of scientific persuasion that replaced the mere providing of information by Ivy Lee, which in turn had supplanted press agentry—the hype and hoopla associated with P. T. Barnum.

Born in Vienna and a nephew of Freud, Bernays once was a press agent—the person who contacts the media to promote theatrical events—for the great tenor Enrico Caruso. A journalist by training, he was called to serve on the American government's Creel Committee for Public Information during World War I, which gave him a better understanding of the workings of propaganda—information deliberately spread to help or hurt the reputation of an individual, organization, or country. His second book, *Propaganda*, published in 1928, was based on the concept that "the conscious and intelligent manipulation of the organized habits and opinions of the masses is an important element in democratic society. Those who manipulate this unseen mechanism of society constitute an invisible government which is the true ruling power of our country."[8]

Bernays coined the phrase "engineering public consent" as a synonym for proactive public relations. He argued that facts and events could be arranged and presented to convince an audience that one course of action was preferable to another. His textbook *Public Relations* was published in 1952, and he continued as a spokesperson and advocate for public relations past his hundredth birthday in 1991.

Edward L. Bernays, the "father of public relations," works in his study. At the age of 100, he was still working for licensing of all public relations practitioners.

Bernays also coined the phrase "public relations counsel" and suggested that it was a profession, not merely a craft or trade.[9] Unlike press agents and publicists, who care only about getting publicity for their clients, Bernays suggested that the public relations counsel should use the techniques of the social sciences to understand how public opinion is created and how public opinions can be swayed through scientific, ethical, and socially responsible techniques.

Development of PR Models

Today's leading public relations scholar and theorist, Professor James E. Grunig, characterizes Bernays as responsible for developing two new models of public relations, which joined two earlier models.[10] P. T. Barnum personified the *press agent/publicity* model, with his shameless promotions based more on fancy than fact. Ivy Lee represented the *public information* model, with his emphasis on one-way (source-receiver, or producer-consumer) dissemination of truthful information.

The writing and practice of Bernays led to the development of what Grunig calls the *two-way asymmetric* model. This model uses formative research—research conducted before beginning an information campaign—to ascertain the attitudes of publics. While the flow of information is imbalanced in favor of the producer, feedback from the consumer can and does influence the producer. The two-way model represents a necessary way of conceiving public relations when the actions

INDUSTRY

Switching Models

Long the dominant auto manufacturer in the United States, General Motors had to acknowledge in the 1980s that many of its customers were switching models—to other American manufactures as well as Japanese and European imports. The firm, long known for its authoritarian control of employees, realized that its labor practices were part of its competitive problems. To survive, the company also had to switch models ... from the two-way asymmetric to the two-way symmetric, or at least closer to the latter. Some examples:

- Establishment of a union-management committee to review all production processes.
- Cosponsorship of a Rose Bowl parade float with union employees.
- Communication seminars to sensitize managers to the need for better exchange of information with employees.
- Employment of a "facilitator" to sensitize top executives to the way their actions were being perceived at lower levels.
- Personal touches such as thank-you letters from the chairman when employees do well.

In order to enact such changes in a large organization, public relations people have to study what other firms are doing, and they must help their company to listen better to employees. It is then the responsibility of the PR department to communicate the new policies effectively to the workers.

Source: Jacob M. Schlesinger and Paul Ingrassia, "GM Woos Employees by Listening to Them, Talking of Its 'Team,'" *The Wall Street Journal*, January 12, 1989, pp. A-1, A-6.

and behaviors of consumer publics affect the actions and behaviors of producers in the competitive business system.

As Bernays worked with educators and professional leaders, he came to realize that in businesses subject to heavy government regulation, or where the activist consumer has as much influence as the producer, balanced communication is necessary to adapt the organization to the realities of society. Grunig calls this fourth situation the *two-way symmetric* model. Examples are an energy utility wishing to open a nuclear power plant, or a pharmaceutical company hoping to introduce an experimental drug.

Table 12.1 summarizes the characteristics of the four models of public relations. Note that the development of the models follows public relations history over the past century, and yet no one model has supplanted the others. All four models coexist today. The astute public relations practitioner is the one who knows how to choose the correct one to fit the situation at hand. Your own college or university, for example, uses publicity to sell football tickets, public information to tell about a research project, two-way asymmetric public relations when dealing with student protesters, and the two-way symmetric model when trying to convince a foundation to fund a major grant.

IDENTIFYING PUBLICS

The two-way models provide means of acknowledging what any good public relations professional knows: The consumer of information can have effects on the producer that are as important as the effects the producer hopes to have on the consumer.

TABLE 12.1 Characteristics of Four Models of Public Relations

Characteristic	Press Agentry/Publicity	Public Information	Two-Way Asymmetric	Two-Way Symmetric
Purpose	Propaganda	Dissemination of information	Scientific persuasion	Mutual understanding
Nature of Communication	One-way; complete truth not essential	One-way; truth important	Two-way; imbalanced effects	Two-way; balanced effects
Communication Model	Source ⟶ Rec.	Source ⟶ Rec.	Source ⟶ Rec. ⟵ Feedback	Group ⟶ Group ⟵
Nature of Research	Little; "counting house"	Little; readability, readership	Formative; evaluative of attitudes	Formative; evaluative of understanding
Leading Historical Figures	P. T. Barnum	Ivy Lee	Edward L. Bernays	Bernays, educators, professional leaders
Where Practiced Today	Sports, theatre, product promotion	Government, nonprofit associations, business	Competitive business; agencies	Regulated business; agencies
Estimated Percentage of Organizations Practicing Today	15%	50%	20%	15%

Source: James E. Grunig and Todd Hunt, *Managing Public Relations* (New York: Holt, Rinehart & Winston, 1984), p. 22.

Because the "mass public" rarely acts in a unified way, "subpublics" must be identified to be targeted for a specific public relations program. This is not a totally new concept: We saw that magazines and radio, responding to the competition of television, learned to aim their messages at "specialized audiences" that have specialized information needs and interests.

Some of the publics a large organization such as a corporation must identify and plan communication programs for include these:

- Employees
- Consumers of products or services
- Other individuals or organizations providing raw materials or services to the organization
- The surrounding business community and local chambers of commerce
- Stockholders in a company or members of an association
- Municipal governments and state and federal regulatory and legislative bodies that can pass laws affecting the organization
- Political and activist groups
- Professional groups that determine norms and standards for a field
- Minorities
- Voters
- The news media
- Trade publications serving a particular industry

INDUSTRY

Top Concerns of Top PR Officers

In order to identify the public relations concerns of the nation's top 500 companies, Public Communications, Inc. of Coral Gables, Florida, has polled the firms' public relations directors periodically over a 25-year period. The surveys indicate that these are the top PR concerns of the major corporations:

1. Improving employee communications to increase loyalty and productivity
2. Enhancing corporate relationships with the financial community
3. Establishing more effective ties with government agencies
4. Improving community relations
5. Improving relations overseas
6. Effectively interpreting technological changes to key constituencies
7. Crisis management, especially related to hazardous waste disposal
8. Positive relations with investors
9. Effective marketing communications
10. Developing and maintaining a consistently positive corporate image

When the studies were begun in 1963, marketing and sales were at the top of the list, and "gaining management acceptance" for public relations programs was a major concern. The shift over the years reflects the growing concern with the diverse publics that can affect an organization. Happily for public relations people, management acceptance of public relations programs is now much more forthcoming.

Source: "Fortune 500 PR Chiefs List Top 10 Concerns," *pr reporter*, Sept. 19, 1988, p. 3.

Each of these categories of subpublic can be further divided. Employees would include part-time workers, blue-collar personnel, clerical staff, managers, and supervisors. Catering to the information needs of every group complicates the job of public relations in an organization.

At your college or university, for example, the alumni are a subpublic that can be further divided by the public relations people working for the administration, the alumni association, and the "foundation" or "development office" (the last two are polite terms for fundraisers). Alumni subpublics might include these:

- Wealthy graduates of 50 years ago who might just come forth with a few million dollars if buildings were named for them
- Football fanatics whose loyalty depends largely on the won-lost record of this year's team
- Parents who are thinking of sending their children to the school from which they graduated
- English majors who now head corporations and think the school should offer a degree in business
- Engineers who work for industry but return to campus occasionally for refresher courses
- Scholars who earned Ph.D. degrees and are now college professors

Each subgroup is potentially helpful or influential. The school may have developed a dozen different publications catering to these subpublics, rather than relying on a single alumni magazine to satisfy everyone's needs and interests.

Harvard's 350th graduation ceremony was an occasion for the college's public information staff to garner national publicity.

Fundraising, if it is to succeed, must target each of the groups separately: an end-of-the-season banquet for the football supporters, seminars and workshops serving those with professional and academic ties, parent groups for those whose children will matriculate, or personal calls from members of the department in which they majored for those who don't fit in any other special category.

Publics also can be categorized according to their behaviors. Some groups readily identify issues, seek information, and are disposed to take action; others don't pay much attention and aren't likely to get involved. Consumers who exhibit "routine" or even "fatalistic" behavior have been identified as audiences that are not likely to have much effect on an organization.[11]

The public relations professional can use survey research techniques to identify those consumers who are highly involved and most likely to engage in behaviors that will affect an organization. Programs are then designed to inform these active publics.

IMPLEMENTING THE PR PROGRAM

Identifying publics and their behaviors is the first step in planning and implementing a public relations program. Another important step is identifying an organization's goals, followed by setting public relations objectives that will help the organization to achieve those goals.

Setting Objectives

Press agent/publicity and public information specialists are concerned mainly with getting information to consumers. Thus their objectives are relatively simple and obvious: "Fill the stadium on Saturday" or "Let people know about the many uses of our products."

In the two-way models, objectives are more complex: "Gain compliance with the new recycling laws" or "Help our employees find educational resources that will promote their career advancement."

Whatever the model, public relations people have to set specific objectives—the number of people reached or the number of consumers behaving in a certain manner—and specific time frames and deadlines so that the effects of the public relations program can be measured and demonstrated to management in numerical terms. (See Figure 12.1.)

Planning the Program

To ensure that they have followed all the steps in implementing a successful public relations program, many professionals follow a plan modeled after John E. Marston's R-A-C-E formula.[12] The letters stand for *research, action, communication,* and *evaluation.* Since evaluation at the end of a program is a kind of research that may lead to modifications or changes in the public relations program, the formula can be seen as a spiral that continually renews the process of analysis, program design, and communication.

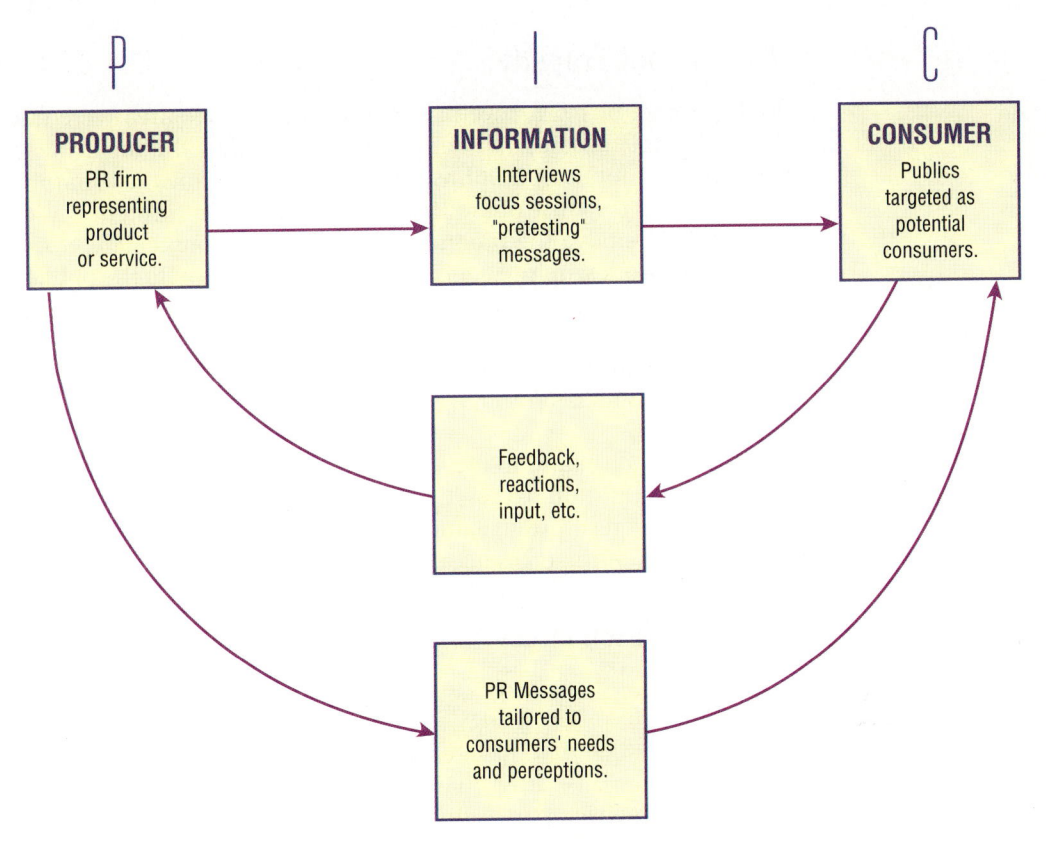

```
      P                    I                    C
  ┌─────────┐         ┌─────────┐          ┌─────────┐
  │PRODUCER │         │INFORMATION│        │CONSUMER │
  │ PR firm │────────▶│ Interviews│───────▶│ Publics │
  │representing│      │focus sessions,│    │targeted as│
  │ product │         │ "pretesting"│      │ potential│
  │or service.│       │ messages. │        │consumers.│
  └─────────┘         └─────────┘          └─────────┘
```

FIGURE 12.1 Two-Way Information Flow Enhances Persuasion Research always precedes implementation of a successful public relations program and continues throughout the process. The producer uses surveys, individual and group interviews ("focus sessions"), and "pretesting" of messages on sample audiences to determine consumers' needs, interests, thoughts, and reactions. With that preparation, the messages sent out to the larger publics have a better chance of achieving the desired goals.

- *Research* includes measuring public opinion, analyzing all information currently available to publics, considering options, pretesting messages, assessing the impact of information channels, and making qualitative assessments of ideas that may prove effective.
- *Action* means laying out the program that will get the message across—planning events and organizing information that will persuade the consumer to accept the views (or product or candidate) put forth by the organization.
- *Communication* means putting the messages into the channels of information.
- *Evaluation* means assessing the effect of those messages on the target audience.

EXAMPLES OF PUBLIC RELATIONS PROGRAMS

To appreciate the diversity of problems public relations people attempt to address, and to understand the wide range of tools available to the public relations department of an organization, let's look at a selection of cases.

The Tylenol Tragedy

In September of 1982, several deaths in the Chicago area were traced to arsenic-laced Tylenol capsules. When it was revealed that the medicine was made by a subsidiary of Johnson & Johnson, the company's stock fell sharply in value.

The swift response of the J&J public relations department was to counsel management to remove the product from the shelves immediately. A team rushed to Chicago to work with the police in getting information to the public, and a national hot line was set up to answer questions from consumers. The chief executive officer of the company served as spokesperson throughout the crisis, and he assured the media and consumers that the company was following the credo initiated by its founder, decreeing that the company would put consumer safety before profits.

Rather than abandon the successful Tylenol brand, the company reintroduced it in tamper-resistant packaging after research showed that consumers trusted the company as a result of its handling of the Tylenol tragedy. Johnson & Johnson's management of the crisis became a model for industry to follow.

Cabbage Patch Dolls

Among the most successful toys of the 1980s were the Cabbage Patch Kids produced by Coleco. The pudgy, homely little people were so popular that parents who wanted them had to sign up on waiting lists at toy stores.

Public relations rather than advertising was the marketing tool that made for gold in the cabbage patch. In fact, Coleco suspended advertising when demand

The quick removal of Tylenol from the shelves after a tampering incident and—more importantly—the speed and candor with which Johnson & Johnson moved to inform the public, was instrumental in restoring confidence in the product when it was reintroduced.

exceeded supply. News releases assured consumers that the company was doing everything it could to fill orders as soon as possible.

The company's public relations consultant used the services of a psychologist, whose research showed that the physical appearance of the dolls inspired a nurturing instinct in children. So the company included "adoption papers" and a "parenting guide" with each doll. Just as real parents have to wait to adopt a child, the children had to wait until supplies of the Cabbage Patch Kids made it possible for them to adopt a doll.

Coleco captured media attention by sending a doll to "Today" show hostess Jane Pauley, who happened to be pregnant. The result was more than five minutes of publicity on that show. Soon Johnny Carson was mentioning Cabbage Patch Kids in his monologue. In addition to press conferences, the public relations people for Coleco set up mass adoption ceremonies to attract news coverage.

Selling Kitchens . . . and Nixon

The American public's opinion of Vice-President Richard Nixon in the 1950s soared when he visited an American exhibition in Moscow. He was shown forcefully lecturing Soviet Premier Nikita Khrushchev about the benefits of the American way of life in front of a model American kitchen.

One might suspect that Nixon's staff arranged the event. But it was the public relations man for the kitchenware firm who created the moment spontaneously. "Right this way . . . right this way!" he shouted at the two leaders as they moved through the exhibit. They moved toward the kitchen, and Nixon made an assertive gesture toward the American hardware. An Associated Press photographer tossed his camera to the public relations man inside the exhibit, who took the famous "Kitchen Debate" photo.[13] The public relations man, William Safire, became President Nixon's speechwriter a decade later, and now is a respected opinion columnist for *The New York Times*.

Overcoming Consumer Reluctance

The Osmose Wood Preserving Company of America, a national marketer of treated wood, found that it faced a number of obstacles in convincing homeowners to use its products. Consumers weren't sure why they should pay more for a quality product, whether or not products treated with inorganic arsenic compounds were safe, and whether they had the expertise to do home construction projects.

The firm's public relations agency conducted focus group interviews with consumers—open-ended sessions in which people could explain how they felt about the products. Osmose found that the obstacles could be overcome if the consumers felt they had a "handyman" to answer their questions and demonstrate the product. It was established that retailers were not able to provide that service.

The public relations firm created a television personality, "The Osmose Handyman," and developed a format in which he could demonstrate home projects as part of a nationally syndicated show with a potential audience of 34 million. In addition, the firm prepared fact sheets that consumers could write for after hearing about them on the show. A toll-free number promoted on the television show enabled consumers to obtain answers to any questions they had.[14]

TECHNOLOGY

Employees Can "Shop" for Information

Following a communication audit showing that employees preferred frequent and efficient messages rather than lengthy articles in the monthly newsletter, the Warner Lambert Company decided to overhaul its publications strategy. Today the firm packages information in brief form for delivery by electronic mail and a weekly "newsline" bulletin. At the end of many of the news items, employees are told where to find more material if they want it—usually from bulletin boards or their supervisors. In effect, this gives the consumer more control and allows employees to shop for the information they want.

The Employee Video Magazine

Like most companies, the LTV Corporation has a monthly newsletter to keep employees informed about the firm's new processes, products, and procedures. But LTV felt there was a gap in its employee communications program because print media didn't bring across the human qualities that make the difference in any business operation.

The firm—a large conglomerate making everything from food to sporting goods to chemicals—restructured at the beginning of the 1980s, and it was felt that many of its 70,000 employees did not have a sense of the size or scope of the company, or where their efforts fit into the big picture. LTV hired a television production firm to produce *LTV Report*, a 15-minute quarterly video magazine that used footage taken at local company plants, interviews with company officials, and other news information with a candid, realistic feeling. The videotapes are played in the company's cafeterias or at meetings of various departments. After the video magazines have been made available to employees, some of the features are reused as marketing films and released to the news media.[15]

RELATIONS WITH THE NEWS MEDIA

The most critical skills for the public relations professional are those necessary for placing stories in the news media. Editors must be convinced that a story is interesting, factual, and relevant. While the advertising agency pays to insert its message in commercial space or time, the public relations counsel ethically cannot pay to control what goes in the news columns. The apparent "newsworthiness" of the item is what wins it credibility.

Not surprisingly, many of today's successful public relations people are former journalists who understand the workings of the newsroom. These are the fundamental skills for dealing with the press:

- Writing an interesting news release following the journalistic format and style used by the news media
- Explaining to a busy editor on the phone in just a few minutes why a story is interesting and important

- Providing the contacts or resources the journalist needs to write a story; helping the journalist get through to the spokespeople for your organization
- Arranging a press conference that is well timed for the media and produces useful information
- Understanding the special needs of the print and broadcast media, which often have different priorities

Two-Way Benefits

When we discussed the creation of news in Chapter 4, we acknowledged the special relationship of the press and public relations people. Former Mobil vice-president for public affairs Herb Schmertz, to whom we referred early in this chapter, counsels public relations professionals to maintain good relations with reporters and editors because "information is currency. If you build a good relationship with a reporter, you may find you'll learn as much from him as he'll learn from you.... When you talk with someone who's well-informed, not all of the information flows in the same direction."[16]

That suggests another use of our P↔I↔C model—to depict the special relationship of journalists and public relations people as simultaneous producers and

INSIGHT

Publicists Seek Influential Media

Some PR practitioners continue to call themselves "publicists" and specialize in getting their clients' names mentioned in the media. The assumption is that publicity creates interest, and interest will translate into sales of clients' products or support for clients' causes.

Publicist Alan Caruba has compiled a list of "Power Media"—those that influence the other media. He advises public relations people to aim for story placements in these outlets in order to trigger further coverage in others. He considers the most influential publicity outlets to be these:

The New York Times

The Washington Post

USA Today

The Wall Street Journal

The Los Angeles Times

People magazine

Associated Press and United Press International

NBC's "Today" show

Cable News Network

Newsweek and Time

Columnists George Will, Liz Smith, and Ann Landers

Advertising Age

The top five are major newspapers with more than just local circulation. People showcases trends and styles; the "Today" show does the same and introduces public affairs issues as well. The wire service set the agenda for smaller media. CNN and the newsmagazines have wide coverage and influence among better-educated and more affluent audiences. Advertising Age is at the cutting edge of trends in marketing. Each of the three columnists is an agenda-setter: George Will in Washington politics, Liz Smith in style and what's "in," and Ann Landers in the concerns of ordinary people.

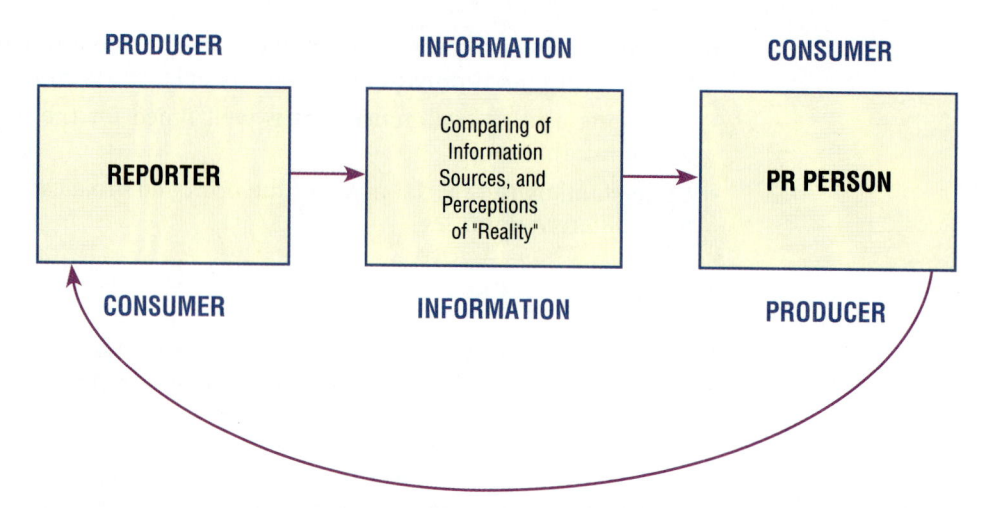

```
PRODUCER           INFORMATION              CONSUMER

                  Comparing of
                  Information
  REPORTER         Sources, and             PR PERSON
                  Perceptions
                  of "Reality"

CONSUMER           INFORMATION              PRODUCER
```

FIGURE 12.2 **Public Relations Talks with the Press** News reporter and public relations professional act simultaneously as producers and consumers of information when the interview reveals new information to both.

consumers of information. For example, a public relations person may have information for a journalist about a company's efforts to comply with new pollution standards set by the state government. The reporter's questions in response to the briefing may reveal what the reporter has heard about another company's efforts to forestall enforcement of the new regulations. That information may help the public relations person to advise management about the climate of opinion surrounding the issue. (See Figure 12.2.)

THE PROFESSION GAINS RECOGNITION

In the early days of public relations, organizations saw it as something of a frill: mere window dressing! Managers weren't sure how much public relations helped, but they thought it couldn't hurt. They hired a few people to give plant tours, plan ribbon-cutting ceremonies, publish a newsletter to make employees feel valued, and help make the annual meeting run smoothly. Unfortunately, when economic times got tough, the "window dressing" is the first thing to go. Public relations was not a secure job.

Today public relations people are rarely among the first fired when an organization cuts back. Recent examples are AT&T after divestiture, the oil and energy companies, and pharmaceutical firms whose patents on profitable drugs expired. All need public relations people to explain the organization's actions to its target publics. Modern management views public relations people as critical to the task of "riding out the storm" of adversity by explaining the organization's policies and by listening to the concerns voiced by its publics.

Before the functions of public relations were viewed this way, PR tended to be a subdivision reporting to the personnel department of an organization. Today the director of public relations is likely to be a vice-president with direct access to the chief executive officer.

Public relations has gained respect and importance because it has learned the importance of research, embraced the concept of "management by objectives," and shown its worth when the organization's very existence is threatened by a crisis.

Management by Objectives

Large organizations have a "mission statement" that explains what their main purpose is—to serve a clientele, to make a profit from manufacture of reliable products, or to win the acceptance of consumers by providing a valued service. The organizations then set goals, which are general, and from those they develop objectives, which are very specific. "Increase the number of people who recycle cans and bottles in Montgomery County by 25 percent" is an example of a specific, measurable objective.

When public relations departments made such promises as to "improve our organization's image" or "celebrate the organization's contribution to the community," they found it difficult to demonstrate their contribution to the "bottom line" of the organization. That is to say, they could not show that they enhanced the making of a profit or, in the case of nonprofit organizations, that they served the main goal of the organization.

However, by adopting the MBO—management by objectives—techniques used by professional managers, public relations people developed the ability to demonstrate the worth of their programs in terms business people can understand. Today a good public relations program begins by stating the organization's goals and objectives, developing PR objectives that relate directly to them, and demonstrating the impact of each PR program through quantitative measurement. Here is an example: "The information project reached 40,000 residents, and over half of them requested our information packet—three times as many as last year, when there was no information program."

Research Applications

The typical public relations person of a generation ago was a former news reporter or editor hired to deal with former colleagues in the press. Today's public relations practitioner needs an important new skill: the ability to use research to understand how a public thinks and behaves in regard to issues that affect a client organization.

Just as the advertising industry became more sophisticated when it learned to measure the consumer's preferences and needs, public relations transcended its "publicity" phase when it learned that understanding the attitudes of consumers was critical if target publics were to be reached with messages that had a chance of persuading them to change their behaviors.

As with advertising, the survey or "public opinion poll" is a major research tool for public relations people. Another is the "focus group interview," in which small groups of selected consumers are interviewed in a formal but open-ended way that allows them to make known to the researchers their interests, preferences, and concerns. Studying behaviors and quantifying them is another valid technique: How many people of what types attended an event, and how many of them subsequently requested information using the phone number provided?

The rise of research by public relations practitioners relates directly to the increase in management by objectives techniques. Research is needed to demonstrate exactly how and why an objective was set, and whether or not it was achieved.

Writing: The Basic Skill

Critics of public relations people assume that the chief talent of the "PR guy" is the ability to talk a good line, coupled with a propensity to "like other people." This limited view assumes that persuasion is accomplished by overwhelming another person with one's personality and depth of conviction.

In truth, persuasion is best accomplished by presenting factual data in a comprehensible, interesting, and believable manner. Consumers of the information should have the opportunity to think about the arguments, weigh the evidence, and persuade themselves that the idea or cause presented is the best one.

That's why *writing* is the basic skill of public relations. And that's why, historically, so many public relations people have come from the ranks of reporters and editors. A premium is put on the individual who can gather information accurately, organize it coherently, and present it in a straightforward manner.

Journalistic writing, both feature articles and hard news reporting, provides the models that public relations people imitate when attempting to place a client's stories in the news media. The closer they come to the ideal, the greater the chances of placement. Because public relations also involves supporting the marketing of products and services, promotional writing modeled after advertising copy is a specialized writing skill that may prove helpful. Similarly, writing for the ear and following tight time formats are desirable specialized skills for public relations people who target the broadcast media.

Crisis Management

In the last decade, one of the most important contributions PR departments have made to many large organizations is to develop a *crisis management plan.* Mindful that it took two or three days for the federal government and the operators of the Three-Mile Island nuclear power plant to get their stories straight after the 1979 accident at the Pennsylvania facility, most corporations have spelled out how quickly media requests for information must be met, and which officer will serve as spokesperson for the company when a catastrophe occurs.

In addition to Johnson & Johnson's Tylenol tragedy, instances of the chairman of a company being prepared by PR people to meet the press almost immediately include the cases of Union Carbide Corp. after the plant explosion in Bhopal, India, and Ashland Oil Inc. after the oil spill near Pittsburgh.

Despite these shining examples of how effective public relations planning can win support for an organization by showing its willingness to talk openly about its mistakes, not every company has learned the lesson. After the Alaskan oil spill in 1989, when one of its tankers ran aground, Exxon Corp. was slow to respond to press inquiries, partly because it also was slow to begin measures to clean up the spill. Worse, its chairman was defensive and elusive when he finally met reporters. Television viewers saw clips of company officers walking out of a press conference when they couldn't or wouldn't answer questions. Ten days after the oil spill, Exxon finally ran a defensive-sounding newspaper ad that included the

Chapter 12   Public Relations

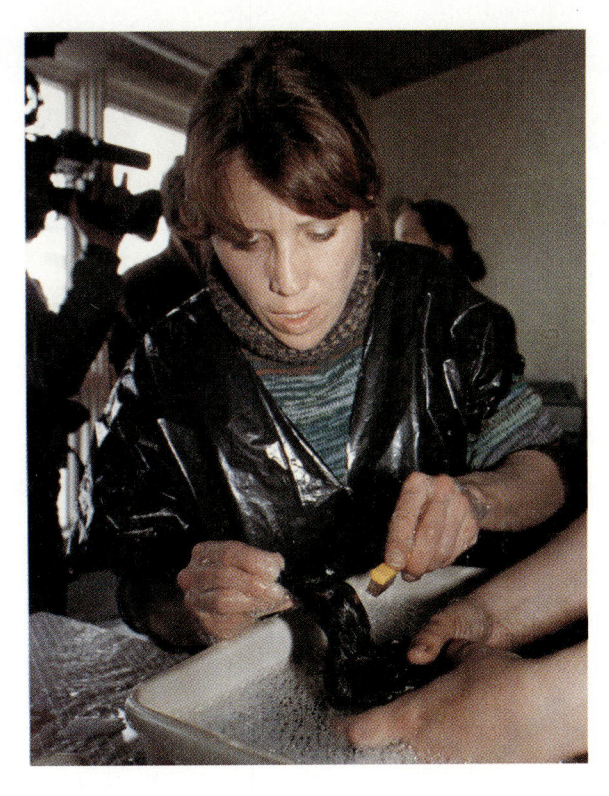

355

A volunteer cleans oil off of a sea bird after the Exxon *Valdez* spill in Alaska, one of the biggest public relations disasters in history.

chairman's apology. But a poor PR response when the crisis began meant the company had already lost the public's trust.

Public relations people have learned that crisis communication breaks down into at least two important phases. The first is called "damage control." It involves finding out what has happened and how it has negatively affected the public's perception of the organization. The immediate task is to demonstrate that the organization is taking responsibility and has the means of solving the crisis.

The second phase involves moving the organization from the "crisis" footing to one of "issues management." While it may not be possible to undo the effects of the crisis or make it go away, it is possible to demonstrate to the public that the organization is working to solve or alleviate the problem through cooperation or negotiation with other organizations.

An example is the exposure of a charity whose executive director has been discovered misappropriating contributions and putting them to personal use. The "damage control" phase consists of showing that the wrongdoing has been stopped and the wrongdoer has been relieved of duty. The "issues management" phase consists of a program to reassure contributors that their money is being applied to the charitable programs for which it was intended, and that those programs continue to be worthy of public support.

Types of Organizations Using PR

Different types of organizations need different types of programs. Public relations people with different areas of specialization may work for any of these:

INSIGHT

Traits for Success

Public relations expert Bill Cantor, who consults management in executive searches, has developed a profile of the successful public relations personality as a guide for measuring job candidates. The winning traits are these:

1. Ability to handle tension and work under pressure
2. Willingness to take the initiative to solve a problem
3. Curiosity and the desire to learn
4. Energy, drive, and ambition—willingness to take a risk
5. Objective thinking and good judgment
6. Flexibility—the ability to see things from another's viewpoint
7. The desire to help people
8. The ability to develop and maintain a wide range of personal contacts
9. Versatility—ability to function as "a generalist with a specialty"
10. Willingness to work in the background and to suppress one's ego

More important than any single trait, according to Cantor, is the public relations person's ability to "fit in" to the organization he or she serves.

Source: Bill Cantor, "Winning Personality Traits," *Public Relations Journal,* June, 1983, pp. 30–31.

- Business organizations—corporations or firms that produce a product or deliver a service for profit. The public relations department must consider the consequences of all actions in terms of the bottom line—the return paid to the owners or stockholders.
- Trade associations—groups formed to advance and protect the concerns of manufacturing and service organizations. The focus again is on the "bottom line," but for an entire industry rather than one company.
- Government agencies—departments overseen by elected or appointed executives and responsible for serving the needs of the public. The public relations department performs a public information function, explaining programs and decisions to affected citizens.
- Nonprofit groups—charities, cultural entities, and organizations whose main purpose is information and fundraising to support health programs, alleviate social problems, or educate the citizenry on public affairs.

The Role of the Agency

Some organizations handle all public relations "in-house," meaning they put together their own publications, do their own lobbying with legislative bodies, and prepare campaigns aimed at diverse external publics, from stockholders to customers to community groups.

Most corporations, however, and also many government bodies and trade associations, give several important segments of their public relations work to specialized agencies. While a manufacturing company may handle relations with its own employees, stockholders, and the investment community, it turns to agen-

> ### MINORITIES/WOMEN
> ## The Field Attracts Women and Minorities
>
> More than half of the approximately 160,000 people working in the field of public relations are women, and 12 percent are members of minority groups, according to the Bureau of Labor Statistics.
>
> The Public Relations Society of America expects the number of minorities to grow: "Employment opportunities for minorities in the fastest growing and highest-paying service-related career are increasing—despite the lack of knowledge about the profession by minorities and the absence of visible role models working in the field. . . . As minorities become increasingly involved in political, economic and social institutions, the skills of minority public relations professionals will continue to be in growing demand."
>
> The PRSA statement points to the growing economic clout of minorities as one reason for the improved employment picture. Minorities are particularly being sought to develop improved relationships with minority communities.
>
> *Source: Opportunities for Minorities in Public Relations*, booklet published by the Public Relations Society of America, 1988.

cies for campaigns aimed at promoting specific products, lobbying, community relations, and media relations.

Some agencies specialize by topic: politics and public affairs, health care, insurance, environmental concerns, or new-product introductions. Other agencies specialize in types of service: video news releases, special events, publications, or crisis communication. Small agencies consisting of a principal and one or two assistants or freelancers may handle only two or three accounts; the largest agencies, with dozens of account teams, serve dozens of clients in a variety of ways.

Should Practitioners Be Accredited?

The issue of licensing or accrediting journalists or those in magazine and book editing has not been mentioned in previous chapters because it is not a major issue in those fields. Journalists reject licensing and accreditation as threats to freedom of the press and the independence of newsgatherers. In the broadcast media, engineers and others involved in transmission of signals are licensed because they must be certified as competent to perform technical tasks, but on-air performers are not.

In public relations, the quest for credibility has raised questions about the need to accredit or even license practitioners, much as lawyers are admitted to the bar, doctors are licensed to practice, and accountants must pass exams in order to pursue their trade.

Accreditation exams are offered by the Public Relations Society of America (PRSA) and the International Association of Business Communicators (IABC). However, because accreditation is not necessary to practice public relations and because the majority of practitioners do not join either organization, professional status is not yet as meaningful as it is in the fields of law, medicine, and accounting.

Accredited or not, today's public relations practitioners find that the field is maturing, gaining acceptance, and taking an increasingly important role in the management of complex organizations that depend on the support of consumers in order to survive.

FUTURE FILE

✓ A small but rapidly growing manufacturing firm that has contracted with outside public relations agencies for all its communication services has decided to set up its own public relations department because it senses the need to have a more direct relationship with its publics. You are interviewing for the position of director. How do you describe the commitment you will bring to the organization as it strives for "two-way symmetric communication"?

✓ You have agreed to serve on the committee that is working for the reelection of the mayor of your city, but only on the condition that the "press agentry" of past campaigns is replaced with what you consider to be more effective and honest public relations techniques. What kind of campaign will you help run?

✓ You have left the newspaper business and started your own small public relations agency. The manufacturer of a new environmentally conscious line of frozen diet meals in paper pouches comes to you and says, "We can't afford to spend millions on advertising. What can public relations do to help us get our message across to consumers who want products that are safe, nutritious, and recyclable?" Explain the role of public relations as opposed to advertising.

NOTES

1. Herb Schmertz, *Good-bye to the Low Profile* (Boston: Little, Brown, 1986).
2. Scott M. Cutlip and Allen H. Center, *Effective Public Relations* (Englewood Cliffs, NJ: Prentice-Hall, 1978), pp. 66–67.
3. James E. Grunig and Todd Hunt, *Managing Public Relations* (New York: Holt, Rinehart & Winston, 1984), p. 15.
4. Scott Cutlip, "Public Relations and the American Revolution," *Public Relations Review*, Winter 1976, pp. 11–24.
5. Fred F. Endres, "Public Relations in the Jackson White House," *Public Relations Review*, Fall 1976, pp. 5–12.
6. Edward L. Bernays, *Public Relations* (Norman: University of Oklahoma Press, 1952), p. 70.
7. Ray E. Hiebert, *Courtiers to the Crowd* (Ames: Iowa State University Press, 1966), p. 48.
8. Edward L. Bernays, *Propaganda* (New York: Liveright, 1928), p. 9.
9. Edward L. Bernays, *Crystallizing Public Opinion* (New York: Liveright, 1923).
10. Grunig and Hunt, pp. 22ff.
11. Grunig and Hunt, pp. 147–160.
12. John E. Marston, *Modern Public Relations* (New York: McGraw-Hill, 1979) pp. 185ff.
13. Art Stevens, *The Persuasion Explosion* (Washington: Acropolis Books, 1985), pp. 70–71.
14. Brian Hickey, "Petrified Wood," *Public Relations Journal*, June 1986, pp. 11–12.
15. Julie Price, "Employee Video Magazines," *Public Relations Journal*, May 1986, pp. 11, 14.
16. Schmertz, p. 126.

SUGGESTED READINGS

Botan, Carl, and Vincent Hazleton, *Public Relations Theory* (Hillsdale, NJ: Erlbaum, 1989).
Brody, E. W., *Public Relations Programming and Production* (New York: Praeger, 1988).

Broom, Glen M., and David M. Dozier, *Using Research in Public Relations* (Englewood Cliffs, NJ: Prentice Hall, 1990).
Grunig, James E., and Todd Hunt, *Managing Public Relations* (New York: Holt, Rinehart and Winston, 1984).
Lesly, Philip, *Lesly's Handbook of Public Relations and Communications* (Chicago: Probus, 1990).
Newsom, Doug, and Bob Carrell, *Public Relations Writing* (Belmont, CA: Wadsworth, 1986).
Pavlik, John V., *Public Relations: What Research Tells Us* (Newbury Park, CA: Sage, 1987).
Wilcox, Dennis L., Phillip H. Ault, and Warren K. Agee, *Public Relations: Strategies and Tactics*, 3rd ed. (New York: HarperCollins, 1992).

WOMEN IN MEDIA INDUSTRIES: THE ISSUES

ELIZABETH L. TOTH

Elizabeth L. Toth is an associate professor of public relations at Syracuse University's S. I. Newhouse School of Public Communications. She is the author of more than 25 scholarly articles and papers, and coauthor of The Velvet Ghetto *and* Beyond the Velvet Ghetto, *benchmark research reports on the impact of the increasing percentage of women entering the fields of public relations and organizational communication.*

In the past decade, women in the communication industries have increasingly analyzed the way their gender contributes to and is perceived by the professional fields. Women's interest groups in most of the communication academic organizations have focused their attention on the unequal treatment of women and have worked to rectify the inequalities. Acknowledging the depth and pervasiveness of the problems women face in mass communication jobs is an important first step in changing those realities.

Women in the Work Force

Of the 122 million workers now in the American labor force, 55 million are women. By the year 2000, women will account for almost two-thirds of the labor force growth. Women now hold the majority of all professional media jobs in the United States and have come to dominate several professions, including editing and reporting.[1]

However, women in journalism earn an average of 71 percent of their male colleagues' earnings.[2] According to the Bureau of Labor Statistics, female public relations specialists earn 58 percent of what their male counterparts earn. Female managers in public relations, marketing, and advertising earn 63 percent of what their male counterparts earn.[3]

Women seeking mass media occupations must confront the issue of pay inequity. Some researchers believe that employers have preconceived ideas about how women and men will perform on the job. Women are not hired, or they are denied advancement, because of stereotypes reinforced by custom, tradition, and law. As L. F. Rakow puts it, "Man came to stand for rationality, competition, aggression, individualism. Woman came to stand for emotionality, nurturing, cooperation, community. Of course none of this was or is biologically determined. In fact, at different times in Western history, man and woman have meant very different things."[4]

Resegregation of the Work Force

Some believe that as more and more women move into the higher-paying jobs and occupations, the pay gap will close. However, women are not choosing to enter all occupations: They are seeking jobs for which they have received training because sex inequality exists in the choice of college curricula. Schools of journalism and mass communication report disproportionate numbers of women in specializations such as news-editorial, television-radio-film, advertising, and public relations because women choose to enter fields where there are other women who will provide them with role models.

Women entering the fields of reporting, editing, advertising, and public relations have effectively lowered the overall salaries for those fields. As a result, all working in those fields will find that their work is less valued by society. A 1987 Census Bureau study concluded

Continued

Continued from page 360

that, ironically, "the earnings of a person, regardless of sex, will be lowered as the ratio of women in his or her occupation increases."[5]

Barriers Facing Women Managers

In the 1986 Velvet Ghetto report,[6] the authors found evidence that women perceived themselves as filling the technician rather than the managerial role in organizational communication. Cited were such barriers to management as bias (both blatant and subtle), women not being "part of the gang," women not seen as good managers, and women as nurturers. Women will not break through these "glass ceiling" barriers because men at the top feel uncomfortable with women beside them; "the result is that in spite of the extraordinary progress women have made in terms of numbers, a caste system of men at the top and women lower down still prevails in corporate America."[7]

Happily, the authors of those words do identify communication as a field in which the caste system will crumble more quickly than in others. Some are concerned, however, that although women will move into top communication spots, these areas—in corporations at least—will be seen as of secondary value and will not lead to the most powerful top management posts.[8]

What's to Be Done?

Writing about women in public relations, Pamela J. Creedon suggested that cultural biases, myths, and misperceptions associated with gender values be studied in order to devise a strategy for emphasizing the appropriateness of diversity.[9]

Beyond the Velvet Ghetto concluded with these recommendations for women who aspire to managerial positions in the mass communication industries:

1. Accept that the segregation of women is real,
2. Learn to play the game,
3. Develop a career plan,
4. Define success,
5. Accept your limitations, and
6. Celebrate your triumphs.[10]

It may be, as many say, only a matter of time before the inequities of pay, advancement, and power are resolved. If we clearly remember what a powerful predictor gender has been, then we, as producers and consumers of mass communication information, should be better able to find the solutions.

Notes

1. M. Winkleman, "Percentage of Professional Women Rises," *Public Relations Journal*, July 1986, p. 6.
2. D. H. Weaver and G. Cleveland Wilmot, *The American Journalist* (Bloomington: Indiana University Press, 1986).
3. V. Russell, "Salary Survey," *Public Relations Journal*, June 1988, p. 28.
4. L. F. Rakow, in Pamela J. Creedon, ed., *Women in Mass Communication—Challenging Gender Values* (Newbury Park, CA: Sage Publications, 1989).
5. R. Deigh, "Mystery of the Closing Pay Gap," *Insight*, October 1987, p. 44.
6. C. G. Cline, E. L. Toth, J. V. Turk, L. M. Walters, N. Johnson, and H. Smith, *The Velvet Ghetto: The Impact of the Increasing Percentage of Women in Public Relations and Business Communication* (San Francisco: IABC Research Foundation, 1986).
7. C. Hymowitz and T. D. Schellhardt, "The Glass Ceiling," *The Wall Street Journal*, March 24, 1986, pp. 1D, 4D.
8. K. Blumenthal, "Room at the Top," *The Wall Street Journal*, March 24, 1986, pp. 7D, 9D.
9. Pamela J. Creedon, "Teaching 'Feminization' by Reframing the Perspective," *Teaching Public Relations*, No. 13, June, 1989.
10. E. L. Toth and C. G. Cline, *Beyond the Velvet Ghetto* (San Francisco: IABC Research Foundation, 1989).

CHAPTER 13

Advertising

AT A GLANCE

✓ As America expanded, its new information media were supported by income from the sale of advertising space. The practice of separating advertising from editorial material developed to help consumers distinguish between the two.

✓ Advertising agencies were founded to help clients prepare their commercial messages and to aid them in purchasing space from the media. The ad agency serves the interests of both the client and the media.

✓ Mergers of smaller agencies into international super-agencies have been the trend as the industry looks to the emerging world market that requires global marketing strategies.

✓ Consumer response to advertising shapes the messages that producers prepare and disseminate. Millions are spent on judging consumer preferences for products and information about those products.

✓ Direct mail is the fastest-growing area of advertising, gaining quickly on newspaper and television advertising.

✓ Government regulators, consumer groups, and the courts monitor advertising to maintain standards for accuracy and fairness. The industry attempts to show that it is capable of guarding against abuses of the public trust.

More than $25 billion is spent annually in the United States to persuade consumers to choose one product or service over another. Those advertising expenditures enable the news and entertainment media to offer their products at a low cost. Like public relations, the field of advertising can be praised for facilitating the flow of information or it can be criticized for distorting reality.

A NATURAL ADJUNCT TO COMMERCE

In a small village, where everything to be bought or bartered for can be found in the square where consumers gather to buy directly from the producers, advertising is not necessary. But as soon as there is trade between communities, cities, or states, there is a need to capture the attention of prospective customers, to describe the goods for sale, and to persuade the buyers to try the product.

Early Forms of Advertising

Rudimentary advertisements can be found as early as 300 B.C., when inscriptions describing goods such as ointments and wines, and services such as shoemaking, were found on Babylonian clay tablets.[1] Signs found in the ruins of Pompeii indicate that shopkeepers used symbols to indicate what wares were available inside—an early form of advertising because it lured passersby into the stores. Signs promoting political candidates and inviting travelers to visit an inn on the road to another town also were found at Pompeii.

The ancient Greeks relied on town criers to let people know that ships had arrived with goods. Musicians accompanied these criers to help keep them in key.[2] One could say, then, by a little stretch of the imagination, that jingles and the use of music—two devices commonly used in radio and television advertising today—date back to before the birth of Christ.

British innkeepers refined the art of attracting patrons by erecting fanciful and elaborate tavern signboards. In the colonies, the *Boston Newsletter* carried what might be called advertising messages as early as 1704. However, the paid notices dealt not so much with trade as with personal matters, such as rewards to be paid for the capture of a thief and the return of stolen goods. A simple caption in bold or fancy letters, such as "Reward" or "Notice," was the only visual embellishment in the early ads.

America and Advertising Grow Together

Expansion was explosive in the new United States of America. During the first century after independence, the 3000-mile-wide continent was linked first by trails, then roads, and finally the railroads, which created a vast market for goods. The population of the country doubled from one generation to the next, fueled by continuing immigration.

As we saw in the chapters on the print media, advertising provided the financial underpinning for the new information vehicles, especially newspapers that sold for only pennies and popular magazines costing only a dime. At first there were no standards for where ads were placed or what format they followed. A

TIME CAPSULE

Advertising

1704	First newspaper advertisements appear in *The Boston News-Letter*.
1842	First U.S. ad agency opened in Philadelphia by Volney B. Palmer.
1865	G. P. Rowell agency founded, develops "commission" system for ads.
1869	N. W. Ayer & Son becomes first full-service ad agency.
1871	Rowell founds *Advertiser's Gazette*, first industry trade paper.
1879	Ayer conducts first marketing survey to test ads.
1906	Pure Food and Drug Act ends era of patent medicine claims.
1910	Association of National Advertisers founded to improve advertising.
1914	Federal Trade Commission established, issues advertising guidelines.
1914	Audit Bureau of Circulations formed to verify print media circulation.
1916	Woodrow Wilson is first president to speak to an advertising convention.
1917	American Association of Advertising Agencies founded.
1922	First radio commercial broadcast on New York station.
1928	*Advertising Age* founded, covers world of marketing.
1942	War Advertising Council formed to offer ad assistance to government.
1968	Federal Highway Beautification Act restricts highway advertising.
1971	Cigarette advertising banned from broadcast media.
1978	FTC gains authority to require corrective advertising.
1986	Supreme Court upholds ad bans on products with "serious harmful effects."
1991	FCC regulates number of minutes of ads per hour in children's programming.

INSIGHT

Caveat Emptor ... American Style

This is your very own winning number. You may have won your choice of a microwave oven or a color television. All you have to do is visit Sunset Estates by the date on your personalized invitation. See why your friends are calling Sunset Estates "heaven on earth!"

Anyone who has received a mail promotion that guarantees a prize and overpraises the value of a lodge in the Poconos, a retirement home in Sarasota, or a condominium in Carmel might think that "hype"—short for hyperbole, or gross exaggeration—represents a new extreme in advertising's persuasive techniques. But the technique is as old as the first advertising gimmick used to sell Americans real estate and the dream of a new life. As social critic Daniel Boorstin points out, "Never was there a more outrageous or more unscrupulous or more ill-informed advertising campaign than that by which the promoters for the American colonies brought settlers here." Immigrants to the New Land were told "gold-in-the-street" tales of the riches and comforts to be had. The reality, of course, proved to be much harsher.

Source: Daniel Boorstin, "Advertising and American Civilization," in *Advertising and Society* (New York: New York University Press, 1974), p. 11.

Signboards from pubs in Boston reflect the "advertising" of the colonial era.

paid notice often was used to fill out a column. Some newspapers gave over part or all of the front page to those willing to pay a premium. But publishers soon realized the need to differentiate between the news or editorial matter and the ads, since the ads often made claims that the publisher would find difficult to defend. Eventually it became standard practice to group advertisements together, separated from the news by borders and boxes.

The first national media that appeared in the late 1800s—the mass circulation magazines—were bought as much for their advertising information as their editorial content. Full-page ads depicting scores of household items or entire lines of wearing apparel were common, and they served the same functions as catalogs for people living far from the main cities. Where newspapers served mainly local merchants within their circulation area, the mass circulation magazines spurred the growth of national products and services.

A Fancy for Patent Medicines

Americans have always been independent people who like to fend for themselves. That makes us natural customers for patent medicines—medicines sold in a drugstore or available from sales outfits without a doctor's prescription. Such remedies depend on advertising and promotion to put them in the public's eye.

Newspapers and magazines since the 1860s have carried ads for cure-alls, nostrums, aids to increasing vigor and potency, and wonder drugs to vanquish any ills. Many people, especially the elderly, perceive of health care as expensive

Chapter 13 Advertising

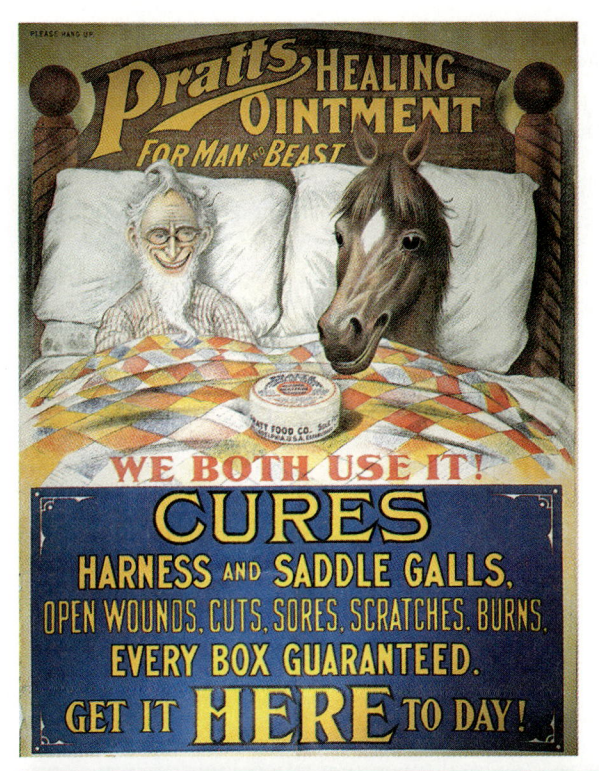

A patent medicine ad of the 1880s seems ludicrous by today's standards . . . or does it? Think of the Energizer bunny!

INSIGHT

Peruna: The Miracle Elixir

In 1900, Americans had a wonderful range of elixirs from which to choose. The choice didn't depend on what was ailing you, since all the products promised to do . . . everything! The most popular cure-alls were Lydia E. Pinkham's Vegetable Compound ("It Keeps Women Strong"), Dr. Mott's Nervine Pills, Dr. Williams' Pink Pills for Pale People, and Dr. Hartman's Peruna.

The magic formula for Peruna wasn't much of a mystery to some: It consisted of 27 percent alcohol. No wonder most people felt "marvelous effects" after consuming a few tablespoons or a small glass of the remedy.

What made Peruna one of the best-selling patent medicines in American history was the strength of the testimonials offered by the users quoted in the advertisements: "My wife was about to die of consumption, but after a few bottles of Peruna, she was able to get up and work again."

Advertisements for Peruna made outlandish claims: "What bread and meat are to the hungry, Peruna is to the sick."

Peruna eventually faced the competition that any highly advertised product must expect. Fly-by-night salesmen sold cheap imitations under similar-sounding names. Some even refilled Peruna bottles with water colored by rusty nails.

---

and consider personal hygiene a taboo topic of conversation. Thus, advertising is turned to by many as the main source of information about treatment of the body's aches and pains, as well as for hope that potency and youth can be regained through the use of special potions and pills.

Eventually newspaper and magazine publishers realized that unscrupulous advertising could bring their publications into disrepute with consumers who were being misled. Some began to reject all advertisements for patent medicines. During the muckraking era of the 1890s, many publications ran exposés of the very products that had sought to use their advertising columns.

DEVELOPMENT OF THE ADVERTISING INDUSTRY

The forerunner of the advertising agency as we know it today was founded in 1841 by Volney Palmer, whose Philadelphia brokerage service specialized in buying advertising space from newspapers at a volume discount, then selling parts of that space to individual advertisers at a markup. To this day advertising agencies gain part or all of their compensation through the discount they receive from publishers for bringing in ads. It is a service to the publishers to have large blocks of ads coming in without having to work with individual merchants or manufacturers.

It was not until the 1870s that advertising agencies emerged to serve manufacturers who needed advice on how to package their products and promote them to consumers. The N. W. Ayer and Son Agency, also of Philadelphia, was among the first to provide the service of studying a product and developing a "campaign," or strategy, for making that product familiar and desirable. Today, the Ayer firm's directory of periodicals is an aid to those who are trying to find the most effective media for advertising their wares.

Another firm that replaced publishers in representing advertising clients was founded in the 1870s by James Walter Thompson. He convinced magazines that they could benefit from advertising and manufacturers that they needed advertising to sell their products, so he deserves some of the credit for shaping the modern advertising industry. Today the J. Walter Thompson agency, with all its branches and subsidiaries, remains as one of the top 10 U.S. agencies as well as a leading international agency.

The Modern Advertising Agency

Eventually the practice of financing the services of an ad agency through commissions from the publishers caught hold and was expanded to other media. Agencies could argue that they serve both the manufacturers' and the publishers' interests, much as a real estate agent claims to work on behalf of both the buyer and the seller.

Despite the fact that remuneration comes from the standard commission or discount offered to the agency by the media, the advertising agency's strongest relationship is with the client who pays the bill. The manufacturer of a product or the provider of a service finds an advertising agency by announcing that it is seeking bids. Usually the amount of the bid is stated in terms of the amount of "billing" expected—the amount that will be spent in advertising dollars paid to the media. Thus, the agency that wins the account can expect to make approximately 15 percent of the total projected billings.

To win a new client, agencies must "pitch an account," meaning that they make a competitive presentation to the client, showing their creative ideas for the

---

INSIGHT

The Purpose of an Advertising Agency

David Ogilvy, who founded Ogilvy and Mather in 1948, is known as one of the most creative people in the history of advertising. But he told his employees: "When I write an advertisement, I don't want you to tell me you find it 'creative'! I want you to find it so interesting that you *buy the product.*"

At the beginning of the 1990s, his agency, which serves 3500 clients in 271 offices throughout 51 countries, listed six goals under the heading, "Our purpose, now and always":

1. To serve our clients more effectively than any other agency.
2. To maintain high ethical and professional standards.
3. To run our agencies with a sense of competitive urgency—to strive to exceed in all disciplines.
4. To earn a significant increase in profits each year.
5. To be the most exciting agency in which to work, and to offer outstanding career opportunities.
6. To earn the continued respect of the community.

Source: Ogilvy and Mather recruiting brochure, 1990.

campaign that the client needs in the near future. Some agencies seek to demonstrate their track record with other clients, showing a portfolio of print ads and the "company reel" of television spots they have produced. Others stress their expertise in a particular area, such as health products or engineering services. The largest firms emphasize that they are "full-service" agencies, meaning that they can handle all media and they can provide everything from graphics to television production to international marketing. Smaller agencies, or "boutiques," emphasize a specialty such as direct mail promotion, or perhaps a "star" account executive with many successes or the services of a talent whose humorous spots for radio are well known.

Relationships between clients and agencies typically last for years, because familiarity with a manufacturer's products and style of marketing is built up over the long haul. However, when sales lag or competition threatens, clients may decide to "put an account up for review," inviting other agencies to show what they might be able to do. When a large account is won or lost, many employees may be hired or fired by the agency.

Another hallmark of the industry is that while smaller agencies may specialize in food, electronics, or apparel advertising, larger agencies diversify. Moreover, the largest agencies try to represent only one of each type of product: an automobile, a soft drink, an airline, an insurance company, a breakfast cereal, and so forth. In order to obtain a big new auto account, the large agency would be expected to resign its current automobile client. The assumption is that a large agency is expected to pour all of its creativity and marketing energy into the campaign of only one client per major competitive category.

Some manufacturers use only one advertising agency; others spread the work around, putting one product with one agency and other products with other agencies. Often this puts the agencies in the position of coordinating parts of campaigns with competing agencies. Still other clients do part of their advertising work "in-house," using agencies for only parts of their campaign.

Advertising's World Gets Smaller

Two trends have characterized the changing world of advertising at the beginning of the 1990s. First is the merging of already large agencies into even larger agencies, resulting in a continuous shake-up in the size and order of the world's largest advertising agencies. Second is the emergence of a global market for products and services and for advertising information about those products and services.

At the end of 1985, the world's top six agencies ranked by revenues were Young & Rubicam (United States), the Ogilvy Group (United States), Dentsu Inc. (Japan), Ted Bates Worldwide (United States), J. Walter Thompson (United States), and Saatchi and Saatchi Compton Worldwide (Great Britain). Within six months, the new largest agency had been formed from the merger of Saatchi and Saatchi with Ted Bates. By the beginning of 1990, Dentsu Inc. had emerged as the top agency, Saatchi and Saatchi Advertising Worldwide was second, and the others had shuffled in order, reflecting, among other things, further mergers and sell-offs.

The rankings of the top advertising agencies will continue to shuffle as the move toward a world market accelerates with the unification of Europe and the emergence of new economic powers in the Far East and the Third World. Predictions abound that, if the trends continue, there may be one or two super-agencies

INDUSTRY

The Largest Advertising Agencies

How do advertising agencies stack up? *Advertising Age*, in its annual agency report, ranked U.S. agencies this way, measured by their worldwide gross income:

U.S. Agencies Ranked by Worldwide Gross Income

Rank 1991	Rank 1990	Agency, Headquarters	Gross Income 1991	Gross Income 1990	% Chg
1	1	Young & Rubicam, New York	$980.8	$1001.4	−2.1
2	2	Saatchi & Saatchi Advertising Worldwide, New York	829.2	814.6	1.8
3	4	McCann-Erickson Worldwide, New York	811.6	757.0	7.2
4	3	Ogilvy & Mather Worldwide, New York	794.9	775.3	2.5
5	6	BBDO Worldwide, New York	772.8	723.8	6.8
6	5	Lintas: Worldwide, New York	729.7	736.2	−0.9
7	7	J. Walter Thompson Co., New York	727.0	690.7	5.3
8	8	DDB Needham Worldwide, New York	698.4	625.2	11.7
9	9	Backer Spielvogel Bates Worldwide, New York	630.4	618.9	1.9
10	11	Foote, Cone & Belding Communications, Chicago	616.0	543.4	13.4

The order of agencies shifts when the focus is put only on income earned within the United States, with Young & Rubicam on top again, followed by BBDO Worldwide and then Saatchi & Saatchi. When U.S. agencies are ranked by their non-U.S. income, McCann-Erickson Worldwide leads Young & Rubicam followed by Lintas:Worldwide. When agencies are ranked by their billings in 14 different media categories, Ketchum Communications leads in business publications, Leo Burnett leads in syndicated television as well as outdoor advertising, and Nationwide Advertising Service is tops in newspaper advertising.

Most United States agencies are affiliated with worldwide companies. The WPP Group based in London—1991's top worldwide agency—is parent to three U.S.-based companies: Ogilvy & Mather Worldwide, J. Walter Thompson Co., and Scali, McCabe, Sloves. Two Tokyo agencies—Dentsu Inc. and Hakuhodo Inc.—are among the top ten worldwide agencies, and speculation is that they may merge with one or more top western agencies to form a worldwide superagency.

Source: Advertising Age annual report on agency income, April 13, 1992, pp. S-1–S-42.

based in the United States competing with similar mega-groups, one in Japan and one in Europe.

The immediate reaction to the mergers on the part of many advertisers was to switch their business to unmerged firms. Colgate didn't want to be handled by the same agency Proctor and Gamble uses, Honda and Dodge suddenly were represented by the same agency, and the people responsible for advertising General Mills's Wheaties found they also had Nabisco Shredded Wheat as an account. The shuffling hasn't ended, and today it is typical for an ad agency to resign one account if it accepts a more lucrative contract with a competitor.

INSIGHT

Ads Don't Always Travel Well

To an American, a green hat is just that: a green hat. To the Chinese, it's the equivalent of a dunce cap. That means Peter Pan peanut butter is sure to flop in China unless it changes its packaging.

Throughout this book we have shown that the world is becoming one market, and communication—advertising in particular—has contributed to the emergence of the "global village." Nonetheless, American advertisers must work with local agencies in other countries to prevent such blunders as these:

One company tried to convince people in India to use its toothpaste to keep their teeth white and bright . . . not knowing that the natives, who chew betel nuts, see stained teeth as a status symbol.

A major campaign flopped in Malaysia because it emphasized the color green, which we associate with the outdoors and naturalness, but to Malaysians symbolizes death and disease.

Animals are often used in American ads: laughing cows, dancing piglets, and Exxon's Tony the tiger. In Arab countries such representations are offensive because animals are viewed as unclean.

Source: Memo circulated to clients by the public relations firm of Lobsenz-Stevens Inc.

One of the reasons that international super-agencies are now possible is that advertising techniques used in other countries have become similar to those in the United States. Once foreign cultures were thought to be different enough that specialized local agencies were needed to cater to the sensibilities of the natives. But the exporting of American products, life-styles, and business methods—ranging from blue jeans to "le weekend" to trade shows—has contributed much to what communication theorist Marshall McLuhan called the "Global Village."

Pepsi Cola, for example, finds that American rock star Tina Turner is so well known that she can be used in television ads in scores of countries. Playtex films a dozen different versions of an ad at one time, merely changing the name of the product and the words spoken by the native tongue announcer, but using the same music, models, and setting. The images in the Timex and Adidas ads we see on our television screens have been made culturally unspecific so that they can be used throughout Europe as well.

HOW ADVERTISING WORKS

Advertising holds a mirror up to society. It defines, distills, shapes, and focuses our basic values in a very powerful way. Good advertisers are perceptive about what people believe. Agencies that appeal to our basic needs are going to be successful because they give us what we want. We reward that by buying the product.

Advertising itself cannot create values but relies on those already present in the culture, which are remarkably consistent over time.[3]

This upbeat view of the role of advertising appeared in an *Advertising Age* special issue with the resounding title "The Power of Advertising: A Unifying Force for the 21st Century." It reflects the way the majority of people in the advertising industry prefer to feel about their field.

But *Advertising Age* is not averse to admitting that advertising is often criticized for society's ills, as two other quotes from that trade publication attest:

> Advertising will be seen in the history books as one of the real evil things of our time. It is stimulating people constantly to want things, want this, want that . . . [and] it gets more and more phony all the time.[4]

And:

> The overwhelming majority of Americans distrust advertising and find it both offensive and insulting to their intelligence. So what does the American Association of Advertising Agencies do? It launches an ad campaign to improve that image . . . [It] might do a better job for itself and its clients if it really respects the intelligence of consumers by giving them accurate and balanced information.[5]

Whatever its "image," the advertising industry is responsible for an information flow that costs its clients—and thus consumers—more than $25 billion a year and, as we have noted earlier, keeps the cost of the mass media low.

Advertising Is Not "All-Powerful"

Department store owner John Wanamaker is alleged to have said: "I know only half of our advertising works . . . but I can't tell which half it is." His quip is at the heart of the dilemma of advertising. Bombarded by messages, consumers "tune out" much of what they hear and see. They simply can't recall many of the hundreds of advertisements they encounter every day.

But they do remember some advertisements. Of those they remember, at least a few interest them enough to cause them to recognize the product in the marketplace. A few advertisements may even create a desire strong enough to cause the consumer to put an item on the shopping list, or to add a store to the itinerary for Saturday's shopping expedition. Advertisers don't really expect to reach or convince 100 percent of the target audience, just enough people to maintain or increase traffic in the stores and achieve the desired volume of sales.

Information packaged for the media by advertising agencies is not so powerful that it can sell products the public doesn't want or trust. Despite a heavy advertising blitz in 1989, sales of a new baldness remedy by a leading pharmaceutical company were disappointing. The ballyhoo surrounding the introduction of "New Coke" didn't dissuade consumers from demanding the return of the Coca-Cola they loved, and the company was forced to reintroduce it as "Coca-Cola Classic." Ford's all-out campaign for the ill-fated Edsel couldn't compensate for the fact that its research had completely missed the coming trend away from boxy family cars toward sportier "personal" cars.

Some products sell well without advertising—Hershey candy bars, for example—because they have been available for generations, they are of predictably high quality, and they are purchased more or less on the spur of the moment.

Advertising Performs Many Functions

We saw in the previous chapter that public relations can be used in many situations ranging from reacting to a crisis to helping market a product. Advertising, too, is a versatile field—much broader than merely "selling" consumers on the

ECONOMICS

TV Spots Are Expensive to Make

How much could it cost to make a 30-second film? Probably somewhere around $150,000 if the film happens to be a television commercial. That was the median figure in 1988. Those glamorous automobile ads in exotic locations run still more. And the splashy, quick-cutting soda and beer commercials? They're more likely to cost a quarter-million dollars to make—unless, of course, they feature a well-known rock singer or movie star, in which case the cost of talent alone may run several millions.

Commercial Production Costs

Average Commercial Costs by Product Category for TV Spots of All Lengths Produced During 1991

Product Category	
Automotive	$339,000
Beauty/fashion	258,000
Consumer services/travel/corp. image	121,000
Fast-food/beer/soft drinks	352,000

Source: American Association of Advertising Agencies figures, 1991.

---

idea of purchasing what a manufacturer wants them to buy. Notice the special function of each of these varied types of advertising:

National consumer advertising makes the consumer aware of the product or service and builds an interest in purchasing it. The 30-second spot during a baseball game showing the speed and handling of a Pontiac Grand Am, for example, makes you think about how nice it would be to have a sporty little car, and it implants in your mind the concept that Pontiac builds such a car.

Retail (local) advertising informs the consumer about where products can be purchased, and what special deals are being offered. For example, this week Honest Motors in your town has 50 Grand Ams on the lot, and all must go at $100 over cost!

Institutional advertising builds consumer trust in the company that makes the product. When you were mulling over that purchase of the Pontiac, you may have remembered the advertisement that showed how much research goes into perfecting all General Motors products.

Goodwill or public service advertising is a form of institutional advertising in which the sponsor does not even mention products or services, but hopes instead to create good feelings that may translate into support later. American Express took full-page ads to explain that during a certain period leading up to the centennial of the Statue of Liberty, for every purchase made on their charge cards the company was making a donation to the restoration of the statue.

Trade and industrial advertising is aimed at other manufacturers, and is seen mainly in specialized trade publications rather than mass media consumer channels. "Trade" advertising is aimed from manufacturer to retailer, while "industrial" advertising is one manufacturer selling goods or supplies to another manufacturer. The Beckett Paper Company's "We enhance your image" industrial ads in media magazines show designers of brochures and catalogs how photographs reproduce on the company's line of printing stock.

Issue or political advertising gives voters reasons to support a candidate, or provides information meant to persuade citizens to support a cause such as recycling or the rights of homeless people. United Technologies is one of several companies

Chapter 13 Advertising **375**

Advertising messages are most effective when they are placed where their target audience will see them—in the case of this public service ad, on the street.

that regularly runs ads in newsmagazines and on the op-ed pages of leading newspapers arguing for the free enterprise system and against any government measures that hamper American industry's ability to compete in world markets.

Informational advertising provides special consumer information concerning recalls of products, and responds to questions or charges raised by consumer advocates, health authorities, or competitors, in which case it is called "counteradvertising." After the Tylenol tampering incidents, Johnson & Johnson ran ads telling consumers what code numbers appeared on the batches involved. When the incident was over and the product was reintroduced, the company's ads showed consumers how the packaging could be checked for the triple seal ensuring that it had not been tampered with.

Corrective advertising, when required by a government agency, repudiates unsupportable claims by earlier ads that may have misled customers. The manufacturer of the leading throat gargle was forced to retract the statement that its product *"cures* the common cold" and replace that phrase with *"relieves symptoms associated with* the common cold" (italics added).

Definitions and Theories of Advertising

The root *advert-* comes from the Latin for "to turn toward." Thus advertising is promotional and persuasive in nature. The American Marketing Association defines the field this way:

Advertising is any paid form of nonpersonal presentation of ideas, goods, or services by an identified sponsor.

If we break that definition down, we find that there are four properties of an advertisement:

1. The message is *paid for* by the client;
2. The message appears as *to-whom-it-may-concern* information, even though the appeal is made to look personal;
3. The information *promotes* ideas, goods, or services, and
4. The *client is identified*.

If one of those elements is missing, the message may not be an advertisement at all but part of the editorial matter of the medium.

A leading advertising text simplifies the definition: "Advertising is a message paid for by an identified sponsor and delivered through some medium of mass communication."[6] It places advertising as one of the four branches of marketing communication, with the others being public relations, personal selling (face-to-face), and sales promotion (incentives such as coupons, free samples, and contests to provide buyers with rewards).

"Theories" of advertising have developed out of observation of the practice and are made operative by maxims that have stood the test of time. Some of these precepts that govern what advertising does include the following:

The AIDA model represents *attention, interest, desire,* and *action,* the four steps of the process through which a consumer supposedly goes when first learning of a product or service. The model is an adaptation of a precept of psychology called the attitude-behavior continuum, which many social scientists now question. It works fairly well when the product, service, or idea is inexpensive: AIDA explains why most of us are willing to try a new snack treat, soft drink, or toiletry product that we hear about. But the consumer stops at "desire" if the product is too expensive, such as a sports car or a vacation on the Riviera, or if an idea is taboo or contrary to other attitudes, such as supporting a candidate who does not appear to stand for widely held values.

The Unique Selling Proposition (USP) concept suggests that the purpose of advertising is to identify and clarify one specific benefit or characteristic of a product or service that differentiates it from its competitors. Advertisers say that they try to "position" the product or service so that it can be the logical choice for the segment of the market that is looking to fill a particular need. One automobile's USP may be high horsepower that makes it sporty and a good highway car. Another may offer the best fuel efficiency in the field, which makes it ideal for people on a budget. Still another car might position itself as the right choice for people who are concerned about the safety of their family.

The hierarchy of needs developed by psychologist Abraham Maslow holds that individuals first have a need for survival, then for security, then for love and a sense of belonging, next for esteem, and finally for self-actualization (achieving life goals). Advertisers can infer from that scheme that their messages should identify and aim at the need that is most basic, or that matches best with the properties of the product or service they wish to promote. AT&T's "Reach out and touch someone" campaign plays on the need for love and belonging, depicting families keeping in contact while separated, thanks to phone service. Phones are used for

> ## RESEARCH
> ## What Bonds a Consumer to a Product?
>
> Market research developed in the 1950s focused mainly on *quantitative* research—surveying thousands of consumers and analyzing the resulting data to try to discern purchasing patterns. The advertising messages then were tailored to the perceived patterns of use.
>
> Today, partly because research has become prohibitively expensive, the focus is shifting to *qualitative* research that involves interviews with individual consumers or "focus group interviews" with small groups. The aim is to find out what bonds a consumer to a product—not just who uses it, but why, for what purpose, and with what kind of satisfaction.
>
> Another reason for shifting to qualitative research methods is that recent studies show the majority of consumers think all beers, soaps, potato chips, coffees, and paper towels are pretty much the same. Advertisers hope that more personalized research methods will enable them to figure out ways to position a product as the one that really is different in the way it satisfies the consumer's needs.
>
> *Source:* Randall Rothenberg, "Ad Research Shifts from Products to People," *The New York Times*, April 6, 1989, pp. D-1, D-10.

security, and owning a cellular phone for use in the car could bring esteem. But rather than confuse us with multiple reasons for needing phones, the advertiser tries to peg the right level on the hierarchy.

Reinforcement theory explains why advertising is repetitious and constant, not just one-shot in nature. Just as mothers have to remind children 10 times a day to "take off your dirty shoes when you come in the house," advertisers cannot assume that a lesson once learned is learned forever. The beer manufacturer knows that it is not enough to place one ad at the beginning of a televised ball game: Spots are scheduled throughout the event to keep the thirst alive. Unless consumers have developed brand loyalty over a long period of time, there is always the chance that someone else's ad will seduce them away. That's why some manufacturers bolster advertising with sales promotions that give the shopper incentive to stick with a brand once it has been sampled.

Media-placement formulas and equations have been developed to help agencies know where, when, and how often to use certain media to reach target groups with greatest effect, and how to allocate advertising dollars to best advantage.

The Consumer's Role

William Weilbacher, a marketing professor as well as an advertising industry manager, says that successful advertising should be viewed not as a one-way process, but rather as communication between manufacturer and consumer:

> The consumer is a participant in the advertising process. Advertising that ignores the necessity of consumer involvement in its success will more than likely fail. And an understanding of the consumer's criteria for relevance, credibility, and usefulness for all the information received, including advertising, will surely help to make advertising both more successful and profitable.[7]

```
      P                          I                         C
```

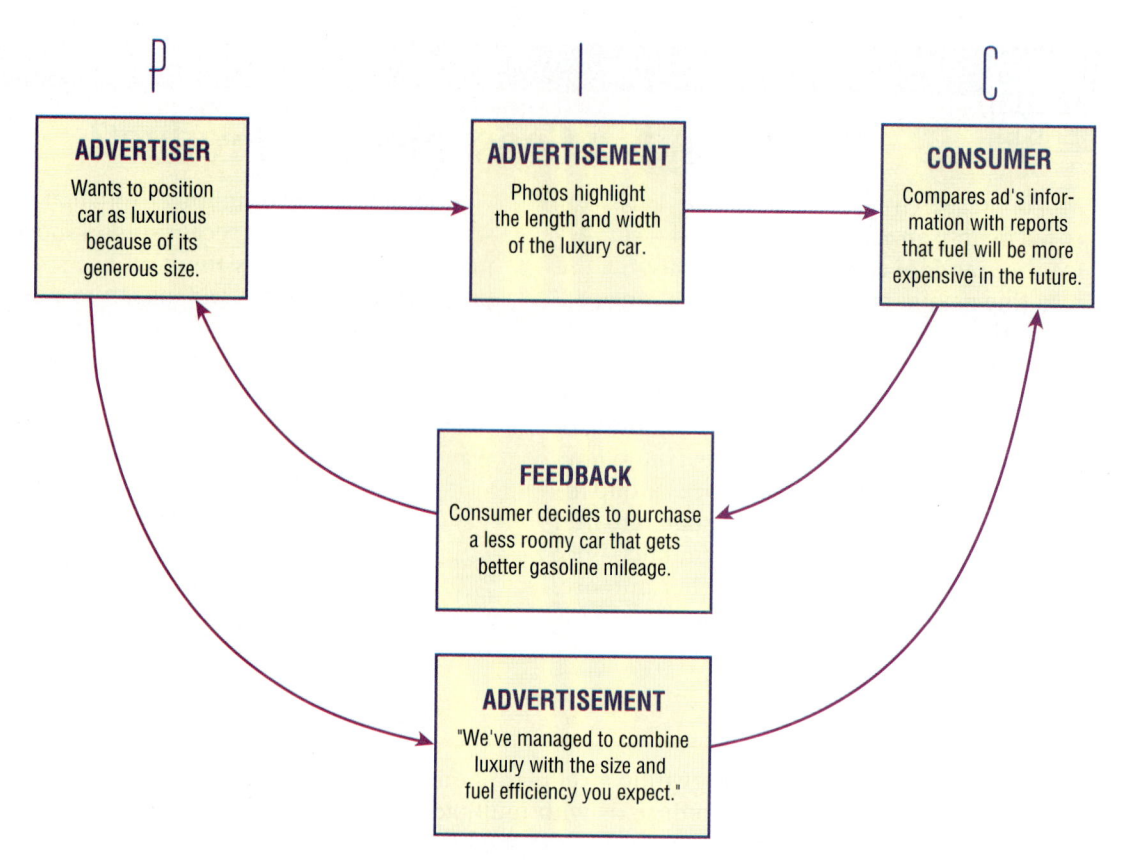

ADVERTISER	ADVERTISEMENT	CONSUMER
Wants to position car as luxurious because of its generous size.	Photos highlight the length and width of the luxury car.	Compares ad's information with reports that fuel will be more expensive in the future.

FEEDBACK
Consumer decides to purchase a less roomy car that gets better gasoline mileage.

ADVERTISEMENT
"We've managed to combine luxury with the size and fuel efficiency you expect."

FIGURE 13.1 The Consumer's Preference Defines the Ad Appeal Producer and consumer participate in the advertising process. Product and the advertising for it must be adjusted to the consumer's response based on all available and relevant information.

Important to this concept is the notion that advertising occurs in a context where the consumer receives considerable information not only from the advertiser, but also from competitors, critics, consumer advocates, news sources, friends, neighbors, and co-workers. The information received by the consumer does not fall on a blank slate: It is assigned a value according to the other information being received.

Thus, most people in the advertising business understand that the information they prepare cannot trigger consumer behavior unless there is a perceived need for the product or service. Sometimes, of course, the consumer's need is abstract: to be attractive, to be accepted, to be successful. Advertising tries to link the product with some concrete aspect of that need (Figure 13.1).

Advertising communicates about life-styles, thus satisfying many of the entertainment and information needs of individuals. Flipping through the pages of advertising in *Gentlemen's Quarterly, Glamour, House & Garden, Town & Country,* or *Travel & Leisure* can be a delightful end in itself, even if only to promote fantasies about the possibilities of achieving the status depicted in the illustrations.

JUSTIFYING THE EXPENSE OF ADVERTISING

Century 21, the nationwide real estate sales company, and its advertising firm, McCann-Erickson, wanted to make sure that their new Unique Selling Proposition was memorable: "No one moves real estate like Century 21." So they spent nearly a half-million dollars for a 30-second television spot that appears to depict several dozen Century 21 sales agents literally lifting a typical suburban home from its foundation.[8]

Half a million dollars for a 30-second spot! Could it possibly be worth the expense?

In a country where one out of five families moves in any one year and real estate commissions total in the billions of dollars, the competitive edge makes the campaign worthwhile. The visual image of all those Century 21 agents in their distinctive yellow blazers straining hard to do an apparently impossible task may well stick in the brain cells of thousands of people who will be selling their houses soon.

Targeting the Audience

Advertisers constantly must question who is being reached by the media, and with what cost efficiency. Market research data are being collected on a weekly, daily, and even hourly basis to find out which people are noticing which advertisements. Ratings and shares are determined for broadcast audiences, and readership of print media is determined through audited circulation figures. Advertisers then use the

RESEARCH

Pretesting: Will It Play in Peoria?

Many advertisements are pretested with sample groups to determine how mass audiences are likely to respond. One of the most famous advertisements in American political history—President Reagan's 1984 "There's a bear in the woods" spot—was tested as thoroughly as any commercial for Coke or Pepsi.

While a grizzly bear lumbered through the wild, an ominous voice said: "For some people, the bear is easy to see. Others don't see it at all. Others say it is vicious and dangerous. Since no one can really be sure who's right, isn't it smart to be as strong as the bear?" The tagline was: "President Reagan—prepared for peace!"

The $80,000 spent filming the commercial and the perhaps million more to air it would be wasted if the average American didn't understand that the bear represented the Soviet threat and that Reagan's defense policies were being discussed metaphorically, making use of the visual shorthand of television. More than 100 focus group interviews were run with voters who were asked to view the commercial and discuss how they felt about it. The spot also was aired in test markets prior to national use, and it scored a high recall of 75 percent based on telephone interviews. Only then was it budgeted for widespread use.

Source: E. Diamond and S. Bates, "The Ads," in M. Robinson and A. Ranney, eds., *The Mass Media in Campaign '84* (Washington: American Enterprise Institute for Public Policy Research, 1985), p. 51.

time or space rates charged by the media to calculate CPM, or cost per thousand consumers reached (the "M" is from the French *mille*, meaning thousand).

Knowing the raw figure of how many consumers are in the audience may satisfy the advertiser of popular products such as soft drinks and toothpaste, but specialized products aimed at target audiences call for more specific data. If you are selling colorful, kicky Swatch watches, then CPM isn't very meaningful. Out of every thousand consumers who watch TV or read the popular magazines, fewer than a hundred are members of your target audience: affluent urban young people who are likely to buy such products.

To meet the need for more specific information about the makeup of media audiences, market researchers since the 1950s have been providing segmented demographic data. *Demographics* refers to the breakdown of an audience by age, income, education, size of community, marital status, and other variables that may influence buying decisions.

It is possible for the advertiser who buys such research to learn that one magazine has a much larger concentration of single women, aged 18 to 25, who have purchased at least one watch in the past year. The research can be so specific as to note past and anticipated buying habits. As we noted in the chapter on magazines, advertisers segment consumers according to behavior patterns that include values and life-styles (VALS) and use that research to match their information to the mind-sets of those who prefer, say, wine rather than beer, or a sensible four-door sedan to a hot little sports coupe.

Cutting Costs and Increasing Efficiency

On the one hand, advertisers occasionally justify great expense in order to make a big splash and be noticed, as Mitsubishi did with eight-page, full-color magazine spreads to introduce its new 35-inch television screens, or the lavish magazine-within-a-magazine inserts Apple used to introduce its new Macintosh line of computers. Coke and Pepsi feel they must spend millions to mount extravaganza-type

---

RESEARCH

Zeroing In on the Consumer's Habits

In the 1980s, advertising researchers learned how to determine the values and life-styles (shortened to "VALS") that lead certain consumers to choose one product over another. The VALS psychological profile enables advertisers to tailor their information more closely to the needs and interests of the consumer.

In the 1990s, a new and more sophisticated approach holds even more promise: single-source research that tracks and correlates *all* of the media habits and buying patterns of selected target consumers. Using a combination of methods—meters on the television, forms to be filled out when shopping, and interviews by researchers—the saturation approach is able to detect nuances such as men who buy certain snack foods to enjoy in conjunction with certain types of television programming, or women whose purchase of cosmetics relates to their choice of soap operas.

Source: Joanne Lipman, "Single-Source Ad Research Heralds Detailed Look at Household Habits," *The Wall Street Journal*, February 16, 1988, p. 39.

commercials featuring the biggest rock stars because they are selling "image" as much as product, and they feel they must keep the name and image of their products on consumers' minds no matter what the cost.

But as rates for advertising skyrocket, agencies are directed to make ad budgets go farther. The chair of General Motors, which spends a billion dollars a year on advertising, says that "the man who stops advertising to save money is just like the man who stops the clock to save time."[9] Nevertheless, GM uses its clout to get the most favorable rates in return for its heavy advertising schedule.

In the early years of television, sponsors often chose to be the exclusive advertiser on a popular show in order to associate their name with a pleasant viewing ritual. The Hallmark Hall of Fame was a leading dramatic program, and the General Electric College Quiz Bowl was a Sunday fixture on television for years. But television advertising became so expensive and audience loyalty to a program so unpredictable that advertisers had to question the wisdom of single sponsorship.

Eventually, cost forced the 1-minute television spot of the early days to give way to the 30-second spot, which is now being replaced by the 15-second spot as the standard. Of course that means that as many as a dozen ads are being clustered around a commercial break, instead of just one or two. That "clutter" puts pressure on advertisers to make their information more intensely urgent and distinctive.

Another solution is to find fresh locations for ads: in paperback books, at the beginnings and ends of videotape cassettes, stuffed in the packaging of other products, and even on lines of clothing—both Coke and Pepsi have marketed their logo and slogan on youth-oriented T-shirts and sweatshirts.

Every medium of mass communication is caught in a bind when it comes to setting its rates for advertising. Rates must be raised when the size of the audience rises. That makes sense both to advertiser and advertising medium, but it has the effect of pricing some advertisers out of the market. Some media try to control the number of subscribers in order to keep the "rate card" steady and maintain the relationship with long-time advertisers.

Media in trouble are forced to offer discounts in order to keep advertisers interested. In the late 1980s, many magazines were rate-cutting to make up for lagging readership and revenues, and network television had to bargain to keep advertisers from drifting to cable. Some newspapers were challenging the organizations that audit their circulations, claiming that artificially low figures were costing them revenue.

When everything is going smoothly, auditing organizations demonstrate to advertisers that the expected number of consumers are being delivered per dollar, and the media stick to their rate cards. When consumers begin to change their habits and alter their choices, the system is disrupted, the system gets complicated, and some media are forced out of the market.

Even public television, which is supposed to be free from the pressures of marketing economics, finds itself scrambling to attract "underwriting support" to pay its bills. That is why a series like "Dining in France" came to be. The show catered to the interests of viewers who wanted information on what to expect when they visited the great restaurants of Europe. It also served as a vehicle for marketing messages. The "Dining in France" series was produced by an American public television station in conjunction with the makers of French products such as yogurt and wine that were happy to have the names of their products mentioned.[10]

MINORITIES/WOMEN

Why Blacks Are More Visible on TV

For more than three decades, television relegated African-Americans to what one black advertising agency called the three C's—comedy, crooning, and criminality. But they rarely showed up in the fourth C—commercials.

The social consciousness of the 1970s prompted advertisers to include what one black critic called the "hand-wavers"—a single ethnic face dropped into every scene to give minorities token visibility. For many years advertisers were content to reach minorities through specialized media, such as magazines and radio stations catering to ethnic groups. Television was considered too expensive to target a small segment of the general audience.

That began to change when the ratings revealed that blacks watch more television than whites (as much as 40 percent higher than the average in the daytime). Studies also showed that blacks are more brand-loyal, especially toward the types of products advertised on television. Clearly it was time to reassess advertising practices.

The breakthrough that brought blacks front and center on the television screen was the emergence in the 1980s of black-run advertising agencies that developed the ability to portray blacks believably in a way that blacks found realistic and that whites could empathize with. Companies that use black agencies to ensure that some of their ads appeal specifically to minorities include Coca-Cola, McDonald's, Pepsi, Ford Motor Co., Proctor & Gamble, and Sears.

OUR LOVE-HATE RELATIONSHIP WITH COMMERCIALS

In the four decades that advertisements have made commercial television possible, viewers have perfected the art of tuning out the paid messages. In recent years the remote control mechanism has made "zapping" commercials simple, and the fast-forward button makes it easy to jump over the ads when viewing copies of programs on videocassette.

When the pay movie channels on cable television show a movie that runs more than three hours, they insert a two-minute break. The screen is blank except for the title of the movie, the word "intermission," and a count-down clock that ticks off the seconds until the movie resumes. Taking that as a cue, NBC decided to find out how a "dark minute" with no information would be used by viewers who had committed themselves to sit through the five to six hours of Super Bowl XX. Late in the pregame show, the network signaled time out and offered the audience 60 seconds in which they could leave the set without missing anything, not even a commercial. A telephone survey conducted for J. Walter Thompson USA found that about a third of the viewers said they would like a similar break in other programs they watch. Over 40 percent said they left the room during the dark minute. Only 2 percent said they used the time to "channel-hop" around the dial. One out of three used the free time to simply enjoy the blank TV screen![11]

Viewers resent being pitched at constantly and harassed into buying a product with which they are already familiar. Most complain that TV ads are intrusive, are louder than other programming, and often insult the intelligence.

Creativity Captures Attention

Despite their reservations about advertising, consumers still pay attention to and actually enjoy the commercials that break new ground or provide anything from a smile to an outright laugh. Even if the bulk of advertisements we see each day are familiar and repetitive, a few display the genius of creativity and command our attention. In their attempts to make us forget that we are watching a commercial message, here are a few of the devices advertisers have used successfully:

The one-shot super commercial, when promoted in print before showing on television, can have great impact. One of the most-discussed examples was the "1984" spot for Apple's Macintosh, aired one time only during the 1984 Super Bowl game. Based on the George Orwell book and employing a large cast in an eerie depiction of future life, the spot won top prize at an advertising film festival. While shown only once, it was so ballyhooed in the trade publications and the popular media beforehand, and received so much comment after the single airing that it had as much impact as an ad repeated hundreds of times.

The delayed-identification advertisement does not reveal the sponsor's name until after the consumer's interest has been teased. The maker of a leading brand of sports shoes lets the montage of motion run for all but the last few seconds of the ad, when the name of the shoe appears over a freeze-frame of the last bit of action. In print, a campaign may run for days in the local newspaper without identifying the sponsor until curiosity has been built.

The charitable tie-in appears to be a "public service" message. Until the final three or four seconds, the viewer learns about the great work being done by a community organization, or one is warned about the evils of a social ill such as addiction to alcohol or drugs. The final frame and the voice-over reveal that the message is "made possible by" a company that usually tries to sell us its products directly. Examples are General Foods Corporation's spots for Mothers Against Drunk Driving and Maxwell House Coffee's commercials benefiting the Muscular Dystrophy Association. In print, the format usually places the name of the sponsor in an understated—but visible—position at the bottom of the advertisement.

The sports tie-in links an advertiser with sporting events, either as a direct sponsor, or in a special relationship. For years Gillette sponsored the fights on radio,

RESEARCH

Which Ads Get Attention on Campus?

A poll of college students in 1990 by *Advertising Age* showed that the old advertising admonition "sex sells" is true on campus. Three of the students' six highest-rated print ads were for Calvin Klein fragrances and jeans—ads that feature handsome nude or seminude young people.

The favorite ad, however, was devoid of sex: Absolut vodka's creative variations on the shape of its bottle. Three of the top ads were for alcoholic beverages.

Students also were asked to say which ads represent their age group best. The Levi 501 and Nike ads rated highest. The remainder of the top 10 were the soft drink and beer ads that show lively young people bouncing around.

Source: Advertising Age Special Report on The College Market, Feb. 5, 1990.

and local beers had a tie-in with baseball teams. But sports sponsorship took off in the 1970s when cigarette advertising was barred from television. By linking their names to sporting events, cigarettes could still get exposure—the view of the scoreboard at many stadiums cannot be televised without taking in the name of the cigarette that sponsors the scoreboard! Beer companies link themselves to special events: the Bud Light Ironman triathlon competition, the Miller 500, the Coors rodeo series, and even the Strohs Light Salmon Derby. With sports reaching a saturation point on television, about the only new sources of revenue appear to be advertising tie-ins. Ad executives are not joking when they talk about the possibility of an "Anheuser-Busch Super Bowl" or the "Winston World Series" in the near future.

Is There a Hidden Message?

Surely one of the most pervasive hoaxes of the twentieth century is the notion that "subliminal" advertising is used to make people desire an alcoholic drink, buy a certain make of car, or dash off to a restaurant lusting for a plate of clams. Gullible people with little understanding of psychology—including some state legislators who have introduced bills that would ban "subliminal" ads—fall prey to books and articles suggesting that words hidden in ice cubes, shapes concealed in the folds of a garment, or symbols worked into pictures of food have the power

Absolut has fun with our suspicions about subliminal advertising by hiding its message in the ice cubes. (Key: ABSO/LUT/VODKA) The Absolut ads are among those most recalled by college students.

to make the consumer jump up and rush to the store, controlled by some unknown force.

In fact, in certain New Jersey theaters in the 1950s, movie audiences were exposed to images superimposed over the last scenes of films, exhorting them to "Drink Coca-Cola" and "eat popcorn." That caused newspaper editorialists to raise a hue and cry against the "alarming and outrageous" mind-fooling technique they supposed would put consumers in a trance.[12] But it doesn't take much to stimulate a movie audience to get up and move to the refreshment stand during intermission. The "subliminal" trickery was hardly necessary.

Psychological research indicates that intense stimuli have a much greater effect than subtle stimuli. Messages hidden within other images certainly are far too subtle to equal the effects of obvious and overt advertising techniques. Advertisers know from experience and past research that the use of vivid hues or colors that create the appropriate mood, sex appeal, and motherhood and manhood images, and the use of high-quality photographs of appealing products can attract our attention sufficiently and heighten our interest in the advertising message. So why bother with messages that appeal to the subconscious?

Moreover, advertising agencies have to prove to their clients that each of the elements in an advertisement has high recall—that the average member of the target audience retains and remembers information from the advertisement. There is no way to test for the recall of anything "subliminal," since the supposed symbol can't be discerned in the first place.

Advertising is not trickery: It is basic persuasion, laid out for all to see.

THE TREND TOWARD DIRECT MARKETING

When early Americans pushed westward, first by wagon train and later by rail, they often left the commercial centers behind as they forged a new rural society. In order to obtain clothing, housewares, and farm implements, they depended on catalogs put out by retailers. The thick Montgomery Ward and Sears, Roebuck catalogs were the "wish books" of the prairies.

As America urbanized in the second half of the twentieth century, marketing changed once more. The assumption was that the purpose of advertising messages was to stimulate consumers to visit the nearby retail centers. After information received through the mass media had prepared the consumer for the transaction, it was up to the attractive displays of merchandise and the skills of salespeople to "close the deal."

That assumption has changed in recent years, for a number of reasons. Consumers are increasingly too busy to find time to visit the retail centers. In urban areas that offer great choice in places to buy, the time spent getting to the giant shopping malls on clogged highways may be daunting. If the consumers do visit the stores, they may discover a shortage of sales personnel that means they have to wait in line to make a purchase, or they may have to deal with salespeople who are not knowledgeable about the merchandise.

Many consumers have discovered that obtaining the necessary information about a product, making the decision, and arranging for delivery can be done in the comfort and convenience of the home, thanks to innovations such as the bank charge card and the toll-free 800 number.

The Fastest-Growing Form of Advertising

Estimates are that nearly $100 million is now spent annually in the United States and Canada on the form of advertising called telemarketing—selling by phone. A similar amount is spent on catalogs and direct mail advertising—the information we love to call "junk mail," even though we make increasing use of the convenience and services it provides.

The Direct Marketing Association estimates that the number of mail-order catalogs more than doubled in the 1980s and continues to grow into the 1990s. Most of the new catalogs do not try to sell everything to everyone, as did the Sears, Roebuck and Montgomery Ward catalogs of an earlier era. Instead they target affluent consumers with specific interests: cooking, gardening, physical fitness, handicrafts, camping, or home decorating. Thus, lists of magazine subscribers are important to direct mail advertising, along with lists of credit card users, members of professional associations, and groups of hobbyists.

The yellow pages—now offered not only by the phone company serving the immediate area, but by other firms as well—have become a direct marketing tool rather than just a "listing" of merchants. Ads in the yellow pages may contain coupons and special numbers for obtaining consumer information.

Cable television is emerging as the newest hot spot for direct marketing. Home shopping adds the excitement of studio hosts demonstrating products and interviewing consumers who call in to place orders. Telephone agents provide the link that makes cable home shopping easy. Time Warner has been especially successful in marketing its magazines with one- and two-minute commercials on cable TV that offer premium incentives such as free binoculars, watches, and calculators.

Shifting Boundaries Between Media

Boundary lines between the different media are shifting continually. "60 Minutes," one of the most popular shows on television, packages itself as a video "magazine" with headlines, bylines, and even letters to the editor. Similarly, the boundary line between magazines and catalogs, once quite distinct, has been blurred by modern marketing concepts. It's not uncommon to find an "advertising supplement" bound into your favorite magazine that turns out to be a small catalog. The theory is that you'll be more attentive if you find the catalog conveniently mixed in with the editorial material that interests you.

Similarly, many catalogs now include articles and service features that provide interesting and useful information alongside the products. Slick catalogs aimed at those with "upscale life-styles" are even being sold on newsstands alongside the magazines they have come to resemble so closely. This gets the catalogs into the hands of those who may not have qualified by virtue of their ZIP-code or by inclusion in a targeted mailing list. (See Table 13.1.)

Sears, Roebuck and the large Spiegel mail-order service now charge for their huge catalogs, refunding the cost with the customer's first purchase. Marketers have found that consumers will pay for information they find useful and interesting, even if it's a commercial message aimed at getting them to spend more.

The boundary line between a brochure and a television commercial was effectively erased by the manufacturer of the Soloflex weightlifting machine. Marketing the Soloflex was difficult because the print brochure couldn't get across the special qualities that made the system different from similar-looking devices. Sales-

TABLE 13.1   1990 Advertising Dollar Expenditures[a]

Rank	Medium	Dollars Spent (billions)[b]	% of Ads[b]
1	Newspapers	$32 billion	25
2	Television	$28 billion	22
3	Direct mail	$23 billion	18
4	Yellow pages	$ 9 billion	7
5	Radio	$ 9 billion	7
6	Magazines	$ 7 billion	5
7	Business publications	$ 3 billion	2
8	Outdoor	$ 1 billion	1
9	Miscellaneous	$16 billion	12

[a]Compiled from industry data.
[b]Figures are rounded off for simplicity.

Note: Newspapers still are the leading national advertising medium, mainly because of the vast numbers of weeklies that augment the dailies. Note that after newspapers and television, the leading media in terms of share of advertising revenue are not news and entertainment media but direct mail and the yellow pages. Because the growth rate of direct mail is greater than that of television or newspapers, it is possible that direct mail could supplant one or both of them at the head of the list in a matter of years.

The entry of the telephone companies into the information business, however, is another variable that could reshape the allocation of advertising dollars to the media in the coming decade.

people at retail outlets were not adept at demonstrating the machine, and a one-minute TV commercial couldn't convince the viewer of all the machine could do. So Soloflex tried a "video brochure"—a 20-minute cassette showing a young athlete demonstrating each of the machine's two dozen exercises. Each copy of the "brochure" cost $6 to produce and mail, but nearly a third of those who sent for it bought the $600 machine—far more effective than the print brochure.[13] Cadillac used the video brochure concept when it introduced its Allante model. Spiegel produces a fashion video that enables women to view the season's new styles in the convenience of their home. (See Tables 13.2 and 13.3.)

TABLE 13.2   Top 15 Advertisers on Network Television

		1990	1989	% Change
1	General Motors Corp.	$598.4	$506.5	18.1%
2	Procter & Gamble Co.	557.6	404.8	37.7
3	Philip Morris Cos.	402.2	368.4	9.2
4	Kellogg Co.	301.3	324.8	−7.2
5	Sears, Roebuck & Co.	253.8	187.5	35.4
6	AT&T Co.	244.9	162.7	50.5
7	McDonald's Corp.	231.0	252.1	−8.4
8	Johnson & Johnson	211.4	169.9	24.4
9	Ford Motor Co.	196.9	201.4	−2.2
10	PepsiCo	193.4	168.8	14.6
11	Chrysler Corp.	190.0	140.6	35.1
12	Grand Metropolitan	183.1	148.2	23.5
13	Toyota Motor Sales USA	170.9	110.8	54.2
14	Unilever U.S.	162.9	190.4	−14.4
15	American Home Products Corp.	150.5	161.9	−7.0

Note: Dollars in millions.

Source: Advertising Age, May 13, 1991.

TABLE 13.3 Top 15 Brands Advertised on Cable

Data gathered from the various ratings service by *Advertising Age* show a very different profile for cable advertising contrasted with network television. The top ten cable advertisers in the first half of 1990 were:

1. Sports Illustrated subscriptions
2. Time-Life books
3. McDonald's restaurants
4. Sports Illustrated videocassettes
5. Time-Life videocassettes
6. Budweiser beer
7. Sears, Roebuck & Co.
8. Burger King restaurants
9. Bud Light beer
10. Wall Street Journal subscriptions.

Note: While two beers and two fast-food chains that advertise heavily on networks are on the cable list, autos and food products that lead the network lists are not as important to cable. Information products, particularly those offered by Time Warner companies, are the ads you're most likely to see while watching cable.

Source: Advertising Age, Dec. 10, 1990.

Even the venerable yellow pages are likely to find a new format in the near future. MIT's Media Lab, funded by several corporations, is exploring the concept of putting all commercial phone listings on a compact videodisc, known as CD-ROM. The consumer who fast-forwards on the disc to a category such as "sporting goods" would view not only the listing and telephone information, but also video ads from those merchants who paid extra for the service.[14]

MONITORING ADVERTISING INFORMATION

At the beginning of this chapter, we saw that newspapers and magazines eventually realized that unscrupulous advertising could bring their publications into disrepute with consumers who had been duped or misled, so publishers began to reject advertisements for products of dubious reputation, including most patent medicines. Fed up with hucksters, the medical community joined with consumers and publishers to press Congress for the passage of the Pure Food and Drug Act in 1906. The law prohibited claims of undocumented cures, forbade manufacturers to misrepresent the efficacy of their products, and required all ingredients to be identified on the product label. Many of the patent medicines relied on alcohol or drugs such as morphine for their apparently miraculous effects, meaning that more serious problems of addiction or complications were likely to follow the initial relief.

The balance of this chapter will look at how Americans have monitored advertising using a mixture of government surveillance, consumer advocacy, media self-regulation, and industry self-regulation.

Government Restraints

The Federal Trade Commission (FTC) was established in 1914, and the agency was empowered to regulate advertising and prevent deceptive practices. The outright hucksters soon were exposed. The FTC monitors and corrects claims of products that "cure" the common cold, guarantee "permanent weight loss," and "reverse baldness." With each passing decade, the FTC became more proactive in its supervision of advertising practices; rather than merely handling complaints, the agency studied abuses and issued reports that attacked deception and the dissemination of misleading information.

In the 1950s, the FTC began to crack down on "bait and switch" ads that lure consumers with a "low-ball" price. The FTC charged that many merchants used pressure sales tactics to convince the consumer to "move up" to higher-priced products, often claiming that the advertised items were out of stock or not really of satisfactory quality. The FTC also investigated the misuse of the word *free* in advertisements for products that weren't really free but required the purchase of other goods in order to receive a premium. Beginning in the 1970s, the FTC began to take a hard look at "Brand X" ads that compared a sponsor's product with an unnamed competitor. The government agency pushed advertisers to (1) name the competitor, so the consumer would know which two products were being compared; and (2) cite impartial research data as proof that one product was better or more effective than another.

The FTC can issue a "cease and desist" order, or it can levy a fine against advertisers whose messages it feels have injured another firm or a consumer. In the 1970s, the agency began to require "corrective advertising" to offset the effects of long-running campaigns that had misled the public. Profile bread was required to explain to consumers that its claim of having fewer calories per slice was true only because its slices were thinner than those of the competitor, and that using the product would not cause weight loss.

More than 20 U.S. government agencies are empowered to regulate one or more forms of advertising. The U.S. Postal Service screens catalogs and other direct mail advertising for information that would constitute "using the U.S. mails to defraud." The Securities and Exchange Commission keeps an eye on any claims that would tend to create undue expectations for the rise in the value of a stock. The Food and Drug Administration oversees the dissemination of any information concerning foodstuffs, health care products, cosmetics, and drugs. A current area of concern for the FDA is the proliferation of health claims that seek to take advantage of the public's concern about fitness and dieting. In 1991, the agency announced new rules that would curb claims like that of Quaker Oat Bran that it "reduces cholesterol" unless such claims could be substantiated by independent authorities such as the Surgeon General or the National Academy of Sciences.

State legislatures also are active in passing laws that affect advertising. Abuses of telemarketing that constitute invasions of privacy have prompted the majority of states to consider passing laws that would put limits on the "harassment" of telephone solicitation.

It appeared through most of the 1970s and 1980s that the U.S. Supreme Court was committed to expanding the protection of commercial speech. In 1988, for example, it permitted lawyers to use direct mail to solicit clients, a practice forbidden by state bar associations. But the Court does not always protect commercial information. In the summer of 1986 it upheld a lower court's ruling that Puerto Rico can ban advertising for casinos aimed at residents of the Commonwealth, and could permit casino ads to be directed only at tourists. The decision alarmed advertisers because it was the first time in American history that truthful advertising for a legal product had been banned by a legislature and upheld by the courts. Earlier decisions, for example, had upheld the right to advertise contraceptives because they are legal.

Manufacturers and the advertising industry constantly pressure government agencies for fear that regulations will become as stringent as they are in some other countries. In Malaysia, television ads that show a car driving fast and even flying through the air—a common way of demonstrating the handling of an automobile in American ads—are prohibited because unsophisticated viewers might emulate the behavior. Malaysia's strict code controlling TV ads also stipulates that speakers in commercials must use the correct pronunciation of the official Maylay language, not dialects of Chinese or Indian.[15]

Most Americans value their right to receive information without interference. They would not welcome or tolerate government control of entertainment or educational information for reasons of cultural purity or protecting the unsophisticated. On the other hand, they place great value on receiving accurate information, especially about health and personal products. That is why there has been little or no protest from citizens as, increasingly, legislative and regulatory bodies have become more stringent with advertisers.

The Attack on Cigarette and Liquor Advertising

Because of the health problems caused by cigarette smoking and the inhaling of smoke by nonsmokers, cigarettes have been under attack in the United States for a generation. A series of findings by the Surgeon General led in 1965 to the warnings required on all cigarette packages and advertisements.

In 1971, after a long congressional debate, cigarette advertising was prohibited from the broadcast media by the federal government, which has more direct control over broadcast media than over print media. The tobacco industry and the broadcast industry maintained—and continue to argue—that the ban is unconstitutional. The temporary setback in advertising revenues for the broadcasters was a gold mine for the print media, which had lost billions of dollars to television over the preceding decade.

INSIGHT

Supreme Court Upholds Truthful Ads

Gary E. Peel, an Illinois attorney, wanted to advertise his legal specialty despite a state rule against such practice. He took his case all the way to the U.S. Supreme Court, which ruled that "truthful advertising related to lawful activities is entitled to First Amendment protection." As long as advertising isn't misleading, said the Court, it cannot be banned.

The decision raised doubts about bills that would restrict advertising for tobacco and alcohol products on the grounds that the products are harmful to society. Because the products are legal, advertising information about them, as long as it isn't misleading, would be legal under the Peel decision.

The court's decision came by the narrowest possible margin, 5 to 4. It is inconsistent with other Supreme Court decisions, such as the 1986 ruling that upheld the Puerto Rican prohibition of gambling information aimed at its own residents, even though casino gambling is legal in Puerto Rico. All of this suggests that the controversy over control of advertising information will continue to be on the nation's legal agenda through the 1990s.

Pushed by the American Medical Association, in the mid-1980s Congress debated whether cigarette ads should be banned from print media as well. The growing number of regulations imposed by industry on smoking in the work place and the decision by the military to restrict smoking helped fuel the spread of antismoking information. The industry responded with its own arguments that smokers should be allowed to choose whether to use the product and whether to receive information about it.

Lawyers for the R. J. Reynolds Tobacco Company, for example, successfully fought the Federal Trade Commission's decision that one of the firm's "issues" advertisements misrepresented the results of a government study of smoking. The ad said that the results of the study were inconclusive, and Reynolds contended that this interpretation was corporate opinion, and was thus protected by the First Amendment. The FTC simply saw the issue as one of making false claims about a scientific study.[16] Reynolds prevailed in a series of hearings before the commission.

Research shows that today more college women than college men smoke cigarettes, which researchers attribute to the fact that the tobacco industry is successfully linking smoking by women with images of glamour, success, and equality, as well as a means of staying thin and attractive. All of these charges are denied by the tobacco industry, which maintains that cigarette advertising is now directed only at people who already smoke.

The drive to prohibit all advertising of harmful substances such as tobacco and alcoholic beverages is being spearheaded by the medical community. Ironically, it comes shortly after the medical professional societies finally altered their own ethical standards to permit "tasteful and restrained" advertising for doctors and medical institutions—a practice long prohibited by the profession.

In 1989, Canada passed a Tobacco Products Control Act that bans all advertising of tobacco products, including billboards and store displays as well as the distribution of free samples. The only way tobacco companies can get publicity now in Canada is through sponsorship of cultural and sporting events, and even there the brand names of cigarettes cannot be used, only the name of the company.[17]

The national debate over the effects of advertising on people who abuse substances has become heated and emotional. A former "Winston man" quit smoking and testified before Congress that "My job was to encourage, entice and lure. I became a high-priced accessory to murder."[18] The National Association to Prevent Impaired Driving, a coalition of a hundred traffic safety, health, and public policy groups, issued a study titled "Beer and Fast Cars" that criticized the brewing companies for sponsoring auto races and putting their emblems on the cars. The practice, said the report, targets young blue-collar men, the group with the highest incidence of auto accidents and arrests for driving under the influence of alcohol.[19]

A study conducted for *The Wall Street Journal* on its centennial anniversary in 1989 showed that U.S. citizens overwhelmingly oppose the illegalization of alcoholic beverages and tobacco products, but their attitudes toward dissemination of information about the substances are quite different. By substantial majorities, the respondents favored banning beer and wine ads from television (hard liquor is already banned), and banning all alcohol and tobacco advertising from print media as well.[20]

The momentum against the tobacco companies' use of advertising was slowed somewhat in 1989 when the Surgeon General's report—"Reducing the Health Consequences of Smoking: 25 Years of Progress"—stated that "There is no scientifically rigorous study available to the public that provides a definitive answer to the basic question of whether advertising and promotion increase the level of tobacco consumption." The report suggested that the true extent of the influence of advertising might be "unknowable." Advertising industry leaders had testified before the Surgeon General's hearings that in countries where tobacco advertising was banned, no reduction in tobacco consumption resulted.[21]

Consumers Pressure Advertisers

In 1989 advertisers including Ralston Purina, General Mills, and Domino's Pizza canceled their advertising on the irreverent "Saturday Night Live" at the urging of a religious group that assailed the show as objectionable. "It's a difficult time for advertisers," said an NBC spokesperson. "There are a lot of pressure groups out there."

Pepsi discovered the truth to that when it presented a commercial featuring the singer Madonna at the same time that her controversial song "Like a Prayer" appeared. Pepsi canceled the ad in response to pressure from the same group that was attacking "Saturday Night Live," only to find its soft drinks boycotted by another group that identifies itself as "victims of fundamental religion."

Mennen was in a similar position when it pulled its ads from a medical drama that some contended was "anti-Christian." Mennen was accused by a gay and lesbian group of having canceled the advertising because one of the characters on the show was openly homosexual.

Irate individual consumers have always fired off letters complaining about ads. In 1989 a mother in Bloomfield Hills, Michigan, managed single-handedly to mount a campaign against the adult-oriented "Married . . . With Children" that attracted the attention of the national news media and struck fear into advertisers. Audiences and advertisers did not flee the show, however. Several advertisers did pull their messages from "thirtysomething" when it showed a homosexual couple in bed, but the "boycott" was only for the one episode.[22]

Today more than ever, advertisers have to walk a fine line in order to avoid offending one or another side of almost any issue. Consumerism has become organized and effective. The Reverend Donald Wildmon heads an organization he calls the American Family Association, and he has called for boycotts against companies that advertise on shows with violence and sexual content. The threat of consumer boycotts is a sure-fire story for the news media, but few boycotts against advertisers because of the television shows they sponsor have been particularly long-lived or effective. (Boycotts prompted by company policies, however, have been prolonged, such as the campaign against Nestlé because of its promotion of infant formulas in underdeveloped countries.)

The practice of inserting advertising messages into entertainment films also has come under scrutiny. The executive director of the Center for Science in the Public Interest used the op-ed page of *The New York Times* as a forum for alerting the public to the amount of advertising that is finding its way into the movies we pay to see. In one movie, "Bull Durham," he counted the presence of Miller beer products or signs 21 times, along with obvious plugs for a soft drink, a brand of bourbon, and even Oscar Meyer weiners—a total of 50 brand names on screen for an average of one every two minutes.[23]

Action for Children's Television, which had a long record of representing to legislative bodies the concerns of parents about advertising aimed at their children, acted as a consultant to the Consumers Union's holiday special that educated parents on the seduction of kids by ads. "Buy Me That!", shown on Home Box Office, dissected several misleading techniques, including the implication that toys can walk and talk, the suggestion that a toy house or gas station comes with all the people and cars shown in the ad, and the failure to make clear that "some assembly required" may mean that an adult has to build a toy from parts before a child can play with it. The show also revealed how ads that show children happily bouncing around on Pogo Balls and tossing Flip Balls with the ease of Olympic athletes are the results of editing, and it is unlikely that most kids will be able to perform with the same happy satisfaction as those depicted on the screen.[24]

The Consumers Union program ended with a call for Congress to pass a bill reinstating a limitation on the number of commercial minutes per hour aimed at children on television. Such limits were removed by the FCC in 1984 as part of the deregulation of television. In 1991, new limitations were imposed.

As early as the 1970s, Action for Children's Television argued in testimony before Congress that small children do not understand the role and function of an advertisement. As they grow up and realize that products do not perform the miracles that the advertisements appear to promise, they become disillusioned or even cynical, which may carry over into a distrust of other institutions as well. Despite these warnings, the FCC and Congress have been reluctant to set permanent rules to eliminate questionable practices in advertising aimed at children. Rules concerning mixing ads and program content as well as using actors from entertainment programs to "pitch" products at children have been tested and enacted by government agency and media standards and practices departments, but they do not seem to have enough teeth or to stay in place long enough to dissuade the advertisers from returning to the tried-and-true techniques of persuasion that work so well on the young.

Media Self-Regulation

Mass media producers usually exercise their rights to refuse advertising that is in bad taste or that makes questionable claims. In 1986, several general-interest magazines refused to run an ad for a men's fragrance because the text of the ad, representing the thoughts of an assertively masculine model, included a "four-letter word." Men's magazines ran the ad, however, finding it acceptable for their audience.

In addition to screening advertisements for taste and validity of claims, television networks frequently have rejected spots that touch on political issues. On the night of the 1984 presidential election, the W. R. Grace Company began running an "issues" spot on network television that depicted a baby crying when it was handed a bill for $50,000—the child's share of the national deficit. Two of the networks accepted the ad, but one rejected it. In 1986, Grace submitted a new version of the ad to the networks depicting an elderly man on trial in the year 2017 for failing to do anything to halt the growing national debt. This time all three networks would not accept the ad, saying that it was too controversial and exposed the networks to possible complaints under the Fairness Doctrine, then in force.

J. Peter Grace, chairman and chief executive officer of the firm, responded: "They sell commercial time to advertise detergents, lingerie, hamburgers, appliances and beer. Can it really be argued that selling time for conveying facts or ideas on important public issues will be detrimental to the interests of the country or the three networks?"[25] Grace scoffed at the networks' contention that their news departments could do a better job of covering political issues than could business interests using advertising as a tool of information.

Most of the American advertising industry agreed with Grace and saw the network move as an attempt to pressure the Congress to do away with the Fairness Doctrine. In other words, the issues ads were being used as bargaining chips by the networks in their quest for less regulation. In 1987, the FCC finally did abolish most provisions of the Fairness Doctrine, but the regulatory body announced that it would continue to enforce the provision stating that issues currently the subject of voter referenda come under the Fairness Doctrine. Thus, opponents have to be given free air time to respond to statements made by another side on the issue.

For a long time the National Association of Broadcasters code was another media mechanism that affected what advertisers could do. First drafted in 1929, the code did not have the force of law; it was accepted by individual stations as a condition of membership in the NAB. When a suit resulted in the 1982 court decision that such a code unduly restricted the freedom to communicate information through advertising, the NAB withdrew it. Nevertheless, many of its provisions had been adopted as part of the standards and practices followed by individual stations, and thus they survive today.

The NAB code prohibited or limited the presentation of some products, which is why you never see hard liquor in commercials, and nobody actually *drinks* the beer or wine being advertised. Actors in commercials are permitted to be shown only lifting the glass or bottle toward or away from their lips. (The film editor cuts away from the action during the moment when the liquid ostensibly is being guzzled.) The practice appears to be rather hypocritical when the actors in the program that surrounds the wine or beer advertisement are free to slug down all the alcohol they want in plain view.

Without the authority of the NAB code, broadcast stations are finding it more and more difficult to explain what messages are acceptable for commercials or public service announcements, and why. Here are some examples:

- A station had a long-standing policy of refusing messages advocating birth control, explaining that "controversial issues" were not suitable for ads and were more properly covered by public affairs discussion programs. The station decided to accept condom ads, however, if they were presented as part of a campaign to slow the spread of acquired immune deficiency syndrome, AIDS.

- A station refused ads mentioning condoms both for birth control and AIDS prevention on the grounds that "we prefer not to deal with such issues in short snippets of 30 seconds." However, the station gladly accepts advertising messages from candidates for public office that discuss in short snippets of 30 seconds the issues on which they hope to be elected—including AIDs prevention and birth control measures.

- A consortium of health and welfare groups concerned with the three million unwanted pregnancies in the United States each year, half of which end in abortion, argued that their ads merely called for "intelligent choices of birth control, including abstinence." They were willing to pay for the ads, reasoning that public service announcements run infrequently and at times of low viewing. Their tasteful ads—and their money—were turned down by most stations because of the fear of controversy.

Most media will not accept an anonymous advertisement that discusses a public issue or in any way takes a political stand; the name of at least one sponsoring person must be placed in the ad, and the media will refuse the ad if they cannot verify that the sponsoring name is a valid one. The media also reject advertisements they feel may open them to libel suits; in the eyes of the law it is the media who publish the defamation and thus share responsibility for it, even if the damaging words were written by the sponsor.

Industry Self-Regulation

In order to forestall regulation, the business community and the advertising industry try to prevent abuses that might lead to public outrage and government interference.

Most advertisers support their local Better Business Bureaus in the campaign to warn consumers about fraudulent claims and deceptive practices. The local telephone company's yellow pages will not accept advertising it deems to be misleading, and merchants must prove claims they are the "best" or the "only" before the telephone book will carry those words.

The National Advertising Review Council (NARC) was formed by the national Better Business Bureau, the American Advertising Federation, the American Association of Advertising Agencies, and the Association of National Advertisers—in short, the major forces in the advertising industry—for the purpose of self-regulating advertising. The investigative body of the NARC is the National Advertising Division (NAD), which is empowered to initiate inquiries into deceptive or misleading advertising and to hear complaints from both consumers and advertisers.

In a typical complaint to the NAD, Orville Redenbacher popcorn charged that General Mills's Pop Secret Cheese Flavored microwave popcorn claimed consumers preferred its product to Orville Redenbacher's cheese-flavored popcorn, but the test was taken before Redenbacher had reformulated its product, although the ad was run after the new product was on the market. In a later test, Redenbacher claimed, its popcorn scored higher. General Mills said its ad had completed its run, and new ads would not be run until after further testing. Case closed.

A more exotic complaint was lodged by the Children's Advertising Review Unit of the NAD against a copying machine company whose ads showed frustrated business people throwing their copiers out of windows. The complaint said that the dangerous act of throwing things out windows might lead impressionable children to imitate the practice, and the scenes of copying machines crashing on the sidewalk might cause anxiety in young children. The sponsoring firm agreed to consider those concerns when planning new ads.

The NAD does not have the power to censor ads, impose fines, or bring any other sanctions. As in the examples above, campaigns in question often have already run their course before the NAD decision is rendered. (The NAD took moves in 1989 to shorten the review process from six months to under two months.) But both the act of review and the publication of the results in the leading trade publications are instructive to the advertising community and help prevent future abuses or excesses. In practice, the NARC and NAD have been effective forces in serving the information needs of the consumer.

Still another form of self-control is the criticism offered by columnists and writers for *Advertising Age* and *Ad Week*. Bob Garfield's weekly "Ad Review" for

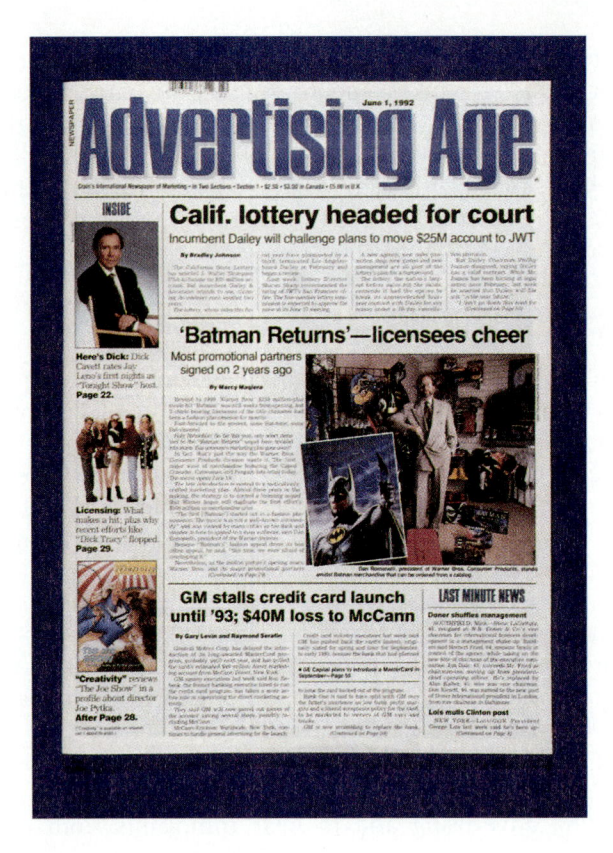

Advertising Age is an important resource not only for the advertising industry, but for everyone involved in any aspect of marketing goods and services.

Advertising Age reads like film or drama criticism and awards from one to four stars according to the quality and effectiveness of the ad being judged. Individuals also can write letters to the editor of those publications to complain about ads. One of *Advertising Age*'s most popular categories of letter is captioned "Ads We Can Do Without"—usually advertisements that exploit women with cheap, vulgar sexual references.

FUTURE FILE

✓ The most powerful advertising tool by the year 2000 may be the personal home computer, receiving information through telephone lines. Assuming that the interests of each subscriber to a computer service are part of the data in the information system, how can advertising messages effectively be "targeted" to the individual?

✓ In the future, everything will be sponsored. What event or institution that now has no link with advertising might lend itself to commercial exploitation?

✓ Advertising can be a great force for good, especially when the creative services of the industry are donated to nonprofit causes. What social concern of today could benefit from a hitherto untried advertising campaign?

NOTES

1. Otto Kleppner (Thomas Russell and Glenn Verrill), *Advertising Procedure* (Englewood Cliffs, NJ: Prentice-Hall, 1986), p. 3.

2. Kleppner, p. 3.
3. Michael Marsden, professor of popular culture at Bowling Green State University, quoted in Richard Edel, "American Dream Vendors," *Advertising Age*, Nov. 9, 1988, p. 153.
4. S. Shapiro, "Muggeridge on the Warpath," *Advertising Age*, April 7, 1986, p. 63.
5. S. Prakash Sethi, "Advertising's Image Problem," *Advertising Age*, March 3, 1986, p. 18.
6. Kleppner, p. 23.
7. William M. Weilbacher, *Advertising* (New York: Macmillan, 1979), p. 15.
8. H. White. "An Uplifting Experience for Century 21," *Advertising Age*, June 30, 1986, p. 39.
9. Philip Dougherty, "GM Puts Stress on Efficiency," *The New York Times*, May 29, 1986, p. D-23.
10. John J. O'Connor, " 'Dining in France' on 13, 'Gourmet Tour' Series," *The New York Times*, May 22, 1986, p. C-26.
11. R. Kaatz, "Super Bowl XX and the 'Dark Minute,' " *Advertising Age*, June 30, 1986, pp. 18, 24.
12. Timothy E. Moore, "Subliminal Advertising: What You See Is What You Get," *Journal of Marketing*, Spring 1982, pp. 38–47.
13. David Arnold, "Video Puts Muscle into Sales Efforts," *Advertising Age*, Oct. 11, 1984, p. 48.
14. Lenore Skenazy, "A Personal Look into the Future," *Advertising Age*, Aug. 8, 1988, p. 26.
15. Jack Burton, "Malaysia Clamps Down on TV Advertising," *Advertising Age*, Sept. 6, 1984, pp. 26–27.
16. Floyd Abrams, "A Chilling Effect on Corporate Speech," *The New York Times*, July 6, 1986, sec. 3, p. 2.
17. Alan Freeman, "Tobacco Firms in Canada Grapple with Ban on Ads," *The Wall Street Journal*, May 2, 1989, p. B-1.
18. Elizabeth Anderson, "One Man's Crusade Against Smoking," *The New York Times*, Nov. 12, 1989, p. 8.
19. Ronald Smothers, "Beer Opponents Start Their Engines," *The New York Times*, May 29, 1990, p. A-13.
20. Alix M. Freedman, "Rebelling Against Alcohol, Tobacco Ads," *The Wall Street Journal*, Nov. 14, 1989, p. B-1.
21. "Koop Surprises Admen," *Advertising Age*, Jan. 16, 1989, p. 8.
22. Geraldine Fabrikant, "Ads Reportedly Lost Because of Gay Scene," *The New York Times*, Nov. 14, 1989, p. D-21.
23. Michael F. Jacobson, "The Bull in 'Bull Durham,' " *The New York Times*, Dec. 23, 1988, p. A-39.
24. Walter Goodman, "Cautionary Guide for Little Customers," *The New York Times*, Dec. 3, 1989, p. 33.
25. J. Peter Grace and J. A. Califano, "End the Curbs on Public Debate," *USA Today*, June 17, 1986, p. 14A.

SUGGESTED READINGS

Arlen, Michael J., *Thirty Seconds* (New York: Farrar, Straus & Giroux, 1980).
Engel, Jack, *Advertising: The Process and the Practice* (New York: McGraw-Hill, 1980).
Gargett, T. F., *Corporate Advertising: The What, the Why and the How* (New York: McGraw-Hill, 1981).
Kleppner, Otto (Thomas Russell and Glenn Verrill), *Advertising Procedure*, 9th ed. (Englewood Cliffs, NJ: Prentice-Hall, 1986).
Ogilvy, David, *Ogilvy on Advertising* (New York: Crown, 1983).
Pope, Daniel, *The Making of Modern Advertising* (New York: Basic Books, 1983).
Weilbacher, William M., *Advertising* (New York: Macmillan, 1979).

CHAPTER 14

Music, Movies, Theater

AT A GLANCE

✓ The entertainment industry performs many of the same roles as the news media—informing, marketing, correlating society, and serving the ritual needs of consumers.

✓ The music recording industry, in addition to providing much of the content for the radio medium, has important links with the film industry and provides powerful marketing tools for other products.

✓ Advances in technology have the effect of constantly renewing interest in the music industry and broadening the audience for recorded music.

✓ The film industry protects itself from government controls and censorship by offering parents a rating system. The music industry has adopted warning labels to perform a similar function.

✓ Filmmaking by business conglomerates results in a "blockbuster" mentality that leads to the production of "presold" films meant to capture a large segment of the audience by offering popular stars and familiar stories.

✓ Because they are "one-to-many" in nature and part of the marketing mix, live theater, sports events, and theme parks also function as mass communication institutions.

The music recording industry, the movies, and live stage performances offer much more than entertainment: They mirror and comment on society, they encapsulate small slices of cultural history, and they provide models for understanding values and life-styles. As we examine these producers and the ways we consume their information, we realize that there are more channels of mass communication than we may have realized, and that these channels are becoming more and more interrelated.

ROLES PLAYED BY THE ENTERTAINMENT INDUSTRY

At first glance, one might assume that music, movies, and theater play an entirely different role in society from the news media. But as we revisit several terms and concepts we used to describe the roles of the news media, we can find many parallels in the consumer's uses of the entertainment media.

Surveillance. Entertainment information can have news value. The film *Rain Man* informs the audience about a particular kind of mental illness and the attitude of various people in society toward it.

Correlation. The films of Oliver Stone, including *Wall Street* and *Platoon*, go beyond entertainment. Stone uses his stories to criticize American values and to examine the conflict of personal and institutional ethics in society. The consumer

A scene from Oliver Stone's "Platoon," a film that helped to start Americans rethinking the Vietnam War.

Chapter 14   Music, Movies, Theater   401

> ### INSIGHT
> # Transcending Media: "A Chorus Line"
>
> At the very beginning of this book, we pointed out that there is a convergence of mass communication media, with information quickly adapting itself to myriad forms and technologies. The Broadway box office hit *A Chorus Line* is an example of information designed for one medium that eventually found itself adapted to other media. As with many musical comedies, it became a record album and a movie; for many consumers who never saw the play, the versions in those media were *their* Chorus Line, and the recorded versions live on and on even after the long-running play closed on Broadway.

sitting in the theater is forced to ask; "How would I behave in this situation? What's the right thing for a citizen, a soldier, or a business person to do?"

Transmission of Social Heritage.   A film like *The Cotton Club*, which depicts music and nightlife in Harlem's heyday, is meant to evoke an era and increase appreciation of a slice of history.

Marketing.   From the beginning, *Batman* was conceived not merely as a film, but as the linchpin for a national mania that would sell T-shirts, cereal, games, hats, and buttons. *Teenage Mutant Ninja Turtles* began as a comic, then a television series, then "the movie," followed by the live stage show and appearances in the Macy's Thanksgiving Day Parade and during the halftime show at a bowl game.

Hard News/Soft News.   Producers of popular culture categorize some items as "serious" and others as pure escapism. Stung by criticism that his songs were merely "pretty," Phil Collins went out of his way to make his lyrics relevant to social issues in his album shrewdly titled ". . . But Seriously." In hopes of avoiding a reputation as the producer of popular entertainment, Steven Spielberg tries to balance his contributions by making serious films like *The Color Purple*.

Follow the Leader.   Just as "pack journalism" and following the lead of certain newspapers of national stature leads to sameness in the news, the field of entertainment is a copycat's delight. In the late 1980s, not just one but half a dozen films were based on the notion that through some mishap, a boy and his father switched identities, leading to all sorts of embarrassing mix-ups. A trip to the "Exercise and Health" section of the video store reveals that although Jane Fonda may have been the first star with a workout video, there are now dozens, including one by Dolph ("Masters of the Universe") Lundgren.

Ritual.   Just as news editors go automatically for standard stories, the entertainment industry relies on old formulas: the rising star who makes it in show business against all odds, the buddies whose friendship enables them to carry off a seemingly impossible caper, the cowboy-pilot-athlete who defies injury or death to win against a dastardly enemy in order to get revenge, the public figure who sinks into the depths of dope addiction or alcoholism and then makes a comeback.

PRESSURES ON THE PRODUCERS

Another parallel with the news media is that producers of music, movies, and theater must deal with pressure from consumers.

Financial Pressure. Movie and theater producers must seek financial backing for their ventures. The support will not be forthcoming from bankers or individual Broadway investors if they aren't convinced that an audience exists for the proposed entertainment vehicle. The cost of putting on a major concert tour is so great that rock stars get financial support from sponsors such as Coke, Pepsi, and Budweiser.

Criticism. Criticism of the arts and entertainment media is in itself an important information product provided by the news media. Critics are "leading consumers" who help the rest of us decide what is worthwhile. No matter how successful the publicity campaign for a film or play, universally negative criticism in the media will turn audiences away. Occasionally an entertainment is critic-proof by virtue of being "presold" to the audience. Interest in *Jaws 12* or *Rocky 10* may be so great that the product can survive a "thumbs down" from Siskal and Ebert. The tele-

INDUSTRY

Profiles of Music, Film, and Theater Audiences

- Rock music recordings have been the favorites of consumers for decades. But whereas 43 percent of each dollar spent on records in 1980 went to rock, by 1990 it was only 34 percent, with easy listening and country and western gaining most. (Source: Recording Industry Association of America survey, 1990.)

- Gift purchases account for about one in four records and cassettes sold in the United States. (Source: Record Industry Association of America, 1989.)

- Music, film, and theater are not the best value for the family's entertainment dollar, according to a nationwide Roper survey. "A nice dinner at a restaurant," tops the list, followed by rental movies, paperback books, and sports events. (Source: *The Wall Street Journal*, 1990.)

- Movie attendance is regular—at least once a month—for only 24 percent of the audience. Another 24 percent say they go only once a year. And 44 percent don't go to the movies at all. (Source: Newspaper Advertising Bureau survey, 1990.)

- Teenage moviegoers constituted 40 percent of the audience through the 1980s, but at the beginning of the 1990s the youth trend seemed to have crested. Older audience members began to attend movie theaters in increasing numbers as themes of films turned to subjects that interested them. (Source: Motion Picture Association of America, 1990.)

- The top three Broadway musicals (*Cats, Phantom of the Opera,* and *Les Miserables*) together grossed $1.5 million a week during the 1990–1991 season. (Source: *The New York Times*, 1990.)

vision rights to *Scarlett*, the sequel to *Gone with the Wind*, were quickly purchased, despite lukewarm critical reception.

Political Pressure. Parents frequently organize to bring pressure against the producers of entertainment they consider harmful to children. When producers of entertainment offend a segment of their audience, the consequences may be public demonstrations. A New York theater was emptied by bomb threats at the opening of a play perceived by Cuban refugee groups as pro-Castro. Gay rights groups have picketed films they see as homophobic, and women's groups boycott films that they feel demean women.

THE MUSIC RECORDING INDUSTRY

Despite the strong link of popular music to the medium of radio, it is a disservice to popular music to study it only as a subsidiary of the broadcasting business. Today, recorded music is heard in elevators, airports, dentists' offices, and the ears of joggers running through the park. Songwriting today is closely linked with the film industry, with many major hit songs being written to fit the needs of the movie soundtrack. As reflected in the popularity of the Grammy Awards show, music has come into its own as a major entertainment medium.

Development of the Music Recording Industry

Could Thomas Edison ever have imagined in 1877, when he built the first recording device in his Menlo Park, New Jersey, laboratories, that the legacy of his

Thomas Edison working on the development of his recording device.

inventive mind would be compact discs, MTV, the GM-Delco auto sound system, Dolby theater stereo, and the Sony Walkman? Certainly John Philip Sousa, the March King, realized by 1906 that recording devices would change the way people enjoyed music. He proclaimed that the day would come when nobody would sing or play the piano because it was easier just to listen to a professional perform on a recording.[1]

In the early days of recorded music, the bulky "Victrola" took up one corner of the living room and became a center of family entertainment. Later it was supplanted by suitcase-like portable equipment with a phonograph in the bottom half and the speaker in the top. The inexpensive portable phonograph made it possible for young people to buy records for playing in their own rooms. This development expanded the market for records, and the sound-recording revolution was under way.

Bell Improves on Edison's Invention. The Edison Speaking Phonograph Company was formed in 1878, just a year after Edison invented his machine, by a group of businessmen that included one of Alexander Graham Bell's relatives. Demonstrations of the marvelous new machine were held in theaters, concert halls, and tents at county fairs.[2]

There were no "practical applications" for the machine, however, since nobody had yet produced information to be played on it. Edison was preoccupied with his work on the electric light, so it was up to Bell's family to continue development of the concept of recording and playing back sound. As the work of the Bell group progressed, Edison's interest was rekindled, and both parties poured their separate energies into perfecting the phonograph.

Still, the new invention was viewed mainly as a novelty, with early phonographs being set up in rows at carnivals and penny arcades so that people could hear recordings at a nickel a play. Each machine held one tune, and so listeners moved from machine to machine with their nickels if they wanted to hear several numbers.

By 1900, however, the home phonograph came on the market with the familiar configuration of a turntable on a box, a tone arm, and an amplifying horn—the device made familiar by Victrola's "His master's voice" logo with the attentive little dog. The device was "acoustical," meaning that it involved no electric power. The turntable was run by a spring that had to be hand-wound.

Early Recordings. Edison's recordings were cut into wax cylinders in so-called hill-and-dale grooves, and his system was adopted by the preeminent Columbia Phonograph Record Company. Emil Berliner, who also worked in New Jersey, where many sound recording innovations arose, developed disc recordings with "zig-zag lateral-cut grooves." Berliner formed the National Gramaphone Company to market disc players, and in 1901 he was the founder of the Victor Talking Machine Company, a forerunner of RCA Records.

Consumers had to choose between the cylinder and the disc, and gradually they moved toward the easy-to-handle though breakable shellac discs. Edison continued to stick by his cylinder, even after Columbia saw which way the market was heading and dropped the cylinder. Thus he closed himself out of the market he had created.

It is interesting to note parenthetically that the concept of "dual technologies" battling it out in the marketplace is one we discussed before in the chapter on television, with CBS and NBC stubbornly pushing different color television systems. Similarly, incompatible Beta and VHS formats confounded consumers in the early years of videocassette recordings. The introduction of compact discs, discussed later in this chapter, was a rare instance of the industry achieving consensus before introducing a new technology.

By the 1920s, music was pressed on both sides of the Victor discs, the prices of recordings came down, and the public clamored for popular music.

Radio and Records. After the original patents on recording machines elapsed during the 1920s, production mushroomed and records became the most popular form of home entertainment. But a competitor loomed on the horizon: radio. When radio replaced records as the preferred form of home entertainment, records had to adapt. Reluctantly at first, but then quickly in order to keep pace with the new technology, the recording industry changed over from *acoustical* (mechanical amplification) recordings and playback systems to *electric* systems that were compatible with radio. (Again, we can see parallels today, as the industry gears up for the switch to "digital" information that brings new fidelity to recordings of both aural and visual information.)

Because not everybody could afford electric playback equipment for their homes, in the 1930s companies began to introduce jukeboxes for playing records in public places such as bars and restaurants. For a nickel a play, the huge Wurlitzer next to the door would put on quite a show: the light tubes bubbled with color, the moving arm selected the records, and the full range of the sound spectrum

Wurlitzer jukeboxes were the ultimate in delivery of music to be enjoyed in public places.

boomed from the huge speakers. Even after personal, portable phonographs became the vogue, jukeboxes continued to be popular because they livened up public places.

As radio increasingly became the outlet for delivering recorded music to the public, musicians became alarmed because their livelihoods were in jeopardy. At one time the radio networks maintained studio bands to provide theme music for the shows. The live "Big Band" variety shows were among the most popular programs on the air. But radio soon discovered that it could dispense with the live musicians and use recordings over and over again. The American Federation of Musicians demanded restrictions on the use of recorded music, but neither the recording companies nor the radio networks and stations were willing to agree. In 1942, the union went on strike and forbade its musicians to make recordings.

The musicians' strike came at a time when World War II created a need for solidarity. As the strike dragged into its second year, President Franklin D. Roosevelt issued a plea for the musicians to return in order to help the nation's morale. But union leader James C. Petrillo was adamant. He demanded recording royalties that would compensate musicians for work lost because of jukeboxes and the use of recorded music on the radio. Eventually the recording companies were forced to comply.

One of the casualties of the strike was the Big Band era. But one of the benefits was the tradition of donations of free music by local unions for nonprofit community events, paid for by funds from the musicians' recording royalties.

ASCAP and BMI License Use of Music. The American Society of Composers, Authors, and Publishers (ASCAP) began collecting fees for the playing of its members' music in 1914, before the advent of radio. In the early 1940s, when some radio stations began to play recorded music all day as the main part of their programming, ASCAP doubled its fees. Many radio stations refused to pay the higher price, even though it meant not playing the works of ASCAP artists. That created the climate for a rival licensing organization, and Broadcast Music, Incorporated

Jitterbugging to music from the jukebox in 1940.

(BMI) was formed for the sole purpose of developing new artists to provide music "product" for the radio industry. ASCAP became the licenser of "old" artists and BMI developed the "new." By the 1950s BMI had become such a dominant force in licensing music for radio play that its near-monopoly status was investigated by Congress.

Ever-Improving Technology. In addition to the effects of the strike, the recording industry was dealt two other economic blows. The Great Depression that began in 1929 meant that records became an unaffordable luxury for many people. Then World War II in the first half of the 1940s made it impossible to get the materials necessary to make records or to manufacture phonographs.

Despite these setbacks, the producers continued to improve the technology. In 1948, Columbia Records introduced the 33⅓ revolutions per minute "long-play" record (as opposed to the industry standard of 78 rpm). The vinyl discs were unbreakable and had 23 minutes of information on each side. Albums of 78 rpm records had consisted of several discs, meaning the program had to be interrupted periodically so that records could be turned over or dropped onto the turntable. Now it was possible to put on one record an album with several songs by one artist or a complete symphony. At the same time, the small 45 rpm disc was introduced, primarily for selling single recordings of hit songs to young people, who played them on portable machines they kept in their own bedrooms and hauled around to parties—the beginning of a concept we now take for granted: that every teenager and college student needs a personal recorded music system.

At about the same time, "hi-fidelity" equipment that approximated studio or concert-hall sound was being introduced. In 1958, a decade after the introduction of the long-play album, stereophonic records with two separate channels recorded in the same groove appeared on the market. It was almost another decade before multichannel tape cassettes appeared, and just about another decade passed before compact discs were introduced.

Thus each decade brought a quantum jump in the quality of sound reproduction and the convenience of using the product. Sound recording, perhaps more than any other information industry, seems to have been able to capture consumers' interest with continuous development of its technology.

When the compact disc, or CD, was introduced in 1983, the $1000 pricetag for a player suggested that it was not aimed at the ordinary consumer. However, the quality and flexibility of the system helped build a market, and the price came down in just a few years.

The format was established as a world standard, meaning any disc can be played on any player. Each digitally encoded disc is less than five inches in diameter, and the information on it is read by a laser beam rather than a needle. There is no contact between disc and player, eliminating wear, damage, and distortion. In addition to unparalleled sound reproduction, it offers the listener random song selection—a distinct advantage over both tape and phonograph records.

Three years after their introduction, only 2 percent of American homes owned CD players.[3] But in the 1990s, the CD is becoming the reigning system for music reproduction. The switch from phonograph records to CDs has meant a shot in the arm for the classical music branch of the industry as collectors decide to replace their worn records with CDs.

Auto companies still install mostly cassette players in their sound systems, but the availability of CD players in luxury cars is another signal that they are the system of the future—technology tends to "trickle down" from products aimed at the wealthy to those intended for the mass audience.

The Impact of Popular Music

Sound recording encompasses many categories of information, including not only specialized types of music such as classical, folk, and jazz, but the spoken word as well. "Talking books" are a means for the blind to enjoy literature. Some people use records or tapes to learn languages, hear poetry recited, receive religious inspiration, or develop such business-related skills as listening, speaking, and motivating others. The televised Grammy Awards sponsored by the National Academy of Recording Arts & Sciences take a few minutes to honor excellence in these special categories.

But popular music cannot merely be lumped in with other forms of information because it is pervasive in American and world culture. While it is often transmitted in other media, especially radio and television, it is also piped into public places, from the supermarket to the airport terminal and the doctor's office, as "background" and mood-setter. It is part of the live entertainment scene, it provides the context for films, and it follows us to the streets, to beaches, and on public transportation, when individuals carrying portable equipment inflict their personal choice of music on others.

The Selling of Music Videos. Are video recordings of artists performing their musical numbers a consumer product in themselves, or are they merely promotions for the sound recordings—and often the movies—from which the songs are

Music mirrors society and sometimes reflects social problems. Rap singer Ice-T's lyrics for "Cop Killer" were criticized by some as causing unrest and disrespect for authority. Others argued that the music sent a powerful message about repression in the inner city.

taken? Are the video music channels really nothing more than wall-to-wall advertising, as some critics have charged?

Rock groups made videotapes of their work as early as the 1970s, mainly as a way of showing themselves to recording companies and agents. With the appearance of MTV in 1981, music videos were prepared as programming material. In 1984, MTV's companion cable outlet, VH-1, was introduced to cater to older viewers who wanted the soft rock and music they grew up with, but not the heavy metal sounds that sometimes throb on MTV.

Throughout the 1980s, advertisements on broadcast and cable television began to look more like music videos, and videos began to look more like advertisements. Not surprisingly, the same directors were being called on to produce both music videos and ads. The style that binds the two together is a nervous, quick cutting of images matched to the beat of the music.

Music videos can catapult some artists from oblivion to popularity overnight, and the new format was hailed by some in the record industry as the ticket to fame for new talent. But other artists, especially those who are established, have top records without exposure through videos.

Videos have helped record sales, but they have not caused a stampede to the video stores for videocassette versions. Sales of music videos for home use have been limited because of quickly changing tastes and the relatively high cost of a video album.

The music video helps promote not only the album, tape, or disc from which it is taken, but movies as well. Film producers now publicize the content of upcoming movies through trade channels and invite composers and artists to submit songs that might fit the theme. At the same time, the hits of yesteryear are reexamined by the film producers to see what "golden oldies" might help capture the mood of the movie's period. Either the original artists or new musicians are given the opportunity to freshen the song and fit it to the requirements of the motion picture.

It should be no surprise, then, that the longest section of the credits at the end of a film usually is devoted to the names of the musicians. The ads and the videos got people interested in seeing *Dirty Dancing*, and then the experience of seeing the film got people interested in buying the album. So successful was the whole interrelated marketing scheme that a second album was produced from songs not used in the first, and a short-lived television series based on the title of the film (and little else) was attempted. Tom Cruise's film career—from *Risky Business* through *Top Gun*, *Cocktail*, and *Rain Man*—may have been boosted by the mutual effect of music videos promoting the movies and Cruise's impish good looks decorating the videos, which helped the songs to hit the number 1 spot in the Top 40 lists.

The fusion of advertising and music has been guaranteed by superstars such as Michael Jackson and Madonna who sometimes make two versions of some of their songs: one for Pepsi and one for MTV.

Evolution of the Parental Advisory Label. The concern among parents and authority figures about the effects of contemporary music ebbs and flows. In the mid-1980s a group of congressional wives headed by Tipper Gore, wife of the senator from Tennessee, formed the Parents Music Resource Center and announced a drive to spur Congress to do something about references in rock lyrics to sex and drugs. The move drew the support of religious groups and passing

> ## INDUSTRY
>
> # The Return of the "Single"
>
> In the 1930s and 1940s, the "single" record with one hit tune (plus a second song on the "flip side") was the backbone of the recorded music industry. In the 1950s the long-playing record made albums of music more practical: Previously, several singles had to be stacked on a player, with interruptions each time a new record dropped into place. By the 1970s, single records accounted for only a small fraction of sales, with the cassette album, later joined by the compact disc, accounting for the bulk of profits.
>
> But in 1990 the single recording began a comeback, this time in cassette format. Over 45 million single cassettes were sold that year. While sales of cassette albums showed little growth over the previous years, singles took off as the booming new area of recorded music. (And music videos, although they sold only about 4 million units, had an even faster growth rate.) Clearly the recording industry's hope for continued success lies in producing innovative formats that capture the interest of consumers.
>
> *Source:* Record Industry Association of America figures.

attention from the media, but it withered as a national issue when Senator Gore became a presidential candidate and his wife's efforts took a back seat to other concerns. Nonetheless, bills calling for mandatory labeling of record albums with explicit lyrics were introduced before the legislatures of 19 states.

As in other media industries, there is a trade association representing the U.S. sound recording industry: the Recording Industry Association of America (RIAA). While it polices pirating of records and protects the creative rights of its members, it has no code like the movie industry's rating system or the broadcasting industry's self-imposed standards. In fact, despite the occasional outcry about the content of song lyrics, the industry has never felt so threatened that it has had to protect itself with a set of self-regulations prohibiting certain subject matter, words, or phrases.

In 1985, however, the RIAA did reach an agreement with parental groups that called for record companies to put warning labels on albums with potentially objectionable material. Wording and placement of the labels was left to the discretion of the record companies. In 1990 the industry agreed on a uniform warning label carrying the words "Parental Advisory—Explicit Lyrics," and a standard placement of the black-and-white label in the lower right-hand corner of record packaging. The use of the label is voluntary, with the artists and their record companies given the decision of what to warn parents about. The National PTA and Tipper Gore's group gave their approval, and 16 of 19 states withdrew their labeling bills, satisfied that the industry move was sufficient.

The Industry Protects Itself

We saw in the case of the pressures for record-labeling that the music business, like any other industry, protects and promotes itself in order to succeed. It also develops marketing tools to extend its influence.

INSIGHT
Urban Nuisance: Consumer as Producer

Radios and tape decks are personal equipment, but when the owner hoists his "boom box" on his shoulder, turns up the volume, and walks down Main Street, he becomes not only a consumer but a producer . . . of sounds that may annoy others on the street. As a result, some cities have passed ordinances that prohibit musical "noise pollution." Questioned about the individual's right to listen to music, legislators suggest that earphones can be used by the listener. The trouble is, some municipalities earlier passed laws against using earphone-type radios and tape players on the street because they may render pedestrians deaf to horns, sirens, and other warning devices.

In New Brunswick, New Jersey, as part of an urban renewal project, speakers were installed along the main shopping street to entertain shoppers with music played by the local radio station. The "service" annoyed many people who already get enough unrequested music in elevators and shopping centers. And it only caused the "boom box" specialists to turn their volume up higher. So the downtown music speakers were turned off, except for two weeks in December when they play Christmas carols.

Charting Success. Just as ratings spell success for television shows, the recording industry lives by the "charts" prepared by three weekly publications—*Billboard, Cash Box,* and *Radio & Records.* The latter depends on reports from radio stations regarding frequency of airplay, while the other two depend more heavily on reports of sales from retailers. *Billboard's* "Hot 100" chart, probably the most quoted in the industry, is noted for the concept of the song that places "with a bullet," meaning that its rise on the charts has been rapid and suggests a hit in the making.

All of the charts, along with the weekly Top 40 countdown shows on radio, are susceptible to manipulation by the overenthusiastic reporting of deejays and retailers who feel that a new song has the makings of a hit. The "Payola" scandal of 1959 revealed that some disc jockies were taking payments to give extra airplay to certain songs to help guarantee their success. The industry's self-monitoring has made the practice less blatant, but with the stakes so high, record promoters find myriad ways to make it worthwhile for stations and deejays to help the process of making a record into a hit.

Battling Piracy. The record industry is concerned that profits are being drained off by unauthorized copies and bogus editions of the work of musical artists. The loss is estimated at $300 million or more every year. The problem is so great that the industry divides it into three categories:

Counterfeiting is the unauthorized duplication of the sound and packaging of the original recording in an attempt to dupe the consumers who think they are buying the real thing, often at a discount.

Piracy is the unauthorized duplication of sound for the purpose of packaging it differently from the original version in order to offer consumers what appears to be a different product, one on which the pirates pay no royalties.

Bootlegging is the unauthorized recording of a performance as it is being broadcast or performed live, for the purpose of offering consumers an "underground" recording of their favorite artists in concert.

Congress passed the Sound Recording Act in 1971 to give copyright protection to recordings and provide criminal penalties for infringement. Revisions were passed in 1974 and 1978, and in 1982 the much stronger Piracy and Counterfeiting Amendments became effective. First-time offenders can get up to five years in prison and fines of $250,000. The RIAA has a full-time antipiracy unit operating nationwide to work with law enforcement agencies.

THE FILM INDUSTRY

Since before the first feature film, *The Great Train Robbery* in 1903, movies have existed mainly to provide the entertainment of escape, thrills, unexpected sights and sounds, and daring behavior.

Film is also an important documentary medium. We have only drawings of Napoleon and still photographs of Abraham Lincoln—but we have General Douglas MacArthur in the Philippines on film, John F. Kennedy's inauguration and funeral on film, and film records of the Beatles' first appearance in the United States with lines of policemen trying to restrain mobs of ecstatic fans.

Film can be literature in its own right, or it can be a way of representing and recording written literature so that it is more accessible to a mass audience. *Gone with the Wind* is more than just one of the most-read novels of all time in the English language; it is also one of the most-seen movies. Dubbed or subtitled, the film transcends English and becomes a memorable visual experience for audiences around the world.

Development of the Film Industry

Although work on capturing the moving image began in Europe, once again it was the tinkering of America's Thomas Edison that advanced commercial use of the new medium.

Experimenting with the Moving Image. In 1839, Daguerre's copper plate photography had begun the drive to reproduce the same image the eye can see. By 1870 projection of still pictures was fascinating audiences. During the 1870s, inventors were working on the problem of how to project several still pictures taken less than a second apart so that the illusion of motion was created. The most famous example was Eadweard Muybridge's 24-camera sequence of still pictures of a running horse, showing that at a certain point the horse had all four feet off the ground at the same time.

Edison and his assistants came up with the idea of creating motion pictures by using a long roll of film and pulling it through a projector with the aid of sprocket holes and a mechanical claw. Each still picture was flashed on the screen, then an opaque disc covered the aperture momentarily and the next still shot was pulled into place. A phenomenon known as "persistence of vision"—the eye retaining the image even as it is changed—gave the illusion of fluid action on the screen.

The first films produced by Edison in the 1890s for his new "kinetoscope" machine were less than three minutes long and made for projection in "peep show" devices into which one viewer at a time could look. This device provided experiences such as seeing an exotic dancer at a carnival tent. In the 1890s, kinetoscope parlors were opened in major cities for the purpose of projecting the images for a small group of people to watch simultaneously.

By the middle of the decade, the Lumiere brothers in Paris were producing movies for projection to larger audiences. The early Edison and Lumiere movies used hand-drawn images rather than photographs. Edison, working in the "Black Maria," his tarpaper-covered building that could be rotated to follow the sun as needed for light, moved beyond the kinetoscope and developed the Vitascope projector for showing photographic images.

Still the movies were only a minute long, and they amounted to little more than vignettes or moments that documented a baby being fed, a train arriving, tourists viewing a monument, firefighters dashing to put out a fire, a circus strongman, a tapdancer, or, in another famous first—a prolonged kiss.

Frenchman George Melies was one of the first to tell a story with film. His *Voyage to the Moon* was as astounding to the audience of 1896 as *Star Wars* pictures were more recently, although his special effects were all theatrical illusions recorded by a single camera. Melies pioneered the development of a "film language," using optical effects such as the fade, dissolves, and cuts in the action to signify the passage of time.

In 1903, Edwin S. Porter's *The Great Train Robbery* moved film storytelling along with editing techniques that included "cross-cutting," so that the audience's point of view could shift back and forth between the exterior shot of the train arriving and the interior shot of the station waiting room. Movies began to be more than just an amusing collection of visual surprises. They began to convey emotion, tension, suspense, and other dramatic values.

Accompanied by a Piano: The Silents. Once filmmakers began telling stories, it became apparent that the sounds of the projector and the audience detracted from the quieter moments in the film. The answer was to have a pianist playing Mozart, Chopin, or Tin Pan Alley to complement the action on the screen.

D. W. Griffith envisioned a full orchestra accompanying the sweep and the large-screen majesty of his *Birth of a Nation* in 1915. The first great epic, it featured flashbacks, large crowd scenes, and highlighting of themes. These effects were achieved through quick-cut editing from sweeping views to close-up reaction shots. An inherently racist film with its sympathetic view of the Ku Klux Klan, it nevertheless is still acknowledged as a masterpiece of cinema.

Griffith next produced *Intolerance*, a picture of incredibly sweeping spectacles that interwove four stories of man's inhumanity to man. It was so visually and thematically complex that it confused audiences of the time, but still engages students of film storytelling. Griffith's films employ elements that are familiar to us today but were ahead of his own time, when he was largely misunderstood. After his brief glory, Griffith was unable to find financing for his films. He was supplanted by those who used film to make people laugh and forget their cares.

The lessons of Edison's early one-minute films were not lost on later producers: People love to laugh at the idiosyncracies of life. Mack Sennett learned his craft working for D. W. Griffith, but he applied what he knew in a totally different way. Working for the Keystone Film Company, he created a group of silly policemen, the "Keystone Kops," who became the prototype for film comedies that kept audiences laughing. At the same time, another Keystone staple was the "Little Tramp" character created by Charlie Chaplin. Both Sennett's and Chaplin's char-

A battle scene from "Birth of a Nation."

acters were filmed at the silent film speed of 18 frames per second and were projected at the sound speed of 24 frames per second, resulting in the herky-jerky movement that made the hijinks even more hilarious.

The period of 1915 until the advent of the talkies in 1927 was the heyday of film comedy. Buster Keaton, "The Great Stone Face," brought perpetually frozen expressions to his confrontations with modern machinery. Laurel and Hardy were two hapless souls who always managed to get into an impossible predicament and then make it worse with their bumbling antics. The audience of working-class immigrants could empathize with these situations, and their amusement at the unrestrained chaos depicted on the screen brought them temporary relief from their everyday problems and frustrations.

The movies did not come of age, however, until the newly emerging film studios added sound to the visual montage. Throughout the 1920s, inventors worked to match sound recording technology to film projection. There were earlier full-length sound movies, but 1927's *The Jazz Singer* starring Al Jolson was the event that captured movie audiences. Soon they came to expect realistic synchronized sound, and the era of the silent movies accompanied by the live pianist was over.

Studios and Their Stars. In the 1930s, the studios became big business operations, and each organized a stable of stars, directors, and technicians to turn out films in quantity to meet the growing demand for movies. Because there was no television and no home air-conditioning, moviegoers happily trooped off to the "refrigerated" cinemas with regularity. Local movie houses were able to change

ECONOMICS

Dividing Up the Production Costs

The editors of the *International Motion Picture Almanac* estimate that the production budget for the typical motion picture is divided as follows:

Cost of the story, script	5%
Production and direction costs	5%
Set, props, and other physical properties	35%
Stars and cast	20%
Studio overhead	20%
Income taxes	5%
Contingency fund	10%

Source: Richard Gertner, ed., *International Motion Picture Almanac—1988* (New York: Quigley Publishing Company, Inc., 1988), p. 32A.

---

their bill three times a week and many people saw every feature that played at the neighborhood cinema.

Each studio had its leading ladies, its dashing men, its comics, its heavies, and its character actors. Rudolph Valentino, Douglas Fairbanks, Lillian Gish, Mary Pickford, Charlie Chaplin, and Laurel and Hardy made the transition from the silents to the talkies. Ginger Rogers and Fred Astaire, James Cagney, Bing Crosby, Clark Gable, William Powell, and Myrna Loy gained stardom in the early talkies and dominated picture-making for the next two decades.

The businesslike studios realized that while the titillating fare of the early years helped to attract an audience, clean and wholesome fare would be more likely to build and hold an audience. They formed a self-regulating commission, the Motion Picture Producers and Distributors Association, and established a rigid self-censorship system that prohibited depictions of sexual conduct and unrestrained violence. (Self-regulation will be discussed later in this section when we look at the movie rating system.)

INSIGHT

25 Films Designated as "National Treasures"

Congress passed the National Film Preservation Act in 1988 and decreed that 25 films should be designated by vote of several leading film organizations as "national treasures," and that additional films should be named in succeeding years. All such films must, by law, be preserved for posterity, and exhibitors must notify audiences if the films have been cut, colorized, or otherwise altered.

The oldest film on the initial list is D. W. Griffith's *Intolerance*, from 1916; the most recent is *Star Wars*, the 1977 movie directed by George Lucas. Many of the films are not familiar to modern audiences. Among the better known are *Casablanca, Citizen Kane, Gone with the Wind, High Noon, Singin' in the Rain, Snow White and the Seven Dwarfs, Sunset Boulevard,* and *The Wizard of Oz.*

The United States Library of Congress is the official repository of the cinematic treasures.

During this "clean" era, America's film industry created its most enduring classics. In the period of just a few years, Hollywood gave the world *Gone with the Wind* (1939), *Citizen Kane* (1940), and *Casablanca* (1942). Each was different: *Gone with the Wind* brought epic historical fiction to the screen, *Citizen Kane* was Orson Welles's riveting psychoprofile of an American business tycoon modeled after the newspaper publisher William Randolph Hearst, and *Casablanca* was the quintessential detective tale, not to mention a smashingly intense love story.

Postwar TV Era Films. After World War II, television did what Marshall McLuhan said all new information technologies do: It gobbled up the information of previous technologies. With the advent of television in the late 1940s and early 1950s, people could see Lassie, John Wayne, Lucille Ball, and Bob Hope in their own homes—so why bother to go to the movies?

The studios were sent reeling. They tried to offer what television could not. The wider screens of CinemaScope and VistaVision projection systems presented spectacles and adventure stories of a breadth not imaginable on television. Audiences were asked to put on special cardboard and cellophane glasses to view three-dimensional horror and adventure movies in which scripts and direction were aimed at giving viewers the feeling that people and objects were coming off the screen and into their laps. Stereo sound enhanced the "you are there" feeling of such epics as the spectacular wide-screen version of Jules Verne's *Around the World in Eighty Days*. Even as the studios embraced these gimmicks, they cut back production and lost their control of Hollywood-style film production.

Orson Welles (center), in this still from "Citizen Kane," directed and starred in this classic story of the rise of a newspaper tycoon.

Eventually "adult" films from France, Italy, and Sweden—with their nudity, frank language, and easy morality—became the model for a new wave of world cinema. The studios reacted with trepidation, but independent American producers and a new generation of directors found eager audiences for the new films. Film schools gained in popularity, and graduates such as Martin Scorcese began to define the limits of the new cinema.

During the 1960s, with middle-aged, middle-class people comfortably at home watching television, the consumers of films shown in urban theaters became a younger and more educated audience. Critic Stanley Kauffman, in his 1966 essay titled "The Film Generation," described the new film audience as "the first generation that has matured in a culture in which film has been of accepted serious relevance."[4]

Films such as *The Graduate, Midnight Cowboy, Easy Rider,* and *2001: A Space Odyssey* were to the film generation what Hemingway and Fitzgerald novels were to the previous generation. Discussions in high school and college English classes were more likely to center on the film of *Women in Love* than the D. H. Lawrence novel from which it was adapted. Personal explorations in super-8 or 16-millimeter film replaced the quest of youth to create the Great American Novel.

A new generation of film critics emerged to satisfy the new audience's desire for serious discussion of films. Pauline Kael, Judith Crist, and Rex Reed were the most-read critics in magazines and newspapers. Crist and Reed also appeared on television news and talk shows with their reviews. Andrew Sarris in *The Village Voice* imported the "auteur theory" from France and argued that the director was the "author" of the contemporary film and that his or her contribution should be analyzed in the same manner that Faulkner or Steinbeck might be discussed.

Finding New Film Formulas

The movie business constantly changes, and often that change takes the form of returning to the formulas that have worked before. The period of enlightenment that began in the 1960s dissipated by the mid-1970s. The auteurs had their day and, like the novelists of the preceding generation, ran out of things to say, seemingly losing the power to offer fresh insights.

A two-tiered film production system emerged. Studios continue to be the major source of motion pictures, but many directors and producers choose to work as independents, outside the studio system. That way they have the artistic freedom to take the risk of making quality films that appeal to a smaller, more sophisticated audience. These producers release their films selectively in carefully chosen markets and hope that the reputation of a film will build until it finds its audience. A measure of the success of the independent producers is that many of the Oscar nominations and awards now go to their films; previously, the studios dominated the Oscar ceremony.

Most of the major studios now are owned by conglomerates, huge parent companies that keep their eyes on the bottom line of profit. Paramount became a division of Gulf & Western, United Artists was bought by Australia's Qintex Group, the Coca-Cola Company acquired Columbia Pictures (and later sold the studio to SONY of Japan), and Universal is owned by MCA, Inc., the record and music publishing company.

The new managements believe that the difference between profit and loss depends on whether the studio has at least one major "blockbuster" film each

INDUSTRY

Conglomerates Own the Big Film Studios

Studio	Owner	Country	Other Interests
Warner	Time Warner	U.S.	HBO, cable systems, magazines, records, books
20th Century Fox	News Corp.	Australia	Fox network, TV stations, books
Columbia Pictures	Sony	Japan	Consumer electronics, CBS Records
Universal	MCA	U.S.	MCA Records, Universal studio tours, movie theaters
Paramount	Paramount Communications	U.S.	Television stations, movie theaters, cable networks, books
Disney	Disney	U.S.	Theme parks, cable network
MGM/UA	Kirk Kerkorian	U.S.	None

Source: Company reports.

With the exception of MGM/UA, the top U.S. film studios are owned by international conglomerates that are involved in several areas of the entertainment business.

---

year. The blockbusters are "formula" films that are calculated to find the largest possible audience, and thus recoup the huge expenditures for their production. They usually require one or more major stars, whose fees per picture may be as high as $5 million and perhaps a share in the ownership of the picture. Big studios, following the market mentalities of their parent companies, spend lavishly to promote their blockbuster films and blanket the nation with hundreds or even thousands of prints of the new movie on a selected date in hopes of making a big splash in the news media.

A new generation of directors and producers, most notably George Lucas and Stephen Spielberg, showed they could deliver the blockbusters: *Jaws, Star Wars, Friday the Thirteenth, Raiders of the Lost Ark,* and *Animal House.* Each of these successful escapist entertainment films spawned numerous sequels and imitators, such as the seemingly never-ending *Porky's* and *Police Academy* series that cloned *Animal House*'s raw, rude, prankish, boys-will-be-boys humor.

Using our P↔I↔C model, Table 14.1 shows how the executives at a movie studio we'll call "Rival Pix" must be aware of the trends in films and the availability of literary properties from which next year's hit movie might come. They must find musical artists whose songs link with the information and with the audience's current tastes. Like editors who "assemble" a magazine from many parts, the movie producers try to assemble a package that is more than just a film: It must be a montage of images, ideas, sounds, and symbols that will attract the interest of consumers.

Shifting Industry Patterns. When the Coca-Cola Company took over Columbia Pictures in 1982, it appeared ready to do for the movies what it had done for the soft drink: increase market share by multiplying the available variations of the product.[5] But instead Columbia reduced the number of pictures it produced, pinning its hopes on making blockbusters like *Tootsie,* its big hit in 1983.

TABLE 14.1 PRODUCERS and CONSUMERS in the Evolution of a Major Motion Picture

Producers	Information	Consumers
Various movie studios	Movies that were big hits during the summer season	Executives at another studio—Rival Pix—who hope to have a hit with a similar film
Author of a best-seller that fits in the current genre of popular films	Best-selling novel	Executives at Rival who are looking for a new script
Script writer	Script for Rival Pix based on best-selling novel	Rival executives; author of book, who has approval rights
Top recording artists such as Whitney Houston, George Michael, Sting, Prince, the Beach Boys	Hit songs	Rival producer, who has advertised in *Billboard* for artists interested in writing and recording songs for a new movie
Director and recording studio hired by movie producers	Music video with movie theme performed by top artist—includes shots from the forthcoming film	MTV programmers who must decide if the video will be used, and if it gets special treatment
MTV	Special contest built around the movie	MTV viewers, who are the target audience for the movie
Advertising agency hired by Rival Pix	Ad campaign on MTV and other television watched by the target audience	Young moviegoers

Jack Valenti, the head of the Motion Picture Association of America (MPAA) described the industry in the 1980s as "embattled."[6] He put part of the blame on the videocassette recorder, which he labeled "a parasitic instrument" because it is used to record and show films in ways that deny income to their producers, both by individuals at home and international film pirates. Also to blame, he said, were the skyrocketing costs of making movies in Hollywood. Industry analysts blame Hollywood's woes, however, on the failure to produce the required big hits—the films that make consumers say "I've got to see that one!"

Despite the risks of filmmaking, the most successful media producers of the day are attracted to movies. Rupert Murdoch of News Corp. bought into 20th Century Fox and Metromedia Inc., a chain of broadcast stations, in hopes of building the Fox Network into television's fourth major outlet. Clearly Murdoch saw benefits in producing movies both for showing in theaters and on television.

Similarly, Atlanta media entrepreneur Ted Turner, owner of the Cable News Network who once bid to take over CBS, arranged a merger with MGM/UA, which gave him access to filmmaking resources that could supply his television outlets. Turner also raised the ire of many in the film world when he used computers to "colorize" old black-and-white movies from the MGM vaults in hopes that they would appeal to a new generation of television viewers who expect color entertainment. Directors such as Woody Allen, many of whose movies are shot in black and white to create an urban mood, are not amused at the idea of computer technicians daubing color over their artistic endeavors. Allen, testifying before congressional hearings on the matter, likened colorization to "improving" the Mona Lisa by colorizing her drab garment. The clash of artistry and business usually is resolved in favor of profits, since most artists do not retain control over the information they create once it is handed over to the producers and distributors.

In the 1940s, the federal government forbade "vertical integration"—meaning top-to-bottom ownership of an industry—under antitrust laws. The studios were forced to divest themselves of their theater chains. Now that the climate has changed, the studios are buying theaters again in order to control the distribution of their products to the consumer.

The studio-owned chains are developing theater videotape projection systems that will be of film quality, so that "film" can actually be shot as "videos," meaning that the technologies of movies and TV will have merged. General Electric, working with a Japanese company, has developed a system that simultaneously feeds movies electronically to several different theaters. No print has to be sent to the individual theater, and no "projectionist" is needed. The system also makes it possible to offer a variety of movies on different days of the week instead of locking the theaters into repeat showings of the same film for a week or more.

One film distributor has even experimented with using credit cards to buy movie tickets from a machine, eliminating the need for a box office. These are signs that the film industry has awakened to economic reality and has begun to think more like big business.

Censorship and Self-Regulation

America's first filmmaker, Thomas Edison, caused an uproar with one of his early short films, a recording of the gyrations of the bellydancer Little Egypt, the dancing sensation of the Chicago Exposition of 1893. Responding to complaints of lewdness, Edison censored his film by placing white lines over parts of the dancer's body, which only made the movie seem naughtier.

The Supreme Court's 1915 *Mutual Film Corporation* v. *Ohio* decision concerning the racial overtones of *Birth of a Nation* held that movies were a business not a form of communication, and were therefore not protected by the First Amendment. That ruling held until 1952, when the Supreme Court decided in the case of *The Miracle*—a film considered blasphemous by some because of its treatment of the virgin birth—that movies had become "a significant medium for the communication of ideas" and were entitled to First Amendment freedom of speech protection.

The Motion Picture Producers and Distributors Association of America (MPPDAA) was formed in 1922 because the industry feared that government regulation and censorship would be the result of growing public dismay over the morals of the movie community. The Fatty Arbuckle affair of 1921, which was played up in the newspapers, scandalized Americans with sordid details of the rape and murder of a starlet by a leading film comedian.

The MPPDAA was run by Will Hays, a former Republican leader, cabinet member, and elder in the Presbyterian church. The Hays Office was not so much a censorship mechanism as a means for policing the industry and convincing the public that Hollywood had standards, even if those standards consisted only of punishing evil or realizing repentance at the end of a 75-minute film.

> **INDUSTRY**
>
> ## U.S. Films Are International Hits
>
> For Christmas week of 1991, the biggest week of the year for filmgoing, the entertainment weekly *Variety* charted the top-grossing films in world capitals this way:
>
> *Hot Shots!*, a comedy spoofing the American military, was number 1 in Amsterdam, Brussels, Copenhagen, Germany, Helsinki, and Zurich.
>
> *The Addams Family* was tops in Australia and Britain. *Terminator 2: Judgment Day* held the lead in Madrid, *Robin Hood: Prince of Thieves* was Italy's favorite film, and in Tokyo audiences flocked to *Cape Fear*.
>
> The only world capitals where locally made non-American films topped the charts were Paris and Stockholm—and in both those cities Warner Brothers' *The Rescuers Down Under* came in a close second.
>
> Source: *Variety*, Jan. 2, 1992, p. 71.

The MPPDAA's informal lists of "no-no's" published in the 1920s were replaced by a Production Code in 1930 requiring, among other things, that "no picture shall be produced which will lower the moral standards of those who see it" and that "the sympathy of the audience shall never be thrown to the side of crime, evil or sin." Several words were forbidden (although "damn" was allowed in Rhett Butler's famous exit line in *Gone with the Wind*). Deep kisses, shots of brothels, the sound of toilets flushing, and couples sleeping in the same bed were some of the many items prohibited by the code.

Industry measures did not satisfy some groups, and the bishops of the American Roman Catholic Church founded the Legion of Decency in 1933 to rate films *Unobjectionable for all*, *Objectionable in part*, and *Condemned*—the last meaning that Catholics were not permitted to see the picture. The ratings were available in every parish and were displayed prominently in local libraries.

To avoid offending audiences, most of the movies produced in the 1930s through the 1950s were squeaky clean. But as we saw earlier, competition from television put pressure on the industry to produce films that were "adult" enough to lure people away from the home screen and back into the theaters.

Supreme Court decisions also changed the climate of opinion. *Roth* v. *United States* in 1957 protected ideas and expressions having "even the slightest redeeming social importance." *Miller* v. *California* in 1973 set up three tests to determine whether a work was obscene:

1. Whether the average person, applying contemporary community standards, would find that the work, taken as a whole, appeals to the prurient interest;
2. Whether the work depicts in a patently offensive way conduct that is specifically defined by state law prohibiting it; and,
3. Whether the work, taken as a whole, lacks serious literary, artistic, political, or scientific value.

The Supreme Court decisions did spell out the situations under which a work could be found obscene and thus removed from circulation. That might have appeared to be a victory for the censors, but the wording had the effect of making censorship very difficult. Works had to be judged "as a whole," meaning that one nude scene could not render a serious film obscene. In subsequent rulings, the Court held that community standards need not mean just the standards of the people living in a particular town where a film is shown; the community could be construed to mean a large area, a subgroup of society that seeks certain types of information, or even the "moviegoing community." In its *Pope* v. *Illinois* ruling in 1987, however, the Court ruled in a 5-4 decision that the standards of a "reasonable person" were to be followed by juries rather than "community standards."

The industry, represented by Jack Valenti as head of the MPAA (which succeeded the MPPDAA), feared, however, that state and local censors would find ways to interpret the decisions to permit encoding of stiffer local standards. Valenti convinced the film producers that they needed an effective form of self-regulation to protect against censorship.

The Voluntary Ratings System. Jack Valenti always refers to the MPAA mechanism set up in 1968 as the *"voluntary* movie rating system" to emphasize that the industry rates its own products as a guide for parents who want to control what kinds of films their children may see.[7] Valenti's stress on the word *voluntary* is intended to remind the public that the industry doesn't think it should be controlled by government codes or regulations. It also acknowledges that films are rated by various religious groups. (The Catholic Legion of Decency system has been replaced by another system publicized in diocesan newspapers to warn parents if films are morally objectionable.)

The film rating system that has functioned successfully in the United States for more than 20 years is sponsored not only by the MPAA but also by the theater owners' organization and the importers' and distributors' organization, making it an industry system rather than just the producers' system. The decisions of the Classification and Rating Administration that decides on the film ratings, which is headed by Professor Richard D. Heffner of Rutgers University, cannot be overruled by Valenti or the MPAA.

The members of the Rating Board are a diverse group of citizens. The only requirement is that they be parents, because the purpose of the rating system is to provide information enabling parents to make judgments on movies they want their children to see or not to see.

The original G, M, R, and X ratings have been modified during the run of the system. Because many parents thought "M," meaning mature, signified that a movie was only for adults, the category was changed to PG for "parental guidance." In 1984 PG-13 was added to indicate the recommended age level of 13 for material deemed not requiring an R rating, but still requiring maturity. In the early years films with nudity, simulated sex acts, and harsh language were likely to get the X rating, but now they usually can qualify for an R.

The X rating, indicating material of an unusually explicit nature, was changed in 1990 to NC-17, meaning "no children under 17 years of age admitted." The change was made because the "X" rating had been misappropriated by pornographers, who changed it to "XXX"—not to warn parents but simply to promote the salaciousness of their material.

The current MPAA ratings categories are as follows:

G—All ages admitted; general audiences

PG—Parental guidance suggested; for mature audiences

PG-13—Parents are strongly cautioned to give special guidance to children under 13

R—Restricted; children under 17 must be accompanied by a parent or other adult

NC-17—No children under 17 admitted

The Rating Board members are not supposed to exercise their personal judgment on the merits of a movie. Instead they follow guidelines that help them determine the age groups for which the film may be considered suitable. The use of certain language, the depiction of nudity, excessive violence, and discussion or depiction of various behaviors virtually automatically move a film toward a certain rating. The rating is decided by a majority vote of the board.

Getting a movie rated is not a one-shot process. The producer submits a print, learns what the rating will be, and has the option of cutting parts of scenes that will get the film a more acceptable rating. Many films have been negotiated down from an X to an R, or from an R to PG-13 by resubmitting the product with the necessary cuts.

Pedro Almodovar's *Tie Me Up! Tie Me Down!*, which contained racy bathtub and bedroom scenes, was well received by the critics. But its producers contend that it was given an X (the debate preceded the NC-17 designation) because it was made by an obscure independent artist rather than a big studio. The movie was released without the rating, which is an option open to the producer.

While artists and critics debated the use of the NC-17 rating in 1990, parents were more exercised over the awarding of a PG rating to the film *Teen-age Mutant Ninja Turtles*, which was wildly popular with subteens. Because no blood was spilled, the movie did not trip the code's violence alert. But the karate kicks and rowdy behavior of the characters were readily imitated by the older children, while younger children cowered in fear over the frenzy and the menacing behavior on screen. Many parents complained that they had not been sufficiently warned and that the film should have been rated at least PG-13.

The Economics of Film

The era of blockbuster movies changed movie distribution patterns. The cost of making films has increased astronomically, so fewer are produced. With fewer movies to show, theaters must play the same film for several weeks. People no longer go to the movies two or three times a week. In fact, many go only once or twice a year.

The once-a-year movie audience is most likely to show up at one of two times, according to the annual "box office barometer" published by *Variety* in its Show Business Annual edition.[8] If they don't come between Memorial Day and Labor Day, then they're most likely to make their annual trek to a movie theater during Christmas week.

The summer bulge in film attendance is so pronounced—twice the number attending compared with the winter months, and three times the attendance during the lean fall season—that Hollywood has taken to gearing the release of major films to catch the wave in June and try to ride it through August. The studio that does not have a summer blockbuster must hope to have a December hit to capture the huge Christmas week crowds. Another reason for the December release date

ECONOMICS

The Top-Grossing Films of All Time

Eleven films have earned more than $200 million at the box office. The figures, expressed here in millions, are not adjusted for inflation, which means that perennial favorites like *Gone with the Wind* and *The Wizard of Oz* are not on the list. The figures are for domestic distribution only.

E.T.	(Universal, 1982) $360[a]
Star Wars	(Fox, 1977) $322.7
Home Alone	(Fox, 1990) $281.5
Return of the Jedi	(Fox, 1983) $263.7
Batman	(WB, 1989) $251.2
Raiders of the Lost Ark	(Par, 1981) $242.4
Beverly Hills Cop	(Par, 1984) $234.8
The Empire Strikes Back	(Fox, 1980) $223.1
Ghost	(Par, 1990) $217.4
Ghostbusters	(Col, 1984) $214.1
Terminator 2	(TriStar, 1991) $204.3

[a] *Estimated.*
Source: *Variety*, Jan. 6, 1992, p. 7.

may be to make the film eligible for an Academy Award, which could add to its successful run in the spring.

The *Star Wars* and *Animal House* copies of the mid-1980s were aimed at capitalizing on the huge audience of young people attending movies, but by 1990, a new trend was being felt: the aging of the audience. The MPAA estimates that the number of over-40 moviegoers is approaching the number of under-20 patrons, and today producers are gearing as many films to adults as to young people.[9] As the president of Universal Pictures analyzed it:

> The percentage of teenagers who go to the movies is as high as ever. It's just that there are fewer [teenagers]. And there are a lot more people over 40. . . . The philosophy of most studios over the last decade was to make movies for people between the ages of 15 and 35. Now we can try to get two audiences into *Dragnet*. . . . We can make *Dragnet* for the teens who want to see Tom Hanks and Dan Akroyd and the older audience that remembers the old *Dragnet* series [on TV].[10]

Pretests and Advisers Aid Decision-Making. The cost of making a movie has gotten so high—and the cost of promoting a $30 million film can run another $10 million—that the studios are understandably nervous about whether consumers will like the product. So, like the manufacturers of toothpaste and soap, they conduct surveys to pretest their films.

Audiences representing the demographics of the filmgoing public are selected at random in public places. After the film is screened for them, each individual fills out a multiple-choice form rating the actors and indicating which scenes were liked most and liked least. Some audience members are asked to participate in focus interview sessions that try to get at their underlying reasons for liking or not liking characters and scenes.

As a result, films today are being reedited, and sometimes new scenes are shot to compensate for criticisms or confusion on the part of consumers. The ending of *Fatal Attraction*, for example, was reshot because adult audiences thought Glenn

> ### INDUSTRY
> ## Exhibitors Face Hard Times
>
> The owners of movie theaters, mostly medium to large chains, face an even tighter squeeze than the studios that produce the films. The studios can make a profit if they have one or two blockbuster hits each year. The exhibitors need movies with "legs"—the ability to build an audience and bring in revenue over several weeks of showings.
>
> Because the distributors require up to 12-week bookings on the films that they expect to do best, exhibitors lose on films that fail to maintain a steady flow of moviegoers over several weeks. Moreover, in the pressure to get the best films for their chains, the exhibitors engage in bidding wars. The result is that they may give the studios as much as 90 percent of the gross receipts during the first week or two when attendance is highest.
>
> The trend is toward larger chains of theaters, with more than half the theaters today owned by the top 10 chains. The biggest problem for the large chains is overbuilding of multitheater complexes at a time when rising ticket prices are hurting attendance. The use of on-screen advertising as a revenue source is being tried by the theater-owners, but it has met with resistance from consumers who don't expect ads as part of the show they paid for.
>
> *Source:* Brian Bremner, "Coming Soon to a Theater Near You: Recession," *Business Week*, Dec. 3, 1990, pp. 127–128.

Close's character should be punished more strongly. The opening scenes of *Mannequin* were reedited and tightened because young viewers felt that the film dragged.

Because of the importance of cable and videocassettes as a secondary outlet for films after the initial theater showings, producers are using an important new technician on the movie set: the video adviser. The video adviser has two primary concerns: frame composition and lighting. Since the television screen is not as wide as the one in a movie theater, the video adviser notes when action is too far to one side or another and suggests reshooting or a second version for video. Dimly lighted scenes that are effective when shown on a high-density theater system may be thoroughly muddy on the home screen unless the video adviser suggests additional illumination. Sound also comes in for scrutiny. Most theaters are equipped with state-of-the-art sound systems, while television sets have tiny speakers that can't handle a wide range of sound.[11]

The World Wants American Movies. Despite the ups and downs of Hollywood producers, America continues to dominate the world market for films. The United States captures 90 percent of the British film market, 70 to 80 percent in many other countries, and more than half the market even in a major film-producing country like France.[12] (Conversely, only one of France's top 10 films in a recent year was distributed in the United States.)

The films that do best abroad are not necessarily those that were the biggest hits in America. In fact, many movies make more money in Europe than they do at home. Movies that Americans consider B-grade and relegate to sleazy downtown cinemas or drive-ins outside of town (kung-fu bloodbaths, for example) get top play in the Far East.

> **INSIGHT**
>
> ## Films Project Canadian Image
>
> A special Oscar was presented in 1989 to honor Canada's National Film Board (NFB) for 50 years of achievement. The NFB has the unique responsibility of "interpreting Canada to Canadians and to other countries," according to the act of Parliament that created the film unit.
>
> The NFB has accomplished its task by giving innovative filmmakers free reign to experiment with animation and documentary techniques. They create information, but more important to the NFB concept, they express an outlook and a style that is different from the commercial products of Hollywood.
>
> The NFB film *If You Love This Planet*, which described the horrors of nuclear war and its effects on people, was seen by millions around the world and won the 1983 Oscar. (It was classified as propaganda by the U.S. Justice Department!)
>
> One of the reasons Canada's government decided to fund the NFB was that it felt a small country without a major film industry needed a special way to express itself. Ironically, many Hollywood studios today are shooting their films in Canada to take advantage of lower production costs and locations that can pass for U.S. cities and towns.

The purchase of 20th Century Fox in 1985 and United Artists and Columbia in 1989 by foreign companies signaled the beginning of a new perspective in the film business. While many films still will be produced with the U.S. market in mind, the international market is so important that financial support for a film often depends on predictions of how it will do abroad as well. In fact, the "sure deal" in Hollywood today is the film that is guaranteed a profit from foreign distribution, cable TV, and home video rights before the first customer even has a chance to see it in an American movie theater.

LIVE PERFORMANCE: THE AUDIENCE PARTICIPATES

Live performances of plays and concerts are different from other mass communication events. The producer of the information is producing at the same time the audience is consuming. Thus the audience can affect the production. To be sure, plays are scripted and rehearsed to proceed according to plan. Musicians know which numbers they intend to do, in what order, and in what style. But the presence of the live audience means that applause, laughter, silence, nervous coughing and sighing, or the ominous shuffling of feet can cause the performer to alter the performance.

Live music performances, from rock concerts to symphonies, have much in common with live theater when it comes to the role of the consumer. Obviously it takes much more of a commitment to purchase a ticket to a live performance, to show up, and to help the performer create the event than it does to sit passively in a chair at home and attend to previously packaged information.

Because of the extra work it takes on both sides of the stage, because of the extra risks of failure resulting from having to stage a performance anew each night,

> ### INSIGHT
> ## Is It Live, or Is It . . . ?
>
> The biggest controversy in the rock concert world in 1990 was the augmentation of "live" performances with taped music to which the artists "lip-sync" or mimic. Defenders say the practice is necessary to duplicate the sound and look of videos, in which a star may sing several parts simultaneously, all the while dancing without getting out of breath. Critics of the practice say that the audience is getting cheated. Several state legislatures have considered laws that would require concert promoters to reveal whether lip-sync is being used.
>
> The issue came to a head when the Grammy awarded to Milli Vanilli as the best new group of 1990 was taken away: The two stars hadn't even provided the real voices on their own recordings.

and because of the great cost of re-creating information again and again, live shows usually are far more expensive for the consumer than prerecorded entertainment. And because much more involvement is demanded of the audience member, the audience for live performance is much smaller than the audience for prerecorded material. But the cost and the effort are what can make the experience special, and therefore more rewarding, for the consumer.

The Development of American Theater

Theater is entwined with American history. The information that theater producers present to consumers tells us much about the values and interests of the people at each stage of the nation's development.

Theater was available almost as soon as the colonies were formed. But opposition to the theater was immediate, because "entertainments" violated the Puritan ethic that underlaid the very reasons for leaving Europe to come to the colonies. Among the 13 original colonies, only Virginia and Maryland did not, in reaction to the complaints of religious groups, enact legislation prohibiting the theater.[13]

Despite the bans on theater, traveling families of actors from England were given permission to perform in New York in the 1750s, and by the 1760s playhouses were opened in New York as well as Virginia. Patriotic plays were written and performed in the 1770s. One example is the popular *Battle of Bunker Hill* in 1776.[14] Following the American revolution, a frontier theater developed. Traveling companies played towns of every size, and riverboats carried theater companies to stops along the river.

Present-day visitors to the old mining towns of the West are surprised to find sumptuous opera houses built in the 1800s by mine owners who wanted to bring culture to the places where they were making their fortunes. Shakespeare was brought to Americans by their own great actors of the 1800s—Edwin Forrest and Edwin Booth, as well as Ira Aldridge, the first great black actor of the English-speaking theater.[15]

Minstrels, Vaudeville, and Burlesque

Nineteenth-century Americans of means and education hungered for culture in order to show that they were as civilized as Europeans. The new country also developed its own forms of popular theater to meet the needs of the ordinary working-class people.

Slaves on southern plantations devised entertainments for themselves that included humorous monologues, clog dances, shuffles, and songs for an entire troupe of performers.[16] In the 1840s, the format was appropriated by touring groups of whites who performed in blackface makeup. The most famous of the groups was Edwin Christy and the Christy Minstrels, who devised the traditional three-part format of the minstrel show, as well as the convention of seating the performers in a semicircle with a master of ceremonies called the interlocutor in the center.[17]

The minstrel shows presented black music and black humor in a nonthreatening way at the time of the nation's debate over slavery. They remained popular until as late as the 1940s, when social consciousness decreed that they were degrading to blacks. The minstrel shows had an effect on entertainments that were to follow, including the American musical comedy.

Vaudeville consisted of variety shows that included singers, dancers, comics, jugglers, and dog acts in a fast-moving show. The format flourished through the second half of the nineteenth century and up to the advent of movies. Originally vaudeville was attended mainly by men because many of the acts were tinged

George Burns and Gracie Allen began on the vaudeville stage, and then successfully made the transfer to television.

WHAT'S PLAYING AT THE APOLLO?

From billboards posted throughout Harlem, everyone knew who was performing [at the Apollo Theater] and when. These billboards seemed to be manufactured by the same marketing mavens who posted notices for the prize-fights at Madison Square Garden. Major figures' names were in giant type, lesser names in type not so large, and newcomers' names were printed small. The billboards lent Harlem a sense of community, of intimacy. And it made the Apollo an even more special place than one simply of top-flight entertainment. The Apollo united audience and performer in a way that I have never seen duplicated.

This excerpt from the autobiography of noted sociologist Irving Louis Horowitz captures a sense of the

culture of Harlem in the late 1930s, and the role of mass communication—the Apollo Opera house and billboards—in creating and maintaining that culture.
Source: Irving Louis Horowitz, *Daydreams and Nightmares: Reflections on a Harlem Childhood* (Jackson: University Press of Mississippi, 1990), pp. 22–23.

with double-entendres and vulgar gestures, but "wholesome bills of family entertainment" were presented by producers eager to appeal to a larger audience.

Burlesque, with its scantily clad girls and rowdy comics, definitely was not a family attraction. The original burlesque consisted of sketches that mocked familiar plays, even Shakespeare. From 1870 until 1900 the burlesque circuit spread through the country, and many vaudeville producers incorporated some of the elements of burlesque, especially the naughty ladies, into their shows. By the 1930s, burlesque was beginning to be synonymous with striptease artists performing in seedy theaters for audiences of men. Radio and movies had replaced live variety entertainment as the media suitable for families.

The American musical comedy grew out of a combination of the operettas imported from Europe—light stories that mixed songs with dialogue—and the turn-of-the-century musical revues staged by George M. Cohan and others that sometimes had a slim story line weaving together the singing and dancing. As we saw earlier, musical comedy was also influenced by the black culture.

Oscar Hammerstein II and Jerome Kern's *Show Boat* in 1927, based on the best-selling Edna Ferber novel of the previous year, hinted at the new era of musical theater to come by telling the story of many quintessentially American characters over a period of half a century. The great Gershwin musicals dominated the New York stage in the 1930s, culminating with the opening of *Porgy and Bess* in 1935, a classic that is performed by grand opera companies today. After World War II the Rogers and Hammerstein musicals created a national audience for Broadway-style musical theater.

Drama Reflects Social Concerns

The world's best-selling book of the nineteenth century—*Uncle Tom's Cabin*—also became the most-produced play in the United States for the second half of that century. At any one time hundreds of companies were performing the play across the United States. The black roles, played by whites in early productions, were stereotypes with which any white member of the audience could be comfortable.[18] The play fit into the then-popular genre called melodrama, with broadly drawn bad guys that the audience could hiss and boo, along with dashing young men and faint-hearted young ladies they could wave their hankies at. It was unsophisticated . . . but so were the poorly educated immigrants who watched it with great enjoyment.

In the 1921–1922 Broadway season, another enduring American hit appealed to the instincts of the "lowest common denominator" of consumers. *Abie's Irish Rose* began a career that would carry it through hundreds of productions across the nation and bring it to the eyes and ears of 11 million people.[19] *Abie's Irish Rose* concerned a Jewish boy who fell in love with an Irish girl. Again the characters, right down to their heavy ethnic accents, offered the stereotypes that popular audiences found appealing and amusing. The play was based on one of the most standard plot devices in dramatic history: the Romeo and Juliet love story. The 1950s hit musical *West Side Story* is, in effect, yet another telling of the familiar tale, albeit with much more artistry.

The Broadway musical was a phenomenon that reflected the needs for a newly affluent society to be entertained with escapist fare. *Oklahoma* in 1943 ushered in an era of more than 30 years when Americans plunked down expense account money or personal savings for a lavish night on the town guaranteed to "send them out whistling the hit tune."

Broadway's Influence

Broadway became the mainstream of American theater, giving the country a dozen or more big musical comedies each year, as well as straight comedies and serious drama. Theatergoers from all over the country either came to Broadway or waited for national touring companies to bring the Broadway hits to their cities. But as costs soared and other entertainments including television, sports, and popular music concerts drew audiences away, Broadway became known as "the fabulous invalid"—still fascinating a dwindling audience, but no longer the centerpiece for the American entertainment world.

Today Broadway produces only one or two big musical hits each year, and those are likely to have been developed in the London theater before producers take the gamble on the Great White Way. Nonetheless, Broadway is still the epitome of theater in America for most people. Its sheer energy powers American theater with a standard of polish, perfection, and pizzazz. Actors, playwrights, and producers don't feel they have really made it until they have had a Broadway success. Hollywood, whose problems in recent decades parallel those of Broadway,

"Cats" whose slogan is "Now . . . and forever" is an example of the long-running blockbuster Broadway musical that depends on stunning stage effects to dazzle the audience.

Chapter 14   Music, Movies, Theater   **431**

ECONOMICS

The Decline of Broadway

Broadway	Current Season	1990–1991 Season	1981–1982 Season
Shows playing last week	18	22	31
Total playing weeks to date	439	550	831
Theater occupancy last week	51.4%	62.9%	—
Theater occupancy to date	41.4%	52.4%	—
Paid attendance last week	167,122	185,661	196,445
(% of capacity last week)	(90.7%)	(86.4%)	
Total attendance to date	3,834,294	4,281,887	6,002,341
(% of capacity to date)	(85.0%)	(82.3%)	
Total receipts last week	$7,140,907	$7,432,625	$4,790,021
Season total receipts to date	$157,410,295	$158,489,589	$130,555,678
Average paid admission last week	$42.72	$40.03	$24.38
New productions to date	12	14	26
Road			
Shows reported last week	24	21	22
Total playing weeks to date	670	667	722
Total receipts last week	$10,135,375	$8,631,634	$3,785,711
Season total receipts to date	$296,535,498	$258,008,789	$138,056,848
Combined Totals			
Total playing weeks	1,109	1,217	1,553
Total receipts to date	$453,945,793	$416,498,378	$268,612,526

Source: Variety, Jan. 2, 1991, p. 95.

decrease in the number of Broadway shows contrasted with the previous year and 10 years earlier, for the final full week of the calendar year. The bright spot for Broadway-style shows is that the number of productions touring the country remains steady. Indeed, the income from former Broadway shows out on the road is double that earned on the Great White Way.

still looks east for stage hits that can be translated onto film for audiences that will never be able to make it to New York to see "what everybody is talking about."

The Role of Regional Theater

The Pulitzer Prize for drama was instituted to reward the most significant contribution to the American theater each year. The majority of the awards in recent

> **PRODUCER IS HIS OWN BEST CONSUMER**
>
> My own tastes happen to be in tune with what the public wants. I think that's the reason my batting average is so high, not because I've discovered some brilliant formula.
>
> Cameron Mackintosh, Broadway producer of *Cats, Phantom of the Opera, Les Miserables,* and *Miss Saigon*.
>
> *Source:* Mervyn Rothstein, "The Musical Is Money to His Ears," *The New York Times Sunday Magazine*, Dec. 9, 1990, p. 84.

years have gone not to original Broadway productions, but to works that originated in one of the country's 70 regional professional theaters.

The League of Regional Theaters (LORT for short) now provides more work for the members of Actors Equity than Broadway does.[20] The Louisville Actors' Theater, the Mark Taper Forum in Los Angeles, the Long Wharf Theater in New Haven, the Tyrone Guthrie in Minneapolis, the Crossroads Theatre in New Brunswick (New Jersey), and the Arena Stage in Washington are typical of the regional professional theaters that have sent productions to New York, and then to the rest of the country.

On Broadway, producers plunge millions into "make or break" productions that come and go in quick succession. But the regional professional theaters can nurture a play and its playwright until they are ready for a national debut. The works of today's most promising playwrights—David Mamet, Sam Shepard, Beth Henley, Wendy Wasserstein—appear first in LORT theaters, and later, perhaps, in New York.

LORT actors, directors, and staff are all paid professionals, not amateurs as in "community" theater. Community theater is an outlet for local talent, priced reasonably because of the unpaid volunteers, and readily accessible to all because it is located nearby, not in the urban cultural centers. A light comedy like Neil Simon's *The Sunshine Boys*, made popular first on Broadway and then in the film, is

Publicity stills for the play "Paul Robeson" give editors the opportunity to select the shot that they feel best captures the essence of the production. The work produced by the regional Crossroads theater played in New York and went on national tour.

typical of the type of play that ends up in a tent, barn, or high school auditorium, starring your dentist and the local librarian in the lead roles.

Dinner theaters and summer stock or "straw-hat" theaters give local, semi-professional, and emerging professional talent a chance to bring popular plays and musicals at reasonable prices to consumers who want to be guaranteed enjoyable entertainment with proven hits.

The Fragile Economy of Live Theater

The move to the suburbs and the increasing diversity in entertainment and recreation activities available to Americans spelled trouble for the theater. So, too, did an economy in which entertainment industry employees demanded and got increasingly higher wages, and a business environment in which every specialty in the world of theater was represented by a trade union.

As recently as the 1950s, Broadway theater tickets could be bought for a top price under $5. Today the hit shows cost $50 or more. A "night on the town" for two, including a good restaurant meal, can cost almost as much as a videocassette recorder or a color television set! Put in those terms, it is easy to see that Broadway has priced itself into a special category: the "once a year experience" for many couples, or the "expense account evening" for people doing business.

Just as Hollywood depends on the "blockbuster" film to keep the studios solvent, Broadway producers who invest $5 million or more in a show must use publicity and slick television advertising to build excitement about a new show. They also depend on marketing techniques that include preselling many seats to theater clubs and other organizations on a block basis. But unlike Hollywood, which can recoup some or all of its investment from a movie that plays in secondary locations for a short period and then has sufficient foreign sales, Broadway

INDUSTRY

Theaters Use Telemarketing

Until recently, theaters depended on advertising, reviews, and word of mouth to bring people into the theater. Lagging theater attendance in the face of competition from electronic entertainment convinced two New York producers that the old marketing methods no longer worked. They formed a telemarketing firm to stimulate consumers toward the theater.

For an annual membership fee of $75, theatergoers can forget the hassle of finding out which shows are available at what prices, and they won't have to stand in line at the box office for the hits. The "Advance Entertainment New York" service calls its patrons to advise them when a show is opening, when seats will be available, and whether it is possible to attend a preview performance. Tickets frequently are offered at a discount because producers of some shows are happy to build their audience using the telemarketing service.

Source: Louis Botto, "Passing Stages" column, *Playbill*, January, 1989, p. 20.

loses its entire investment if the reviews and early word of mouth are poor and the audiences fail to show up at the box office.

Broadway is a place for wealthy "angels" who invest in shows and risk it all on the whims of public favor. Dance companies, symphony orchestras, opera, and LORT theaters, on the other hand, are supported by grants from all levels of government and by patrons of the arts and community leaders. Those engaged in the not-for-profit theatrical entertainment sector typically draw approximately 60 percent of their income from the box office and seek the other 40 percent of "unearned income" from benefactors. Most cities and states have arts councils to make such grants, and the National Endowment for the Arts is also a large supporter of live performance.

Thus a minority of consumers create a special situation where not-for-profit producers need not depend on the majority of consumers if they can demonstrate that their performances enhance the cultural life of a city or region and provide a special service to society.

EXPANDING THE CONCEPT: SPORTS AND THEME PARKS

Some people might not be able to conceive of theater as an example of mass communication. After all, they are in the same room with the performer, and the performer speaks to them without a mediator. But the performer cannot really interact in a personal way with each audience member, and the performance is a message aimed by the playwright and the director not at an individual but at an audience—which is to say, at a mass public.

Once we understand the nature of mass communication—the one-to-many situation—it is not difficult to see that sporting events and theme parks really function as mass communication enterprises.

Sports as Theater

It can be an artificial distinction to separate commercial sports events from theatrical events. The same dynamic applies to both situations: An audience of consumers comes to be entertained and to see a winning performance. The home team's loss is analogous to the play or concert that fails to live up to expectations.

Most professional sports teams have added the trappings of theater to keep their consumers involved and interested. Thus we have not only the game, but halftime spectaculars, cheerleader/dancer squads, electronic scoreboards with computer graphics displays, fireworks when the home team scores, Old Timers' Day, Banner Day, T-Shirt Day, fan free-throw contests, prizes for the best tailgate picnic in the parking lot, and a rock star to sing the national anthem.

Even in the television booth, one member of the announcing team is assigned to do the straight play-by-play, but "color commentators" are hired to spark things during the dull moments by offering critiques and commentary . . . and adding a touch of show business to the proceedings.

The audience makes the same use of sporting events as it does of news. The events provide common identity with other members of the mass public, and they provide something to talk about with individuals we meet each day.

Theme Parks as Mass Communication Media

When we pack the family off to the Disney World or Universal Studios theme parks, we may conceive of the adventure as purely one of escape and entertainment. But leaving it at that oversimplifies the experience. We also sign ourselves on as recipients of mass communication messages.

At the Disney theme parks in Florida and California, we learn about our cultural heritage in Frontierland, we discover other cultures as we wander through the villages representing foreign countries, and we receive none-too-subtle information about the shape of the future as envisioned by corporate America when we tour the Epcot and Tomorrowland displays. When we visit the movie studios for their tours, we are treated to a vision of what America was and is, and we are given a heavily commercial message about the excitement of consuming a particular medium: film.

FUTURE FILE

✓ The ultimate media experience would be a film and music *environment* so realistic that consumers would feel transported in time and space. How could the latest technology be adapted to make a theater, your home entertainment center, or even your mass communication classroom into such a media experience—assuming that cost was no object!?

✓ Technological advances in film, music, and theater dazzle us so that we may not notice that nobody seems to have anything new to say. Would a moratorium on technology result in a renaissance of creative expression?

✓ Miniaturization has made it possible for people to hear symphonies in speakers worn over their ears and to watch films on tiny screens mounted on the backs of airplane seats. How close are we to electronic "chips" that can be placed in or near the brain for the purpose of receiving aural and visual information? What kinds of information would we want to have piped directly *into* our bodies? How would producers or entertainment products bill us for such services?

NOTES

1. Will Crutchfield, "Why Can't Johnny Play the Piano?" *The New York Times*, July 31, 1986, p. C-20.
2. The historical information in this section and the data about the recording industry are from the sourcebook *Inside the Recording Industry: An Introduction to America's Music Business*, copyright 1985 by the Recording Industry Association of America, Inc.

3. David E. Sanger, "Compact Discs: Audio Industry's New Hope," *The New York Times*, Jan. 11, 1986, p. 1.
4. Stanley Kauffman, *A World on Film: Criticism and Comment* (New York: Harper and Row, 1966).
5. Geraldine Fabrikant, "A Shift at Columbia Pictures," *The New York Times*, Nov. 11, 1985, p. D-1.
6. Peter W. Kaplan, "Are Movies a Fabulous Invalid Too?" *The New York Times*, May 5, 1985, Arts & Leisure section, p. 1.
7. Valenti's opinions in this section are based on a position paper, "The Voluntary Movie Rating System," by Jack Valenti, provided by the MPAA, and on personal correspondence with Richard D. Heffner, chairman of the Classification and Rating Administration.
8. "Box Office Barometer for 1985," *Variety*, Jan. 11, 1985, p. 9.
9. Wayne Walley, "Why Movies Are Booming," *Advertising Age*, Jan. 30, 1989, p. 80; Aljean Harmetz, "Funny Meant Money at the Movies in 1988," *The New York Times*, Jan. 17, 1989, p. C-15.
10. Aljean Harmetz, "The Figures Don't Lie: Hollywood's Audience Is Older and Pickier," *The New York Times*, March 7, 1988, p. C-13.
11. Hans Fantel, "Bringing Movies to the Video Screen," *The New York Times*, Feb. 24, 1986, p. C-14.
12. Richard W. Stevenson, "Hollywood Takes to the Global Stage," *The New York Times*, April 16, 1989, Business section, p. 1; R. Grenier, "When It Comes to Movies, the World Looks to America," *The New York Times*, Sept. 25, 1985, Arts & Leisure section, p. 27.
13. Hugh F. Rankin, *The Theater in Colonial America* (Chapel Hill: University of North Carolina Press, 1965), p. 7.
14. B. Donald Grose and O. Franklin Kenworthy, *A Mirror to Life: The History of the Western Theatre* (New York: Holt, Rinehart & Winston, 1985), pp. 476–479.
15. Grose and Kenworthy, pp. 476–477.
16. Emory Lewis, *Stages: The Fifty-Year Childhood of the American Theatre* (Englewood Cliffs, NJ: Prentice-Hall, 1969), p. 147.
17. Grose and Kenworthy, pp. 479–480.
18. Lewis, p. 148.
19. Howard Taubman, *The Making of the American Theatre* (New York: Coward McCann, 1965), p. 159.
20. A. Eisenberg, "LORT Contracts Pointed Up How Equity Is Not Just Broadway," *Variety*, Jan. 8, 1986, p. 225.

SUGGESTED READINGS

Allen, R. C., and D. Gomery, *Film History: Theory and Practice* (New York: Alfred A. Knopf, 1985).

Denisoff, R. S., *Solid Gold: The Popular Record Industry* (New Brunswick, NJ: Transaction, Inc., 1975).

Ellis, J. C., *A History of Film* (Englewood Cliffs, NJ: Prentice-Hall, 1979).

Grose, B. Donald, and O. Franklin Kenworthy, *A Mirror to Life: A History of Western Theatre* (New York: Holt, Rinehart & Winston, 1985).

Kindem, G. A., ed., *The American Movie Industry: The Business of Motion Pictures* (Carbondale: Southern Illinois University Press, 1982).

May, M., *Screening Out the Past: The Birth of Mass Culture and the Motion Picture Industry* (New York: Oxford University Press, 1980).

McCue, G., ed., *Music in American Society, 1776–1976: From Puritan Hymn to Synthesizer* (New Brunswick, NJ: Transaction, Inc., 1977).

Palmer, T., *All You Need Is Love: The Story of Popular Music* (New York: Viking, 1976).

Toll, Robert C., *The Entertainment Machine: American Show Business in the Twentieth Century* (New York: Oxford University Press, 1982).

PEOPLE OF COLOR IN MASS COMMUNICATION

MARILYN KERN-FOXWORTH

Marilyn Kern-Foxworth is an associate professor in the Department of Journalism at Texas A&M University. Her research focuses on the portrayal and employment of people of color in the mass media. In 1988 she was the recipient of the Pathfinder Award from the Institute of Public Relations—the first woman and the first person of color to receive the honor.

This is who I am not. I am not a crack addict. I am not a welfare mother. I am not illiterate. I am not a prostitute. I have never been in jail. My children are not in gangs. My husband doesn't beat me. My home is not a tenement. None of these things defines who I am, nor do they describe the other black people I've known and worked with and loved and befriended over these 40 years of my life. Nor does it describe most of black America, period. Yet in the eyes of the American news media, this is what black America is: poor, criminal, addicted and dysfunctional. Indeed, media coverage of black America is so one-sided, so imbalanced that the most victimized and hurting segment of the black community—a small segment, at best—is presented not as the exception but as the norm. It is an insidious practice, all the uglier for its blatancy.

Patricia Raybon[1]

Newsweek essayist Patricia Raybon's statement is typical of the reaction of many ethnic groups to the way they are presented in the mass media and of the perceptions that whites have of them as a result of that presentation. Such pejorative images will not be eliminated from the media until more nonwhites are hired in policymaking positions.

The mass media are among the most powerful and pervasive institutions in American society. Unfortunately, multiethnic groups and people of color are not fully integrated into the media industries. Yet progress, although slow, and in some cases minuscule, has been made since the issuance of the Kerner Commission Report in 1968 and the two reports issued subsequently by the United States Commission on Civil Rights ("Window Dressing on the Set: Women and Minorities in Television" and "Window Dressing on the Set: An Update," issued in 1977 and 1979).

Television

Anyone asked to cite accomplishments made by people of color in the mass media will readily make note of the phenomenal progress of Bill Cosby, Oprah Winfrey, Geraldo Rivera, and Arsenio Hall. For years "The Cosby Show" was ranked number 1; approximately 30 million viewers tuned in each week to see what the Huxtable family was doing. Advertisers paid a hefty $300,000 for each 30 seconds of commercial time for the privilege of touting their wares during this prime-time show.[2]

A year after the Oprah Winfrey Show became nationally syndicated, it became the country's top-ranked syndicated talk show, beating out Phil Donahue and Geraldo Rivera.[3] In 1989 *The Wall Street Journal* listed Winfrey as one of the 28 rising stars in the business world. Dubbed the richest woman on television, in 1989 she purchased a television and movie studio in Chicago and founded Harpo Productions, Inc., thus becoming the third woman and the only black woman in American history to own her own production company.[4]

Continued

Chapter 14   Music, Movies, Theater

Continued from page 438

Television talk show host Oprah Winfrey exemplifies people of color who have risen to the top of the communications industry.

Although it is easy to rattle off the names of four or five African-Americans who make lucrative salaries in television, it is not an easy task to do this for members of other racial groups. After Geraldo Rivera it is difficult to name another major Hispanic television personality. On a positive note, the California Chicano Media Association and other groups have been instrumental in placing more Hispanics in broadcasting positions.

A few television series have Asian characters. Native Americans appear rarely on television, usually in the news. A content analysis of newscasts from 1979 to 1982 by Television News Index and Abstracts showed that Native Americans made the news 44 times during the four-year span.[5]

Newspapers

On October 23, 1989, viewers were stunned as television showed the grisly scene of Charles and Carol Stuart who, while sitting in a car in Boston, had both suffered gunshot blasts from a lone assailant. Carol Stuart's murder became news around the world and Charles Stuart became the heroic survivor of a tragic attack. On December 28, the Boston police arrested William Bennett, a black male, as a suspect in the killings after he was identified by Charles Stuart as the man "most like" the alleged gunman.[6]

Racial tension erupted. Following the revelation that it was, in fact, Charles Stuart who had killed his wife and shot himself in an attempt to collect insurance money, Boston's two major daily newspapers were boycotted for their coverage of the murder. Protestors argued that media portrayals of multiethnic neighborhoods had lent credibility to Stuart's story. "The reason why Charles Stuart was able to do what he did was people believe the stereotypes in our community," said Tony Van Der Meer, an organizer of the Boston Boycott Committee. "The imagery was demeaning, it was racist."[7]

For decades African-Americans and other racial groups have objected to their portrayal in the mass media. In 1990, protestors picketed *The Dallas Morning News* and WFAA-TV every week for two months to denounce the use of photographs of a partially clothed African-American woman giving birth to illustrate a story about rising taxes used to support the county hospital. In addition to the news coverage's demeaning the woman, the protestors felt that it held blacks responsible for depleting county resources.

Such images will continue until more people of color are employed on American newspaper staffs. But change will be slow. Only 7.54 percent of newspaper personnel were multiethnic in 1988. The percentage edged up to 7.86—or 4500 of the 56,900 professionals working in the nation's newsrooms—according to a 1990 survey by the American Society of Newspaper Ed-

Continued

Continued from page 439

itors.[8] Few multiethnic people are in policy-making positions on newspaper staffs: 95 percent of all newsroom managers are white, and 54 percent of daily U.S. newspapers do not employ any people of color.[9]

The newspaper industry has been trying to find ways to make staffs more diverse, including job fairs, training programs, internships, mentoring programs, and guidebooks to assist newspapers in their recruiting efforts. Newspapers are aware that they must encourage more multiethnic students to pursue careers in journalism and must also help them secure jobs. To assist newspapers, San Francisco State University's journalism department has created the Center for Integration and Improvement of Journalism to recruit, train, and place minorities in newsrooms nationwide, and to sensitize reporters and media managers to the need for improved coverage of multiethnic groups.[10]

Magazines

Only a handful of people of color have been able to secure positions in the magazine publishing industry, particularly in editorial departments and advertising sales. Kathleen Andres of the University of Akron found that 2.2 percent of 374 employees responding to a demographic survey were multiethnic personnel: three African-Americans, four Hispanics, and one Asian.[11] Few students from multiethnic groups choose career paths in magazine publishing—only about two dozen a year, according to statistics compiled annually by the Association for Education in Journalism and Mass Communication.

Several reasons are given for the small numbers of nonwhites employed in the magazine industry: (1) recruitment is not a top priority for many firms, (2) younger members of multiethnic communities do not find role models to serve as mentors and to encourage them to choose magazine careers, (3) training for magazine work is not offered on many college campuses, and (4) the fact that relatively few magazines are published by multiethnics desensitizes students to career opportunities in magazine publishing.

In 1988 the only two African-Americans in major positions at general-circulation magazines were Marcia Ann Gillespie, executive editor of *MS.* and Audreen Ballard, executive editor of *Lear's*—both women's magazines. A factor contributing to this situation is that neither the Magazine Publishers Association (MPA) nor the Association of Business Publishers (ABP) has adopted official policies pertinent to increasing the number of multiethnic members on the staffs of magazines.[12]

Advertising

The portrayal and employment of blacks in advertising have been critically examined ever since a group of blacks became trademarks and symbols for companies during the 1930s and 1940s—Aunt Jemima being the most famous example. Today critics are scrutinizing more intensely than ever the social effects of advertising on racial groups.

Sparks ignited in 1990 when R. J. Reynolds announced an advertising campaign targeting blacks as smokers of "Uptown" cigarettes. Blacks were outspoken against the product, and the company abandoned the brand after spending $10 million to develop it.[13] Because of the abundance of billboard advertising for tobacco and alcoholic products, African-American communities in New York, Chicago, Detroit, Philadelphia, and Dallas began a campaign to whitewash billboards following the announcement of the Reynolds campaign. Hispanics contemplated the same actions.[14]

No one would argue with the fact that there are definitely more People of Color shown in commercials today than there were as recently as the 1970s. The question that needs to be

Continued

Continued from page 440

addressed today is: Are some advertising practices having a detrimental effect on multi-ethnic communities and, if so, what can be done to rectify the situation?

Mass Media Diversity and the Future

Turn on the television or radio, pick up a magazine or newspaper, and you are likely to see more People of Color than in past years. In fact, the line-up for the 1990 season had more African-Americans on prime-time television than ever before in the 50-year history of the medium. However, the participation of racial groups in American mass communication systems is not yet comparable with their representation in the population. This issue becomes critical as we move into the 21st century. By the year 2000, racial groups in America will comprise 30 percent of the American consumer market and will have total combined disposable income of $1 trillion annually. Media conglomerates must be prepared to communicate with a diverse population where multiethnic communities will be a majority of the subscribers, viewers, readers, listeners and consumers of mass communication information and entertainment. Without People of Color in positions of authority in the media, the images portrayed will continue to be stereotypical and obsolete. Mass communication institutions must encourage young people to pursue careers in the media, and they must offer moral and financial support to multiethnic media entrepreneurs. Only then will People of Color begin to achieve full participation in American society.

Notes

1. Patricia Raybon, "A Case of 'Severe Bias'," *Newsweek*, October 2, 1989, p. 11.
2. D. Narine, "Black TV and Movie Scriptwriters: The Write Stuff," *Ebony*, March, 1988, pp. 92–98.
3. Charles Whitaker, "Oprah Winfrey: The Most Talked-About TV Show Host," *Ebony*, March, 1987, pp. 38–44.
4. Andrew Feinberg, "The Richest Woman on TV? Oprah!" *TV Guide*, August 26, 1989, pp. 2–7.
5. J. P. Danky, M. E. Hady, and R. J. Morris, eds., *Native American Press in Wisconsin and the Nation* (Madison: University of Wisconsin Press, 1982).
6. Larry Martz, "The Boston Murder: Unraveling a Grisly Hoax," *Newsweek*, January 22, 1990, pp. 16–20.
7. Lori Stahl, "Pressing the Point: Minorities Protest News Media Images," *The Dallas Morning News*, October 18, 1990, p. 8J.
8. "ASNE Survey: Grim News on Minority Hiring," *NABJ Journal*, April 1990, p. 1.
9. David Lawrence, "Making Staff Diversity Top Priority," *Minorities in the Newspaper Business*, Spring 1990, p. 3.
10. Jon Funabiki, "Changing the Face of the Newsroom," *Minorities in the Newspaper Business*, Spring 1990, p. 4.
11. Marcia Ann Gillespie, "Where Are the Minorities in Publishing?" *Folio*, August 1988, pp. 19–20.
12. Gillespie, pp. 19–20.
13. Robyn Griggs, "RJR's 'Uptown' May be Down, But It's Not Out—Yet," *Adweek*, January 19, 1990, p. 4.
14. Robyn Griggs, "Tobacco, Alcohol's Foe: Black Ministers Target Ads," *Adweek*, March 12, 1990, p. 1; Ken Smikle, "Post No Bills: Whitewashing Brigades Take on Controversial Ads," *Emerge*, March 1990, pp. 25–26.

CHAPTER 15

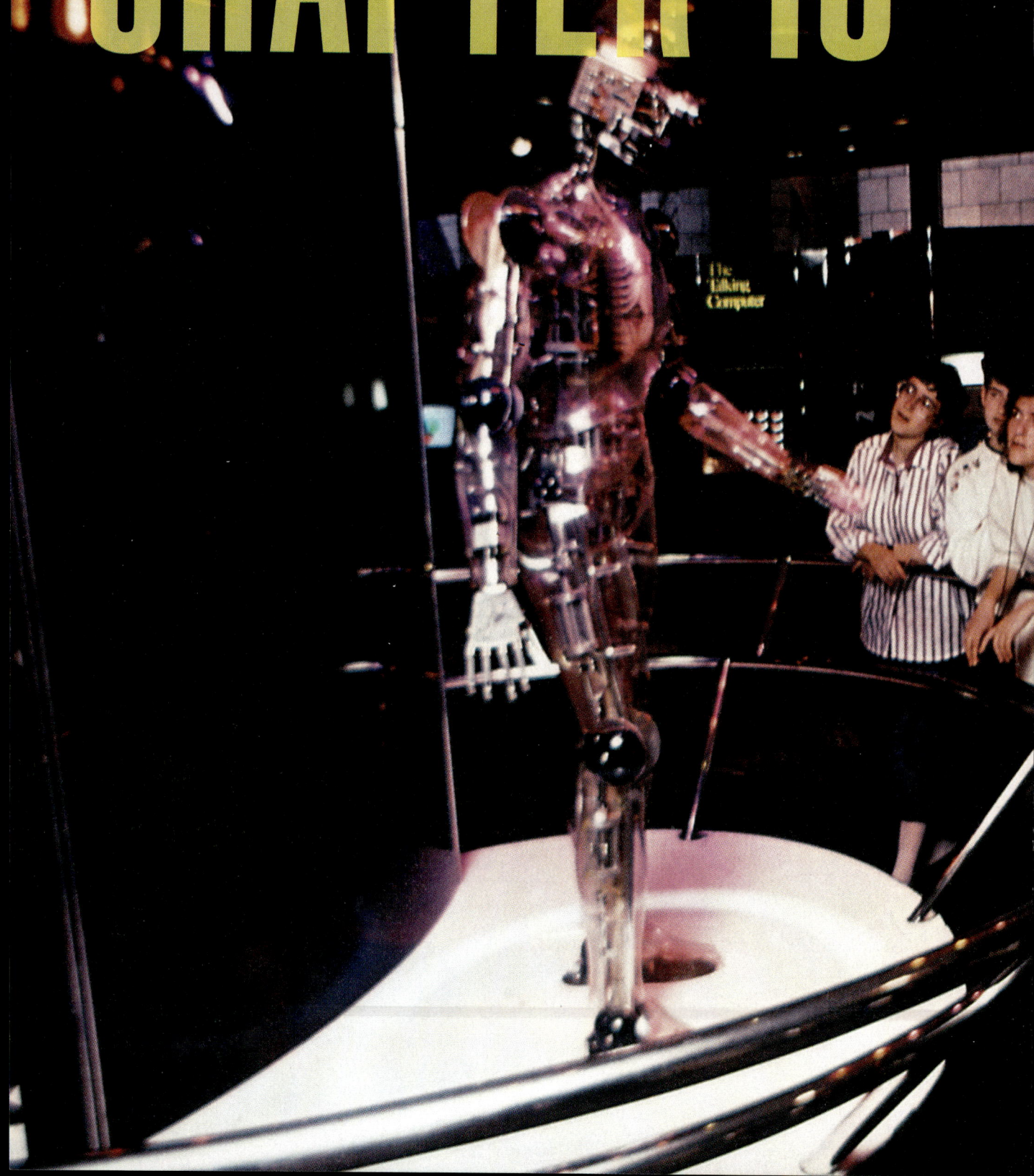

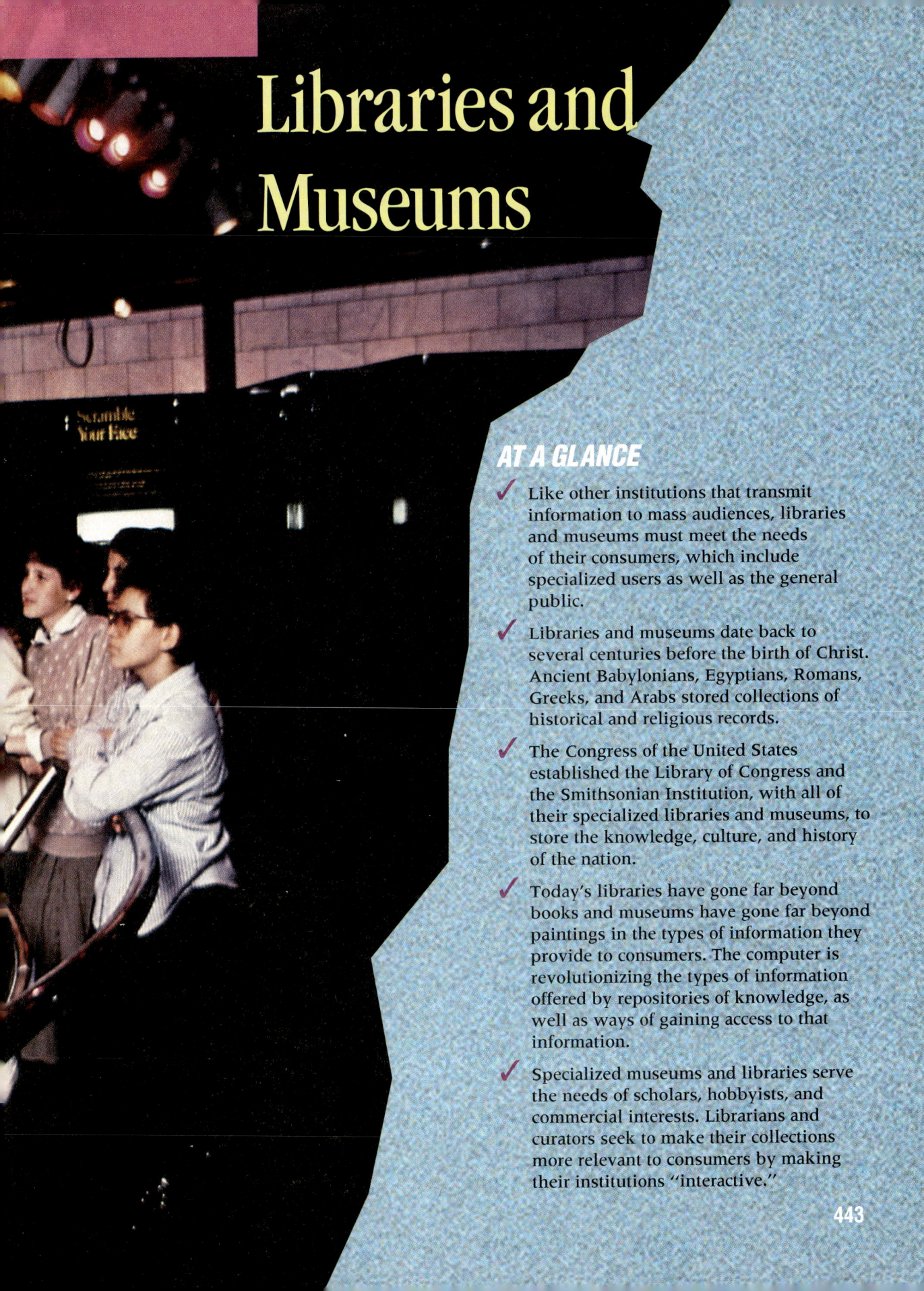

Libraries and Museums

AT A GLANCE

✓ Like other institutions that transmit information to mass audiences, libraries and museums must meet the needs of their consumers, which include specialized users as well as the general public.

✓ Libraries and museums date back to several centuries before the birth of Christ. Ancient Babylonians, Egyptians, Romans, Greeks, and Arabs stored collections of historical and religious records.

✓ The Congress of the United States established the Library of Congress and the Smithsonian Institution, with all of their specialized libraries and museums, to store the knowledge, culture, and history of the nation.

✓ Today's libraries have gone far beyond books and museums have gone far beyond paintings in the types of information they provide to consumers. The computer is revolutionizing the types of information offered by repositories of knowledge, as well as ways of gaining access to that information.

✓ Specialized museums and libraries serve the needs of scholars, hobbyists, and commercial interests. Librarians and curators seek to make their collections more relevant to consumers by making their institutions "interactive."

> I dreaded the assignment to visit the art museum because I figured it would be nothing but old paintings in gold frames. But, much to my surprise, I thoroughly enjoyed the videotape and the demonstration of Japanese paper-making arts and crafts.
>
> Student in Rutgers mass communication course

Museums no longer are dusty, musty repositories of dead and lifeless objects, and libraries have changed from the days when pursed-lipped guardians of silence went about hushing patrons. If they have kept up with the times, both institutions are lively centers of mass communication.

If you didn't already realize it, you will discover now that libraries and museums have a great deal in common with all the forms of mass communication we have discussed so far. That includes the requirement that they must understand and meet the information needs and behaviors of the consumers they serve in order to survive and thrive.

MORE THAN JUST REPOSITORIES

The information producers we have discussed so far are concerned primarily with the *selling* of information: providing products that they hope large numbers of consumers will *pay* to use or see. Libraries and museums differ from the media of mass communication in that they are usually supported by government or non-profit organizations as a benefit to the public. Their services may be provided at no cost, for a nominal fee, or through taxation. With the exception of the admission charge paid to certain museums, we think of access to the information stored in libraries and museums as a right of citizenship.

Libraries and museums deal with large numbers of people, but their consumers come in and use the facilities one by one, not as a mass audience. While libraries and museums try to cater to popular tastes, they have the special role of providing information to individuals who may have unique needs and interests. The university library is willing to store and maintain a book that may interest only one scholar in a lifetime. A museum with public displays also works behind the scenes with individual researchers whose interests may be esoteric and specialized.

Archive or Active Institution?

Many libraries and museums are charged by the groups that fund them—corporations, governments, universities, or wealthy benefactors—with an archival responsibility. That is, they are supposed to collect, organize, and store every available bit of information of interest within a certain realm of human knowledge. It is assumed that having all of this information saved for future use provides certain benefits, however abstract or minimal the importance may seem to the lay person.

The librarian in a metropolitan newspaper, for example, clips each item that appears in the publication and files it for possible future reference. The fact that most items are never sought out again is unimportant. The fact that any piece of historical background will be there if needed is what is important to reporters and editors who must research their stories under deadline pressure.

Chapter 15 Libraries and Museums

TABLE 15.1 Functions and Audiences Served by Libraries and Museums

Producers	Information	Consumers
Libraries		
General	Novels, reference works, nonfiction, biographies, periodicals, videos, records	General public
Research	Journals, reference works, periodicals, microfiches, databases, special collections	Professors, students, scientists
Corporate/special	Trade publications, technical books, business books, specialized databases	Employees, managers, research scientists
Museums		
Art	Classic paintings/sculpture, contemporary art, crafts, ethnic art	General public, artists, art historians, "The Art World," students, teachers
Historical	Artifacts, recreations of cultures, films and other records	General public, historians, students, teachers
Technical/science	Displays of tools, recreation of scientific developments, archives, demonstrations	General public, technicians, scientists, students, teachers
Corporate	Products of the past, portraits of founders, demonstrations of manufacturing techniques	General public, employees, corporate guests

Other institutions must prove their value, perhaps to overseers or elected officials, by ascertaining the interests of consumers, catering to them, and demonstrating certain levels of circulation or attendance in order to ensure continued funding. We'll see later in the chapter how these "active" libraries and museums with this pressure to "build traffic" use innovative measures to match their services with the interests and needs of the community.

Revisiting our P↔I↔C model, we can see that the jobs of the librarian and museum curator are the same, at least at a generic level, as the job of the editor—*selecting, organizing, and displaying information for the individual use of members of a mass audience.* Table 15.1 shows the many functions and audiences of specialized institutions. As we shall see, libraries and museums today produce information as well as store it. And, as with any other institutions of mass communication, they use advertising and public relations to attract audiences to special events, develop funding support, and inform consumers about the services they provide.

LIBRARIES

The forerunners of the library and museum may well have been the tombs of the pharaohs. Inside the crypts were stored artifacts associated with the dead ruler, many documenting his daily life as well as his triumphs as a leader. On the outside of the burial vaults, inscriptions told the stories of the ruler's life and times. Of course ordinary people never saw these artifacts. The contents of the tombs were

TIME CAPSULE

Libraries and Museums

2100 B.C.	First libraries established in ancient Babylonia.	1887	First library school established at Columbia University by Dewey.
300 B.C.	Alexandria, Egypt, establishes library for world scholars.	1893	World's Columbian Exhibition held in Chicago highlights history.
300 B.C.	First museum also established in Egypt.	1900	Hall of Fame at New York University honored famous Americans.
1653	First library in Colonies established in Boston.	1929	Museum of Modern Art established in New York City.
1732	First public lending library established in Philadelphia.	1937	National Gallery of Art established by Congress in Washington.
1759	British Museum opened in London.	1969	Exploratorium opens in San Francisco, pioneering hands-on science education.
1773	First museum in America opened in Charleston, South Carolina.	1970	National Library consortia develop cooperative information distribution networks.
1800	Library of Congress established in Washington, D.C.	1976	National Air and Space Museum, most popular in the world, opens in Washington.
1824	Franklin Institute of Science museum opened in Philadelphia.	1983	Library of Congress implements new electronic information systems and closes card catalog.
1836	National Library of Medicine established in Bethesda, Maryland.	1984	*Museum for a New Century* appears, advocating outreach, education, and collaboration.
1846	Smithsonian Institution established by Congress.	1990s	Proliferation of reference works using CD-ROM (compact disc) technology.
1870	Library of Congress required to store all books published in United States.		
1880	Metropolitan Museum of Art opened in New York City.		

supposed to accompany the deceased on the final journey instead of serving scholars who might come along centuries later.

Development of Libraries

Libraries developed concurrently with the invention of writing, for one of the purposes of writing was to make possible the storage of information.[1] The word *library* means "a place for books," but the first libraries in ancient Babylonia, in the twenty-first century B.C., consisted of clay tablets. The earliest Roman and Egyptian collections, containing inscriptions pertaining to historic and religious events, were kept on scrolls and parchments as well as tablets.

About 300 B.C., a library was established at Alexandria, Egypt, to gather a huge collection of documents and make them available to scholars who traveled

A nineteenth century German engraving reconstructs one of the halls in the great library at Alexandria, Egypt, founded at the beginning of the third century B.C.

from all over the ancient world. Libraries of the Roman Empire were "public" in the sense that anyone who could read had access to them. The Greeks as well as the Arabs housed book collections in permanent institutions.

Libraries were essentially private, restricted to the use of the learned classes, through the Dark Ages. But the invention of movable type in the fifteenth century stimulated a wider literacy and a desire for exposure to printed information. The first library in Europe was assembled at the Vatican. Great collections also were amassed at the Sorbonne in Paris, the British Museum in London, and Oxford University. The modern library—consisting of a reading room, stacks of shelves where volumes were kept, and an organizing system based on alphabetic coding—had emerged by the end of the Renaissance.

The first public library in the colonies was established in Boston in 1653, and the first library that permitted patrons to take books home was opened in Philadelphia in 1732. Andrew Carnegie urged the establishment of "free libraries" in every community to assist those who would improve their education and thus increase their chances of success in life. To this day, "Carnegie free libraries," established in part by funds from the steel magnate turned philanthropist, are found in many American communities.

The Library of Congress. The U.S. national library is the Library of Congress, established in Washington in 1800. Supported primarily by appropriations from Congress, it serves mainly as a reference library. An 1870 act requires that a copy of every book copyrighted in the United States be in the repository of the Library of Congress. The system developed there for coding the collection of books with a combination of letters and numbers to assist in their location is widely used as an alternative to the Dewey Decimal System (named for Melvil Dewey, who established the first library school at Columbia University in 1887).

The reading room of the Library of Congress.

The Expanding World of the Library

A 1987 Gallup study showed that 44 percent of the volumes purchased by those who *buy* books were fiction, while 40 percent were nonfiction. That finding contrasted with a similar study in 1983 showing that the balance tipped slightly in favor of nonfiction. But a 1987 study by the American Library Association showed that those who *borrow* books from libraries are much more likely to seek information to satisfy specific interests than they are to browse for reading material meant to be used in leisure time.[2]

Librarians note such trends when deciding which types of books to purchase. Faced with limited budgets and storage space, librarians must consult their usage data to determine whether to purchase two copies of each novel on the best-seller list, or to put more money into nonfiction books of interest to hobbyists, thereby forcing fiction readers to put requests on file and wait their turn. Librarians also have to decide whether a book is the best way to present information, or whether consumers would prefer a videotape on the subject of car repair, gardening, or flattening the tummy.

Librarians organize their collections by period, subject matter, utility to specialized researchers, interest to the general public, and usage patterns. The most heavily used categories, such as reference works and current popular literature, are placed near the entrance to the library to help patrons find what they want at once. Specialized collections of interest to scholars are tucked away in corners of higher or lower floors. Vast and bulky collections of periodicals more often than not are stored in the basement. Special display cases near the entrance to the library show off works of historical interest or items arranged around a seasonal theme to intrigue patrons as they enter the library.

Libraries are not subjected to regular criticism in the media, nor are they often the target of pickets. Nonetheless, reference librarians handle many requests that indicate gaps in the collection, and the circulation desk hears and records complaints about missing books, items perpetually in the bindery, and inability to get access to special collections. If the library's collection has few volumes about minorities, minor religions, or groups formed to defend sexual preference, a library or museum may find itself pressured by those special interest groups. Tactics include letter-writing, attending administrative meetings, demonstrations, or symbolic gestures such as book-burnings.

The head librarian, no less than the editor or broadcaster in the same community, knows that the consumer's needs and attitudes must be monitored constantly if the institution is to remain useful and successful in its mission.

Beyond Books. For most of their long history, libraries were almost exclusively paper-oriented. The works they stored were printed on paper. The catalog systems for finding those works also were stored on paper. Communication with patrons of the library was carried out on paper, starting with the personal library card. Today's library is growing increasingly less dependent on paper, partly because paper deteriorates and is costly to maintain, partly because it is bulky and takes thousands of square feet to store, and partly because people now are interested in information that is created and stored in other ways.

For decades now, libraries have been offering films for use by groups and phonograph recordings for the pleasure of individual patrons. Now the lending

The librarian's job is changing as the collection changes from mostly books to a wider range of materials that may even include video games.

service has been expanded by many libraries to include paintings, sculpture, and other prints or original works of art. In the 1980s, responding to the popularity of the neighborhood video store, a great number of public libraries stocked videocassettes, including instructional tapes and classic movies that aren't available in all stores.

Innovative libraries have expanded the list of items that can be borrowed to include toys, games, audiovisual equipment, computers, tools, sewing machines, and even pets. Services now offered by libraries may include literacy programs, materials for the blind, bilingual aids, and child care referral centers.[3] Not to be overlooked is the use of photocopiers and other duplicating machines, which is the sole reason some people set foot inside a public library.

Reference librarians have continued the tradition of providing answers to any question patrons might ask, even if only to settle a bet or satisfy curiosity. People who move into a new community and don't know where to find local services—be it a doctor, a veterinarian, or a plumber—often depend on the public library to help get them oriented.

Thousands of people each year who come to the great New York Public Library building on Fifth Avenue do so for the express task of tracing their family's lineage in the Genealogy Room. The library accommodates these patrons by providing sample "family trees" and offering the assistance of librarians who specialize in genealogical research.

Reaching Out. Urban libraries have provided branches to serve neighborhoods for more than a century, and research libraries at large universities also place books in reading rooms around the campus. To contend with urban sprawl and suburban development, many public libraries began bookmobile service in the 1950s, with a mobile selection of popular titles that came to set locations once every week or two.

More innovative libraries, realizing that use drops off in the summer, have managed to follow their patrons to the beach or the parks, setting up temporary libraries stocked with light vacation reading in community centers, parks, and recreation facilities, or even station wagons in beach communities.

One of the most popular locations for branch libraries today is in the suburban shopping mall. Reasoning that many people will not go out of their way to seek information or use the facilities of a library, the libraries moved to the high-traffic areas in the malls.

Senior citizen centers are becoming increasingly important places of communication and information-sharing as the population grows older. Many senior citizens are not willing or able to read for long periods, so librarians who make weekly visits to their centers bring audiovisual materials, pamphlets, or speakers to make receiving information easy and enjoyable. Story hours, once provided mainly in schools as a means of interesting children in books and libraries, today are equally popular at senior citizen centers.

Another place where a library may be located to meet the special needs of a captive audience is the jail or prison, where, in addition to escapist literature, the inmates may have an interest in legal books. Bus and railway stations are home to small libraries catering to commuters, who may want a novel to read or a self-help book to study on the way to work. The Readington, N.J., public library is the former train station—rail commuters there buy their monthly tickets by mail, so

> **INDUSTRY**
>
> ## Teenagers' Reading Habits
>
> Teenagers spend twice as much time with electronic media as with print media, according to a Gallup poll of 13- to 17-year-olds in 1987. Over half the teenagers sampled say they read less than their parents. The breakdown:
>
> | | |
> |---|---|
> | Viewing television | 2 hours, 24 minutes |
> | Listening to radio | 2 hours |
> | Reading books | 1 hour, 6 minutes |
> | Reading magazines | 24 minutes |
> | Reading newspapers | 18 minutes |
>
> The information habits of teenagers have implications for librarians who must select the media that appeal to the needs and interests of their patrons.
>
> *Source:* Leonard Wood, "Teenagers' Reading Habits," *Publishers Weekly,* July 29, 1988, p. 132.

the ticket window became the librarian's desk and the waiting room benches now are surrounded by stacks of books.

The Specialized Library. Just as we saw that there are general-interest magazines for everybody and special-interest magazines that target audiences with specific needs, the public library is only one type of institution. Your college library is a "special-interest" facility in that it probably doesn't offer many novels, cookbooks, and travel volumes for browsers, but it may have hundreds of books on Chinese history if your college has a Chinese department or there is a Far East scholar in the history department.

Corporate libraries can be quite extensive and can contain collections that go into great depth on some topics. A pharmaceutical company's library, for example, will carry many medical journals in addition to the lore of medical history. Most corporate libraries also have sections for books and other resources pertaining to marketing, accounting, and other business practices; research and development; and commercial law.

Government agencies also maintain their own collections of volumes they use on a regular basis. A specialized library at one Navy base in New England, for example, has a large collection of books about the Antarctic because the base is the staging area for the military's expeditions to that chilly climate. Several engineering books in the collection focus on the performance of machinery in sub-zero temperatures.

The specialized library is different from the public library in two very important respects. Its staff, unlike the many generalists at a public library, must be knowledgeable about the subject matter. It is not unusual for the librarian at a major government contractor to have a degree in engineering, business, or some other specialized field. Law librarians are at an advantage if they have a law degree.

The other difference has to do with the relationship of the library and its patrons. Purchasing decisions may be made by committees that include several representative consumers of information. Managers of a corporation or directors of a government agency may have annual budgets for the purchase and maintenance of books and materials on their behalf by the librarian.

NEXT: "ARTIFICIAL INTELLI-GENCE"

Advanced thinking about libraries tends to look toward a time when computerized knowledge systems will begin to interact directly with human beings by sharing, in one form or another, the use of natural language. This form of artificial intelligence depends upon building into the computer the power not merely to reason in an abstract way, but to analogize, absorb and use metaphorical links, and to suggest connections between patterns and ideas in the way that scientists do in their most creative moments. . . .

Source: Anthony Smith, "Books to Bytes: The Computer and the Library," *Gannett Center for Media Studies, Occasional Paper No. 7*, November 1988.

The Electronic Library. The first attempt by libraries to escape from under a mountain of paper began around World War II, when it became common to store back issues of newspapers and government documents on microfilm, thus vastly cutting down on the amount of storage space. The next development was the microfiche, which could reduce an entire telephone book to a dozen or fewer thin pieces of plastic on which images of the pages were stored in miniature.

Both microfilm and microfiche, while saving space, require machines to enlarge their images. Loading the machine and searching for the desired pages of information can be as laborious as turning the pages of a book, and eyestrain occurs after a half hour or so of work. Another machine may have to be used to print out desired copies, at a cost of 10 cents per page—if the one machine many libraries have is working and not being used by another patron. The "miniature image" systems provided more benefits to the library than to the consumer.

Today's library hums electronically with computer terminals that work 24 hours a day to keep track of information. While nobody doubts the value of keeping printed volumes for historic value, the preferred means of storing and finding information is electronic because of speed, flexibility, and ease of use.

Libraries first used computers for their own purposes, and many have been slow to make them available to patrons.[4] First, checking out a book was made into

The bulky old card catalog system has been rendered obsolete by computer databases that help patrons find anything in the library.

TECHNOLOGY

Computer Index Replaces Card Catalog

Many libraries have phased out the endless rows of wooden cases containing one locator card for each item in the collection. In their place is the indexing computer, where patrons can use a keyboard to call information up on the screen.

The CD-ROM (compact disc—read only memory) technology offers speedy access to information about the library. The "user-friendly" computer program guides the first-time patron with a set of questions that help locate the desired information.

Elsewhere in the library, CD-ROM technology may be used to provide a multimedia encyclopedia that includes pictures and sound as well as text. A student researching a paper on Shakespeare might select a disk that not only provides historical data, but also shows a picture of Richard Burton as Hamlet and a recording of Burton's rendition of the "To be or not to be" soliloquy.

Librarians envision the day when students will put questions in their home computers, connect with the library's computer, and wait for the information they want to appear on their screen.

---

an electronic transaction, using library cards coded with electronic strips identifying the user and book cards coded electronically to identify the volume. This way, the library could find where the book was more readily, and it could issue a recall to the person who was holding onto the book in order to provide it to the person who was requesting it. Eventually, many libraries made computer terminals available at the main desk to allow patrons to find out if a book was available in a branch library, if the book was in the bindery, or when the current user was due to return it. Some universities have wired their campuses so that students in dorms, fraternities, and other remote locations can extract the information they need from the library's central computer without leaving the comfort of their living units.

In the 1980s many libraries provided their patrons with terminals that duplicated the functions of the card catalog. But where the card catalog may require jostling other patrons to get at the desired drawer, then flipping endlessly through cards squeezed tightly in the tray, the computer allows for much quicker access to information about volumes in the collection. The "user-friendly" program in the computerized catalog walks the patron through the process of providing enough information (author? title? subject?) so that the computer can display the possible volumes of interest.

Personal computers now are provided by many libraries as a note-taking and information-organizing system for the patrons, or as a means of using software from a growing collection that may include games, vocabulary tests, sample college entrance examinations, tax preparation assistance, and language lessons. The 1987 American Library Association survey indicates that half of the libraries serving communities of more than 25,000 people now provide microcomputers for whatever use patrons might want to make of them.[5]

The most exciting innovation in library service is the availability of the computer database system that allows the patron to find, examine, and print out the information itself working entirely at a computer station. By feeding key phrases into the computer and requesting various types of search, the user can locate larger amounts of information much more quickly.

Undergraduates at many universities can now request discs on subjects such as American history or abnormal psychology, insert them into a computer, and conduct a search for the information needed to produce a term paper, thus saving endless walking from card catalog to the Reader's Guide to Periodical Literature to the stacks, and finally to the photocopying machines. Restricting lower-level students to the use of discs assures the library of keeping costs under control. Graduate students and faculty researchers who have research budgets registered with the library, however, are given passwords to use "on-line" database services that enable them to have access to hundreds of databases all over the world.

Libraries are just beginning to wrestle with the complexities of the electronic information age, not the least of which is the increasing cost. It is now possible for authors to update books electronically whenever they wish, thus confounding the concepts of "editions" and "copyright." Publishers may have to earn their profits by charging patrons for electronic access, since theoretically only one "copy" of a book would be necessary to make it available electronically to the entire world.

Planning the Library of the Future. A Harvard scholar writing for *Academe*, the bulletin of the American Association of University Professors, noted that during the 1980s, campus researchers were so busy learning how to use their personal computers that they neglected to work with librarians to ensure that library computer systems met the needs of scholars: "The usefulness of the facility depends in part upon the information within it, but *also* upon how the on-line system was designed to interact with the personal microcomputer systems that have become the basic tools of scholarly work."[6] Clearly, consumers must be included on library planning committees when decisions are made about the configuration and the services libraries provide in the future.

French President François Mitterand has announced plans for a new 17-acre library in Paris, set to open in the mid-1990s, that will house works created since 1945 in an all-electronic library. It may even use robots to patrol the stacks, relieving patrons of the task of searching for materials.[7]

Libraries now are studying the electronic copying and storing of documents the institutions already hold. Storage on microfilm and microfiche has several drawbacks: the materials get brittle and dry, the surface becomes scratched to the point where the information is illegible, copies can get lost or stolen, and only one user at a time can take advantage of the materials. "Imaging"—storing documents so they can be displayed on a computer screen—would solve all of those problems, because the discs on which the information is stored are never physically touched and are made to last virtually forever.

MUSEUMS: ARCHIVES AND ACTIVITY

Like an iceberg, only one-eighth of which floats above the surface of the water, museums display a fraction of their collections to the public in a combination of permanent installations and changing exhibits. The vast majority of what they have collected remains in storage rooms awaiting future use. Any piece of infor-

> **THE CAMPUS LIBRARY OF THE FUTURE**
>
> The research library of the near future will place less emphasis on the sheer number of volumes arrayed on its shelves . . . A clearinghouse of new demands from diverse and largely remote constituencies, it will be judged by its performance as a site of information transfer. No longer contained within its four walls, the increasingly decentralized library must meet the individualized demands of . . . professors and students who use a bewildering array of commercial and self-devised software to search catalogs, review bibliographies, and store information.
>
> Editor's introduction to a special issue on "The Electronic Library," *Academe—Bulletin of the American Association of University Professors*, July-August, 1989, p. 7.

mation tucked away in a library might be sought and used at any moment, according to the needs and interests of the consumers, but the usage of museum artifacts depends on the focus of researchers or the entrepreneurship of curators who find a means to display the stored treasures.

Every museum director must chart a program that includes specializing in some categories so that researchers will know and respect the fact that the collection offers something unique. At the same time, the director must be concerned with serving a broader public that needs to be given a fresh reason to visit the facility. Some museums have the luxury of catering only to scholars; others are charged with amusing and informing the masses.

Development of Museums

The history of museums parallels that of libraries. The first was found in ancient Egypt about 300 B.C. However, the real flourishing of the institution came at the end of the Renaissance when the collections of historical artifacts belonging to the noble families were opened to the public. The British Museum, also a library, opened in 1759, more than 75 years after the vast collections of the antiquarian Elias Ashmole were first displayed at the Ashmolean Museum at Oxford University.[8]

Museum comes from the Greek word for the temple of the Muses, the goddesses of the arts and sciences. The word literally means "a place to study." This definition may not reflect the experience of most of us, who think of museums as places we are taken for an hour's visit by teachers or parents. But just as libraries cater to individual scholars, museums provide access to their collections for researchers with specialized interests.

The first museum displaying artifacts in America was established at Charleston, S.C., in 1773 in order to show the intellectual independence of that colony from New England.[9] Art museums began to appear in the United States in the mid-nineteenth century. At the same time, the leading cities decided to use public funds to document not only the art that reflected their heritage, but also the natural history and the social history of their individual regions.

The Smithsonian Institution was established by an act of Congress in 1846 to conduct scientific research. As a result, the National Zoo, the National Gallery of Art, the Museum of National History, and many other important collections were assembled in the nation's capital. Early in the twentieth century, the first museums of science and industry were opened in Chicago and Philadelphia to document the growth and contributions of American inventiveness.

Types of Museums

Just as there are many types of libraries, museums serve varied purposes. The Smithsonian in Washington is so vast that it is not a single museum, but several. One branch is charged with displaying only American popular culture, and it has a number of novelties including the red sequined shoes that Judy Garland wore in *The Wizard of Oz*, a turn-of-the-century schoolroom, Burma Shave advertising signs from alongside a 1930s highway, and the ballgowns worn by each of the First Ladies of the United States. Another branch of the Smithsonian—the popular

Air and Space Museum containing planes, rockets, and spacecraft—can be viewed as having a propaganda function, creating as it does the feeling that Americans want to explore the skies (even if at great cost) to expand our horizons and to demonstrate the indomitable American spirit.

Many cities and states sponsor historical museums to record the deeds, events, and modes of living of earlier generations. Most larger communities also support one or more art museums, through taxation as well as with gifts from wealthy citizens. The largest cities have the resources to maintain museums of natural history, science and technology, commerce, and perhaps even a planetarium. Universities often find the resources to support not only major art museums but also museums of geology, anthropology, zoology, horticulture, and archeology.

Specialized arts, crafts, and hobbies are preserved and documented in small museums such as the Museum of Woodworking. The Museum of the American Indian is just one of many that tell the story of an ethnic group. Entire sports are celebrated in the various halls of fame, such as the one for baseball in Cooperstown, N.Y., and the one for football in Akron, Ohio. The Green Bay Packer Museum in a field house across from Packer stadium contains uniforms worn by past greats, film showings of the great championship games, and troves of memorabilia ranging from photographs to souvenir pennants.

Static, Interactive, or Environmental?

Early museums were static: they displayed artifacts on walls or in cases for observation by passive patrons. Animosity against museums has been cultivated in gen-

Every major sport has its Hall of Fame that enshrines memorabilia and allows visitors to rekindle memories of the great games.

A child examines the workings of the human heart at the Museum of Science and Industry in Chicago, which uses interactive exhibits to intrigue young visitors.

erations of schoolchildren who were trooped past "famous" paintings and "important" historical objects that seemed lifeless to the untutored mind.

In an attempt to win over the mass audience, museums realized that they had to offer involvement with the information they presented. The new concept, developed in the 1950s, was called the *interactive* exhibit. The Chicago Museum of Science and Industry's exhibit on tool-and-die operations was made memorable to visiting schoolchildren who could pay a dime to operate a large press that stamped out a souvenir disc emblazoned with the child's name. An exhibit on color at the Allentown, Pa., Art Museum invited children to set huge disks spinning in order to create various combinations of the primary colors, making that basic lesson one of action instead of passive learning. Today many exhibits offer the viewer a chance to participate by pressing buttons that illuminate displays and set machinery in motion to demonstrate some kind of activity.

Even more exciting than the interactive exhibit is the *environmental* exhibit that puts the visitor in a realistic context recreating a moment in history or a different way of life from the one he or she knows. The Mud Island Museum on the Mississippi River in Memphis is such a museum. Visitors walking aboard a Union battleship anchored in the river can hear and see the explosions of the cannons aboard the ship and in the Confederate fort above. Then they climb to the fort and look down on the ship they have just left, all the time hearing the shouts of the combatants. A few minutes later, leaving the Civil War behind, they find themselves not merely looking at artifacts from the Elvis Presley era, but standing in a facsimile of the recording studio where "The King" cut his first records.

The Corporate Museum: Goodwill and More

More than a century ago, companies began to open exhibits at their headquarters buildings or big city office buildings to display inventions and innovations for which they could take credit.

Henry Ford spurred the development of the Dearborn Museum, near the spot where his first assembly line once stood, to show succeeding generations not only the Model T and other Ford innovations, but everything else mechanical and manufactured that was the result of American genius. On the occasion in 1929 of the fiftieth anniversary of Thomas Edison's invention of the light bulb, Ford, with the help of public relations man Edward Bernays, got together Edison, President Herbert Hoover, Luther Burbank, Harvey Firestone, and hundreds of other American businessmen and government leaders at the Dearborn Museum to open a new exhibit that featured the actual laboratory in which Edison accomplished his feat. After decades of distrust, "Light's Golden Jubilee" marked the day when Americans' attitudes toward the contributions of "big business" became more positive.[10]

The corporate museum in America has evolved from the historical archive that merely shows off the company's products through the years to an important marketing device that helps the visitor appreciate the firm's contribution to society, and thus encourages the public to value and trust the company.[11]

INSIGHT

InfoQuest: The Personalized Exhibit

You're not just a face in the crowd when you visit AT&T's InfoQuest Center on Madison Avenue in New York City. By typing your name into a computer as part of the registration process, you create your own personalized "Access Card" before an elevator whizzes you up to the top floor.

Every time you insert your card in an interactive exhibit, the demonstration is personalized to include your name: "Welcome, Johnny, to the wonderful world of fiber optics!" In some cases, video cameras also use your image to show you how visual information is stored and transferred by electronic systems.

Insert your card, for example, and a robot arm builds your name in blocks. A computer invites you to engage in a "conversation" to demonstrate how artificial intelligence is created. Another electronic genie presents you with your own face as a scrambled puzzle, then coaches you if you make too many wrong moves as you try to reassemble your image.

The InfoQuest Center deals with some very heavy concepts: lightwave communications, microelectronics, and computer software. But because it is interactive, personalized, and presented as a fun trip through the Information Age, children and most adults find it not only comprehensible but loads of fun as well.

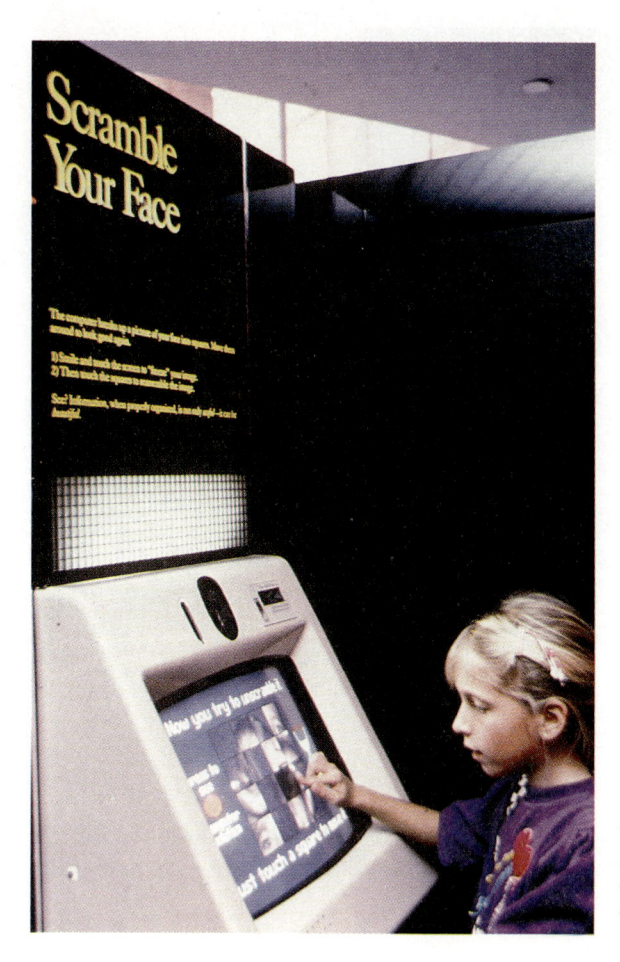

Visitors to AT&T's InfoQuest exhibits can interact with robots, computers, artificial intelligence systems, and picturephones.

AT&T's InfoQuest exhibit at corporate headquarters in New York City depicts how telecommunications affect the modern family. Visits by school and recreational groups are encouraged. The midtown Manhattan location also makes it a place that office workers on their lunch hour, shoppers, and tourists discover as a diverting and free attraction.

Other examples of corporate museums include these:

- TRW's corporate headquarters exhibit demonstrating the broad range of technologies in which the company is involved—similar to the point made by its television commercials.
- The General Foods exhibit that shows how the firm fits into worldwide food production.
- The exhibit documenting the development of computers that is maintained in Boston by several computer firms located in that area.
- Squibb's art gallery at its Princeton, N.J., headquarters that has an impressive permanent collection in addition to offering visiting shows like a public art museum.

Historic old airplanes and the first rockets are on display at the Air and Space Museum in Washington, along with memorabilia from the "Star Trek" series.

- The ground-floor exhibit space purposely designed into the Lever Tower on Park Avenue in New York to provide exposure in a high-traffic area to shows of arts and crafts.

Criticisms of Museums

Museums have their critics, and one of the issues is whether science and technology museums are tools of corporate science, and whether their exhibits serve commercial goals. We mentioned earlier that the Smithsonian's Air and Space Museum on the Capitol Mall serves a heavy propaganda function for American exploration of the skies. Major corporations underwrite many exhibits at science and technology museums with the expectation that the return for their investment will be a message showing the audience the benefits of the free enterprise system. That offends those audience members who resent the self-serving nature of a message that supposedly is serving the public good.

Similarly, art museums often come under attack from groups that believe certain political or social views affect the choice of shows. The controversial photographic images of Robert Mapplethorpe caused government agencies to withdraw support and citizens' groups to protest showings in Washington, D.C., and Cincinnati in 1989 and 1990. In reaction, art critics and civil libertarians rallied to the cause, arguing that the public should be allowed to view any information that curators considered art, and decide for themselves what its worth might be. Like any other mass communication enterprise, selecting information for showing a museum is not value-free. The curator always runs the risk of misjudging the needs, interests, and tolerance of the consumers.

Marketing the Museum

The Louvre in Paris could put the Mona Lisa near the front door, because that's what most people come to see. Instead, the portrait of the enigmatic lady is hung where it will facilitate a constant traffic pattern through vast galleries. Just as broadcasters select certain stories from the evening news to "promo" all day long in hopes of attracting a large audience, museum curators plan special shows that can be promoted in the media to ensure that people will come in droves. A blockbuster Picasso retrospective may generate commemorative posters, T-shirts, tie-in promotions with department stores, school tours, and cocktail parties for the museum's major patrons—in short, much the same ballyhoo that surrounds a media event like the Super Bowl or the political nominating conventions.

Museums have had to learn from business how to use advertising and promotions to building interest in their "products." Often that means working with a large corporation to sponsor a showing. "The Treasure Houses of Britain" in 1985–1986, the largest exhibit ever mounted by the National Gallery of Art in Washington, with over 700 objects borrowed from private estates, was funded by a grant from Ford Motor Company.

Interest in the exhibit was created through three hour-long shows carried by the Public Broadcasting System. To keep the public from surging through the exhibits, an intricate electronic system was used to distribute free tickets in advance to groups and individuals and to ensure that they would be able to move through the many rooms without crowding. Conventions meeting in Washington during the more than four-month period were accommodated through special evening hours, with receptions in the court of the East Building to entertain guests while they waited for the assigned time to visit the show.

Even the venerable Victoria and Albert Museum in London has changed its official name to the National Museum of Art and Design in order to appeal to a larger constituency, including the business community. The museum increased its hours to allow patrons to visit in the evening, and it added contemporary art and design exhibits to help overcome its stuffy image. The moves prompted an outcry from long-time members of the museum's board of directors, but museum attendance increased, and the resulting support from the business community assured it of solvency in the face of diminishing government help.[12]

The Minneapolis Institute of Art began using an advertising agency on a regular basis in the 1970s, with the agency donating its services as a contribution to the museum. By the end of the 1980s, other Minnesota arts and cultural institutions, aware of the visibility and success of the Institute, were aiming to develop the same relationships with advertising agencies.

Almost every museum has a small shop where patrons can buy postcards, books, art reproductions, and jewelry. But today the museum shop can be big business. One can enter the shops of New York's main art museums from the street without even visiting the exhibits. The Metropolitan Museum of Art has branch stores in Macy's and in malls in wealthy suburban areas, as well as a catalog mailed nationally. The Smithsonian also gains revenue from a lavish catalog featuring reproductions of art, archeological artifacts, and jewelry. Marketing museum merchandise has become such an important fundraising device that the Internal Revenue Service is looking into the tax-free status of some museums.[13]

While most public-supported museums try to keep admission free or to charge a nominal entrance fee, some museums depend on the occasional blockbuster show with a special admission charge—a Picasso retrospective or a King Tut's Tomb exhibit—to attract new visitors and to realize a budget surplus.

FUTURE FILE

✓ One thinks of *going to* a library or museum to avail oneself of the information stored there. How can libraries and museums, working with the latest telephone, television, and computer technologies, make their collections available to more people?

✓ Museums have evolved to store and display information about everything ranging from art to popular culture to sports. If you were a philanthropist wishing to do something innovative, what fresh concept might you develop for a museum?

✓ Libraries are faced with skyrocketing costs for purchasing and storing the millions of documents, publications, and books required by their consumers. Take the role of the entrepreneur and identify services that libraries might develop as "profit centers" by charging consumers for information that they find valuable.

NOTES

1. David Davidson and Richard W. Budd, "Libraries: Relics or Precursors?" in R. W. Budd and Brent D. Ruben, eds., *Beyond Media* (Roselle Park: Hayden Book Company, 1979), p. 138.
2. Lena Williams, "Studies Find More Reading for Information and Less for Fun," *The New York Times*, May 2, 1988, p. D-10.
3. Lena Williams, "American Libraries: A World Far Beyond Books," *The New York Times*, Sept. 21, 1988, p. A-10.
4. Anthony Smith, *Books to Bytes: The Computer and the Library*, Gannett Center for Media Studies, Occasional Paper No. 7, November 1988.
5. Andrew L. Yarrow, "Electronics Reshaping U.S. Public Libraries," *The New York Times*, June 7, 1988, p. C-15.
6. Timothy Weiskel, "The Electronic Library and the Challenge of Information Planning," *Academe*, July-August 1989, pp. 8–12.
7. James M. Markham, "Mitterand Orders a Library for the Ages," *The New York Times*, April 26, 1989, pp. C-15, C-22.
8. Victor J. Danilov, "The Transmission of Cultural Heritage: Museums," in Budd and Ruben, *Beyond Media*, p. 162.
9. Danilov, p. 167.
10. Warren Sloat, *1929—America Before the Crash* (New York: Macmillan, 1979).
11. Victor Danilov, "Museum Pieces," *Public Relations Journal*, August 1986, pp. 12–16, 30–31.
12. Terry Trucco, "The Victoria and Albert Tries to Catch Up," *The New York Times*, Feb. 25, 1989, p. 13.
13. Teri Agins, "Growth of Museum Shops Stirs Debate on Tax Status," *The Wall Street Journal*, Feb. 27, 1989, p. B-1.

SUGGESTED READINGS

Alexander, E. P., *Museum Masters: Their Museums and Their Influences* (Nashville, TN: American Association for State and Local History, 1983).

Harris, M. H., *History of Libraries in the Western World* (Metuchen, NJ: Scarecrow Press, 1984).
Katz, H., *Museum Adventures: An Introduction to Discovery* (New York: Coward-McCann, 1969).
Schroeder, F. E. H., ed., *Twentieth-Century Popular Culture in Museums and Libraries* (Bowling Green, OH: Bowling Green University Popular Press, 1981).
Schwartz, A., *Museum: The Story of America's Treasure Houses* (New York: Dutton, 1967).

CHAPTER 16

New Electronic Services

AT A GLANCE

✓ When an interpersonal channel such as the telephone is used to send messages to many people at one time instead of to one person at a time, it becomes a mass communication channel.

✓ Transmission of information to and from earth-orbiting satellites makes instantaneous communication around the world possible.

✓ AT&T was given a monopoly on phone service when the aim was ease of connection between systems, but it gave up that monopoly in 1984 in order to take part in the telecommunications revolution that allows many firms to provide electronic services using telephones, computers, and satellites.

✓ Computers have changed the work place by moving information electronically to many consumers, networking them with others inside and outside their organizations.

✓ Databases permit multiple users to gain access simultaneously to information stored all over the world and to use the power of the computer to search out desired documents quickly.

The new electronic services have taken traditional *communication* media and changed them into *mass communication* media. Channels once used primarily for interpersonal communication now are used to carry messages that are "one-to-many" or "to whom it may concern" in nature.[1] In this chapter we shall see how devices such as computers, satellites, and telephones are changing our lives.

CONVERGING TECHNOLOGIES CHANGE COMMUNICATION

When Alexander Graham Bell worked on the telephone, he envisioned a mechanism that would allow two people to speak across long distance—*interpersonal* communication. When Thomas Edison worked on motion pictures, he envisioned the ability to capture a performance on film and re-create it for theaters full of people—*mass* communication. The development of the typewriter and later the xerographic copying machine made it possible to prepare and disseminate multiple copies of letters, memos, and reports within the work place—*organizational* communication.

Telephone, film, typewriter, and copier were all separate machines. The telephone could not be hooked to the typewriter. Copiers could not make still pictures from movies. In the last decades of the twentieth century, however, because electronic technology was behind many of the improvements made on earlier mechanical technologies, a *convergence* occurred. Suddenly those in charge of creating, storing, and disseminating information, whether "producers" as we have used the term before or "consumers" as we have understood the concept, began to see the linkage between systems originally designed primarily for one mode of human communication: interpersonal, organizational, or mass.

Today, in the workplace more rapidly than in the home, we find it useful to analyze every available technology in terms of its *mass* communication applications, even if it is presented as something else. We then discover that technologies have blurred the lines between interpersonal, organizational, and mass communication, and that there are mass communication uses for every technology.

THE IMPORTANCE OF SATELLITES

For many years, the shape of the planet Earth and the mechanical problems caused by transmitting information over wires or through the lower atmosphere seemed to prohibit instantaneous transmission of information around the world. Beaming information up to satellites high above the earth, then between satellites, and finally down to earth receiving stations answered these mechanical problems.

In the late 1950s, the Soviet Union and the United States placed satellites in orbit around the earth. By the 1970s, both countries were routinely placing satellites in fixed positions relative to the earth, so that transponders aboard them

Dow Jones uses satellite dishes to receive and send the information that consumers find in *The Wall Street Journal*, the Dow Jones NewsRetrieval service, and other publications and databases offered by the firm.

could receive and send signals to and from below. The sending stations on the planet are called *uplinks* and the receiving stations are called *downlinks*.

Today all sorts of information are transmitted through uplink stations and back down to downlink stations: a long distance telephone call, the movie being shown on Home Box Office at any particular moment, the facsimile page layouts for tomorrow's edition of *USA Today* that will be printed in plants all over America, the Dow Jones News Retrieval database to which any owner of a personal computer can subscribe. Most residents of technologically advanced countries receive information via satellite every day, usually without realizing that the information has made the long trip to and from a satellite in a fraction of a second.

Closer to the surface of the earth, the same information may be moved from station to station by microwave. Indeed, the position of a microwave dish tells the observer whether it is receiving from a satellite (tilted upward) or from another earthbound microwave dish (horizontal to the plane of the earth).

Satellite transmissions are used in education, perhaps even in the high school you attended. For example, Oklahoma State University offers a German course for students in 50 high schools across a two-state area. Usually the schools are so small that they cannot afford language teachers. The televised language instruction is not just a lecture; it shows the language being used in a cultural context. To keep the lessons interesting, they are broken into five-minute modules. On-site teachers provide supplementary materials and answer questions.[2]

**Thursday,
June 29, 1989**
On your desk
weekdays by 5 p.m.

Courant FaxPaper
Ahead of Tomorrow

**Dow Jones Average
Today's close** —
30 Industrials 2458.27
Down 46.47

Business

■ **Commercial real-estate sales,** little noticed by much of the public, are where the last-minute, avoid-the-tax-increase action is. Car dealers, appliance salesmen and bankers expect to be fairly busy as consumers buy now... ■ **As former workers** look for jobs elsewhere and its new owner tries to find a buyer, the old Emhart complex begins to shut down... ■ **The SEC files** a securities fraud suit against corporate raider Paul A. Bilzerian, shopping center developer Edward J. DeBartolo Sr. and three others in connection with several stock deals. DeBartolo and two others immediately settle the charges without admitting or denying guilt... ■ **Federal bank regulators** estimate they will spend $2 billion to rescue MCorp of Dallas. They forsee no failures rivaling it in the immediate future. Meanwhile... ■ **Banc One Corp.** of Columbus, Ohio, agrees to take over 20 failed banks of MCorp... ■ **Sales of new homes** edge up 2.7 percent in May as interest rates continue to fall, but analyst say sales will remain slow because of the weakening economy... ■ **The U.S.,** already the world's largest debtor country, strengthens its hold on that title in 1988 as its total foreign debt surged by 41 percent to $532.5 billion... ■ **Growth in Americans'** living standards lagged behind other major industrialized nations last year despite a big surge in U.S. export sales, a new report says... ■ **Paramount Communications** says seven banks have agreed to serve as co-agents in the syndicate being formed to finance the company's $12.2 billion hostile tender offer for Time Inc. The disclosure comes the day before Time's annual shareholders meeting... ■ **Integrated Resources,** the cash-strapped investment concern, announces a plan to refinance its $955 million short-term debt... ■ **The chairman** of a key House subcommittee says he will introduce legislation restricting dual trading in the nation's futures markets and giving regulators the power to conduct undercover investigations of market corruption... ■ **Shareholders of Koito** Manufacturing vote overwhelmingly against giving American corporate raider T. Boone Pickens three seats on the company's board.

Closing stocks

Aetna	55⅛	–½	Steam Boiler	42¾	–¾
Advest	6⅞	0	ITT	57½	–1½
Ames	16⅛	–¼	Kaman	12¾	–½
Bank of Boston	28⅛	–¼	Loctite	44⅜	+⅜
NEB	21½	–⅛	NU	21⅝	+⅛
Cigna	56⅝	–¼	Shawmut	27⅛	–½
CNG	17¼	0	SNET	75	–¾
Dexter	24	–¾	Stanley	34¾	–¾
Emhart	39¾	0	Travelers	40½	–½
Fleet	27	–¾	UTC	50	–1⅛

Opinion

Courant editorial: ■ **The anti-abortion protesters** in West Hartford are using flamethrower rhetoric that hurts their credibility. It would take a lot more evidence than has been shown so far by the protesters to persuade the public that West Hartford police have violated the human rights of the occupiers of the Summit Women's Center... Other views:
■ **Higher fuel taxes** won't do much to avert the greenhouse effect, writes Wesleyan University economics professor Gary Yohe... ■ **Columnist Don Noel** says U.S. Rep. Bruce Morrison is past the big-toe stage in his testing of the gubernatorial waters.

State government/Politics

■ **Gov. O'Neill visits** Advanced Pulmonary Technologies, a small high-tech firm in Glastonbury, to sign a bill creating a new economic development agency intended to support innovations in technology... ■ **The state Gaming Policy Board** gives Hartford Jai-Alai owner Buddy Berenson permission to run 51 extra performances this year, more than making up for 47 he lost last year to the jai alai players' strike. The state will add about $1 million to its treasury from the performances... ■ **Workers at three group homes** for the mentally retarded threaten to strike July 11 if the state does not increase their wages... ■ **Leaders of a PAC** dedicated to electing women to higher office bring their campaign to Hartford tonight, meeting with 45 to 50 people at Barbara Kennelly's home. Among them, Rosa DeLauro, who is considering a run for Congress from the 3rd district.

Connecticut news

■ **The July Fourth holiday** does not create a three-day weekend this year, but tourism is expected to be brisk, and some businesses are giving employees the 3rd off anyway Other folks are creating their own four-day weekends with personal days... ■ **The marine radio frequency** used in an attempt to warn the captain of the oil tanker World Prodigy that he was off course is often cluttered with chatter and frequently abused by pleasure boaters. It's a serious problem, the Coast Guard says... ■ **OSHA opens hearings** on new lift-slab construction regulations as part of a multi-year process of improving safety rules for lift-slab construction. Critics say the new rules would put lift slab companies out of busines.

National

■ **The much-anticipated** Supreme Court decision on abortion is delayed without explanation until at least Monday, disappointing hundreds of anxious protesters who jammed the steps of the Supreme Court building. Meanwhile,... ■ **The High Court** places new limits on the Constitution's free-speech protections when commercial expression is involved. The instant case involves the sale of cookware on State University of New York campuses... ■ **President Bush moves** to clean up campaign-finance provisions — such as those allowing congressmen to save contributions from one campaign to the next and to accept huge PAC donations — that have helped keep most incumbents in office. But he also says he will "work with Congress" on obtaining pay raises... ■ **The House prepares** to adopt limited new sanctions against China in response to the brutal crackdown against pro-democracy demonstrators, ignoring objections from the Bush administration that the move will limit the president's flexibility... ■ **Oil hunt ban?** The House Appropriations Committee, citing concerns about a possible oil spill, approves legislation imposing a year-long moratorium on oil or gas exploration in Alaska's Bristol Bay, one of the nation's premier fishing areas. The legislation also would extend existing prohibitions against oil or gas exploration along vast stretches off the coasts of California, Florida and New England, and impose a new moratorium on leases along a coastal stretch from Rhode Island to Maryland. Meanwhile... ■ **The captain of the tanker** that spilled oil in Narragansett Bay is confined to his ship, charged with violating federal clean water laws. He did not testify at a NTSB hearing.

International

■ **Premier Li Peng,** responding to international condemnation of China's suppression of dissent, warns Thursday of an "anti-China adverse current" and said people made unwarranted accusations against China "under the banner of human rights."... ■ **Gen. Wojciech Jaruzelski** says the Communist Party's automatic leading role in Poland "already is history" and it will never return to the monopoly rule of the past. He also praised the "realism" of Solidarity leader Lech Walesa, and said Poland would seek "friendly American support," not "charity," during the upcoming visit by President Bush.

Sports/Entertainment

■ **Pete Rose** could be threatened with jail if the IRS can prove allegations by a former associate that he tried to hide income from his gambling, memorabilia sales and card shows... ■ **Dino Radja,** a center on Yugoslavia's national basketball team drafted by the Boston Celtics, will not be allowed to join the NBA, his Yugoslavian coach says... ■ **Boris Becker** and 17-year-old French Open winner Arantxa Sanchez ease into Wimbledon's third round. John McEnroe survives a run-in with the umpire and a balky serve to advance... ■ **Ken Green's** public links behavior may be ill-suited for the PGA Tour. The Connecticut native will play in the GHO next week... ■ **"Great Balls of Fire,"** is a hard driving, feverishly paced biography of rock star Jerry Lee Lewis. Our critic gives it three stars.

Weather

■ **Tonight:** Tonight clear, lows 45 to 50. Light northwest winds.
■ **Tomorrow:** Mostly sunny, highs 75 to 80. Outlook for Saturday: fair, highs in the 80s.

An executive digest prepared by the editors of The Hartford Courant. Copyright 1989.
FaxPaper, 285 Broad St., Hartford, CT 06115; Phone (203) 241-3858

> **INSIGHT**
>
> ## Campus Is Computer Testing Ground
>
> Stanford University is just one of many campuses where new uses of computer technology are being put to the test in everyday situations. The spring 1989 election of student governing association officers was conducted using Macintosh computers instead of paper ballots or mechanical voting machines. County and state election officials observed the process, interested in whether the system could be adapted eventually for their use.
>
> On the same campus, only weeks before the computer balloting, a controversy broke out when it was discovered that a database service used by Stanford students offered a file of ethnic, racial, and sexual jokes. When the university decided to close down the joke file because many found it offensive, faculty members petitioned the president of the university to argue against what they saw as censorship of a means of communication.
>
> *Sources:* Katherine Bishop, "New Campus Test: Computer Voting," *The New York Times*, May 9, 1989, p. A-18; "Stanford Official Bans Computer Joke File," *The Chronicle of Higher Education*, Feb. 22, 1989, p. A3.

TELEPHONES MAKE THE CONNECTION

In 1915, American Telephone and Telegraph president Theodore N. Vail made the first coast-to-coast call to inaugurate his company's transcontinental service. A decade later, AT&T was using public opinion polls to determine what customers thought of their service and what they wanted from the telephone company.[3] "Ma Bell" has always been in the forefront of the development of communication technologies. The company's executives sensed the many uses to which telephones could be put in the coming years.

AT&T Enters the Information Business

Early telephone systems made it difficult, if not impossible, to connect customers of various small telephone companies with customers who were using incompat-

> **TIME CAPSULE**
>
> ## Electronic Services
>
> | | | | |
> |---|---|---|---|
> | 1876 | Alexander Graham Bell takes out first patent on telephone. | 1981 | IBM's personal computer becomes the industry standard. |
> | 1915 | First coast-to-coast telephone call made by AT&T. | 1984 | Divestiture of AT&T begins new era of telephone service competition. |
> | 1950s | Soviets and United States put satellites in orbit around earth. | 1991 | Apple and IBM agree to join technologies. |
> | 1980s | Introduction of cellular telephone technology. | | |

The telephone is a link to the rest of the world.

ible equipment. Because consumers wanted to be interconnected with others in their region and the rest of the nation, the U.S. government allowed AT&T to become a telephone service monopoly. "*The* phone company" was allowed to provide local and long distance service, and also to make and lease telecommunication equipment to its customers. Local operating companies were all subsidiaries of the nationwide telephone company.

The monopoly made sense until after World War II, when rapidly developing technologies changed the picture. Clearly telecommunications and computers were going to vastly expand the types of information carried over phone lines. New entrepreneurs wanted the opportunity to offer broad services in conjunction with telephones. AT&T wanted to produce computers and offer other products and services that were forbidden to it because it enjoyed monopoly status.

The government brought antitrust suits against AT&T in the 1970s, charging that the company had control over every aspect of telephone service and related technologies to the detriment and exclusion of other producers. The parties agreed to a divestiture that took place on January 1, 1984. At that time AT&T gave up its local operating companies, which were then formed into regional companies. AT&T was allowed to keep its research laboratories and long-distance business—not as a monopoly, but in competition with the new firms offering long-distance services.

AT&T employees accustomed to working for a giant with no competitors had to learn new attitudes. Suddenly the huge company had to market its goods and services like any other firm. The new, lean AT&T had to sell aggressively to the individual consumer as well as to America's businesses. (The company's sales efforts were hampered by several factors: it could no longer use the name "Bell," which was reserved for the regional operating companies; some consumers were confused by the host of new names for former AT&T divisions; others were confused by the introduction of new long-distance companies such as Sprint and MCI.) The FCC required that new telecommunications companies be allowed to lease their lines from AT&T, which had built them as a monopoly but now manages them in the new competitive arena. Television spots for AT&T during the years after divestiture advised consumers to "stay with the name you've learned to trust."

Within six months after divestiture, AT&T had introduced the first in a new line of personal computers for home and business. By the end of its first year, the new AT&T had introduced almost 70 new products and services. At the same time, IBM acquired companies involved in the telephone business, and other firms such as ITT, RCA, and Xerox moved to broaden their bases to include all facets of telecommunications. Every major producer wanted to offer the consumer complete information services.

Fiber Optics: The New Information Transmitter

The technology of transmission also was changing. Both AT&T and its competitors were busy laying a new kind of cable over land and under sea. Unlike early sound transmitters that used copper wires to transmit electrons, the new fiber optics systems used thin strands of glass to transmit information in the form of light.

Fiber optics have several advantages over copper cables. They are more resistant to water and corrosion. Because they do not carry electrons, they cannot spark or ignite, and they don't need heavy protective shielding. Thus they are flexible and easy to install over rough terrain, and they are not affected by electromagnetic interference.

Fibre optics are being used to wire the nation for transmission of phone messages, cable television, and other electronic services.

Because light travels faster than electrons, fiber optics systems can carry more information faster and more cheaply than copper cables. Computer services depend on fiber optics to transmit millions of words per hour. Fiber optics are also used in stores and businesses, because the information moves from machine to machine with virtually no distortion or loss of data.

"Baby Bells" Seek Wider Markets

In the first few years after divestiture, the seven Bell operating companies—"Baby Bells"—organized themselves in the spirit of competition. Consumers initially were confused when Bell companies from outside their region offered Yellow Pages in competition with the local company. The rival books contained not only listings and the usual advertisements, but coupons, listings of government agencies, maps, ZIP code directories—in short, any information the producers thought might be of use or interest to consumers. The Baby Bells saw the Yellow Pages as lucrative mass communication media in themselves, not just an adjunct to the local telephone company's service. Local Bell companies found themselves having to increase their advertising budgets on radio and television to convince people to use their directories.

The Baby Bells felt that the judge who set down the guidelines for divestiture favored AT&T because he excluded the operating companies from offering long distance service. The judge reviews the effects of telephone divestiture every three years and, in response to suggestions from all the affected companies, issues modifications. The Baby Bells, arguing that the FCC should not have the jurisdiction to limit their competition with each other, are pushing for entry into the long distance field.[4]

The operating companies also see electronic publishing—creating and arranging all text and graphic elements on a computer screen—as a field with great potential. They are pressuring Congress and the courts to allow them to enter the information-services business, possibly in conjunction with other information producers. A bill introduced in the House of Representatives in 1989 would require the FCC to oversee the Baby Bells' entry into electronic publishing to make sure they don't gain monopoly control over the phone-information market.[5]

In August 1989, the judge presiding over the divestiture allowed the ban on electronic publishing by AT&T to expire, and the company immediately began to plan its entry into the field. At the 1989 convention of the American Newspaper Publishers Association (ANPA), the nation's newspaper publishers finally acknowledged that the phone companies were likely to enter the field. Arthur Ochs Sulzberger, chair of the ANPA as well as publisher of *The New York Times*, conceded that he and other publishers could not prevent the phone companies from entering electronic publishing. He and other leaders of the print field acknowledged that the future of the newspaper might well lie in cooperating with the phone companies as delivery vehicles for the information produced by newspapers.[6] (As we saw in an earlier chapter, the FCC already has granted the telephone companies entry into the cable business.)

800, 900 Numbers Offer Many Services

Another way in which the long-distance phone companies have broadened their involvement as a medium of mass communication—or, more correctly, as a *carrier* of mass communication information—is the development of 800 and 900 numbers. Unlike other area codes that represent a region, the special area codes denote numbers that provide marketing and information services used by businesses and other organizations to communicate with consumers. Some of the communication is interpersonal—a voice on the other end of the line talks to the consumer. But much of it involves prerecorded messages to which the consumer listens, or, in some cases, with which the consumer can interact to leave personal information on a tape recording.

A call to an 800 number is free to the consumer. Thus the 800 number is used by business for two purposes: (1) to complete a sale after information about a product or service is advertised in another medium, or (2) to provide information to the consumer about the product or service that has already been purchased. Many over-the-counter health products now carry 800 numbers on the package so that consumers can call if they are confused about the dosage, or to find out what they should do if they have had an adverse reaction to the product. Insurance and investment companies list 800 numbers on their policies and statements so that customers can get advice on their financial status.

AT&T, which handles 75 percent of all toll-free calls, processed seven billion 800-number calls in 1989, up from about two billion calls only five years earlier.[7] General Electric alone spends $10 million a year on its GE Answer Center service. The company feels that the expenditure is worthwhile not only in terms of customer satisfaction, but also because the three million calls each year present an opportunity for research on consumer preferences. After answering an inquiry, the service representative may ask: "How long have you been using the product? What product did you use before? Where do you buy the product? What is your reason for choosing this product? Do you have any suggestions for how the product might be improved?"

Buying Information by Phone

Whereas the 800 service is free to the consumer, a call to a 900 number is billed to the caller by the minute. By placing the call, the consumer is, in effect, purchasing the information that is included in the recorded message. Everything from Dial-a-Joke to Dial-a-Prayer and even Dial-Porn are carried by the 900 service. The vendor sets the charge for the service, and the phone company collects the money as part of the monthly bill.

INSIGHT

No Puzzle at All . . .

The New York Times now offers its crossword puzzle devotees a 900-number to call if they're stuck for a word. By hitting "a" for across or "d" for down and the clue number, the caller gets the puzzling answer. Why did the *Times* decide to provide assistance? "It's a way we can interact with readers," said a spokesperson for the paper.

Source: The Wall Street Journal, Feb. 1, 1990, p. A9

Fans of D. J. Jazzy Jeff and Fresh Prince, for example, paid $2 for the first minute and 45 cents for an additional minute to hear a two-minute tape in which the rap duo talked about their music, their tours, and their personal lives. The messages were changed daily.[8] Supporters of Jim and Tammy Bakker could support the television preacher after he lost his ministry by placing a call to 1-900-660-HOPE at a cost of $1.50 for the first minute and 35 cents for each minute thereafter. The Bakkers got 25 cents for each call.[9] The Bakkers resorted to the phone service not only to make money but also because they felt they were being denied access to the news media to refute charges made against them by others.

Advertising Age reported that the 900-number concept is fast becoming "an ad medium in its own right" as marketers find innovative ways to combine its services with other traditional media.[10] In the summer of 1990, movie marketers used contests on 900 lines to build interest in *Dick Tracy*, *Total Recall*, and other blockbuster films.

Information companies are finding new uses for the numbers. American Express and AT&T joined to form Call Interactive, a service that links 900-line callers to voice-activated computers at the American Express service center. Journal Phone (dial 1-900-Journal) allows consumers access to news from *The Wall Street Journal*. Once connected, the caller uses four-digit codes to select information: 1000 for the stock market, 4200 for sports, 4500 for weather.

A Phone in Every Briefcase?

The 1980s saw the introduction of cellular phone technology. By dividing metropolitan areas into areas called "cells" and equipping each battery-operated remote phone to send and receive radio signals within the zone, the phone companies are able to link drivers into their system. The service is promoted in drive-time radio advertisements aimed at commuters who are cut off from their places of business and their customers while they are on the road. Subscribers buy or lease the equipment and pay a monthly charge for the service in addition to the cost of the calls. By 1990, there were three million cellular subscribers in the United States, with 25 million forecast by 1998.[11]

The first hand-held cellular phones for use in cars weighed from 5 to 15 pounds. But in 1989 Motorola introduced Micro Tac, a cellular unit weighing 12 ounces and not much larger than a billfold or pack of cigarettes. That meant it could be carried in a pocket and fit easily in a corner of the briefcase. This miniaturization is the key to the forecast of 25 million users within the next decade, as the $2500 price tag has plummeted to the $400 range.

In the early years, cellular transmissions were often of marginal quality. But as the phone companies have moved from analog systems (wherein information is transmitted mechanically) to digital systems (wherein information is converted to numbers and then back to information), the quality is improving dramatically. When digital systems are the standard, cellular phones—now used mainly for interpersonal communication—are more likely to be used in conjunction with battery-powered computers so that subscribers can access any information, voice or print, from any location through their "body phones."

One of the technological limitations of cellular phones has been the number of calls that can be made simultaneously in one area. Current systems can handle just 832 channels. In 1990 the FCC granted licenses for experimental cellular networks of approximately 25,000 subscribers in Houston and Orlando that will

---

NO ESCAPE FROM THE OFFICE?

Today we leave the resources of our office behind when we leave the office. But that may well change with miniature cellular phones. Wherever I go, the whole intellectual environment of the office will come with me.

Richard Adler, director of teleservices for the Institute for the Future thinktank, Menlo Park, California.

Source: Frank E. James, "Battle of Miniature Cellular Telephones Heats Up with Launch of Motorola Model," *The Wall Street Journal*, May 5, 1989, p. B-1.

vastly increase the number of subscribers who can place calls at one time. Still the United States is behind Britain, which is moving toward a nationwide system.

The cellular phone is another example of an interpersonal medium that is having profound effects on the people who work in communication industries. In a page 1 feature, *The Wall Street Journal* profiled a typical cellular phone user:

> It's a typical morning on the Santa Monica freeway. Bumper-to-bumper traffic grinds to a halt. Barbara Stewart, busy president of an advertising agency, is trapped in her 1988 silver Dodge Ram van. Is she frantic?
>
> Quite the contrary. Cellular phone in hand, Ms. Stewart talks with a client 90 miles away about a new ad campaign. She hangs up, revises the ad layout, then zaps him a copy over her van's portable fascimile machine, linked to the cellular phone. During the two hours it takes her to creep from Irvine to downtown Los Angeles, the car phone rings steadily: A client calls to change the publication date of an ad; a prospective customer asks about fees; Ms. Stewart's office faxes an ad layout and a brochure for her approval.[12]

COMPUTERS REVOLUTIONIZE MASS COMMUNICATION

Mathematicians and statisticians long dreamed of machines that would speed their calculations. By the late 1800s, the U.S. Bureau of the Census was developing a punch-card system for tabulating data that was the forerunner of a computer. While the early systems were mechanical, by the 1930s developments in the field of electronics made electric-powered computers possible. Still the systems basically used electricity to power mechanical systems that read punched cards. Computers that did little more than what today's personal computer can achieve were so large they took up an entire room.

The evolution of the electronic computer accelerated in the 1940s and 1950s with the development of the transistor, and then the introduction of integrated circuits on microchips. These innovations made it possible to reduce the size of computers as well as the cost of producing them. By the 1970s, personal computers were being marketed by Tandy-Radio Shack, Apple, and other pioneering small firms. In 1981, the giant computer firm IBM had moved into the market with models that shortly would become the industry standard.

The automobile and the radio were innovations that took at least a generation to enter the economic and cultural mainstream, but the complex technology of the computer took less than half a generation to go from novelty to necessity for many people.

Miniaturizing the Computer

Early data-processing machines took up an entire room. The personal computer, however, is hardly more bulky than the typewriter it replaced in many homes and offices, and the trend is toward even smaller computers, many of which perform limited special functions. If you have a recent-model car, for example, the on-board computer monitors the electronic systems so that a mechanic can readily diagnose difficulties and make repairs. In luxury models, some of the information displayed on the control panel to advise driver and passengers of fuel usage and weather conditions is created by a small computer. Since the mid-1980s drivers

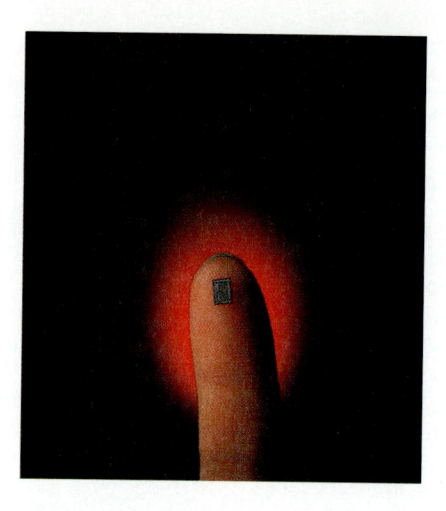

The computer chip, with its ability to store the information that formerly occupied several bookshelves, is the key to modern communication technology.

for some delivery companies have used dashboard computers to log in driving time, expenses, delivery times—virtually everything about their job performance. Auto manufacturers soon will introduce dashboard screens that display electronic maps to help drivers plan trips and keep track of mileage.

The Changing Work Place

At the New York World's Fair of 1939 and again at another New York World's Fair 25 years later, exhibits by General Motors and other transportation companies portrayed rocketlike cars and multitiered people-mover systems whisking people around domed skyscraper cities at breathtaking speeds. As it turned out, the cars of today move at speeds not much greater than the cars of past decades, and they run conventionally on four wheels. But the automobile has become much more trouble-free and automatic to maintain and drive. In computer terms, it has become more "user-friendly."

The computer, too, was predicted as liberating us from everyday concerns by doing such wonderous things as running our household appliances and maintaining all of our records. But the first generation of personal computers proved difficult for the average person to master: the operating manuals ran hundreds of pages, and most users had to ask a computer expert for help when they got into trouble. Until more user-friendly personal computers came along, most people used them for rather basic tasks: to write more easily, to maintain records, to do fairly simple computations, or to play games. The cost of the computer has kept it from being a helper in every phase of household management for the average family, but it has become a fixture in the typical office.

With that historical perspective, we shall see now that the work place gradually is being reshaped by the new computer technologies, often in conjunction with new telephone applications. In an *evolutionary*, rather than revolutionary, way we are depending more and more on electronic processing of information in the work place.

A Computer on Every Desk. Beginning with the Class of 1990, every student at the U.S. service academies was required to have and use a computer. The Army, Navy, and Air Force assume that it will be impossible to perform managerial work without computer skills. Many colleges do not yet require computer literacy, but most make computer facilities available.

Similarly, industry does not have an immediate goal of a computer on every employee's desk, but the introduction of the IBM PC in 1981 and its marketing as a standard piece of office equipment accelerated the interest of business in computing as a means for nearly everybody to complete everyday tasks. As we have seen with other media, the immediate reasons for introducing the technology were not necessarily to facilitate *mass* communication. But people with mass communication as their aim quickly saw applications in every new technology for reaching large numbers of people.

It is not a far stretch of the imagination to see that the software—the programming packages—prepared for computer users are an example of a new kind of mass communication. The creators of the program packages function as editors who must analyze the information needs of a large audience. Just as the textbook you are reading will have new editions when information changes, computer programs are constantly being updated and reissued with the new types of information that consumers tell producers they need.

Predictions of a "Paperless" Office. An agent for the Travelers Insurance Companies who was already using a personal computer to keep his own records asked the company to provide him with prices of policies on a computer diskette rather than in huge volumes of paper. Another employee of the company with an interest in computers assembled the information and prepared it for computer use. When agents in the field heard about it, they clamored for the simpler way of "accessing" information. (In computer jargon, nouns often become verbs!) A few years later, Travelers had 9000 personal computers, half of them in the field.[13]

A computer on every desk seemed futuristic just a few years ago, but today the worker without a computer lacks the up-to-the-minute information needed to make decisions.

By the mid-1980s, the American automobile industry had been revolutionized by the small computer. Personal computers were used to move information almost instantaneously between the auto companies and their parts suppliers. A spokesperson for an auto trade group predicted a "paperless environment" by 1990 and warned that suppliers who didn't use personal computers to keep in contact with the rest of the industry might be out of business.[14]

The prediction about needing a computer to do business was on the mark. However, the prediction of a "paperless" society has not been realized. Most users prefer to augment the electronic data with a paper copy for record-keeping purposes or for "back-up" in case the electronic system is not functioning. More important, the ease of creating data with a computer has resulted in a glut of data, and much of it is printed out because of the user's need to see "proof" of the work.

Networking: The Electronic Link. The primary use people in the work place make of their desktop computers is to process information and to create documents. They organize and store data for later use. They also use programs that can both reorganize the data according to their various needs, and search for correlations between bits of information. When people use computer programs to compose memos, letters, and reports, the function is called "word processing."

All of these are personal uses of the small computer. But when wiring connects all of the personal computers in one office, or when a simple device called a "modem" (for modulator/demodulator) is used to link two or more computers over phone wires, a "network" is created. The result is that information can be shared widely.

At first PCs were not necessarily compatible with each other, with peripheral equipment, or with phone systems. But the world's major manufacturers of com-

TECHNOLOGY

New Technology Joins "Hands"

Trying to organize thousands of volunteers to run the one-day fundraising event to fight world hunger in May 1986—"Hands Across America"—was a massive undertaking. "Three or four years ago this event could not have been done," its national director told the press. "Computers, TV, teleconferencing—the technology has come together."

Organizers of the event, which linked millions of Americans hand to hand in a line stretching from coast to coast, realized that many of the pieces would fall into place only days or hours beforehand. Mail service would be too slow for keeping track of donations and assigning volunteers where they were needed.

So, a mail-order firm donated the use of its mainframe computers, and GTE Telenet Communications provided its network to link the central computer with personal computers in the offices and homes of volunteers around the country. Information about where there were too many or too few people assigned to the line could be updated and shared instantly.

The success of the "Hands Across America" communication system suggests that similar links might be used in the future not only for fundraising, but perhaps for voter registration the day before an election or for coordination of disaster relief.

Source: Peter H. Lewis, "New Technology Linking Hands Across America," *The New York Times,* May 25, 1986, p. 18.

puters and associated equipment, along with the phone companies, have been working to increase compatibility and to set industry standards. The agreement between IBM and Apple in 1991 to work together in developing joint systems signaled the beginning of a new era of compatibility. The phone companies developed a system in the mid-1980s that enables home and office computers to "talk" with other computers in banks, stores, and database services by using short "bursty" transmissions that carry a large amount of information in a second or even a fraction of a second. The new digital phone systems will enable all phone lines to serve any telecommunication function. Networking is becoming more of a reality all the time.

Electronic Pathways. Surely one of the most vexing and wasteful processes in the work place is the writing and routing of memos, many of which are mass communication messages in that they are "one-to-many" and "to whom it may concern" in nature. Having composed a memo, the manager would like to have quick responses from its recipients, or at least would like to know whether the message has been received and acted on. But if a secretary must type and duplicate the memo, distribute it through an internal mail system that depends on footwork, and then wait for each member of the distribution list to respond in writing, it may take a week or more before all the replies have been received.

Electronic mail, usually shortened to "E-Mail," provides a way of getting ideas out fast and receiving responses within 24 hours, whether dealing with people in one location or with locations scattered across the country. Memos are created on the computer video display, then routed electronically through the computer network, with codes ensuring security and proper distribution. Every worker who is part of an E-Mail network quickly gets into the habit of checking the E-Mail file first thing in the morning, when returning from meetings or lunch, and before going home at night.

Using a laptop computer small enough to fit in a briefcase, the worker who is at a remote location can plug into any phone with a pinch-type connector, dial the computer at the home office, and access the E-Mail file on the screen of the laptop computer. Thus, members of an organization need not be delayed in receiving mail simply because their work has taken them away from the office for the day.

Many systems allow the sender to note whether the addressees have checked their files, and at what time. If the sender notes that an addressee has not checked the file, a phone follow-up is in order.

As with most technologies, the cost of using E-Mail has been dropping rapidly in recent years while the number of users tripled. Because external E-Mail links carried over telephone lines are offered by many different companies, compatibility of systems was a problem for E-Mail users in the 1980s. But the nine major services in the United States—including subsidiaries of AT&T, MCI, and the CompuServe database service—are cooperating in the move toward a worldwide standard, called X.400, which will interconnect all systems to make E-Mail the fastest way to send a memo to anyone in the world.[15]

Voice mail, which also uses the telephone system, works like E-Mail but carries the speaking voice of the sender rather than a written memo. Anyone can phone into a voice mail system using any phone. The receiving system has the capability of routing hundreds of messages up to 10 minutes in length.

The most important application of voice mail has been in business situations where buyers, suppliers, and sales personnel need to get information quickly to someone, and they must explain it carefully . . . but they do not really need to speak personally. It's like talking into a phone-answering machine, but voice mail has much greater ability to interact with and guide the caller and then route the information to the proper destination in an organization.

As with all the other systems we have discussed, voice mail can be adapted nicely to mass communication situations. Some members of Congress, for example, inform their constituents through newsletters and personal visits to community centers that assistance can be obtained from the legislator or his or her staff by calling a number designated to route requests using voice mail. A tape asks questions of callers about the nature of their request. The callers respond by touching the appropriate keys on the phone. Their message is then routed to the staff member with the answer, or directly to the government agency that can help. Similarly, customers who call a large wholesaler needing information about products, warranties, or prices will have their requests routed by voice mail, and a representative will call back later with the desired information. The special number for the service is featured prominently in the wholesaler's literature, letterhead, and billheads.

Computer database bulletin boards enable subscribers of computer database services (which will be described more completely later in this chapter) to "post" notices that will be seen by all other subscribers to the system. Any one of those subscribers can then choose to leave a return message—aimed at the individual enquirer, but seen by all who choose to look at the bulletin board. The authors of this book, for example, if they wanted to know whether other teachers were using essay or multiple-choice formats for the final exam in the mass communication course, could pose the question on a bulletin board designated to serve college instructors of communication. They would use their home computers to check the bulletin board from time to time for responses, suggestions, and perhaps further inquiries from other interested instructors of introductory mass communication courses.

Facsimile machines, now popularly called "fax" (used interchangeably as a verb and a noun), were invented in the 1840s, and by the 1920s they were carrying weather maps and wirephotos for newspapers. For decades, magazines edited in New York but printed in Chicago have used facsimile transmission to move page layouts from one place to the other in minutes. The fax machine scans information electronically, looking at each dot of space for a millisecond. It converts all dark marks to digital pulses that then are converted to audible information for transmission over phone lines. The receiving machine reverses the process and prints out a copy a scant minute later.

After 1980, the cost of fax machines dropped, and 1988 saw an explosion of the fax machine market. Fax phone numbers now are printed on letterheads and business cards under ordinary phone numbers, suggesting two ways to communicate with the individual or office.

When fax machines became a standard piece of equipment in offices and even homes, the use of them for mass communication purposes exploded. As *Advertising Age* told its readers in 1988: "Far beyond fax's original purposes—to send urgent correspondence between major businesses—the compact, simple, and versatile machines now constitute a truly 'direct' ad medium."[16] Some advertisers believe an advantage of fax is that because no envelope has to be opened, the message is most likely to catch the eye of the recipient. The problem remains that the recipient pays the cost of the fax paper and is billed for the time the receiving machine is connected with the phone system. So, unlike other advertising media in which the producer pays the bill, with fax the consumer does. Many new owners of fax machines have been angered to find huge quantities of paper used up by what quickly came to be called "junk fax." Some companies that were originating fax messages instructed their staff to send information only to clients who requested it. But other firms eagerly assembled lists of fax numbers in order to increase their use of the machines as delivery systems for promotional messages.

In 1989, only months after the fax explosion, more than a dozen states were considering legislation that would make it illegal to send fax messages to people who did not request them. The Direct Marketing Association, however, claimed that a ban on faxed advertising might violate freedom of speech. Constitutional lawyers argue that a total ban on junk fax probably would not be upheld by the courts. However, regulations that limit transmissions of unsolicited information to a one-page length and require junk fax to be sent at nonbusiness hours might be more likely to be accepted.[17]

Realizing that many of its business customers were growing accustomed to receiving information quickly by fax, the Hartford *Courant* began a new service in 1989: the *Courant FaxPaper*. The one-page publication carries news items that ordinary subscribers will read the next day, but it is delivered electronically to the desks of fax subscribers at around 4 P.M., giving them a head start on the next business day. Nearly a hundred items are fit into the summary by condensing and using typography to highlight the most important facts. The *FaxPaper* began as an experiment, but it suggests that office technology may hold the key to the delivery system of the future for all newspapers.

The work station represents the concept of bringing together in one unit, managed by one computer, all of the electronic services available to the office. The work station enables an individual to assemble an "electronic desktop" within the memory of his or her own computer that includes a directory, dictionary, files, documents in preparation, a calendar, a mailbox, and even an electronic wastebasket for information no longer needed. Information produced elsewhere is brought into the work station computer, assigned a file number, and fit into the consumer's system of organization for later reference and use.

Computer-aided meetings put each employee at a terminal and require that participants, instead of speaking, type their comments and suggestions onto the document that the group creates. The document not only records the meeting, it *is* the meeting. IBM has built 18 electronic meeting rooms at its sites and plans dozens more. Experience with the system shows that employees who attend computer-aided meetings are much more likely to participate—even shy people who often are silent at regular meetings—and they are also much more likely to criticize with brutal honesty rather than "going along" with what they perceive to be group consensus.[18]

Electronics Change Employee Communication. Most employees find it difficult to get information from the personnel or payroll office about their taxes, benefits, and retirement plans. It usually involves several telephone calls before the employee finds out where to get the information, and then there is the hassle of going in person because the information can't be given over the phone.

The solution is a computer kiosk—a free-standing booth in the employee lunchroom where anybody can step inside for privacy, type his or her social security or employee identification number on the keyboard, and watch as pay records, information about retirement plans, and personal data maintained by the company are displayed on the screen. At some companies, the system is interactive, and the employee can use it to change tax withholding status, request a switch in benefits or beneficiaries, or initiate an inquiry about any item that is of concern.

Following a communication audit showing that employees preferred frequent and efficient messages rather than lengthy articles in the monthly newsletter, the Warner Lambert Company decided to overhaul its publications strategy. Today the firm packages information in brief form for delivery by electronic mail and a weekly "newsline" bulletin. At the end of many of the news items, employees are told where to find more material if they want it—usually from bulletin boards or their supervisors. In effect, this gives the consumer more control and allows employees to shop for the information they want.

Desktop Publishing Saves Time and Money. It can be frustrating to work with a printer. First there is the long lag time between sending off the material for a newsletter or brochure and getting the material back in the form of proofs that have to be read for accuracy. Then there is the disappointment that some things do not look the way you intended and others do not take up the amount of space you estimated they would. Changes are made, and then it all must be sent off again to the printers. Another round of frustration awaits the return of the first page proofs. The process is not only time-consuming, but expensive as well, and there will be extra charges if too many changes have to be made in the text or the layout.

Computers and the printing machines that work in conjunction with them have changed this picture, enabling almost anyone to produce "camera ready" (ready for production and printing) layouts for simple publications that can be produced in the office using xerography or sent out for printing by a professional outfit. Routine publications such as fact sheets and reports can be produced literally on the top of a desk—hence the term *desktop publishing.*

Software programs have been developed for the personal computer that will produce book-quality type set in neat columns, and the columns can be arranged by a program such as Pagemaker into pages with the desired margins, borders, page numbers, and other graphic elements including headlines and gray shading. Fancier devices called sheet image scanners can take photographs and other images and fit them electronically to page layouts. The best-quality laser printers (as opposed to the dot matrix and daisy wheel printers used for simple office work) turn out crisp, high-contrast work equivalent to that produced by a print shop.

Electronic publishing's greatest leap forward came with the introduction of the user-friendly Macintosh personal computer and the Apple LaserWriter printer to accompany it. The system is so simple to operate and turns out such professional typography and graphics that many small newspapers, as well as the slick *USA Today*, have turned to it to speed production and cut costs.[19] Computer giant IBM also has a special division to develop and market hardware and software for com-

Personal computers, with programs designed especially for students, the home and the workplace, have revolutionized the way we organize our lives for the purpose of communication.

puter-aided publishing—CAP in industry jargon. Xerox is a leader in production of work stations geared to desktop publishing and also increases its market share because it is a leader in the production of the photocopying machines that are used to duplicate electronic publications.

Many small newsletters and magazines have sprung up and become economically viable in recent years because their publishers—part-time producers who want to exchange information owing to their own interest in a hobby or field rather than a desire to make a profit—were able to keep costs down by setting their own type and laying pages out on the computer screen. One example is *Balloon Life*, a 2500-circulation magazine for hot-air balloon enthusiasts.[20]

The rise of desktop publishing doesn't threaten to run professional printers out of business because printers specialize in quality papers, odd folds, stapling, gluing, and assembling operations that cannot be duplicated in the office. Instead the effect of desktop publishing has been to "dress up" reports, internal publications, small newsletters, and flyers in a way that tends to impress the mass audience accustomed to lesser quality in "homemade" information. While content still is important, the impressive packaging achieved with the personal computer has helped bring credibility and impact to information produced by the consumers themselves.

New Information Channels: Databases and Videotex

Looking for information—whether for a term paper, a financial report, a news story, or just personal curiosity—until recently has involved a tedious, laborious, and fatiguing process.

With computer technology, it is possible today to sit down at a keyboard and display screen, then simply enter some phrases in code and plain English to gain access to the information you want. The information begins to stream past on the screen. You may stop and pause if you wish. You may decide to print out the information on paper for later reference. All of this happens not in hours, but in minutes.

Increasingly, consumers of information are leaving the world of libraries, books, and card catalogs for the world of databases and videotex, which they use at personal work stations. This section will examine how the electronic systems work, what kinds of information producers provide, and how consumers make use of the new bounty of information.

Database Services: A Computerized Library. To understand the use of electronic storage and retrieval systems by individual consumers, it is important first to distinguish between a *database* and a *database service*.

A *database* is a collection of information stored electronically by a producer, or a repository of information, and made available for use by other individuals and organizations who pay for access from their personal computers through the phone lines. Many databases are electronic versions of information also prepared in print form by the producer. Here are some examples of databases.

Academic American Encyclopedia—A standard reference work with more than 32,000 concisely written articles arranged in alphabetical order.

American Express Advance—Billing statement information, travel-planning services, and a merchandise catalog for use by American Express cardholders. (Contains much of the same type of information traditionally transmitted as "bill-stuffers" with the member's monthly statement.)

Cineman Movie Reviews—Current movie reviews and others dating back to 1926, as well as box office rankings of current hit films.

Dow Jones Historical Quotes—Summaries of past performance of stocks and the stock market.

Medical and Drug Reference—Treatments for more than a thousand ailments, and information on prescription drugs used to treat those ailments.

Merrill Lynch Research Service—Market analysis of stocks and recommendations for investment.

Official Airline Guide—Schedules and fare information for domestic and international flights.

Peterson's College Selection Service—Descriptions, locations, majors offered, and admissions requirements for colleges.

There are nearly 4000 databases available in the United States. Some are very specific, such as those that cover medicine or financial markets in depth. Others are very broad, such as those that contain general news and information on all academic subjects in the sciences or the humanities.

Rather than trying to locate each individual database producer and arranging to be billed for receiving that particular information, the consumer subscribes to a *database service*. The consumer makes the selection based on the variety of databases included in the offerings of the database service. (It is analogous to the many channels offered by a cable television company. But whereas you are obliged to subscribe to the cable company that has the franchise to serve your community, you can select any database service that meets your needs.)

Some database services, such as Dow Jones NewsRetrieval, cater to investors, entrepreneurs, and managers who are interested in business and the stockmarket. Other services, such as Dialog, which offers 250 databases, are more general and cater to information professionals and academics. Still others, such as CompuServe, provide a mixture of databases to interest both professionals and general consumers.

To show the range of offerings from a general database service, here are some of the databases included in the basic CompuServe package:

Bulletin boards—electronic mail, want ads and classified listings, a public kiosk of announcements, and interactive on-line conferencing that permits a group of users to "converse" back and forth with their computers.

Personal computing support—information from computing publications that can help users get more out of their computer and the database system, as well as forums where users with questions or problems can seek answers from others who have more expertise.

News, weather, and sports—The Associated Press news, sports, and business wires, as well as the National Weather Service city, state, and marine forecasts.

Electronic shopping—Discount home shopping with catalog information from leading national merchants including Sears, Bloomingdale's, and Waldenbooks.

Financial transaction services—Banking, American Express services, stock portfolio evaluation, and on-line purchase and sale of stocks.

Travel services—Information on hotels, resorts, tours, cruises, and air reservations.

Entertainment and games—Trivia, sports, board, and fantasy games, as well as an entertainment newswire and interactive forums for hobby and special-interest groups such as auto racers, skiers, and science fiction fans.

Home, health, and family—Fitness and nutrition information, recipes and party planning, wine tips, hobbies, and personal finance suggestions, including a list of free government publications.

What Does a Database Service Cost? The subscriber needs three compatible devices: a computer, a telephone, and a modem for connecting them. A one-time fee of about $35 (or in some cases, an annual fee) is paid to the database service in return for a password that enables the user to "log on" to the system. When a connection is made, there is, of course, the phone company's charge for the use of its line. The database service charges for "connect time" when you are "accessing" databases. The charge may be by the minute or by the hour, and it varies according to the speed at which the user's modem works to channel the information to the personal computer. Most services offer lower rates outside of business hours, so home users often wait until the evening to go on-line. Information extracted from the database can be stored in the user's personal computer for later use. Subscribers who stay on-line to engage in interactive communication can run up a bill of $50 to $200 a month, while users who merely check various databases for 5 or 10 minutes a day may pay as little as $30 a month for the service.

Using the Database for Research. Business managers and professionals find that many of the databases they use are organized and indexed to facilitate finding the information they need. Lawyers can search under standard topic headings or by the names of particular cases. Doctors can search by name of disease or by symptoms. "Menus" that go from general headings to much more specific headings help the user to progress toward the desired information.

Academic researchers usually have a topic they want to gather information about, but they may not know who has written about the topic or in which publications. With about a half-day's training, the scholar learns to manage search strategies that involve the creation of index words and phrases. The computer then literally searches every word of every document stored in the system and informs the researcher where the key words and phrases were used. Searches that took days in the traditional library are completed in as little as an hour or two.

Journalists also find databases a godsend for investigative reporting. Former Providence, R.I., *Journal-Bulletin* reporter Elliot Jaspin, now a journalism professor at the University of Missouri, built a library of computer databases that included all of the state criminal court records, drivers' license records, land transfer records, and corporate records. He taught other reporters to use the computer to sift quickly through the voluminous records, find the desired facts, and cross-index and organize them so the reporter could analyze them. The technique resulted in exposés of wrongdoing that otherwise probably would have gone undetected.[21]

Videotex and Teletext Services. The database services have been aimed primarily at academic or business consumers, and they are flourishing. Videotex and teletext services, on the other hand, are aimed more at ordinary consumers who want to receive information either on their television screen or on the monitors of personal computers. Although the majority of homes now have cable and a great many have personal computers, videotex and teletext have not yet proved successful.

Teletext is print and graphic information that has been carried through the air or through a cable for display on a television screen. The consumer uses a keypad to turn from the usual television programming to the teletext "magazine" of news, announcements of community events, sports, weather, and shopping information. It is a one-way system, meaning that the producer simply offers the information for the consumer to receive and view.

Videotex also offers print and graphic information carried by cable or over telephone lines, but it is a two-way interactive system. Whether consumers use a single-function videotex terminal or a home computer, they are linked to the main computer and can send information to it. That means they can respond to a poll, order from an advertisement, check items they want from catalog pages, or play games with the main computer's software. Unlike databases, which transmit original documents in lengthy form that must be "scrolled" up and down to be read in their entirety, Videotex, like Teletext, is formatted in "screens" that include one electronic page of information designed specifically for viewing as a coherent unit of information. (See Figure 16.1.)

Newspaper companies experimented in the 1980s with videotex services in the expectation that many subscribers would want to receive a brief news capsule, sports, and weather reports, along with this week's supermarket specials, on their home screens. The newspapers were anticipating that videotex might be the key to their survival as information producers.

In 1986 the Miami-based Knight-Ridder Newspapers and the Times Mirror Company in Los Angeles abruptly dropped the two most ambitious attempts to market videotex services. Home consumers did not appear to be ready to pay for the equipment necessary to interface their computers with the videotex services.

Chapter 16 New Electronic Services

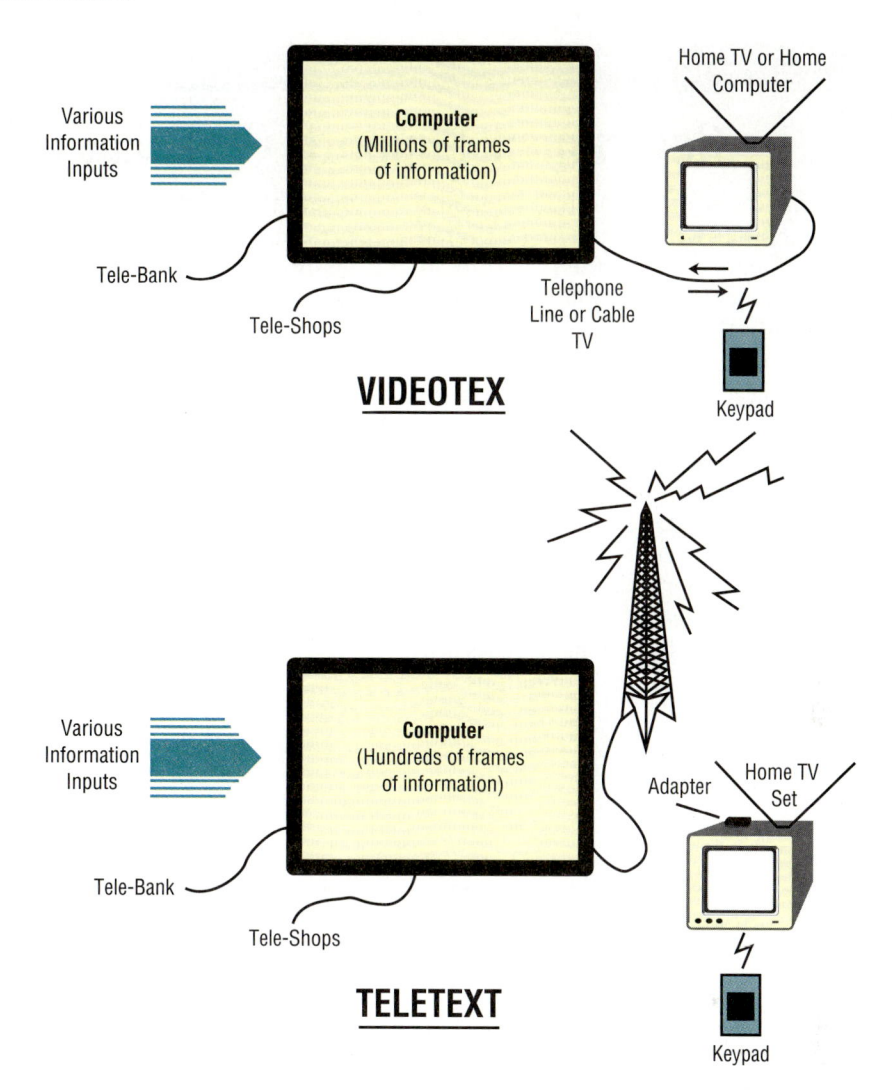

FIGURE 16.1 How Videotex and Teletext Operate Videotex and Teletext are two types of interactive information services. Source: Everett M. Rogers, *Communication Technology: The New Media of Society* (New York: Free Press, 1986), p. 46.

They were also not ready to pay the monthly fee plus per-minute fees for actual use of information. And apparently many were not interested in the extra effort needed to activate the system, because watching television or browsing through a newspaper is comparatively effortless.

Still, the feeling persists among information producers and marketing companies that videotex can find a place in the American home, as it already has in England and other European countries where there is far less information available on television and readership of newspapers is not as great.

In 1989, Sears and IBM joined to introduce Prodigy. The videotex service expects to succeed where others failed because it is priced at a flat $9.95 a month, and because Sears has more expertise in service marketing than did the newspapers in the earlier experiments. Nynex announced the introduction of its Infolook

> ### INDUSTRY
> # Government Supports Canadian Videotex
>
> The standards for North American videotex and teletext graphics were set not in the United States but in Canada, where the government spurred development of electronic text services by funding research on the Telidon system. Private manufacturers in Canada, thus assured of a standard technology, created the software for receivers and page-creation equipment. Major American firms including AT&T, CBS, and Time, Inc. then followed suit, as did the French government. (Britain has its own standards, and its electronic text technology is not compatible with North America's.)
>
> Drivers' exams in one Canadian province are now administered with videotex, requiring drivers to view simulated road conditions, interact with the motion on the screen, and indicate their responses to various situations by pressing buttons. "Grassroots," a system for getting weather and crop information to farmers by videotex that is now used in the United States, was developed in Canada.
>
> Two of Canada's largest publishers formed Infomart, a videotex system that offers many services including *Teleguide* kiosks placed in hotels, shopping malls, and transportation centers to provide directory services, restaurant listings, dates and times of cultural events, and other information of use to shoppers and travelers—all supported by advertising messages.
>
> *Source:* Jerome Aumente, *New Electronic Pathways* (Beverly Hills, CA: Sage, 1987), pp. 39–41.

system later in 1989, signaling the interest of the telephone companies in exploring the possibilities of videotex.

Despite the new attempts to gain acceptance for videotex, critics still believe that the expense and the bother are too great for the average consumer. Over the years, columnists for *Advertising Age*, the influential weekly journal of marketing, have argued that no information vehicle is successful until and unless advertising support makes access to it simple and the cost insignificant. At present, the consumer pays time charges when ordering goods or services by videotex. *Ad Age* argues that retailers should pay the cost, and should expedite ordering by providing the consumer with simple equipment at little or no cost. (In France, the government postal-telegraph monopoly plans to give every telephone owner in the country a free videotex terminal.[22])

One area where videotex has caught on in America is agriculture, because farmers often operate in remote locations far from information sources, and suppliers who can't call on them personally are eager to get information about products and services to them. The electronic technology benefits farmer and supplier alike, giving both quicker and more specific information about the specialized needs of individual farmers according to the crops or livestock they choose to grow, weather conditions, price supports, and other variables. A farmer contemplating putting a field into winter wheat, for example, might query the supplier electronically about moisture requirements or pest-resistance before using the videotex system to place an order for seed.

Consumer interest in teletext is likely to increase as a new generation of television sets is designed to make receiving the service simpler, and as the producers

Phone technology knows no geographic boundaries.

of cable services learn better how to package information so that consumers find it appealing and different from what they already receive through other media.

Videophones Are on the Horizon. Almost a generation ago, American telephone customers were being told that "picturephone" was just around the corner and that the visual component would allow callers to see each other. Although industry has embraced the idea of teleconferencing—holding meetings that combine live television and phone connections—the picturephone for home use has not yet caught on. Most people have second thoughts about a telephone that allows the caller to see what you are doing. The added expense did not seem to warrant the innovation.

But the concept is not dead. In France, the government has invested heavily in "videophone" systems that carry voice and picture transmissions over fiber optics. In a pilot project in the city of Biarritz, videophone owners can see each other, they can show each other documents or pictures, and they can walk around the room transmitting pictures of family and friends using a hand-held camera.[23] In America, AT&T now offers a videophone for under $2000, but sales so far are limited.

As we have seen with so many other technological innovations, what begins as novelty and is used for interpersonal communication eventually finds mass communication applications. Videophone obviously could be a powerful sales tool, with the marketer able to show and demonstrate products and services while talking to the customer over the phone. Estimates for carpeting or redecorating a room could be given over the phone instead of requiring a visit by the merchant. Homeowners whose appliances were not functioning properly might not have to wait a day or two for an expensive house-call if the problem could be diagnosed with some "show-me-the-problem" consulting over the videophone. The videophone could even be used to provide "living yellow pages" ads!

FUTURE FILE

✓ You didn't really relish struggling out of bed today to attend the review session for your mass communication final exam. How could the new electronic services ease the task of studying for your college courses?

✓ Presuming that by the year 2000 most homes have computers that are linked with the main computer at the work place, what information will employees want to receive, and what kinds of information can organizations send their employees more efficiently than they do now?

✓ Will this textbook be a "book" a decade from now, or will your little sister "access" it through a database? If so, how will the role of the authors change?

NOTES

1. The concept of *communication* media designed for interpersonal uses being modified for *mass communication* uses is explored in Lee Thayer's essay "On the Media and Mass Communication: Notes Toward a Theory," in Richard W. Budd and Brent D. Ruben, eds., *Beyond Media* (Rochelle Park, NJ: Hayden Book Co., 1979), pp. 53–83.
2. Jo Joggerst, "Satellite Scholastics," *Satellite Orbit*, March, 1986, pp. 31–34.
3. James E. Grunig and Todd Hunt, *Managing Public Relations* (New York: Holt, Rinehart & Winston, 1984), pp. 35–36.
4. Leigh Ornstein, "Baby Bells Ring for More," *Business Today*, 24:3 (Fall 1987), pp. 68–70.
5. Patrick Reilly, "Hungry 'Baby Bells,' " *Advertising Age*, May 1, 1989, p. 4.
6. Patrick Reilly, "Newspapers Eye Electronic Future," *Advertising Age*, May 1, 1989, p. 4; Joe Sharkey, "Newspaper Publishers Debate Pros, Cons of Allying with Phone Firms," *The Wall Street Journal*, April 26, 1989, p. B-6.
7. Brent Bowers, "For Firms, 800 Is a Hot Number," *The Wall Street Journal*, Nov. 9, 1989, p. B-1.
8. Stephen Holden, "The (900) Numbers to the Stars," *The New York Times*, Jan. 24, 1989, p. C-15.
9. Jack Kelley, "Call Bakkers, Where Talk Isn't Cheap," *USA Today*, Sept. 29, 1987, p. A-1.
10. Wayne Walley and Alison Fahey, " '900' Numbers, Ad Tie-ins Connect," *Advertising Age*, June 5, 1989, p. 12.
11. Frank E. James, "Battle of Miniature Cellular Telephones Heats Up with Launch of Motorola Model," *The Wall Street Journal*, May 5, 1989, p. B-1.
12. Julie Amparano Lopez, "Once High-Tech Toys, Cellular Phones Are Becoming Staples," *The Wall Street Journal*, Aug. 11, 1989, p. 1.
13. Ron Winslow, "Everybody with a PC," *The Wall Street Journal*, Sept. 16, 1985, p. 28-C.
14. Andrew Pollack, "Doing Business by Computer," *The New York Times*, July 10, 1986, p. D-2.
15. Jeffrey A. Tannenbaum, "Speed, Cost and Cachet Aid Growth of Electronic Mail," *The Wall Street Journal*, July 27, 1988, p. 19; Peter H. Lewis, "E-Mail Searches for a Missing Link," *The New York Times*, March 12, 1989, Business section, p. 6.
16. "Fax Fixation," *Advertising Age*, Aug. 15, 1988, p. 1.
17. Michele Manges, "Junk Mail in the Age of Fax," *The Wall Street Journal*, May 3, 1989, p. B-1.

18. Jim Bartimo, "At These Shouting Matches, No One Says a Word," *Business Week*, June 11, 1990, p. 78.
19. Stuart Silverstone and Craig L. Webb, "Many Newspapers, Small and Large, Turn to 'The Mac,' " *Presstime*, April, 1986, p. 23.
20. Andrew Pollock, "Computers Let a Thousand Publishers Bloom," *The New York Times*, Oct. 8, 1987, pp. D-1, D-4.
21. Elliot Jaspin, "Out with the Paper Chase, In with the Data Base," speech to participants in a technology studies seminar, Gannett Center for Media Studies, New York, March 20, 1989.
22. Alvin Achenbaum, "Videotex Misses Consumer Mark," *Advertising Age*, March 6, 1989, p. 50; Anika Michalowska and Dennis Chase, "French Finding Ways to Make Videotex Work," *Advertising Age*, March 24, 1986, p. 4.
23. Paul Lewis, "Biarritz Enjoys 'Videophone,' " *The New York Times*, April 21, 1986, p. D-12.

SUGGESTED READINGS

Aumente, Jerome, *New Electronic Pathways* (Beverly Hills, CA: Sage, 1987).
Condry, J., and D. Keith, *Educational and Recreational Uses of Computer Technology* (Beverly Hills, CA: Sage, 1983).
Haigh, R. W., G. Gerbner, and R. B. Byrne, *Communications in the Twenty-First Century* (New York: Wiley, 1981).
Kelleher, K., and T. B. Cross, *Teleconferencing: Linking People Together Electronically* (Englewood Cliffs, NJ: Prentice-Hall, 1985).
Tydeman, J., et al., *Teletext and Videotex in the United States: Market Potential, Technology and Public Policy Issues* (New York: McGraw-Hill, 1982).
Weaver, D. H., *Videotex Journalism* (Hillsdale, NJ: Erlbaum, 1983).

Credits

Text, tables, and figures

Chapter 5 Page 142, Table 5.1, "100 Leading Media Companies," *Advertising Age*, August 10, 1992. Reprinted by permission.

Chapter 6 Page 167, "AAP Estimated Industry Sales 1989–1990," *Publishers Weekly*, August 9, 1991, p. 10. Copyright © 1991 Publishers Weekly. Reprinted by permission.

Chapter 7 Page 187, Table 7.1, "Top 25 Newspapers By Circulation," *Advertising Age*, November 4, 1991. Reprinted by permission; p. 200, "Diverse Work Force Can Benefit Readers" by Barbara Reynolds, *USA Today*, 6/6/89. Copyright © 1989 USA Today. Reprinted by permission.

Chapter 8 Page 213, Table 8.1, "The Top 25 Magazines By Circulation" from *Advertising Age*. Reprinted by permission; p. 223, Figure 8.2, "Magazine Outlets," *The New York Times*, October 29, 1990. Copyright © 1990 by The New York Times Company. Reprinted by permission.

Chapter 9 Page 249, Table 9.1, "Top Billing Stations" from 1990 Edition of Duncan's Radio Market Guide. Reprinted by permission of James H. Duncan, Jr.

Chapter 10 Page 291, "Charting the Nielsen Ratings," *Variety*, January 6, 1992, p. 26. Reprinted by permission; p. 294, "Tapping the Hispanic Market," *The New York Times*, July 7, 1988. Copyright © 1988 by The New York Times Company. Reprinted by permission.

Chapter 11 Page 304, Figure 11.1, "How Cable Systems Operate" from *Communication Technology: The New Media of Society* by E. M. Rogers, p. 56. Copyright © 1986 by The Free Press. Reprinted with the permission of The Free Press, a division of Macmillan, Inc.; p. 309, "An Advertiser's Guide to Cable," *Advertising Age*, February 24, 1992, p. C-2. Reprinted by permission; p. 310, "Cable Penetration Accelerating; Reaches 54%," Nielsen figures from *Advertising Age* supplement, February 20, 1989. Reprinted by permission; p. 314 "Ted Turner's CNN Gains Global Influence & Diplomatic Role," *The Wall Street Journal*, 2/1/90. Copyright © 1990 Dow Jones & Company, Inc. Reprinted by permission of The Wall Street Journal. All Rights Reserved Worldwide; p. 331, Figure 11.2, "Time Spent with Cable is Growing" from Cabletelevision Advertising Bureau. Reprinted by permission.

Chapter 12 Page 343, Table 12.1, "The Four Models of Public Relations" from *Managing Public Relations* by James E. Grunig and Todd Hunt. Copyright © 1984 by Holt, Rinehart, and Winston, Inc. Reprinted by permission of the publisher.

Chapter 13 Page 371, Table 13.1, "U.S. Agencies Ranked by Worldwide Gross Income," *Advertising Age*, April 13, 1992. Reprinted by permission; p. 374, "Commercial Production Costs" from American Association of Advertising Agencies Inc. Reprinted by permission; p. 387, Table 13.2, "Top 15 Advertisers on Network Television," *Advertising Age*, May 13, 1991. Reprinted by permission; p. 388, Table 13.3, "Top 15 Brands Advertised on Cable," *Advertising Age*, December 10, 1990. Reprinted by permission.

Chapter 14 Page 431, "The Decline of Broadway," *Variety*, January 2, 1991, p. 95. Reprinted by permission; p. 438, "A Case of 'Severe Bias'" by Patricia Raybon, *Newsweek*, 10/2/89. Copyright © 1989 Patricia Raybon. Reprinted by permission of the author.

Chapter 15 Page 452, *Books to Bytes: The Computer and the Library* by Anthony Smith, November 1988, Occasional Paper No. 7. Reprinted by permission of Gannett Center for Media Studies, now known as The Freedom Forum Media Studies Center, New York, NY; p. 455, "The Campus Library of the Future: 'The Electronic Library'" from *Academe: Bulletin of the American Association of University Professors*, July/August, 1989, p. 7, Reprinted by permission.

Chapter 16 Page 475, "Once High Tech Toys, Cellular Phones Are Becoming Staples" by Julie A. Lopez, *The Wall Street Journal*, 8/11/89. Copyright © 1989 Dow Jones & Company, Inc. Reprinted by permission of The Wall Street Journal. All Rights Reserved Worldwide; p. 487, Figure 16.1, "How Videotext and Teletext Operate" from *Communication Technology: The New Media of Society* by E. M. Rogers, p. 46. Copyright © 1986 by The Free Press. Reprinted with the permission of The Free Press, a division of Macmillan, Inc.

Photos

Chapter 1 Pages 2–3, © Granitsas/The Image Works; p. 5, Copyright USA Today, reprinted with permission; p. 6, © Sidney, Stock, Boston; p. 8, © Granitsas/The Image Works; p. 11, Granitsas/The

Credits

Image Works; p. 13, Daemmrich, Stock, Boston; p. 20, © 1989, Pasley, Stock, Boston; p. 21, © Snider/The Image Works; p. 22, © Sulley/The Image Works.

Chapter 2 Pages 32–33, © Freeman, PhotoEdit; p. 35, © Schwerzel, Stock, Boston; p. 36, © Vohra, Picture Cube; p. 37, © 1991, Borkoski, Stock, Boston; p. 40, © Fleck, Liaison; p. 42, © Bourg, Liaison; p. 47, Savino/The Image Works; p. 48, Culver; p. 52 © 1989, Pasley, Stock, Boston; p. 55, © 1989, Horsman, Stock, Boston.

Chapter 3 Pages 60–61, © Levy, Liaison; p. 63, Antman/The Image Works; p. 68, © Zweig, Liaison; p. 73, Nielsen Media Research; p. 77, Globe.

Chapter 4 Pages 94–96, © Brenner, PhotoEdit; p. 101, De Keerle, Liaison; p. 103, © 1989, Siteman, Stock, Boston; p. 105, UPI/Bettmann; p. 109, © 1988, Gupton, Stock, Boston; p. 110, UPI/Bettmann; p. 117, PR Newswire; p. 122, Brissaud, Liaison; p. 125, © Daemmrich/The Image Works.

Chapter 5 Pages 128–129, © Neubauer, Monkmeyer Press Photo; p. 131, © Marcotte, Picture Cube; p. 133, © Stepanowicz, Picture Cube; p. 134, © Stepanowicz, Picture Cube; p. 138, Wildenberg-Figaro Magazine, Liaison; p. 141, Reuters/Bettman.

Chapter 6 Pages 154–155, © Brenner, PhotoEdit; p. 158, Granger; p. 160, Granger; p. 166, B. Dalton; p. 170 © Giboux, Liaison.

Chapter 7 Pages 176–177, © Snider/The Image Works; p. 182, Granger; p. 183, Granger.

Chapter 8 Page 215, © Grant, Picture Cube; p. 217, *Rolling Stone* magazine, by Straight Arrow Publishers, Inc., © 1992 Straight Arrow Publishers, Inc. All rights reserved. Reprinted by permission.

Chapter 9 Pages 226–227, © Howell, Liaison; p. 229, Bettmann Archive; p. 231, UPI/Bettmann; p. 232, Culver; p. 233, Bettmann Archive; p. 234, Culver; p. 237, UPI/Bettmann; p. 238, UPI/Bettmann; p. 241, UPI/Bettmann; p. 248, © Howell, Liaison; p. 251, Radio Advertising Bureau.

Chapter 10 Pages 254–255, Coletti, Picture Cube; p. 259, UPI/Bettmann; p. 261, UPI/Bettmann; p. 267, © 1989, Sander, Liaison; p. 275, Gifford, Liaison; p. 286, UPI/Bettmann; p. 289, Bettmann Archive; p. 292, Globe.

Chapter 11 Pages 300–301, © 1985, Siteman, Stock, Boston; p. 313, C-SPAN; p. 315, © 1991, CNN, Inc.; p. 319, © 1988, Lawfer, Picture Cube; p. 324, © Gallery, Stock, Boston; p. 328, © 1988, Kirn, Liaison; p. 330, Edinger, Liaison.

Chapter 12 Pages 334–335, © Alpher, Stock, Boston; p. 339, Granger; p. 341, UPI/Bettmann; p. 345, Harrison, Stock, Boston; p. 348, Greenwood, Liaison; p. 355, Reuters/Bettmann.

Chapter 13 Pages 362–363, Granger, Pepsi Cola International; p. 366, Hackel, © Coletti, Stock, Boston, Mazzaschi, Stock, Boston; p. 367, Granger; p. 375, Snitzer, Stock, Boston; p. 384, Absolut Vodka logo and bottle, ™ of V&S Vin & Spirit AB, Carillon Importers Ltd.; p. 396, *Advertising Age*.

Chapter 14 Pages 398–399, Rangefinders, Globe; p. 400, Neveu, Liaison; p. 403, Granger; p. 405, © Barnwell, Stock, Boston; p. 406, Culver; p. 408, Guboux, Liaison; p. 414, Culver; p. 416, Culver; p. 428, Culver; p. 430, © Kaiser, Picture Cube; p. 432, Crossroads Theater Co.; p. 438, © 1991, Ferguson, Globe.

Chapter 15 Pages 447, Granger; p. 448, © Crandall, Stock, Boston; p. 449, The Bridgewater, New Jersey Courier News, January 30, 1990. Photo reprinted with permission; p. 452, © Pedrick/The Image Works; p. 456, Baseball Hall of Fame; p. 457, © Cameramann/The Image Works; p. 459, AT&T InfoQuest; p. 460, National Air and Space Museum © 1992 Smithsonian Institution.

Chapter 16 Pages 464–465, © Herwig, Picture Cube; p. 467, courtesy Dow Jones and Co., Inc.; p. 468, The Hartford Courant; p. 470, © Isaacs, Liaison; p. 471, Sprint; p. 476, © 1989, Spahr, Liaison; p. 477, IBM; p. 483, Apple Computer, Inc.: Chase/Greenleigh; p. 489, © Greenlar/The Image Works.

Note: An attempt has been made to obtain permission from all suppliers of photographs used in this edition. Some sources have not been located, but permission will be requested from them upon notification to us of their ownership of the material. Material not credited was supplied by the authors.

Name Index

Abelman, Robert, 58
Abrams, Floyd, 397
Achenbaum, Alvin, 491
Adams, John, 338
Adams, R.C., 58
Adams, Samuel, 338
Adelson, Andrea, 253, 262
Adhikarya, Ronny, 92
Adler, Richard, 474
Agins, Teri, 462
Akroyd, Dan, 424
Aldridge, Ira, 427
Alexander, E. P., 462
Alger, Horatio, Jr., 157, 160
Allen, Gracie, 428
Allen, R. C., 436
Allen, Woody, 419–420
Almodovar, Pedro, 423
Alsop, Joseph, 121
Anderson, Elizabeth, 397
Andres, Kathleen, 440
Aristotle, 16–17
Arlen, Michael J., 397
Armstrong, Edward, 230
Arnaz, Desi, 261
Arnett, Peter, 315
Arnold, David, 397
Ashmole, Elian, 455
Astaire, Fred, 415
Astor, David, 202
Atkin, David, 297
Aumente, Jerome, 202, 488, 491
Ayer, N. W., 365

Baensch, Robert D., 174
Bagdikian, Ben H., 143, 202
Bakker, Jim, 474
Bakker, Tammy, 474
Baldwin, Thomas F., 332–333
Ball, Lucille, 261, 416
Ball, Samuel, 92
Ball-Rokeach, Sandra, 83, 92
Ballard, Audreen, 440
Bandura, Albert, 79, 92
Bantz, Charles R., 58
Banzhaf, John, III, 121
Baran, Stanley J., 92
Barbato, Joseph, 174
Barnouw, Eric, 253, 297
Barnum, Phineas Taylor, 339, 341–342
Barron, Jerome, 143
Bartimo, Jim, 491
Barwick, L., 30
Bates, Johnny, 15
Bates, S., 379
Beach Boys, The, 419
Beatles, The, 259
Becker, Samuel L., 57
Bell, Alexander Graham, 404, 469
Bennett, James Gordon, 180–181
Bennett, Tony, 114
Bennett, William, 439
Benny, Jack, 234

Berelson, Bernard, 80, 92
Bergen, Candice, 237
Bergen, Edgar, 237
Berkowitz, Leonard, 92
Berle, Milton, 259
Bernays, Edward, 340–341, 358, 458
Bert, B., 151
Bettey, Emily Verdery, 180
Billings, Victoria, 92
Bishop, Katherine, 469
Blasko, Vincent J., 92
Blau, Eleanor, 253
Block, Martin P., 333
Blumenthal, K., 361
Blumenthal, Norman, 294
Blumler, Jay, 92
Bly, Nellie, 183
Bobbin, Ray, 41
Bocuse, Paul, 138
Bogart, Leo, 190, 202
Boorstin, Daniel, 115, 160, 365
Booth, Edwin, 427
Botan, Carl, 358
Botto, Louis, 433
Bowers, Brent, 490
Boyer, Ernest, 54
Boyer, Peter J., 296
Bradsher, Keith, 193
Brady, Matthew, 182
Bremner, Brian, 425
Bricklin, Malcolm, 329
Broadbent, D. E., 57
Brody, E. W., 358
Broom, Blen M., 359
Brown, Les, 296
Brown, M. E., 30
Brown, Merrill, 296
Bryant, Jennings, 59
Budd, Richard D., 30, 93, 462, 490
Burbank, Luther, 458
Burger, Warren, 143, 307
Burgoon, Judee K., 58
Burgoon, Michael, 58
Burnett, Carol, 137
Burns, George, 428
Burton, Jack, 397
Burton, Richard, 453
Bush, George, 105, 112, 174, 285
Butler, Rhett, 420
Butterfield, Fox, 78
Buxton, Frank, 253
Byrne, R. B., 491

Caesar, Julius, 17
Cagney James, 415
Califano, J. A., 397
Campbell, K. K., 127
Campell, John, 180
Canby, Vincent, 333
Cantor, Bill, 356
Cantril, Hadley, 80, 92, 93
Capriati, Jennifer, 47
Carley, William M., 127

Carmody, Deirdre, 214
Carnegie, Andrew, 447
Carnevale, Mary Lu, 253
Carson, Johnny, 349
Caruba, Alan, 351
Caruso, Enrico, 229, 341
Cathcart, Robert, 58
Caxton, William, 157–158
Center, Allen H., 358
Cerf, Bennett, 162
Chancellor, John, 202
Chaplin, Charlie, 413, 415
Charren, P., 333
Chase, Dennis, 491
Cheney, Michael, 202, 298
Chopin, Frédéric, 413
Christopher, Maurine, 332
Christy, Edwin, 428
Cline, C. G., 3, 61
Clinton, Bill, 77
Close, Glenn, 425
Cohan, George M., 429
Cohen, Daniel, 283
Cohen, Morris, 64
Cohen, Roger, 174
Collins, Phil, 401
Combs, James E., 14, 30
Compaine, Benjamin M., 174, 225
Condry, J., 491
Corry, John, 296
Cosby, Bill, 438
Costner, Kevin, 320
Couzens, Michael, 297
Cox, Meg, 294
Craig, Robert T., 57
Creedon, Pamela J., 361
Crist, Judith, 417
Cronkite, Walter, 276
Crosby, Bing, 415
Cross, T. B., 491
Crouse, Timothy, 127
Crutchfield, Will, 435
Csikszentmihalyi, Mihaly, 58, 284, 297
Cunningham, Linda Grist, 200
Curley, John, 191
Cutlip, Scott M., 358

Dana, Charles A., 181
Danilov, Victor J., 462
Danky, J. P., 441
Davidson, David, 462
Davis, Bob, 297
Davis, Jim, 170
Day, Benjamin, 181
DeFleur, Melvin L., 81, 83, 92–93
De Forest, Lee, 229
Deigh, R., 361
DeJong, William, 49
Dembart, L., 202
Denisoff, R. S., 436
Dennis, Everette E., 7, 30, 197
Denver, John, 245
Dessauer, John P., 175

494

Name Index

Dewey, Melvil, 447
Diamond, E., 379
Dione, E. J., 253
Dizard, Wilson P., 30
Dizier, David M., 359
Doig, C., 127
Doig, I., 127
Donahue, Phil, 285, 439
Donaton, Scott, 333
Dougherty, Philip H., 224, 397
Downey, Morton, Jr., 285
Dukakis, Michael S., 78
Dumont, Allen B., 256

Easterbrook, Gregg, 127, 285, 296
Ebert, Roger, 68, 402
Eckert, Toby, 296
Eckholm, Erik, 63
Edison, Thomas, 403, 412–413, 420, 458, 466
Eichler, Glenn, 333
Eisenbery, A., 436
Elek, Janos, 9
Elliott, Deni, 148
Ellis, J. C., 436
Elson, R. T., 225
Emshwiller, John K., 202
Endres, Fred F., 358
Engel, Jack, 397
Epstein, E. J., 127
Estep, Rhoda, 14
Ettema, James S., 92

Fabrikant, Geraldine, 332, 397, 436
Fahey, Alison, 490
Fairbanks, Douglas, 415
Falwell, Jerry, 121
Fantel, Hans, 436
Farnsworth, Philo, 258
Feather, Frank, 39
Feinberg, Andrew, 441
Fields, Howard, 174
Firestone, Harvey, 458
Fish, Sandra L., 12, 58
Fisher, John, 198
Fiske, John, 58
Fitzgerald, F. Scott, 417
Fitzgerald, Kate, 333
Fonda, Jane, 401
Ford, Henry, 458
Fornatale, Peter, 253
Forrest, Edwin, 427
Foster, Eugene S., 253, 294, 332
Frank, J. F., 30
Franklin, Benjamin, 140, 157, 159, 180–181, 202, 338
Franklin, James, 180–181
Freedman, Alix M., 397
Freeman, Alan, 202, 397
Frish, Karl von, 57
Funabiki, Jon, 441
Fust, Johann, 157

Gable, Clark, 415
Gans, Herbert J., 13, 127
Garfield, 170
Gargett, T. F., 397
Garland, Judy, 455
Gartner, Michael, 189
Gates, G. P., 253

Gaudet, Hazel, 80, 92
Gay, Verne, 297
Gerbner, George, 76, 91, 491
Gertner, Richard, 415
Gillespie, Marcia Ann, 440–441
Gillmor, Donald, 143
Gish, Lillian, 415
Gitlin, Todd, 296–297
Glasser, Theodore, 123, 127
Godfrey, Arthur, 259
Goldberg, Bernard R., 262
Goldberg, Robert, 295, 297
Gomery, D., 436
Goodes, Melvin, 326
Goodman, Walter, 126, 397
Gore, Tipper, 409–410
Gowler, E., 333
Graber, Doris A., 58
Grace, J. Peter, 393–394, 397
Graham, Judith, 333
Greeley, Horace, 180–181
Greenberg, Bradley S., 92
Greenfield, Jeff, 297
Greenhouse, Linda, 202
Griffith, D. W., 413
Griggs, Robyn, 441
Grose, Donald B., 436
Gross, Larry, 91
Gross, Lynne S., 252–253, 297, 332
Grunig, James E., 343, 340, 342, 358, 490
Grunwald, Henry A., 211, 224
Gumbel, Bryant, 77
Gumpert, Gary, 12, 58
Gurevitch, Michael, 92
Gutenberg, Johann, 156, 158
Guy, Pat, 202

Hadden, Briton, 210
Hady, M. E., 441
Haigh, R. W., 491
Haley, Alex, 137
Hall, Arsenio, 438
Hamilton, Alexander, 181
Hammerstein, Oscar, II, 429
Hancock, Ellen M., 4
Hanks, Tom, 424
Hanson, Jarice, 332–333
Harmetz, Aljean, 436
Harris, Benjamin, 180
Harris, M. H., 463
Hawthorne, Nathaniel, 161
Hays, Will, 420
Hazleton, Vincent, 358
Hearst, William Randolph, 105, 180, 184, 416
Heffner, Hugh, 208
Heffner, Richard D., 422, 436
Hemingway, Ernest, 417
Henley, Beth, 432
Henry VIII, 159
Hensley, John E., 92
Hertz, Heinrich, 228
Heuvel, Jon Vanden, 30
Hewitt, Don, 276, 296
Hickey, Brian 358
Hiebert, Ray E., 358
Hill, Anita F., 139, 140
Holahan, C., 202
Holden, Stephen, 490

Hoover, Herbert, 234–235, 458
Hoover, Stewart M., 12
Hope, Bob, 416
Horowitz, Irving Louis, 11, 30, 232, 430
Houston, Whitney, 419
Hovland, Carl I., 58, 74, 94
Huffman, John, 87
Hume, Ellen, 115
Hunt, Morton, 44, 58
Hunt, Todd, 91, 127, 202, 343, 358, 490
Hymowitz, C., 361

Ice-T, 408
Ingrassia, Paul, 342
Innis, Harold Adams, 78, 91

Jackson, Andrew, 338, 340
Jackson, Lynn M., 64
Jackson, Michael, 331
Jacobson, Michael F., 397
James, Frank E., 474, 490
Jamieson, Kathleen, 127
Janis, Irving L., 91
Jaspin, Elliot, 491
Jay, John, 181
Jeff, D. J. Jazzy, 474
Jefferson, Thomas, 133, 160, 338
Jesuale, N., 333
Joggerst, Jo, 490
Johnson, Bradley, 219
Johnson, J. H., 215
Johnson, N., 361
Johnston, Jerome, 92
Jolson, Al, 414
Jones, Alex S., 202, 124
Jones, Dylan, 25

Kaatz, R., 397
Kael, Pauline, 417
Kaplan, Michael, 333
Kaplan, Peter W., 436
Katz, Elihu, 47, 58, 92
Katz, H., 463
Kauffman, Stanley, 417, 436
Keaton, Buster, 414
Keillor, Garrison, 247
Keith, D., 491
Kelleher, K., 491
Kelley, Harold H., 91
Kelley, Jack, 490
Kendall, Amos, 340
Kennedy, John F., 276, 285, 296, 412
Kensinger, Jones, 333
Kenworthy, Franklin O., 436
Keppler, Joseph, Jr., 183
Kern, Jerome, 429
Kern-Foxworth, Marilyn, 438
Khrushchev, Nikita, 349
Kindem, G. A., 436
King, Alan, 168
King, Larry, 241
Kitross, John, 253
Klapper, Joseph T., 79, 92
Kleppner, Otto, 396–397
Konrad, Walecia, 201
Koppel, Ted, 27
Kostelanetz, André, 236
Kreighbaum, Hillier, 127
Kubey, Robert, 58, 281, 284, 296–297

Laakaniemi, Ray, 202
Lamphier, Gary, 202
Landers, Ann, 351
Landro, Laura, 18–19, 30, 332
Lawrence, D. H., 417
Lawrence, David, 441
Lazarsfeld, Paul, 47, 58, 80, 92
Lederer, L., 92
Lee, Ivy Ledbetter, 340–341
Lembart, Lee, 193
Lesley, Philip, 359
Lessershon, Jim, 202
Lewin, Kurt, 102
Lewis, Emory, 436
Lewis, Paul, 491
Lewis, Peter H., 478
Lewis, Sinclair, 157
Lievrouw, Leah, 31
Lincoln, Abraham, 10, 412
Lindbergh, Charles, 232
Lindsey, R., 333
Lipman, Joanne, 224, 333, 380
Lippmann, Walter, 76, 91
Litman, Barry, 297
Locke, John, 136
Loftus, Elizabeth, 58
Loftus, Geoffrey, 58
Lopez, Julie Amparano, 490
Lowenstein, Ralph L., 91
Lowery, Shearon, 81, 93
Loy, Myrna, 415
Luce, Henry, 202, 210

MacArthur, Douglas, 412
McCabe, Peter, 297
McCombs, Maxwell E., 76, 91
McCormick, Ken, 162
McCroskey, James C., 58
McCue, G., 437
McDowell, Edwin, 174
McGehee, Scott, 202
McGrath, James, 253
Mackintosh, Cameron, 432
McLuhan, Marshall, 78, 91, 228, 252–253, 282, 372
McVoy, D. Steven, 332–333
Madison, Charles G., 175
Madison, James, 181
Madonna, 46
Mailer, Norman, 172
Main, J., 333
Malamuth, Neil M., 92
Malloy, Michael T., 202
Manges, Michele, 490
Mapplethorpe, Robert, 131, 146, 458
Marc, David, 257, 297
Marcom, John, Jr., 332
Marconi, Guglielmo, 228–230
Markham, James M., 462
Marsden, Michael, 397
Marston, John E., 346, 358
Martz, Larry, 441
Maslow, Abraham, 58, 376
Maxwell, Robert, 198
May, M., 437
Mayur, Rashmi, 39
Mears, Walter R., 202
Medill, Joseph, 182
Melies, George, 413
Melville, Herman, 161

Mendelson, Lee, 41
Merrill, John C., 91, 143
Merton, Robert, 75
Met, David, 432
Metzger, Nancy J., 58
Meyers, Janet, 202
Meyrowitz, Joshua, 79, 91–92
Michael, George, 331, 419
Michalowska, Anika, 491
Miller, Cyndee, 329
Mills, Joshua, 253
Millward, Emelia, 92
Milton, John, 136
Miranda, Carmen, 286
Mitchell, George, 313
Montana, Joe, 114
Moore, Timothy E., 397
Morris, R. J., 441
Mott, Frank Luther, 210–211, 224–225
Mowlana, Hamid, 30
Mozart, Wolfgang, 413
Murdoch, Rupert, 118, 164, 184, 198, 419
Murrow, Edward, 233
Muybridge, Eadweard, 412

Nader, Ralph, 121, 240
Napoleon Bonaparte, 412
Narine, D., 441
Nelson, Harold, 144
Neuhart, Allen, 191
Newcomb, Horace, 297
Newsom, Doug, 359
Nimmo, Dan, 14, 30, 92
Nixon, Richard, 276, 349
Noelle-Neumann, Elizabeth, 77, 91
Norris, Floyd, 143
North, Oliver, 110

Ochs, Adolph, 184
O'Connor, John J., 397
Ogilvy, David, 369, 397
Ong, Walter, 79, 91
Ornstein, Leigh, 490
O'Toole, John, 75
Owen, Bill, 253

Paine, Tom, 160
Paley, William S., 231
Palmer, Patricia, 92
Palmer, T., 437
Parker, Edwin, 30
Parton, Dolly, 245
Pauley, Jane, 349
Pavlik, John V., 359
Pearl, David, 92
Penn, Mark, 42
Percy, Susan, 84
Peterson, Theodore, 136, 144, 225
Petrillo, James C., 406
Phillips, David, 92
Phillips, Gerald M., 58
Phillips, Lisa E., 332
Picasso, Pablo, 462
Pickford, Mary, 415
Piirto, Rebecca, 174
Pinkham, Lydia E., 368
Pollack, Andrew, 242, 490–491
Pool, Ithiel de Sola, 31, 130, 143
Pope, Daniel, 397

Porter, Wedwin S., 413
Post, Emily, 157
Postman, Neil, 181, 256, 283, 296–297
Powell, William, 415
Pratt, Catherine, 145
Prescott, Eileen, 294
Presley, Elvis, 240, 458
Prince, Fresh, 474
Price, Julie, 358
Prince, 419
Pulitzer, Joseph, 180, 182–183
Pytte, Alyson, 332

Quayle, Dan, 7, 285

Rakow, L. F., 361
Rankin, Hugh F., 436
Rankin, W. Parkman, 202
Rather, Dan, 107, 285
Raybon, Patricia, 438, 441
Raymond, Henry, 180
Reagan, Ronald, 237–238, 276
Reed, Rex, 417
Reeves, Byron, 59
Reilly, Patrick M., 202, 224, 490
Revzin, Phillip, 39
Reynolds, Barbara, 202
Reynolds, R. J., 440
Riggio, Len, 174
Rivera, Geraldo, 285, 438
Rivers, William, 202
Roberts, Johnnie, 200, 202
Roberts, W. Rhys, 30
Rochter, Larry, 127
Rockefeller, John D., 340
Rockwell, Norman, 209
Rogers, Everett M., 58, 92, 487
Rogers, Ginger, 415
Rogers, Karen Helmer, 92
Roosevelt, Franklin Delano, 230, 237–238, 406
Rose, Ernest D., 143
Rosen, Richard, 168
Rosenthal, Andrew, 332
Rothenberg, Randall, 377
Rothmyer, K., 202
Rothstein, Mervyn, 432
Routt, Edd, 253
Rowell, G. P., 365
Ruben, Brent D., 30, 59, 93, 490
Ruben, Robbi L., 30
Rubin, Alan M., 58
Russell, V., 361
Ryan, Meg, 46

Sachsman, David, 201
Safire, William, 120
Salmas, Eileen Becker, 332
Salvaggio, Jerry L., 59
Sandler, M. W., 333
Sanger, David E., 333, 436
Sarnoff, David, 229, 231, 332
Scardino, Albert, 196
Schellhardt, T. D., 361
Schement, Jorge R., 31
Schiller, Herbert I., 16, 30–31, 76, 143
Schlesinger, Jacob M., 342
Schmertz, Herb, 336, 351, 358
Schramm, Wilbur, 136, 144
Schulz, Charles, 41
Schwartz, A., 463

Name Index

Scott, Willard, 286
Scripps, E. W., 105, 180
Selnow, Gary W., 13
Sennett, Mack, 413
Serrano, Andres, 146
Sethi, S. Prakash, 397
Shapiro, S., 397
Sharkey, Joe, 201–202, 490
Shaw, Donald L., 76, 91, 107
Shepard, Sam, 432
Sherman, Barry L., 253
Sherman, Ted, 332
Shoemaker, Floyd, 92
Siebert, Fred S., 136, 144
Signorielli, Nancy, 294
Silverstone, Stuart, 491
Simon, Neil, 432
Sims, Calvin, 297
Sinatra, Frank, 168
Sinclair, Upton, 157
Siskel, Gene, 68, 402
Skenazy, Lenore, 397
Sloat, Warren, 201, 462
Smikle, Ken, 441
Smith, Alfred G., 39
Smith, Anthony, 455, 462
Smith, H., 361
Smith, Liz, 351
Smith, R. L., 333
Smith, Ted J., III, 124, 127
Smolla, R. A., 144
Smothers, Ronald, 397
Snider, Paul B., 127
Sousa, John Philip, 404
Spielberg, Stephen, 418
Stahl, Lori, 441
Steffen, Lincoln, 184
Sterling, Christopher, 253
Stevens, Art, 358
Stevenson, Richard W., 294, 436
Stone, Oliver, 400
Stuart, Carol, 439
Stuart, Charles, 439
Sturken, Peter, 294
Sullivan, Ed, 259

Talese, Gay, 202
Tannenbaum, Jeffrey A., 490
Tarbell, Ida, 184
Taubman, Howard, 436
Tebbel, John, 175, 225
Teeter, Dwight, 144
Teinowitz, Ira, 201, 225, 333
Telander, Rick, 15
Thayer, Lee, 92, 490
Thomas, Clarence, 139–140
Thomas, Eugene, 15
Thompson, James Walter, 369
Toggerson, Steve K., 58
Toll, Robert C., 437
Toscanini, Arturo, 236
Toth, Elizabeth L., 360–361
Trauth, Denise, 87
Travis, Randy, 245
Trost, Cathy, 202
Trucco, Terry, 462
Tuchman, Gaye, 127
Turk, J. V., 361
Turner, Ted, 314
Turner, Tina, 372
Tyler, Ralph, 174
Tyndeman, J., 491
Tyson, Mike, 139

Udell, Jon G., 195, 202

Vail, Theodore, 338, 340
Valenti, Jack, 419, 422, 436
Valentino, Rudolph, 415
Van Der Meer, Tony, 439
Verne, Jules, 184, 416

Wallace, DeWitt, 209
Walley, Wayne, 332, 436, 490
Walsh, Calvin, 15
Walters, L. M., 361
Wannamaker, John, 373
Wartella, Ellen, 59
Washington, George, 211
Wasserstein, Wendy, 432
Waterman, David, 143

Wayne, John, 416
Weaver, D. H., 361, 491
Webb, Craig L., 491
Weilbacher, William M., 377, 397
Weiskel, Timothy, 462
Weiss, Fredrich, 253
Weiss, P., 201
Weiss, W., 58
Welles, Orson, 230, 416
Wennberg, Kristin, 332
Westheimer, Ruth, 12
Wheeless, Lawrence R., 58
Whitaker, Charles, 441
White, David Manning, 127
White, H., 397
White, William Allen, 182
Whitney, D. Charles, 119
Wicklein, John, 294
Wilcox, Dennis L., 359
Wildmon, Donald, 392
Wilkinson, Miriam, 58
Will, George, 351
William, Grant, 333
Williams, Andy, 237
Williams, Frederick, 31, 315
Williams, Jerry, 240
Williams, Lena, 462
Wilmot, G. Cleveland, 361
Wilson, Woodrow, 365
Winfrey, Oprah, 438
Winleman, M., 361
Winslow, Ron, 490
Winsten, Jay A., 49
Wolseley, Roland E., 225
Wood, Leonard, 451
Wright, Charles R., 30, 75, 91, 93

Yarrow, Andrew L., 462
Yovovich, B. G., 201, 224

Zassoursky, Yassen, 30
Zenger, John Peter, 180
Zimbardo, Phillip, 58
Zuckerman, L., 201
Zworykin, Vladimir, 256, 258

Subject Index

AAA World, 13
Action for Children's Television (ACT), 121
Advance Publications, 142
Advertising, 15, 25, 41–42, 47, 69, 122, 187–188, 222, 231, 250–252, 364–396
   agencies, 368–372
   and the ancient Greeks, 364
   attention to, 383–384
   audiences, 377–380, 382–383
   the Audit Bureau of Circulation (ABC), 365
   and the Boston *Newsletter*, 364–365
   and cable television, 309, 388
   cigarette, 13, 365, 390–392
   consumer pressures, 392–393
   consumers, 377–380, 382–383
   corrective, 375
   costs, 370–381
   credit card, 13
   definitions, 375–377
   directed toward blacks, 382
   directed toward college students, 382
   direct marketing, 385–386
   economics, 67, 370, 374, 379–381
   ethics, 149–150
   expenditures, 387
   and the Federal Communications Commission (FCC), 365
   functions, 373–374
   government regulation, 288–290
   history, 364–369
   house ads, 102
   how it works, 372–379
   impact, 373
   industrial, 374
   industry, 368–372
   informational, 374
   international, 372
   issue, 374–375
   and lifestyle, 378
   liquor, 390–392
   and mass communication, 12
   and media regulation, 393–395
   minorities in, 441
   monitoring and regulation, 388–396
   N. W. Ayer & Son, 365
   national, 374
   and news, 101–102
   and newspapers, 187–188
   patent medicines, 366–368
   political, 374–375
   pressures, 117
   products, 377
   public service, 374
   radio, 228
   research, 379–380
   retail, 374
   self-regulation, 395–396
   subliminal, 384–385
   and the Supreme Court, 390
   television, 266–268, 374, 382–383, 387
   theories, 375–377
   time capsule, 365
   trade, 374
   truth in, 390

Advertising Age, 216, 365, 396
Advertising agencies, 368–372
   Backer Spielvogel Bates Worldwide, New York, 371
   BBDO Worldwide, New York, 370–371
   DDB Needham Worldwide, New York, 371
   Foote, Cone & Belding, New York, 371
   J. Walter Thompson, 368–371
   Lintas Worldwide, New York, 371
   McCann-Erickson Worldwide, New York, 370–371
   N. W. Ayer & Son, 365, 368
   Ogilvy and Mather, 368–371
   Saatchi & Saatchi Advertising Worldwide, New York, 370
   Ted Bates, 370–371
   Young & Rubicam, 370
Agenda setting, 74, 76
American Advertising Federation, 395
American Antiques, 215
American Association of Advertising Agencies, 395
American Association of Retired Persons (AARP), 214, 223–224
American Baby, 214
American Broadcasting Company (ABC), 231
American Glass Review, 218
American Legion Magazine, 213
American Legion Magazine, The, 214
American Library Association (ALA), 448, 453
American Newspaper Publishers Association (ANPA), 185–186, 472
American Radio Company, 247
American Society of Composers, Authors, and Publishers (ASCAP), 69, 406–407
American Society of Newspaper Editors (ASNE), 185–186, 200
American Telephone & Telegraph (AT&T), 229–231, 338, 458–459, 469–472
American Way, The, 215
American Zionist, The, 214
"America's Most Wanted," 25
"Amos 'n' Andy," 237, 239
Ampersand's Guide to College Entertainment, 218
Anonymity, 56
Anti-trust legislation, 139
Apollo Theater, The, 427
Apparel Industry Magazine, 218
Arbitron ratings, 69, 289
Architectural Digest, 212
Aristotle, 16–17
Arizona Republic, 187
Armour's Farmer's Almanac, 206
Around the World in Eighty Days, 184, 415
Arts & Entertainment Network, 312
Associated Press, The (AP), 104–106, 180–181
Associated Press Stylebook, 108
Association of American Publishers, 166–167, 170
Atlanta Constitution, The, 185

Atlantic Monthly, The, 121, 207
Audience(s), 7, 20–25, 27–28, 50–53, 62–74, 80–84, 100, 125, 172, 220–221, 235, 239, 247, 264
   access, 62
   access research, 66, 70
   advertising, 377–380, 382–383
   attitude, 62–63
   attitude research, 70–72
   awareness, 62–63
   awareness research, 66, 70–72
   behavior, 62–63
   behavior research, 66, 70–72
   book, 161
   cable television, 302, 310–312, 316
   characteristics, 63–65
   college, 218
   couples, 100
   demographic research, 66, 70
   demographics, 64–65
   economics, 67
   effects on, 73–91
   elite, 65
   exposure, 62
   exposure research, 66, 70
   families, 100
   feedback systems, 65–73
   film, 402, 418–419
   general, 65, 68
   groups, 100
   individuals, 100
   knowledge, 62–63
   knowledge research, 66
   library, 445
   live performance, 426–427, 432
   magazine, 211–214, 216, 219–221
   measurement, 62–65, 248–250
   music, 402, 411
   newspaper, 187
   opinion, 62–63
   opinion research, 70–72
   organizations, 100
   perceptions, 124
   psychographic research, 66, 70
   psychographics, 64–65
   public relations, 343–347, 351–352
   radio, 228, 239–240, 244–246, 248–250
   research, 54, 62–63, 65–73
   size, 64
   societies, 100
   specialized, 65
   support, 67
   television, 264, 280–284
   theater, 402
   types, 65
   video, 321
   women, 218–219
Audit Bureau of Circulation (ABC), 69, 219, 365
Auteur theory, 415
Auto Laundry, 218

"Baby Bells," 472
Barnum, P. T., 339
Battle of Bunker Hill, 427
BBDO Worldwide, New York, 370–371
Bernays, Edward, 341–342

Subject Index

Better Homes & Gardens, 213
"Beverly Hills, 90210," 6
Bias
   conservative, 123
   liberal, 123
   in mass media, 123
   minority, 126
   news, 126
Billboard, 69, 411
"Birth of a Nation," 413
Black, Gordon S., Corporation, 75
Black-oriented radio, 244
Black publishers, 215
Bon Appetit, 212
Book industry, 162–167
Book publishers, 163–164
   general, 168–169
   specialized, 168–169
Book publishing economics, 67, 163–167
Books, 69, 156–174
   in America, 159–162
   audiences, 161
   children's, 169
   coffee-table, 173
   in England, 158–159
   erotica, 169
   hardcover, 162–163
   hobby, 169
   how-to, 169
   law, 169
   and literacy, 160–161
   marketing, 168, 169–171
   paperback, 162–163
   professional, 169
   publishing, 162–169
   readers, 172
   reference, 169
   religious, 169
   sales, 167
   scientific, 169
   self-publishing, 169
   as status symbols, 168
   technical, 169
   textbooks, 166–167, 169
   uses, 172–173
Bookselling, 165–166
Bookstores, 165–166
"Boom boxes," 411
Boston *Globe,* 187
Boston *Herald,* 187
Boston *News-Letter,* 180
Bride, 212
British Museum, 446
Broadcast media, 156–174
Broadcast Music, Inc. (BMI), 406
Broadcasting, 130
   Chain Regulations, 236
   public, 246–248
   spectrum allocation, 257
   UHF (ultra high frequency), 242
   VHF (very high frequency), 242
Broadsheets, 178–179
Broadway, 430–431
Burson-Marsteller, 340
Business Week, 212
Business Week Careers, 218

Cabbage Patch Dolls and public relations, 348–349
Cable advertising, 388
Cable Communication Act of 1984, 306
Cable News Network (CNN), 8–9, 71, 268, 312, 314–315, 327

Cable television, 5, 87, 302–318
   and advertising, 309
   audiences, 302, 310–312, 316
   consumers, 310, 312, 316
   deregulation, 306–308
   economics, 67, 308–313
   interactive, 317–318
   Knight-Ridder, 194–195
   Qube, 194
   regulation, 304–308
   services, 313–316
   sports, 317
   subscription fees, 314, 316–317
   technology, 303–304
   and the telephone companies, 308
   time capsule, 306
California Business, 214
Cameras in the court room, 139
Campus Voice, 218
Canadian videotex, 488
Canons of Journalism, 185
Capital Cities/ABC, 141–142
Carnegie free libraries, 447
Casablanca, 415
Categories of news, 100, 111–113
Cats, 430
CATV, 306
CBN Family Channel, 312
CD-ROM, 446
Censorship and film, 420–422
Century, 207
"Charlie McCarthy," 237
Chicago *Sun-Times,* 186–187
Chicago *Tribune,* 182, 185, 187
Children's Advertising Review Unit, 395
Children's Playmate, 214
Chorus Line, A, 401
Christian Athlete, The, 214
Christian Bookseller, 218
Christian Science Monitor, The, 42, 185
Citizen Kane, 184, 415
Cleveland *Plain Dealer,* 187
Colliers, 208
Columbia Broadcasting System (CBS), 141, 230–233, 256
Columbia Journalism Review, 121
Columbia Pictures, 418
Columbia Record Company, 231, 407
Commercial broadcast television economics, 67
Common carriers, 130
Communication
   contexts of, 36–38
   dynamics, 38
   group, 36–37
   human, 34
   impersonal, 36–37
   interpersonal, 36–38
   intrapersonal, 36–38
   mass, 36–38
   media, 4
   modes of, 36–38
   organizational, 36–38
   personal, 36–37
   private, 36–37
   process of, 36–38
   public, 36–37
   reciprocity in, 34
   technology, 4, 8, 39
Community antenna television (CATV), 303–304
Compact discs (CDs), 407–408, 446

Compuserve, 485
Computer(s), 5–7, 469
   bulletin boards, 480
   and employee communication, 481–482
   and mass communication, 55, 475–490
   and news, 192–194
   and newspaper, 192–194
   and the workplace, 476–483
   work stations, 481
Computer-aided meetings, 481
Consumer(s), 7, 20–25, 27–28, 50–53, 62–74, 80–84, 100, 125, 172, 220–221, 235, 239, 247, 264, 343–347, 351–352
   action, 120–123
   advertising, 377–380, 382–383
   attitudes of, 51–52
   behavior, 65
   cable television, 310, 312, 316
   capabilities of, 52
   characteristics, 45–48, 50–53
   communication style, 53
   context, 53
   decision making, 29, 66
   experiences, 53–54
   film, 402, 418–419, 423–424
   goals of, 52
   habits, 53–54, 380
   individual, 122
   interests, 168
   libraries, 445
   live performances, 426–427, 432
   magazine, 223–224
   music, 402, 411
   needs of, 51
   penetration, 222–223
   as producers, 411
   public relations, 343–347, 351–352
   radio, 228, 239–240, 248–250
   resistance, 349
   television, 280–284
   theater, 402
   utilities, 53
   values of, 51–52
   video, 321
Consumer News Business Channel (CNBC), 313
Consumers Union, The, 393
Consumption, 23–24, 36–57, 66, 239
   information, 36–57
   magazines, 223–224
   radio, 228
Continental Cablevision, 142
Cooking Light, 212
Copyright, 137
Copyright Act, 166
Corporation for Public Broadcasting (CPB), 246–247, 258, 270
Cosmopolitan, 213, 222
Council of Better Business, National Advertising Division, 122
Courier News, 72, 83
Courier-Journal, 182
Cox Enterprises, 142
Credibility, 46–47
Crisis management and public relations, 353–354
Critics, 67–68, 121
C-SPAN, 306, 313–315
Cultivation theory, 74, 76

Cultural information, 10–11
Culture, 10–16, 70
  distribution of, 10
  and information, 10–16
  on prime-time television, 14
  packaging of, 10
  popular, 24
Czechoslovakia, mass communication in, 9

Daily Record, The, 200
Dallas *Morning News*, 187
Database(s), 197, 483–486
  Academic American Encyclopedia, 484
  American Express Advance, 484
  Cineman Movie Reviews, 484
  Compuserve, 485
  costs, 485
  Dow Jones Historical Quotes, 484
  and libraries, 484
  Medical and Drug Reference, 484
  Merrill Lynch Research Service, 484
  Official Airline Guide, 484
  Peterson's College Selection Service, 484
  and research, 485–486
Database services, 10
DDB Needham Worldwide, New York, 371
Democracy, 21
Desert Storm, 8
Desktop publishing, 482–483
Des Moines Register, The, 185
Detroit *Free Press*, 187
Detroit *News*, 187
Diffusion of innovations, 74, 82
Digital radio, 242
Disinformation, 115
Disney Studios, 418
Donnelley, R. R., Company, 213
"Doogie Howser, M.D.," 7
"Doonesbury," 178
Dorm, 218
Dow Jones NewsRetrieval service, 194–195, 467–468

Easy Rider, 415
Ebony, 208, 215
Economics, 25, 39
  advertising, 379–381
  book publishing, 163–167
  databases, 485
  entertainment industry, 401
  film, 415, 423–426
  magazines, 222–223
  mass communication, 12–13
  radio, 250–252
  theater, 433–434
Education, 88–89
Educational television economics, 67
Effects of mass communication, 18–19, 73–91
  consumer perspective, 74, 80–84
  producer perspective, 74–80, 83–85
Egypt, mass communication in, 17
Elections and radio, 237
Electronic information services, 466
Electronic ministry, 11
Electronic publishing, 472
Electronic services
  fiber optics, 471–472
  time capsule, 469

EM, 215
E-mail, 479
Endorsements, 137–138
Entertainment, 6, 11–12, 24, 41–42, 68, 400–401
  and correlation, 400–401
  economics, 401
  financial pressures, 401
  and hard news, 401
  marketing, 401
  and "pack journalism," 401
  political pressure, 402
  and ritual, 401–402
  roles played by, 400–411
  and social heritage, 401
  and soft news, 401
  surveillance, 400–401
  theater, 401
Entertainment industry, 400–412
Entertainment media ethics, 150
"Entertainment Tonight," 266
Entertainment Weekly, 212
Erie County voting study, 74, 80, 82
ESPN, 312
Ethics, 135–136, 148–151
  codes, 135–136
Europe, mass communication in, 9, 39
Experimental attitude change studies, 74–75

Face-to-face communication, 19
Facsimile (FAX) machines, 480–481
Fairness Doctrine, 393
Family Circle, 213
Family values, 12
Farm Futures Magazine, 218
Farm Journal, 214
Fax and mass communication, 21
Federal Communications Commission (FCC), 121–122, 230, 240–241, 235–236, 246, 257, 271–273, 295, 306, 365
Federal Radio Act, 230
Federal Trade Commission (FTC), 388–389, 391
Federalist Papers, 181, 340
Feedback, 120, 126
  in mass communication, 7
  verbal, 66–67
Feedback systems
  market-based, 66–70
  in mass communication, 65
  research-based, 66, 70–73
Fiber optics, 471–472
Field research, 73
Film(s), 39, 69, 402, 412–426
  audiences, 418–419
  auteur theory, 415
  Canadian, 426
  and censorship, 420–422
  consumers, 418–419
  economics, 67, 415, 423–426
  formulas, 417–418
  international, 421
  international demand, 425–426
  "national treasures," 415
  pretesting, 424–425
  production costs, 415
  research, 83
  and self-regulation, 420–422
  stars, 414–416
  studios, 414–416, 418–420

  and the Supreme Court, 421–422
  top-grossing, 242
  voluntary rating system, 422–423
Film industry, 412–426
  development, 412–420
  studios, 414–416
Film studio ownership, 418–420
"Financial Interest and Syndication Rules," 272
First Amendment, 130, 132, 145–147
First for Women, 213
Flexography, 196–197
Food and Drug Administration (FDA), 389
Foote, Cone & Belding, New York, 371
Forbes, 212, 214
Fortune, 212, 214
Freedom of Information Act, 119, 132, 135
Freedom of speech, 145–147
Freedom of the press, 145–147
Freedom's Journal, 180
Front Page, The, 185
Functional analysis, 74–76

Gag rules, 139
"Gangbusters," 238
Gannett Company, 142, 180, 191–192
Gannett News, 199
"Garbage analysis," 72
Gatekeeper, 102
Gatekeeping, 107
Gender roles and television, 262
General Electric, 141–142, 229, 256
General Motors, 342–343
Gentlemen's Magazine, The, 206–208
Gentlemen's Quarterly, 212, 221
Glamour, 212
Global communication, 39
Global village, 39
Godey's Lady's Book, 208
Gone with the Wind, 412, 416
Good Housekeeping, 213, 222
Graduate, The, 415
Great Train Robbery, The, 413
Greece, mass communication in, 16–17
Group communication, 36–37
Group W Cable Inc, 310
Gutenberg, Johann, 156–157

Hackensack (New Jersey) *Record*, 189
Hardware Age, 218
Harper's Monthly, 207–208
Harper's Weekly, 209
Hate speech, 138
Hearst Corp, 142
Hill and Knowlton, 340
Hippocrates, 214
Hollywood Reporter, 215
Home Box Office, 306
Home office, 212
Home Shopping Network, 206
House and Garden, 212, 215
House Beautiful, 215
House Plants and Porch Gardens, 215
Human information consumption, 36–57
Hungary, mass communication in, 9
Hypodermic-needle approach, 18

Illiteracy, 173–174
Imitative effect, 63
Impersonal communication, 36–37

Subject Index

Influence, 41–42
Infoquest, 458–459
Information, 22, 24, 34
 advertising, 374
 business, 469–471
 buying by phone, 473
 channels, 483–490
 consumption, 36–57
 context, 53
 creation of, 34
 decay, 43
 distribution and libraries, 444–445
 economics, 39
 entertainment, 6
 factors that influence, 45–57
 filtering, 40–41
 flow and public relations, 336–337, 347
 freedom of, 132–135
 free flow of, 135
 interpretation, 38, 41–42
 literacy, 28–29
 manipulation, 100, 113–123
 overload, 28–29
 processing, 4, 34, 36–37, 43–44
 processing cycle, 43–44
 producers, 45–48, 66
 production, 45
 retention, 38
 selection, 38–41
 transmission of, 34
 uses of, 43–44
Information Age, 4, 7, 9, 28–29, 135
Information consumers, 50–53, 66
 attitudes of, 51–52
 capabilities of, 52
 characteristics, 45–48, 50–53
 communication style, 53
 context, 53
 experiences, 53–54
 goals of, 52
 habits, 53–54
 needs of, 51
 utilities, 53
 values of, 51–52
Information producers
 attractiveness, 46
 authority, 46
 characteristics, 45–48
 credibility, 46–47
 intent, 47–48
 motivation, 47–48
 similarity of consumer to, 46
Information products, 23, 26–27, 29, 45, 48–50, 68, 74, 100
 characteristics, 45, 48–50
 media, 48
 novelty, 50
 organization, 49
 physical characteristics, 49
Information services, 23, 26–27, 45, 68, 74, 100
 characteristics, 45
 economics, 67
 electronic, 466
Informational programming, 11–12
In Health, 214
"Inner Sanctum," 238
INTELSAT V, 306
Interactive media, 21–22
Interactivity, 29
 and museums, 455–458

International Association of Business Communicators (IABC), 135, 357
International communication, 7–10, 21, 39
International mass communication, 7–10, 243
International media, 7–10
International News Service (INS), 180
International radio, 243
Interpersonal communication, 36–38
 and technology, 27
Interpersonal messages, 20
Intrapersonal communication, 36–38
Inverted pyramid, 49, 106
Investigative reporting, 100

J. Walter Thompson, 368, 370–371
Jazz Singer, The, 413
Jet, 215
Journalism, 17, 185–186
 conflicts of interest, 119–120
 quality of, 9
 research, 124
 yellow, 184
Journalist(s), 102
 changing role of, 116
 conflicts of interest, 119–120
Journal of Commerce, 198
Jukeboxes, 405–406

KABC-AM, Los Angeles, 249
KDKA, Pittsburgh, 230
KGO-AM, San Francisco, 249
KIIS-AM/FM, Los Angeles, 249
Kinkos, 166–167
Kiwanis, 214
KLOS-FM, New York, 249
KMOX-AM, St. Louis, 249
Knight-Ridder, 142
Knight-Ridder Free Press, 199
KNX-AM, Los Angeles, 249
KOST-FM, Los Angeles, 249
KPWR-FM, Los Angeles, 249
KRTH-AM/FM, Los Angeles, 249
KVIL-AM/FM, Dallas, 249

Ladies' Home Journal, 208, 213, 222
Lasswell's approach to mass communication, 18–19
Lear's, 219
Lee, Ivy, 340
Legal issues, 118–123
 and mass media, 136–139, 145–147
Legal threats, and news, 100
Leisure, 212
Leisure, 56–57
Libel, 137
Libel laws, 118
Libraries, 70, 444–454
 audiences, 445
 campus libraries of the future, 454
 consumers, 445
 economics of, 67
 electronic, 452–454
 functions, 445
 future, 454
 history, 445–447
 and mass communication, 4, 444–445
 role of, 448–451
 specialized, 448
 time capsule, 446
Library of Congress, 446–448

Life, 208–210, 212
Lifeline, 312
Limitations of mass communication, 54–57
Limited communication modes of mass communication, 54–55
Lintas Worldwide, New York, 371
Literacy, 28–29, 160–163
Live performances, 426–435
 audiences, 426–427, 432
 burlesque, 428–429
 consumers, 426–427, 432
 minstrels, 428–429
 sports, 434–435
 theater, 427–434
 theme parks, 434–435
 vaudeville, 428–429
Long Island *Newsday*, 187, 199
Look, 209–210
Los Angeles Times, 185, 187, 189, 191
 NewsFax, 198
"Lux Radio Theatre," 238

Magazine Publishers Association (MPA), 136, 220
Magazine(s), 69, 206–224
 and advertising, 216
 alumni, 214
 association, 214
 audiences, 213, 219, 221
 Black-oriented, 215
 business, 214
 categories, 214–216
 children's, 214
 circulation, 213, 215, 223–224
 club, 214
 college, 214, 217
 computer, 220
 craft, 215
 creating, 220
 economics, 222–223
 ethnic, 214
 financial, 214
 fraternal, 214
 functions, 211
 the future, 220–224
 garden, 215
 health, 214
 history, 206–211
 hobby, 215
 home, 215
 in-flight, 215
 and lifestyle, 220
 literary, 206–207, 216
 mass appeal, 208
 men's, 216
 minorities in, 440
 religious, 214
 sales, 223
 selective binding, 213–214
 services, 211
 special-interest, 211–212
 target audiences, 211–214
 and television, 210
 time capsule, 208
 trade, 216, 218
 university, 214, 217
 women's, 216, 218–219
Manipulation of information, 113–123
Marketing, 385–386
 museums, 461–462
Market penetration, 222–223

"Marketplace," 247
Mass communication, 10, 36–38
   and anonymity, 56
   commercializing function, 15–16
   and concerts, 22
   consumption, 12–13, 23–24, 36–57, 66, 83–84
   context, 53
   and culture, 10–16
   definition, 10
   distribution, 24
   in Eastern Europe, 9
   effects, 18–19, 73–91
   and family values, 12
   functions of, 10–16
   and gender roles, 12
   and imitation, 63
   institutions, 8–10, 23
   international, 7–10
   inventories, 26
   and justice, 25
   and lifestyles, 12
   limitations of, 54–57
   and limited communication modes, 54–55
   and mass communication, 88–89
   and mass media, 8–9
   and minorities, 126
   origins of the concept, 16–17
   organizations, 23, 25–26, 140–143
   and people of color, 438–441
   and politics, 14, 77–78
   popularizing function of, 11–15
   and pornography, 86–88
   process, 24–25
   and public opinion, 86
   and public speaking, 16–17
   research, 66
   role of, 10–16
   and sex, 11, 14, 86–88
   and socialization, 89–90
   sources, 124
   in the Soviet Union, 9
   and sports, 14
   and suicide, 63
   and theme parks, 16
   and transportation, 56–57
   uses of, 23
   validating function of, 11–15
   values in, 13
   and violence, 11, 85–86
   and women, 126
Mass communication consumers, 7, 20–25, 27–28, 50–53, 62–74, 80–84, 100, 125, 172, 192, 216, 219–221, 235, 239, 247, 264
   action groups, 120–123
   attitudes of, 51–52
   books, 172
   capabilities of, 52
   characteristics of, 45, 50–53
   college students, 218
   communication style, 53
   context, 53
   experiences, 53–54
   goals of, 52
   habits, 53–54
   influence of, 172, 192
   interest, 168
   magazines, 211–214, 220–221
   measurement, 249–250
   newspapers, 179, 187
   perceptions, 124
   and regulation, 132
   research, 62–63, 65
   television, 264
   utilities, 53
   values of, 51–52
   women, 218
Mass communication producers, 7, 22–25, 67–68, 74–80, 100, 171–172, 192, 220, 235, 247, 264
   attractiveness, 46
   authority, 46
   characteristics, 45–48
   credibility of, 46–47
   decision making, 172
   intent, 47–48
   motivation, 47–48
   and regulation, 132
   similarity of consumer to, 46
Mass communication production, 23–24, 66
Mass communication products, 23, 26–27, 29, 67–68, 74, 100, 172, 192
   characteristics of, 48–59
   media, 48
   magazines, 220
   novelty, 50
   organization, 49
   physical characteristics, 49
   repetition, 50
   television, 264
Mass communication regulation, 130–132
Mass communication services, 23, 26–27, 68, 74, 100
Mass communication sources, attention to, 38, 40–41
Mass communication technology, 256
Mass media, 10, 29, 156–174, 386–388
   advertising pressure, 117
   anti-trust legislation, 139
   bias, 123
   cameras in the court room, 139
   commercial control, 115–118
   competition, 116–117
   concept, 17–23
   conflicts of interest, 119–120
   copyright, 137
   criticism, 123–126
   critics, 121
   definition of, 10
   endorsements, 137–138
   ethics, 148–151
   four theories of the press, 136
   gag rules, 139
   and government pressure, 118–119
   hate speech, 138
   and information, 124–125
   laws, 118
   legal and political threats, 118–123
   legislation, 118
   legislative coverage, 139
   libel, 137
   marketplace pressures, 141–143
   and mass communication, 8–9, 26
   minorities in, 197, 215
   ownership, 140–143
   privacy, 126
   radio, 228–252
   regulation, 130–132
   sensationalism, 125
   Shield laws, 138–139
   slander, 137
   and society, 125
   sources, 124
   sponsorship, 117
   women in, 360–361
Mass media consumers, 125
Mass media cycle, 107
Mayflower Decision, 230
MCA, 69
McCall's, 213
McCann-Erickson Worldwide, New York, 370–371
McClure's, 184, 208
Meaning, 34–36, 41–42
Media
   broadcasting, 9
   communication, 4
   convergence of, 5–7, 386–388
   critics, 66–68
   hybrid, 5–7, 386–388
   interactive, 21–22
   news, 4, 8
   reviewers, 67–68
Media regulation, and advertising, 393–395
Media system dependency, 74, 83
Memory, 43–44
   decay, 43
   long-term, 43
   short-term, 43
Men's Fitness, 214
"Mercury Theater of the Air," 238
Message reception, 34
Message sending, 34
Metropolitan Museum of Art, 446
Metropolitan Opera House, 229
MGM/UA Studios, 418–419
Miami *Herald*, 185, 187, 196
Microwaves, 218
Middle East, mass communication in, 7, 9
Midnight Cowboy, 415
Minneapolis *Star-Tribune*, 199
Minneapolis–St. Paul *Star Tribune*, 187
Minorities
   in mass communication, 438–441
   and mass media, 126, 197, 200–201
   in public relations, 357
Mirabella, 219
Model Railroader, 215
Modeling theory, 74–79
Modern Maturity, 213–214, 223–224
Money, 206
Morality, 148–151
"Moscow Meets Main Street," 124
Motion Picture Association of America (MPAA), 136, 419, 422
Motion Picture Producers and Distributors Association of America (MPPDAA), 415, 420–421
Movie(s), 39, 69, 402, 412–426
   audiences, 418–419
   auteur theory, 415
   Canadian, 426
   and censorship, 420–422
   consumers, 418–419
   economics, 67, 415, 423–426
   formulas, 417–418
   international, 421
   international demand, 425–426
   "national treasures," 415
   pretesting, 424–425

Subject Index

production costs, 415
research, 83
and self-regulation, 420–422
stars, 414–416
studios, 414–416, 418–420
and the Supreme Court, 421–422
top-grossing, 242
and VCRs, 320–321
voluntary rating system, 422–423
"Mr. and Mrs. North," 238
Ms., 208, 218
MTV, 8, 230, 312, 409
Muckraking, 184
Multimedia, 6
Munsey's, 208
"Murphy Brown," 7, 12
Museum for a New Century, 446
Museums, 70, 444–446, 454–462
    corporate, 458–460
    criticisms, 460
    development, 455
    economics, 67
    environmental, 455–458
    interactive, 455–458
    marketing, 461–462
    sports, 455
    static, 455–458
    time capsule, 446
    types, 455–460
Music, 402
    American Society of Composers, Authors, and Publishers (ASCAP), 406–407
    Broadcast Music, Inc. (BMI), 406
    compact discs (CDs), 407–408
    Grammy Awards, 403
    Parental Advisory label, 409–410
    piracy, 411–412
    popular, 408–410
    radio, 234–235
    rock, 402
    technology, 406–407
    videos, 230, 408–409
Musicals, 402
Music industry, 403–412, 419
    history, 403–408
    monitoring audiences, 411
Mutual Broadcasting System, 230–231

The Nashville Network (TNN), 312
National Academy of Recording Arts & Sciences, 408
National Advertising Division (NAD), 395
National Advertising Review Council (NARC), 395
National Advisory Commission on Civil Disorders, 121
National Air and Space Museum, 446
National Association of Broadcasters (NAB), 136, 234, 241
National Association of Broadcasters code, 394
National Broadcasting Company (NBC), 141, 240
National Educational Network (NET), 268–269
National Enquirer, 137, 184, 213
National Film Board of Canada (NFB), 426
National Gallery of Art, 446
National Geographic, 213, 224

National Library of Medicine (NLM), 446
National Newspaper Association, 199
National Public Radio (NPR), 247–248
National Television Systems Committee, 257
Network(s)
    American Broadcasting Company, 231
    Blue, 231
    economics, 273–274
    and the FCC, 272–274
    "Financial Interest and Syndication Rules," 272
    National Broadcasting System (NBC), 231
    ownership, 273
    pressures, 278–279
    radio, 230–232
    Red, 231
    television, 271–274
Newark *Star-Ledger*, 120, 186–187, 189
New electronic services, 466–490
New England *Courant*, 180
News, 11–12, 13, 24, 41–42, 68
    and advertising, 101–102
    analysis, 103–104
    and business, 101–102
    categories, 100
    characteristics of, 100, 109–111
    commentary, 103–104
    commercial control, 100, 115–118
    and computers, 192–194
    conflict, 100, 111
    conflicts of interests, 100
    consequence, 100, 110
    consumer action, 100
    copy editors, 100
    database, 100, 112
    disaster, 100, 110, 111
    enterprise news, 100
    event-centered, 103–104
    as events, 103–104
    exclusive, 111
    feature treatment, 111
    "frames," 195
    gatekeeper, 102
    hard, 100, 111, 401
    human interests, 100, 110
    inverted pyramid, 106
    investigative reporting, 100
    lead, 110
    legal and political threats, 100
    local, 189–190
    "news hole," 102
    novelty, 100, 111
    obituaries, 100, 112–113
    objectivity, 106–107
    packaging, 107
    packaging considerations, 100
    peg, 109
    photographers, 100
    pressures, 100
    as process, 103–104
    producers, 100
    production, 100–102
    production manager, 100–101
    prominence, 100, 111
    proximity, 100, 110
    radio, 232–233
    reporters, 100
    rewriters, 100
    soft, 100, 111, 401
    spot news, 100, 111

    staff artist, 100
    straight news, 100, 111
    syndicates, 106
    television, 257–258, 274–278
    television and print, 276–278
    timeliness, 100, 109–110
    utility, 102
    videotapes, 322
    wire services, 105
News Corp., 142
News media, 4, 8
    and the bandwagon, 123–124
    ethics, 150–151
    and public relations, 350–352
News packaging considerations
    departmentalization, 100, 108
    illustrations and graphics, 100, 108
    newsworthiness, 100, 107–108
    proof, 100, 109
    style, 100, 108–109
Newspaper(s), 69, 178–201
    and advertising, 187–188
    audience preferences, 190
    audiences, 179, 187
    changing times for, 186–195
    circulation, 186–188
    circulation data, 187, 199
    city editor, 99
    Civil War, 182
    classified ads, 193
    colonial, 180–181
    and computers, 192–194
    consumers, 179
    copy editors, 100
    correction policies, 119
    coverage of local issues, 189
    dailies, 186
    economics of, 67
    editing, 21
    editorial page, 98–99
    extras, 188
    future, 195–201
    hispanic, 197
    interactive, 194–195
    "metros," 188–190
    minorities in, 439–440
    minority hiring, 200
    the opinion function, 185
    organizational chart, 99
    ownership, 198–199
    paperless, 194–195
    photographers, 100
    photography, 182–183
    "pms," 188
    the popular press, 181–182
    publisher, 99
    readers, 192
    readership, 179
    research, 119, 190
    rewriters, 100
    the role of minorities in, 200–201
    the role of women in, 200–201
    Spanish-language, 197
    staff artists, 100
    "suburbans," 188–190
    Sunday papers, 186–187
    and television, 190–191
    time capsule, 180
Newspaper Advertising Bureau, 190
Newspaper Guild, 185–186
Newspaper Preservation Act, 199
News producers, 98–107

Newsroom, structure, 98–100
Newsweek, 210, 213–214
Newsweek on Campus, 218
New York *Daily News*, 187, 189
New York *Herald*, 180–181
New York *Journal*, 180
New York *Post*, 187, 189, 198
New York *Sun*, 180–181
New York Times, The, 21, 42, 106, 122, 141, 180–181, 184–185, 187, 265
   TimesFax, 198
New York Times Book Review, The, 168
New York Times Company, 142
The New York Times crossword puzzle, 473
New York *Tribune*, 180
New York *World*, 180, 183
Nickelodeon, 312
Nielsen ratings, 69, 287–292, 321
Nuevo Herald, El, 196
Nutshell, 218
N. W. Ayer & Son, 365, 368

Objectivity
   myth of, 106
   and news, 106
Obscenity, 133
Oglivy and Mather, 368–370
Orange County Register, 187
Organizational communication, 36–38
Ownership
   mass media, 140
   newspapers, 198–199
Oxford *Gazette*, 180

P↔I↔C Model, 23–27, 29–30, 45, 66, 68, 74, 84, 100, 172, 192, 220, 235, 247, 264
   and advertising, 378
   and film, 418–419
   and public relations, 347, 351–352
Packaging news, 107
"Pack journalism," 401
Paramount Communications, 141
Paramount Studios, 418
Parental Advisory label, 409–410
Parenting, 212
Pay television, 268
Pennsylvania Gazette, 181
Penthouse, 222
People, 206, 208, 212, 213, 221
"People meters," 288–289
People of color in mass communication, 438–441
Personal communication, 36–37
Peterson's Magazine, 207
Philadelphia *Inquirer*, 187
Physiological arousal, 86
Picture Week, 212
Playboy, 208, 213, 221–222
Playboy Enterprises, 213
Poland, mass communication in, 9
Police, 41
Political issues, 118–123
Political threats and news, 100
Politics, 237
   and radio, 241
   and television, 275–276
   and video, 327
Pool reporters, 104
Poor Richard's Almanac, 159
Popular culture, 70
Pornography, 86–88

"Portia Faces Life," 238
Portland *Oregonian*, 182
Press
   agents, 338–339
   associations, 104–106, 232
   freedom of speech, 145–147
   theories of, 136
Prevention, 213, 214
Print media, 156–174
Print revolution, 157–158
Privacy, 126, 132–135
Private communication, 36–37
PR (public relations) newswire, 117
Prodigy, 219
Producer perspective, evolution of, 79–80
Producers, live performances, 432
Propaganda, 341
Pseudo events, 115
Public broadcasting, 118, 246–248, 268–271, 298–299
Public Broadcasting Act, 270
Public Broadcasting Service (PBS), 247, 270, 299
Public communication, 36–37
Public interest, 235
Public opinion research, 71, 86
Public radio, 246–248
Public relations, 41–42, 117, 135–136, 336–358
   and accrediting, 357
   and agencies, 356–357
   audiences, 343–347, 351–352
   P. T. Barnum, 339
   Edward Bernays, 341–342
   Burson-Marsteller, 340
   and Cabbage Patch Dolls, 348–349
   cases, 348–350
   and consumer resistance, 349
   consumers, 343–347, 351–352
   and crisis management, 353–354
   and employee communication, 350
   ethics, 151
   and the *Federalist Papers*, 340
   Hill and Knowlton, 340
   industry priorities, 345
   and information flow, 336–337, 347
   Ivy Lee, 340
   and management, 353
   and minorities, 357
   models, 342–343
   and news media, 350–352
   objectives, 346, 353
   origins of, 338–343
   practitioners, 357–358
   producers, 347, 351–352
   profession, 352–358
   program planning, 346–357
   programs, 346–350
   and propaganda, 341
   and the P↔I↔C model, 347, 351–352
   publicists, 351
   publics, 343–346
   research applications, 353–354
   skills needed, 353, 356
   "spin control," 340
   theories, 342–343
   time capsule, 240
   and the Tylenol tragedy, 348
   types of organizations, 355–356
   and women, 357
   and writing, 356

Public Relations Society of America (PRSA), 135, 357
Public Telecommunications Financing Act, 270
Publick Occurrences Both Foreign and Domestick, 17, 180
Publishers, Black-oriented, 215
Publishing industry, 4

"Q-Rating" system, 292–293
Qube cable system, 194
Quill, The, 121

Radio, 228–252
   advertising, 231, 250–252
   affiliate stations, 246
   all-news, 244
   all-talk, 244
   AM, 230, 240–243
   American Broadcasting Company (ABC), 231
   "Amos 'n Andy," 232
   and anonymity, 56–57
   audiences, 248–250
   baseball, 232
   Black-oriented, 244
   Blue network, 231
   careers, 252
   citizen's band (CB), 230
   classical, 244–245
   Columbia Broadcasting System (CBS), 230, 231
   Communications Act of 1934, 235
   competition, 240
   consumers, 248–250
   country and western, 244–245
   deejays, 240
   digital, 242
   economics, 67, 249, 250–252
   educational, 246
   and elections, 237, 241
   Federal Communications Commission (FCC), 230
   Federal Radio Act, 230
   "fireside chats," 230, 237
   FM, 230, 239–243
   formats, 240, 244–247
   Golden Age of, 236–239
   history, 230
   KDKA, Pittsburgh, 230
   licensing, 235–236
   Mayflower Decision, 230
   middle of the road, 245
   most listened to stations, 249
   music, 234–235, 240
   and the music industry, 240
   Mutual Broadcasting System, 230, 231
   National Association of Broadcasters, 234
   National Association of Broadcasters code, 234
   National Broadcasting System (NBC), 231
   network affiliation, 246
   networks, 230–232
   news, 232–233
   and politics, 237, 241
   programming, 231–232
   public, 246–248
   Radio Act of, 1912, 234
   Radio Act of, 1927, 235

Subject Index

Radio Corporation of America (RCA), 231
  and records, 405–406
  Red network, 231
  regulation, 233–236
  religious, 245
  salaries in, 252
  shock radio, 245
  spectrum, 242
  talk, 230, 240
  time capsule, 230
  top-40, 245
  transnational, 243
  Voice of America, 230
  "War of the Worlds," 230
Radio Act of 1912, 234
Radio Act of 1927, 235
Radio Advertising Bureau, 228
Radio audiences
  AGB ratings, 248
  arbitron ratings, 248–249
  dayparts, 249
  measurement, 249–250
  Nielsen ratings, 248
  ratings, 250
  share, 250
Radio Corporation of America (RCA), 229–231, 256–257
Ranger Rick's Nature Magazine, 214
Rating system
  film, 422–423
  television, 285–292
RCA records, 404
Reader's Digest, 208–209, 213, 221–223
Reader's Guide to Periodical Literature, 211
Readership surveys, 69
Readers' perceptions, 124
Reading habits, 451
Real Estate, 212
Recording Industry Association of America (RIAA), 410
Recordings, 69
Records
  and radio, 405–406
  "singles," 410
Redbook, 213
Religious radio, 245
Reporters, 100
  pool, 104
  Shield laws, 138–139
Reporting, investigative, 100
Research
  advertising, 71–72, 220–221, 379–380, 383
  audience, 54, 62–63, 65–73
  consumer, 62–63, 65
  database, 485–486
  environments, 72–73
  feedback, 66, 70–73
  field, 73
  film, 83
  journalism, 124
  mass communication, 66, 83
  movie, 83
  naturalistic, 73
  newspaper, 119, 190
  public opinion, 71, 86
  public relations, 353–354
  readability, 71
  recall, 71–72
  recognition, 71
  self-report technique, 71

television, 13–14, 25, 41, 49, 63, 64, 78, 84, 90, 283–284
  television effects, 90
  unobtrusive, 73
  violence, 84
Retention, 43–45
Reviewers, 67–68
"Rock in America," 236
Rocky Mountain News, 187
Rolling Stone, 208, 216–217
"Romance of Helen Trent, The," 238
"Roots," 137

Saatchi & Saatchi Advertising Worldwide, New York, 370–371
St. Louis *Post-Dispatch*, 180, 182, 187
St. Paul *Pioneer Press*, 199
St. Petersburg *Times*, 199
San Francisco *Chronicle*, 187
Satellites, 466–468
Saturday Evening Post, 208–210
Saudi Arabia, mass communication in, 21
Savvy, 212, 218
Scholastic Teen Network, 213
Scott's Monthly Stamp Journal, 215
Scribner's, 207
Scripps, E. W., 142
"Section 315," 235
Securities and Exchange Commission (SEC), 114
Selective attention, 38, 40–41
Self, 212, 218
Self-publishing, 169
Self-regulation
  advertising, 395–396
  and film, 420–422
  media, 393–395
"Sesame Street," 6
Sex
  and advertising, 383
  and mass communication, 11–12, 14, 86–88
  telephone, 133–134
  on television, 14
"Shadow, The," 238
Shield laws, 138–139
Show Boat, 429
Sigma Delta Chi, 185
Signals, 34–36
Simons Market Research Bureau, 69
"60 Minutes," 233
Slander, 118, 137
S→M→C→R perspective, 17–18, 23, 79
  deficiencies of, 18
Smithsonian Institution, 214, 446
Soap operas, 12, 238
Socialization, 89–90
Social learning theory, 79
Society for Professional Journalists, 185
Sound Recording Act, 412
Source similarity, 46
Southern Living, 212, 213
Soviet Union, mass communication in, 8–9
Spanish-language newspapers, 197
Spanish-language television, 293–294
Special-interest groups, 120
"Spin control," 340
Spiral of silence, 74, 77
Sports, 22
  and mass communication, 280

as mass communication, 434–435
and museums, 455
programming, 14
Sports Illustrated, 206, 208, 212–213
SportsChannel, 313
Star, The, 184, 213
Suicide, 63
Symbols, 34–36
Syndicates
  feature, 106
  news, 106

Tampa *Tribune*, 199
Technological convergence, 5–7
Technological school, 74, 77–79
Technology, 8–9, 21–22, 28, 130–132, 289, 475–490
  communication, 4
  converging, 466
  HDTV, 295–296
  music, 406–407
  and newspapers, 192–194
  and public relations, 350
  television, 293–296
  VCR recording, 320–323
Ted Bates, 370–371
Teen-Age Mutant Ninja Turtles, 6
Telecommunication, 10
Tele-Communications Inc., 141–142, 310
Teleconferencing, 325
Telemarketing and theater, 433
Telephone(s), 469–475
  800 and 900 numbers, 64, 472–474
  and mass communication, 5–6, 25, 41, 56, 469–475
  and work, 474–475
Teletext, 486–489
Television, 11–13, 14–15, 22, 39, 41, 69
  advances, 293–295
  advertising, 266–268, 280, 374, 387
  audiences, 280–284, 298
  cable, 87, 256–295, 302–318
  commercials, 382–383
  and confrontation, 284
  consumers, 280–284, 298
  docudrama, 264–265
  economics, 266–269, 273–274
  "Financial Interest and Syndication Rules," 272
  game shows, 261–262
  and gender roles, 262
  high-definition (HDTV), 293–296
  history, 256–263
  immediacy, 284
  "infomercials," 265–266
  "infotainment," 265–266
  interactive, 25
  and leisure time, 281
  licenses, 256–257
  and loneliness, 284
  low-power, 293
  and magazines, 210
  markets, 257
  minorities in, 438–439
  and the national character, 283
  network ratings, 14
  networks, 264, 271–274
  news, 257–258, 274–278
  and newspapers, 190–191
  and politics, 275–276
  prime-time, 264

Television (Continued)
  programming, 259–268, 276–282, 299
  public, 268–271
  public broadcasting, 298–299
  ratings, 264, 285–292
  remote control, 11, 64
  research, 13–14, 25, 49, 63–64, 78, 84, 90, 283–284
  satellites, 258
  soap operas, 26, 263
  Spanish-language, 293–294
  and sports, 280
  sweeps week, 112
  time capsule, 258
  ultra high frequency (UHF), 257
  uses, 256
  video applications, 318–331
  women on, 262
Television rating system
  deficits, 290–292
  development, 286–288
Textbooks, 166–167
Theater, 69, 402, 427–434
  The Apollo, 427
  Broadway, 430–431
  economics, 433–434
  regional, 431–433
  and social concerns, 429–430
  and telemarketing, 433
Theme parks
  and mass communication, 16
  as mass communication, 434–435
Thomson Corporation, 142
Time, 206, 209–211, 213, 221
Time capsules
  advertising, 365
  cable television, 306
  electronic services, 469
  libraries and museums, 446
  magazines, 208
  newspapers, 180
  public relations, 340
  radio, 230
  television, 258
Time Inc., 141–142, 212
Time Warner, 141–142
Times, The, 181
Times-Mirror Company, 141–142
Transportation, and mass communication, 56–57
Tribune Company, 142
"Truth or Consequences," 239
Turner Broadcasting System (TBS), 142, 311
Turner's Cable News Network, 311

TV-Cable Week, 212
TV Guide, 208, 210, 213, 222–223
TWA Ambassador, 215
Twentieth Century Fox Studios, 418–419
Two-step flow, 47
Tylenol tragedy, and public relations, 348

UNESCO (United Nations Educational, Scientific, and Cultural Organization), 16, 30
United Press International (UPI), 105–106, 180
Universal Studios, 418
"Unsolved Mysteries," 25
USA Network, 312
USA Today, 4–5, 29, 113, 180, 187, 191–192, 197–198, 200, 210, 222
User group, 27
Users, 27
Uses and gratifications, 74, 82–83
U.S. News & World Report, 210

VALS research, 220–221
Values, 13
Vanity press, 169
Variety, 69
Variety industry reports, 69
VCR Plus, 323
VCRs, 316–331
  economics of, 67
  sales, 319
Verbal feedback, 66–67
Vertical integration, 420
Viacom International, 142, 310
Video, 318–331
  applications, 324–328
  audiences, 321
  consumers, 321
  ratings, 321
  recording codes, 323
Video Business, 216
Video games, and mass communication, 14–15
Videoconferencing, 325
Videodisc(s), 4, 326
Videophones, 489–490
Videotapes
  and news, 322
  specialized uses, 322
Video technology
  advances, 323–331

  applications, 324–328
  growth of, 318–321
Videotex, 5, 486–490
  Canadian, 488
Violence
  and mass communication, 85–86
  in mass communication, 12
Violence research, 84
Voice mail, 479–480
Voice of America, 230, 243
Voxbox rating system, 289

Wall Street Journal, The, 4, 122–123, 127, 185, 187, 191
War Advertising Council, 365
Warner Amex, 310
Warner Communications, 141
Warner Studies, 418
"War of the Worlds," 74, 80–81, 230
Washington Journalism Review, The, 121
Washington Post, The, 108, 180, 185, 187, 142
WCBS-FM, New York, 249
WCCO-AM, Minneapolis, 249
WCVG-AM, Cincinnati, 240
Westinghouse, 229, 256
WFAN, 243
WFAN, New York, 240
WFAN-AM, New York, 246
WGN-AM, Chicago, 249
Whittle Communications, 268
WHTZ-FM, New York, 249
WINS-AM, New York, 249
Wire services, 105, 232
WJR-AM, Detroit, 249
WLTW-FM, New York, 249
WNBC, New York, 243
Woman's Day, 213, 222
Women
  and mass media, 126, 200–201
  in media industries, 360–361
  in public relations, 357, 360–361
  on television, 262
Women in Love, 417
Women's Sports & Fitness, 212
Work, 56–57
Working Woman, 212, 218
World's Columbian Exhibition, 446
Writer's Market, 168
WRKO-AM, Boston, 240

Yellow journalism, 183–184
Young & Rubicam, 370–371
"Your Hit Parade," 236